CIVIL AVIATION:
STANDARDS AND LIABILITIES

AVIATION PRACTICAL GUIDES

Air Cargo Claims
by Rex C. Tester
1998

CIVIL AVIATION:
STANDARDS AND LIABILITIES

by

TIM UNMACK

LONDON   HONG KONG
1999

LLP Professional Publishing
(a trading division of the Informa Publishing Group Ltd)
69–77 Paul Street
London EC2A 4LQ
Great Britain

EAST ASIA
LLP Asia
Room 1101, Hollywood Centre
233 Hollywood Road
Hong Kong

First Published in Great Britain 1999
© Tim Unmack, 1999

British Library Cataloguing in Publication Data
A catalogue record
for this book is available
from the British Library

ISBN 1–85978–633–2

Text set in 10/12pt Plantin by
Interactive Sciences Ltd,
Gloucester
Printed in Great Britain by
MPG Books Ltd,
Bodmin, Cornwall

DEDICATION

This book is dedicated to Mike Griffin and Roger Hoyle who were both overtaken by sudden severe illnesses and died before this book came to print. I am indebted to them both.

ACKNOWLEDGEMENTS

I am grateful to Dr Ludwig Weber, Director, Legal Bureau, ICAO, to Mr Andrew Charlton, Director, Legal Department—Geneva, IATA, and to my friends and colleagues for their assistance.

TIM UNMACK

ABOUT THE AUTHORS

TIM UNMACK

Solicitor. Former Partner and Senior Partner of Beaumont and Son. He is currently a consultant at Shadbolt & Co. Member of Royal Aeronautical Society.

DR D A RYDER (Chapter 17)

A former Principal Scientific Officer at the Royal Aircraft Establishment, Farnborough, and former Senior Lecturer in metallurgy at the University of Manchester, Institute of Science and Technology.

THE LATE CAPTAIN ROGER HOYLE (Chapter 18)

Pilot with British United Air Ferries and Training Captain both with British Caledonian and British Airways. After retiring from British Airways he flew as Captain with British Mediterranean Airways.

PHIL HOSEY (Chapter 19)

Served in the Aircraft Engineering branch of the Royal Air Force. Was formerly Technical Services Director, Dan Air Engineering Ltd and is currently Director of FLS Aerospace Ltd.

THE LATE CAPTAIN MICHAEL GRIFFIN (Chapter 20—joint author)

Served in the Royal Navy as Engineering Officer and Pilot. He joined Bristow Helicopters Ltd in 1973 as a pilot and became their Company Flight Safety Officer.

CAPTAIN MICHAEL BETTS (Chapter 20—joint author)

Served in the Royal Air Force as Operational Pilot, Instructor Pilot and Test Pilot. He joined Bristow Helicopters Ltd in 1980 where he is Chief Test Pilot and Chief Training Captain. He is a CAA authorised examiner.

CONTENTS

TABLE OF CASES

TABLE OF LEGISLATION

*Page numbers in **bold** indicate where the legislation is quoted or discussed in detail*

li

TABLE OF TREATIES AND CONVENTIONS

*Page numbers in **bold** indicate where the Treaty or Convention is quoted or discussed in detail*

GLOSSARY OF DEFINITIONS AND ACRONYMS USED IN THIS BOOK

Act:	Legislative Act, statute or other legal enactment of a State.
Aeroplane:	A power-driven heavier-than-air aircraft, deriving its lift in flight chiefly from aerodynamic reactions on surfaces which remain fixed under given conditions of flight. (Definition).
Aircraft:	Any machine that can derive support in the atmosphere from the reactions of the air other than the reactions of the air against the earth's surface. (Definition).
Annex:	Any annex to the Chicago Convention 1944 drawn up pursuant to Article 37.
ANO:	UK Air Navigation (No 2) Order 1995 or replacement Order.
AIS:	Aeronautical Information Services.
ATS:	Air Traffic Services.
Authority:	Any regulatory or government authority responsible for the administration of civil aviation in a State.
Aviation Law:	Civil Aviation law, excluding law on military operations.
CC Cargo:	IATA Conditions of Carriage for Cargo
CAA:	The Civil Aviation Authority of the United Kingdom.
Chicago Convention:	Chicago Convention on Civil Aviation 1944.
Civil Law:	Laws and legal systems based on ancient Roman law.
Court:	Any court including tribunal carrying out the judicial process.
Defined:	Defined in the Definitions
Definitions:	Definitions in ICAO publication "International Civil Aviation Vocabulary" (doc. 9713) which combines the ICAO Lexicon, ICAO Definitions and List of ICAO Bodies.
Domestic Law:	The law or legal system of any State, otherwise known as "internal", "national" or "municipal" law.
Enterprise:	Any entity, company or corporation carrying on business.
EC:	European Economic Community.
EU:	European Union.
FAA:	Federal Aviation Administration of the USA.
GCC Pax:	IATA General Conditions of Carriage for passengers and baggage.
IATA:	International Air Transport Association.
ICAO:	International Civil Aviation Organization.
International Law:	Public International Law.
Market:	International Aviation Insurance Market.
Private Law:	That part of domestic law regulating the private rights and duties of individuals, legal persons and governments.

SARPS:	Standard Procedures and Recommended Practices in any Annex to the Chicago Convention.
SDR:	Special Drawing Right.
State:	Any Sovereign State and its dependencies, otherwise called "nation" or "country".
state (used in a political sense):	Any member of any federal State or similar constitution.
State of Design:	The State having jurisidiction over the organisation responsible for the type design. (Definition).
State of Manufacture:	The State responsible for the certification as to the airworthiness of the prototype. (Definition).
State of Operator:	The State in which the operator has his principal place of business or if he has no such place of business his permanent residence. (Definition).
State of Registry:	The State on whose register the aircarft is entered. (Definition).
UK:	The United Kingdom of Great Britian and Northern Ireland.
USA, US:	The United States of America.

PRINCIPAL PUBLICATIONS, REPORTS CITED AND MATERIAL REPRODUCED

PRINCIPAL PUBLICATIONS AND REPORTS, AS CITED

AHM: International Air Transport Association (IATA), *IATA Airport Handling Manual* (19th edition), reprinted by permission of IATA

Air Law: *Journal of Air and Space Law*, Kluwer Law International

AVI: AVICAS (Aviation Cases Reported by Commercial Clearing House)

Black: *Black's Law Dictionary*, West Publishing Co., St Paul, Minnesota

Buergenthal: Buergenthal, *Law Making in the International Civil Aviation Organization* (1st edition), Syracuse University Press, Syracuse, New York

Dicey: Dicey & Morris, *Conflict of Laws* (12th edition), Sweet & Maxwell, London

Giemulla: Giemulla & Schmid, *Warsaw Convention* (1st edition), 1994, reproduced with the kind permission of Kluwer Law International

Halsbury: *Halsbury's Laws of England* (4th edition), Butterworths Tolley

Margo: Margo, *Aviation Insurance* (2nd edition), reproduced by permission of The Butterworths Division of Reed Elsevier (UK) Ltd

McWhinney: *Aerial Piracy and International Terrorism*: "The Illegal Diversion of Aircraft and International Law" by Edward McWhinney QC, Martinus Nijhoff Publishers

RFDA: *Revue Française de Droit Aerien et Spatial*

S&B: Shawcross & Beaumont, *Air Law* (4th edition), reproduced by permission of The Butterworths Division of Reed Elsevier (UK) Ltd

Starke: Shearer, *Starke's International Law* (11th edition), reproduced by permission of The Butterworths Division of Reed Elsevier (UK) Ltd

Wade: Wade and Forsyth, *Administrative Law* (7th edition), 1994, reprinted by permission of Oxford University Press

lxvi Principal Publications, Reports Cited and Material Reproduced

The extracts from Annexes 1–18 to the Chicago Convention 1944 are reproduced with the permission of the International Civil Aviation Organization (ICAO). Readers who wish to obtain original copies of the Annexes can contact ICAO directly at the following address: International Civil Aviation Organization, Attn: Document Sales Unit, 999 University Street, Montreal, Quebec, Canada H3C 5H7.

The "Area/Aerodrome Qualification Certificate and Route Check Report" (revision 6) on pages 500–501 is the copyright of British Airways plc and is reprinted with permission. (Please note that this form was used by British Airways plc until April 1999, since which time it has been replaced by an electronic form.)

The London Aircraft Insurance Policy AVN 1C (in Appendix 5) is reproduced by kind permission of Lloyd's Aviation Underwriters' Association.

INTRODUCTION

This book is about operational standards and obligations in civil aviation, and the consequences of failure to comply with them. It also deals with risk management, insurance of risk and claims arising from accidents.

The book is a handbook and part of the Aviation Practical Guide series. It is not a detailed analysis of all aspects of the legal and technical questions considered, which are often dealt with briefly.

It does not deal with:

(i) Criminal law in relation to civil aviation except for Annex 17 to the Chicago Convention and the treaties summarised in Chapter 12;
(ii) The rights and liabilities arising as between employer and employee;
(iii) Rights and liabilities in relation to hybrids such as air cushion vehicles;
(iv) Property rights in aircraft;
(v) Commercial topics such as air services and anti-trust issues.

Legal cases and comments are usually given as examples of the general principle under consideration and not as a comprehensive survey of a subject or of all relevant sources.

While every effort has been made to make sure the book is up-to-date at the time it went to print, it is essential, when using it, that a careful check is made as to whether there are any subsequent changes or developments, and as to whether the particular matter under consideration raises questions not dealt with in this book.

CHAPTER 1

LEGAL FRAMEWORK OF AVIATION LAW

Law sets the minimum standards of behaviour in a society and establishes consequential rights and obligations. Failure to comply with such standards in domestic law may result in a court ordering that, under private law, damages should be paid or certain obligations performed; breach of criminal law may result in the imposition of a fine or imprisonment (or in extreme cases in certain States), the death penalty; for example, in the USA if anyone is killed in the course of aircraft piracy or hijacking (49 US Code 46502).

Laws are established by the relevant law-making process, which may be:

    (i) legislative acts such as an international treaty or domestic Act; and

    (ii) decisions of international and domestic courts.

The law-making process in a particular society, whether international or domestic, gives force of law to those minimum standards, thus distinguishing the activity concerned from a mere social habit or a theorem of physics.

For example, it is a principle of physics that air passing over an aerofoil surface will in certain conditions create the lift essential for aircraft flight. It is therefore necessary that an aeroplane wing must be designed in a certain way if lift is to be achieved. It is a rule of law that an aircraft wing must be designed and constructed in accordance with technical specifications if a certificate of airworthiness is to be issued in respect of the aircraft. It is usually a breach of law if an aircraft is flown without a valid certificate of airworthiness.

Civil aviation is an international activity regulated mainly by international treaties.

It is necessary to distinguish between international law, sometimes called public international law, and the system of law within a State, referred to as domestic, municipal or national law. In this book that system is called "domestic law".

CHAPTER 2

INTERNATIONAL LAW

"International law may be defined as that body of law which is composed for its greater part of the principles and rules of conduct which States feel themselves bound to observe, and therefore, do commonly observe in their relations with each other, and which includes also:

(a) The rules of law relating to the functioning of international institutions or organizations, their relations with each other, and their relations with States and individuals; and
(b) certain rules of law relating to individuals and non-State entities so far as the rights or duties of such individuals and non-State entities are the concern of the international community.

. . .

It is a very good practical working rule to regard international law as mainly composed of principles whereby certain rights belong to, or certain duties are imposed upon, States" (*Starke*, pages 3–4).

WORLDWIDE AND REGIONAL RULES OF INTERNATIONAL LAW

Rules of international law may be worldwide, such as those controlling the activity of ICAO, or regional as in the case of the EU.

STATES

Recent political changes emphasise the importance of whether a group of people in a particular place constitutes a State or not. Article 1 of the Montevideo Convention 1933 on the Rights and Duties of States (signed by the USA and certain Latin American countries) provides that

"the State as a person of international law should possess the following qualifications:

(a) a permanent population;
(b) a defined territory;
(c) a government;
(d) a capacity to enter into relations with other States."

While a particular group of people may possess the necessary elements of Statehood, it cannot exist in a political vacuum; in order to carry on business it must be recognised by other States within the international community. The group may be denied recognition by other States because the circumstances of its creation offend fundamental laws of the international legal order (*Starke*). The United Nations plays a crucial role in influencing recognition of Statehood.

State recognition and its effect on private rights in property in civil aviation are considered in the decision of *Civil Air Transport Inc* v. *Central Air Transport Corp* [1953] AC 70. The UK Judicial Committee of the Privy Council held that

"a contract entered into by the Nationalist Government of China, at a time when it was recognised by the UK Government as the de jure government of China, for the sale of civil aircraft belonging to the Chinese Government, and which by the date of the contract had been flown by employees of the Nationalist Government to Hong Kong, was effective to pass title to the aircraft to the purchasers, and operated to defeat a claim to the aircraft by the succeeding Communist Government of China which, after the date of the contract, had been recognised by the UK Government as the de jure government of China."

For *Dicey* a "State" means the whole of a territory subject to one sovereign power.

Note: The Privy Council originated as the Council of the Norman Kings. The functions of the Judicial Committee of the Privy Council include the hearing of appeals from Colonial territories and certain Commonwealth States. The Committee is made up of those Privy Councillors who hold, or have held, high judicial office in the UK, such as those judges sitting in the House of Lords, the highest court of appeal in the UK.

SOURCES OF INTERNATIONAL LAW

Starke considers that the material sources of international law fall into five principal categories:

    (1) Custom;
    (2) Treaties;
    (3) Decisions of judicial or arbitral tribunals;
    (4) Juristic works;
    (5) Decisions of the organs of international institutions.

Article 38 of the Statute of the International Court of Justice directs the Court to apply the same sources except that it replaces sources (3) and (5) above with "the general principles of law recognised by civilised nations" and extends (4) to include judicial decisions and teachings of the various countries.

Domestic judicial decisions interpret treaties. See extract from New South Wales Court of Appeal in *Kotsambasis* v. *Singapore Airlines Ltd* (page 249 below).

TREATIES

The rules of international law concerning treaties were to a large extent codified and reformulated in the Vienna Convention on the Law of Treaties concluded on 23 May 1969. The US Department of State declared in 1971 that the Vienna Convention was "recognised as the authoritative guide to current treaty law and practice".

Article 2 of the Vienna Convention defines a treaty as an, "International agreement concluded between States in written form and governed by international law, whether embodied in a single instrument or in two or more related instruments and whatever its particular designation". The Supreme Court of the USA stated in *Trans World Airlines Inc* v. *Franklin Mint* (see Chapter 7, Part 3, below): "A treaty is essentially a contract between or among sovereign nations. The great object of an international agreement is to define the common ground between sovereign nations".

Treaties have a number of names which may indicate a difference in procedure or degree of formality. The principal categories are:

(1) Convention—This is a formal instrument of a multilateral character. The term includes an instrument adopted by an international institution, for example the Assembly of ICAO adopting the Chicago Convention in 1944. Another example is the Warsaw Convention for Unification of Certain Rules relating to International Carriage by Air 1929 ("The Warsaw Convention 1929").

(2) Protocol—This is less formal than a convention. Its purpose may be subsidiary to a convention or it may be an ancillary instrument to a convention but of an independent character. An example is the Hague Protocol 1955 which amended the Warsaw Convention 1929.

(3) Other categories of treaty include Agreements, Arrangements, and *Procès-Verbal*.

Treaties will normally only apply to those States who are parties to them. Article 34 of the Vienna Convention provides that a treaty does not create either obligations or rights for a third State without its consent. A third State means a State not party to the treaty. This is similar to the common law rules on privity of contract in domestic law referred to in Chapter 3 below.

CONCLUSION AND ENTRY INTO FORCE OF TREATIES

Starke (at page 407) lists eight steps in the creation of obligations by treaty:

(1) The accrediting of persons who conduct negotiations on behalf of the Contracting States;

(2) Negotiation and adoption;

(3) Authentication, signature and exchange of instruments;
(4) Ratification;
(5) Accessions and adhesions;
(6) Entry into force;
(7) Registration and publication;
(8) Application and enforcement;

For practical purposes the main questions are:

(1) What does the treaty say?
(2) Is a particular State party to it?
(3) Has that State taken those steps required under its constitution to incorporate the treaty into its domestic law?

Article 2 of the Vienna Convention defines "ratification" as, "the international act . . . whereby a State establishes on the international plane its consent to be bound by a treaty". *Starke* (at page 413) points out that the development of constitutional systems giving Parliament the function of ratification has increased the importance of ratification. Procedures differ from State to State.

Once a treaty has come into force, the constitution of each State establishes how the provisions of the treaty are incorporated into domestic law. In UK incorporation must generally be by domestic legislation, whether primary (Act of Parliament) or delegated legislation (*Maclaine Watson & Co Ltd* v. *International Tin Council* [1990] 2 AC 418).

In USA, treaties are usually self-executing, i.e. no act of incorporation is necessary. In *Trans World Airlines* v. *Franklin Mint Corp* the US Supreme Court said " . . . the (Warsaw) Convention is a self-executing treaty. Though the Convention permits individual signatories to convert liability limits into national currencies by legislation or otherwise, no domestic legislation is required to give the Convention the force of law in the United States".

There are similar provisions in Article 7 of the Russian Civil Code.

The Warsaw Convention 1929 is an example of how a treaty comes into operation:

(a) The preamble to the Convention lists the States who are recited to have nominated their respective plenipotentiaries (authorised representatives) who were duly authorised and who have concluded and signed the Convention.

(b) Article 36: "This Convention is drawn up in French in a single copy which shall remain deposited in the archives of the Ministry for Foreign Affairs of Poland and of which one duly certified copy shall be sent by the Polish Government to the Government of each of the High Contracting Parties."

(c) Article 37(1): "This Convention shall be ratified. The Instruments of ratification shall be deposited in the archives of the Ministry for Foreign Affairs of Poland who shall give notice of the deposit to the Government of each of the High Contracting Parties."

(d) Article 37(2): "As soon as this Convention shall have been ratified by five of the High Contracting Parties it shall come into force as between them on the ninetieth day after deposit of the fifth ratification. Thereafter it shall come into force between the High Contracting Parties which shall have ratified and the High Contracting Party which deposits the instrument of ratification on the ninetieth day after the deposit."

(e) Article 37(3): "It shall be the duty of the Government of the Republic of Poland to notify the Government of each of the High Contracting Parties of the date on which this Convention comes into force as well as the date of the deposit of each ratification."

(f) Article 38(1): "This Convention shall, after it has come into force, remain open for adherence by any State."

(g) Article 38(2): "The adherence shall be effected by a notification addressed to the Government of the Republic of Poland which shall inform the Governments of each of the High Contracting Parties."

(h) Article 38(3): "The adherence shall take effect as from the ninetieth day after the notification made to the Government of the Republic of Poland."

(i) Article 39: Provides for denunciation, see page 286. Any one of the High Contracting Parties may denounce the Convention.

(j) The UK incorporated the Convention into its own domestic law by the Carriage by Air Act 1932.

When checking whether a treaty is in force or who are the parties to it, sources of information are:

(1) The depository State or institution, for example Poland in the case of the Warsaw Convention 1929.

(2) ICAO, which keeps details of civil aviation treaties and the parties as notified by other depositories. ICAO also keeps details of the parties to any treaty where it is the depository, for example Tokyo Convention 1963 (Chapter 12 below) dealing with offences on board aircraft.

(3) Registration of Treaties Department of UN.

(4) The government of a party State.

Interpretation of treaties by domestic courts depends on the applicable domestic law which in turn may apply treaty law such as that found in the Vienna Convention. The question may arise whether the court is free to consider the *travaux préparatoires* (working papers) of the meetings leading to the finalisation of any treaty. See Articles 31 and 32 of the Vienna Convention referred to in *Fothergill* v. *Monarch Airlines* [1981] AC 251, and the Belgian Court of Cassation decision of *Tondriau* v. *Air India* (1977) *Pasicrisie Belge 1*, 574 where the court consulted the *travaux préparatoires* in interpreting Article 25 of the Amended Warsaw Convention (see page 270 below).

Termination or suspension of a treaty depends on its express terms, the Vienna Convention and public international law generally.

McWhinney makes the following points with regard to public international law treaties:

(1) There will often be a substantial time-lag between treaty signing and the necessary follow-up of ratification.

(2) The more States who are parties to a multi-lateral treaty, the less bite it may have. It may therefore be "declaratory" or a restatement of an existing law.

(3) There may be a perverse tendency to assume that in making a treaty on a particular subject, such treaty automatically displaces already existing customary international law on that subject so that States not parties to the treaty are, on their non-signature or non-ratification, automatically released from their obligations to adhere to existing customary international law.

TREATIES AND SUCCESSION

Recent political changes make it important to check that a particular treaty binding on a State will continue to apply to a new sovereign State made up of all or part of the domestic territory of the former State.

In *Starke*'s view (at page 291) the two main questions relate to:

(1) The passing of rights and obligations upon *external* changes of sovereignty over territory.

(2) The passing of rights and obligations upon *internal* changes of sovereignty irrespective of territorial changes, see for example decision of the International Court of Justice in *Territorial Dispute* (Libyan Arab Jamahiriya/Chad February 1994) where the party States remained bound by the Treaty of Friendship and Good Neighbourliness between France and the United Kingdom of Libya 1955 on frontiers.

Each case of State succession must be considered on its own facts.

CUSTOMARY LAW

In the UK and USA customary international law, insofar as it is consistent with domestic law, is accepted as part of domestic law under the doctrine of incorporation.

INTERNATIONAL TRIBUNALS

In aviation international tribunals include:

(1) International Court of Justice.
(2) EU Court of Justice.
(3) ICAO Council: Settlement of disputes and Arbitration Procedures (Articles 84 and 85 of the Chicago Convention).
(4) Special Arbitral Tribunals.

CHAPTER 3

STATE DOMESTIC LAW

Each State has its own system of domestic law. However, diversity in legal systems is limited because:

(1) Domestic laws of many States are derived either from the English common law or from the Roman civil law;

(2) The international community is continuously harmonising and codifying laws.

COMMON LAW

Following the Norman Conquest in 1066, the Norman and Angevin kings in England centralised administration of justice, extending the powers of the King's courts over courts of local lords. Common law was the unwritten law made by the King's judges as opposed to Statute law. It has, however, come to mean the domestic legal system generally applied, not only in England but also for example in Australia, Canada, New Zealand, Singapore and the USA.

"ROMAN" CIVIL LAW

While Roman law continued to be applied in parts of Western Europe after the barbarian invasions of the Roman Empire, its renaissance was due largely to the efforts of the Italian universities in the 12th century. It formed the basis of law in many European States and their overseas territories. It was codified by Napoleon Bonaparte into the French Civil Code. It is applied in States such as France, Italy, Germany and Spain. It is used in Latin America and also in Louisiana, USA and Quebec, Canada.

In this book law derived from Roman civil law is called "civil law".

In certain States where either common law or civil law was imposed on the original local law, the latter may also continue to apply particularly in the sphere of family law.

In some States former Communist law has been replaced by Codes drafted to meet contemporary needs.

FEDERAL CONSTITUTION

Certain States have a federal constitution where the State consists of a number of states or provinces. In such instances there is usually a federal legal system applicable overall to all states or provinces and an individual system for each state.

Distinctions in law between parts of a State, whether a state or province, may concern questions such as jurisdiction, limitation and exercise of private rights.

In the USA there are important differences between federal law and state law. Rules govern the respective jurisdictions of federal courts and state courts in aviation litigation involving a foreign element. Both federal and state courts have their own appeal systems. The US Supreme Court is the final court of appeal from federal courts, and from state courts where a point of federal law is involved. There may in certain cases be concurrent jurisdiction in lower courts. Some private rights may be affected by the Federal Preemption Doctrine: where an action is begun in a state court, it may be removed to a federal court which must create a private right of action and must preempt state law.

There are references in this book to English, Scottish and UK law. English law is a common law system. Early Scottish law was influenced by civil law. UK law applies to the UK as a whole. The leading UK case on negligence, *Donoghue* v. *Stevenson* ([1932] AC 562), was a Scottish case where the senior appellate court in the UK, the House of Lords, laid down the principles of the tort of negligence applicable both to England and Scotland (see page 370).

SOURCES OF DOMESTIC LAW

Sources of domestic law include legislative Acts, delegated legislation, decisions of courts and custom. In common law systems, previous judicial decisions are legally binding on certain other courts under the rule of precedent, obliging such courts to apply the legal principle on which those earlier decisions were based.

While civil law systems are not bound by precedent, earlier court decisions are important, as footnotes in commentaries on the French Civil Code indicate.

Legislative Acts are laws enacted in accordance with the constitution of the State concerned. Examples are US Acts of Congress, UK Acts of Parliament and *Loi* of the French "Assemblée".

Power is often delegated by an Act to a government department or some other body to make regulations and laws in accordance with the Act. These delegated powers must be exercised in the manner required by the Act. See *Rocky Mountain Helicopters Inc* v. *FAA* where the US Court of Appeals, 10th Circuit (971 F 2d 736 (1992)), held that the FAA had acted in an improper manner when it sought to impose a rule prohibiting an emergency medical evacuation service from allowing its pilots to use night vision goggles (24 AVI 17,113 1992–5).

States can surrender sovereignty over making of domestic law. For example, in the EU, Regulations of the Commission have direct effect automatically within a Member State. See page 214.

PUBLIC AND PRIVATE LAW

Most legal systems distinguish between (a) private or civil law which applies to private rights and duties of natural persons (individuals), and legal persons (for example commercial corporations) in their dealings with each other and with governments and other authorities; and (b) public law, which includes criminal law, constitutional and administrative law.

The 7th edition of Wade's *Administrative Law* states "A first approximation to a definition of administrative law is to say that it is the law relating to the control of governmental power. This, at any rate, is the heart of the subject" (page 4).

In this book, private or civil law is referred to as "private law". The reference here to civil law must not be confused with "Roman" civil law as defined in the Glossary.

Many legal situations involve questions of private and of public law. For example, if an aircraft operator operates an aircraft without the aircraft having a valid certificate of airworthiness, as a result of which passengers are killed in an accident:

(1) The passengers and their families will have a claim in private law for damages.

(2) The operator will almost certainly have breached a criminal law for which it will incur a penalty.

(3) An official inquiry will usually be held on the accident in accordance with Annex 13 principles (see page 154).

Private law interests may seek to control abuse of public law duties by methods such as English judicial review or by application of the French *droit administratif.*

Judicial review is one of the weapons with which the courts in England have equipped themselves in the absence of a written constitution against the improper exercise of governmental powers. See Comment on page 192 at the end of Annex 16 on *R* v. *Secretary of State for Transport ex parte Richmond-upon-Thames London Borough Council* which illustrates:

(1) The English remedy of judicial review to control executive government; and

(2) The executive steps taken to control aircraft noise at London's airports.

LEGAL LIABILITY

Legal liability arises in private law when one person, the wrongdoer, has committed a breach of a legal obligation owed to another person who is injured by the breach.

If the wrongdoer does not accept that he has committed a breach, it may be necessary for the injured person to start legal proceedings (plaintiff) before the appropriate court to enforce his rights against the alleged wrongdoer (defendant).

If the court is satisfied that the defendant is in breach of the obligation it may award the plaintiff monetary damages or make an order requiring the defendant to desist from the wrongful conduct. In certain jurisdictions legal costs may be awarded to the successful party. The nature of damages is dealt with in Chapter 14, which considers certain aspects of litigation.

While terminology between States may differ, the concepts of liability arising from a breach of contract or in tort has wide application.

CONTRACT

Halsbury (Volume 9, para 201) states "Whilst it is probably impossible to give one absolute and universally correct definition of a contract, the most commonly accepted definition is a promise or set of promises which the law will enforce". The expression "contract" may, however, be used to describe any or all of the following:

(1) That series of promises or acts themselves constituting the contract;
(2) The document or documents constituting or evidencing that series of promises or acts, or their performance;
(3) The legal relations resulting from that series.

Each State has its own domestic law as to what constitutes a valid contract. In England, *Halsbury* continues that there must be:

(1) Two or more parties to the contract;
(2) Agreement between the parties arising out of an offer and acceptance;
(3) Intention of the parties to create a legal relationship;
(4) Consideration: the party who benefits from the obligation undertaken by the other party must give a benefit in return. There must be a bargain.

In France, Article 1101 of the Civil Code provides that the contract is an agreement under which one or more persons bind themselves to one or more others to give, to do or not to do something.

Article 1108 of the French Civil Code states that the four essential conditions for the validity of a contract are:

(1) Consent of the party undertaking the obligation;
(2) Capacity to contract;
(3) Certainty of subject matter of the commitment;
(4) Lawful purpose of the obligation.

Capacity and Legality are also important elements in English law of contract, having far reaching consequences where either is absent. However, they are not included in *Halsbury*'s four essential constituents.

In common law many types of contract need not be in writing in order to be valid although it is usual and advisable to record them in writing, particularly where they concern complex matters in aviation.

Where domestic law applies the doctrine of privity of contract, generally speaking only a party to the contract can have the legal right to benefit from it.

TORT OR DELICT

Black describes tort as a legal wrong committed upon the person or property independent of contract.

Halsbury describes tort as "those civil rights of action, which are available for the recovery of unliquidated damages by persons who have sustained injury or loss from acts, statements or the omissions of others in breach of duty or contravention of right imposed or conferred by law rather than by agreement, are rights of action in tort".

Similar concepts are found in civil law where the wrong is called a delict (*délit*). The French Civil Code provides:

Article 1382: Any act whatsoever of man which causes damage to any other person, obliges him by whose fault it occurred to make reparation.

Article 1383: Each one is liable for damage he has caused not only by his act, but also by his negligence or imprudence.

An important tort is negligence. While it is described in Chapter 11 in relation to products liability it applies also to the negligent provision of services. It is therefore relevant in considering the application of SARPS to Private law rights and duties in domestic law.

Contractual rights can only arise out of an intended relationship. Rights in tort or delict arise independently of a contract.

The same circumstances can give the right to claim for breach of contract and in tort. Whether the injured party is entitled to exercise both rights of action against the same wrongdoer depends on the applicable domestic law. Important differences can exist between the two different causes of action, for example the applicable limitation period (Chapter 14).

Some relationships do not fall easily into the definitions of contract and tort but nevertheless are supported by law. For example Article 1371 of the French Civil Code provides "Quasi-contracts are purely voluntary acts of man from which there results, no matter what, engagement towards another, and some-times, a reciprocal engagement of both parties".

Defences in the English law of tort include contributory negligence and voluntary assumption of risk.

In the USA common law principles of contract and tort are based on state law only; federal courts are obliged to apply the law of the state in which the relevant federal court sits. An exception to this is "federal common law" which has developed under treaties such as the Warsaw Convention 1929.

VICARIOUS LIABILITY

This is the common law name for the legal rule that a person will be liable for the tort of another person even though he has neither authorised nor ratified that tort.

Vicarious liability arises through the wrongful acts or omissions of employ-ees. While there appears to be vicarious liability in respect of acts or omissions of independent contractors, such liability in fact may arise in English law in respect of non-delegable duties of the principal.

BREACH OF STATUTORY DUTY

Domestic law may impose a public law duty on a person or institution. For example, an international airport operator must provide a properly equipped and trained fire service. (See Annex 14 and Conditions of Aerodrome Licence (Public Use) UK CAP 168 Licensing of Aerodromes.) If failure to carry out the duty injures an individual, the following questions arise:

(1) Can that individual sue the party on whom the public duty was imposed?
(2) If so, is the liability strict, or must negligence or breach of some other duty of care be proved?
(3) If the failure is a crime, does that give the injured party a private right to claim damages?

It may be that breach of statutory duty merely constitutes evidence of a commission of some other private wrong, for example the tort of negligence; alternatively the breach may give the injured party the right to claim damages for breach of statutory duty as a separate wrong.

Answers to these questions are determined by domestic law. In order to establish a separate cause of action, the essential elements are:

- Duty must be owed to the plaintiff. The duty imposes a liability to a private law action by the plaintiff.
- Injury must be of the type which the Act is designed to prevent.

- The defendant must be guilty of a breach of his statutory obligation: "The measure of the defendant's obligation in every case must be found in the Act itself and no single standard of conduct exists."
- Breach of duty must have caused the damage.

CONFLICT OF LAWS

Conflict of laws which is also called private international law is that branch of the domestic law concerned with cases having a foreign element:

(i) Contract

For example, in a case where there is a foreign element the question may arise whether a contract has been formed. *Dicey* states, "The formation of a contract is governed by that law which would be the proper law of the contract if the contract was validly concluded". The "proper law" is the particular domestic law. This rule then requires the court to make a decision as to which is the proper law of the contract.

The court must analyse the facts, apply its domestic law principles in deciding the law of which legal system governs the contract, and then decide whether under that law, a valid contract has been made.

Such a question can arise where there is a foreign element in the sale and delivery of equipment from a seller in one State to a buyer in another. Often the contract will specify the applicable law.

(ii) Tort

Conflict of laws can arise for example in litigation in State A involving a possible tort in State B arising out of an accident where nationals of State B were injured. In England, for example, the original rule was that where a tort was committed abroad, an action could only be brought in the English court if it was both actionable according to the law of the State where it was committed and was a tort according to English law. This "double actionability" rule has been abolished by the Private International Law (Miscellaneous Provisions) Act 1995 which still leaves the court having to decide whether there is a tort and what is the applicable law.

Examples of conflict of laws in aviation were considered in the first edition of *S&B on Air Law* (1945, page 10):

"A German travelling in an English aeroplane is killed in an accident in Belgium. The ticket under which he was travelling was bought in Poland for a journey from there to Scotland via Germany. His widow brings an action in the English courts against the owners of the aircraft, claiming damages for his death. Without the international law which now exists there might be a conflict between the different laws of Germany, Poland, Belgium, Scotland and England resulting in almost hopeless confusion."

For an example of interstate conflict of laws in the USA see *Poindexter* v. *USA* (9th Circuit, 5 November 1984), 18 AVI 18,353 1983–5, where the plaintiff widow of the co-pilot sued the USA under the Federal Tort Claims Act for allowing the pilot to fly after too little rest. The Ninth Circuit Court of Appeals held that Nevada state law would apply as Nevada was the site of the accident and not Arizona law. The co-pilot was resident in Arizona and worked for an Arizona corporation which supplied fire-fighting services to the government under contract. The Court of Appeals remanded the case to the trial court to determine Nevada law.

APPEALS

Most legal systems give the unsuccessful litigant the opportunity to appeal from the decision of the lower court. The higher the court of appeal, the more likely it is that only important questions of law will be the subject of appeal. For example, where a passenger argues that there is no limit of liability of the carrier pursuant to Article 25 of the Amended Warsaw Convention (see page 270) on the grounds that the carrier has acted recklessly and with the knowledge that damage would probably result in a particular case, the question of what happened in the accident is a question of fact while the question of whether the provisions of Article 25 are satisfied is a question of law.

CHAPTER 4

THE CHICAGO CONVENTION 1944

The Chicago Convention establishes the international basis of civil aviation. It consists of 96 Articles referred to in this chapter as "Articles". It exists in the English, French and Spanish languages.

At the time of writing 185 States are party to the Chicago Convention.

Among its provisions the Chicago Convention:

(1) Creates ICAO (Article 43).
(2) Recognises that every State has complete and exclusive sovereignty over the airspace above its own territory (Articles 1 and 2).
(3) Adopts the international standards and procedures in the Annexes to Chicago Convention (Article 37).
(4) Performs the functions imposed on it by the International Air Services Transit Agreement and the International Air Transport Agreement Chicago 7 December 1944 (Article 66).

The first three topics are dealt with below. The fourth falls outside the ambit of this book.

Article 3 provides that the Chicago Convention shall apply only to civil aircraft and not to State aircraft. Aircraft used in military, customs and police services shall be deemed to be State aircraft. No State aircraft shall fly over or land in another State without authorisation. States when issuing regulations for State aircraft will have due regard to safety of navigation of civil aircraft.

PART 1. ICAO

Article 43 provides that an organisation to be named the International Civil Aviation Organization is formed by the Chicago Convention. It is made up of an Assembly, a Council and such other bodies as may be necessary.

By an agreement which came into force on 13 May 1947 ICAO became a Specialised Agency of the United Nations Organisation.

ICAO has six working languages: Arabic, Chinese, English, French, Russian and Spanish.

Objectives

Article 44 provides that the aims and objectives of ICAO are to develop the principles and techniques of international air navigation and to foster the planning and development of international air transport so as to:

   (a) ensure the safe and orderly growth of international civil aviation throughout the world;

   (b) encourage the arts of aircraft design and operation for peaceful purposes;

   (c) encourage the development of airways, airports, and air navigation facilities for international civil aviation;

   (d) meet the needs of the peoples of the world for safe, regular, efficient and economical air transport;

   (e) prevent economic waste caused by unreasonable competition;

   (f) ensure that the rights of contracting States are fully respected and that every contracting State has a fair opportunity to operate international airlines;

   (g) avoid discrimination between Contracting States;

   (h) promote safety of flight in international air navigation;

   (i) promote generally the development of all aspects of international civil aeronautics.

Membership

Articles 91 to 95 deal with membership of the Convention and its amendment. Article 93bis provides for automatic cessation of membership in the circumstances specified.

Legal capacity

Article 47 provides that ICAO shall enjoy in the territory of each Contracting State such legal capacity as may be necessary for the performance of its functions. Full juridical personality shall be granted wherever compatible with the constitution and laws of the State concerned.

   Starke comments (page 549) "that this formula seems to leave States parties free to grant or withhold the privilege of legal personality if their municipal domestic law so permits, whereas the corresponding provisions in most other constitutions of international bodies binds State members fully to recognise such personality".

   Article 59 provides that the President of the Council, the Secretary General, and other personnel shall not seek or receive instructions in regard to the discharge of their responsibilities from any authority external to ICAO. Each Contracting State undertakes fully to respect the international character of the responsibilities of the personnel of ICAO and not to seek to influence any of its nationals in the discharge of their responsibilities.

Article 60 provides that

"each State undertakes, so far as possible under its constitutional procedure, to accord to the President of the Council, the Secretary General and other personnel of the Organization the immunities and privileges which are accorded to corresponding personnel of other public international organizations. If a general international agreement on the immunities and privileges of international civil servants is arrived at, immunities and privileges accorded to the President, the Secretary General, and other personnel of the organization (ICAO) shall be immunities and privileges accorded under that general international agreement."

In view of the functions of ICAO concerning operational standards, the question of immunity from suit is important.

In 1947 the UN General Assembly adopted a convention for the coordination of the privileges and immunities of the specialised agencies with those privileges and immunities already provided to the United Nations under the Convention on the Privileges and Immunities of the United Nations 1946.

For further consideration of this subject see *Starke*, page 210.

ICAO maintains close contact with regional agencies such as ECAC (see Chapter 6 below), Civil Aviation Council of Arab States, Latin American Civil Aviation Commission and Africa Aviation Commission.

PART 2. SOVEREIGNTY OVER AIRSPACE

Article 1 provides that Contracting States recognise that every State has complete and exclusive sovereignty over the airspace above its territory.

Article 2 states: "For the purposes of this Convention the territory of a State shall be deemed to be the land areas and territorial waters adjacent thereto under the sovereignty, suzerainty, protection or mandate of such State."

Articles 5 to 8 deal with non-scheduled air services, prohibition of scheduled air services without permission, sabotage and pilotless aircraft. Scheduled services are dealt with in the Transit and Air Transport Agreements referred to on page 22.

Article 68 provides that each Contracting State may, subject to the provisions of this Convention, designate the route to be followed within its territory by any international air service and the airports which any such service may use.

PART 3. INTERNATIONAL STANDARDS AND RECOMMENDED PRACTICES

Article 37 is headed "Adoption of International Standards and Procedures" and provides:

"Each Contracting State undertakes to collaborate in securing the highest practicable degree of uniformity in regulations, standards, procedures, and organization in relation to aircraft, personnel, airways and auxiliary services in all matters in which such uniformity will facilitate and improve air navigation.

To this end the International Civil Aviation Organization shall adopt and amend from time to time, as may be necessary, international standards and recommended practices and procedures dealing with:

(a) communications systems and air navigation aids, including ground marking;
(b) characteristics of airports and landing areas;
(c) rules of the air and air traffic control practices;
(d) licensing of operating and mechanical personnel;
(e) airworthiness of aircraft;
(f) registration and identification of aircraft;
(g) collection and exchange of meteorological information;
(h) log books;
(i) aeronautical maps and charts;
(j) customs and immigration procedures;
(k) aircraft in distress and investigation of accidents;

and other such matters concerned with the safety, regularity, and efficiency of air navigation as may from time to time appear appropriate."

The 11 items listed in Article 37 have now been extended to 18 and are considered in Chapter 5.

Article 38 provides that

"Any State which finds it impracticable to comply in all respects with any such international standard or procedure, or to bring its own regulations or practices into full accord with any international standard or procedure after amendment of the latter, or which deems it necessary to adopt regulations or practices differing in any particular respect from those established by an international standard, shall give immediate notification to ICAO of the differences between its own practice and that established by the international standard."

Article 38 continues that

"In the case of amendments to international standards, any State which does not make the appropriate amendments to its own regulations or practices shall give notice to the Council [of ICAO] within 60 days of the adoption of the amendment to the international standard, or indicate the action which it proposes to take. In any such case, the Council shall make immediate notification to all other States of the difference which exists between one or more features of an international standard and the corresponding national practice of that State."

Therefore while there is no absolute obligation on any Contracting State to comply with the international standards and procedures as such, nevertheless there is an absolute obligation to give notice to ICAO and a corresponding obligation on ICAO to notify this to other Contracting States. The requirement for notification expressly refers to international standards and does not include the recommended practices.

Buergenthal considers two express exceptions where there is an obligation imposed by specific Articles to comply: these are Rules of the Air for flights over the high seas (Article 12) (see comment (1), page 47) and journey log book requirements (Articles 29 and 34); see page 63 and also Comment (1) under Annex 1 on the application of Article 33 on page 40.

Each Annex draws attention to the requirements of Article 38 for notification.

Article 90 deals with the Adoption by the Council of any Annex and the coming into effect of an Annex or any amendment. The textual discrepancy between the wordings in Articles 38 and 90 was dealt with by the Council first in 1947 and as subsequently modified and adopted in Revised Form of Resolution of Adoption of an Annex, ICAO Council 18 Session doc. 7361 1953 (*Buergenthal* page 88 onwards).

Contracting States are invited to extend notification to differences between national regulations and national standards on the one hand, and recommended practices on the other, when the notification of any such difference is important for the safety of air navigation.

Each Contracting State should comply with Articles 37 and 38 by way of its constitution. In the UK section 60 of its Civil Aviation Act 1982 provides that the Crown may make an Order in Council (a type of delegated legislation) that will implement the Chicago Convention, any Annex relating to international standards or recommended practices, and any amendment of the Chicago Convention or of such Annex. This is an example of (a) the incorporation of an international obligation into domestic law and (b) of delegated legislation resulting in ANO. Other examples are given by *Buergenthal* which comments on the extent to which the SARPS (Standard Procedures and Recommended Practices) are directly applicable in a domestic court. It cites two older civil law cases:

(1) The Court of Appeals, Dakar, Senegal (then French West Africa) held that Annex 9 (Facilitation) was directly applicable law which individuals could invoke in French territorial courts (*Ministère Publique* v. *Schreiber* 11 RFDA 355, (1957)).

(2) The Belgian Supreme Court held in 1957 that without special implementing legislation the provisions of an Annex could not be relied on in Belgian courts (*Etat Belge* v. *Marquise de Croix de Maillie de la Tour Landry* (1958) *Pasicrisie Belge 1*, 88).

A useful analysis of the common law position is set out by the New Zealand Court of Appeal in *New Zealand Air Line Pilots Association Inc* v. *Attorney General* [1997] 3 NZLR 269 (see Chapter 13 below).

Details of the notification by States of non-compliance is given in the relevant Annexes and should be published in the Aeronautical Information Publication in accordance with the SARPS of Annex 15, see page 177.

In addition to the SARPS, ICAO promulgates PANS and SUPPS.

(i) (a) PANS are Procedures for Air Navigation Services. The ICAO Booklet *Memorandum on ICAO* states: "The PANS are developed by the Air Navigation Commission. Following consultation with all Contracting States, they are approved by the Council and recommended to Contracting States for worldwide application. The PANS comprise, for the most part, operating practices, as well as material considered too detailed for SARPS.

PANS often amplify the basic principles in the corresponding SARPS to assist in the application of those SARPS."

Paragraph 3 of the Foreword ("Status") to *PANS—OPS* (see page 76) states that PANS do not have the same status as SARPS. While SARPS are adopted by Council in pursuance of Article 37 and are subject to the full procedure of Article 90, PANS are approved by Council and are recommended to Contracting States for worldwide application.

Implementation of PANS is the responsibility of Contracting States; they are applied in operations only after, and insofar as States have enforced them.

(b) *Publication of differences*

Article 38 (Requirements to notify differences) does not apply. However see Annex 15 on the publication of differences

Promulgation of information as specified should be in accordance with the provisions of Annex 15.

(ii) SUPPS are Regional Supplementary Procedures. These establish operating procedures designed for application in specific air navigation regions.

Buergenthal comments that the Annexes, PANS and SUPPS make up an integrated air navigation code, supplemented by the Regional Air Navigation Plans.

These Plans are recommendations approved by the ICAO Council setting out the requirements for adequate air navigation facilities and services in the nine air navigation regions established by ICAO, formulated at Regional Air Navigation Meetings, and approved under Article 69.

The Chicago Convention does not mention PANS or SUPPS or enact them.

Compare Articles 37 and 38 with Article 28 which is headed "Air Navigation Facilities and Standard Systems" and reads as follows:

"Each Contracting State undertakes, so far as it may find it practicable, to:

(a) provide, in its territory, airports, radio services, meteorological services and other air navigation facilities to facilitate international air navigation, in accordance with the standards and practices recommended or established from time to time, pursuant to this Convention;

(b) adopt and put into operation the appropriate standard systems of communications procedure, codes, markings, signals, lighting and other operational practices and rules which may be recommended or established from time to time, pursuant to this Convention;

(c) collaborate in international measures to secure the publication of aeronautical maps and charts in accordance with standards which may be recommended or established from time to time, pursuant to this Convention."

Article 28 is restricted to air navigation facilities and standard systems which however cover much of the contents of the 18 Annexes. The Article imposes an obligation on each Contracting State to provide, adopt and collaborate "so far as it may find practicable". Articles 37 and 38 have a similar "let-out".

ICAO standards do not preclude the development of national standards which may be more stringent than those contained in the relevant Annex. In all phases of aircraft operations, minimum standards are the most acceptable compromise as they make commercial and general aviation viable without prejudicing safety (ICAO Booklet *The Convention on Civil Aviation Annexes 1–18*, page 11 on Annex 6).

Article 54 sets out the mandatory functions of the ICAO Council, which include the following:

"(e) establish an Air Navigation Commission, in accordance with the provisions of Chapter X;

  . . .

(i) request, collect examine and publish information relating to the advancement of air navigation and the operation of international air services, including information about the costs of operation and particulars of subsidies paid to airlines from public funds;

(j) report to Contracting States any infraction of this Convention, as well as any failure to carry out recommendations or determinations of the Council;

(k) report to the Assembly any infraction of this Convention where a Contracting State has failed to take appropriate action within a reasonable time after notice of the infraction;

(l) adopt, in accordance with the provisions of Chapter VI of this Convention, international standards and recommended practices; for convenience designate them as Annexes to this Convention; and notify all Contracting States of the action taken;

(m) consider recommendations of the Air Navigation Commission for amendment of the Annexes and take action in accordance with the provisions of Chapter XX;

(n) consider any matter relating to the Convention which any Contracting State refers to it."

Article 55 sets out the permissive functions of the Council, which include the creation of subordinate air transport commissions and the conduct of research into all aspects of air transport and navigation of international importance.

Article 57 states that the Air Navigation Commission shall:

"(a) consider and recommend to the Council for adoption, modifications of the Annexes;

(b) establish technical sub-committees on which any Contracting State may be represented;

(c) advise the Council concerning collection and communication to the contracting States of all information which it considers necessary and useful for the advancement of air navigation."

Article 69 provides that

"If the Council is of the opinion that the airports or other air navigation facilities, including radio and meteorological services, of a Contracting State are not reasonably adequate for the safe, regular, efficient and economical operation of international air services, present or contemplated, the Council shall consult with the State directly concerned and other States affected with a view to finding means by which the situation may be remedied, and may make recommendations for that purpose. No Contracting State shall be guilty of an infraction of this Convention if it fails to carry out these recommendations."

Article 70 provides that

"A Contracting State, in the circumstances arising under the provisions of Article 69, may conclude an arrangement with the Council for giving effect to such recommendations. The State may elect to bear all of the costs involved in any such arrangement. If a State does not so elect, the Council may agree, at the request of the State, to provide for all or a portion of the costs."

Article 71 provides that

"If a Contracting State so requests, the Council may agree to provide, man, maintain and administer any or all of the airports and other air navigation facilities, including radio and meteorological services, required in its territory for the safe, regular, efficient and economic operation of the international air services of the other Contracting States, and may specify just and reasonable charges for the use of the facilities provided."

With the exceptions referred to on page 24, it therefore appears that the only strict obligation imposed on a Member State with regard to compliance with operational standards is the duty to notify ICAO pursuant to Article 38 of non-compliance.

The "liberal" wording of these Articles which are of universal application should be compared with the strict regional legislation of the EU.

Concern over low standards of compliance with SARPS and failure to notify under Article 38 by certain States party to the Chicago Convention, or their airlines, led in recent years to the establishment by ICAO of a voluntary Safety Oversight Programme under which ICAO provided safety oversight assessment as requested by the State concerned. As a result of the assessment the State would undertake to provide an action plan. Direct assistance could be provided by ICAO on a cost recovery basis.

As a result of decisions taken at recent Assembly Meetings ICAO has introduced a universal safety oversight audit programme consisting of mandatory audits. It looks to Articles 54 and 38 as a legal basis of action, with some assistance from Article 55.

Professor Bin Cheng states in Volume 10 (1957) of *Current Legal Problems* that a State which fails to notify ICAO in accordance with Article 38 is in breach of the Convention, and "would be liable to another Contracting State if the latter, or one of its nationals, suffers damage as a result of a mistaken belief, induced by lack of notification, that the former Contracting State was complying with a given international standard".

In November 1997 ICAO signed a Memorandum of Understanding with European Civil Aviation Conference ("ECAC") on Coordination of Flight Safety (ICAO *Bulletin* article by Chairman Assad Kotaite, May 1998).

In this respect the following steps are also being taken in Europe and the USA:

(i) Europe

(a) ECAC has developed the Safety Assessment of Foreign Aircraft Programme (SAFA) based on the powers of search given under Article 16 of the Chicago Convention 1944. Data obtained from the search is passed on to other ECAC member States.

(b) EU: EU has drawn up a proposed Council Directive "Establishing a Safety Assessment of Third Countries Aircraft using Community Airports". The proposal covers inspection, information exchange (between EU members and commission) and measures to be taken. The proposal is pending.

(c) ECAC urges its member states in Recommendations ECAC/21–2 to include in their Bilateral Agreements an aviation safety clause as suggested in such Recommendations.

The UK for example can prohibit aircraft registered outside the UK from flying within the UK on the grounds specified in Articles 10 and 107 of the ANO.

There are currently provisions in the UK Air Service Agreements whereby the aeronautical authorities of each Contracting State may require the airline designated by the other Contracting State to satisfy such authorities that it is qualified to fulfil the conditions prescribed under the laws and regulations normally and reasonably applied by such authorities in conforming with the provisions of the Chicago Convention. There is no express requirement that this right can only be exercised at the time of the original designation.

(ii) USA

The FAA has developed a Safety Oversight Programme under which blacklisted operators can be banned from flying to the USA.

PART 4. DISPUTES

Under Article 84 the Council has compulsory jurisdiction for settlement of disputes between States. Such jurisdiction is subject to four conditions:

(1) There must be disagreement between the parties.

(2) The disagreement must relate to the interpretation or application of the Chicago Convention or its Annexes.

(3) Only a contracting State "concerned in the disagreement" can refer the case to the Council for adjudication.

(4) The disagreement cannot be settled by negotiation.

Where one party State is in material breach of a treaty, the other party or parties may terminate the treaty either against the party in breach or as between all parties. However, in "Appeal Relating to the jurisdiction of ICAO Council", the International Court of Justice held that "a dispute between India and Pakistan as to termination or suspension of the Chicago Convention between them for an alleged material breach was a disagreement relating to the interpretation on application of the Convention vesting the ICAO Council with jurisdiction to entertain the dispute".

PART 5. APPEALS

Article 86 provides that:

    (1) unless the Council decides otherwise, its decision on whether an airline is acting in conformity with the Convention shall remain in effect unless reversed;

    (2) any Council decision on other matters shall be suspended until the appeal is decided. Appeal decisions shall be final and binding.

Article 87 provides that each State shall not permit an airline to operate through its airspace if the airline does not conform to any final decision given under Article 86.

Article 88 provides that the voting right of any State in default of the provisions of Articles 84 to 88 shall be suspended.

The Council also has dispute jurisdiction under the Transit and Transport Agreements, referred to on page 21 and under certain other international treaties or agreements such as the Rome Convention on Damage Caused by Foreign Aircraft on the Surface 1952, see Article 15(7), and under certain bilateral State aeronautical agreements.

CHAPTER 5

THE ICAO ANNEXES

FORM OF ANNEX

The Foreword of each Annex explains the nature of the information provided and its status. For example, the Foreword of Annex 13 on Aircraft Accident and Incident Investigation contains the following:

1. Historical background to the Annex, that is, when the SARPS were drawn up, adopted by ICAO, and amended.

2. Applicability.

3. Relationship between Annex 13 and Article 26.

4. *Action by Contracting States*
   This draws the attention of Contracting States to the obligation to notify of differences imposed by Article 38 (above page 24).

   Contracting States are invited to extend such notification to any difference from the Recommended Practices, and any amendments thereto, when the notification of such differences is important for the safety of air navigation. Contracting States are invited to keep ICAO currently informed of any differences which may subsequently occur, of withdrawal of any differences previously notified. Request for notification of differences will be sent to Contracting States immediately after the adoption of each amendment to the Annex.

   Attention is drawn to Annex 15 which provides for the publication of differences between States' regulations and practices and SARPS through the Aeronautical Information Service in addition to action under Article 38.

   Attention is drawn to ICAO Council Resolution of 13 April 1948 on the desirability of using in national regulations the precise language of the ICAO Standards of regulatory character, and also of indicating departures from Standards, including additional regulations important for safety or regularity of air navigation.

   This makes clear the importance of definitions; see Appendix 1 to this book.

5. *Status of Annex components*

An Annex is made up of the following component parts, not all of which, however, are necessarily found in every Annex; they have the status indicated:

(1) Material comprising the Annex proper:

(a) *Standards* and *Recommended Practices* adopted by the Council under the provisions of the Convention. They are defined as follows:

Standard: Any specification for physical characteristics, configuration, material, performance, personnel or procedure, the uniform application of which is recognised as necessary for the safety or regularity of international air navigation and to which Contracting States will conform in accordance with the Convention; in the event of impossibility of compliance, notification to the Council is compulsory under Article 38.

Recommended Practice: Any specification for physical characteristics, configuration, material, performance, personnel or procedure, the uniform application of which is recognised as desirable in the interest of safety, regularity or efficiency of international air navigation, and to which Contracting States will endeavour to conform in accordance with the Convention.

(b) *Appendices* comprising material grouped separately for convenience but forming part of the Standards and Recommended Practices adopted by the Council.

(c) *Provisions* governing the applicability of the Standards and Recommended Practices.

(d) *Definitions* of terms used in the Standards and Recommended Practices which are not self-explanatory in that they do not have accepted dictionary meanings. A definition does not have independent status but is an essential part of each Standard and Recommended Practice in which the term is used, since a change in the meaning of the term would affect the specification.

(e) *Tables* and *Figures* which add to or illustrate a Standard or Recommended Practice and which are referred to therein, form part of the associated Standard or Recommended Practice and have the same status.

Author's Note: (e) is not found in current Annex 13 but in other Annexes.

(2) Material approved by the Council for publication in association with the Standards and Recommended Practices (SARPS):

(a) *Forewords* comprising historical and explanatory material based on the action of the Council and including an explanation of the obligations of States with regard to the application of the Standards and Recommended Practices ensuing from the Convention and the Resolution of Adoption;

(b) *Introductions* comprising explanatory material introduced at the beginning of parts, chapters or sections of the Annex to assist in the understanding of the application of the text;

(c) *Notes* included in the text, where appropriate, to give factual information or references bearing on the Standards or Recommended Practices in question, but not constituting part of the Standards or Recommended Practices;

(d) *Attachments* comprising material supplementary to the Standards and Recommended Practices, or included as a guide to their application.

6. *Selection of language*

This lists the languages in which the Annex has been adopted. Each Contracting State is requested to select one of the texts for national implementation through direct use of or translation into its national language.

7. *Editorial practices*

These include the printing of Standards in light face Roman and Recommended Practices in light face italics. Recommended Practices are indicated by the prefix "Recommendation". Notes are printed in light face italics preceded by prefix Note.

Annex 13 has at its end a summary headed "ICAO Technical Publications". These are described as:

(1) International Standards and Recommended Practices (SARPS);
(2) Procedures for Air Navigation Services (PANS);
(3) Regional Supplementary Procedures (SUPPS);
(4) Technical Manuals;
(5) Air Navigation Plans;
(6) ICAO Circulars.

The ICAO Publications Catalogue lists the various publications ancillary to the Annexes.

In this chapter each Annex is dealt with below as follows:

- Title
- Relevant Articles in Chicago Convention
- Summary of the Contents of the Annex
- Author's comments

Each summary is selective. It is not comprehensive. Some provisions are omitted, dealt with briefly, summarised, or paraphrased. The summary is intended as a pointer both to the contents of each Annex and as to what should be included in the corresponding domestic law.

The phrase "as specified" in the summaries and elsewhere in this book signifies that there are specifications, material and lists which are of significance but which are not summarised in this book.

Where Recommended Practices are referred to in the summaries, they are, as in the Annexes, printed in italics.

Any reader who is interested in or who wishes to use any information in an Annex is strongly advised to refer to the text of the relevant Annex and any related material.

ICAO is continuously updating the Annexes and ancillary documents.

While each Annex nearly always refers to parties to the Chicago Convention as "Contracting States", this chapter, for brevity's sake, refers to "States" only. There are, however, a few references in the texts of the Annexes to "States" as opposed to "Contracting States", for example in Annex 13. While the omission should be kept in mind, it does not generally alter the sense of the Annexes.

While the Chicago Convention is an international treaty imposing operational duties on a Contracting State by way of SARPS, these SARPS should become part of the State's domestic law and in many cases constitute private law obligations. For example, disregard in certain circumstances of the provisions of Annex 6 by a carrier may give rise to unlimited liability under Article 25 of the Warsaw Convention (see page 306).

The Definitions, some of which are given in each Annex, are important.

The Comments section illustrates the fact that the SARPS applied in domestic law raise legal and operational questions in everyday civil aviation life.

ANNEX 1.   PERSONNEL LICENSING—8TH EDITION (JULY 1988)

(i) Articles

Article 32—Licences of personnel

(a) The pilot of every aircraft and the other members of the operating crew of every aircraft engaged in international navigation shall be provided with certificates of competency and licences issued or rendered valid by the State in which the aircraft is registered.

(b) Each Contracting State reserves the right to refuse to recognise, for the purposes of flight above its own territory, certificates of competency and licences granted to any of its nationals by another Contracting State.

Article 33—Recognition of certificates and licences

Certificates of Airworthiness and certificates of competency and licences issued or rendered valid by the Contracting State in which the aircraft is registered, shall be recognised as valid by the other Contracting States, provided that the requirements under which such certificates or licences were issued or rendered valid are equal to or above the minimum standards which may be established from time to time pursuant to the Convention.

Article 39—Endorsement of certificates or licences

(b) Any person holding a licence who does not satisfy in full the conditions laid down in the international standard relating to the class of licence or certificate which he holds shall have endorsed on or attached to his licence a complete enumeration of the particulars in which he does not satisfy such conditions.

Article 40—Validity of endorsed certificates or licences

No aircraft or personnel having certificates or licences so endorsed shall participate in international navigation, except with the permission of the State or States whose territory is entered. The registration or use of any such aircraft, or of any certified aircraft part, in any State other than that in which it was originally certified shall be at the discretion of the State into which the aircraft or part is imported.

Article 42—Recognition of existing standards of competency of personnel

The provisions of this chapter shall not apply to personnel whose licences are originally issued prior to a date one year after initial adoption of an international standard of qualification for such personnel; but they shall in any case apply to all personnel whose licences remain valid five years after the date of adoption of such standard.

(ii) Summary

Chapter 1—Definitions and general rules concerning licences

Definitions include:

"Aeroplane" and *"Aircraft"*: See Glossary page lxiii.
Aircraft Avionics: A term designating any electronic device—including its electrical part—for use in an aircraft including radio, automatic flight control and instrument systems.
Flight crew member: A licensed crew member charged with duties essential to the operation of an aircraft during flight time.

Other definitions include "Flight Time", "to certify as airworthy" and "to sign a maintenance release".

1.2: Note 1 draws attention to Resolution A23–13 and refers to the situation where the State of Registry may be unable to fulfil its obligations where aircraft are leased, chartered or interchanged—in particular without crew—by operator of another State. In such a case the Resolution applies until Article 83bis enters into force and the State of Registry may delegate in certain circumstances certain of its functions to the State of Operator. The text of the Resolution is given in Appendix 2. For further consideration of this question, see Comments on Annex 7.

Note 2: SARPS are established for licensing the following personnel:

  (a) Flight crew
    — private pilot—aeroplane;
    — commercial pilot—aeroplane;
    — airline transport pilot—aeroplane;
    — private pilot—helicopter;
    — commercial pilot—helicopter;
    — airline transport pilot—helicopter;
    — glider pilot;
    — free balloon pilot;
    — flight navigator;
    — flight engineer.
  (b) Other personnel
    — Aircraft maintenance (technician/engineer/mechanic);
    — Air traffic controller;
    — Flight operations officer;
    — Aeronautical station operator.

1.2.1: A person shall not act as a flight crew member in an aircraft unless a valid licence is held showing compliance with the specifications of the Annex and appropriate to the duties to be performed by that person. The licence shall have been issued by the State of Registry of that aircraft, or by any other State and rendered valid by such State of Registry.

1.2.2 sets out the methods of rendering a licence valid by one State of a licence issued by another State.

1.2.3: A State shall not permit the holder of a licence to exercise privileges other than those granted by that licence.

1.2.4: Medical fitness. This sets out the various procedures regulating the issue by the Licensing Authority to the licence holder with an appropriate Medical Assessment.

Note 1 states that guidance material is published in the Manual of Civil Aviation Medicine (doc. 8984).

Note 2 deals with the medical requirements which are specified as three classes of Medical Assessment.

Medical Assessment is defined as the evidence issued by a State that the licence holder meets specific requirements of medical fitness. It is issued following the appropriate examination of the licence applicant.

Flight crew members or air traffic controllers shall not exercise the privileges of their licence unless they hold a current Medical Assessment.

1.2.5: Validity of licences.

1.2.5.1: A State having issued a licence shall ensure that its privileges or those of related ratings are not exercised unless the holder maintains competency and meets the requirements for recent experience established by that State.

Note the reference to proficiency flight checks for commercial air transport crew completed in accordance with Annex 6, the keeping of records and use of synthetic flight trainers.

1.2.5.2 states the intervals at the end of which a report of medical fitness shall be submitted in respect of the licences concerned.

1.2.5.2.2 Intervals when licence holders are over 40.

1.2.6: Decrease in medical fitness.

1.2.6.1: Holders shall not exercise the privileges of their licences and related ratings when they are aware of the decrease in their medical fitness which might render them unable to safely exercise these privileges.

1.2.6.1.1 Each State should, as far as is practicable, ensure the licence holders do not exercise the privileges of their licences and related ratings during any period in which their medical fitness has, from any cause, decreased to an extent that would have prevented the issue or renewal of their Medical Assessment.

1.2.7: Use of psychoactive substances.

1.2.7.1–1.2.7.2: Holders of licences shall not:

    (a) exercise the privileges of their licences and ratings while under the influence of any psychoactive substance which might render them unable to safely and properly exercise these privileges;

    (b) engage in any problematic use of substances.

See also 1.2.7.3 *Recommendations* and guidance notes.

"Psychoactive substances" are defined as alcohol, opioids, cannabinoids, sedatives and hypnotics, cocaine, other psychostimulants, hallucinogens, and volatile solvents, whereas coffee and tobacco are excluded.

"Problematic use of substances" is defined as the use of one or more psychoactive substances by aviation personnel in a way that:

    (a) constitutes a direct hazard to the user or endangers lives, health or welfare of others; and/or

    (b) causes or worsens an occupational, social, mental or physical problem or disorder.

1.2.8: Approved training shall provide a level of competence at least equal to that provided by the minimum experience requirements for personnel not receiving such training. See Note.

Chapter 2—Licences and Ratings for Pilots

2.1: General rules.

2.1.1.1: A person shall not act as pilot-in-command or co-pilot of an aeroplane, helicopter, glider or free balloon unless he holds a licence issued in accordance with the provisions of this chapter in the categories—aeroplane, helicopter, glider, free balloon.

2.1.1.2 requires the aircraft category to be stated on the licence as specified.

2.1.1.3 requires the applicant to meet the necessary requirements and to demonstrate the required knowledge and skill as specified.

2.1.2 deals with Category ratings.

2.1.3–2.1.5: These provisions establish aircraft class and type ratings, e.g. multi-engine, land, the circumstances in which they are required, and their requirements.

2.1.6 deals with the use of synthetic flight trainers for demonstrations of skill. These trainers comprise a flight simulator, a flight procedures trainer and a basic instrument trainer. (See Definitions.)

2.1.7 sets out the circumstances in which an instrument rating is required, i.e. where the holder acts as a pilot-in-command or co-pilot of an aircraft under IFR.

2.1.8 deals with circumstances in which authorisation to conduct flight instruction is required. It specifies the proper authorisation.

2.1.9 deals with the crediting of pilots' flight times.

2.1.10: 60th birthday. States shall not permit holders of pilot's licences to act as a pilot-in-command of aircraft engaged in scheduled international air services or non-scheduled international air transport operations for remuneration or hire on attaining their 60th birthday.

2.2: Student pilot.

2.2.1: Must meet prescribed requirements.

2.2.2: May only fly solo under supervision or as authorised, and on international flights by arrangement between States.

2.2.3: Must hold specified Medical Assessment.

2.3, 2.4, and **2.5** specify the requirements and privileges for the Private Pilot's Licence—Aeroplane, Commercial Pilot's Licence—Aeroplane, and Airline Transport Pilot's Licence—Aeroplane, respectively. These requirements include: required age, knowledge, experience, instruction, skill and medical fitness.

2.6 sets out the requirements and privileges for Instrument Rating —Aeroplane.

2.7–2.10 deal with the corresponding requirements and privileges for helicopter pilots.

2.11 deals with requirements and privileges for Flight Instructor rating appropriate to aeroplanes and helicopters.

2.12 and **2.13** deal with glider and free balloon pilots' licences.

See the references throughout to ICAO Training Manual (doc. 7192).

Chapter 3—Licences for other flight crew members

This chapter deals with the requirements for licences for flight crew members other than licences for pilots, namely Flight Navigator, Flight Engineer and Flight Radiotelephone Operator.

For the Radiotelephone Operator, see reference in Note 1 to International Telecommunication Convention.

Chapter 4—Licences and ratings for personnel other than flight crew

This chapter deals with the requirements for licences and ratings for personnel other than flight crew members.

4.1 sets out general rules on requirements.

4.2 deals with aircraft maintenance (technician/engineer/mechanic) and the relevant requirements and privileges where an approved maintenance organisation (Defined) authorises non-licensed personnel to exercise such privileges. Such personnel shall meet the specified requirements.

See also:

(a) Chapter 19 of this book;

(b) reference to ICAO Training Manual (doc. 7192).

4.3: Air traffic controller licence.

4.3.1 sets out the licence requirements of age, knowledge, experience and fitness, which include demonstration by the applicant of a level of knowledge appropriate in respect of the language or languages nationally designated for use in air traffic control and the ability to speak such language or languages without accent or impediment which would adversely affect radio communication.

4.4.1 sets out air traffic controller ratings which cover:

(a) aerodrome control;

(b) approach control;

(c) approach radar control;

(d) approach precision radar control;

(e) area control;

(f) area radar control.

Note: The World Meteorological Organisation has specified requirements for personnel making meteorological observations which apply to air traffic controllers providing such a service.

4.4.2 sets out requirements for air traffic controller ratings.

4.5 deals with flight operations officer/flight dispatcher licence.

4.6 deals with the aeronautical station operator licence. Note reference to ICAO Circular 211 Aerodrome Flight Information Service (AFIS).

Chapter 5—Specifications for personnel licences

This chapter deals with the specifications for contents and make-up of personnel licences, such as detail, material, colour and language.

Chapter 6—Medical provisions for licensing

This chapter sets out SARPS to be applied in carrying out medical assessments covering physical, mental, visual and hearing requirements for the Classes 1, 2 and 3 medical assessments. See references to the Manual of Civil Aviation Medicine (doc. 8984).

The Attachment to Annex 1 sets out in four column format the SARPS for the various pilots' licences and instrument ratings for easy comparison.

(iii) Comments

(1) *Buergenthal* comments that the effect of Article 33 is to enforce compliance with the relevant SARPS by any State wishing to engage in international air navigation. Unfortunately, in some cases, sub-standard performance or assessment may become evident too late.

(2) Flight crew training in the UK is described in Chapter 18.

(3) The following US cases are examples of domestic law:

(a) *Tur* v. *FAA*, US Court of Appeals, 9th Circuit No. 92–70094 September 1993; 24 AVI 17,685 1992–5. FAA revoked a pilot's licence where he flew his helicopter within 100 feet of a fire and interfered with fire-fighters. On a previous occasion he had operated his helicopter in formation with a rescue flight helicopter, causing the latter to bypass his landing site.

(b) Medical certification is carried out by FAA. While the US courts give limited redress in certain cases to dissatisfied applicant crew, the most important remedy is review by the National Transportation Safety Board of the FAA decision. See however *Delta Airlines* v. *US*, 490 F Supp 907 (ND Ga, 1980) 16 AVI 17,278 1980–2 where the airline obtained an order against the US ordering it not to: (i) issue medical certificates to airmen who possessed absolute disqualifying conditions; (ii) place any limitations on the medical certificate of an airman that describes the flight functions he may perform, for example, "not valid for pilot-in-command duties"; and (iii) exempt airmen from disqualifying provisions without the proper finding that such exemption is in the public interest.

(c) In *Berman* v. *USA*, No. 080–1479 A F Supp (ND Ga, 4 January 1985) the court held that USA could be liable for negligence for the acts or omissions of a designated medical examiner and a pilot examiner in the area of operational decisions and could not escape liability on the grounds of discretionary decision. See comments on *Swanson* case, (page 78), *Varig* case (page 97), and *West* case (page 173).

(4) For application of licensing procedures in UK under ANO, see *Pike* v. *CAA* ((1978) *Air Law*). An appeal to the county court (court of minor jurisdiction) is available only where the CAA decides a person is not a fit person to hold a licence, and not against a decision of the CAA that the person is not qualified, by reason of a deficiency in knowledge, experience, competence, skill, physical or mental fitness.

(5) For developments on licensing procedures in Europe, see for example JAR-FCL 1 Aeroplane, which came into effect on 1 July 1999.

ANNEX 2.   RULES OF THE AIR—9TH EDITION (JULY 1990)

(i) Articles

Article 3bis

Interception of civil aircraft

(a) The Contracting States recognise that every State must refrain from resorting to the use of weapons against civil aircraft in flight and that, in case of interception, the lives of persons on board and the safety of aircraft must not be endangered. This provision shall not be interpreted as modifying in any way the rights and obligations of States set forth in the Charter of the United Nations.

(b) The Contracting States recognise that every State, in the exercise of its sovereignty, is entitled to require the landing at some designated airport of a civil aircraft flying above its territory without authority or if there are reasonable grounds to conclude that it is being used for any purpose inconsistent with the aims of this Convention; it may also give such aircraft any other instructions to put an end to such violations. For this purpose, the Contracting States may resort to any appropriate means consistent with relevant rules on international law, including the relevant provisions of this Convention, specifically paragraph (a) of this Article. Each Contracting State agrees to publish its regulations in force regarding the interception of civil aircraft.

(c) Every civil aircraft shall comply with an order given in conformity with paragraph (b) of this Article. To this end each Contracting State shall establish all necessary provisions in its national laws or regulations to make such compliance mandatory for any civil aircraft registered in that State or operated by an operator who has his principal place of business or permanent residence in that State. Each Contracting State shall make any violation of such applicable laws or regulations punishable by severe penalties and shall submit the case to its competent authorities in accordance with its laws or regulations.

(d) Each Contracting State shall take appropriate measures to prohibit the deliberate use of any civil aircraft registered in that State or operated by an operator who has his principal place of business or permanent residence in that State for any purpose inconsistent with the aims of this Convention. This provision shall not affect paragraph (a) or derogate from paragraphs (b) and (c) of this Article.

Article 9—Prohibited areas

(This deals with prohibited areas and the restriction or prohibition of flying. It is not set out here.)

Article 12—Rules of the Air

Each Contracting State undertakes to adopt measures to insure that every aircraft flying over or manoeuvring within its territory and that every aircraft carrying its nationality mark, wherever such aircraft may be, shall comply with the rules and regulations relating to the flight and manoeuvre of aircraft there in force. Each Contracting State undertakes to keep its own regulations in these respects uniform, to the greatest possible extent, with those established from time to time under this Convention. Over the high seas, the rules in force shall be those established under this Convention. Each State undertakes to insure the prosecution of all persons violating the regulations applicable.

(ii) Summary

The Foreword provides that:

(a) the Standards in Annex 2, together with the SARPS of Annex 11 (ATS) govern the application of the "Procedures for Air Navigation Services—Rules of the Air and Air Traffic Services", and the "Regional Supplementary Procedures—Rules of the Air and Air Traffic Services" in which latter document will be found subsidiary procedures of regional application; and

(b) the Annex constitutes the Rules relating to the flight and manoeuvre of aircraft within the meaning of Article 12. Therefore over the high seas these rules apply without exception.

Chapter 1—Definitions

Definitions include:

Altitude: The vertical distance of a level, a point or an object considered as a point, measured from mean sea level (MSL).

Flight level: A surface of constant atmospheric pressure which is related to a specific pressure datum, 1013.2 hectopascals (hPa) and is separated from other such surfaces by specific pressure intervals.

(Note 1: A pressure type altimeter calibrated in accordance with the Standard Atmosphere:
(a) when set to a QNH altimeter setting, will indicate altitude;
(b) when set to a QFE altimeter setting, will indicate height above the QFE reference datum;
(c) when set to a pressure of 1013.2 hectopascals (hPa) may be used to indicate flight levels.
Note 2: The terms "height" and "altitude" used in Note 1 above, indicate altimetric rather than geometric heights and altitudes.)

Instrument meteorological conditions (IMC): Meteorological conditions expressed in terms of visibility, distance from cloud, and ceiling, less than the minima specified for visual meteorological conditions.
Visual meteorological conditions (VMC): Meteorological conditions expressed in terms of visibility, distance from cloud, and ceiling equal to or better than specified minima.

(Note: the specified minima are contained in Chapter 4 of this Annex.)

Chapter 2—Applicability of the Rules of the Air ("rules")

2.1: Territorial application of the rules of the air.
2.1.1: The rules apply to aircraft bearing Nationality and Registration Marks of a Contracting State, wherever they may be, and to the extent they do not conflict with the rules published by the State having jurisdiction over the territory overflown. The Note provides that the rules apply over the high seas without exception.

2.1.2: This deals with the position with regard to the provision of ATS over the high seas in the case of an applicable Regional Air Navigation Agreement. Such agreement refers to an agreement approved by ICAO Council normally on the advice of a Regional Air Navigation Meeting.

("High seas" in international law means all parts of the sea not included in the territorial sea and internal waters of any State (Convention on the Territorial Sea and the Contiguous Zone, Geneva 1958).

2.2: Compliance. Operation of the aircraft either in flight or on the movement area of an aerodrome shall comply with the General Rules, and in addition when in flight either with VFR or IFR.
2.3: Responsibility for compliance.
2.3.1: The pilot-in-command is responsible for the operation of the aircraft in accordance with the rules. He may depart from the rules in circumstances such as to render such departure absolutely necessary in the interests of safety.

2.3.2: The pilot-in-command shall become familiar with all available information appropriate to the intended operation as specified.

2.4: The pilot-in-command has final authority for the disposition of the aircraft while in command.

2.5: No person whose function is critical to the safety of aviation (safety sensitive personnel) shall undertake that function while under the influence of any psychoactive substance, by reason of which human performance is impaired. No such person shall engage in any kind of problematic use of substances.

Chapter 3—General Rules

The main headings are listed below:

3.1: Protection of persons and property
3.1.1: An aircraft shall not be operated in a negligent or reckless manner so as to endanger life or property of others.

3.1.2: Except where necessary for landing or take-off, aircraft shall not be flown over congested areas of cities etc. or over an open-air assembly of persons unless at such a height as in an emergency will permit landing to be made without undue hazard to persons or property on the surface.
3.1.3 specifies terms of cruising levels.

Note reference to Procedures for Air Navigation Services—Aircraft Operations (doc. 8168) (page 68 below).

3.1.4–3.1.10 deal with dropping and spraying, towing, parachute descents, acrobatic flights (Defined), formation flights, unmanned free balloons, and prohibited and restricted areas.

3.2: Avoidance of collisions.
See Note: it is important that vigilance for the purpose of detecting potential collisions be not relaxed on board an aircraft in flight, regardless of the type of flight or the class of airspace in which the aircraft is operating, and while operating on the movement area of an aerodrome.

3.2.1 Proximity: aircraft shall not be operated in such proximity to other aircraft as to create a collision hazard.

3.2.2 sets out the rules of the right-of-way in flight, landing and surface movement of aircraft. The initial paragraph states that the aircraft that has the right of way shall maintain its heading and speed, but nothing in these rules shall relieve the pilot-in-command from the responsibility of taking such action, including collision avoidance manoeuvres based on resolution advisories provided by Anti Collision Avoidance System (ACAS) equipment, as will best avoid collision.

Notes 1 and 2 refer to ACAS operating procedures in PANS—OPS (doc. 8168) and to Annex 8. The rules then follow in this paragraph.

3.2.3: Lights to be displayed by aircraft. The Notes refer to:

- Annexes 6 and 8 (see below);
- The meaning of "operating";
- Aircraft on water;
- Airworthiness Technical Manual (doc. 9051). (See page 96).

The SARPS then follow.

3.2.4: Simulated instrument flights. Note the requirements for dual control and qualified safety pilot.

3.2.5: For operations on and in the vicinity of aerodromes;

(a) observe traffic to avoid collisions,
(b) conform with or avoid pattern of traffic,
(c) make all turns to the left on approach to landing or take-off unless otherwise instructed,
(d) carry out landing and take-off into the wind unless safety or runway configuration or air traffic conditions determine different direction is preferable.

3.2.6 Water operations. This deals with the rules for avoiding collisions and also specifications for lights. See reference to International Regulations for Preventing Collisions at Sea.

3.3: Flight plans.
These are Defined as "Specified information provided to ATS units relative to an intended flight or portion of a flight of an aircraft".

3.3.1: Submission of flight plan.

3.3.1.1: Information relative to a flight, to be provided to ATS units, shall be in the form of a flight plan.

3.3.1.2: A flight plan shall be submitted prior to operating:

(a) any flight where ATS is to be provided;
(b) IFR flight within advisory airspace;
(c) any flight within or into designated areas or routes as required by ATS authority to facilitate provision of flight information, alerting and SAR services;
(d) any flight within or into designated areas or routes as required by ATS authority to facilitate co-ordination with military units or ATS units of adjacent States;
(e) any flight across international borders.

3.3.1.3–3.3.1.4 deal with submission of flight plan before flight to the specified agency and with prior notice as specified.

3.3.2: Contents of flight plan.

3.3.3: Completion of flight plan.

3.3.4: Changes to flight plan.

3.3.5: Closing a flight plan. Note the reference to Arrival Report.

3.4 refers to the signals given in Appendix 1, their observation, receiving and meaning.

3.5: Time is Coordinated Universal Time (UTC). See the requirements for obtaining a time check.

3.6: Air traffic control services. The SARPS are set out under the subsequent headings.

3.6.1: ATC clearance, re-clearance, obtaining priority clearance, and taxiing at a controlled airport.

3.6.2: Adherence to flight plan.

3.6.3: Position Reports; see reference to SSR Mode C transmission and PANS—RAC, Part II (doc. 4444).

3.6.4: Termination of control.

3.6.5: Communications. This applies to controlled flights and deals with maintenance of listening watch, establishment of two-way communication and procedures on communication failure.

3.7 Unlawful interference. ATS unit to be notified if possible. See reference to Annex 11, PANS—RAC (doc. 4444), PANS—OPS (doc. 8168), Attachment B to this Annex, and *Manual of ATS Data Link Applications* (doc. 9694).

3.8: Interception.

3.8.1: Interception of civil aircraft shall be governed by the appropriate regulations and administrative directives issued by States in compliance with the Chicago Convention and in particular Article 3(d) under which States undertake, when issuing regulations for their State aircraft, to have due regard for the safety of navigation of civil aircraft. See Appendices to this Annex.

3.8.2 deals with response of intercepted pilot-in-command. In this context interception does not include intercept and escort services provided on request to an aircraft in distress in accordance with the *Search and Rescue Manual* (doc. 3333).

Chapter 4—Visual Flight Rules (VFR)

This chapter sets out the conditions which make up VFR flight and when and how VFR flights are flown.

Special VFR flights are defined in Definitions.

Chapter 5—Instrument Flight Rules (IFR)

5.1 sets out the rules applicable to all IFR flights dealing with equipment, minimum levels and change from IFR to VFR flight.

5.2 sets out the rules applicable to IFR flights within controlled airspace.

5.3 sets out the rules applicable to IFR flights outside controlled airspace.

"Controlled airspace" is defined as an airspace of defined dimensions within which ATC service is provided in accordance with the airspace classification.

Appendices

Appendix 1 sets out the following signals:

(1) Distress and emergency signals;
(2) Signals for use in the event of interception;
(3) Visual signals used to warn an unauthorised aircraft flying in or about to enter a restricted, prohibited or danger area;
(4) Signals for aerodrome traffic;
(5) Marshalling signals.

Appendix 2 deals with the interception of civil aircraft.
Appendix 3 sets out tables of cruising levels.
Appendix 4 deals with unmanned free balloons.

Attachments

Attachment A deals in greater detail with interception of civil aircraft.
Attachment B deals with unlawful interference.

(iii) Comments

(1) The effect of Article 12 is that the ICAO Rules of the Air are mandatory for flights over the high seas and any discretion given by Article 37 does not apply. For a full consideration see *Buergenthal* page 80 onwards.

(2) Article 3bis was enacted into the Convention following the shootdown of Korean Airlines 007 in 1983.

(3) In *Re Korean Airlines disaster of 1 September 1983* (District Court, District of Columbia, 1985) 19 AVI 17,758 1985–6, the court briefly considered Annex 2 and its Appendix 2 dealing with interception. This case was an unsuccessful attempt by the plaintiffs to claim against Boeing and Litton on the grounds of defective inertial navigation systems. The court held that the missile attack was unforeseeable by the designers and manufacturers and was also an intervening and independent cause relieving them of legal responsibility.

(4) *Steering Committee et al* v. *USA and Aeromexico* (US Court of Appeals, 9th Circuit, 1993) 24 AVI 17,707 1992–5 discusses the duty of care of crew in a mid-air collision between a commercial jet and a single-engined aircraft. The crew of the jet acted as a reasonably prudent crew in attempting to see and avoid the other aircraft and in the circumstances did not act negligently by failing to see the other aircraft until it was too late to see such aircraft.

(5) For practical advice on interception procedures see CAA General Aviation Safety Sense Leaflet 11: Interception of Civil Aircraft.

ANNEX 3.   METEOROLOGICAL SERVICE FOR INTERNATIONAL AIR NAVIGATION—12TH EDITION (JULY 1995)

(i) Articles

Articles 28, 69, 70, 71

See Chapter 4 above.

(ii) Summary

The Foreword points out that:

(1) The SARPS govern the application of the Regional Supplementary Procedures (doc. 7030, Part 3—Meteorology) which contains regional choices where permitted.

(2) In accordance with a similar provision in Annex 6 Part II, the responsibility which devolves on an operator in accordance with Annex 3, falls on the pilot-in-command in the case of international general aviation.

(3) Regulatory material in Annex 3 is, except for a few differences, identical with that found in the Technical Regulations (Chapter 3.C.1) of the World Meteorological Organisation. See reference to aeronautical meteorological code forms.

Chapter 1—Definitions

These include *World Area Forecast System (WAFS)* (see page 49 below).

Chapter 2—General provisions

The following are covered in the Introductory notes:

(1) The provisions of the Annex with respect to meteorological information are subject to the understanding that the obligation of a State is for the supply, under Article 28, of such information and that the responsibility for its use is that of the user.

(2) The allocation of responsibilities in the situation envisaged in Resolution A23–13.

(3) International operations effected jointly with aeroplanes not all of which are registered in the same State.

2.1.1: The objective of meteorological services for international air navigation shall be to contribute towards the safety, regularity and efficiency of international air navigation.

2.1.2: This objective is achieved by the supply to operators, flight crew, ATS units, SAR units, airport management and others concerned with the conduct or development of international air navigation of the meteorological information necessary for the performance of their respective functions.

2.1.3: Each State shall determine the meteorological services it will provide to meet the needs of international air navigation.

2.1.4: An appropriate authority shall be designated as the meteorological authority.

2.2 deals with the supply and use of meteorological information which shall be up to date and in forms which require a minimum of interpretation.

2.3.1: An operator requiring meteorological services or changes in the service shall notify the meteorological authority/office(s) sufficiently in advance.

2.3.2: See instances when notification is required, e.g. planning of new routes.

2.3.3: Aerodrome or other meteorological office shall be notified of the specified flight details.

2.3.4: Information to be provided by operator for individual and scheduled flights.

Chapter 3—WAFS and meteorological offices

WAFS is defined as "A world-wide system by which world and regional area forecast centres provide aeronautical meteorological en-route forecasts in uniform standardised formats".

3.1: WAFS objectives are to supply the forecasts and information as specified to:

- meteorological offices for direct operational use;
- meteorological authorities and other users.

The objectives shall be achieved through a comprehensive worldwide uniform system in a cost, effective manner.

3.2.1: A State, having accepted responsibility for providing a WAF Centre (WAFC) within the system shall make the designated arrangements for the Centre to provide, issue and amend the forecasts as specified.

3.2.2–3.2.14 are all Recommendations dealing with WAFCs' activities except 3.2.8 which specifies as standard procedures that WAFCs shall adopt uniform forms and codes for supply of forecasts and amendments.

3.3 lists the functions of and defines a Regional Area Forecast Centre (RAFC), where a State which has accepted, by regional air navigation agreement, the responsibility for providing an RAFC. These functions include the collection of data from WAFC and preparation of charts.

3.4: Meteorological offices.

3.4.1: Each State shall establish one or more aerodrome and/or other meteorological offices which shall be adequate for the provision of the meteorological service required to satisfy operational needs.

3.4.2 lists the functions to be carried out by an aerodrome meteorological office, which include preparing and obtaining forecasts and other relevant information, and briefing flight operations personnel.

3.4.3–3.4.4 and 3.4.6: Recommendations.

3.4.5: The extent to which an aerodrome meteorological office prepares forecasts and uses products from WAFCs and RAFCs and other sources shall be determined by the meteorological authority concerned.

3.4.7: For aerodromes without meteorological offices the meteorological authority shall designate the meteorological office who will supply the meteorological information as required.

3.5: Meteorological watch offices.

States responsible for providing ATS shall establish meteorological watch offices to watch over meteorological conditions and supply SIGMET and AIRMET and other specified information.

AIRMET information is Defined as "Information issued by a meteorological watch office concerning the occurrence or expected occurrence of specified en-route weather phenomena which may affect the safety of low-level aircraft operations and which was not already included in the forecast issued for low-level flights in the flight information region concerned or sub-area thereof".

SIGMET information is Defined as "Information issued by a meteorological watch office concerning the occurrence or expected occurrence of specified en-route weather phenomena which may affect the safety of aircraft operations".

Chapter 4—Meteorological observations and reports

4.1.1: Each State shall establish at aerodromes and other points of significance to international air navigation in its territory, such aeronautical meteorological stations as it determines necessary. An aeronautical meteorological station may be a separate station or combined with a synoptic station.

4.1.2: Recommendation dealing with meteorological stations for helicopter operations.

The rest of the chapter sets out the SARPS for the making of observations and provision of reports. The section headings are:

4.1.3: Routine observations at meteorological stations and aerodromes and supplementary special observations also at aerodromes.

4.1.4–4.1.10 are all Recommendations.

4.1.11: The observations form the basis of preparation and dissemination of reports.

4.1.12: The specific values in any report shall be understood by the recipient to be the best approximation to the actual conditions at the time of observation.

4.2–4.12 deal with routine and special observations and reports, observations and reports for take-off and landing, surface wind, visibility, runway visual range, present weather, cloud, air temperature and dew-point temperature, pressure values and supplementary information.

4.13: Contents of reports.

4.14: Format of reports.

4.15: Observing and reporting of volcanic activity.

These are followed by examples of reports.

Chapter 5—Aircraft observations and reports

5.1: Each State shall arrange for observations and recording and reporting to be made by aircraft of its registry operating on international air routes.

5.2: Such observations are (a) routine and (b) special or otherwise non-routine in the circumstances and manner specified.

5.3: Observations shall be reported by air-ground data link, and, where not available, by voice communications, during flight or as soon as practicable thereafter.

5.4–5.8 specify form, content and other aspects of the observations, including **5.7** which deals with exchange of air reports.

Chapter 6—Forecasts

6.1.1: Specific value of any elements given in a forecast shall be understood by the recipient to be the most probable value the element is likely to assume during the period of the forecast. A similar principle applies to time.

6.1.2: The issue of a new forecast by a meteorological office, such as a routine aerodrome forecast, shall be understood to cancel automatically any forecast of the same type in the same place and period of validity or part thereof.

The chapter then deals with specific forecasts for:

6.2: Aerodrome.

6.3: Landing.

6.4: Take-off.

6.5: Area and route, other than forecasts issued by regional area forecast centres.

6.6: sets out the SARPS for area forecasts for low-level flights to support issuance of AIRMET information.

Chapter 7—SIGMET and AIRMET information, aerodrome warnings and wind shear warnings

7.1: SIGMET information—general provisions

7.1.1: SIGMET information shall be issued with the information and in the form specified for flight:

    (a) at subsonic cruising levels;

    (b) at transonic and supersonic cruising levels.

The relevant phenomena and codes for the two levels are listed, for example:

- Thunderstorm—Squall Line   —   SQL TS
- Hail   —   GR

7.1.2–7.1.3 deal with the content and cancellation of SIGMET.

7.2 gives the format and exchange of SIGMET messages with an example.

7.3: AIRMET information.

7.3.1: AIRMET information shall be issued in accordance with a regional air navigation agreement as specified. The information shall be indicated as specified for example:

- mountain wave—moderate—MOD MTN

7.3.2 and **7.3.3** deal with content and cancellation.

7.4 gives the form and exchange of AIRMET messages with an example.

7.5: Aerodrome warnings. This section concerns meteorological conditions which could adversely affect aircraft on the ground including aerodrome facilities and services.

7.6: Wind shear warnings. This specifies how and when warnings should be given.

    Notes 1:   Wind shear conditions are normally associated with the phenomena as listed.

          2:   Refers to ICAO Wind Shear Circular (186).

          3:   Information to be included in routine, special and selected special reports.

Chapter 8—Aeronautical climatological information

Note: This deals with cases where it is impracticable to meet requirements on a national basis.

8.1.1: Aeronautical climatological information required for planning of flight operations shall be prepared in the form of aerodrome climatological tables and summaries. Such information shall be supplied to aeronautical users as agreed between the meteorological authority and those users.

The chapter deals with aerodrome climatological tables and summaries, and the provision of meteorological observational data.

Chapter 9—Service for operators and flight crew members

9.1: General Provisions

9.1.1: Meteorological information shall be supplied to operators and flight crew members for:

    (a) pre-flight planning by operators;
    (b) use by flight crew before departure;
    (c) aircraft in flight.

9.1.2: Information supplied shall cover the flight for the time, altitude and geographical extent required.

9.1.3 deals with content of the information.

9.1.4 covers forecasts for aerodromes of departure, intended landing and alternatives.

9.1.5–9.1.7 Recommendations.

9.1.8 deals with coordination between States.

9.1.9 specifies the five methods of supply of information:

    (a) written/printed material;
    (b) grid point data in digital form;
    (c) briefing;
    (d) consultation;
    (e) display.

9.1.10: The meteorological authority shall determine type and format of information and method of its supply in consultation with the operator.

9.1.11 deals further with supply of information.

9.2: Information for pre-flight planning by operators.

9.2.1 specifies information to be included in the pre-flight planning:

    (a) wind, temperature and tropopause height;
    (b) significant en route weather phenomena and jetstream information;
    (c) take-off forecast;
    (d) aerodrome reports and flight forecasts.

9.2.2: Reports for supersonic aircraft.
9.2.3: Reports for helicopter operators.
9.2.4: Supply in chart form of upper-air information.

9.3: Briefing, Consultation and Display.

9.3.1–9.3.6 set out the SARPS for briefing and/or consultation and provision, on request, of supply of latest information as specified.

9.3.7 deals with briefing arrangements.

9.3.8: To assist in flight preparation and briefing, the Meteorological Office shall display the latest:

(a) routine and selected special reports;
(b) aerodrome and landing forecasts;
(c) local aerodrome warnings;
(d) take-off forecasts;
(e) SIGMET/AIRMET information and special reports;
(f) current and prognostic charts;
(g) satellite photographs, mosaics, and/or nephanalyses;
(h) ground-based weather radar information.

9.4: Flight documentation—general.
9.4.1–9.4.12: Recommendations on form and content.
9.4.13: The meteorological authority shall retain a copy of the flight documentation supplied to flight crew for at least 30 days from the date of issue. This information shall be made available for inquiries or investigation and shall be retained until completion of the same.

9.5: Flight Documentation—upper wind and upper-air temperature information. This gives SARPS for supply of information in chart or tabular form.

9.6: Flight documentation—significant weather charts.
9.6.1 lists what shall be shown on such charts, as appropriate to the flight, for example:

(a) thunderstorms;
(k) tropopause heights;
(l) jetstreams.

See also Notes and *Recommendations.*

9.7: Flight documentation—aerodrome forecasts.
9.7.1: The documentation shall include forecasts for aerodromes of departure, intended landing and one or more alternates.

Forecasts received from other meteorological offices shall be included without change in substance.

9.8: *deals with flight documentation—supplementary charts and other forms of presentation.*

9.9: Information for use by aircraft in flight.
9.9.1–9.9.2: This information shall be supplied by a meteorological office to its associated ATS unit in accordance with Chapter 10 and through VOLMET broadcasts. Information for planning by operators shall be supplied on request, as agreed.

VOLMET broadcast is defined as "routine broadcast of meteorological information for aircraft in flight".

Chapter 10—Information for ATS, SAR and AIS

This chapter deals with information for ATS, search and rescue services and aeronautical information services.

10.1: Information for ATS units.

10.1.1: The meteorological authority shall designate a meteorological office to be associated with each ATS unit. Such office shall supply up-to-date meteorological information to the unit as necessary for the conduct of its functions.

10.1.3: The associated meteorological office for a flight information centre or an area control centre shall be a meteorological watch office.

10.1.5, 10.1.6 and **10.1.7** list the meteorological information to be supplied as necessary to:

- an aerodrome control tower;
- an approach control office;
- flight information centre or area control centre.

10.1.8: Information received on pre-eruption volcanic activity and/or a volcanic eruption shall be supplied as necessary to an ATS unit as agreed between the meteorological and ATS authorities.

10.1.9: Any meteorological information requested by an ATS unit in connection with an aircraft emergency shall be supplied as rapidly as possible.

10.1.11: Where necessary for flight information purposes, current reports and forecasts shall be supplied to designated aeronautical telecommunication stations and copied if required to flight information or area control centre.

10.1.10, 10.1.12 and **10.1.13** are Recommendations.

10.2: Information for search and rescue services units.

10.2.1: Designated meteorological offices shall supply search and rescue service units with information as required. A designated office shall maintain liaison with SAR units throughout a SAR operation.

10.2.2 lists the information to be supplied to a rescue coordination centre concerning the conditions existing at last known position and intended route of missing aircraft.

10.2.3 Recommendations on provision to meteorological office of flight documentation supplied to missing aircraft.

10.3: Information for aeronautical information service units.

This deals with the supply of information as specified to such units being:

(a) information on meteorological service for international air navigation intended for inclusion in the AIPs concerned;

(b) information necessary for the preparation of NOTAM;

(c) information necessary for the preparation of aeronautical information circulars.

Chapter 11—Requirement for and use of communications

This sets out the SARPS under which States shall supply suitable telecommunications facilities to permit the meteorological services to perform their obligations for the supply of the required information to the various agencies, for example ATS, SAR units and to meteorological offices, authorities and other users.

The section headings are:

11.1: Requirements for communications.
11.2: Use of aeronautical fixed service communications—meteorological bulletins in alphanumeric format.
11.3: Use of aeronautical fixed service communications—world area forecast system products.
11.4: Use of aeronautical mobile service communications.
11.5: Use of aeronautical broadcast service—contents of VOLMET broadcasts.

Appendix

This sets out flight documentation, model charts and forms (see 9.4–9.8 of the Annex).

Attachments

Attachment A: Guidance on Area Forecasts in Abbreviated Plain Language.
Attachment B: Operationally Desirable and Currently Attainable Accuracy of Measurement and Observation.
Attachment C: Selected Criteria Applicable to Aerodrome Forecasts.
Attachment D: Conversion of Transmissometer Readings into Runway Visual Range.
Attachment E: Operationally desirable Accuracy of Forecasts.
Attachment F: SIGMET and AIRMET.

(iii) Comments

(1) The Annex is headed "Meteorological Service for *International* Air Navigation", suggesting the SARPS do not apply to non-international navigation. It would however be unacceptable for one standard to be applied to international navigation and another to domestic.

(2) In the domestic law case *Webb et al* v. *USA* (US District Court, 1994, CD Utah; 24 AVI 17,957 1992–5), the pilot was 60 per cent at fault for a

crash for failing to obtain complete weather information and in attempting special VFR approach under adverse conditions. The air traffic controllers' failure to warn of possibility of white out and of reported reduced visibility was negligent and a proximate cause of the accident; accordingly FAA employees were 40 per cent to blame. See also Comments for Annex 11. This case is an example of operational mistakes where the FAA can be legally liable.

(3) Commercial aircraft were severely damaged by a hailstorm on approach to Munich Airport on 12 July 1984. The airlines claimed damages from the German government because of the failure of the German Meteorological Service to warn. The German Supreme Court held there was no public liability because the Service has only duties to the public but not to third parties (Bundesgerichtshof 16 February 1995, 1996 ZLW 85; *Air Law* Vol XXI (Number 4/5/1996)).

ANNEX 4. AERONAUTICAL CHARTS—9TH EDITION (JULY 1995)

(i) Articles

Article 28—Air navigation facilities and standard systems

See Chapter 4 above.

(ii) Summary

Chapter 1—Definitions, applicability and availability

"*Aeronautical Chart*" is defined as "A representation of a portion of the earth, its culture and relief, specifically designated to meet the requirements of air navigation".

1.2: Applicability. The specifications in the Annex apply on and after 9 November 1995.

1.3: Availability.

1.3.1: Information. Information on territories, as specified, shall be provided on request between States.

1.3.2: States shall when so specified, ensure availability of charts in whichever way is appropriate for a particular chart or single sheet of a chart series.

1.3.2.1: The State having jurisdiction over the relevant territory to which the chart exclusively relates shall either:

(1) produce the chart itself, or
(2) arrange for its production by another State or agency;
(3) provide another State accepting an obligation to produce the chart with the necessary data.

1.3.2.2: This requires States to determine how the charts shall be made available in the case of territory of two States being included on the same chart.

Regard shall be given to Regional Air Navigation Agreements and any allocation established by the ICAO Council.

1.3.3: States shall take all reasonable measures to ensure that the information and charts they provide are adequate and accurate and that they are
adequately maintained up to date.

*1.3.4: Recommendations on States making available to other States appropriate
charts free of charge.*

See Note on guidance material in Aeronautical Chart Manual (doc.
8697).

Chapter 2—General specifications

2.1: Operational requirements for charts. The initial note states that the total
flight is divided up into six phases:

    (1) taxi from aircraft stand to take-off point;
    (2) take-off and climb to en-route ATS route structure;
    (3) en-route ATS route structure;
    (4) descent to approach;
    (5) approach to land and missed approach;
    (6) landing and taxi to aircraft stand.

The requirements include the following:

2.1.1: Each type of chart shall provide information relevant to its
function.

2.1.2: Each type of chart shall provide information appropriate to the phase
of flight, to ensure the safe and expeditious operation of aircraft.

2.1.3: The presentation of information shall be accurate, free from distor-
tion and clutter, unambiguous and be readable under all normal operating
conditions.

2.1.4: Colours, tints and type size shall permit easy reading and
interpretation.

2.1.5: Information shall be in adequate form.

2.1.6: Presentation of information on each type of chart shall permit
smooth transition from chart to chart as appropriate.

2.2–2.18: The headings only are set out below.

2.2: Titles.

2.3: Miscellaneous information.

2.4: Symbols.

2.5: Units of measurement.

2.6: Scale and projection.

2.7: Date of validity of aeronautical information.

2.8: Spelling of geographical names.

2.9: Abbreviations (see reference to Procedures for Air Navigation
Services—ICAO Abbreviations and Codes (doc. 8400)).

2.10: Political boundaries.

2.11: Colours.

2.12: Relief.

2.13: Prohibited, restricted and danger areas (see reference to doc. 7910 Location Indicators).

2.14: ATS airspaces.

2.15: Magnetic variation.

2.16: Typography (see reference to Aeronautical Chart Manual, doc. 8697).

2.17: Aeronautical data.

2.18: World Geodetic System—1984 (WGS–84).

Chapters 3–19—Specific charts

These chapters deal with the following specific charts (see the first paragraph in each chapter headed "Function"):

Chapter 3: Aerodrome Obstacle Chart—ICAO type A (Operating Limitations).

       4: Aerodrome Obstacle Chart—ICAO Type B.

       5: Aerodrome Obstacle Chart—ICAO Type C.

       6: Precision Approach Terrain Chart—ICAO.

       7: En-route Chart—ICAO.

       8: Area Chart—ICAO.

       9: Standard Departure Chart—Instrument (SID)—ICAO.

     10: Standard Arrival Chart—Instrument (STAR)—ICAO.

     11: Instrument Approach Chart—ICAO.

     12: Visual Approach Chart—ICAO.

     13: Aerodrome/Heliport Chart—ICAO.

     14: Aerodrome Ground Movement Chart—ICAO.

     15: Aircraft Parking/Docking Chart—ICAO.

     16: World Aeronautical Chart—ICAO 1:1 000 000.

     17: Aeronautical Chart—ICAO 1:500 000.

     18: Aeronautical Navigation Chart—ICAO Small Scale.

     19: Plotting Chart—ICAO.

Appendices

The Appendices are as follows:

(1) Marginal note layout.

(2) ICAO chart symbols.

(3) Colour guide.

(4) Hypsometric tint guide.

(5) Sheet layout for the world aeronautical chart ICAO 1:1 000 000.

(iii) Comments

(1) In the US case of *Brocklesby* v. *USA and Jeppesen & Company* (US Court of Appeals, 9th Circuit, 1985; 19 AVI 17,215 1985–6), the plaintiffs claimed damages for wrongful death and property damage arising from an aircraft accident in Alaska.

The US Court of Appeals 9th Circuit affirmed the court of first instance and held:

(i) The chart was a defective product for which Jeppesen was strictly liable although the defective data was supplied by the FAA (USA);

(ii) Jeppesen was liable in negligence for failing to detect a defect in the product it marketed;

(iii) Public policy defences were not available to Jeppesen because it converted government procedure from text into graphic form and represented that the chart contained all necessary information.

Prior to the hearing at first instance the USA had settled with the plaintiffs and had been dismissed from the suit.

(2) See Annex 6, Part I:

(i) 4.2.6: concerning inaccuracies in charts;

(ii) 5.3.2: operator shall take account of charting accuracy in assessing compliance with 5.2.8 (take-off).

ANNEX 5.   UNITS OF MEASUREMENT TO BE USED IN AIR AND GROUND OPERATIONS—4TH EDITION (JULY 1979)

(i) Articles

Article 28—Air navigation facilities and standard systems

See Chapter 4 above.

(ii) Summary

Chapter 1—Definitions

This chapter sets out Definitions of units of measurement, e.g. Nautical Mile, Pascal (used in Chapter 17 of this book on Materials and Structures) and Radian.

Chapter 2—Applicability

The introductory note states that the Annex contains specifications for the use of a standardised system of units of measurement in international civil aviation air and ground operations. The standardised system is based on the International System of Units (SI) and certain non-SI units considered necessary to meet the specialised requirements of international civil aviation. Attachment A gives details concerning the development of the SI.

2.1: The Standards shall be applicable to all aspects of international civil aviation air and ground operations.

Chapter 3—Standard application of units of measurement

3.1.1: The International System of Units developed and maintained by the General Conference of Weights and Measures (CGPM) shall, subject to the provisions of 3.2 and 3.3, be used as the standard system of units of measurement for all aspects of international civil aviation air and ground operations.
    3.1.2 deals with prefixes and symbols.
3.2 deals with non-SI units and sets out those for permanent use in Table 3.2 and for temporary use in Table 3.3.
3.3: Application of specific units.
The application of units of measurement for certain quantities used in international civil aviation air and ground operations shall be in accordance with Table 3.4.
    Table 3.4 sets out the standard application of specific units of measurement listing the primary unit symbol and the non-SI alternative to unit (symbol), if any, for example:

	Primary	*Non-SI alternative*
1.1 altitude	m	ft

Chapter 4—Termination of use of non-SI units

This chapter deals with the termination of use of non-SI alternative units: the knot, nautical mile, and foot. The termination date has not yet been established.

Attachments

Attachment A sets out the development of the SI. The system evolved from units of length and mass created by members of the Paris Academy of Sciences and adopted by the French National Assembly in 1795.
    The International Metric Convention in 1875 established the CGPM and The International Bureau of Weights and Measurements (BIPM). BIPM ensures worldwide unification of physical measurements and operates under the supervision of the International Committee of Weights and Measures (CIPM) which itself comes under the authority of CGPM.
    The International Standards Organisation is the worldwide federation of national standards institutes which, although not part of the BIPM, provides recommendations for the use of SI and certain other units. ICAO liaises with ISO concerning the standardised application of SI units in aviation.

Attachment B sets out guidance on the application of the SI.

Attachment C sets out unit conversion factors.

Attachment D deals with Coordinated Universal Time (UTC) which has replaced Greenwich Mean Time (GMT) as the accepted international standard for clock time.

Attachment D states that the basis for all clock time is the time of apparent rotation of the sun. This is a variable quantity and a mean value of this time is known as Universal Time. A different time scale, based on the definition of the second, is known as the International Atomic Time (TAI). A combination of these two scales results in Coordinated Universal Time. This consists of TAI adjusted as necessary by the use of leap seconds to obtain a closer approximation (always within 0.5 seconds) of Universal Time.

Attachment E sets out presentation of date and time in all-numeric form, and examples of presentation.

(iii) Comments

It is essential that clarity is achieved and accuracy is applied in drawing up and interpreting technical documents. See for example Brunei Aircraft Accident Report DCA 200/1/82 where it was found that the maintenance personnel had wrongly interpreted the amount of allowable debris contaminating the main gearbox magnetic plug of a helicopter, due to the mistaken interpretation of an unfamiliar metric term. Following the accident CAA issued Airworthiness Notice 12 entitled "The Use and Interpretation of Unfamiliar Units".

ANNEX 6.   OPERATION OF AIRCRAFT

Part I   International Commercial Air Transport—Aeroplanes (7th edition, July 1998).

Part II   International General Aviation—Aeroplanes (6th edition, July 1998).

Part III   International Operations—Helicopters (4th edition, July 1998).

(i) Articles

Article 4—Misuse of civil aviation

Each Contracting State agrees not to use civil aviation for any purpose inconsistent with the aims of this Convention.

Article 28—Air navigation facilities and standard systems

See Chapter 4 above.

Article 29—Documents carried in aircraft

Every aircraft of a Contracting State, engaged in international navigation, shall carry the following documents in conformity with the conditions prescribed in this Convention:

(a) its certificate of registration;

(b) its certificate of airworthiness;

(c) the appropriate licences for each member of the crew;

(d) its journey log book;

(e) if it is equipped with radio apparatus, the aircraft radio station licence;

(f) if it carries passengers, a list of their names and places of embarkation and destination;

(g) if it carries cargo, a manifest and detailed declarations of the cargo.

Article 34—Journey log books

There shall be maintained in respect of every aircraft engaged in international navigation a journey log book in which shall be entered particulars of the aircraft, its crew and of each journey in such form as may be prescribed from time to time pursuant to this Convention.

Article 35—Cargo restrictions

(a) No munitions of war or implements of war may be carried in or above the territory of a State in aircraft engaged in international navigation, except by permission of such State. Each State shall determine by regulations what constitutes munitions of war or implements of war for the purpose of this Article, giving due consideration, for the purposes of uniformity, to such recommendations as the International Civil Aviation Organisation may from time to time make.

(b) Each Contracting State reserves the right, for reasons of public order and safety, to regulate or prohibit the carriage in or above its territory of articles other than those enumerated in paragraph (a) provided that no distinction is made in this respect between its national aircraft engaged in international navigation and the aircraft of the other States so engaged; and provided further that no restriction shall be imposed which may interfere with the carriage and use of aircraft of apparatus necessary for the operation or navigation of the aircraft or the safety of the personnel or passengers.

Article 36—Photographic apparatus

Each Contracting State may prohibit or regulate the use of photographic apparatus in aircraft over its territory.

(ii) Summary

Author's Note: The ICAO booklet on the Annexes states on page 10 that the purpose of Annex 6 is to contribute to the safety of international air navigation by providing criteria for safe operating practices, and to contribute to the efficiency and regularity of international air navigation by encouraging Contracting States to facilitate the passage over their territories of commercial aircraft belonging to other countries that operate in conformity with these criteria.

PART I (7th edition, July 1998)

The significance of Annex 6, Part I is demonstrated by the list of publications given in the Annex (page vii).

See also the list of abbreviations and symbols (page vi).

Chapter 1—Definitions

Definitions include:

> *Air Operators Certificate (AOC)*: "a certificate authorising an operator to carry out specified commercial air transport operations".
> *Commercial air transport operation*: "an aircraft operation involving the transport of passengers, cargo or mail for remuneration or hire".
> *Crew member*: "a person assigned by an operator to duty on an aircraft during flight time".
> *Flight crew member*: see page 35.
> *General Aviation Operation*: "an aircraft operation other than a commercial air transport operation or an aerial work operation".
> *Operator*: "a person, organisation or enterprise engaged in or offering to engage in an aircraft operation".
> *Operational Control*: "The exercise of authority over the initiation, continuation, diversion or termination of a flight in the interests of the safety of the aircraft and the regularity and efficiency of the flight".

Chapter 2—Applicability

The SARPS shall apply to the operations of aeroplanes by operators authorised to conduct international commercial air transport operations.

Chapter 3—General

Notes 1: Refers to Resolution A23–13 and Article 83bis (see page 81).
2: Deals with joint international operations where not all the aeroplanes are registered in the same Contracting State.

3.1: Operator shall ensure that all employees when abroad know they must comply with the laws, regulations and procedures of those States in which operations are conducted.

3.2: An operator shall ensure that flight crew are familiar with the laws, regulations and procedures pertinent to the performance of their duties prescribed for the areas to be traversed, and aerodromes and air navigation facilities to be used.

3.3: An operator or a designated representative shall have responsibility for operational control.

3.4: If an emergency situation which endangers the safety of an aeroplane or persons necessitates the taking of action which involves a violation of local regulations or procedures, the pilot-in-command shall notify the appropriate local authority without delay. If required by the State in which the incident occurs, the pilot-in-command shall submit a report on any such violation to the appropriate authority of such State; in that event, the pilot-in-command shall also submit a copy of it to the State of the Operator. Such reports shall be submitted as soon as possible and normally within ten days.

3.5: The pilot-in-command shall have on board all essential search and rescue information for areas overflown.

3.6: An operator shall establish and maintain an accident prevention and flight safety programme. Guidance on accident prevention is given in the Accident Prevention Manual (doc. 9422) and Manual for Preparation of an Operations Manual (doc. 9376).

3.7: Dangerous goods; see Annex 18 and Article 35.

3.8: Use of psychoactive substances; see Annex 2, 2.5.

Chapter 4—Flight operations

4.1: Operating facilities.

4.1.1: The operator shall ensure by every reasonable means of ascertainment that the ground/water facilities available and required for safe operation of the flight are adequate. The Note provides that "reasonable means" is intended to denote the use, at the point of departure, of information which is available to the operator either through official information published by the aeronautical information services or is readily obtainable from other sources.

4.1.2: Inadequacy of facilities to be reported by operator.

4.1.3: Subject to the published conditions of use, aerodromes shall be kept continuously available for operations during published hours of operations, irrespective of weather considerations.

4.2: Operational certification and supervision.

4.2.1.1: The operator shall not engage in commercial air transport operations without a valid AOC or equivalent document issued by State of Operator.

4.2.1.2: The AOC or equivalent document shall authorise the operator to conduct commercial air transport operations in accordance with such conditions and limitations as may be specified.

4.2.1.3: The issue of the AOC shall be dependent on the operator demonstrating an adequate organisation, method of control and supervision of flight operations, training programmes and maintenance arrangements consistent with the nature and extent of the operations specified.

4.2.1.4: Continued validity of an AOC shall depend on the operator maintaining requirements of 4.2.1.3 under supervision of State of Operator.

4.2.1.5: Minimum contents of AOC:

(a) operator's identification;
(b) date of issue and period of validity;
(c) types of operation authorised;
(d) types of aircraft authorised;
(e) authorised areas of operation or routes.

4.2.2: Operations manual. An operator shall provide an Operations Manual (Defined) for use and guidance of operator's personnel and keep it up to date. State of Operator shall be provided with a copy. The manual shall contain the mandatory material required by the State of Operator.

4.2.3: Operating instructions—general.

4.2.3.1: All operations personnel must be properly instructed in their duties and responsibilities.

4.2.3.2: No aeroplane shall be taxied on the movement area without the person at the controls being authorised and competent as specified.

4.2.3.3: Recommendation on climb performance.

4.2.4: No in-flight simulation of emergency or abnormal situations shall be performed when passengers or cargo are being carried.

4.2.5: Checklists provided in accordance with 6.1.3 shall be used during and after operations, and in emergency, to ensure compliance with the operating procedures contained in the Aircraft Operating Manual and the Flight Manual or other documents associated with the Certificate of Airworthiness and otherwise in the Operations Manual. The design and utilisation of checklists shall observe human factors principles.

Note: Guidance material on the application of human factors principles can be found in the specified Circulars.

4.2.6: Establishment of minimum flight safety altitudes by operator. The six Recommendations on factors to be taken into account include possible inaccuracies in charts.

4.2.7: Establishment of aerodrome operating minima. See factors to be taken into account and reference to Manual of All-Weather Operations (doc. 9356).

4.2.8: Establishment of procedures relating to threshold (Definition) crossing height for precision approaches. (Definition.)

4.2.9: Fuel and oil records shall be maintained and retained for three months.

4.2.10: Crew.

4.2.10.1: Pilot-in-command shall be designated for each flight.

4.2.10.2–4.2.10.3: An Operator shall:

> (i) formulate rules to limit flight time and duty periods and for provision of rest periods; and
>
> (ii) maintain records.

(see also Attachment A). Such rules shall be in accordance with regulations of or approved by State of Operator and be included in the operations manual.

4.2.10.4: Records for cosmic radiation doses to be kept (see Circular 126 Guidance Material for SST Aircraft Operations).

4.2.11: Passengers.

4.2.11.1: Operator shall ensure passengers are made familiar with location and use of:

> (a) seat belts;
> (b) emergency exits;
> (c) life jackets;
> (d) & (e) oxygen and other equipment.

4.2.11.2–4.2.11.4 deal with emergencies, and also the use of seat belts and harnesses.

4.3.1–4.3.2: Flight preparation. A flight shall not be commenced until flight preparation forms have been completed certifying that the pilot-in-command is satisfied on the seven items as specified; forms to be kept for three months. Items include airworthiness, load distribution and maintenance release.

4.3.3: Operational flight plan must be completed in accordance with the operations manual.

4.3.4 deals with take-off, en route and destination alternate aerodromes.

4.3.5: Weather: specifies preconditions for VFR and IFR flights and flights in expected icing conditions.

4.3.6: Sufficient fuel and oil to be carried as specified.

4.3.7: Requirement for refuelling with passengers on board. Note reference to Airport Services Manual (doc. 9132).

4.3.8: Oxygen supply requirements.

4.4: In-flight procedures. This section deals with:

> (1) Aerodrome operating minima;
> (2) Meteorological observations;
> (3) Hazardous flight conditions;
> (4) Flight crew members at duty stations;
> (5) Use of oxygen;

(6) Loss of pressurisation: "safeguarding of cabin attendants and passengers";
(7) In-flight operational instructions;
(8) Instrument flight procedures;
(9) Aeroplane operating procedures for noise abatement.
(See reference to PANS—OPS (doc. 8168) (page 76)).

4.5: Duties of pilot-in-command. The pilot-in-command shall be responsible for:

(1) the operation and safety of the aeroplane and the safety of all persons on board during flight time;
(2) compliance with check lists in detail;
(3) notifying the appropriate authority by quickest means of any accident resulting in serious injury or death or substantial damage to the aeroplane or property;
(4) reporting known or suspected defects in the aeroplane to the operator on termination of flight;
(5) the journey log book or general declaration containing the information listed in 11.5.1. (See reference to Assembly Resolution A10–36, 1956.)

4.6 specifies the duties of flights operations officer/flight dispatcher.

4.7 specifies the additional requirements for extended range operations by aeroplanes with two turbine power-units.

4.8: Carry on baggage shall be adequately and securely stowed.

Chapter 5—Aeroplane performance operating limitations

5.1.1: Aeroplanes shall be operated in accordance with a comprehensive and detailed code established by State of Registry in compliance with the applicable standards.

5.1.2 sets out the operational limitations for single-engined aeroplanes.

5.2 sets out the Standards applicable to aeroplanes certificated in accordance with Part III of Annex 8. See requirements in 5.2.2 to 5.2.11, in particular:

5.2.3: Aeroplane shall be operated in compliance with the terms of its Certificate of Airworthiness and within approved operating limitations contained in its Flight Manual.

5.2.4: The State of Registry shall take such precautions as are reasonably possible to ensure that the general level of safety contemplated by these provisions is maintained under all expected operating conditions, including those not covered specifically by the provisions of this chapter.

5.2.5: A flight shall not be commenced unless the performance information in the Flight Manual indicates that the Standards of 5.2.6–5.2.11 can be complied with for the flight to be undertaken. These Standards deal with:

5.2.6: Factors affecting performance shall be taken into account. See list.

5.2.7: Mass limitations.

5.2.8: Take-off.

5.2.9–5.2.10: En route: one or two power-unit(s) inoperative.

5.2.11: Landing.

5.3.1: Obstacle data shall be provided for development of procedures for take-off to comply with 5.2.8.

5.3.2: Operator shall take account of charting accuracy in assessing compliance with 5.2.8.

Chapter 6—Aeroplane instruments, equipment and flight documents

6.1.1–6.1.2: In addition to the minimum equipment necessary for the issue of the Certificate of Airworthiness, specific documents, equipment and instruments shall be carried or installed as specified in this section and a minimum equipment list (MEL) shall be included in the Operations Manual. The MEL (Defined) enables the pilot-in-command to determine whether a flight can be undertaken.

6.1.3: The operator shall provide an aircraft operating manual to the operations staff and flight crew containing normal/abnormal operating procedures and details of systems and checklists.

6.2.1: All aeroplanes on all flights shall carry: instruments necessary to control the flight path, carry out required procedural manoeuvres and observe operating limitations of the aeroplane as specified.

6.2.2: An aeroplane shall be equipped with:

(a) medical supplies as specified;
(b) portable fire extinguishers;
(c) seats, seat belts and harnesses;
(d) method of ensuring certain information and instructions as specified are conveyed to passengers;
(e) spare necessary fuses.

6.2.3: Aeroplanes shall carry:

(a) Operations Manual;
(b) Flight Manual;
(c) necessary charts.

6.2.4 deals with marking of break-in points.

6.3: Flights recorders. Flight recorders comprise two systems, Flight Data Recorders and Cockpit Voice Recorders. The section deals with type, duration, construction and installation, operation, serviceability, and other requirements which depend on the take-off mass of the aircraft and the date of its individual Certificate of Airworthiness.

6.4–6.19 sets out the instruments, equipment and documents as respectively specified which shall be carried on aeroplanes for the following flights, operations and conditions.

6.4: VFR flights.

6.5: Flights over water.

6.6: Flights over designated land areas.

6.7: High altitude flights.

6.8: In icing conditions.

6.9: Operation in accordance with IFR.

6.10: Night operations.

6.11: Pressurised aeroplanes when carrying passengers—weather radar.

6.12: Operations above 15,000 metres (49,000 ft)—radiation indicator.

6.13: Aeroplanes complying with noise certification standards in Annex 16, Vol 1.

6.14: Mach number indicator to be carried by aeroplanes with speed limitations expressed in Mach number.

6.15: Aeroplanes required to be equipped with ground proximity warning systems (GPWS). This specifies which aircraft should be equipped with GPWS and what warnings should be provided.

6.15.4: GPWS shall provide automatically a timely and distinctive warning to the flight crew when the aeroplane is in potentially hazardous proximity with the earth's surface.

6.15.5: After 1 January 1999 GPWS shall provide listed minimum additional information.

6.16: Aeroplanes carrying passengers—cabin attendants' seats.

6.17: Emergency locator transmitter (ELT).

6.18: Aeroplanes required to be equipped with airborne collision avoidance systems (ACAS).

6.19: Aeroplanes required to be equipped with pressure altitude reporting transponders.

6.20: Requirement for flight crew to use boom or throat microphones below transition level/altitude.

6.21 sets out two Recommendations on equipment of specified turbo-jet aeroplanes with wind shear warning system.

Chapter 7—Aeroplane communication and navigation equipment

7.1.1 specifies the required communications equipment capable of: two-way communication for aerodrome control purposes; receiving meteorological information; conducting two-way communication at any time with at least one aeronautical station and with other stations and on frequencies as prescribed.

7.1.2: Such equipment shall provide for communications on emergency frequency 121.5 MHz.

7.2 specifies the required navigation equipment to enable the aeroplane to proceed in accordance with (a) flight plan; (b) RNP types; (c) requirements of ATS.

It also refers to

- Manual on Required Navigation and Performance (RNP) (doc. 9613).
- Regional Supplementary Procedures (doc. 7030).
- Manual on Implementation of a 300m (1,000 ft) Vertical Separation Minimum between FL 290 and FL 410 inclusive (doc. 9574) (FL—Flight Level).

7.3 deals with installation, and also failure of any single unit required for communications and/or navigation.

Chapter 8—Aeroplane maintenance

8.1: Operator's maintenance responsibilities.

8.1.1: Operators shall ensure that in accordance with specified procedures:

(a) each aeroplane is maintained in an airworthy condition;
(b) the necessary operational and emergency equipment is serviceable;
(c) the Certificate of Airworthiness for each aeroplane remains valid.

8.1.2: Operator shall not operate an aeroplane unless it is maintained and released to service by an organisation, approved as specified.

8.1.3 deals with licensing of person signing the maintenance release.

8.1.4: Operator shall employ person(s) to ensure all maintenance is carried out in accordance with the maintenance control manual.

8.1.5: Maintenance shall be performed in accordance with the maintenance programme.

8.2 deals with the provision and amendment of the Maintenance Control Manual. Copies shall be provided to States of Operator and Registry. It shall incorporate such mandatory materials as either of such States may require.

8.3: The operator shall provide a maintenance programme approved by State of Registry containing the information required by 11.3. The design and application of the programme shall observe human factors principles. Amendments shall be furnished promptly.

8.4: Maintenance records.

8.4.1 requires the operator to keep records of:

(a) total time in service;
(b) status of compliance with mandatory continuing airworthiness information;
(c) modifications and repairs;
(d) time in service since last overhaul;
(e) status of compliance with maintenance programme; and
(f) maintenance to show in detail all requirements for signing a maintenance release have been met.

8.4.2 deals with minimum periods of keeping of records.

8.4.3 deals with availability and transfer of records to new operator.

8.5 deals with the responsibilities of the operator in respect of continuing airworthiness information concerning aeroplanes over 5,700 kg maximum certificated take-off mass.

8.6: Modifications and repairs shall comply with requirements acceptable to State of Registry. Procedures shall be established for retention of substantiating data.

8.7 deals with the following aspects of an approved maintenance organisation:
   8.7.1: Issue of approval.
   8.7.2: Maintenance Organisations Procedures Manual.
   8.7.3: Maintenance procedures and assurance control system.
   8.7.4: Facilities (environment, data, equipment, tooling, material and storage).
   8.7.5: Personnel.
   8.7.6: Records.
   8.7.7: Maintenance release.

Chapter 9—Aeroplane flight crew

9.1: Composition of flight crew. This deals with the number of flight crew, radio operator, flight engineer and flight navigator. See reference to Operations and Flight Manuals.
   9.2: Flight crew emergency duties shall be assigned to flight crew as specified.
   9.3: Flight crew members' training programmes. These shall be established and maintained by the operator and approved by the State of Operator and shall be as specified.

9.4: Qualifications.
9.4.1: Requirements for recent experience of pilot-in-command.
   9.4.2: Requirements for recent experience of co-pilot.
   9.4.3: Pilot-in-command: route and airport qualification.
   9.4.4: Pilot proficiency checks, see reference to flight simulator approved by the State of Operator and also Manual of Criteria for the Qualification of Flight Simulators (doc. 9625).

9.5: Flight crew equipment: spare pair of correcting lenses must be available when lenses are worn.
   9.6: Flight time, flight duty periods and rest periods: the State of Operator shall establish regulations. See guidance in Attachment A.

Chapter 10—Flight operations officer/flight dispatcher

10.1: A flight operations officer/flight dispatcher, when employed in conjunction with an approved method of flight supervision requiring the services of licensed flight operations officers/flight dispatchers, shall be licensed in accordance with the provisions of Annex 1.

See also note.

10.2–10.3: Recommendations on qualification flight, knowledge and familiarisation.

Chapter 11—Manuals, logs and records

11.1: Note: the Flight Manual contains the information specified in Annex 8.

The Flight Manual shall be updated with mandatory changes.

11.2: Operators Maintenance Control Manual provided in accordance with 8.2 shall contain the 12 specified descriptions.

11.3: Maintenance programme required by 8.3 shall contain:

(a) maintenance tasks and their intervals;
(b) when applicable, a continuing structural integrity programme;
(c) procedures for changing or deviating from (a) and (b); and
(d) when applicable, condition monitoring and reliability programme descriptions for aircraft systems, components and power plants.

11.3.2: Maintenance tasks and intervals specified as mandatory shall be identified as such.

11.3.3: Maintenance programme should be based on the information as specified.

11.4: Maintenance Organisations Procedures Manual provided in accordance with 8.7.2 shall contain the 11 items of specified information.

11.5: The aeroplane journey log book should contain the 12 listed items in the manner specified.

11.6: Operators shall at all times have available for immediate communication to rescue coordination centres, list containing information on the emergency and survival equipment (as specified) carried on board any of their aeroplanes engaged in international air navigation.

11.7: Operators shall ensure to the extent possible preservation of flight recorder records and recorders in the case of an accident or incident as specified.

Chapter 12—Cabin attendants

12.1: This sets out the SARPS for cabin attendants under the following headings: The minimum number of attendants for safe and expeditious evacuation of the aircraft, and the assignment of their functions.

12.2: Emergency evacuation stations.

12.3: Protection of cabin attendants during flight.

12.4: Training.

12.5: Flight time, duty periods and rest periods.

Chapter 13—Security

The word "security" is used in the sense of prevention of illicit acts against civil aviation.

This sets out the SARPS under the following headings:

13.1: Security of flight crew compartment: door capable of being locked from within.

13.2: Aeroplane search procedure checklist and guidance.

13.3: Training programmes to be established and maintained.

13.4: Reporting acts of unlawful interference.

13.5.1: *Miscellaneous Recommendations dealing with the provisions of special-ised means of attenuating and directing bomb blast for use at the least-risk bomb location.*

13.5.2: *Recommendation on stowage of weapons.*

Appendices

1: Lights to be displayed by aeroplanes.

2: Contents of an Operations Manual.

Attachments

Attachment A: Flight time and flight duty period limitations;

Attachment B: First aid medical supplies;

Attachment C: Aeroplane performance operating limitations;

Attachment D: Flight recorders;

Attachment E: Extended range operations by aeroplanes with two turbine power-units;

Attachment F: Air operators certificate or equivalent document;

Attachment G: Minimum equipment list (MEL).

PART II (6th edition, July 1998)

This establishes the SARPS for international general aviation aeroplanes. They include some of the material in Annex 6, Part I.

Chapter 1—Definitions

For "General Aviation" see Chapter 8 of this book.

Chapter 2—Applicability

These SARPS shall apply to international general aviation operations with aeroplanes.

Chapter 3—General

These SARPS are similar but not identical to those in Annex 6, Part I.

Chapter 4—Flight preparation and in-flight procedures

This gives the SARPS for 17 items.

Chapters 5–9

These chapters give the SARPS for the following subjects—aeroplane performance operating limitations, instruments and equipment, communication and navigation equipment, maintenance and aeroplane flight crew—and are headed accordingly.

Appendix

Lights to be displayed.

Attachments

Attachment A: Flight recorders.
Attachment B: Carriage and use of oxygen.

PART III (4th edition, July 1998)

This establishes the SARPS for international operations—helicopters. It consists of three sections:

(I) General;
(II) International commercial air transport;
(III) International general aviation.

Section I—General

Chapter 1—Definitions

Definitions include:

Helicopter: A heavier-than-air aircraft supported in flight chiefly by the reactions of the air on one or more power-driven rotors on substantially vertical axes.
Night: The hours between the end of evening civil twilight and the beginning of morning civil twilight or such other period between sunset and sunrise, as may be prescribed by the appropriate authority. See Note on civil twilight.

Chapter 2—Applicability

These SARPS apply to all helicopters engaged in international commercial air transport operations, or in international general aviation operations, except that these SARPS are not applicable to helicopters engaged in aerial work.

Section II—International commercial air transport

The relevant chapter headings are identical to those in Part I. Many parts of this section are similar to the corresponding parts of Part I, subject to obvious differences.

Section III—International general aviation

The relevant chapter headings are identical, except in one case, to those in Part II of the Annex.

Appendix

Contents of an Operations Manual.

Attachments

Attachment A: Helicopter performance and operating limitations.
Attachment B: Flight recorders.
Attachment C: Flight time and flight duty period limitations.
Attachment D: Medical supplies.
Attachment E: Minimum equipment list.
Attachment F: Air operator certificate or similar document.

PANS—OPS

A summary of the publications ancillary to Annex 6 is beyond the scope of this book except for a brief consideration of doc. 8168—OPS/611 "Procedures for Air Navigation Services—Aircraft Operations" (PANS—OPS).

The legal status of PANS has been considered on page 26 above.

PANS—OPS consists of two volumes:

Volume I : Flight Procedures (4th edition 1993).
Volume II: Construction of Visual and Instrument Flight Procedures (4th edition 1993).

The Foreword to Volume I states:

"*Volume I—Flight Procedures* describes operational procedures recommended for the guidance of flight operations personnel. It also outlines the various parameters on which the criteria in Volume II are based so as to illustrate the need for operational personnel including flight crew to adhere strictly to the published procedures in order to achieve and maintain an acceptable level of safety in operations.

Volume II—Construction of Visual and Instrument Flight Procedures is intended for the guidance of procedures specialists and describes the essential areas and obstacle clearance requirements for the achievement of safe, regular instrument flight operations. It provides the basic guidelines to States, and those operators and organizations producing instrument flight charts that will result in uniform practices at all aerodromes where instrument flight procedures are carried out."

Both volumes present coverage of operational practices that are beyond the scope of the SARPS but with respect to which "a measure of international uniformity is desirable".

PANS—OPS explain the important procedures concerning: departure, approach, holding, noise abatement, altimeter setting, simultaneous operations on parallel or near parallel runways, and secondary surveillance radar (SSR) transponder operation.

(iii) Comments

(1) For further consideration of flight crew training, aircraft maintenance procedures and helicopters operations, see Chapters 18, 19 and 20 of this book.

(2) ICAO Manual of Procedures for operations inspection, certification and continued surveillance (doc. 8335—AN/879) establishes the procedures for State regulation of operators.

Para 1.2.5 of the ICAO Manual states that considerable merit exists in a State regulatory system which should:

(a) represent a well-balanced allocation of responsibility between the State and the operator for the safety of operations;

(b) be capable of economic justification within the resources of the State;

(c) enable the State to maintain continuing regulation and supervision of the activities of the operator without unduly inhibiting the operator's effective direction and control of the organisation; and

(d) result in the cultivation and maintenance of harmonious relationships between the State and the operator.

Para 1.2.6 states that an essential element in the regulatory system is the certification of operators. The Manual goes on to explain how application is made for an AOC, the inspections and requirements prior to issue of the AOC, and continuing surveillance of certificated operators.

Chapter 2: "State Regulatory System" states that the two prerequisites of a regulatory system are:

(a) the provision, in the basic aviation law of the State, for a code of air navigation regulations; and

(b) the establishment of an appropriate State body (referred to as the civil aviation authority) with regulatory powers.

All aspects of the operator's structure and activities come under scrutiny. For example:

(a) Chapter 4 deals with the assessment of financial, economic and legal matters including insurance arrangements;

(b) Chapter 6 deals with maintenance inspection; and

(c) Chapter 10 deals with lease, charter and interchange operations.

(3) Council Regulation (EEC) No. 2407/92. In addition to the requirements of holding an AOC, all air carriers established in the EU (as specified) who operate for "remuneration and/or hire" within the territory of the Community must hold the appropriate operating licence in accordance with Council Regulation (EEC) No. 2407/92 ("the operating licence"). As *S&B* point out: "The operating licence gives the holder the status of Community air carrier who thereby gains near automatic access to almost all routes within the Community . . . ".

In order to have this route access, Community air carriers in addition to holding the AOC must also demonstrate to the authority of the licensing Member State that they can meet their obligations and costs (Article 5 of the Council Regulation).

Article 7 requires an air carrier to be insured against liability.

Article 10.1 provides that for the purpose of ensuring safety and reliability standards a carrier using an aircraft from, or providing an aircraft to, another undertaking shall obtain prior approval from the appropriate authority. The condition of approval shall be included in the lease agreement.

Article 10.2 provides that a Member State shall not approve any lease agreement unless it is satisfied the specified safety standards are met.

(4) In appreciating Annex 6 useful publications include the following:

(i) The ICAO Manual of Procedures (doc. 8335);

(ii) "The Safety Performance of United Kingdom Airline Operators Special Review" published by UK Board of Trade in 1968;

(iii) "Safe skies for Tomorrow—Aviation Safety in a Competitive Environment", published by Congress of the United States Office of Technology Assessment in 1988.

(iv) Final Report of White House Commission on Aviation Safety and Security 1997 (Gore Report).

(5) In the Canadian case of *Swanson & Others* v. *R* (Federal Court of Canada 31.10.89–7290 and Federal Court of Appeal of Canada, Feb/May 1991; *S&B* AvR 191), the plaintiffs who were relatives of passengers killed in an air crash brought proceedings against the Federal Crown of Canada (that is the Canadian State) alleging negligence of its agent, Transport Canada, who was the regulatory authority of commercial air transport. The Federal Court of Appeal in their judgment given in 1991 upheld the decision of the judge at first instance ruling:

(i) The Crown owed a civil (private law) duty to the plaintiffs in the exercise of their regulatory duties and those duties were breached through negligence.

(ii) Although the Crown was liable in tort for damages as if it were a private person, it would only be liable for negligent operational decisions and not for negligent policy decisions. The Crown's response to complaints and reports about the safety of the operator Wapiti Aviation Limited was an operational decision. The Crown owed a civil duty to exercise reasonable care to the families of the passengers.

(iii) Transport Canada's failure to take any meaningful steps to correct the situation which it knew existed at Wapiti amounted to a breach of duty of care.

(iv) There was a clear causal link between the failure to take care and the loss since the incidents of negligence of Transport Canada were so numerous that they provided more than ample evidence that this negligence caused much of the unsafe environment at Wapiti Airlines before the crash.

The judgment is relevant to a number of topics in this book:

(i) It describes the regulatory framework in which Transport Canada's representative should have worked.

(ii) It describes the shortcomings both of the regulatory authorities and of the organisation and operation of a small commuter airline operating in a competitive environment.

(iii) It analyses the distinction between an operational decision, and a policy decision by a government (see comments on US case law at the end of Annexes 1, 8 and 14).

(iv) It is a statement of the rights of the travelling public against the Regulatory Authority.

(v) It analyses causation and negligence.

(vi) It is an example of the court in one common law country (Canada) being guided by case law from other common law countries (the UK and the USA). The court quotes the majority view in *Dalehite* v. *US* (1953) 346 US 15 (see page 98 below), where the dissenting judge, Jackson J, claimed that "the ancient and discredited doctrine 'that the King can do no wrong' has not been uprooted; it has merely been amended to read 'the King can do only little wrongs' "; that is the executive government will be liable for operational acts and not for policy or discretionary acts.

(6) In the UK case *Philcox* v. *Civil Aviation Authority* (February 1994 and May 1995) the trial judge held that the CAA as regulatory authority did not owe a duty of care in tort to the aircraft owner in respect of economic loss in exercising supervisory duties in maintenance. He held that generally CAA did not owe a private law duty of care for the reasons stated in the judgment. The Court of Appeal confirmed the judgment. The CAA's role was to protect the public. The CAA did not owe a duty of care to the aircraft's owners to ensure

they had maintained the aircraft properly. The Appeal Court commented that there was no universal rule that a supervising body could not owe a duty of care but referred to four recent (non-aviation) cases where the courts had held that even third parties could not recover for the failure of a supervisory authority. In view of the particular circumstances of *Philcox* it is suggested that it can be "distinguished" as a precedent and that the question of liability of CAA as a regulatory authority in other circumstances remains open. The UK Civil Aviation Act 1982 does not contain a provision similar to section 2860(a) of the US Federal Tort Claims Act (see page 97).

(7) In *Hawke* v. *Waterloo Wellington Flying Club Ltd* (1971) 22 DLR (3rd) 266, it was held that maintenance engineers owe a duty of care in respect of certificates of airworthiness given by them in log books or records which become part of log books. The duty of care is owed to the current owners of the aircraft and other persons who may operate the aircraft as subsequent purchasers or with the permission of the owners.

(8) Recent developments in airline management has led to the AOC holder becoming separated from critical safety functions such as airworthiness and crew training. This puts increasing responsibilities on regulatory authorities.

ANNEX 7. AIRCRAFT NATIONALITY AND REGISTRATION MARKS—4TH EDITION (JULY 1981)

(i) Articles

Article 12—Rules of the Air

See Annex 2, page 47.

Article 17—Nationality of aircraft

Aircraft have the nationality of the State in which they are registered.

Article 18—Dual registration

An aircraft cannot be validly registered in more than one State, but its registration may be changed from one State to another.

Article 19—National laws governing registration

The registration or transfer of registration of aircraft in any Contracting State shall be made in accordance with its laws and regulations.

Article 20—Display of marks

Every aircraft engaged in international air navigation shall bear its appropriate nationality and registration marks.

Article 21—Report of registrations

Each Contracting State undertakes to supply to any other Contracting State or to the International Civil Aviation Organisation, on demand, information concerning the registration and ownership of any particular aircraft registered in that State. In addition, each Contracting State shall furnish reports to the International Civil Aviation Organisation, under such regulations as the latter may prescribe, giving such pertinent data as can be made available concerning the ownership and control of aircraft registered in that State and habitually engaged in international air navigation. The data thus obtained by the International Civil Aviation Organisation shall be made available by it on request to the other Contracting States.

Article 77—Joint operating organisations permitted

Nothing in this Convention shall prevent two or more Contracting States from constituting joint air transport operating organisations or international operating agencies and from pooling their air services on any routes or in any regions, but such organisations or agencies and such pooled services shall be subject to all the provisions of this Convention, including those relating to the registration of agreements with the Council. The Council shall determine in what manner the provisions of this Convention relating to nationality of aircraft shall apply to aircraft operated by international operating agencies.

Article 79—Participation in operating organisations

A State may participate in joint operating organisations or in pooling arrangements, either through its government or through an airline company or companies designated by its government. The companies may, at the sole discretion of the State concerned, be State owned or partly State owned or privately owned.

Article 83bis

Transfer of certain functions and duties.

(a) Notwithstanding the provisions of Articles 12, 30, 31 and 32(a), when an aircraft registered in a Contracting State is operated pursuant to an agreement for the lease, charter or interchange of the aircraft or any similar arrangement by an operator who has his principal place of business or, if he has no such place of business, his permanent residence in another Contracting State, the State of Registry may, by agreement with such other State, transfer all or part of its functions and duties as State of Registry in respect of that aircraft under Articles 12, 30, 31 and 32(a). The State of Registry shall be relieved of responsibility in respect of the functions and duties transferred.

(b) The transfer shall not have effect in respect of other Contracting States before either the agreement between States in which it is embodied has been registered with the Council and made public pursuant to Article 83 or the existence and scope of the agreement have been directly communicated to the authorities of the other Contracting State or States concerned by a State party to the agreement.

(c) The provisions of paragraph (a) and (b) above shall also be applicable to cases covered by Article 77.

Author's note

Article 83 deals with notification of any arrangement and its registration with the Council by the State concerned.

(ii) Summary

1: Definitions include:

"*Common Mark*": A mark assigned by ICAO to the common mark registering authority registering aircraft of an international operating agency on other than a national basis.

2: Nationality. Common and registration marks to be used.

2.1: The nationality or common mark and registration mark shall consist of a group of characters.

2.2: The nationality or common mark shall precede the registration mark.

2.2–2.4 deal with selection of nationality and common marks. See reference to International Telecommunication Union.

2.5: Registration mark specification.

2.6 deals with avoidance of confusion.

3: Location of nationality, common and registration marks. These SARPS set out general requirements for affixing marks on both lighter-than-air and heavier-than-air aircraft.

4: Measurements of nationality, common and registration marks.

5: Type of characters for nationality, common and registration marks.

6: Register of nationality, common and registration marks.

7. Certificate of registration.

7.1: The certificate of registration shall be in the form as set out.

7.2: The certificate of registration shall be carried in the aircraft at all times.

8: Identification plate.

9: General. The Annex does not apply to meteorological pilot balloons and unmanned free balloons as specified.

Table 1 sets out classification of all aircraft including the seldom seen amphibian ornithopter.

Supplement I dated August 1997: Part A lists notified State differences and lists aircraft nationality marks, national emblems and common marks. See examples of emblem (Switzerland) and Common Mark 4YB for Arab Air Cargo established by Jordan and Iraq.

(iii) Comments

(1) For rights in aircraft refer to the Convention on the International Recognition of Rights in Aircraft—Geneva Convention 1948.

(2) While the coming into force of Article 83bis was pending, ICAO Assembly passed Resolution A23–13 acknowledging that the Chicago Convention does not adequately specify the responsibilities of the State of Operator where an aircraft of the State of Registry is leased, chartered or interchanged to the State of Operator. It urges (i) delegation by the State of Registry to the State of Operator of its duties under Annex 6, (ii) the State of Operator to review its regulations. It invites all Contracting States to remove any inhibition on lease, charter or interchange of aircraft and also to extend their powers in order to exercise the new functions imposed on them as State of Operator. The problem addressed in Resolution A23–13 should not arise in the EU, at least in respect of leased aircraft where Article 10 of Regulation 2407/92 of 23 July 1992 applies. However, the problem otherwise remains where the State of Registry is not able to exercise its functions under Annex 6 and the State of Operator may not have the legal power to do so.

(3) See also ECAC (see Chapter 6) Recommendation ECAC/21 on leasing of aircraft. ECAC recommends that for the purpose of ensuring safety and reliability standards and compliance with any applicable economic conditions, all leasing arrangements entered into by air carriers should receive prior approval from the appropriate authorities. The Recommendation specifies the information which should be obtained by the authorities. The Recommendation differentiates between a dry lease and a wet lease. In the case of a dry lease safety functions and duties under Articles 12, 30, 31 and 32(a) of the Convention should normally be transferred to the authorities in the State of the lessee in accordance with Article 83bis.

In the case of a wet lease ECAC's Recommendation is that the aeronautical authorities shall be satisfied, if necessary by means of an audit, that the lessor meets the safety standards equivalent to those which its own airlines are required to meet under their AOC. An air carrier should only be permitted to lease in an aircraft type not on its own AOC if its authority considers this will not affect its required safety standards. Recommendations follow, including (f) wet leased aircraft should not be used as a means of circumventing applicable laws, regulations and international agreements; (h) consumers, i.e. passengers, should be informed beforehand as to the actual operator of any wet leased aircraft. ECAC States are urged to cooperate with the provision of information concerning leases, particularly in connection with the ECAC action programme for the safety assessment of foreign aircraft.

(4) Article 83bis has now come into force. At the time of going to press it has been ratified by 109 States out of a total of 185. Resolution A23–13 remains in force for those parties to the Chicago Convention who have not ratified Article 83bis.

The Resolution is less effective than Article 83bis because:

(1) it refers only to Annex 6;
(2) it contains no provisions for binding third party States;
(3) it does not have the same legal force as the Protocol of Amendment introducing Article 83bis.

(5) An example of the effect of registration is provided by ANO Article 112 which applies the provision of ANO worldwide to UK registered aircraft and to foreign registered aircraft when within the UK.

ANNEX 8.   AIRWORTHINESS OF AIRCRAFT— 8TH EDITION (JULY 1988)

(i) Articles

Article 29—Documents carried in aircraft

Every aircraft of a Contracting State, engaged in international navigation, shall carry documents in conformity with the conditions prescribed in this Convention; these documents include its Certificate of Airworthiness.

Article 31—Certificates of Airworthiness

Every aircraft engaged in international navigation shall be provided with a Certificate of Airworthiness issued or rendered valid by the State in which it is registered.

Article 33—Recognition of certificates

Certificates of Airworthiness issued or rendered valid by the Contracting State in which the aircraft is registered, shall be recognised as valid by the other Contracting States, provided that the requirements under which such certificates or licences were issued or rendered valid are equal to or above the minimum standards which may be established from time to time pursuant to this Convention.

Article 39—Endorsement of certificates or licences

(a) Any aircraft or part thereof with respect to which there exists an international standard of airworthiness or performance, and which failed in any respect to satisfy that standard at the time of its certification, shall have endorsed on or attached to its airworthiness certificate a complete enumeration of the details in respect of which it so failed.

Article 40—Validity of endorsed certificates and licences

See page 35.

Article 41—Recognition of existing standards of airworthiness

The provisions of this chapter shall not apply to aircraft and aircraft equipment of types of which the prototype is submitted to the appropriate national authorities for certification prior to a date three years after the date of adoption of an international standard of airworthiness for such equipment.

(ii) Summary

PART I

Definitions include:

> "*Appropriate airworthiness requirement*": The comprehensive and detailed airworthiness codes established by a Contracting State for the class of aircraft under consideration (see 2.2 of Part II of this Annex).
> "*Rendering (a certificate of airworthiness) valid*": The action taken by a Contracting State, as an alternative to issuing its own Certificate of Airworthiness, in accepting a Certificate of Airworthiness issued by any other Contracting State as the equivalent of its own Certificate of Airworthiness.
> "*Performance Class 1 Helicopter*": A helicopter with performance such that, in case of engine failure, it is able to land on the rejected take-off area or safely continue the flight to an appropriate landing area.
> "*Performance Class 2 Helicopter*": A helicopter with performance such that, in case of engine failure, it is able to safely continue the flight, except when the failure occurs prior to a defined point after take-off or after a defined point before landing, in which cases a forced landing may be required.
> "*Performance Class 3 Helicopter*": A helicopter with performance such that, in case of engine failure at any point in the flight profile, a forced landing must be performed.
> "*Power-Unit*": A system of one or more engines and ancillary parts which are together necessary to provide thrust, independently of the continued

operation of any other power-unit(s), but not including short period thrust-producing devices.

"*Standard Atmosphere*": See Definition.

PART II—ADMINISTRATION

See note on Council Resolution A23–13 (see page 83).

Chapter 1—Certificate of Airworthiness

Note: Certificate of Airworthiness as used in these standards is the Certificate of Airworthiness referred to in Article 31.

Chapter 2—Applicability

2.1 deals with the applicability of the Standards of Part II to the aircraft types as specified.

2.2: A Contracting State shall not issue or render valid a Certificate of Airworthiness for which it intends to claim recognition pursuant to Article 33 of the Convention, unless the aircraft complies with a comprehensive and detailed national airworthiness code established for that class of aircraft by the State of Registry or by any other Contracting State. The national code shall be such that compliance with it will ensure compliance with:

  (a) the Standards of Part II of this Annex;
  (b) where applicable, with the Standards of Part III or Part IV of this Annex.

See provisions where Parts III or IV are inapplicable.

See reference to Airworthiness Technical Manual (doc. 9051).

Chapter 3—Proof of compliance with appropriate airworthiness requirements

3.1: The Certificate of Airworthiness shall be issued by the Contracting State approving the aircraft on the basis of satisfactory evidence of compliance with the appropriate requirements.

3.1.1–3.1.3 deal with the nature and provision of such evidence including test flying.

3.2: Where an aircraft has a valid Certificate of Airworthiness issued by one Contracting State, another Contracting State, when entering the aircraft on its register, may accept the valid Certificate of Airworthiness as satisfactory evidence of airworthiness and need not follow the procedures in 3.1.1–3.1.3.

3.3: Contracting States shall take whatever further steps are necessary to ensure the Certificate of Airworthiness is withheld if the aircraft is known or suspected to have dangerous features not specifically guarded against by the applicable airworthiness requirements.

Chapter 4—Continuing airworthiness of aircraft

4.1 requires the State of Registry to determine continuing airworthiness and to adopt and develop requirements to ensure such continuing airworthiness. Notes:

(1) the requirements will cover maintenance requirements of Annex 6 (Aircraft Operations);

(2) guidance on continuing airworthiness requirements is contained in the Continuing Airworthiness Manual.

4.2: Information relating to the continuing airworthiness of aircraft.

4.2.1–4.2.9 set out the procedures applicable to the State of Design and State of Registry for exchange of information relating to continuing airworthiness of aircraft. Note in particular the obligations in respect of "mandatory continuing airworthiness information".

Note 1 to 4.2.2: The term "mandatory continuing airworthiness information" is intended to include mandatory requirements for modification, replacement of parts or inspection of aircraft and amendments of operating limitations and procedures. Among such information is that issued by the Contracting State in the form of airworthiness directives.

See also references to ICAO Circular 95—"The Continuing Airworthiness of Aircraft in Service" and to "The Airworthiness Technical Manual" (doc. 9051).

4.2.9: Where the State of Manufacture is other than the State of Design, there shall be an agreement acceptable to both States to ensure that the manufacturing organisation co-operates with the organisation responsible for the type design in assessing information received on experience with operating the aircraft.

Chapter 5—Validity of the Certificate of Airworthiness

5.1: A Certificate of Airworthiness shall be renewed or remain valid subject to the laws of the State of Registry which must provide that continuing airworthiness shall be determined by periodical inspection at appropriate intervals or by an approved system of inspection producing an equivalent result.

5.2 deals with the method to be adopted by State of Registry rendering a Certificate of Airworthiness of another State valid instead of issuing its own Certificate of Airworthiness.

Chapter 6—Temporary loss of airworthiness

6.1: Failure to maintain an aircraft as required in an airworthy condition shall render it ineligible for operation until restored to airworthy condition.

6.2 deals with damage to the aircraft both inside and outside the territory of State of Registry, the loss of airworthiness and relevant procedure.

Chapter 7—Standard form of Certificate of Airworthiness

This requires that there shall be a standard form of Certificate of Airworthiness containing the required information which is shown in Figure 1 to the chapter.

Chapter 8—Aircraft limitations and information

This states that each aircraft shall be provided with a Flight Manual, placards or other documents stating the approved limitations within which the aircraft is considered airworthy as defined by the appropriate airworthiness requirements and other instructions and information necessary for the safe operation of the aircraft.

PART III—AEROPLANES

Chapter 1—General

1.1.1–1.1.2 deal with applicability of Standards to aircraft as specified.

The Note deals with amended Standards relating to fire protection, crash survival and provisions for emergency.

1.1.3: These Part III Standards apply to aeroplanes of over 5,700 kg maximum certificated take-off mass intended for the carriage of passengers or cargo or mail in international air navigation.

1.1.4 requires that the level of airworthiness defined by the national code referred to in 2.2 of Part II above shall be at least substantially equivalent to the overall level intended by the broad standards of Part III.

1.1.5: Unless otherwise stated the Standards apply to the complete aeroplane including power-units, systems and equipment.

1.2: Number of power-units. The aeroplane shall have not less than two power-units.

1.3.1–1.3.2: Limitations. Limiting conditions and ranges shall be established for the aeroplane, its power-units and its equipment as specified.

See also Notes which include 3: the maximum operating mass may be limited by application of Noise Certification Standards. (See Annexes 16 and 6, Parts I and II.)

1.4: The aeroplane shall not possess any unsafe features and characteristics.

1.5: Proof of Compliance shall be based on tests, calculations and calculations based on tests.

Chapter 2—Flight

2.1: Compliance with Standards set out in Chapter 2 shall be established by flight or other tests as specified for the applicable combinations and configurations.

2.2: Performance.

2.2.1: General.

2.2.1.1: Sufficient performance data shall be determined and scheduled in the Flight Manual to enable operators to determine the total mass of the aeroplane on the basis of the values, peculiar to the proposed flight, of the relevant operational parameters, in order that the flight may be made with reasonable assurance that a minimum performance will be achieved.

2.2.1.2: The performance scheduled for the aeroplane shall not require exceptional skill or alertness on the part of the pilot.

2.2.1.3: Scheduled performance shall be consistent with compliance with 1.3.1 and with the operation in logical combinations of those of the aeroplane's systems and equipment, the operation of which may affect performance.

2.2.2: Minimum performance shall be established at the maximum mass scheduled as specified for:

> *Take-off:* dealing with power unit failing on take-off and also minimum performance under conditions departing slightly from idealised conditions scheduled in 2.2.3;
>
> *Landing:* deals with critical power unit inoperative, missed approach, and balked landing where all power units are operating.

2.2.3: Scheduling of performance. Performance data shall be determined and scheduled in the aeroplane Flight Manual so that their application by means of the operating rules to which the aeroplane is to be operated in accordance with 5.2 of Annex 6, Part I, will provide a safe relation between the performance of the aeroplane and the aerodromes and routes on which it is capable of being operated. Performance data shall be determined and scheduled for the following stages for the range of mass, altitude or pressure-altitude, wind velocity, gradient of the take-off and landing surface for landplanes, water surface conditions, density of water and strength of current for seaplanes, and for any other operational variables for which the aeroplane is to be certified.

The section then deals specifically with:

2.2.3.1: Take-off.

2.2.3.1.1: Accelerate—stop distance.

2.2.3.1.2: Take-off path.

2.2.3.2: En route.

2.2.3.3: Landing.

2.3: Flying qualities. The aeroplane shall comply with the Standards of 2.3 at all altitudes up to the maximum anticipated altitude relevant to the particular requirement in all temperature conditions relevant to the altitude in question and for which the aeroplane is approved.

The section then sets out requirements for the aspects as headed:

2.3.1: Controllability:

(1) On surface;
(2) During take-off;
(3) Take-off safety speed.

2.3.2: Trim.
2.3.3: Stability.
2.3.4: Stalling:

(1) Stall warning;
(2) Behaviour following stall;
(3) Stalling speeds.

2.3.5: Flutter and vibration. The parts of the aeroplane shall be free from flutter and excessive vibration in all configurations under all speed conditions within the operating limitations of the aeroplane (see 1.3.2). There shall be no buffeting severe enough to interfere with control of the aircraft, to cause structural damage or to cause excessive fatigue to the flight crew.

Note: buffeting as a stall warning is considered desirable and discouragement of this type of buffeting is not intended.

Chapter 3—Structures

3.1: General. These Standards apply to the aeroplane structure consisting of all portions of the aeroplane, the failure of which would seriously endanger the aeroplane.

3.1.1–3.1.3 deal with:

3.1.1: Mass and mass distribution.

3.1.2: Limit loads (defined as "the maximum loads assumed to occur in the anticipated operating conditions").

3.1.3: Strength and deformation.

3.2: Airspeeds.

3.2.1: Design airspeeds shall be established for which the aeroplane structure is designed to withstand the corresponding manoeuvring and gust loads in accordance with 3.3. In establishing the design airspeeds, consideration shall be given to the speeds as specified in the subsection.

3.2.2: Limiting airspeeds based on design airspeeds with safety margins shall be included in the Flight Manual as part of the operating limitations (see 9.2.2).

3.3: Flight loads. The flight load conditions of 3.3.1, 3.3.2, and 3.5 shall be considered for the range of mass and mass distributions prescribed in 3.1.1 and at airspeeds established in accordance with 3.2.1. Asymmetrical as well as symmetrical loading shall be taken into account. The air, inertia, and other loads resulting from the specified loading conditions shall be distributed so as to approximate actual conditions closely or to represent them conservatively.

3.3.1–3.3.2 deal with manoeuvring loads and gust loads respectively.

3.4: Ground and water loads. The structure shall be able to withstand all the loads due to reactions of the ground and water surface which are likely to arise during taxiing, take-off and landing.

3.5: Miscellaneous loads. In addition to other loads as specified loads such as flight control, cabin pressures, engine operations, changes of configuration should be considered.

3.6: Flutter, divergence and vibration. Structure shall be designed to be free of flutter, structural divergence and loss of control due to structural deformation at speeds specified. Structures shall withstand vibration and buffeting in anticipated operating conditions.

3.7: Fatigue strength. The strength and fabrication of the aeroplane shall be such as to ensure that the probability of disastrous fatigue failure of the aeroplane's structure under repeated loads and vibratory loads in the anticipated operating conditions is extremely remote.

Chapter 4—Design and construction

4.1: General. Details of design and construction shall be such as to give reasonable assurance that all aeroplane parts will function effectively and reliably in the anticipated operating conditions. They shall be based on practices which experience has proven to be satisfactory or which are substantiated by special tests or by other appropriate investigations or both.

4.1.1: Substantiating tests. The functioning of all moving parts essential to the safe operation of the aircraft shall be demonstrated by suitable tests.

4.1.2: Materials. All materials used in the aeroplane essential for its safe operation shall conform to approved specifications. Materials accepted as complying with the specifications will have the essential properties assumed in the design.

4.1.3: Fabrication methods. Fabrication and assembly methods shall be such as to produce a consistently sound structure which shall be reliable with respect to maintenance of strength in service.

4.1.4: Protection. The structure shall be protected against deterioration or loss of strength in service due to weathering, corrosion, abrasion, or other causes, which could pass unnoticed, taking into account the maintenance the aeroplane will receive.

4.1.5: Inspection provisions. Adequate provision shall be made to permit any necessary examination, replacement, or reconditioning of parts of the aeroplane periodically or after unusually severe operations.

4.1.6: Design features. Special consideration shall be given to design features affecting the ability of the flight crew to maintain controlled flight. This shall include at least:

(a) controls and control systems;

(b) systems survivability (as of 12 March 2000);

(c) crew environment;

(d) pilot vision;

(e) provision for emergencies;

(f) fire precautions;

(g) fire suppression;

(h) incapacitation of occupants;

(i) protection of flight crew compartment from smoke and fumes (as of 12 March 2000).

4.1.7: Emergency landing provisions.

4.1.7.1: Provisions shall be made in design to protect the occupants in the event of emergency landing, from fire and from the direct effects of deceleration as well as from injuries resulting from deceleration forces on the aeroplane's interior equipment.

4.1.7.2: Facilities shall be provided for rapid evacuation.

4.1.7.3: Interior layout and position and layout of emergency exits shall be such as to facilitate rapid evacuation.

4.1.7.4: On aeroplanes certificated for ditching conditions, provisions shall be made in design to give maximum practicable assurance for safe evacuation.

4.1.8: Provision of ground handling. Adequate provisions shall be made in design to minimise the risk of damage during ground handling operations, e.g. towing or jacking.

Chapter 5—Engines

5.1: Scope. Standards of Chapter 5 shall apply to engines of all types which are used on aeroplanes as primary propulsion units.

5.2: Design, construction and functioning. The engine complete with accessories shall be designed and constructed so as to function reliably within its operating limitations under the anticipated operating conditions when properly installed in the aeroplane in accordance with Chapter 7 and if applicable fitted with a suitable propeller.

5.3: Declared ratings, conditions and limitations. Power ratings and the conditions of the atmosphere and all operating conditions and limitations, as specified, shall be declared.

5.4: Tests. Engines of the type shall satisfactorily complete necessary tests which shall include at least the following:

(a) power calibration;

(b) operation;

(c) endurance.

Chapter 6—Propellers

6.1: Scope. Standards in this chapter apply to all types.

6.2: Design, construction and functioning. This sets out provisions similar to 5.2 but applicable to propellers.

6.3: Power ratings, conditions and limitations shall be declared.

6.4: Tests. A propeller of the type shall complete satisfactorily necessary tests including at least:

(a) Operation;
(b) Endurance.

Chapter 7—Powerplant installation

7.1.1: The powerplant installation shall comply with the Standards of Chapter 4 and this chapter.

7.1.2 deals with capability of use in anticipated operating conditions and compliance with engine and propeller limitations.

7.1.3 deals with control of rotation of a failed engine.

7.1.4 deals with engine restarting.

7.2: Arrangement and functioning.

7.2.1: Independence of power units. Powerplant shall be arranged and installed so that (a) each power-unit (Defined) and associated systems can be controlled and operated independently, (b) there is at least one arrangement of powerplant and systems in which any failure, unless its probability is extremely remote, cannot result in a loss of more power than that resulting from complete failure of the critical power unit.

7.2.2: Propeller vibrations. Vibration stresses shall be determined and shall not exceed values as specified.

7.2.3: Cooling systems. System shall be capable of maintaining power plant temperatures as specified. Maximum and minimum temperatures shall be scheduled in Flight Manual.

7.2.4: Associated systems. Fuel, oil, air induction and other systems associated with the power plant shall be capable of supplying engine as required.

7.2.5: Fire protection. Where for regions of the power plant fire hazards are particularly serious because of proximity of ignition sources to combustible materials the following shall apply in addition to Standard 4.1.6 (e):

(a) Isolation: such regions to be isolated;
(b) Flammable fluids: adequate containment;
(c) Fire protection: sufficient detectors to be provided;
(d) Fire extinguishment: capable system to be supplied.

Chapter 8—Instruments and equipment

8.1: The aeroplane shall be provided with approved instruments and equipment necessary for the safe operation of the aeroplane in the anticipated operating conditions. These shall include the instruments and equipment necessary to enable the crew to operate the aeroplane within its operating limitations.

See Note: Instruments and equipment additional to the minimum necessary for the issuance of a Certificate of Airworthiness are prescribed in Annex 6 Parts I and II for particular circumstances or particular routes.

8.2: Installation shall comply with Chapter 4 Standards.

8.3: Safety and survival equipment shall be reliable, accessible and method of operation plainly marked.

8.4 deals with navigation and anti-collision lights.

Chapter 9—Operating limitations and information

9.1: General. The operating limitations within which compliance with the standards of this Annex is determined, together with other necessary information for the safe operation of the aeroplane, shall be made available by means of an aeroplane flight manual, markings and placards, and such other means as may effectively accomplish the purpose. The limitations and information shall include at least those prescribed in 9.2, 9.3 and 9.4.

9.2: Operating limitations. Limitations which there is a risk of exceeding in flight and which are defined quantitively shall be expressed in suitable units and corrected if necessary for errors in measurements so that the flight crew can by reference to the instruments available to them, readily determine when the limitations are reached.

9.2.1: Loading limitations shall include limiting mass, centres of gravity positions, mass distributions, and floor loading (see 1.3.2).

9.2.2: Airspeed limitations shall include all speeds (see 3.2) which are limiting from the standpoint of structural integrity, flying qualities, or other considerations.

9.2.3: Powerplant limitations shall include limitations for its various components as installed. (See 7.1.2 and 7.2.3).

9.2.4: Limitations shall apply to equipment and systems as installed in the aeroplane.

9.2.5: Miscellaneous limitations concerning conditions prejudicial to the safety of the aeroplane (see 1.3.1).

9.2.6: Flight crew limitations. This includes minimum number of flight crew. See Annex 6, Parts I and II.

9.2.7: Flight time limitation after system or power-unit failure. Limitations shall include maximum flying time for which reliability has been established in relation to approval of operations with two turbine power-units beyond the threshold time established in accordance with 4.7 of Annex 6, Part I. See Note.

9.3: Operating information and procedures.

9.3.1: Types of eligible operations shall be listed, as specified.

9.3.2: Loading information shall include certain information as specified. See Note on what is excluded from, and included in, empty mass.

9.3.3: Operating procedures. Description shall be given of normal and emergency operating procedures peculiar to the particular aeroplane and necessary for its safe operation. These include procedures to be followed in the event of failure of one or more power units.

9.3.4: Handling information. Sufficient information shall be given of any significant or unusual features of the aeroplane characteristics. This includes stalling and minimum steady flight speeds required to be established by 2.3.4(3) which shall be scheduled.

9.4: Performance information of the aeroplane shall be scheduled in accordance with 2.2. Information as specified shall be included.

9.5: An aeroplane Flight Manual shall be made available. It shall identify clearly the specific aeroplane or series of aeroplanes. It shall include at least limitations, information and procedures specified in this chapter.

9.6: Markings and placards.

9.6.1: Markings and placards on instruments, equipment, controls, etc. shall include such limitations and information as necessary for the direct attention of flight crew during flight.

9.6.2: Markings and placards shall provide essential information to ground crew to avoid mistakes in ground servicing which could pass unnoticed and jeopardise the safety of the aeroplane in subsequent flights.

Chapter 10—Continuing airworthiness—maintenance information

10.1: Information for use in developing procedures for maintaining the aeroplane in an airworthy condition shall be made available and shall include:

10.2: Maintenance information; which shall include description of the aircraft and recommended methods of accomplishing maintenance tasks and guidance on defect diagnosis.

10.3: Maintenance programme information which shall include maintenance tasks and the recommended intervals for performance of these tasks.

10.4: Maintenance tasks and frequencies that have been specified as mandatory by the State of Design in approval of the type design shall be identified as such.

Chapter 11—Security

As of 12 March 2000:

11.1: Consideration shall be given during the design of the aeroplane to the provision of a least-risk bomb location.

11.2: In all aeroplanes equipped with a flight crew compartment door, this door and the flight crew compartment bulkhead shall be designed to minimise penetration by small arms fire and grenade shrapnel.

11.3: Consideration shall be given to design features which will deter the easy concealment of weapons, explosives or other dangerous objects on board aircraft and which will facilitate search procedure for them.

PART IV—HELICOPTERS

Chapters 1–9 deal with corresponding provisions of airworthiness for helicopters.

In Chapters 1–5 the chapter headings are the same as for aeroplanes. The subsequent four chapters are:

Chapter 6: Rotor and power transmission systems and powerplant installation.

Chapter 7: Instruments and equipment.

Chapter 8: Electrical systems.

Chapter 9: Operating limitations and information.

(Author's Comment: The above summary on aeroplanes gives some guidance on the corresponding SARPS for helicopters. Space does not permit a corresponding summary for helicopters.)

Airworthiness Technical Manual (doc. 9051—AN/896 2nd edition, 1987)

The Foreword to the Airworthiness Technical Manual gives a useful explanation of the views of ICAO Council:

"The Council, on 15 March 1972 adopted a policy which included a declaration that States' obligations, for the purposes of Article 33, should be met by their compliance with the broad Standards in Annex 8. Each State should either establish its own comprehensive and detailed Code of Airworthiness or select such a Code established by another State. To assist States to develop detailed Codes, ICAO would develop Airworthiness Technical Guidance material which would have no mandatory status."

The Manual is not intended to be a complete Code of Airworthiness. Comprehensive airworthiness requirements are published in a number of national and multinational Codes such as the (then) USSR Civil Airworthiness Requirements, the USA Federal Aviation Regulations and the European Joint Airworthiness Requirements (JAR).

The Manual is short, dealing in outline with a specific number of topics. It is divided into four parts as follows:

- Part I—Definitions (which include the different "probabilities of occurrence");
- Part II—Administration (which includes "Continuing Airworthiness");
- Part III—Aeroplanes;
- Part IV—Helicopters.

The contents of the Manual are useful but are not summarised in this book. In view of Chapter 17 on Structures and Materials (below page 469) see the section in the Manual on Strength under Flight Loads and Damage Tolerance and Fatigue Evaluation of Structures.

Page III—1–1 lists and defines the nomenclature of the various operational speeds such as V_1 (decision speed).

(iii) Comments

(1) Each State can develop its own code of airworthiness with minimum requirements based on the broad standards of Annex 8 or it may borrow the airworthiness code established by another State.

See also Chapter 6 below on Regulation of Civil Aviation in Europe.

(2) The judgment of the US Supreme Court (1984) in *US* v. *SA Empresa De Viacao Aerea Rio Grandense (Varig Airlines) et al* and *US* v. *United Scottish Insurance Co et al*, 18 AVI 17,960 1983–5 concerns an effort to sue certifying authorities for negligent certification in respect of wrongful death and hull losses. The actions were brought under the Federal Tort Claims Act which authorises suits against the USA for damages for injury or loss of property or personal injury or death caused by the negligent or wrongful act or omission of any government employee while acting within the scope of his office or employment under circumstances where the USA, if a private person, would be liable.

However, the Federal Tort Claims Act section 2860(a) provides that "The Act does not apply where any claim is based on the exercise or performance or the failure to exercise or perform a discretionary function or duty on the part of a Federal agency or an employee of the government whether or not the discretion involved be abused".

The Supreme Court held that the actions were barred. The discretionary function exception precludes a tort action based on negligent conduct. The legislative history of the Act indicates that Congress wished to prevent judicial "second-guessing" of legislative and administrative decisions grounded in social, economic and political policy through the medium of an action in tort.

The Secretary of Transportation has the duty to promote safety in air transportation by promulgating reasonable rules and regulations governing the inspection, servicing, and overhaul of civil aircraft. The FAA, as the Secretary's designee, has devised a system to review compliance with safety standards that involves certification of aircraft design and manufacture at several stages of production. The implementation of a mechanism for compliance review is plainly discretionary activity of the nature and quality protected by the discretionary function exception. The acts of FAA employees in executing the "spot-check" compliance programme in accordance with agency directives are protected by the discretionary function exception as well.

The Court considered the earlier case of *Dalehite v. US*, 346 US 15, 20–36 (1953), involving a government decision to institute a fertiliser export programme, where there was alleged failure to experiment with a fertiliser on the drafting of a basic plan of manufacture, and the failure to police storage and loading of fertiliser. The court in that case held that the discretionary function exception applied.

However, among further cases considered were *Indian Towing Co v. US*, 350 US 61 (1955) and *Eastern Airlines Inc v. Union Trust Co*, 95 US App DC 189, 221 Fd 62, affirmed 350 US 907 (1955). In the first of those cases the government conceded that the discretionary function was not implicated where the plaintiffs alleged that the Coastguard had been negligent in inspecting and maintaining and repairing the light of a lighthouse prior to a vessel running aground. (Compare with the UK Coastguard cases considered in the Comments at the end of Annex 12 (page 154).) In the second case the US District Court of Appeals for the District of Columbia Circuit permitted the suit against the US government asserting negligence of Air Traffic Controllers in a mid-air collision of two aircraft when attempting to land at Washington National Airport.

The *Varig* decision does not mean that a certifying authority cannot be negligent, it merely classifies the certifying function in *Varig* as discretionary and therefore immune from suit. In other circumstances or jurisdictions the decision may be different.

(3) In *Wilson v. Piper Aircraft Corporation* (April 1978, Sup Court of Oregon) it was held that neither FAA approval of the general model design of the aircraft nor FAA approval of the airworthiness of a particular aircraft is a complete defence to a claim for civil liability for faulty design against the manufacturer.

(4) For a UK example, see *Philcox v. CAA* (Comment (6) in Annex 6). However, in *Perrett v. Collins* [1998] 2 Lloyd's Rep 255 the Court of Appeal held that Popular Flying Association who had issued a certificate of fitness for flight owed a duty of care to a passenger who was injured in a subsequent test flight. The Association was authorised by the CAA to issue such certificates under section 3 of the Civil Aviation Act 1982. This case concerned personal injury, not economic loss, and the role of the inspector was not a subsidiary one.

ANNEX 9.   FACILITATION—10TH EDITION (APRIL 1997)

(i) Articles

Article 10—Landing at customs airport

Except in a case where, under the terms of this Convention or a special authorisation, aircraft are permitted to cross the territory of a Contracting State without landing, every aircraft which enters the territory of a Contracting State shall, if the regulations of that State so require, land at an airport designated by that State for the purpose of customs and other examination. On departure from the territory of a Contracting State, such aircraft shall depart from a similarly designated customs airport. Particulars of all designated customs airports shall be published by the State and transmitted to the International Civil Aviation Organization established under Part II of this Convention for communication to all other Contracting States.

Article 11—Applicability of air regulations

Subject to the provisions of this Convention, the laws and regulations of a Contracting State relating to the admission to or departure from its territory of aircraft engaged in international air navigation, or to the operation and navigation of such aircraft while within its territory, shall be applied to the aircraft of all Contracting States without distinction as to nationality, and shall be complied with by such aircraft upon entering or departing from or while within the territory of that State.

Article 13—Entry and clearance regulations

The laws and regulations of a Contracting State as to the admission to or departure from its territory of passengers, crew, or cargo of aircraft, such as regulations relating to entry, clearance, immigration, passports, customs and quarantine shall be complied with by or on behalf of such passengers, crew or cargo upon entrance into or departure from, or while within the territory of that State.

Article 14—Prevention of spread of diseases

Each Contracting State agrees to take effective measures to prevent the spread by means of air navigation of cholera, typhus (epidemic), smallpox, yellow fever, plague, and such other communicable disease as the Contracting States shall from time to time decide to designate, and to that end Contracting States will keep in close consultation with the agencies concerned with international regulations relating to sanitary measures applicable to aircraft. Such consultation shall be without prejudice to the application of any existing international convention on this subject to which the Contracting States may be parties.

Article 15—Airport and similar charges

Every airport in a Contracting State which is open to public use by its national aircraft shall likewise, subject to the provisions of Article 68, be open under uniform conditions to the aircraft of all the other Contracting States. The like uniform conditions shall apply to the use, by aircraft of every Contracting State, of all air navigation facilities, including radio and meteorological services, which may be provided for public use for the safety and expedition of air navigation.

Any charges that may be imposed or permitted to be imposed by a Contracting State for the use of such airports and air navigation facilities by the aircraft of any other Contracting State shall not be higher;

(a) as to aircraft not engaged in scheduled international air services, than those that would be paid by its national aircraft of the same class engaged in similar operations, and

(b) as to aircraft engaged in scheduled international air services, than those that would be paid by its national aircraft engaged in similar international air services.

All such charges shall be published and communicated to the International Civil Aviation Organization: provided that, upon representation by an interested Contracting State, the charges imposed for the use of airports and other facilities shall be subject to review by the Council, which shall report and make recommendations thereon for the consideration of the State or States concerned. No fees, dues or other charges shall be imposed by any Contracting State in respect solely of the right of transit over or entry into or exit from its territory of any aircraft of a Contracting State or persons or property thereon.

Article 16—Search of aircraft

The appropriate authorities of each of the Contracting States shall have the right, without unreasonable delay, to search aircraft of the other Contracting States on landing or departure, and to inspect the certificates and other documents prescribed by this Convention.

Article 22—Facilitation of formalities

Each Contracting State agrees to adopt all practicable measures, through the issuance of special regulations or otherwise, to facilitate and expedite navigation by aircraft between the territories of Contracting States, and to prevent unnecessary delays to aircraft, crews, passengers and cargo, especially in the administration of the laws relating to immigration, quarantine, customs and clearance.

Article 23—Customs and immigration procedures

Each Contracting State undertakes, so far as it may find practicable, to establish customs and immigration procedures affecting international air navigation in accordance with the practices which may be established or recommended from time to time, pursuant to this Convention. Nothing in this Convention shall be construed as preventing the establishment of customs-free airports.

Article 24—Customs duties and ancillary documents

(a) Aircraft on a flight to, from, or across the territory of another Contracting State shall be admitted temporarily free of duty, subject to the customs regulations of the State. Fuel, lubricating oils, spare parts, regular equipment and aircraft stores on board an aircraft of a Contracting State, on arrival in the territory of another Contracting State and retained on board on leaving the territory of that State shall be exempt from customs duty, inspection fees or similar national or local duties and charges. This exemption shall not apply to any quantities or articles unloaded except in accordance with the customs regulations of the State, which may require that they shall be kept under customs supervision.

(b) Spare parts and equipment imported into the territory of a Contracting State for incorporation in or use on an aircraft of another Contracting State engaged in international air navigation shall be admitted free of customs duty, subject to the compliance with the regulations of the State concerned, which may provide that the articles shall be kept under customs supervision and control.

Article 29—Documents the aircraft is required to carry (see page 69 above)

(f) if it carries passengers, a list of their names and places of embarkation and destination;

(g) if it carries cargo, a manifest and detailed declaration.

(ii) Summary

Chapter 1—Definitions and applicability

A. Definitions

Definitions include:

"*Airline*": As provided in Article 96 of the Chicago Convention, any air transport enterprise offering or operating a scheduled international air service. (Author's Comment: Article 96(c) omits the word "scheduled".)

"*Cargo*": Any property carried on an aircraft other than mail, stores and accompanied or mishandled baggage.

"*Security equipment*": Devices of a specialised nature for use, individually or as part of a system, in the prevention or detection of acts of unlawful interference with civil aviation and its facilities.

"*Mail*": Dispatches of correspondence and other objects tendered by and intended for delivery to postal administrations.

"*Narcotics Control*": Measures to control the illicit movement of narcotics and psychotropic substance by air.

"*Stores*": Articles of a readily consumable nature for use or sale on board an aircraft during flight including commissary supplies.

B. *Applicability*

The SARPS apply to all categories of aircraft operation except where a particular provision specifically refers to one type of operation without mentioning other types of operations.

Chapter 2—Entry and departure of aircraft

A. *General*

2.1: Governmental regulations and procedures applicable to the clearance of aircraft shall be no less favourable than those applied to other forms of transportation.

2.2: Contracting States shall make provision whereby procedures for the clearance of aircraft, including those normally applied for aviation security purposes, will be applied and carried out in such a manner as to retain the advantage of speed inherent in air transport.

2.3: No documents other than those provided for in this chapter shall be required from aircraft operators for departure and entry of aircraft.

2.4: Regulations of World Health Organisation concerning interruption of flights.

B. *Description, purpose and use of aircraft documents specifically: general declaration, passenger manifest, cargo manifest and AV7*

2.5–2.6: General declaration procedures and information on crew. See also Appendix 1 of the Annex.

2.7–2.9: Passenger and cargo manifests.

2.10: Mail. Only AV7 shall be required (see Chapter 7, Part 6 on mail).

2.11: Stores. Written declaration may only be required of stores laden on or unladen from an aircraft and not in respect of stores remaining on board.

2.12: Presentation of list of number of pieces of accompanied baggage shall not be required. Information shall be provided by operators where not otherwise provided by passengers on customs clearance.

C. *Outbound procedures*

2.13–2.15 deal with documentation required for outbound procedures and use of standard baggage weights.

D. *Inbound procedures*

2.16–2.17 deal with documentation for inbound procedures: general declaration, cargo manifest and stores list.

E. *Consecutive stops*

2.18 deals with documentation and procedures for consecutive stops at two or more international airports (Defined) in the same Contracting State.

F. *Completion of aircraft documents*

2.19–2.23: No visa or fee required in connection with the use of documentation required for entry or departure. Note the position with regard to errors in documentation and their correction. Operator or his agent shall not be subject to penalties if he satisfies the public authorities the error was inadvertent and not of a serious nature.

G. *Disinsecting of aircraft*

2.24–2.33: See reference to recommendations of the World Health Organisation and also to ICAO's Technical Instructions for the Safe Transport of Dangerous Goods by Air (doc. 9284) in respect of aerosol dispensers.

H. *Disinfection of aircraft*

2.34: States shall define the types of animals and animal products requiring the aircraft to be disinfected. Disinfection shall be limited to the relevant container or compartment and shall be expeditious. Inflammable compounds or solutions likely to damage aircraft structure shall not be used.

I. *Other arrangements*

2.35–2.47: Arrangements concerning international general aviation and other non-scheduled flights.

(I) General

2.35: States shall publish their regulations concerning the advance notices and applications for permission referred to in 2.36 and 2.41, and communicate them to ICAO.

(II) Advance notification of arrival

2.36: In the case of aircraft registered in other States not engaged in scheduled international services and making flights either in transit non-stop across territory of a State or stopping there for non-traffic purposes, such State shall not require more advance notice of such flights than is necessary to meet the requirements of ATC, and of the public authorities concerned. The Note makes clear that this provision is not intended to prevent the application of appropriate narcotics control measures.

   2.37: Information contained in a flight plan provided at least two hours in advance of arrival will be adequate advance notification as specified. Responsibility for notification rests with the appropriate authority of the State concerned.

   The Note draws attention to flight plan specifications given in Annex 2.

   2.38–2.39 deal with a single agency through which Notices may be routed and the appropriate addresses for such notification.

(III) Special permission for operations

2.40: If a State for flight safety reasons requires special permission for flights referred to in 2.36, application shall not be required to be filed more than three working days in advance of the intended arrival of the aircraft or its non-stop transit flight; and no information other than that in the flight plan shall be required.

   2.41: In the case of carriage by aircraft for remuneration or hire on a non-scheduled international service, if the State requires its special permission for taking on or discharging passengers, cargo or mail, it shall not require such permission to be applied for through diplomatic channels and shall establish effective procedures to deal with the application for permission promptly and without payment. Where possible permission will be for a specific length of time or number of flights.

   2.42: States should not require more than the details as listed in 2.42 in applications referred to 2.41.

   2.43–2.44 deal with agency for applications and the relevant addresses.

(IV) Clearance and sojourn of aircraft

2.45–2.46 set out recommended practices for inspection and clearance of general aviation services.

2.47: An aircraft which is not engaged in scheduled international air services and is admitted to an airport, as specified, temporarily free of duty in accordance with Article 24 shall be allowed to remain within the State for the established period without security for customs duty being required.

Chapter 3—Entry and departure of persons and their baggage

A. General

3.1–3.2: Regulations and Procedures applied to persons travelling by air shall be no less favourable than those applied to persons travelling by other means of transport and shall retain the advantage of speed inherent in air transport.

See reference to narcotics control, aviation security and Annex 17.

3.3: Only documents provided for in this chapter shall be required.

B. Entry requirements and procedures covering:

   (I) Passenger identity documents

3.4: States shall not require from visitors travelling by air any documents of identity other than a valid passport.

3.4.1–3.6 deal with further provisions on passports and their prompt issue. See reference to "A passport with Machine Readable Capability" (ICAO doc. 9303).

   (II) Visas

3.7–3.8: Note in particular: 3.7 Visas, if required, shall be issued without charge through reciprocal or other arrangements.

   (III) Additional documentation

3.9–3.10: Additional documentation to be limited to embarkation and disembarkation cards in accordance with Appendix 5.

   (IV) Public health requirements

3.11–3.12: Note reference to Vaccination or Revaccination Certificate.

   (V) Clearance procedure

3.13–3.21: These procedures include:

    (i) procedures for examination of identity documents;
    (ii) dual channel clearance systems as recommended by the Customs Cooperation Council;

(iii) baggage clearance (including mishandled baggage); and
(iv) system of Advance Passenger Information and Guideline of the Joint World Customs Organisation (IATA) on such Information.

(VI) Crew and other operators' personnel

3.22–3.27: Set out the SARPS for crew and other operators' personnel.

(VII) Civil aviation flight operations and cabin safety personnel

3.28–3.31: The only SARPS are Recommended Practices.

C. Departure requirements and procedures

3.32: Contracting States shall not require exit visas for own nationals or residents to tour abroad nor from visitors at end of stay.
   3.33–3.36 deal with documentation, baggage and taxes.

D. Completion of passenger and crew documents

3.37: Recommended Practice on names.

E. Custody and care of passengers and crew and their baggage

   (A) General provisions

3.38: The public authorities shall, without unreasonable delay, accept passengers and crew for examination for admissibility into the State.
   3.38.1: The operator shall be responsible for the custody and care of passengers and crew until they are accepted for such examination. This includes custody of passengers and crew between the aircraft and the terminal building and within the terminal building transit area. The Contracting State may relieve the operator from this responsibility.
   3.38.2: The responsibility of the public authorities after acceptance for examination.

   (B) Particular provisions

3.39: Upon refusal of admission of any person, the public authorities shall ensure that he shall be transferred back into the custody of the operator, who shall be responsible for promptly removing him to the point where he commenced his journey or any other place where the person is admissible. Operator shall be advised and consulted regarding departure.
   3.39.1: States shall accept for examination a person being returned from his point of disembarkation after having been found inadmissible if this person previously stayed in their territory before embarkation, other than in direct transit. States shall not return such a person to the country where he was earlier found to be inadmissible.

3.39.2 deals with a substitute document where the inadmissible person has lost or destroyed his travel document.

3.39.3 deals with security precautions to be taken by the operator on the return flight.

3.39.4: The obligation of the carrier to transport any passenger away from the territory of a State shall terminate from the moment such person has been definitely admitted into that State.

3.39.5: Where a person found inadmissible is returned to the operator for transport away from the territory of the State, the operator shall not be precluded from recovering from such person transportation costs arising from his inadmissibility.

3.40: Operators shall take precaution at embarkation to the end that the passengers possess any control documents prescribed by States.

3.40.1: States shall not fine operators if passengers are found inadmissible unless there is evidence to suggest that the carrier was negligent in taking precautions to the end that passengers complied with the documentary requirements for entry into the receiving State.

3.40.2 deals with Recommended Practice for Mitigation of any such fine.

3.40.3: States and operators shall cooperate where practical in establishing the validity and authenticity of passports or visas.

3.41: Each State shall ensure that public authorities shall seize fraudulent, falsified or counterfeit travel documents of inadmissible persons. Such documents shall be removed from circulation and returned to the appropriate authorities. In place of the documents a covering letter should be issued by the removing State and attached to it will be a copy of the forged travel documents as well as any other important information. The letter and attachments shall be handed over to the operator responsible for removal of the inadmissible person. It will serve as information to the authorities at transit and/or original point of embarkation.

3.41.1: The letter will be accepted by other States without production of the offending document.

3.41.2: This deals with notice of a removal order being given to the authorities of the countries of transit and where advisable of final destination of the trip planned. The notice should contain the information as specified, including risk assessment.

3.42: On transfer back of an inadmissible passenger pursuant to 3.39, the travel documents shall be delivered to the operator or escort for delivery to the State of destination.

3.43: Where operator has taken the precautions in 3.40 but the passenger is not admitted for reasons beyond the control of the operator, the operator should not be held directly responsible for any costs related to official detention of the passenger.

3.44: A State shall respond within a reasonable time (not more than 30 days) to the request by the returning State for travel documents to be issued to one of its nationals.

3.45–3.46 develop the provisions of 3.44.

3.47: A State shall not thwart the return of one of its nationals by rendering that person stateless without the approval of the State from which that person has been ordered to be removed.

3.48: Operators shall be informed when persons are obliged to travel because they have been formally ordered by public authorities of a Contracting State to be removed from that State.

3.49: Each State shall ensure that public authorities ordering the deportation inform the public authorities of transit countries, and if advisable, those of destination countries of the planned transport.

3.50: In States where the operator is under obligation to the customs authorities for safeguarding baggage until customs clearance, he shall be free from his obligation and from liabilities for duties and taxes when it is taken into charge by the customs authorities and is under their sole control.

Chapter 4—Entry and departure of cargo and other articles

A. General

4.1–4.2: These provisions correspond to those in "General" in Chapters 2 and 3.

4.3: States shall examine with operators and trade organisations all possible means of simplifying clearance of goods and introduce such means as soon as possible.

B. Electronic data-processing techniques

4.4–4.8: This deals with their use for cargo facilitation and documentation. References include UN standards (UN/EDIFACT) and Guidelines for Expedited Clearance of World Customs Organisation.

4.9: When planning use of electronic data-processing techniques, States should endeavour to apply specified principles.

4.10: When introducing such techniques, States should consider optionality regarding participation by operators and others.

C. Clearance of export cargo

4.11: Contracting States should waive as far as possible presentation of individual documents for cargo shipments. See reference to UN Layout Key for Trade Documents.

4.12: A Contracting State requiring such documents for export clearance shall, where possible, limit its requirements to a single export declaration.

4.13: Arrangement(s) shall be made to accept cargo up to the time of departure, subject to security and narcotics control. Cargo includes unaccompanied baggage and stores.

4.14: States shall establish simple procedures for export licences and permits where required.

4.15.1: *Contracting States shall not normally require physical examination of cargo and unaccompanied baggage to be exported by air except for security reasons.* However, see subsequent Note and 4.15.2 requiring sealing.

4.16: deals with procedures where physical examination cannot be waived completely.

4.17: Cargo shall be permitted to be presented for clearance at any approved customs office. See provisions on subsequent procedures which should be kept simple, subject to aviation security and narcotics control.

4.18 deals with export of tax-free goods.

D. Clearance of import cargo

4.19: Contracting States shall endeavour to simplify documentary requirements for clearance of import cargo and minimise the forms and information to be shown.

4.19.1: Alignment of documents with UN layout for Trade Documents.

4.20: Commercial invoice is the basic document for accomplishment of customs and other government formalities.

4.21: Format.

4.22: Where an Air Waybill is required for inspection for cargo clearance, States shall not require consignor and/or operator to put special information on it for customs or other governmental purpose.

4.23: No consular formalities, charges or fees in respect of documents for cargo clearance are to be required.

4.24: A State which continues to require import licences and requirements for certain goods shall establish simple and rapid procedures for their issue and renewal.

4.25: States should arrange that imported low value or weight consignments should be exempt from import duties and taxes and from declaration procedures.

4.26: Simplified documentation procedures shall be used for cargo in excess of the criteria of 4.25, and upper limits of value or weight shall be established for such documentation.

4.27: Prompt release procedures shall be established for consignments not falling within 4.25 and 4.26.

4.28: Procedures shall be developed for submission of pre-import information to customs prior to arrival of cargo to facilitate process of entries.

4.29: Subject to national restrictions, aviation security and narcotics control, States shall arrange immediate clearance or release of special consignments, e.g. disaster relief shipments and perishables (livestock etc.).

4.29.1: General cargo requiring only a normal inspection should be released not more than four hours, or as soon as practical thereafter, after presentation of proper documentation or electronic equivalent.

4.30 deals with procedures where clearance agencies are involved.

4.31 requires cooperation of interested parties to reduce to a minimum the dwell-time of cargo in airport terminals.

4.31.1: Release of part shipments.

4.32: Physical examination shall be accomplished on a sampling or selective basis. Physical means of rapid examination shall be devised.

4.33: Cargo including unaccompanied baggage which has been unloaded at an international airport shall be allowed to be transferred to any authorised customs office within the State for entry and clearance as simply as possible.

4.33.1: Cargo opened for a physical examination and sealed according to 4.15 shall be handled and cleared in the same way as cargo which has not been opened.

4.34: If the volume justifies it, States in cooperation with interested parties should promote handling facilities for accompanied and unaccompanied courier baggage; see guidance material in the Attachment to the Annex. These arrangements must be fully consistent with security requirements and should include: (a) a more advanced notification of large number of bags, (b) a more advanced deadline for check-in, (c) distinctive baggage tag for courier baggage, (d) identification of check-in facilities, see also the source of these procedures, Recommendation B-12 of FALS/10.

E. Containers, pallets and their loads

4.35: States shall, subject to compliance with their respective regulations, permit temporary importation of containers, pallets and associated equipment without payment of customs duties and other taxes and charges and shall facilitate the use of this equipment in air traffic.

4.36–4.40 specify further SARPS on facilitation on pallets etc. See Note on such equipment subject to hire purchase, lease or other contract.

F. Limitation of operator's responsibilities

4.41: Unless the operator is, or is acting for, importer/exporter, he shall not be responsible for ensuring requirements on import documents such as commercial invoice or import licence are met, or for inaccuracies on such documents.

4.42: Where the operator is obliged to customs for safeguarding cargo, unaccompanied baggage (Defined), mail, or stores until customs clearance, he will be free from these obligations and from liability for customs duty etc. when they are taken into charge by and under sole control of customs.

4.43: Operators are to be absolved from liability for customs duties, taxes etc. when goods are transferred with the approval of authorities into the possession of a third party, having adequate security or guarantee on file with customs.

4.44: States are not to impede movement of cargo solely to collect statistics. Any necessary documents shall be provided by the declarant as required by the authorities.

G. *Aircraft equipment stores and parts*

4.45: Import of stores provided for in 4.46 should not require ancillary documentation (e.g. certificates of origin).

4.46: Stores imported into the territory of a State by an airline of another State for use in connection with an international service operated by that airline shall be admitted free of customs duties and other taxes or charges subject to compliance with the relevant regulations. Such regulations shall not unreasonably interfere with the necessary use by the airline concerned of such stores.

4.47 deals with tax free sale and use of commissary supplies on board the aircraft.

4.48: Admission of ground equipment (Definition) and security equipment (Definition) should be free of customs duties and as far as possible other taxes and charges, subject to regulations of the State concerned. Such regulations should not unreasonably interfere with the necessary use by the airline of such equipment. See list of relevant items.

4.49 deals with admission of instructional material and aids free of customs duties and other taxes and charges, subject to regulations of the State concerned. See Note for type of instructional material.

4.50: States should arrange for duty free admittance of airline and operators' documents and allow for their expeditious clearance.

4.51: States shall establish procedures for prompt entry into or departure from their territories of aircraft equipment, spares, ground training and security equipment.

4.51.1: Listing of such equipment on manifest.

4.52: States shall not require advance production of documents, e.g. entry or exit permits when aircraft equipment, spare parts, stores, ground, training and security equipment are urgently required by airline or operator of another State to maintain service, provided the airline accepts responsibility to produce those documents after admission or export of those items and provided the State concerned is satisfied the documents will be produced.

4.53: States shall allow non-profit-making loans of equipment and parts between airlines in connection with scheduled international air services without payment of duties, taxes or charges subject to control measures as specified.

H. *Cargo and other articles not entering the country of intended destination*

4.54: When, because of error, emergency, or inaccessibility upon arrival, cargo, unaccompanied baggage or stores are not unladen at their destination, the public authorities at the place of intended unlading shall accept a declaration from the operator that the articles in question have not been unladen and the reasons therefor and no new documentation shall be required from, or fines, penalties etc. imposed on, the operator.

4.55: Goods consigned to a destination within a State but which have not been released for home consumption in that State but subsequently are required to be returned to the point of origin or to be redirected, such State shall allow reforwarding without further licences, if no contravention of law is involved. The Note draws attention to special restrictions.

4.56: When, because of error or handling problems, cargo, unaccompanied baggage or stores are unladen at an international airport without being manifested, the State concerned shall facilitate return to the correct destination or allow normal clearance and delivery provided all requirements are satisfied. In the case of reforwarding the State may impose requirements as specified.

I. Unaccompanied baggage

4.57: Unaccompanied baggage carried by air shall be cleared under the procedure applicable to accompanied baggage or under another simplified customs procedure distinct from that normally applicable to other cargo.

See Note on the intention of this provision.

4.57.1: States shall provide for clearance of unaccompanied baggage by authorised representative for the owner.

J. Animal and plant shipments

4.58: Where States require sanitary certificates or related documents they shall publish details.

K. Mail documents and procedures

4.59: States shall carry out the handling, forwarding and clearance of mail and shall comply with the documentary procedures as prescribed in the Acts in force of the Universal Postal Union.

Chapter 5—Traffic passing through the territory of a State

This deals with:

A.   Traffic arriving and departing on same through-flight;
B.   Traffic being transferred to another flight at the same airport;
C.   Traffic being transferred to another airport;
D.   Cargo traffic being transferred between air and surface transport;
E.   Free airports and free zones.

Chapter 6—International airports—facilities and services for traffic

A. General

6.1: States shall take all necessary steps to secure the cooperation of operators and airport administrations in ensuring that satisfactory facilities and services are provided for rapid handling and clearance of passengers, crew, baggage, cargo and mail at their international airports. Such facilities and services shall be flexible and capable of expansion to meet anticipated growth in traffic volume and increased security measures while permitting narcotic control measures.

6.2: Consultations shall be encouraged between airport administration on the one hand and operators, control authorities, and bodies representing other users at the earliest stage when planning a new or substantially modified terminal building at their international airports.

6.3: Cooperation of operators and airport administrators shall be secured as specified to achieve at international airports best possible airport traffic flow arrangements.

6.3.1 deals with traffic peaking problems.

6.4 deals with facilitation problems caused by the levying of a passenger service charge at international airports and their solution.

6.5 deals with the acceptable use of credit cards.

6.6: Operators should be offered the choice of providing their own services for ground handling operations or the option of having such operations performed by another authorised operator, or by the airport operator, or approved servicing agent.

B. Airport traffic flow arrangements

(I) Common provisions

6.7: States shall ensure particular attention is given to the need for adequate facilities to be made available at international airports and measures are adopted to permit embarkation and disembarkation of passengers without delay.

6.7.1–6.14 are all Recommended Practices dealing with the handling of, and the provision of facilities to, passengers, their handling, and warnings given to them such as the consequences of illegal narcotics trafficking.

(II) Parking and servicing arrangements

6.15: Adequate measures should be taken to ensure convenient parking and servicing of aircraft of all types and categories—regular, non-scheduled and general aviation aircraft—in order to expedite clearance and operations on the apron and to reduce aircraft ground stop time. Several specific recommendations are made in (a)–(g).

(III) Outbound passengers, crew and baggage

6.16–6.25 are all Recommended Practices concerning the arrangements that States should make to enable passengers to complete departure formalities within a reasonable time. States should establish as a goal, as far as is practicable, a total time period

*of 60 minutes for the completion of departure formalities for all passengers requiring
not more than normal inspection on international air transport services calculated
from the time of the passenger's presenting himself at the first processing point at the
airport until the scheduled time of his flight departure, noting that security measures
must be fully carried out. This section also deals with examination of baggage for
security or narcotics control purposes.*

*6.26: Premises which the crew members have to visit for operational purposes
should be readily accessible and, if possible, next to one another.*

(IV) Inbound passengers, crew and baggage

6.27: This Standard requires States to make arrangements for a sufficient
number of control channels so that clearance of inbound passengers and crew
may be obtained with the least possible delay. Additional channels shall be
available if possible to which complicated cases may be directed.

6.28: Particular points of delay.

*6.29: Clearance within forty-five minutes from disembarkation should be estab-
lished as a goal for clearance at major international airports for all passengers
requiring not more than normal inspection.*

6.30–6.32.1 deal with procedures concerning the unloading of baggage and
assistance in its carriage.

(V) Transit and transfer of passengers and crew

*6.33–6.36: See references in particular to refuelling procedures and also the use of
telescopic passageways.*

(VI) Miscellaneous facilities and services in passenger terminal buildings

6.37–6.39 are *Recommended Practices* with the exception of 6.37.2. This Standard provides that international airports shall be equipped with functional
secure storage facilities where unclaimed, unidentified and mishandled baggage will be kept available for clearance until forwarded, claimed or disposed
of in accordance with applicable regulations and procedures. Airline personnel
shall have access to the baggage at least throughout the hours of operation.

*6.38–6.39 deal with non-travelling public in terminal buildings, facilities for
group/tour operators and the sale of duty-free or other goods.*

(VII) Cargo and mail handling and clearance facilities

6.40–6.51 This sets out 12 Recommendations dealing with cargo.
6.52 Recommendation dealing with mail.

C. Facilities required for implementation of public health, emergency medical relief, and animal and plant quarantine measures

6.53: States, in cooperation with airport authorities, shall ensure the maintenance of public health, including human, animal and plant quarantine at international airports.

6.54–6.59 set out SARPS to develop the duties imposed by 6.53.

D. Facilities required for clearance controls and operation of control services

6.60: Space and facilities for the authorities in charge of clearance controls should, as far as possible, be provided at public expense.

6.61: If the space and facilities are not provided at public expense, they shall be provided on terms no less favourable than those applicable to operators of other means of transportation.

Note: 6.62.1 states that under Annex 15—AIS, States are obligated to publish the types and hours of clearance services (customs, immigration, health) at their international airports.

The remainder of D sets out the organisation for the provision of these facilities.

6.64: States should make arrangements whereby one State will permit another State to station representatives of the public authorities in its territory to examine aircraft, passengers, crew, baggage, cargo and documentation for customs, immigration, public health and animal and plant quarantine purposes as specified.

E. Monetary exchange facilities

6.65–6.71 Relevant information shall be displayed and adequate facilities for legal exchange of funds shall be provided.

Chapter 7—Landing elsewhere than at international airports

A. General

7.1: Each State shall take steps to ensure that all possible assistance is rendered by its public authorities to an aircraft, which, for reasons beyond the control of the pilot in command, has landed elsewhere than at one of its international airports and shall keep control formalities and procedures to a minimum.

7.2: The crew shall report such a landing as soon as practicable to the public authorities.

B. Short stopover

7.3 deals with a short stopover, passenger and crew handling, and onward transportation, and any part of the aircraft load which cannot continue the flight.

C. No resumption of flight

7.4.1–7.4.4: These provisions apply where an aircraft is substantially delayed or unable to continue its flight. They relate to:

(i) the taking of emergency measures for health and safety of passengers and crew, and to minimise aircraft loss or destruction;
(ii) the accommodation of passengers and crew;
(iii) the removal of cargo, stores and unaccompanied baggage for safety reasons and their deposit in a nearby area pending completion of formalities;
(iv) disposal of mail as required by the Acts in force of the Universal Postal Union.

Chapter 8—Other facilitation provisions

A. Bonds and exemption from requisition or seizure

8.1: Where a bond is required from an operator to cover liabilities under customs or other similar laws, use of a single comprehensive bond should be permitted whenever possible.

8.2: Recommendation dealing with freedom from seizure of aircraft, ground equipment, security equipment, spare parts and technical supplies of a foreign airline for public use without prejudice to seizure for breach of law of the State concerned.

B. Facilitation of search, rescue, accident investigation and salvage

8.3–8.7 deal with the facilitation for entry of qualified personnel and the entry and removal of aircraft, tools, equipment etc., including removal of damaged aircraft.

C. Relief flights following natural and man-made disasters and accidents which seriously endanger human health or the environment, and similar emergency situations where United Nations assistance is required

8.8–8.9: This sets out the relevant facilitation SARPS for relief flights which shall be commenced as quickly as possible after obtaining agreement with the recipient State.

Note 1: Under the Internationally Agreed Glossary of Basic Terms the UN considers an emergency to be "a sudden and usually unforeseen event that calls for immediate measures to minimise its adverse consequences", and a disaster to be "a serious disruption of the functioning of society, causing widespread human, material or environmental losses which exceed the ability of the affected society to cope using only its own resources".

Note 2 draws attention to Annex 11, the Manual Concerning Safety Measures Relating to Military Activities Potentially Hazardous to Civil Aircraft Operations (doc. 9554) and the Manual concerning Interception of Civil Aircraft (doc. 9433).

D. Marine pollution and safety emergency operations

8.10–8.11: This sets out the two Standards for facilitation for aircraft combatting or preventing marine pollution.

E. Implementation of international health regulations and related provisions

8.12–8.15: The SARPS include compliance with the International Health Regulations of the World Health Organisation.

   8.16: Sickness on board aircraft, other than suspected airsickness, shall be reported promptly.

F. Establishment of national facilitation programmes

8.17–8.18: Each Contracting State shall establish a national facilitation programme based on the Chicago Convention and this Annex. Its objective will be to adopt all practicable measures to facilitate the movement of aircraft, crews, passengers, cargo, mail and stores, by removing unnecessary obstacles and delays.

   8.19: Each State shall establish National Air Transport Facilitation Committees and Airport Facilitation Committees or similar coordinating bodies for the purposes as specified.

   8.20: Close coordination should be established between civil aviation security and facilitation programmes.

G. Facilitation of the transport of passengers requiring special assistance

   (I) General

8.22–8.26 set out five Recommended Practices.

   (II) Access to airports

8.27: States shall take the necessary steps to ensure that airport facilities and services are adapted to the needs of persons with disabilities. *Six Recommended Practices are given.*

   (III) Access to air services

8.34: Contracting States shall take the necessary steps to ensue that persons with disabilities have adequate access to air services. *Four Recommended Practices are given.*

Appendices

The Appendices set out the following aircraft documents forms:

Appendix 1:   General Declaration.

Appendix 2:   Passenger Manifest.
Appendix 3:   Cargo Manifest.
Appendix 4:   Certificate of Residual Disinsection.
Appendix 5:   Embarkation/Disembarkation Card.
Appendix 6:   Recommendation of the Customs Cooperation Council on dual-channel system.
Appendix 7:   Crew Member Certificate.
Appendix 8:   Civil Aviation Safety Inspector Certificate.
Appendix 9:   Suggested Formats for Documents Relating to the return of inadmissible persons.
Appendix 10:   United Nations Layout Key for Trade Documents.
Appendix 11:   Model Outline for a national air facilitation programme.
Appendix 12:   Guidelines for the establishment and operation of National Air Transport and Airport Facilitation Committees.

Attachment

This Attachment sets out guidance material for Chapters 3, 4, 5 and 6. See Note: "This guidance material does not form part of the Annex proper but provides supplementary information concerning methods and procedures for implementing its provisions and facilitation in general." The guidance material deals with specific topics.

(iii) Comments

(1) Chapter 2G, 2.24–2.33. For an example of a passenger claim arising out of disinsecting procedures see page 250 in Chapter 7.

(2) The SARPS in Chapter 3 are reflected in GCC Pax Article 14 which imposes the responsibility and costs of compliance or non-compliance on the passenger.

(3) An example of the contrasting interests of facilitation and narcotics control is found in the English Court of Appeal decision of *Customs and Excise Commissioners* v. *Air Canada* (CA 1990). The court held that under the UK Customs and Excise Management Act 1979 a wide-bodied aircraft was subject to seizure by the State where narcotics were found on the aircraft, without the State having to prove evil intent. The decision was based on strict construction of the Act. The proceedings were civil proceedings *in rem* against the aircraft and the knowledge or motive of the owner or user of the aircraft was not relevant. The aircraft was returned on payment of £50,000. Air Canada appealed to the European Court of Human Rights who held Air Canada's rights had not been violated.

(4) An example of Recommended Practices and national requirements are found in Chapter 2, 2.7 above and in the UK Aeronautical Information Publication ("AIP"). 2.7 recommends that Contracting States should not require the presentation of the cargo manifest when this information can be

readily obtained in an alternative and acceptable manner. The UK AIP GEN 1.7.7 states that the cargo manifest is normally required for general control and anti-smuggling purposes.

ANNEX 10.   AERONAUTICAL TELECOMMUNICATIONS

Vol. I   Radio Navigation Aids (5th edition, July 1996).

Vol. II   Communication Procedures including those with PANS status (5th edition, July 1995).

Vol. III Part I: Digital Data Communication Systems;
Part II: Voice Communication Systems (1st edition, July 1995).

Vol. IV Surveillance Radar and Collision Avoidance Systems (1st edition, July 1995).

Vol. V   Aeronautical Radio Frequency Spectrum Utilization (1st edition, July 1996).

(i) Articles

Article 28—Air navigation facilities and standard systems

See Chapter 4 above.

Article 30—Aircraft radio equipment

(a) Aircraft of each Contracting State may, in or over the territory of other Contracting States, carry radio transmitting apparatus only if a licence to install and operate such apparatus has been issued by the appropriate authorities of the State in which the aircraft is registered. The use of radio transmitting apparatus in the territory of the Contracting State whose territory is flown over shall be in accordance with the regulations prescribed by that State.

(b) Radio transmitting apparatus may be used only by members of the flight crew who are provided with a special licence for the purpose, issued by the appropriate authorities of the State in which the aircraft is registered.

Article 69—Improvement of air navigation facilities

See page 27 above.

Article 83bis

See page 81 above.

(ii) Summary

VOLUME I—RADIO NAVIGATION AIDS

Page 1.

Note 1: All references to "Radio Regulations" are to the Radio Regulations published by the International Telecommunication Union.

Note 2 deals with the SARPS for certain forms of equipment, the necessity for specific installations and the review of the formulation of ICAO opinion and recommendations.

Chapter 1—Definitions

Included in the Definitions are:

> "*Telecommunications*": Any transmission, emission, or reception of signs, signals, writing, images or sounds or intelligence of any nature by wire, radio, optical or other electro-magnetic systems.
>
> "*Radar*": A radio detection device which provides information on range, azimuth and/or elevation of objects.
>
> "*Secondary Surveillance Radar (SSR)*": A system of secondary radar using ground transmitters/receivers (interrogators) and airborne transponders conforming to specifications developed by ICAO.

Definitions also include *Altitude, Elevation, Height, Pressure Altitudes* and *Touchdown*.

Chapter 2—General provisions for radio navigation aids

2.1: Aids to final approach and landing. The standard non-visual aids to final approach and landing shall be the instrument landing system (ILS) and the microwave landing system (MLS) conforming to the specified standards. Alternative non-visual aids can be used on the basis of regional air navigation agreements.

2.1.2–2.1.3 deal with requirements for publication in the AIP of specified differences.

2.1.4: Precision approach radar (PAR) and surveillance radar element (SRE) to be installed as supplement to a non-visual aid as specified.

2.1.5: A non-visual aid should be supplemented by a source or sources of guidance information which include:

> *(a) VHF omni-directional radio range (VOR) or equivalent;*
> *(b) locator(s) or non-directional radio beacon (NDB);*
> *(c) distance-measuring equipment (DME).*

2.2: Short-distance aids. Where, in the localities and on the routes as described, such aids are needed, the standard aids shall be the VHF omni-directional radio range (VOR) of the CW phase comparison type. Where for

ATC or operational reasons a more precise navigation service than VOR is needed, DME shall be used as a complement to VOR.

2.3: Radio beacons. This deals with the non-directional radio beacons (NDB) and en-route VHF marker beacons.

2.4: Long-distance aids. Material under development.

2.5: Secondary Surveillance Radar (SSR). See Volume IV of this Annex.

2.6: Specification for additional distance measuring facility.

2.7.1: Radio navigation aids of the type covered by the specifications in Chapter 3 of this volume and available for use by aircraft engaged in international air navigation shall be the subject of periodic ground and flight tests (Guidance is given in Attachment C to Part 1 and doc. 8071).

2.8: Provision of information on the operational status of radio navigation aids.

2.8.1: Aerodrome control towers and units providing approach control service shall be provided without delay with information on the operational status of air navigation aids essential to approach, landing and take-off at the aerodrome(s) with which they are concerned.

2.9: Secondary power supply. Radio navigation aids and ground elements of communication systems shall be provided with suitable power supplies and means to ensure continuity of services appropriate to the needs of the service provided. See Attachment C.

Chapter 3—Specifications for radio navigation aids

Note: Specifications concerning siting and construction of equipment and installations on operational areas aimed at reducing hazard to aircraft to a minimum are contained in Annex 14, Chapter 8.

Specifications are given for:

3.1: ILS.

3.2: Precision approach radar system comprising precision approach radar element (PAR) and the surveillance radar element (SRE).

3.3: VHF Omni-directional Radio range (VOR).

3.4: Non-directional Radio Beacon (NDB).

3.5: UHF distance measuring equipment (DME).

3.6: En-route VHF marker beacons (75 MHz).

3.7: (Reserved).

3.8: Secondary Surveillance Radar (SSR) system characteristics. (See Volume IV of this Annex.)

3.9: System characteristics for airborne ADF receiving systems.

3.10: (Reserved).

3.11: Microwave landing systems (MLS) characteristics.

Appendix A

Microwave landing system (MLS) characteristics.

Attachments

Attachment A: Determination of integrity and continuity of service objectives using the risk tree method which is described as a graphical method of expressing the logical relationship between a particular failure condition and the causes or failures leading to this condition.

Attachment B: Strategy for introduction and application of non-visual aids to approach and landing.

Attachment C: Information and material for guidance in the application of SARPS for ILS, VOR, PAR, 75 MHz marker beacons (en-route), NDB and DME.

Attachment D: (Reserved).

Attachment E: Guidance material on the pre-flight checking of VOR airborne equipment.

Attachment F: Guidance material concerning reliability and availability of radiocommunications and navigation aids.

Attachment G: Information and material for guidance in the application of the MLS SARPS.
Tables and figures for Attachment G.

(iii) Comment

2.7.1: Where malfunction of an aid may be an element in any accident, its tests records are important.

VOLUME II—COMMUNICATION PROCEDURES

Introduction

The object of the international aeronautical telecommunication service is to ensure the telecommunications and radio aids to air navigation necessary for the safety, regularity and efficiency of international air navigation.

The Procedures for International Aeronautical Telecommunication Service in this volume are for worldwide use. Supplementary regional Procedures may be necessary.

See reference to the Radio Regulations published by the International Telecommunications Union and their application. Communications Procedures are to be used in conjunction with the Abbreviations and Codes of doc. 8400 and with such other codes and abbreviations as may be approved by ICAO. Note the reference to exchange of information and the use of low modulation rates and medium and higher signalling rates.

Chapter 1—Definitions

The numerous Definitions are divided into the following sections:

1.1: Services;

1.2: Stations;

1.3: Communication methods;

1.4: Direction finding;

1.5: Teletypewriter systems;

1.6: Agencies;

1.7: Frequencies;

1.8: Miscellaneous.

Attachment A sets out a list of specialised COM terms and their Definitions related to aeronautical telecommunications planning. They fall into three categories of use: "general", "aeronautical fixed service planning", and "aeronautical mobile service planning".

Definitions include:

> *"Aeronautical Telecommunication Service"*: A telecommunication service provided for any aeronautical purpose.
>
> *"International Telecommunication Service"*: A telecommunication service between offices or stations of different States or between mobile stations which are not in the same State, or subject to different States.

Chapter 2—Administrative provisions relating to the international aeronautical communication service

2.1: Such service is divided into four parts:

(i) aeronautical fixed service;

(ii) aeronautical mobile service;

(iii) aeronautical radio navigation service;

(iv) aeronautical broadcasting service.

All are Defined.

2.2: The exchange of communications necessary for ensuring safety of air navigation and the regularity of air traffic should be handled without specific message charge unless otherwise provided.

2.3: Hours of service and changes shall be notified by the Competent Authority specified. Requests for changes shall be notified as soon as possible. Such changes where necessary shall be promulgated in NOTAM.

2.4: Supervision.

2.4.1: Each State shall designate the authority for ensuring the international aeronautical telecommunication service is conducted in accordance with the procedures in this Annex.

2.4.2–2.4.3 deal with infringements.

2.4.4 deals with the exchange of specified information between the authorities referred to in 2.4.1.

2.5: Superfluous transmissions. Each State shall ensure that there is no wilful transmission of unnecessary or anonymous signals, messages or data by any station within that State.

2.6 deals with the avoidance of interference resulting from tests and experiments.

Chapter 3—General procedures for international aeronautical telecommunications service

3.1: These procedures are general in character and shall be applied where appropriate to the other chapters in this Volume. The procedures are set out in the following headings.

3.2: Extension of services and closing down of stations.

3.3: Acceptance, transmission and delivery of messages.

3.4 applies Universal Coordinated Time (UTC) for use by all stations in aeronautical telecommunication service.

3.5: Record of communications. This requires a record of communications to be kept. See provisions on telecommunication logs, their retention, and contents.

3.6: Establishment of radio communications: all stations shall:

    (i) answer calls;
    (ii) exchange communications;
    (iii) radiate minimum power to ensure satisfactory service.

3.7: Use of abbreviations and codes (refer to ICAO Abbreviations and Codes doc. 8400).

3.8: A station shall cancel messages only with the authority of the message originator.

Chapter 4—Aeronautical fixed service (AFS)

This chapter deals with the aeronautical fixed service (AFS) which is defined as: "A telecommunication service between specified fixed points provided primarily for the safety of air navigation and for the regular, efficient and economical operation of air services."

4.1 provides that the AFS comprises all types and systems of point to point communications in the international aeronautical telecommunications service.

4.1.2 specifies the material permitted in AFS messages.

4.2: Note: Provisions relating to ATS direct speech communications are contained in Chapter 6 of Annex 11.

4.3 deals with the compatibility of meteorological operational channels and meteorological operational telecommunications networks with aeronautical fixed telecommunications network (AFTN).

AFTN is defined as: "A world-wide system of aeronautical fixed circuits provided, as part of the aeronautical fixed service, for the exchange of messages and/or digital data between aeronautical fixed stations having the same or compatible communications characteristics."

4.4: AFTN. This sets out the nature and categories of and procedures for the following messages:

    (a) distress;
    (b) urgency;
    (c) flight safety;
    (d) meteorological;
    (e) flight regularity;
    (f) aeronautical information services (AIS);
    (g) aeronautical administrative;
    (h) service.

4.4.1.1.1–4.4.1.1.9 deal with message priority indicators and certain other aspects of service messages.

4.4.1.2 gives the order of priority of transmission of messages.

4.4.1.3: The routeing of messages.

4.4.1.4: Supervision of message traffic.

4.4.1.4.2.1: When the receiving station detects that a message has been misrouted, it shall either send a service message to the previous station rejecting receipt of such message, or shall assume responsibility for transmission of the message to all addressee indicators.

4.4.1.4.2.3: If the sending station is notified of the misrouted message it shall reassume its responsibility for the message and for the transmission on the correct channel(s).

4.4.1.5 sets out the procedures for failure of communications.

4.4.1.6 and **4.4.1.7** set out the requirements respectively for the long-term and short-term retention of AFTN traffic records.

4.4.2–4.4.6 set out requirements for the form and content of messages.

Figure 4.1: "Message format ITA–2".

4.4.7: Provisions on tape feed in the use of the teleprinter and torn-tape installation.

4.4.8 deals with stripped address.

4.4.9–4.4.11: Teletypewriter procedures.

4.4.12–4.4.13: Correction of errors in conditions specified.

4.4.14: Predetermined distribution system for AFTN messages.

4.4.15: Message format—international alphabet No 5 (IA–5), see Figure 4.4.

4.4.16: Action taken on mutilated messages in IA–5 detected in computerised AFTN relay stations.

4.4.17: Transfer of AFTN messages over code and byte independent circuits and networks.

4.5: Air Traffic Management (ATM) data exchange.

Chapter 5—Aeronautical mobile service

Definitions

> *"Aeronautical mobile service"*: A mobile service between aeronautical stations and aircraft stations, or between aircraft stations, in which survival craft stations may participate; emergency position-indicating radio beacon stations may also participate in this service on designated distress and emergency frequencies.
>
> *"Aeronautical station"*: A land station in the aeronautical mobile services. In certain instances an aeronautical station may be located, for example, on board a ship or on a platform at sea.
>
> *"Aircraft station"*: A mobile station in the aeronautical mobile service, other than a survival craft station, located on board an aircraft.

Note 1 observes that while the provisions of Chapter 5 are based on the use of R/T (radio telephony), the provisions of 5.1 would apply to any mode of communications in the aeronautical mobile service.

Note 2: These communication procedures also apply, as appropriate, to the aeronautical mobile satellite service.

Chapter 5 sets out provisions relating to how aircraft should speak to aircraft or to the ground and vice versa.

5.1.1: In all communications the highest standard of discipline shall be observed at all times.

5.1.1.1: In all situations for which standard radio-telephony phraseology is specified it shall be used.

5.1.1.2: Transmission of messages, other than those specified in 5.1.8, on aeronautical mobile frequencies shall be avoided when the aeronautical fixed services can serve the intended purpose.

5.1.1.3: Consequences of human performance which could affect the accurate reception and comprehension of messages should be taken into consideration.

5.1.2–5.1.3 deal with the making of test signals.

5.1.4: Except as otherwise provided, the responsibility of establishing communication shall rest with the station having traffic to transmit.

5.1.5: Recommendation on elapse of time before second call.

5.1.6: Simultaneous call of an aeronautical station by several aircraft stations—order of priority shall be decided by former.

5.1.7: In communications between aircraft stations, the duration of communication shall be controlled by the receiving aircraft station, subject to intervention of an aeronautical station. If communication is on ATS frequency prior permission of aeronautical station should be obtained, except for brief exchanges.

5.1.8 sets out the six categories of message:

(a) Distress calls, distress messages and distress traffic—the radio-telephony signal MAYDAY;

(b) urgency messages, with the radio-telephony signal PAN, PAN or PAN, PAN MEDICAL;

(c) communications relating to direction finding;

(d) flight safety messages;

(e) meteorological messages;

(f) flight regularity messages.

Note 1 states that messages concerning acts of unlawful interference constitute a case of exceptional circumstances which may preclude the use of recognised communication procedures used to determine message category and priority.

Note 2: a NOTAM may qualify for any of the categories or priorities (c) to (f) inclusive. Its priority will depend on its contents and importance to the aircraft concerned.

Subsequent provisions deal with the six categories of messages in greater detail.

5.1.8.8: Interpilot air-to-air communication shall comprise messages related to any matter affecting safety and regularity of flight. Their category and priority shall be determined on the basis of their content in accordance with 5.1.8.

5.1.9 deals with cancellation of messages, comprising incomplete and complete transmissions.

5.2: Radiotelephony procedures.

5.2.1: General.

5.2.1.1: Language to be used.

5.2.1.1.1: In general, the air-ground R/T communications should be conducted in the language normally used by the stations on the ground.

Note: Language used by such station may not necessarily be the language of the State in which it is located.

Figure 5.1 sets out the radio telephony spelling alphabet.

5.2.1.1.2: Pending development and adoption of a more suitable form of speech for universal use, the English language should be used and should be available on request from any aircraft station unable to comply with 5.2.1.1.1.

See further references on language and use of interpreters.

5.2 continues with the requirements for and examples of the use of radio telephony.

5.3 deals with distress and urgency radiotelephony communication procedures.

5.4: Communications related to acts of unlawful interference.

5.4.1: Station addressed by an aircraft being subjected to an act of unlawful interference, or first station acknowledging a call from such aircraft, shall render all possible assistance as specified.

Chapter 6—Aeronautical radio navigation services

6.1: General.

6.1.1: The aeronautical radio navigation service comprises all types and systems of radio navigation aids in the international aeronautical service.

6.1.2–6.1.3 deal with the putting into operation of an aeronautical radio navigation aid and the provision to the local aeronautical information unit of information on changes in the operational status of non-visual aids.

6.2 sets out the procedure for Direction Finding.

Chapter 7—Aeronautical broadcasting service

This covers: the text of broadcasting materials, frequencies and schedules and radiotelephony broadcasting procedures.

Attachments

Attachment A: List of Specialised COM Terms and their definitions related to aeronautical telecommunications planning.

Attachment B: Development of radiotelephony speech for international aviation.

Attachment C: Guidance Material for AFTN Communications Procedures.

Attachment D: Guidance Material for Transmission of Long Messages on the AFTN.

(iii) Comments

4.4.1.4.2.1: Failure of the receiving station to act as required could in certain circumstances give rise to legal liability.

VOLUME III—COMMUNICATION SYSTEMS

Part I—Digital Data Communication Systems.
Part II—Voice Communication Systems.
First edition—July 1995.

These SARPS are detailed and technical. They are not summarised in this book.

The chapter headings given in the table of contents are:

Part I—Digital Data Communication Systems

(1) Definitions, which include the following:

"*Aeronautical telecommunication network (ATN)*": An internetwork architecture that allows ground, air-ground and avionic data subnetworks to interoperate by adopting common interface services and protocols based on the International Organization for Standardization (ISO) Open Systems Interconnection (OSI) reference model.

"Aircraft earth station (AES)": A mobile earth station in the aeronautical mobile-satellite service located on board an aircraft (see also GES).

"End-user": An ultimate source and/or consumer of information.

"Ground earth station (GES)": An earth station in the fixed satellite service, or, in some cases, in the aeronautical mobile-satellite service, located at a specific fixed point on land to provide a feeder link for the aeronautical mobile-satellite service.

(2) General (to be developed).
(3) Aeronautical Telecommunications Network (to be developed).
(4) Aeronautical Mobile-Satellite Service.
   7 Appendices
(5) SSR Mode S Air-ground Data Link.
(6) Air-ground VHF Digital Link (VDL).
   2 Appendices
(7) Subnetwork Interconnection (to be developed).
(8) AFTN Network.
(9) Aircraft Addressing System.
   Appendix
(10) Point-to-Multipoint Communications.

Part II—Voice Communication Systems

(1) Definitions (to be developed). This cross-refers to Annex 10 Volume 1 as specified.
(2) Aeronautical Mobile Service.
(3) SELCAL System.
(4) Aeronautical Speech Circuits.
(5) Emergency Locator transmitter (ELT) for Search and Rescue.
   Appendix 1 to Chapter 5 ELT Coding.

Attachments

Attachment A to Part I—Guidance material for aeronautical mobile-satellite service. Appendix to Attachment A Performance Analysis.

Attachment B to Part I—Guidance material for the VHF digital link (VDL).

Attachment A to Part II—Guidance material for communication systems.

VOLUME IV—SURVEILLANCE RADAR AND COLLISION AVOIDANCE SYSTEMS

Second edition July 1998.

Chapter 1—Definitions

Definitions include:

> *"Airborne collision avoidance system (ACAS)"*: An aircraft system based on secondary surveillance radar (SSR) transponder signals which operates independently of ground-based equipment to provide advice to the pilot on potential conflicting aircraft that are equipped with SSR transponders.
>
> *"Aircraft address"*: A unique combination of twenty-four bits available for assignment to an aircraft for the purpose of air-ground communications, navigation and surveillance.
>
> *"Secondary surveillance radar (SSR)"*: A surveillance radar system which uses transmitters/receivers (interrogators) and transponders.

See the accompanying notes and also Definition *"Collision avoidance logic"*.

Chapter 2—General

2.1: Secondary surveillance radar (SSR).

2.1.1: When SSR is installed and maintained in operation as an aid to air traffic services, it shall conform with the provisions of 3.1 unless otherwise specified.

2.1.2: Interrogation modes (ground-to-air).

2.1.2.1: Interrogation for air traffic services shall be performed on the modes described in 3.1.1.4.3 or 3.1.2. The uses of each mode shall be:

- Mode A;
- Mode C;
- Intermode;
- Mode S—as specified.

2.1.2.1.1: Administrations should coordinate with appropriate national and international authorities those implementation aspects of the SSR system which will permit its optimum use.

2.1.2.1.2: The assignment of interrogator identifier (II) codes, where necessary in areas of overlapping coverage across international boundaries of flight information regions, shall be the subject of regional air navigation agreements.

2.1.2.2: Mode A and Mode C interrogations shall be provided.

2.1.2.3: In areas where improved aircraft identification is necessary to enhance the effectiveness of the ATC system, SSR ground facilities having Mode S features should include aircraft identification capability.

2.1.2.4 deals with side-lobe suppression control interrogation.

2.1.3 deals with transponder reply modes (air-to-ground).

2.1.4 deals with Mode A reply codes (information pulses).

2.1.5 deals with Mode S airborne equipment capability.

2.1.6 deals with Mode S address (aircraft address).

Chapter 3—Surveillance radar systems; and Chapter 4—Airborne collision avoidance systems

These chapters deal with their respective systems.

Attachment A

This Attachment provides guidance material on ACAS.

VOLUME V—AERONAUTICAL RADIO FREQUENCY SPECTRUM UTILISATION

First edition July 1996.
   Chapter 1 deals with definitions. These include:

"*Duplex*": A method in which telecommunication between two stations can take place in both directions simultaneously.
"*Frequency channel*": A continuous portion of the frequency spectrum appropriate for a transmission utilising a specified class of emission.
"*Simplex*": A method in which telecommunication between two stations takes place in one direction at a time.

Chapter 2 deals with distress frequencies.
Chapter 3 deals with utilisation of frequencies below 30 Mhz.
Chapter 4 deals with utilisation of frequencies above 30 Mhz.
Appendix to Chapter 4 lists assignable frequencies.

Attachments

Attachment A: Considerations affecting the deployment of VHF communication frequencies.
Attachment B: Considerations affecting the deployment of LF/MF frequencies and the avoidance of harmful interference.
Attachment C: Guiding principles for long distance operational control communications.

ANNEX 11.   AIR TRAFFIC SERVICES—12TH EDITION (JULY 1998)

(i) Articles

Article 1—Sovereignty

See page 23 above.

Article 2—Territory

See page 23 above.

Article 28—Air navigation facilities and standard systems

See page 26 above.

(ii) Summary

Chapter 1—Definitions

The Definitions include:

> "*Advisory Airspace*": An airspace of defined dimensions or designated route, within which air traffic advisory service is available.
> "*Air traffic*": All aircraft in flight or operating on the manoeuvring area of an aerodrome.
> "*Air Traffic Control Clearance*": Authorisation for an aircraft to proceed under conditions specified by an air traffic control unit.
> "*Air Traffic Control Service*": A service provided for the purpose of:
> (a) preventing collisions;
> > (1) between aircraft; and
> > (2) on the manoeuvring area between aircraft and obstructions; and
>
> (b) expediting and maintaining an orderly flow of air traffic.
> "*Air traffic service*": A generic term meaning, variously, flight information service, alerting service, air traffic advisory service, air traffic control service (area control service, approach control service or aerodrome control service).
> "*Controlled airspace*": This is defined on page 134.
> "*Flight Information Service (FIS)*": Service provided for the purpose of giving advice and information useful for the safe and efficient conduct of flights.
> "*Human Factors Principles*": Principles which apply to aeronautical design, certification, training, operations and maintenance and which seek safe interface between the human and other system components by proper consideration to human performance.
> "*Uncertainty phase*": A situation wherein uncertainty exists as to the safety of an aircraft and its occupants (INCERFA).
> "*Alert phase*": A situation where apprehension exists as to the safety of an aircraft and its occupants (ALERFA).
> "*Distress phase*": A situation wherein there is reasonable certainty that an aircraft and its occupants are threatened by grave and imminent danger or require immediate assistance (DETRESFA).

Chapter 2—General

2.1.1: States shall determine in accordance with this Annex and for the territories over which they have jurisdiction those portions of the airspace and those aerodromes where air traffic services (ATS) will be provided. They shall arrange for such services to be established and provided in accordance with this Annex except by mutual agreement with another State, delegation of such services may be made to such other State.

See Note on such delegation.

2.1.2: Airspace over high seas or airspace of undetermined sovereignty where ATS will be provided shall be determined on the basis of regional air navigation agreements. A State having accepted responsibility for the airspace concerned will provide such services.

2.1.3: States providing ATS shall designate the responsible authority which may be a State or suitable Agency. See Notes and examples of situations where ATS may be established or provided.

2.1.4: Information on ATS shall be published as necessary.

2.2: Objectives of air traffic services shall be to:

(a) prevent collisions between aircraft;
(b) prevent collisions between aircraft on the manoeuvring area and obstructions on that area;
(c) expedite and maintain an orderly flow of air traffic;
(d) provide advice and information useful for the safe and efficient conduct of flights;
(e) notify appropriate organisations regarding aircraft in need of search and rescue, aid, and assist such organisations as required.

2.3 Specifies that ATS shall comprise three services identified as follows:

2.3.1: Air Traffic Control (ATC) Service which is divided into three parts:

(a) Area Control Service;
(b) Approach Control Service;
(c) Aerodrome Control Service;

so as to accomplish objectives (a), (b) and (c) of 2.2 above.

2.3.2: Flight Information Service—so as to accomplish objective (d) of 2.2.

2.3.3: Alerting Service—so as to accomplish objective (e) of 2.2.

2.4.1: The need for the provision of ATS shall be determined by consideration of the following:

(a) Types of air traffic involved;
(b) Density of air traffic;
(c) Meteorological conditions;

(d) Such other factors as may be relevant.

See Note on elements to be taken into account.

2.4.2: The carriage of Airborne Collision Avoidance Systems ("ACAS") by aircraft in a given area shall not be a factor in determining the need for ATS in that area.

2.5: Designation of the portions of the airspace and controlled aerodromes where ATS will be provided.

2.5.1–2.5.2: When it is determined that ATS will be provided in particular portions of airspace or at particular aerodromes then those portions shall be designated as:

2.5.2.1: Flight information regions, where flight information and alerting services will be provided.

2.5.2.2: Control areas and control zones. Those portions of airspace where ATC service will be provided to IFR flights shall be designated as control areas or control zones.

2.5.2.2.1.1: Portions of controlled airspace where ATC service will also be provided to VFR flights shall be designated as Classes B, C or D airspace.

2.5.2.2.2: Where designated within a flight information region, control areas and control zones shall form part of that flight information region.

2.5.2.3: Controlled Aerodromes. Those aerodromes where ATC service will be provided to aerodrome traffic shall be designated as controlled aerodromes.

2.6: Classification of airspaces. This deals with the classification and designation of ATS airspaces in classes A–G for IFR and VFR flights as described, see Appendix 4.

2.7: Required navigation performance (RNP). RNP is defined as a statement of the navigation performance accuracy necessary for operation within a defined airspace.

This deals with the prescription by States of RNP types. See also Manual on Required Navigation Performance (doc. 9613).

2.8: Establishment and designation of the units providing ATS. ATS will be provided by units as follows:

2.8.1: Flight information centres which shall provide flight information service and alerting services within flight information regions unless responsibility for such service is assigned to an ATC unit having adequate facilities.

2.8.2: ATC units shall be established to provide ATC service, flight information service and alerting service within control areas, control zones and at controlled aerodromes.

2.9: Specifications for flight information regions, control areas and control zones.

2.9.1: The delineation of airspace for provision of ATS should be related to the nature of the route structure and need for efficient service rather than to national boundaries.

See Consequential Notes.

2.9.2 deals with flight information regions which shall be delineated to cover the whole of the air route structure. Such a region shall include all airspace within its lateral limits except as limited by the upper flight information region. See 2.9.2.3 for further information on delineation of the FIRs and UFIRs. See also Note.

2.9.3: Control areas including *inter alia* airways and terminal control areas shall be delineated so as to encompass sufficient airspace to contain flight paths of IFR flights or portions to which it is desired to provide ATC service, taking into account the capabilities of the navigation aids normally used in that area.

Note: In a control area not formed by an airways system, a system of routes may be established to facilitate the provision of ATC.

2.9.3.2 establishes the lower limit of a control area. See also Air Traffic Services Planning Manual (doc. 9426).

2.9.3.3 deals with the circumstances when the establishment of the upper limit of a control area is required.

2.9.4: Flight information regions or control areas in upper airspace should be included within lateral limits of a number of lower FIRs or control areas in certain circumstances as specified.

2.9.5 specifies the lateral and vertical limits of the control zone.

2.10: Identification of ATS units and airspaces.

2.11: Establishment and identification of ATS routes. Identification is by designators. See Appendix 1 to the Annex and also the guidance material in the Air Traffic Services Planning Manual (doc. 9426).

2.12: Establishment of change-over points. "Change-over Point" is Defined as the point at which an aircraft navigating on an ATS route segment defined by reference to very high frequency omni-directional radio ranges is expected to transfer its primary navigational reference from the facility behind the aircraft to the next facility ahead of the aircraft.

See also Attachment A on establishment of change-over points.

2.13: Establishment and identification of significant points. These points shall be established for the purpose of defining an ATS route and/or in relation to the requirements of ATS services for information regarding the progress of aircraft in flight.

"Significant point" is Defined as a specified geographical location used in defining a ATS route or the flight path of an aircraft and for other navigation and ATS purposes. See Appendix 2 to the Annex.

2.14: Establishment and identification of standard routes for taxiing aircraft.

2.15: Coordination between the operator and ATS. These provisions concern primarily the passing of information to operators by ATS units. Note the reference to Annex 6.

2.16: Coordination between military authorities and air traffic services.

2.16.1: ATS authorities shall establish and maintain close cooperation with military authorities responsible for activities which may affect flights of civil aircraft; see 2.16.2–2.16.3 as to how this should be done.

2.17: Coordination of activities potentially hazardous to civil aircraft. These SARPS cover both State territory and the high seas. These activities are not necessarily related to civil aviation apart from the fact that they are hazardous to it. The objective of the coordination shall be to achieve the best arrangements which will avoid hazards to civil aircraft and minimise interference with their normal operation. Promulgation is the responsibility of the ATS authorities.

2.18: Aeronautical data.

2.18.1–2.18.6: deal with the determination and reporting of ATS related aeronautical data, the maintenance of its integrity, the protection of electronic data stored or in transit, determination and reporting of geographical coordinates, and accuracy of field work.

Guidance is given in World Geoditic System—1984 (WGS—84) Manual (doc. 9674) and RTCA Document DO–201A and European Organisation for Civil Aviation Equipment (Eurocae) Document ED–77—Industry Requirements for Aeronautical Information. See cross references to Annexes 4 and 15 and to Appendix 5 of this Annex.

2.19: Coordination between meteorological and ATS authorities.

2.19.1: To ensure that aircraft receive the most up-to-date meteorological information, arrangements shall be made when necessary between these authorities for the reporting procedures as specified. See 4.2.3 regarding transmission of special air reports.

2.19.2 deals with coordination of information on volcanic ash.

2.20: Coordination between aeronautical information services (AIS) and ATS.

2.20.1: To ensure that AIS units obtain information to enable them to provide up-to-date pre-flight information and to meet the need for in-flight information, arrangements shall be made between AIS and ATS authorities for reporting to the responsible AIS unit with the minimum of delay, the information as specified including aerodrome conditions, status of associated facilities, and volcanic activities.

2.20.2–2.20.3 deal with the introduction of changes to the air navigation system and their notification, taking into account the time needed by the AIS for their promulgation. Changes affecting charts and/or computer based navigation systems which qualify to be notified by AIRAC System are particularly important.

2.20.4: ATS responsible for the provision of raw aeronautical information/ data shall take into account required accuracy and integrity as specified in Appendix 5.

See also the Notes 1–4 concerning NOTAMS, SNOTAMS, ASHTAMS, and AIRAC Information (Annex 15) and volcanic activity (Annex 3).

2.21: Minimum flight altitudes. These shall be determined and promulgated for each ATS route. They shall provide minimum clearance above the relevant controlling obstacle.

Publication is dealt with in Annex 15. Obstacle clearance criteria are contained in PANS—OPS (doc. 8168) Vol. II Part VI.

2.22.1: Service to aircraft in the event of an emergency. An aircraft known or believed to be in a state of emergency including being subjected to unlawful interference shall be given maximum consideration, assistance and priority necessitated by the circumstances.

The Note concerns use of SSR transponders.

2.22.1.1: Observance of human factors principles (Defined).

2.22.2 deals with functions of ATS units on occurrence of unlawful interference.

2.23: In-flight contingencies.

2.23.1 deals with strayed and unidentified aircraft.

Note 1 defines (a) "strayed aircraft": an aircraft which has deviated significantly from its intended track or which reports that it is lost; and (b) "unidentified aircraft": an aircraft which has been observed or reported to be operating in a given area but whose identity has not been established.

Note 2: Some aircraft can be both strayed and unidentified at the same time.

2.23.1.1–2.23.1.2 set out the SARPS for strayed and unidentified aircraft respectively.

2.23.2: Interception of civil aircraft.

2.23.2.1: As soon as an ATS unit learns that an aircraft is being intercepted in its area of responsibility it will take the appropriate steps as specified:

(a) and (b) establish two-way communication with the intercepted aircraft and inform its pilot of the interception;

(c) and (d) establish contact with, and inform, intercept control unit; and relay messages between intercepting aircraft or intercept control unit and the intercepted aircraft;

(e) in close coordination with the intercept control unit, take all necessary steps to ensure safety of intercepted aircraft;

(f) inform ATS units serving adjacent flight information regions if it appears the aircraft has strayed from such regions.

2.23.2.2 deals with the functions of an ATS unit learning of an aircraft being intercepted outside its area of responsibility.

2.24: Time in air traffic services. Coordinated Universal Time (UTC) shall be used.

ATS units shall be equipped with clocks which shall be checked as specified. Correct time shall be obtained from a standard time station as specified. Control towers shall prior to taxiing for take-off provide the pilot with correct time. ATS units shall provide correct time to aircraft on request.

2.25: States shall establish requirements for carriage and operation of pressure-altitude reporting transponders within defined airspace.

Chapter 3—ATC service

3.1 sets out the VFR and IFR flights and airspace where ATC service shall be provided. Such service shall also be provided to all aerodrome traffic at controlled aerodromes.

3.2: The parts of ATC service shall be provided by various units as follows:

(a) Area Control Service: by area control centre or the unit providing approach control service in a control zone or in a control area of limited extent as specified.

(b) Approach Control Service: by aerodrome control tower or area control centre or by approach control service as specified; and

(c) Aerodrome Control Service: by aerodrome control tower.

See Note: the task of providing specified services on the apron, e.g. Apron Management Service, may be assigned to an aerodrome control tower or to a separate unit.

These services are Defined.

3.3: Operation of ATC service.

3.3.1: In order to provide ATC service, an ATC unit shall:

(a) be provided with information concerning movement and progress of aircraft as specified;

(b) determine from such information the relative positions of known aircraft to each other;

(c) issue clearances and information for the purpose of preventing collision between aircraft under its control and of expediting and maintaining an orderly flow of traffic;

(d) coordinate clearances as necessary with other units as specified, concerning (1) possible conflict of traffic; (2) transfer of control.

3.3.2: Information on aircraft movements, together with a record of ATC clearances issued, shall be displayed to permit ready analysis in order to maintain efficient flow of traffic with adequate aircraft separation.

3.3.3: Clearances issued by ATC units shall provide separation between flights and in airspace classes as specified.

However, note the exception where a specific portion of the flight is conducted in VMC on request.

3.3.4: Separation by an ATC unit shall be obtained by at least one of:

(a) vertical separation, obtained as described;

(b) horizontal separation, obtained as described;

(c) composite separation, obtained as described.

See guidance in "Manual on Implementation of a 300m (1000 ft) Vertical Separation Minimum between FL 290 and FL 410 inclusive (doc. 9574)", and also "ATS Planning Manual (doc. 9426)".

3.4: Separation minima.

3.4.1 Selection of separation minima for a given portion of airspace shall be:

(a) as prescribed by the PANS—RAC and the Regional Supplementary Procedures applicable. In the circumstances specified, other minima shall be established by (1) the appropriate ATS authority following consultation with the operators, for routes within the sovereign airspace of a State; (2) regional air navigation agreements for routes in airspace over the high seas or in areas of undetermined sovereignty. (See reference to PANS—RAC Rules of the Air and Air Traffic Services (doc. 4444) and Part I of Regional Supplementary Procedures (doc. 7030));

(b) selection of separation minima shall be made in consultation between the ATS authorities responsible for the provision of ATS in the neighbouring airspace when:

(i) traffic will pass from one into the other of the neighbouring airspaces;

(ii) routes are closer to the common boundary of the neighbouring airspaces than the separation minima applicable in the circumstances.

3.4.2: Details of the selected separation minima and their areas of application shall be notified to (a) the ATS units concerned; and (b) to pilots and operators through aeronautical information publications, where separation is based on the use by aircraft of specified navigation aids or techniques.

3.5: Responsibility for control.

3.5.1: A controlled flight shall be under the control of only one ATC unit at one time. ("Controlled flight" is Defined as "any flight which is subject to an ATC clearance").

3.5.2: Responsibility for control of all aircraft within given block of airspace shall be vested in a single ATC unit. Control may be delegated to other ATC units provided coordination between all units is assured.

3.6: Transfer of responsibility for control.

3.6.1: Place or time of transfer. This deals with the three cases of transfer of responsibility between:

3.6.1.1: Two units providing area control service.

3.6.1.2: A unit providing area control service and a unit providing approach control service.

3.6.1.3: A unit providing approach control service and a unit providing aerodrome control service.

3.6.1.3.1 deals with arriving aircraft.

3.6.1.3.2 deals with departing aircraft.

3.6.2: Coordination of transfer.

3.6.2.1: Responsibility for control of an aircraft shall not be transferred from one ATC unit to another without the consent of the accepting unit obtained as specified.

The rest of the section deals with the procedures for coordination between the two units and the use of Radar and ADS data; see reference to the flight plans.

3.7: Air traffic control clearance. Air traffic control clearance is Defined as "Authorisation for an aircraft to proceed under conditions specified by an air traffic control unit".

See the two Notes following the Definition on use of the term "clearance".

3.7.1: ATC clearances shall be based solely on requirements for providing ATC service.

3.7.1.1: An ATC clearance shall indicate:

(a) aircraft identification as shown in the flight plan;
(b) clearance limit;
(c) route of flight;
(d) level(s) of flight for the entire route or part thereof and of changes of levels if required;
(e) any necessary instructions or information on other matters as indicated.

3.7.1.2: Standard departure and arrival routes and associated procedures should be established to facilitate safe, orderly and expeditious flow of air traffic and description of route and procedure in ATC clearances. See reference to Air Traffic Services Planning Manual (doc. 9426) and PANS—OPS Vol II (doc. 8168).

3.7.2 deals with clearance for transonic flights.

3.7.3: Coordination of clearances. ATC clearance shall be coordinated between ATC units to cover the entire route of an aircraft or a specified portion thereof as indicated in 3.7.3.1–3.7.3.4.

3.7.4: Control of air traffic flow. This deals with the procedures when it becomes apparent to an ATC unit that traffic additional to that already accepted cannot be accommodated.

3.8: Control of persons and vehicles at aerodromes.

3.8.1: The movement of persons or vehicles including towed aircraft on the manoeuvring area of an aerodrome shall be controlled by the aerodrome control tower as necessary to avoid hazard to them or to aircraft landing, taxiing or taking-off.

3.8.2: deals with those conditions where low visibility procedures are in operation and relate to restriction on persons and vehicles, minimum separation between vehicles and taxiing aircraft, and the protection of the more restrictive ILS or MLS critical and sensitive areas when mixed ILS and MLS

Category II and Category III precision instrument operations are taking place.

Guidance is contained in the Manual of Surface Movement Guidance and Control Systems (SMGCS) (doc. 9476).

3.8.3: Emergency vehicles proceeding to aircraft in distress shall be afforded priority.

3.8.4 sets out, subject to 3.8.3, the rules concerning vehicles on the manoeuvring area.

3.9 Provision of radar. *Recommendation: Radar systems should provide for the display of safety-related alerts and warnings, including conflict alert, conflict prediction, minimum safe altitude warning and unintentionally duplicated SSR codes.*

3.10: Use of surface movement radar (SMR). The Note states SMR has proven to be useful in assisting monitoring of aircraft and vehicles on the manoeuvring area. It refers to Annex 14 and also Air Traffic Services Planning Manual (doc. 9426) for guidance.

Chapter 4—Flight Information Service (FIS)

4.1.1: FIS shall be provided to all aircraft likely to be affected by the information and which are:

    (a) provided with ATC service;
    (b) otherwise known to the relevant ATS units.

See Note: FIS does not relieve the pilot-in-command of any responsibilities. He has to make the final decision regarding any suggested alteration of flight plan.

4.1.2: Where ATS provides FIS and ATC service the provision of ATC service has precedence over the provision of FIS whenever the provision of ATC service requires.

See also Note recognising that in certain circumstances aircraft on final approach, landing, take-off and climb may require to receive without delay essential information other than that pertaining to the provision of ATC service.

4.2: Scope of FIS.

4.2.1: FIS shall include the provision of information on:

    (a) SIGMET and AIRMET;
    (b) volcanic activity;
    (c) release into the atmosphere of radioactive materials or toxic chemicals;
    (d) changes in the serviceability of navigation aids;
    (e) changes in conditions of aerodromes and associated facilities;
    (f) unmanned free balloons;

and any other information likely to affect safety.

4.2.2: FIS shall include in addition to the information in 4.2.1 the provision of information concerning weather at aerodromes as specified, collision hazards to aircraft operating in specified airspace Classes, and available information for flight over water areas.

4.2.3: Transmission of special air-reports.

4.2.4 deals with additional FIS provided for VFR flights.

4.3: Operational Flight Information Service Broadcasts.

4.3.1: Application.

4.3.1.1: Meteorological and operational information included in the FIS shall, whenever available, be provided in an operationally integrated form.

4.3.1.2 and 4.3.1.3: Transmission and contents of operational flight information.

4.3.2: HF operational flight information service (OFIS) broadcasts.

4.3.2.1: OFIS broadcasts should be provided when regional air navigation agreement has determined a requirement exists.

4.3.2.2 sets out the form and requirements of the broadcast and the information it shall contain.

4.3.2.3–4.3.2.4 deal with use of English language. Where another language is available as well, discrete channels should be used for each language.

4.3.2.5: HF OFIS broadcast messages should contain the information in the sequence as indicated or as determined by regional air navigation agreement. The listed information is:

(a) *en-route weather information;*

(b) *aerodrome information as specified.*

4.3.3: VHF Operational Flight Information Service (OFIS) broadcasts.

4.3.3.1: VHF OFIS broadcast should be provided as determined by regional air navigation agreement. These Recommendations are similar to those on HF OFIS.

4.3.3.2–4.3.3.4 deal with determination of the relevant procedures for the broadcasts and languages.

4.3.3.5: VHF OFIS broadcasts should contain the following information in the sequence indicated:

(a) *name of aerodrome;*

(b) *time of observation;*

(c) *landing runway;*

(d) *significant runway surface conditions and, if appropriate, braking action;*

(e) *changes in the operational state of the navigation aids, if appropriate;*

(f) *holding delay, if appropriate;*

(g) *surface wind direction and speed; if appropriate, maximum wind speed;*

(h) visibility and, where applicable, runway visual range (RVR);

* *(i) present weather;*

*(j) *cloud below 1500 m (5000 ft) or below the highest minimum sector altitude, whichever is greater; cumulonimbus; if the sky is obscured, vertical visibility, when available;*

† *(k) air temperature;*

† *(l) dew point;*

†*(m) QNH altimeter setting;*

(n) *supplementary information on recent weather of operational significance and where necessary wind shear;*

(o) *trend type landing forecast, when available;*

(p) *notice of current SIGMET messages.*

* and †: see footnotes.

4.3.4: Voice Automatic Terminal Information Service (Voice-ATIS) broadcasts.

4.3.4.1: ATIS broadcasts shall be provided at aerodromes where there is a requirement to reduce the communication load on ATS VHF air-ground communications channels. When provided they shall comprise the broadcast services for arriving and departing aircraft as specified.

4.3.4.2–4.3.4.8: The remainder of the sections sets out further details on the form, procedures and content of ATIS. See reference to Circulars 216, 238 and 241 dealing with human factors.

4.3.5 deals with data link-automatic terminal information service (D-ATIS). Guidance is given in Manual of ATS Data Link Applications (doc. 9694).

4.3.6: Automatic terminal information service (voice and/or data link).

4.3.6.1–4.3.6.5 deal with the procedures and dissemination for such service.

4.3.7: ATIS broadcast messages containing both arrival and departure information shall contain the elements of information listed.

4.3.8–4.3.9 list the contents of ATIS broadcasts for arriving aircraft and departing aircraft respectively.

4.3.10 deals with the use of OFIS messages in directed request/reply transmissions.

Chapter 5—Alerting service

This is Defined as "A service provided to notify appropriate organizations regarding aircraft in need of search and rescue, aid, and assist such organizations as required."

5.1: Application.

5.1.1: Alerting service shall be provided:

(a) for all aircraft provided with ATC service;

(b) in so far as practicable, to all other aircraft having filed a flight plan or otherwise known to ATS; and

(c) to any aircraft known or believed to be the subject of unlawful interference.

5.1.2: Flight information centres (Defined) or area control centres shall serve as the central point for collecting information relevant to a state of emergency of an aircraft operating within the flight information region or control area concerned and for forwarding it to the appropriate rescue coordination centre.

5.1.3 deals with notification of a state of emergency arising while the aircraft is under control of aerodrome control tower or approach control office and steps to be taken.

5.2: Notification of rescue coordination centres. Without prejudice to any other circumstances rendering notification advisable, ATS units shall except as prescribed in 5.5.1 notify rescue coordination centres immediately an aircraft is considered to be in a state of emergency in accordance with the following:

(a) Uncertainty phase: When there is no communication with or from the aircraft within the periods as specified or aircraft fails to arrive within 30 minutes of ETA, except where no doubt exists as to safety of aircraft and its occupants;

(b) Alert phase: (1) following uncertainty phase where subsequent attempts to communicate with the aircraft or make other enquiries have failed to reveal news of the aircraft; or (2) aircraft fails to land within five minutes of estimated time of landing following clearance and communication has not been re-established; or (3) information has been received indicating operating efficiency of the aircraft has been impaired but not to the extent that a forced landing is likely; except when evidence exists that would allay apprehension as to the safety of an aircraft and its occupants; or (4) when an aircraft is known or believed to be the subject of unlawful interference.

(c) Distress phase when: (1) following alert phase, unsuccessful attempts to establish communication and unsuccessful enquiries point to probability that aircraft is in distress; or (2) fuel on board is considered to be exhausted or insufficient for safety or; (3) information indicates that a forced landing is likely, due to impaired operating efficiency of the aircraft or; (4) information is received or it is reasonably certain that the aircraft is about to make or has made a forced landing, except where there is reasonable certainty that aircraft and occupants are not threatened by grave and imminent danger and do not require immediate assistance.

5.2.2: The notification shall contain such information as specified in the order listed as is available including the relevant phase of the emergency.

5.2.2.1: Recommendation dealing with information that may not be available.

5.2.3: The rescue coordination centre shall, without delay, be furnished with any useful additional information especially on development of the state of emergency; or information that the emergency situation no longer exists.

Note: Cancellation of action initiated by the rescue coordination centre is the responsibility of that centre.

5.3: Use of communication facilities. ATS units shall use all available communication facilities to communicate with an aircraft in a state of emergency, and to request news of the aircraft.

5.4: Plotting aircraft in a state of emergency. The flight of an aircraft in a state of emergency and other aircraft in the vicinity shall be plotted on a chart to determine probable future positions, range and endurance.

5.5 deals with information to be provided to the operator.

5.5.1: Where area control or a flight information centre decides that an aircraft is in the uncertainty or alert phase it shall, when practicable, advise the operator prior to notifying the rescue coordination centre.

Note: If an aircraft is in the distress phase, the rescue coordination centre has to be notified immediately in accordance with 5.2.1.

5.5.2: Information notified to the rescue coordination centre shall, whenever practicable, be communicated to the operator without delay.

5.6.1 deals with informing other aircraft operating in the vicinity of an aircraft in a state of emergency.

5.6.2: Where ATS knows or believes an aircraft is subjected to unlawful interference, no reference shall be made to it in ATS air-ground communication unless it is certain the reference will not aggravate the situation.

Chapter 6—ATS requirements for communications

6.1: Aeronautical mobile service (air-ground communications); (Defined, page 126).

6.1.1: General.

6.1.1.1: Radio-telephony and/or data link shall be used in air ground communications for ATS purposes.

See Note on maintaining guard on emergency channel 121.5 MHz.

6.1.1.2: Where direct pilot-controller two-way radio-telephony or data link communication is used for the provision of ATC services, recording facilities shall be provided on all such air-ground communications channels.

6.1.2–6.1.5 deal with facilities for:

- FIS;
- area control service;
- approach control service;
- aerodrome control service.

6.2: Aeronautical fixed service (ground-ground communications) see page 124.

6.2.1: General.

6.2.1.1: Direct-speech and/or data link communications shall be used in ground-ground communications for ATS purposes.

See Note on establishment of speed of communication.

6.2.2 deals with the communications within a flight information region under the following headings.

6.2.2.1–6.2.2.2 deal with communications between ATS units, and between ATS units and other units; the latter include for example military units and rescue coordination centres.

6.2.3: Communications between flight information regions.

6.2.4: Procedures for direct-speech communications.

6.3: Surface Movement Control Service.

6.3.1: Communications for the control of vehicles other than aircraft on manoeuvring areas at controlled aerodromes. This deals with the provision of two-way radio-telephony communication procedures unless visual signal system is deemed adequate.

6.4: Aeronautical radio-navigation service. These Recommendations deal with automatic recording of surveillance data.

Chapter 7—ATS requirements for information

This deals with the provision to ATS units, centres and towers, as specified, of the six classes of information as follows:

7.1: Meteorological.

7.2: Aerodrome conditions and the operational status of associated facilities.

7.3: The operational status of navigation aids.

7.4: Unmanned free balloons.

7.5: Volcanic activity.

7.6: Radioactive materials and toxic chemical "clouds".

Appendices

Appendix 1:   Principles governing the identification of RNP types and the identification of ATS routes other than standard departure and arrival routes.

Appendix 2:   Principles governing the establishment and identification of significant points.

Appendix 3:   Principles governing the identification of standard departure and arrival routes and associated procedures.

Appendix 4:   ATS Airspace classifications.

Appendix 5:   Aeronautical Data Quality Requirements.

Attachments

Attachment A: Material relating to a method of establishing ATS routes defined by VOR.

Attachment B: Method of establishing ATS routes for use by RNAV-equipped aircraft.

(RNAV is the abbreviation for Area Navigation defined as "A method of navigation which permits aircraft operations on any desired flightpath within the coverage of station-referenced navigation aids within the limits of the capability of self-contained aids, or a combination of these".)

Attachment C: Traffic information broadcasts by aircraft and related operating procedures.

PANS—RAC

Procedures for Air Navigation Services—Rules of the Air and Air Traffic Services, doc. 4444, 13th edition 1996. As explained in its Foreword these procedures are complementary to the SARPS in Annex 2 and Annex 11. They are supplemented where necessary by regional procedures contained in the Regional Supplementary Procedures (doc. 7030). They specify in greater detail than in the SARPS the actual procedures to be applied by ATS units in providing the various ATS to air traffic. Their status, implementation, publication of differences and promulgation of information in the Foreword correspond exactly to those in doc. 8168—OPS/611 Vol. I (see page 76 above) with differences in paragraph 4: Implementation. The regional supplemental procedures (SUPPS) form the part of the Air Navigation Plan developed by Regional Air Navigation (RAN) meetings; see Foreword N7 030/4.

(iii) Comments

(1) Public law: international agencies. The following regional international agencies are charged with regulation of ATS:

(a) Eurocontrol established by the Convention relating to Cooperation for the Safety of Air Navigation (Eurocontrol) Brussels 1960;

(b) Cooperacion Centroamericana de Servicios de Navegacion Aerea (COCESNA) established by the Convention of Tegucigalpa;

(c) Agence pour la Securité de la Navigation Aérienne en Afrique et Madagascar (ASCNA) established by the Convention of Dakar.

(2) Private law: Case law establishes that ATS and their employees can be legally liable for failure to exercise their duties properly.

Initially it should be checked whether there is any exemption from liability on the grounds that the provision of ATS is discretionary. However, most, if not all, States impose liability for defective provision of ATS. In common law States liability usually arises in tort and is based on negligence; damages are unlimited.

The basis of civil law liability is less clearly established. Alternative bases are strict liability, negligence or gross negligence.

See Article by A. E. du Perron in *Air Law* (Vol. X, no 4/5/1985).

Whether any of the agencies listed in (1) above can be sued depends on their status, domestic law and the functions they perform.

(3) In *Yates* v. *USA* (12 AVI 18,416 1972–4; US Court of Appeals, 10th Circuit, 1974) the court held that the wrongful death of a pilot was proximately caused by the negligence of ATC when it failed to provide adequate separation between aircraft. It advised the pilot to keep his aircraft close behind the preceding 707 jet aircraft, and failed to advise the pilot of the presence and hazard of wake turbulence caused by the preceding aircraft. Landing instructions are not merely advisory and once the pilot has received and followed them he is not free to disregard them and exercise independent initiative.

(4) A number of US cases illustrate the question of apportionment of legal liability between the pilot and ATC, e.g. *Budden* v. *US*, 24 AVI 17,743 1992–5; US Court of Appeals, 8th Circuit, 1993 and *Todd* v. *US*, 13 AVI 17,260 1974–6; US District Court Florida, 1974.

ANNEX 12.   SEARCH AND RESCUE—6TH EDITION (MARCH 1975, REPRINTED 1994)

(i) Articles

Article 25—Aircraft in distress

Each Contracting State undertakes to provide such measures of assistance to aircraft in distress in its territory as it may find practicable, and to permit, subject to control by its own authorities, the owners of the aircraft or authorities of the State in which the aircraft is registered to provide such measures of assistance as may be necessitated by the circumstances. Each Contracting State, when undertaking search for missing aircraft, will collaborate in coordinated measures which may be recommended from time to time pursuant to this Convention.

(ii) Summary

The Annex refers to ICAO Resolution A18–16, replaced by Resolution A23–13.

Chapter 1—Definitions

Definitions include:

"*Emergency phase*"—a generic term meaning, as the case may be, uncertainty phase, alert phase or distress phase.

(See summary on Annex 11 page 132.)

Chapter 2—Organisation

2.1: The establishment and provision of search and rescue ("SAR") service.

2.1.1: States shall arrange for the establishment and provision of SAR services within their territories on a 24-hour basis. Portions of high seas or areas of undetermined sovereignty for which SAR service will be established shall be determined on the basis of regional air navigation agreements.

2.1.2: Assistance to aircraft in distress and to survivors of aircraft accidents shall be provided regardless of the nationality of such aircraft or survivors.

2.2.1: States shall delineate the SAR regions in which they will provide SAR service.

2.3.1: States shall establish a rescue coordination centre ("RCC") in each SAR region.

2.3.2–2.3.3 relate to establishment of rescue sub-centres and description of alerting posts.

2.4.1–2.4.2: Each RCC shall have means of:

- (i) immediate communication with the relevant:
    - (a) ATS unit;
    - (b) rescue sub-centres;
    - (c) direction-finding and position-fixing stations;
    - (d) capable coastal radio station.
- (ii) means of rapid and reliable communication with the six further listed agencies.

2.4.3 deals with means of communication for each rescue sub-centre.

Note 2 deals with use of satellite systems COSPAS and SARSAT.

2.5: Designation of Rescue Units.

2.5.1: States shall designate as rescue units elements of public and private services suitably located and equipped for SAR in each SAR region.

2.5.1.1: Additional rescue units shall be established if units designated pursuant to 2.5.1 are insufficient.

Note: Minimum units and facilities necessary for the provision of SAR within SAR regions are determined by regional air navigation agreements and are specified in appropriate Air Navigation Plan publications.

2.5.2: States should designate as parts of SAR plans of operation, elements of public or private services which do not themselves qualify as rescue units but are qualified to participate in SAR.

2.6: Equipment of rescue units.

2.6.1: Rescue units shall be provided with facilities and equipment for locating promptly and providing adequate assistance at the scene of the accident.

2.6.2–2.6.10 deal with means of communication, ELT and survival equipment.

Chapter 3—Cooperation between States

3.1: Cooperation between States.

3.1.1: States shall coordinate their SAR organisations with those of neighbouring States. See rest of section for further details.

3.2: Cooperation with other services.

3.2.1.1: States shall arrange for all aircraft, vessels and local services and facilities which do not form part of SAR organisation to cooperate fully in SAR and to extend any possible assistance to survivors.

3.2.2: States shall ensure that their SAR services will cooperate fully with those responsible for investigation of accidents and with those responsible for the care of those who have suffered in an accident.

3.2.3: Rescue units should be accompanied by persons qualified in investigation of accidents.

3.2.4: SPOC (SAR point of contact) shall be established for receipt of COSPAS-SARSAT distress data.

3.3: Dissemination of information.

3.3.1: Each State shall publish and disseminate all information necessary for the entry of rescue units of other States into its territory.

3.3.2–3.3.4: Recommendations which deal with the dissemination of information on plans, position of ships and general public directives.

Chapter 4—Preparatory measures

4.1: Requirements for information.

4.1.1 specifies the five items of information which each RCC shall have available concerning its SAR region, for example item (a) rescue units, sub-centres and alerting posts; (b) ATS units, etc.

4.1.2–4.1.3 Recommendations on further information available to RCC.

4.1.4: Large scale map shall be provided at each RCC.

4.2: Plan of operation.

4.2.1–4.2.2: Each RCC shall prepare a detailed plan for the conduct of SAR operations which shall include arrangements for servicing and refuelling air-craft, vessels and vehicles employed in SAR.

4.2.3: Recommendation on detail in plan.

4.3.1: Preparatory procedures for rescue units. Each unit shall:

(a) be aware of plan of operation in 4.2;
(b) maintain in readiness required number of rescue craft and vessels;
(c) maintain required supplies as specified;
(d) keep RCC informed of quantity and preparedness of equipment.

4.3.2: Supply of additional craft or vehicles.

4.4: Training.

4.5.1: Removal of wreckage. Each Contracting State shall ensure that the wreckage within its territory or the SAR regions for which it is responsible is removed or obliterated following completion of the accident investigation, or charted to prevent confusion.

Chapter 5—Operating procedures

5.1: Information concerning emergencies.

5.1.1: States should encourage any person observing an accident or having reason to believe that an aircraft is in an emergency to give immediately all information to the appropriate alerting post or to the rescue coordination centre concerned.

5.1.2: Any authority or element of SAR organisation having reason to believe an aircraft is in an emergency shall immediately give all available information to the RCC concerned.

5.1.3: RCCs shall immediately on receipt of information concerning aircraft in emergency, evaluate such information and determine the extent of operation required.

5.1.4: When information concerning aircraft in emergency is received from sources other than ATS units, the RCC shall determine the emergency phase and apply applicable procedures.

5.2.1–5.2.2 specify the procedures in INCERFA and ALERFA.

5.2.3: The duties of the RCC in the DISTRESFA are:

(a) initiate SAR in accordance with the detailed plan of operation;
(b) ascertain the position of the aircraft and determine area to be searched;
(c) notify and keep informed operator;
(d) notify adjacent RCCs as specified;
(e) notify associated ATS unit when the information on the emergency has been received from another source;
(f) request at an early stage such aircraft, vessels, coastal stations or other services not specifically included in (a) to maintain listening watch, assist aircraft in distress and inform RCC of any developments;
(g) draw up plan of conduct of SAR operation required and communicate such plan for guidance of the authorities immediately directing the conduct of such operations;
(h) amend as necessary the guidance given in (g);
(i) notify State of Registry of aircraft;
(j) notify appropriate accident investigation authorities.

5.2.4: Initiation of SAR action in respect of aircraft whose position is unknown.

5.2.4.1: If an emergency phase is declared where aircraft position is unknown and may be in one of two or more SAR regions, the section sets out (a) the procedures applicable to the RCCs involved; (b) in particular those procedures to be followed unless otherwise decided by common agreement of the RCCs; and (c) the position after declaration of the distress phase.

5.2.5 deals with the passing of information to aircraft in respect of which an emergency phase has been declared concerning the SAR action initiated.

5.3: Where responsibility for conduct of operations extends to two or more States, each State shall take action in accordance with the plan of operation when so requested by the RCC of the Region.

5.4: Procedures for authorities in the field. Authorities immediately directing operations shall give instructions to their units, inform the RCC of such instructions and keep the RCC informed of developments.

5.5: Procedures for RCC—Termination and suspension of operations.

5.5.1: In the case of an uncertainty or alert phase, where the RCC is informed that the emergency no longer exists it will inform the relevant unit or service activated by it.

5.5.2: Distress phase. A higher grade of responsibility as specified applies to the RCC where it is informed that the distress phase emergency no longer exists or any search should be discontinued.

5.6: Procedures for rescue units. When notified by the RCC the rescue unit shall:

(a) act as required in the notification;
(b) and (c) keep the RCC currently informed of the quantity and preparedness of its SAR equipment and of its operations.

5.7: Procedures for person-in-charge of the rescue unit at the scene of the accident.

5.7.1: The person assigned to be in charge of the rescue unit shall act as required by the RCC and shall: (a) protect the aircraft from fire as specified; (b) give aid to survivors and, except as necessary for (b) or when otherwise directed, ensure that the wreckage of the aircraft or marks made by it in landing are not disturbed until all information required for investigation of the causes of the accident has been obtained.

5.8: Procedures for pilots-in-command at the scene of the accident.

5.8.1: When a pilot-in-command observes that another aircraft or surface craft is in distress, he shall, unless he is unable, or in the circumstances of the case considers it unreasonable or unnecessary:

(a) keep the craft in sight until his presence is no longer necessary;
(b) if his position is not known with certainty, take such action as will facilitate its determination;
(c) report to the RCC as much of the specified information as required;
(d) act as instructed by the RCC or ATS unit.

5.8.1.1: If the first aircraft on the scene of the accident is not an SAR aircraft it shall take charge of on-scene activities of all subsequent aircraft until the first SAR aircraft reaches the scene; see further as specified.

5.8.2: When it is necessary for an aircraft to direct a surface craft to the place where the aircraft or surface craft is in distress, the aircraft shall do so by transmitting precise instructions by any means at its disposal including, in the absence of radio, the signals in Appendix A to the Annex.

5.8.3 deals with communication with survivors or surface rescue units by means of dropping communications equipment or message where two-way communication is not available.

5.8.4 deals with response to a ground signal.

5.9: Procedures for pilots-in-command intercepting a distress transmission. Whenever a distress signal and/or message or equivalent transmission is intercepted on radio-telegraphy or radio-telephony by a pilot-in-command, he shall:

(a) record position of the craft in distress if given;

(b) if possible take a bearing on the transmission;

(c) inform the appropriate RCC or ATS unit of the distress transmission, giving all available information;

(d) at his discretion while awaiting instructions, proceed to the position given in the transmission.

5.10 deals with the use of SAR signals of Appendix A and action to be taken.

5.11: Maintenance of records.

Appendix A: SAR signals.

(iii) Comments

(1) The SAR section of the AIP (see Annex 15) gives an example of the application of Annex 12. The UK AIP in GEN 3.6–SAR provides, among other things, the names and addresses of the authorities, delineates the UK SAR region, and describes the types of services, communication frequencies, and signals. Maps show regions, facilities and maritime rescue centres.

(2) Case law:

(i) In *Mooney* v. *USA*, EDNY, 1987; 20 AVI 18,059, the personal representatives of the passenger sued the FAA on the grounds that they had negligently monitored the flight of the aircraft and then failed to carry out a timely air/sea rescue which could have saved the passenger's life. USA applied to strike out the claim but the court refused on the basis of the rule that a complaint was not subject to dismissal unless the plaintiff could not prevail under any state of facts which might be proved to support the complaint. There is no suggestion in the brief judgment that USA was pleading para 2860 of 20 USC, that is, it was performing a discretionary function. There is no further law report on this case in AVI.

(ii) In *Fagundes* v. *State of Idaho*, 19 May 1989 (Idaho Court of Appeals, 1989; 21 AVI 18,536 1988–9) the Idaho Court of Appeals held that the state of Idaho did not owe a duty of care, as claimed, to a pilot, an employee of the helicopter company which the state had hired as an independent contractor, when the pilot died shortly after his helicopter crashed. The state was not negligent in (a) failing to require that the helicopter contained a homing beacon which could have aided rescue efforts, (b) not requiring that radio communications be workable in the event of a crash, (c) not providing adequate medical supplies to save the pilot, and (d) failing to start rescue operations earlier. Even if the state realised or should have realised that it was necessary to require that the helicopters contain homing beacons, powerful radio transmitters and medical supplies, it was not under a duty to supply such equipment. Finally, the state was free to require some safety equipment without incurring a duty to require all potentially helpful safety equipment. The case concerns a common law duty of care. The judgment does not indicate that the state was the designated authority obliged to carry out SAR duties. The pilot died before the state employee concerned initiated the rescue.

(iii) In the English marine case of *Skinner* v. *Secretary of State for Transport*, *The Times*, 3 January 1995, the court held that the Coastguard did not owe a private law duty of care to a mariner when exercising its ordinary functions of watching and listening and its rescue coordination activities, even in an emergency. The judge ruled that the Coastguard Act 1925 was administrative and not directive and did not in terms place a statutory duty on the coastguard.

Under English common law a fire brigade will not generally be liable except for some positive negligent act increasing the risk (*Capital & Counties plc* v. *Hampshire County Council* [1997] 2 All ER 865).

In another English case, *OLL Ltd* v. *Secretary of State for Transport* [1997] 3 All ER 897, the court applied parts of the judgment in *Skinner* v. *Secretary of State for Transport* and also followed *Capital & Counties plc* v. *Hampshire CC*, holding that the Coastguard would only be liable if its negligence amounted to a positive act which directly caused greater injury than would have occurred if it had not intervened at all.

While none of these English cases relate to the application of Annex 12 SARPS they illustrate private law decisions on the SAR area of activity.

(3) For aerodrome fire service SARPS see Annex 14.

ANNEX 13.   AIRCRAFT ACCIDENT INVESTIGATION—8TH EDITION (1994)

(i) Articles

Article 26—Investigation of accidents

In the event of an accident to an aircraft of a Contracting State occurring in the territory of another Contracting State, and involving death or serious injury, or indicating serious technical defect in the aircraft or air navigation facilities, the State in which the accident occurs will institute an inquiry into the circumstances of the accident, in accordance, so far as its laws permit, with the procedure which may be recommended by the International Civil Aviation

Organization. The State in which the aircraft is registered shall be given the opportunity to appoint observers to be present at the inquiry and the State holding the inquiry shall communicate the report and findings in the matter to that State.

(ii) Summary

Certain aspects of aircraft accident investigation are dealt with in Chapter 13 of this book below. The Annex is summarised in this chapter.

Annex 13 also applies to incidents. Attachment D lists examples of serious incidents.

Chapter 1—Definitions

Definitions include:

"*Accident*": an occurrence associated with the operation of an aircraft which takes place between the time any person boards the aircraft with the intention of flight until such time as all such persons have disembarked, in which:

(a) a person is fatally or seriously injured as a result of:
  • being in the aircraft; or
  • direct contact with any part of the aircraft, including parts which have become detached from the aircraft; or
  • direct exposure to jet blast,
  except when the injuries are from natural causes, self-inflicted or inflicted by other persons, or when the injuries are to stowaways hiding outside the areas normally available to the passengers and crew; or

(b) the aircraft sustains damage or structural failure which:
  • adversely affects the structural strength, performance or flight characteristics of the aircraft, and
  • would normally require major repair or replacement of the affected component,
  except for engine failure or damage, when the damage is limited to the engine, its cowlings or accessories; or for damage limited to propellers, wing tips, antennas, tires, brakes, fairings, small dents or puncture holes in the aircraft skin; or

(c) the aircraft is missing or is completely inaccessible.

Notes:

(1) For statistical uniformity only an injury resulting in death within 30 days of the date of the accident is classed as a fatal injury by ICAO.

(2) An aircraft is considered to be missing when the official search has been terminated and the wreckage has not been located.

"Causes": actions, omissions, events, conditions, or a combination thereof which led to the accident or incident.

"Incident": An occurrence, other than an accident, associated with the operation of an aircraft which affects or could affect the safety of operation.

Note: incidents which are of main interest to ICAO for accident prevention studies are listed in ICAO Accident/Incident Reporting Manual (doc. 9056).

"Serious Incident": An incident involving circumstances indicating that an accident nearly occurred.

"State of Occurrence": The State in the territory of which an accident or incident occurs.

Chapter 2—Applicability

2.1: Unless otherwise stated the specifications in this Annex apply to activities following accidents or incidents wherever they occurred.

2.2: The specifications concerning State of Operator apply only where the aircraft is leased, chartered or interchanged and where the State of Operator is not the State of Registry and if it discharges, in respect of this Annex, in part or whole, the functions and obligations of State of Registry.

Chapter 3—General

3.1: The sole objective of the investigation of an accident or incident shall be the prevention of accidents or incidents. It is not the purpose of the investigation to apportion liability.

3.2: The State of Occurrence shall as specified take all reasonable measures to protect evidence and maintain safe custody of the aircraft and its contents for such period necessary for the investigation.

3.3 and **3.4** deal with requests by the State of Registry, State of Operator, State of Design or State of Manufacture that the aircraft and its contents and other evidence remain undisturbed pending inspection.

3.5 deals with release from custody of the aircraft, contents or parts no longer required for the investigation.

Chapter 4—Notification

Note: Attachment B provides a notification and reporting checklist.

Accidents or serious incidents in the territory of a Contracting State to aircraft of another Contracting State

4.1: Responsibility of the State of Occurrence. Notification by State of Occurrence shall be forwarded to State of Registry, State of Operator, State of

Design, State of Manufacture and ICAO (in last case where aircraft is over 2,250 kg).

If the State of Occurrence is not aware of a serious incident, State of Operator or State of Registry shall give notice as specified.

4.2 sets out form and content of notification and information where available:

(a) identification abbreviation for accident or serious incident;
(b) details of aircraft as specified;
(c) name of owner, operator and hirer of aircraft;
(d) name of pilot-in-command;
(e) date and time of accident or serious incident;
(f) last point of departure and point of intended landing;
(g) position of aircraft;
(h) number of crew, passengers and others killed and seriously injured;
(i) nature of accident or serious incident and extent of damage to aircraft;
(j) indication of investigation to be made/delegated by State of Occurrence;
(k) physical characteristics of accident area;
(l) identification of originating authority.

See reference to ICAO Manual of Aircraft Accident Investigation (doc. 6290).

4.3: Notification shall be given in one of the working languages of ICAO.

4.4: Additional Information to be given, as specified.

4.5: On receipt of notification, State of Registry and State of Operator shall provide to State of Occurrence any available relevant information concerning aircraft and crew. Each State shall inform State of Occurrence if they wish to be represented in the investigation.

4.6: On receipt of notification and request by State of Occurrence for participation, each of the State of Design and Manufacture shall, in the case of an accident or serious incident, (a) advise State of Occurrence in respect of the aircraft with maximum mass of over 100,000 kg as to the name of its accredited representative and whether he will be represented at the investigation and his date of arrival, (b) in respect of an aircraft with maximum mass not over 100,000 kg, whether it will appoint an accredited representative giving his name and advising if he will be present at the investigation.

Accidents or serious incidents in the territory of the State of Registry, in a non-Contracting State or outside any State

4.7: When State of Registry institutes investigation of an accident or serious incident involving an aircraft of a maximum mass of over 2,250 kg it shall notify with minimum delay the States of Operator, Design, Manufacture and ICAO.

4.7.1 deals with Notification by State of Registry in respect of accident or serious incident to aircraft of maximum weight of 2,250 kg or less of States of Operator, Design and Manufacture.

4.8: The notified States shall provide on request relevant information as specified and shall inform State of Registry whether they intend to be represented at the investigation.

Chapter 5—Investigation

Responsibility for instituting and conducting the investigation

Accidents or serious incidents in the territory of a Contracting State to aircraft of another Contracting State:

5.1 State of Occurrence shall (i) institute an investigation into the circumstances of the accident, (ii) be responsible for the conduct of the investigation but may delegate the whole or part of the conduct of such investigation to State of Registry or of Operator, (iii) use every means to facilitate the investigation.

5.1.1 deals with investigation by State of Occurrence of a serious incident and delegation of the investigation and facilitation of the investigation.

Accidents or serious incidents in the territory of a non-Contracting State or outside the territory of any State:

5.2: Where the accident or serious incident occurs in a non-Contracting State, the State of Registry should endeavour to investigate accident in cooperation with the State of Occurrence, or otherwise alone.

5.3: For accidents or serious incidents outside territory of any State: State of Registry shall investigate and can delegate.

5.3.1: States nearest the scene in international waters shall provide such assistance as they are able.

Organisation and conduct of the investigation

See Note on use of best technical evidence from any source.

General

5.4: The accident investigation authority shall have independence in the conduct of the investigation and have unrestricted authority over its conduct. The investigation shall include the gathering, recording and analysis of all available relevant information, if possible the determination of causes, and the completion of the Final Report followed, if appropriate, by safety recommendations. When possible the scene of the accident shall be visited, the wreckage examined and statements taken from witnesses.

5.4.1: Recommendation: Any judicial or administrative proceedings to apportion blame or liability should be separate from any investigation conducted under the provisions of this Annex.

5.5–5.6 deal with designation and powers of investigator-in-charge who shall have unhampered access to the wreckage and unrestricted control over it.

5.7–5.8: Effective use of flight recorders shall be made in investigation of accidents, serious incidents and incidents.

5.9: Expeditious and complete autopsies of crew and passengers shall be arranged, as specified. See reference to ICAO Manual of Civil Aviation Medicine (doc. 8984) and ICAO Manual of Accident Investigation (doc. 6920).

5.10: The investigating State shall recognise the need for coordination between the investigator-in-charge and the judicial authorities.

Particular attention shall be given to evidence which requires prompt recording and analysis for the investigation to be successful, such as the examination and identification of victims and readouts of flight recorder recordings.

See Note 2 on solution of possible conflicts on custody of flight recorders and recordings.

5.11: If in the course of investigation it is known or suspected that an act of unlawful interference was involved, the aviation security authorities of the State(s) concerned shall be informed.

5.12: The State conducting the investigation of an accident or incident, wherever it occurred, shall not make the following records available for purposes other than accident or incident investigation, unless the appropriate authority for the administration of justice in that State determines that their disclosure outweighs the adverse domestic and international impact such action may have on that or any future investigations:

(a) all statements taken from persons by the investigation authorities in the course of their investigation;

(b) all communications between persons having been involved in the operation of the aircraft;

(c) medical or private information regarding persons involved in the accident or incident;

(d) cockpit voice recordings and transcripts from such recordings; and

(e) opinions expressed in the analysis of information, including flight recorder information.

These records shall be included in the final report or its appendices only when pertinent to the analysis of the accident or incident. Parts of the records not relevant to the analysis shall not be disclosed.

The Note describes the rationale of 5.12. If information given voluntarily is subsequently used inappropriately for civil, administrative and criminal proceedings, it may no longer be openly disclosed to investigators. Lack of access to such information would impede the investigative process and seriously affect flight safety.

5.13: If after the closure of investigation new and significant evidence becomes available, the investigation shall be re-opened.

5.14: Any State on request shall provide the Investigating State with all relevant available information.

5.15: Any State whose services or facilities have been or would normally have been used by the aircraft prior to the accident/incident shall provide pertinent information on request.

5.16: Flight recorders. Where an aircraft involved in an accident or serious incident lands in a State other than the State of Occurrence, State of Registry or of Operator shall furnish to investigating State flight recorder records and, if necessary, the recorders.

5.17: State of Registry and State of Operator shall provide Investigating State with information on any relevant organisation influencing the operation of the aircraft.

5.18: The State of Registry and State of Operator shall be entitled to appoint an accredited representative to participate in the investigation.

5.19: The State of Registry or State of Operator shall appoint advisor(s) nominated by the operator to assist its accredited representative.

5.19.1: Participation of operator.

5.20: The State of Registry and/or State of Operator shall be obliged to appoint accredited representatives when their participation is requested where the aircraft has maximum mass of over 2,250 kg.

5.21–5.22: Provisions similar but not identical to those in 5.19 and 5.20 apply to States of Design and Manufacture.

Note to 5.21 and Note 1 to 5.22 concern participation by State of Manufacture and State of Design of powerplant or major components in the investigation.

Note 2 to 5.22 concerns assistance by State of Manufacture or Design in investigations where the aircraft does not have a maximum weight of over 2,250 kg.

5.23: Any State which on request provides information, facilities or experts shall be entitled to appoint accredited representatives to participate in the investigation. See Note extending this to States which provide operational base for field investigation or were involved in SAR or wreckage removal.

5.24: A State entitled to appoint accredited representatives is also entitled to appoint advisor(s), who may participate in the investigation as specified.

Note: Any participating State can call upon technical experts from any source and appoint them as advisors.

5.25 sets out important entitlements of those participating in investigations, e.g. obtaining information and making submissions.

5.26 imposes obligations on accredited representatives and advisors (i) concerning their provision of information to the investigating State, and (ii) not to provide information on progress and findings of investigation without express authority of the investigating State.

5.27: Participation of a State having suffered fatalities or serious injuries to its citizens.

Chapter 6—Reporting

See Notes:

(1) Attachment B provides a notification and reporting checklist

(2) Three separate reports may be required:

    (i) Preliminary Report;

    (ii) Accident/Incident Data Report;

    (iii) Final Report.

(3) Guidance is given by ICAO Accident/Incident Reporting Manual (9156)

(4) Format of Final Report.

6.1: Where aircraft has a maximum mass over 2,250 kg the investigating State shall send the Preliminary Report to the various States, as designated, and to ICAO.

6.2: Preliminary Report concerning aircraft weighing 2,250 kg or less.

6.3–6.5 deal with form, language, coding and dispatch of Preliminary Report; dispatch to be within 30 days of accident. Where matters affecting safety are directly involved, such report shall be sent by quickest means available.

6.6–6.8 deal with Accident/Incident Data Report to be sent to ICAO and supply of information additional to such report.

6.9: Final Report. State of investigation shall send draft Final Report to State which instituted the investigation and to all participating States, asking for significant and substantial comments within 60 days. If such comments are received, either the report will be amended or comments will be appended. If no comments are received within 60 days, the report will be issued unless an extension has been agreed.

6.10: Final Report will be sent with minimum delay to:

    (a) State instituting investigation;

    (b) State of Registry;

    (c) State of Operator;

    (d) State of Design;

    (e) State of Manufacture;

    (f) any State suffering fatalities or serious injuries to its citizens;

    (g) any State providing relevant information, significant facilities or experts.

6.11: In the interest of accident prevention, the State of investigation shall publish the Final Report as soon as possible.

6.11.1: Corresponding Recommendation for serious incidents.

6.12: Investigation of accident concerning aircraft of maximum mass over 5,700 kg: Final Report shall be sent to ICAO.

See Note on language and form of report.

6.13 imposes a prohibition on Draft Report and relevant documents being circulated, published or access being given to them without consent of investigating State unless already published or released by such State.

6.14: With regard to investigation by a State of an incident involving matters of interest to other States, Investigating State should forward the information to such other States as soon as possible.

Chapter 7—Accident prevention measures

Note: the specifications in this chapter apply only where an investigation has been conducted. Their objective is to promote accident prevention by prompt exchange of information.

7.1: At any stage of investigation of an accident or incident wherever it occurred, the investigating authority shall recommend any necessary preventive action which needs to be taken promptly to prevent similar occurrences.

7.2: A State conducting investigation of accidents or incidents, wherever they occurred, shall analyse the information contained in its reports to determine the preventive actions required.

7.3: States should establish formal incident reporting systems to facilitate collection of information on actual or potential safety deficiencies.

The Note refers to guidance on mandatory and voluntary systems given in the ICAO Accident Prevention Manual (doc. 9422).

7.4: Establishment of systems including data bases for analysis of information obtained from investigation of accidents and incidents.

7.5: A State conducting investigations of accidents or incidents, and a State maintaining an incident reporting system, shall address appropriate safety recommendations to other States concerned and, when ICAO documents are involved, to ICAO.

7.6: A State which receives a safety recommendation or other proposals for preventive action shall inform the proposing State of action taken or under consideration or the reasons why no action will be taken.

Appendix: format of Final Report

Note in particular:

(1) The factual information to be included;
(2) Analysis;
(3) Conclusion;
(4) Safety Recommendations;
(5) Appendices.

Attachments

Attachment A: Rights and obligations of State of Operator in respect of accidents and incidents involving leased, chartered or inter-changed aircraft.
Attachment B: Notification and reporting checklist.
Attachment C: Exchange of Final Reports between States and publication of a list of Final Reports available in States.
Attachment D: List of examples of serious incidents.

(iii) Comments

(1) While the text of most Annexes refers to "Contracting States" Annex 13 SARPS refer mostly to "State". However, the distinction is not significant as SARPS will, subject to Articles 37 and 38, only bind Contracting States.

(2) While Article 26 applies only to an accident to an aircraft of one Contracting State occurring in the territory of another Contracting State, Sections 2.1 and 4.7 of Annex 13 (8th edition) apply the SARPS to accidents in the State of Registry, in a non-Contracting State or outside the territory of any State.

(3) For certain aspects of accident investigation, see Chapter 13 of this book.

(4) Accident Prevention Manual (doc. 9422) considers methods essential to accident prevention and "rounds out the systems of prevention" deemed fundamental to preventing accidents.

(5) **6.9**: Final Report. Spanish Civil Aviation Accident Report on accident to Boeing 727 G-BDAN on 25 April 1980 is an example of the use of the addendum. The report was published also in UK in 1981 under Number 8/81.

(6) **7.3**: ANO Article 106 imposes mandatory reporting obligations on operators, manufacturers, etc. concerning incidents which if not corrected would endanger aircraft, its occupants and others.

ANNEX 14. AERODROMES

Vol. I: Aerodrome Design and Operations (2nd edition, July 1995).
Vol. II: Heliports (2nd edition, July 1995).

(i) Articles

Article 15—Airports and similar charges (see page 100).
Article 28—Air navigation facilities and standard systems (see page 26).
Article 68—Designation of routes and airports (see page 23).
Article 69—Improvement of air navigation facilities (see page 27).
Article 71—Provision and maintenance of facilities by Council (see page 28).

(ii) Summary

Legal liability aspects of Aerodromes are dealt with in Chapter 9 of this book.

VOLUME I: AERODROME DESIGN AND OPERATIONS (2ND EDITION, JULY 1995).

Author's Note: Volume I is one of the lengthier Annexes. Its table of contents is given in Appendix 3 to this book.

Volume I, page (v), lists, (a) the relevant abbreviations and symbols and (b) the seven manuals related to the specifications of the Annex.

Chapter 1—General

The Introductory Note:

Para 1 explains that the Annex contains the SARPS (specifications) that prescribe the physical characteristics and obstacle limitation surfaces to be provided for at aerodromes, and certain facilities and technical services normally provided at an aerodrome. It is not intended that these specifications limit or regulate the operation of an aircraft.

Para 3 points out that the Annex sets out the minimum aerodrome specifications for aircraft which have the characteristics of those which are currently operating or for similar aircraft that are planned for introduction. See reference to "more demanding aircraft" and guidance in the Aerodrome Design Manual Part 2.

Para 4 refers to specifications for precision approach runways Categories II and III.

Para 5 explains that this volume does not include specifications for overall planning of aerodromes, see Airport Planning Manual Vol I.

Para 6 refers to security being an integral part of aerodrome planning and operations.

1.1: Definitions include:

"*Aerodrome*": A defined area on land or water (including any buildings, installations, and equipment) intended to be used either wholly or in part for the arrival, departure and surface movement of aircraft.

Note: the term "aerodrome" where used in the provisions relating to flight plans and ATS messages is intended to cover also sites other than aerodromes which may be used by certain types of aircraft, e.g. helicopters or balloons.

"*Apron*": A defined area, on a land aerodrome, intended to accommodate aircraft for purposes of loading or unloading passengers, mail or cargo, fuelling, parking or maintenance.

"*Human performance*": Human capabilities and limitations which have an impact on the safety and efficiency of aeronautical operations.

"Manoeuvring area": That part of an aerodrome to be used for the take-off, landing and taxiing of aircraft, excluding aprons.

"Movement area": That part of an aerodrome to be used for the take-off, landing and taxiing of aircraft, consisting of the manoeuvring area and the aprons.

"Runway": A defined rectangular area on a land aerodrome prepared for landing and take-off of aircraft.

"Runway visual range (RVR)": The range over which the pilot of an aircraft on the centre line of a runway can see the runway surface markings or the lights delineating the runway or identifying its centre line.

Other definitions include *"Declared Distance"* and *"Instrument Runway"*.

For the Definition of *"International Airport"* see Chapter 9 of this book, page 317.

1.2: Applicability.

1.2.1 deals with the method of interpretation of some of the specifications.

1.2.2: The specifications apply to all aerodromes open to public use (Annex 15). They apply where appropriate to heliports, but not to stolports. Chapter 3 applies only to land aerodromes.

1.3: Reference code. Introductory note: The intent of the reference code is to provide a simple method for interrelating the numerous specifications concerning the characteristics of aerodromes so as to provide a series of aerodrome facilities that are suitable for the aeroplanes that are intended to operate at the aerodrome. The code is not intended to be used for determining runway length or pavement strength requirements.

The Note goes on to explain the code more fully. The remainder of the section sets out the SARPS for the code. The code is in Table 1–1.

Chapter 2—Aerodrome data

This chapter contains specifications relating to the determination and reporting of aerodrome related aeronautical data. The 12 specific items are listed in 2.2 to 2.13 of Chapter 2—Table of Contents.

Chapters 3–8

These chapters set out the SARPS as listed in the Table of Contents (see Appendix 3 of this book). They are not summarised below.

Chapter 9—Emergency and other services

9.1: Aerodrome emergency planning.

General.

The Introductory Note explains that aerodrome emergency planning is the process for preparing an aerodrome to cope with an emergency. The objective of such planning is to minimise the effect of an emergency particularly in respect of saving lives and maintaining aircraft operations. The aerodrome emergency plan sets out the procedures for coordinating the response of different aerodrome agencies or services and of those agencies in the surrounding community. Guidance is given in the Airport Services Manual, Part 7.

9.1.1–9.1.2: Aerodrome Emergency Plan ("Plan") shall be established commensurate with operations and activities conducted at the aerodrome. It shall provide for the coordination of action to be taken.

The Note gives examples of emergencies: aircraft emergencies, sabotage, unlawfully seized aircraft, dangerous goods occurrences, fires and natural disasters.

9.1.3 deals with coordination of the various agencies, examples are:

(a) on the aerodrome: ATC units, rescue, fire-fighting, medical and ambulance services; and

(b) off the aerodrome: fire departments, police, medical and ambulance services etc.

9.1.4–9.1.10 deal with the Plan, emergency operations centre and command post, and communication systems.

9.1.11–9.1.12 deal with procedures for periodic testing of the adequacy of the plan.

9.2: Rescue and fire-fighting.

Introductory Note: The principal objective of rescue and fire-fighting service is to save lives. The Note stresses the importance of training and effectiveness of equipment, and speed with which personnel and equipment can be put to use.

Requirements to combat building and fuel farm fires, or to deal with foaming of runways are not taken into account.

9.2.1: Rescue and fire-fighting equipment and services shall be provided at an aerodrome.

Note 1: Public or private organisations which can be suitably located and equipped may be designated to provide the rescue and fire-fighting service. It is intended that fire stations housing these organisations be located at the aerodrome although an off-aerodrome location is not precluded provided response time can be met.

Note 2 deals with the provision of suitable rescue equipment and services at an aerodrome located close to water, swampy areas or other difficult environment.

9.2.2–9.2.6: Level of protection to be provided.

9.2.2–9.2.6 set out the SARPS for the level of protection to be provided, principally based on the size of the aeroplanes using the aerodrome and also in certain cases the number of aeroplane movements.

9.2.7–9.2.17 deal with chemical extinguishing agents.

9.2.18: Rescue equipment commensurate with the level of aircraft operations should be provided on the rescue and fire-fighting vehicles. Guidance is given on such equipment in the Airport Services Manual Part 1.

9.2.19–9.2.21: Response time and maintenance of emergency access roads.

9.2.22–9.2.24: Provision of emergency access roads, their bearing strength and marking.

9.2.25–9.2.26 deal with the housing of rescue and fire-fighting vehicles in the fire station, which should be located where access for such vehicles into the runway area is direct and clear, requiring a minimum number of turns.

9.2.27–9.2.28 Communication and alerting systems.

9.2.29 deals with the number of rescue and fire-fighting vehicles depending on the category of the aerodrome.

9.2.30: All rescue and fire-fighting personnel shall be properly trained to perform their duties efficiently and shall participate in live fire drills as specified.

See references to Airport Services Manual and Training Manual in Note 1.

Note 2 defines "pressure fed fuel fires".

9.2.31: During flight operations sufficient trained personnel should be readily available as specified.

9.2.32: In determining the number of personnel to be provided for rescue, consideration should be given to the types of aircraft using the aerodrome.

9.2.33: All responding rescue and fire-fighting personnel shall be provided with protective clothing and respiratory equipment to enable them to perform their duties effectively.

9.3: Disabled Aircraft Removal. This refers to guidance in Airport Services Manual and Recommendations on a plan for removal of disabled aircraft and the equipment, personnel and arrangements to be included in such a plan.

9.4: Maintenance.

9.4.1: A maintenance programme should be established to provide facilities in the condition which does not impair safety, regularity or efficiency of air navigation. See Notes on preventive maintenance and the facilities to be maintained.

9.4.2: Surface of pavements (runways, taxiways, aprons etc.) should be kept clear of any loose stones or other objects that might cause damage to aircraft structures or engines, or impair the operation of aircraft systems.

See Note on surface of shoulders.

9.4.3: Runway surface should be maintained in a condition such as to preclude the formation of harmful irregularities.

9.4.4: Measurement of friction characteristics of a runway surface shall be made periodically with a continuous friction measuring device using self-wetting features.

9.4.5: Corrective maintenance action shall be taken when friction characteristics of all or part of a runway are below minimum friction level specified by the State.

9.4.6: Corrective maintenance action should be considered when the friction characteristics of all or part of a runway are below a maintenance planning level specified by the State.

9.4.7: Assessment of friction characteristics when drainage characteristics of a runway are poor. Corrective action should be taken as necessary.

9.4.8: Where taxiway is used by turbine engined aeroplanes surface of its shoulders should be maintained free of loose stones or other objects which could be ingested by the aeroplane engines; see Aerodrome Design Manual Part 2.

9.4.9: Surface of a paved runway shall be maintained so as to provide good friction characteristics and low rolling resistance. Snow, slush, ice, standing water, mud, dust, sand, oil and rubber deposits and other contamination shall be removed as rapidly and completely as possible to minimise accumulation.

9.4.10–9.4.12 deal with corresponding Recommendations for taxiways and aprons, and set out priority for clearance for the various parts of the movement area.

9.4.13: Use of chemicals to prevent formation of ice and frost where effective. Caution should be exercised so as not to create a more slippery condition. Guidance on use of chemicals is given in Airport Services Manual Part 2.

9.4.14: Harmful or toxic chemicals (as specified) shall not be used. See note on Runway Pavement Overlays.

9.4.15–9.4.18 deal with specifications for runway overlay projects when the runway is to be returned to an operational status before overlay of the entire runway is complete, thus normally necessitating a temporary ramp between the new and old runway surfaces. Guidance is given in the Aerodrome Design Manual Part 3.

9.4.19–9.4.27: Visual aids. The Note observes that these specifications are not intended to define the operational failure of a lighting system.

9.4.19: A light shall be deemed to be unserviceable when the main beam is out of its specified alignment or when its average intensity is less than 50 per cent of the specified value.

9.4.20: A system of preventive maintenance of visual aids shall be employed to ensure lighting and marking system reliability. Guidance is given in Airport Services Manual Part 9.

9.4.21 deals with the objective of preventive maintenance employed for precision approach runway Category II or III.

9.4.22 deals with the objectives of preventive maintenance employed for a stop-bar provided at a taxi-holding position used in conjunction with a runway intended for operations in runway visual range conditions less than a value of 350 m.

9.4.23 deals with preventive maintenance for a taxiway for use in runway visual range conditions less than a value of 350 m.

9.4.24 deals with the objective of the system of preventive maintenance for a precision approach runway Category I.

9.4.25 deals with preventive maintenance employed for a runway meant for take-off in runway visual range conditions less than a value of 550 m.

9.4.26: The system of preventive maintenance employed for a runway meant for take-off in runway visual range conditions of a value of 550 m or greater shall have as its objective that all runway lights are serviceable as specified.

9.4.27: In low visibility procedures the appropriate authority should restrict construction or maintenance activities in the proximity of aerodrome electrical systems.

9.5: Bird hazard reduction.

9.5.1: Bird strike hazard on or in the vicinity of an aerodrome should be assessed through:

   (a) establishment of a national procedure as specified;
   (b) collection of information on presence of birds on or around aerodrome.

Note refers to ICAO Bird Strike Information System (IBIS) in the Manual on the ICAO Bird Strike Information System.

9.5.2: When bird strike hazard is identified, the appropriate authorities should decrease the number of birds constituting a potential hazard by adopting measures for discouraging their presence in the vicinity of an aerodrome. Guidance is given in Airport Services Manual Part 3.

9.5.3: Garbage disposal dumps or similar sources attracting bird activity on or near an aerodrome should be eliminated.

9.6: Apron management service.

9.6.1: It is recommended when volume of traffic and operating conditions warrant, an appropriate apron management service should be provided by aerodrome ATS unit or other authority to:

   (a) regulate movement with the objective of preventing collisions;
   (b) regulate entry of aircraft into and coordinate exit of aircraft from apron with aerodrome control tower;
   (c) ensure safe and expeditious movement of vehicles and appropriate regulation of other activities.

9.6.2: Where the aerodrome control tower does not participate in the apron movement service, transition of aircraft between apron management unit and aerodrome control tower should be established. Guidance is found in Airport Services Manual Part 8 and in the Manual of Surface Movement Guidance and Control Systems (SMGCS).

9.6.3: Apron management service shall be provided with radio-telephony communications facilities.

9.6.4: When low visibility procedures are in effect, persons and vehicles operating on an apron shall be restricted to the essential minimum.

Notes refer to guidance given in the SMGCS.

9.6.5: An emergency vehicle responding to an emergency shall have priority over all other surface movement traffic.

9.6.6: A vehicle operating on the apron shall:

(a) give way to the emergency vehicle, an aircraft taxiing, about to taxi, or being pushed or towed; and

(b) give way to other vehicles in accordance with local regulations.

9.6.7: An aircraft stand shall be visually monitored to ensure the recommended clearance distances are provided to an aircraft using the stand.

9.7: Ground servicing of aircraft.

9.7.1: Fire extinguishing equipment suitable for at least initial intervention in the event of a fuel fire and trained personnel shall be available during ground servicing of an aircraft and there shall be a means of quickly summoning rescue and fire-fighting services in the event of a fire or major fuel spill.

9.7.2: When aircraft refuelling operations take place while passengers are embarking, on board or disembarking, ground equipment shall be positioned so as to allow:

(a) the use of sufficient number of exits for expeditious evacuation; and

(b) the ready escape route from each of such exits to be used in the event of an emergency.

Appendices

Appendix 1:   Aeronautical Ground Light and Surface Marking Colours.
Appendix 2:   Aeronautical Ground Light Characteristics.
Appendix 3:   Information Markings.
Appendix 4:   Requirements Concerning Design of Taxiing Guidance Signs.

Attachments

Attachment A: Guidance Material Supplementary to Annex 14, Volume 1, as specified.
Attachment B: Obstacle Limitation Surfaces. This includes a useful diagram showing such surfaces.
Limited index of significant subjects included in Annex 14, Volume 1.

VOLUME II: HELIPORTS (2ND EDITION, JULY 1995)

Page v gives abbreviations and symbols and lists the relevant manuals.

Chapter 1

The Introductory Note states that the specifications in Volume II modify or complement those in Volume I which, where appropriate, are also applicable to heliports.

1.1: Definitions.

1.2: Applicability.

1.2.1: The interpretation of some of the specifications in the Annex expressly requires the exercising of discretion, the taking of a decision or the performance of a function by the appropriate authority. In other specifications, the expression appropriate authority does not actually appear although its inclusion is implied. In both cases, the responsibility for whatever determination or action is necessary shall rest with the State having jurisdiction over the heliport.

1.2.2: The specifications in Annex 14, Volume II shall apply to all heliports intended to be used by helicopters in international civil aviation. The specifications of Annex 14, Volume I shall apply, where appropriate, to these heliports as well.

1.2.3 deals with colour specifications in both Volumes of this Annex.

Chapter 2—Heliport data

2.1 deals with aeronautical data.

2.2: Heliport reference point shall be established for a heliport not co-located with an aerodrome.

2.3.1: Heliport elevation shall be measured and reported to the AIS authority.

2.3.2: See also further elevations to be reported in respect of heliports used by international civil aviation.

2.4 sets out the dimensions and related information to be reported or described for each facility provided on a heliport.

2.5 specifies the distances to be declared where relevant for a heliport.

2.6 deals with coordination between aeronautical information services and heliport authorities.

Chapter 3—Physical characteristics

This sets out the SARPS applicable to each of the following heliports:

3.1: Surface-level heliports.

3.2: Elevated heliports.

3.3: Helidecks.

3.4: Shipboard heliports.

Chapter 4—Obstacle restriction and removal

The Introductory Note states that the objectives of the specifications in this chapter are to define the airspace around heliports to be maintained free from obstacles so as to permit the intended helicopter operations at the heliports to be conducted safely and to prevent the heliports becoming unusable by the growth of obstacles around them. This is achieved by establishing a series of obstacle limitation surfaces that define the limits to which objects may project into the airspace.

4.1: Obstacle limitation surfaces and sectors. This describes different surfaces, and their characteristics, for example approach surface.

4.2: Obstacle limitation requirements. The Introductory Note states that the requirements for obstacle limitation surfaces are specified on the basis of the intended use of a FATO, i.e. approach manoeuvre to hover or landing or take-off manoeuvre and type of approach, and are intended to be applied when such use is made of the FATO.

In cases where operations are conducted to or from both directions of a FATO, then the function of certain surfaces may be nullified because of more stringent requirements of another lower surface.

FATO is defined as the final approach and take-off area being the defined area over which the final phase of the approach manoeuvre to hover or landing is completed and from which the take-off manoeuvre is commenced. Where the FATO is to be used by performance Class 1 helicopters, the defined area includes the rejected take-off area available.

The section then deals with the various types of heliports as listed in Chapter 3.

The Chapter includes useful figures illustrating application of the SARPS.

Table 4.1–4.4 set out dimensions and slopes of obstacle limitation surfaces and criteria.

Chapter 5—Visual aids

This chapter sets out the SARPS for visual aids:
5.1: Wind Direction Indicators.
5.2: Markings and Markers.
5.3: Lights.

Chapter 6—Heliport services

6.1: Rescue and fire-fighting. The section headings are:

General:
- Level of protection to be provided;
- Extinguishing agents;
- Rescue equipment;

• Response time.

Appendix 1: Aeronautical Data Requirements

(iii) Comments

1. Chapter 9 of this book describes the participants in aerodrome operations, and their rights and duties.

2. Chapter 5, Section 9.5 of Volume 1 of the Annex deals with bird hazard reduction. In the English case of *A/S Fred Olsens Flyelskap* v. *Norwich City Council and Norfolk County Council* ((1980) *Air Law* 35) the court held the defendant airport operators liable for damage caused to an aircraft leased to and operated by the plaintiffs through a forced landing shortly after take-off at Norwich Airport on 12 December 1973.

The court found that the aircraft engines went dead on ingesting gulls which rose from the airport on take-off. The court held that the defendants owed the plaintiffs a duty to take reasonable care in the circumstances which was based on the statutory obligation created by the Occupiers Liability Act 1957 and not under the common law duty of care. The judge held that there was a reasonably foreseeable risk of damage to the aircraft from the presence of gulls; the air traffic controller had failed to keep a proper look-out, had not used his binoculars and had been content to step out of the tower merely to see the state of the weather. The windows of the tower had been wet and dirty. The defendants had not taken action recommended in the Government Advisory Document DAT 14 by using shell crackers to scare birds and by installing SAPPHO, a system emitting simulated distress cries.

3. In the US case of *Screaming Eagle Air Ltd* v. *Airport Commission of Forsyth County* (North Carolina Court of Appeals, 1990; 22 AVI 17,902 1989–90) the airport operator was liable for hull damage caused by dogs on the runway.

4. For operational aspects see *West* v. *FAA* (US Court of Appeals, 9th Circuit, 21 October 1987; 20 AVI 18,269 1986–8). The court held:

  (i) the actions of FAA employees who were responsible for the design of the departure procedures from an airport lying in a deep funnel-shaped valley fell into the discretionary function of the Federal Tort Claims Act and therefore the district court had no subject matter jurisdiction for the surviving relatives' legal action when an aircraft crashed on take-off at night. At first trial the District Court found the cause of the accident was that FAA employees, acting in the scope of their employment, negligently failed to conduct night flight tests of the visual climb departure procedure.

  (ii) the FAA employees used their discretionary judgement in deciding it was not feasible or necessary to make any more tests on the procedure because the costs of doing additional testing greatly outweighed any added safety benefits;

(iii) the FAA employees were entitled to consider in designing the departure procedure that the pilot has the primary responsibility to determine whether conditions are safe enough to use the prescribed procedure.

See Comments in (a) Annexes 1, 6 and 8 for more cases on the discretionary function, and (b) Annex 16 on siting of Brussels International Airport.

5. For helicopter operations see Chapter 20 of this book.

ANNEX 15. AERONAUTICAL INFORMATION SERVICES—10TH EDITION (JULY 1997)

(i) Articles

Article 28—Air navigation facilities and standard systems

See page 26 above.

(ii) Summary

Chapter 1—Introduction

Chapter 1 states that the object of the aeronautical information service (AIS) is to ensure the flow of information necessary for the safety, regularity and efficiency of international air navigation and that guidance on the organisation and operation of AIS is contained in the Aeronautical Information Services Manual (doc. 8126).

See reference to area navigation (RNAV), required navigation performance (RNP) and airborne computer based navigation systems.

Chapter 2—Definitions

Definitions include:

"*Aeronautical Information Circular (AIC)*": A notice containing information that does not qualify for the origination of a NOTAM or for inclusion in the AIP, but which relates to flight safety, air navigation, technical, administrative or legislative matters.

"*Aeronautical Information Publication (AIP)*": A publication issued by, or with the authority of, a State containing aeronautical information of a lasting character essential to air navigation.

"*AIRAC*": An acronym (aeronautical information regulation and control) signifying a system aimed at advance notification based on common effective dates, of circumstances that necessitate significant changes in operating practices.

"*Integrated Aeronautical Information Package*": A package which consists of:

- AIP, including amendment service;
- supplements to the AIP;
- NOTAM and pre-flight information bulletins (PIB);
- AIC;
- checklists and summaries.

"*NOTAM*": A notice distributed by means of telecommunication containing information concerning the establishment, condition or change in any aeronautical facility, service, procedure or hazard, the timely knowledge of which is essential to personnel concerned with flight operations.

"*Pre-Flight Information Bulletin (PIB)*": A presentation of current NOTAM information of operational significance, prepared prior to flight.

See also definition of ASHTAM and SNOWTAM.

Chapter 3—General

3.1: Responsibilities and functions.

3.1.1: Each State shall:

(a) provide an AIS; or

(b) agree with one or more other States for provision of a joint service: or

(c) delegate the provision of AIS to a non-governmental agency, provided the SARPS are adequately met.

3.1.1.1: The State concerned shall remain responsible for the information published.

3.1.1.2: Information/data gathered by the State shall be of the required quality (Defined) and timely.

3.1.1.3 deals with the provision of AIS where a 24–hour service is not provided.

3.1.2: An AIS shall also obtain information to enable it to provide pre-flight and in-flight information:

(a) from the AIS of other States. (See 3.1.3 concerning authority of State of Origin.)

(b) from other available sources. (See 3.1.4 concerning verification.) For one such source see 8.2.

3.1.3: Information obtained under 3.1.2(a) shall be identified as having the authority of the State of Origin.

3.1.4 deals with verification of 3.1.2(b) information.

3.1.5: An AIS shall promptly make available to the AIS of other States information required as specified to enable them to comply with 3.1.6.

3.1.6: An AIS shall ensure that information necessary for the safety, regularity or efficiency of air navigation is available in a form suitable for the operational requirements of:

(a) flight operations personnel as described; and

(b) ATS unit responsible for flight information service and services responsible for pre-flight information.

3.1.7: AIS shall receive and/or originate, collate or assemble, edit, format, publish/store and distribute aeronautical information/data concerning the entire territory of the State as well as areas in which the State is responsible for ATS outside its territory. Such information shall be published as an Integrated Aeronautical Information Package.

3.2: Quality system.

3.2.1: As of 1 January 1998 each State shall take all necessary measures to introduce a properly organised quality system containing procedures, processes and resources necessary to implement quality management at each function stage as outlined in 3.1.7 above. See reference to International Organisation for Standardisation (ISO) 9000.

3.2.2–3.2.10 deal with the established quality system, order of accuracy for aeronautical data, integrity of data and related subjects including audit of compliance. See reference to guidance material in World Geodetic System—1984 (WGS—84) RTCA Document DO–201A and European Organisation for Civil Aviation Equipment (EUROCAE) Document ED–77—Industry Requirements for Aeronautical Information.

3.3: Exchange of aeronautical information.

3.3.1: Each State shall designate the office to which elements of the Integrated Aeronautical Information Package originated by other States shall be addressed. Such office shall be qualified to deal with requests for information.

3.3.2 deals with the position where a State designates more than one international NOTAM office.

3.3.3: An AIS shall arrange for issue and receipt of NOTAM distributed by telecommunication.

3.3.4–3.3.6 deal with direct contact between various AIS and the interchange of aeronautical information on a free basis at least in respect of 1 copy of each of the elements of the Integrated Aeronautical Information Package. See the Recommendation for further copies.

3.4: General specifications.

3.4.1: Each element of the Integrated Aeronautical Information Package for international distribution should include an English text for those parts expressed in plain language.

Further provisions include:

3.4.2: Place names.

3.4.3: Consistency of units of measurements as specified.

3.4.4: World Geodetic System—1984 (WGS—84). (This deals with coordination and geoid undulations (Defined).)

3.4.5: Use of ICAO abbreviations.

3.4.6: Use of automation.

3.4.7: Identification, promulgation and delineation of prohibited, restricted and danger areas. See Article 9 of the Chicago Convention.

Chapter 4—Aeronautical Information Publications (AIP)

Note 1: AIP are intended to satisfy international requirements for the exchange of aeronautical information of a lasting character essential to air navigation.

Note 2: AIP constitute the basic information source for permanent information and long duration temporary changes.

4.1: Contents

4.1.1: The AIP shall contain, in three parts, sections etc. and subsections, referenced to allow for electronic data storage and retrieval, the information referred to in Appendix 1 that appear in Roman type except that where the AIP is designed to facilitate operational use in flight, the precise format and arrangement is left to the discretion of the State.

4.1.1.1: The information in italics in Appendix 1 should also be included in the AIP.

(Author's Note: The AIP contents are summarised in 24 pages in Appendix 1 to the Annex. Its three main parts are:

   (i) General (GEN);
  (ii) En-route (ENR);
 (iii) Aerodromes (AD).

The nature and importance of the information is shown by the headings to the sections within each part.)

4.1.2: The AIP shall include in Part 1—General:

(a) a statement of the competent authority responsible for the air navigation facilities, services or procedures covered by the AIP;

(b) the general conditions under which the services or facilities are available for international use;

(c) a list of significant differences between the national regulations and practices of the State and the related ICAO Standards, Recommended Practices and Procedures given in a form adequate to differentiate between the requirements of the State and the related ICAO provisions;

(d) the choice made by a State in each significant case where an alternative course of action is provided for in ICAO Standards, Recommended Practices and Procedures.

4.1.3 lists those 10 types of chart which shall, when available for designated international aerodromes and heliports, form part of the AIP or are to be distributed separately to AIP recipients.

4.1.4: Charts, maps or diagrams shall be used, when appropriate, to complement or as a substitute for tabulations or text of AIPs.

Note: Charts produced in accordance with Annex 4 (Aeronautical Charts) may be used to fulfil this requirement.

4.2 sets out the General Specifications for AIP and deals with a number of matters such as date, format, binding, amendments and changes.

4.2.5: Each AIP shall be annotated, to indicate clearly:

    (a) identity of AIP;
    (b) territory covered;
    (c) identification of issuing State and producing organisation;
    (d) page numbers/chart titles;
    (e) degree of reliability if information is doubtful.

4.2.6: AIP sheet size.

4.2.7: Changes to AIP or new information on a reprinted page shall be distinctively identified.

4.2.8: Operationally significant changes to the AIP shall be published in accordance with AIRAC procedures and shall be clearly identified by the acronym AIRAC.

4.2.9: AIP shall be amended or reissued regularly as specified.

4.3: Specifications for AIP amendments

4.4: Specifications for AIP supplements, which include:

4.4.4: Where an AIP Supplement replaces a NOTAM, it shall include a reference to the serial number of the NOTAM.

4.5: Distribution shall be expeditious.

Chapter 5—NOTAM

5.1: Origination.

5.1.1: NOTAM shall be originated and issued promptly whenever the information to be disseminated is of a temporary nature and of short duration, or when operationally significant permanent changes, or temporary changes of long duration are made at short notice, except for extensive text and/or graphics.

Note: information of short duration containing extensive text and/or graphics is published as an AIP Supplement.

5.1.1.1: A NOTAM shall be originated and issued whenever the information is of direct operational significance and relates to:

    (a) status of aerodromes or runways;
    (b) operation of aeronautical services as specified;
    (c) aids to air navigation and aerodromes;

(d) visual aids;

(e) major components of aerodrome lighting systems;

(f) procedures for air navigation services;

(g) major defects or impediments in the manoeuvring area;

(h) availability of fuel, oil and oxygen;

(i) SAR facilities and services;

(j) operation of hazard beacons marking significant obstacles to air navigation;

(k) changes in regulations requiring immediate action, e.g. prohibited areas for SAR action;

(l) presence of hazards affecting air navigation, e.g. obstacles or air displays;

(m) significant obstacles to air navigation in the take-off/climb, missed approach, approach areas and runway strip;

(n) status of prohibited, restricted or danger areas;

(o) areas or routes or portions thereof where the possibility of interception exists and where maintenance of guard on VHF emergency frequency 121.5 MHz is required;

(p) status of location indicators;

(q) status of level of protection normally available at an aerodrome for rescue and fire-fighting;

(r) hazardous conditions due to snow, slush, ice or water on movement area; (see reference to SNOWTAM format in Appendix 2 or in NOTAM Code (doc. 8400) and plain language);

(s) outbreak of epidemics;

(t) forecasts of solar cosmic radiation;

(u) volcanic activity;

(v) release into the atmosphere of radioactive materials or toxic chemicals;

(w) establishment of operations of humanitarian relief missions.

5.1.1.2 refers to the origination of NOTAMs where AIP Amendment or Supplement is published in accordance with AIRAC.

5.1.1.2.1: NOTAM should remain in force as a reminder in the PIB until the next checklist/summary is issued.

5.1.1.3: The need for origination of a NOTAM should be considered in any other operationally significant circumstance.

5.1.1.4 sets out nine items of information which shall not be notified by NOTAM.

5.1.1.5: At least seven days' advance notice shall be given of activation of established danger, restricted or prohibited areas and activities requiring temporary airspace restrictions other than for emergency operations.

5.1.1.5.1: Notice of subsequent cancellation of activities or reduction of hours of activity or dimensions of airspace should be given as soon as possible.

5.1.1.6: NOTAM of unserviceability of aids to air navigation facilities or communication services should give estimate of period of unserviceability or time of expected restoration of service.

5.2 sets out the general specifications for NOTAMs. They include, for example:
5.2.3: Each NOTAM shall be issued as a single telecommunication message;
5.2.8 deals with issue of checklists of NOTAMs in force.

5.3: Distribution.
5.3.1: A NOTAM shall be distributed to addressees to whom the information is of direct operational significance, and who would not otherwise have at least seven days' prior notification.
5.3.2–5.3.4 deal with order of information to be contained in NOTAMs, SNOWTAMs and ASHTAMs.
5.3.5: NOTAMs shall be prepared in accordance with the ICAO communications procedures and distributed whenever practicable by the AFTN.
5.3.6 deals with phraseology to be used.
5.3.7: The originating State shall select the NOTAM to be given international distribution.
5.3.8 deals further with exchange and distribution.

Chapter 6—Aeronautical Information Regulation and Control (AIRAC)

This chapter deals with the organisation for dissemination of information concerning the circumstances listed in Appendix 4, Part I under the regulated system (AIRAC).
See also Aeronautical Information Services Manual (doc. 8126).

Chapter 7—Aeronautical Information Circulars (AIC)

7.1.1: An AIC shall be originated whenever it is necessary to promulgate aeronautical information which does not qualify to be included in an AIP or under the specifications for the origination of a NOTAM.
7.1.1.1: An AIC shall be originated whenever it is desirable to promulgate:

(a) a long-term forecast of major changes in legislation, regulations, procedures or facilities;
(b) and (c) information, or in some cases, notification of an explanatory or advisory nature liable to affect flight safety or concerning technical, legislative or administrative matters.

7.1.1.1 lists the 21 items to be included in AIC.

7.1.1.2 sets out the provisions concerning snow plan.

7.2 sets out general specifications for AIC.

7.3 deals with distribution where the States shall give AIC selected for international distribution the same distribution as for AIP.

Chapter 8—Pre-flight and post-flight information

8.1: Pre-flight information

8.1.1 and **8.1.2**: At any aerodrome normally used for international air operations, aeronautical information essential for the safety, regularity and efficiency of air navigation and relative to the route stages which originate at the aerodrome shall be made available to flight operations personnel, including flight crews and services responsible for pre-flight information. This will include elements of the Integrated Aeronautical Information Package, maps and charts.

8.1.2.1 deals with additional current information to be provided.

8.1.3: Current NOTAM and other information of urgent character shall be made available to flight crews in the form of plain language pre-flight information bulletins (PIB).

8.2: Post-flight information. States shall ensure that arrangements are made to receive at aerodromes/heliports information concerning the state and operation of air navigation facilities noted by aircrews and that such information is made available to the AIS for necessary distribution.

Chapter 9—Telecommunication requirements

This deals with the connection of international NOTAM offices to the aeronautical fixed service (AFS). Each such NOTAM office shall be connected through the AFS service to area control centres and flight information centres, and to the aerodromes and heliports within the territory at which an information service is established in accordance with Chapter 8.

Appendices

Appendix 1:   Contents of AIP.
Appendix 2:   SNOWTAM Format.
Appendix 3:   ASHTAM Format.
Appendix 4:   Information to be Notified by AIRAC.
Appendix 5:   Predetermined Distribution System for NOTAM.
Appendix 6:   NOTAM Format.
Appendix 7:   Aeronautical Data Quality Requirements.

(iii) Comments

(1) Chapter 2: Definitions. Some States issue BIRDTAMS on bird avoidance. (CAA General Aviation Safety Sense Leaflet IOA: Bird Avoidance.)

(2) An unusual example of the issue of NOTAMs is considered by Dr Michael Milde in his article, "Aeronautical Consequences of the Iraqi invasion of Kuwait" (*Air Law* Vol. XVI, No 2, page 63).

On 1 February 1991 the international NOTAM office in Jeddah, Saudi Arabia, distributed the NOTAM "All Iraqi and Kuwaiti airspace is a war zone. Any aircraft penetrating and/or within this airspace will be treated as hostile and shot down by allied forces". Dr Milde points out: (i) Article 89 of the Chicago Convention gives belligerents and neutrals freedom of action with no obligation to issue NOTAMs for civil aviation; (ii) States only have the right to issue aeronautical information on territories over which they have jurisdiction; (iii) the NOTAM is too categorical in making no distinction between civil and military aircraft or between aircraft of hostile, neutral or friendly States. All civil aircraft enjoy protection against the use of weapons under the general principle recognised in Article 3bis and additional protection is provided by the Geneva Convention relative to the protection of civilian persons in time of war of 12 August 1949 and to civilian population in general and "ambulance aircraft" in particular.

A subsequent NOTAM was issued by the same office on 18 February 1991 which "replaces the NOTAM of 1 Feb 1991 and corrects those legal elements which could have created difficulties".

(3) The UK AIP in the AD section for London Gatwick is considered in Chapter 9 of this book.

(4) UK AIP entry on SAR is considered briefly in the Comments under Annex 12.

(5) UK AIC 109/1996 explains the UK Confidential Human Factors Incident Reporting Programme (CHIRP). CHIRP's principal aim is to seek to identify human factors related causes of incidents which would not be reported through other systems, but which may, if analysed and compared with similar experiences, lead to changes in procedures or design so that others may learn from the reporter's experience. It is aimed at professional pilots and civilian Air Traffic Controllers.

ANNEX 16.   ENVIRONMENTAL PROTECTION

Volume I: Aircraft Noise—(3rd edition, July 1993)
Volume II: Aircraft Engine Emissions—(2nd edition, July 1993)

(i) Articles

None. Reference should be made to:

(a) Comments (1) below.

(b) Resolution A16–3 on Aircraft Noise in the Vicinity of Airports adopted by ICAO Assembly in 1968.

(ii) Summary

VOLUME I: AIRCRAFT NOISE (3RD EDITION, JULY 1993)

Part I: Definitions

Definitions include:

> *"Associated aircraft systems"*: Those aircraft systems drawing electrical/pneumatic power from an auxiliary power unit during ground operations.
> *"Subsonic Aeroplane"*: An aeroplane incapable of sustaining level flight at speeds exceeding flight Mach number of 1.
> And also *"by-pass ratio"* and *"derived version"* of an aircraft.

Part II: Aircraft noise certification

Chapter 1—Administration

1.1 provides that 1.2–1.5 apply to all aircraft included in the classifications defined for noise certification in the listed chapters where such aircraft are engaged in international air navigation.

1.2: Noise certification shall be granted or validated by the State of Registry on the basis that the aircraft complies with requirements at least equal to the applicable Standards specified in the Annex.

See Note on form of documents attesting noise certification.

1.3–1.4: The documents attesting noise certification shall provide certain minimum information listed (a)–(g), which shall be included (with the exception of 1.3(a)) in the Flight Manual. These items of information in 1.3 are:

(a) State of Registry: nationality and registration marks;
(b) manufacturer's serial number;
(c) manufacturer's type and model designation; engine type/model; propeller type/model (if applicable);
(d) statement of any additional modifications incorporated for the purpose of compliance with the applicable noise certification standards;
(e) maximum mass as specified;
(f) for specified aeroplanes and helicopters the average noise levels at the specified reference points;
(g) the chapter of Annex 16 Volume I according to which the aircraft was certificated.

1.5: States shall recognise as valid a noise certification granted by another State provided that the requirements under which such certification was granted are at least equal to the applicable Standards specified in the Annex.

1.6 deals with suspension or revocation of noise certification of an aircraft if it ceases to comply with the applicable noise Standards. Removal of suspension or granting a new noise certification shall not take place unless compliance with the applicable Standards is shown.

1.7 and **1.8** deal with the date for determining the Standards to be applied.

The following Chapters 2–11 deal with aircraft types and their appropriate noise requirements:

Chapter 2—Subsonic jet aeroplanes: application for certificate of airworthiness for the prototype accepted before 6 October 1977

This sets out the applicable Standards.

2.1.1 lists certain exceptions defined by runway length or engine by-pass ratio.

2.1.2 deals with derived version aeroplanes (Defined).

2.2: The noise evaluation measure shall be the effective perceived noise level in EPNdB as described in Appendix 1 to the Annex.

2.3 sets out the noise measurement points for lateral noise, flyover noise and approach noise, which it Defines.

2.4 establishes the maximum noise levels at the lateral noise, flyover noise, and approach noise measurement points.

2.5 permits the trade-off of excesses of noise levels against reduction of noise levels at different measurement points.

2.6 deals with take-off and approach test procedures. Note the reference to the Environmental Technical Manual on the use of Procedures in the Noise Certification of Aircraft (doc. 9501).

Chapter 3—Subsonic jet aeroplanes and certain categories of propeller-driven aircraft

This chapter refers to:

(1) Subsonic jet aeroplanes—application for certificate of airworthiness accepted on or after 6 October 1977.

(2) Propeller-driven aeroplanes over 5,700 kg—application for certificate of airworthiness for the prototype accepted on or after 1 January 1985 and before 17 November 1988.

(3) Propeller-driven aeroplanes over 8,618 kg—application for certificate of airworthiness for the prototype accepted on or after 17 November 1988.

The section headings are the same as those in Chapter 2 with the addition of noise certification reference procedures, which are quite lengthy (section 3.6). The SARPS of course differ from those in Chapter 2.

Chapter 4—Supersonic aeroplanes

4.1: Supersonic aeroplanes—application of certificate of airworthiness for prototype accepted before 1 January 1975.

4.1.1: The Standards of Chapter 2 apply as specified, except for the maximum noise levels specified in 2.4, to all supersonic aeroplanes in respect of which the application for the prototype certificate of airworthiness was before 1 January 1975 and the grant of the certificate of airworthiness for the individual type was first issued after 26 November 1981.

4.1.2: Maximum noise levels determined in accordance with Appendix 1 shall not exceed the measured noise levels of the first certificated aeroplane of the type.

4.2: SARPS for aeroplanes where application for certificate of airworthiness for prototype is accepted on or after 1 January 1975 are not developed. See Note concerning guidelines.

Chapter 5—Propeller-driven aeroplanes over 5,700 kg: application for certificate of airworthiness for the prototype accepted before 1 January 1985

The section headings are the same as those in Chapter 3 but the SARPS are different.

Chapter 6—Propeller-driven aeroplanes not exceeding 8,618 kg: application for prototype certificate of airworthiness accepted before 17 November 1988

This chapter has only five sections headed as follows:

(1) Applicability;
(2) Noise evaluation measure;
(3) Maximum noise levels;
(4) Noise certification reference procedures;
(5) Test procedures.

Chapter 7—Propeller-driven STOL aeroplanes

SARPS are not yet developed, see guidelines in Attachment B.

Chapter 8—Helicopters

Section headings are:

(1) Applicability;
(2) Noise evaluation measure;
(3) Reference Noise measurement points;
(4) Maximum noise levels;
(5) Trade-offs;
(6) Noise certification reference procedures;
(7) Test procedures (see reference to the Environmental Technical Manual on the Use of Procedures in the Noise Certification of Aircraft (doc. 9501)).

Chapter 9—Installed auxiliary power units (APU) and associated aircraft systems during ground operations

SARPS are not developed, see guidelines in Attachment C which may be used for APUs in the specified aircraft.

Chapter 10—Propeller-driven aeroplanes not exceeding 8,618 kg: application for certificate of airworthiness for the prototype or derived version accepted on or after 17 November 1988

Section headings are:

(1) Applicability;
(2) Noise evaluation measure;
(3) Reference noise measurement points;
(4) Maximum noise levels;
(5) Noise certification reference procedures;
(6) Test procedures.

Chapter 11—Helicopters not exceeding 2,730 kg maximum certificated take-off mass

The section headings are the same as those in Chapter 10 except in 11.3, 11.4 and 11.5 where respectively "points", "levels" and "procedures" are in the singular. The contents are different.

Part III: Noise measurement for monitoring purposes

This Recommendation has been developed to assist States which measure noise for monitoring purposes, until such time as agreement on a single method can be reached. Where measurement of aircraft noise is made for monitoring purposes, the method of Appendix 5 should be used.

Part IV: Assessment of airport noise

The methodology described in "Recommended Method for Computing Noise Contours around Airports" (Circ. 205) should be used in the specified circumstances.

Part V: Criteria for the application of noise abatement operating procedures

The Note states that Part II is aimed at noise certification which characterises the maximum noise emitted by the aircraft. However, noise abatement procedures approved by national authorities and included in operations manuals allow the reduction of noise during aircraft operations.

  (1) Aircraft operating procedures for noise abatement shall not be introduced unless the regulatory authority, based on appropriate studies and consultations, determines that a noise problem exists.
  (2) *Procedures for noise abatement should be developed in consultation with the operators which use the aerodrome concerned.*
  (3) *The factors to be taken into consideration in the development of the appropriate procedures should include:*
      (a) *the nature and extent of the noise problem, including:*
          (i) *location of noise-sensitive areas;*
          (ii) *critical hours.*
      (b) *the types of aircraft affected including aircraft mass, aerodrome elevation, temperature considerations;*
      (c) *the types of procedures likely to be most effective;*
      (d) *obstacle clearance (PANS—OPS (doc. 8168) Volumes I and II).*

Attention is drawn to Annex 6, Part 1, Chapter 4 for aeroplane noise abatement operating procedures.

Appendices

Appendices 1–4 and 6 set out the evaluation method for noise certification of the aircraft as listed.

Appendix 5 sets out provisions for monitoring aircraft noise on and in the vicinity of aerodromes.

Attachments

The Attachments are:

Attachment A: Equations for the calculation of noise levels as a function of take-off mass;

Attachment B: Guidelines for noise certification of propeller-driven STOL aeroplanes;

Attachment C: Guidelines for noise certification of installed auxiliary power units and associated aircraft systems during ground operation;

Attachment D: Guidelines for evaluating an alternative method of measuring helicopter noise during approach;

Attachment E: Applicability of ICAO Annex 16 Noise Certification Standards for Propellor-driven Aeroplanes.

VOLUME II: AIRCRAFT ENGINE EMISSIONS (2ND EDITION, JULY 1993)

Part I: Definitions and symbols

Chapter 1—Definitions

Definitions include:

> "*Smoke*": The carbonaceous materials in exhaust emissions which obscure the transmission of light;
> "*Taxi/ground idle*";
> "*Derivative version*" of a gas turbine engine (which the Note points out is not the same as "derived version of aircraft" in Volume I).

Chapter 2—Symbols

These include, for example, SN representing Smoke Number.

Part II: Vented fuel

Chapter 1—Administration

1.1: This Part applies to all turbine engine-powered aircraft intended for operation in international air navigation manufactured after 18 February 1982.

1.2 and **1.3** deal with certification related to the prevention of intentional fuel venting granted by the certificating authority, and recognition by other States of certification.

Chapter 2—Prevention of intentional fuel venting

Aircraft shall be so designed and constructed as to prevent the intentional discharge into the atmosphere of liquid fuel from the fuel nozzle manifolds resulting from the process of engine shutdown following normal flight or ground operations.

Part III: Emissions certification

Chapter 1—Administration

1.1: The provisions of 1.2–1.4 shall apply to all engines included in the classifications defined for emission certification in Chapters 2 and 3, where such engines are fitted to aircraft engaged in international air navigation.

1.2: Emissions certification shall be granted by the certificating authority on the basis of satisfactory evidence that the engine complies with the relevant requirements; compliance to be demonstrated as specified.

1.3: The document attesting emissions certification for each individual engine shall include at least the following information applicable to the engine type:

    (a) name of certificating authority;

    (b) manufacturer's type and model designation;

    (c) statement of any additional modifications incorporated for the purpose of compliance with the applicable emissions certification requirements;

    (d) rated output;

    (e) reference pressure ratio:

    (f) a statement indicating compliance with Smoke Number requirements;

    (g) a statement indicating compliance with gaseous pollutant requirements.

1.4: States shall recognise as valid certification granted by another State provided that the requirements under which such certification was granted are not less stringent than the provisions of this Volume.

Chapter 2—Turbo-jet and turbo-fan engines intended for propulsion only at subsonic speeds

2.1: General. This deals with the applicability of the provisions of the chapter to the engines as specified, the emissions to be controlled:

    2.1.2:

- Smoke
- Gaseous emissions
  —unburned hydrocarbons (HC);
  —carbon monoxide (CO); and
  —oxides of nitrogen (NO_x).

    2.1.3: Units of measurements. Smoke emission shall be measured and reported in Smoke Number. Mass of gaseous pollutant emitted during the reference emissions landing and take-off cycle, as defined, shall be measured and reported in grams.

2.1.4 and **2.1.5** deal both with reference conditions and test conditions.

2.2 deals with and defines the Regulatory Smoke Number, which applies to all engines manufactured on or after 1 January 1983.

2.3 deals with and defines regulatory levels of gaseous emissions which apply to engines manufactured on or after 1 January 1986 of greater output than 26.7 kN and as further specified for oxides of nitrogen.

2.4: Information required. This consists of:

2.4.1 which lists the eight items of general information to be provided for each engine type for which certificate of origin is sought;

2.4.2 which sets out the test information required for each engine tested for certification purposes;

2.4.3 which sets out the derived information required (dealing with emissions, values and Smoke Number).

Chapter 3—Turbo-jet and turbo-fan engines intended for propulsion at supersonic speeds

3.1: General. The sub-section headings here are the same as found in Chapter 2 with the addition of 3.1.4, "Nomenclature dealing with engines where afterburn is not used and taxi/ground idle thrust setting".

3.2 provides the regulatory smoke number formula.

3.3: Regulatory levels of gaseous emissions.

3.4: Information required, having the same three sub-sections as in Chapter 2: General, Test and Derived.

Appendices

Appendix 1: Measurement of reference pressure ratio. This is defined in Chapter 1 as the ratio of the mean total pressure at the last compressor discharge plane of the compressor to the mean total pressure at the compressor entry plane when the engine is developing take-off thrust rating in ISA sea level static conditions.

Appendix 2 deals with smoke emission evaluation.

Appendix 3 and its Attachments A–F deal with instrumentation and measurement techniques for gaseous emissions.

Appendix 4 sets out the specification for fuel to be used in aircraft turbine engine emission testing.

Appendix 5 and its Attachments A–F deal with instrumentation and measurement techniques for gaseous emissions from afterburning gas turbine engines.

Appendix 6: Compliance procedure for gaseous emissions and smoke.

(iii) Comments

(1) While there are no Articles in the Chicago Convention dealing expressly with environment pollution, *S&B* suggest in Part 111/31 that Articles 6, 9 and 11 are bases for imposition by States of environmental restrictions. It has also been argued that customary international law permits such restrictions.

(2) Noise is regulated in the EU by Council Directive 89/629/EEC, supplemented by Directive 92/14/EEC which limit the operation of aircraft which do not meet the SARPS of Chapter 3 of Annex 16, Part I. The SARPS of Chapter 3 impose higher standards than those in Chapter 2. The Directive is applied in the UK by the Air Navigation (Noise Certification) Order 1990 (SI 1990 No 1514); see also sections 77 and 78 of the UK Civil Aviation Act 1982 and the Aeroplane Noise (Limitation of Operations of Aeroplanes) Regulations 1993.

(3) At the 28th (Extraordinary) Session of ICAO Assembly in October 1990 it was decided that a withdrawal of Chapter 2 Aircraft would take place between 1995 and 2002. It was also decided that there should be no restriction before 1 April 1995 on aircraft less than 25 years old after the date of each first individual certificate of airworthiness on any presently existing wide-bodied aircraft or on any aircraft fitted with high by-pass ratio engines.

(4) In the USA noise is regulated by the Airport Noise and Capacity Act 1990 and regulations. Annex 16, Chapters 2 and 3 requirements are referred to as FAA Stage II and III requirements.

(5) For sleep disturbance see the UK Department of Transport Report of a field study of Aircraft Noise and Sleep Disturbance (December 1992). Pages 36–37 list the reference publications.

(6) The Belgian Court of Appeal's decision, *State of Belgium, Regie der Luchtwegen ("RDL"), Sabena & Others* v. *Robert Brussel & Others* (24 January 1997, RG 1996/AR/2547; (1998) XXIII *Air Law*, No. 1), is important:

  (a) The court at first instance had ordered the State and RDL to stop allowing certain aircraft types to overfly specified cities between 11 pm and 6 am near Brussels National Airport. The court ordered a fine to be paid for each violation.

  (b) The Court of Appeal held:
  (i) Article 25 of the Belgian Constitution giving a constitutional right to a healthy environment was not directly applicable and not sufficient to obtain a night flight prohibition in the subject case.
  (ii) Article 8–1 of the European Convention on Human Rights does not give an absolute right to privacy.
  (iii) There was no violation of:
  (a) Law on aerial navigation, 27 June 1937; and
  (b) EC Directives EEC 89/629 and 92/14.
  (iv) The appellants had instituted special night departure routes to avoid over-flight of urban areas.

(v) The State and RDL are not liable for violation of noise abatement procedures by pilots after clearance for take-off.

(vi) The decision of the State and RDL to build an airport near to Brussels urban area is political and dictated by historic and opportunistic reasons. The court is not allowed to have a personal opinion on a decision of the authorities on public interest.

(vii) The claim based on the alleged abuse of right (also based on the Aquilian Law (Roman civil law of delict)) was not proven.

(viii) Even if the claim based on "no fault" theory of nuisance (Belgian Civil Code Article 544) had been accepted, this would not have authorised the judge to prohibit the activity causing the harm.

(ix) The claimants had chosen to live adjacent to an airport whose development was foreseeable.

(x) The claimants could not prove a real loss of value to their properties.

(7) A further illustration of the application of noise limitation procedures is found in the UK case of *R* v. *Secretary of State for Transport ex parte Richmond-upon-Thames London Borough Council (No 4)* ([1996] 4 All ER 93) and in the application by IATA on behalf of its member airlines in 1996/1997 which are summarised as follows:

(a) In 1993 and 1995 the Secretary of State for Transport issued consultative documents revising the policy under which restrictions were imposed on night flying at London Heathrow, London Gatwick and Stansted Airports under section 78 of the Civil Aviation Act 1982. In August 1995 the Secretary of State made a decision regarding night flying restrictions.

(b) Richmond upon Thames London Borough Council in a series of cases challenged the decision on the flying restrictions by way of an application for judicial review on the grounds that in allowing for increased aircraft movements and noise the decision removed an advantage from local people which could legitimately be expected to continue.

(c) The Borough Council submitted that the consultative documents did not satisfy the necessary legal requirements for such documents in that they failed to give reasons for the change of policy and failed to explain the change and did not maintain a balance between the needs of the local people and those of the airlines, or explain how night noise levels might be expected to change. The Court of Appeal upheld the Minister's decision and ruled that the consultative documents were adequate.

(d) Subsequently IATA acting on behalf of its member airlines challenged the Secretary of State's decision and applied for judicial review. The Department of Transport admitted that there were procedural errors in the consultation process and agreed to launch a fresh consultation. These proceedings continue.

(8) Sonic boom is defined by ICAO Sonic Boom Committee as "the acoustic event which is a manifestation of the shock wave system generated when [an aeroplane] flies at a speed greater than the local sound velocity". The Committee concluded that States have the right to regulate supersonic flights over their own territory but cannot prohibit supersonic flights outside their territory including the high seas (ICAO doc. 9011 SBC/1 1972).

(9) Pollution. See practical application of anti-pollution restrictions, for example in UK in the Civil Aviation Act 1982, Air Navigation (Aircraft and Aircraft Engine Emissions) Order 1986 and Air Navigation (Aeroplane and Aeroplane Engine Emission of Unburned Hydrocarbons) Order 1988.

(10) Insurance: See reference to Aviation Clause 46B "Noise and Pollution and Other Perils Exclusion Clause" page 450.

ANNEX 17. SECURITY—SAFEGUARDING INTERNATIONAL CIVIL AVIATION AGAINST ACTS OF UNLAWFUL INTERFERENCE—6TH EDITION (MARCH 1997)

(i) Articles

Article 4—Misuse of civil aviation

Each Contracting State agrees not to use civil aviation for any purpose inconsistent with the aims of this Convention.

(ii) Summary

Chapter 1—Definitions

Definitions are:

"*Air Side*": The movement area of an airport, adjacent terrain and buildings or portions thereof, access to which is controlled.

"*Regulated Agent*": An agent, freight forwarder or any other entity who conducts business with an operator and provides security controls that are accepted or required by the appropriate authority in respect of cargo, courier and express parcels or mail.

"*Screening*": The application of technical or other means which are intended to detect weapons, explosives or other dangerous devices which may be used to commit an act of unlawful interference.

"*Security*": A combination of measures and human and material resources intended to safeguard international civil aviation against acts of unlawful interference.

"*Security Control*": A means by which the introduction of weapons, explosives and articles likely to be utilised to commit an act of unlawful interference can be prevented.

"*Security Programme*": Measures adopted to safeguard international civil aviation against acts of unlawful interference.

Chapter 2—General

2.1.1–2.1.2: The aim of aviation security shall be to safeguard international civil aviation operations against acts of unlawful interference. Safety of passengers, crew, ground personnel and the general public shall be the primary objective.

2.1.3: Each Contracting State shall establish an organisation, develop plans and implement procedures which together provide a standardised level of security for the operation of international flights in normal operating conditions and which are capable of rapid expansion to meet any increased security threat.

2.2: Wherever possible, security measures and procedures should be arranged to cause minimum of interference and delay to civil aviation.

See also reference to Security Manual for Safeguarding Civil Aviation Against Acts of Unlawful Interference (doc. 8973).

Chapter 3—Organisation

3.1 sets out the SARPS for a national organisation.

3.1.1–3.1.4: Each State shall establish a national civil aviation security programme ("Programme") the objective of which shall be to protect international civil aviation against acts of unlawful interference through regulations and procedures. It shall designate the appropriate authority to be responsible for the Programme. Such authority shall be specified to ICAO.

3.1.5: Each State shall keep under constant review the level of threat within its territory taking into account the international situation and adjust the relevant elements of its Programme accordingly.

Each State shall procure that:

3.1.6: The authority shall coordinate activities between the various organisations etc. of the State concerned with various aspects of the Programme.

3.1.7: The authority shall define and allocate the tasks for implementation of the Programme as between State agencies, airport administrations, operators and others.

3.1.8: Each State shall ensure the establishment of an adequate security programme for each airport serving international aviation.

3.1.9: Each State should make available to its airport administrations, airlines operating in its territory and others concerned a written version of appropriate parts of the Programme.

3.1.10–3.1.15 deal with the SARPS to be applied at each airport serving international civil aviation. These include the establishment of an airport security committee, and the provision of trained staff, facilities and contingency plans.

3.1.16 requires the development and implementation of training programmes to ensure the effectiveness of the Programme.

3.1.17: Each State should ensure persons engaged to implement security controls are subject to pre-employment checks, are capable of fulfilling their duties and adequately trained.

3.1.18: The relevant operators shall implement a security programme appropriate to meet requirements of the Programme of the State concerned.

3.1.19: Promotion of research and development of new equipment.

3.2: International cooperation.

3.2.1 requires inter-State cooperation on any necessary adaptation of Programmes.

3.2.1.1: Inter-State exchange of appropriate parts of the Programme.

3.2.1.2: Each State should include in its bilateral agreement on air transport a clause related to aviation security.

3.2.2: Each State shall ensure that requests from other States for special security measures in respect of specified flights by aircraft operators of such other States, as far as practicable, are met.

3.2.3: States shall cooperate in development and exchange of information on training programmes.

3.2.4: Cooperation in research and development of new equipment.

Chapter 4—Preventive security measures

4.1: General objectives of the measures.

4.1.1: Each State shall establish measures to prevent weapons, explosives or any other dangerous devices which may be used to commit an act of unlawful interference, the carriage or bearing of which is not authorised, from being introduced, by any means whatsoever, on board an aircraft engaged in international civil aviation.

See Note on electric, electronic or battery operated items and reference to the Security Manual (doc. 8973).

4.1.2: Procedures concerning carriage of weapons by law enforcement officers and other authorised persons.

4.1.3: Pre-flight checks of originating aircraft assigned to international flights shall include measures to discover suspicious objects or anomalies that could conceal weapons, explosives or other dangerous devices.

4.1.4: Each State shall establish procedures which include notification to the operator, for inspecting aircraft, when a well-founded suspicion exists that the aircraft may be the object of an act of unlawful interference, for concealed weapons, explosives or other dangerous devices.

4.1.5: Each State shall establish measures to safeguard aircraft where a well-founded suspicion exists it may be attacked on the ground and to provide as much prior notification of the arrival of such aircraft to the airport authorities.

4.1.6: Each State shall arrange for surveys and inspections and testing in relation to security needs, security controls and their effectiveness.

4.2: Measures relating to passengers and their cabin baggage.

4.2.1–4.2.3: Each State shall ensure that:

4.2.1: Adequate measures are taken to control transfer and transit passengers and their cabin baggage to prevent unauthorised articles from being taken on board aircraft as specified;

4.2.2: There is no possibility of mixing or contact between passengers subjected to security control and other persons not subjected to such control after security screening points have been passed; if there is mixing or contact then rescreening is required before boarding;

4.2.3: The aircraft operator and pilot-in-command are informed when passengers are obliged to travel because they have been the subject of judicial or administrative proceedings so appropriate measures can be taken.

4.2.4: Each State should require operators providing service from that State to include in their security programmes, measures and procedures to ensure safety on board when passengers are to be carried who are obliged to travel because they have been the subject of judicial or administrative proceedings.

4.2.5: Measures shall be taken by each State in respect of flights under increased threat to ensure disembarking passengers do not leave items on board at transit stops on its airports.

4.3: Measures relating to checked baggage, cargo and other goods.

4.3.1: Each State shall establish measures to ensure that operators when providing service from that State do not transport baggage of passengers who are not on board the aircraft unless the baggage separated from passengers is subjected to other security control measures.

4.3.2: Measures should be established to ensure that operators transport only baggage authorised for carriage.

4.3.3: Each State should establish measures to ensure that checked baggage is screened before being placed on board the aircraft.

4.3.4–4.3.5: Measures shall be established so that:

- consignments checked-in as baggage by couriers for carriage on passenger flights are subjected to specific security controls in addition to those in 4.3.1;

- baggage intended for carriage on passenger flights and originating from places other than airport check-in counters is protected from the point it is checked-in until it is placed on board an aircraft.

4.3.6: Each State shall ensure implementation of measures at airports serving international civil aviation to protect cargo, baggage, mail, stores and operators' supplies being moved within an airport and intended for carriage on an aircraft to safeguard such aircraft against an act of unlawful interference.

4.3.7: Establishment of security controls for catering supplies, operators' stores and supplies, intended for carriage on passenger flights.

4.3.8: Each State shall establish measures to ensure that cargo, courier and express parcels and mail intended for carriage on passenger flights are subjected to appropriate security controls.

4.3.9: Each State shall establish measures to ensure that operators do not accept consignments of cargo, courier and express parcels or mail for carriage on passenger flights unless the security of such consignments is accounted for by a regulated agent or such consignments are subject to controls to meet the requirements of 4.3.8.

4.3.10: Secure storage areas shall be established at airports serving international civil aviation where mishandled baggage may be held pending further disposal.

4.3.11: Each State should take necessary measures to ensure that unidentified baggage is placed in a protected and isolated area until it is ascertained it does not contain any explosives or other dangerous device.

4.4: Access control. Each State shall establish procedures and identification systems to prevent unauthorised access by persons or vehicles to the airside of an airport serving international civil aviation and to other areas important to the security of the airport. It shall also establish measures to ensure supervision over movement of persons to and from the aircraft and to prevent unauthorised access to the aircraft.

4.5: Airport design. Each State shall ensure that the architectural and infrastructure-related requirements necessary for optimum implementation of international civil aviation security measures are integrated into the design and construction of new facilities and alterations of existing facilities at airports.

Chapter 5—Management of response to acts of unlawful interference

5.1.1: Each State shall take adequate measures for the safety of passengers and crew on an aircraft subjected to an act of unlawful interference.

5.1.2: Each State responsible for providing ATS for an aircraft being the subject of an act of unlawful interference shall collect all pertinent information on the flight of that aircraft and transmit it to States responsible for the ATS units as specified so timely action can be taken en route and at destination.

5.1.3: Timely distribution of information received as a consequence of 5.1.2.

5.1.4: Each State shall provide such assistance to an aircraft subjected to an act of unlawful seizure, including provision of navigation aids, ATS and permissions to land as may be necessitated by the circumstances.

5.1.5: Each State shall take measures, where practicable, to ensure that an aircraft subjected to an act of unlawful seizure which has landed in its territory is detained on the ground unless its departure is necessitated by the overriding duty to protect human life, recognising the importance of consultations, wherever practicable, between the State where the aircraft has landed and State of Operator, and of notification to States of assumed or stated destination.

5.2: Reports.

5.2.1: States should exchange information relating to plans, designs, equipment, methods and procedures etc. for safeguarding international civil aviation against acts of unlawful interference. Such information should be supplied to ICAO.

5.2.2: A State in which an aircraft, subjected to an act of unlawful interference, has landed shall notify by the most expeditious means:

(a) the State of Registry and State of Operator of the landing and shall provide all other relevant information to those States; and also to
(b) each State whose citizens have suffered fatalities or injuries;
(c) each State whose citizens were detained as hostages;
(d) each State whose citizens are known to be on board;
(e) ICAO.

5.2.3: Each State concerned with an act of unlawful interference shall require its appropriate authority to re-evaluate security measures and procedures in respect to international flights which have been the subject of unlawful interference and remedy weaknesses to prevent recurrence.

5.2.4: Each State concerned with an act of unlawful interference shall provide ICAO with all pertinent information concerning the security aspects of the act of unlawful interference as soon as practicable after the act is resolved.

5.2.5: Each State should adopt measures to ensure that persons acting in an official capacity do not divulge confidential information concerning an act of unlawful interference if such information is likely to jeopardise the safety of international civil aviation.

Attachment

Attachment to Annex 17 sets out extracts from other relevant Annexes and procedures, as listed:

Annex 2:   Rules of the Air
Annex 6:   Operation of Aircraft Part I

Annex 9:   Facilitation
Annex 10: Aeronautical Telecommunications Vol. IV (Surveillance Radar and Collision Avoidance Systems)
Annex 11: ATS
Annex 13: Aircraft Accident Investigation
Annex 14: Aerodromes Vol I—Aerodrome Design and Operations
Annex 18: Safe Transport of Dangerous Goods by Air
Doc. 9284—Technical Instructions for the Safe Transport of Dangerous Goods.
Procedures for Air Navigation Services—Rules of the Air and ATS (doc. 4444).
Procedures for Air Navigation Services—Aircraft Operations (doc. 8168) Vol. I—Flight Procedures.

(iii) Comments

(1) The various treaties and other legal aspects of this subject are dealt with in Chapter 12.

(2) GCC 14.6 requires the passenger to submit to any security checks by Government, airport officials or carrier.

(3) 3.2.1.2 above, see Article 9 "Aviation Security" of the UK/Estonia Bilateral Air Service Agreement, 3 March 1993 (Cm 2252).

ANNEX 18.   THE SAFE TRANSPORT OF DANGEROUS GOODS BY AIR—2ND EDITION (JULY 1989)

(i) Articles

None specific.

(ii) Summary

The Foreword states that the provisions of the Annex govern the international transport of dangerous goods by air and the broad provisions of the Annex are amplified by the detailed specifications of the Technical Instructions for the Safe Transport of Dangerous Goods by Air (doc. 9284) ("Technical Instructions").

Chapter 1—Definitions

Definitions include:
"*Dangerous Goods*": Articles or substances which are capable of posing significant risk to health, safety or property when transported by air;

"Unit Load Device (ULD)": Any type of freight container, aircraft container, aircraft pallet with a net, or aircraft pallet with a net over an igloo. This definition does not include an overpack.

"Flammable": Note: The word flammable has the same meaning as inflammable in the English language.

"State of Origin": The State in the territory of which the cargo was first loaded on an aircraft.

The Definitions also include *"Dangerous Goods Accident"*, *"Dangerous Goods Incident"*, *"Package"* and *"Serious Injury"*.

Chapter 2—Applicability

2.1 states that the SARPS shall be applicable to all international operations of civil aircraft. See (a) when exemptions can be granted, e.g. extreme urgency, (b) the four Notes.

2.2.1: Each State shall comply with the Technical Instructions.

2.2.2: Each State should advise ICAO of difficulties in application of Technical Instructions.

2.3: In the interests of safety and minimising interruptions to the international transport of dangerous goods, States should also take the necessary measures to achieve compliance with the Annex and the Technical Instructions for domestic civil aircraft operations.

2.4: Exceptions.

2.4.1: Articles and substances which would be otherwise classed as dangerous goods but are required for airworthiness and operating regulations or for identified specialised purposes shall be exempt from the provisions of this Annex.

2.4.2: Replacements for articles and substances described in 2.4.1 shall be transported in accordance with this Annex except as permitted by the Technical Instructions.

2.4.3: Articles and substances intended for personal use by crew or passengers shall be exempted to the extent specified in the Technical Instructions.

2.5.1: Where a State adopts different provisions from those specified in the Technical Instructions, it shall notify ICAO promptly of such variations for publication in the Technical Instructions.

Note: States are expected to notify a difference to the provisions of 2.2.1 under Article 38 only if they are unable to accept the binding nature of the Technical Instructions. Where States have adopted different provisions from those specified in the Technical Instructions, they are expected to be reported only under the provisions of 2.5.

2.5.2: The State of the Operator should take the necessary measures to ensure that when an operator adopts more restrictive requirements than those specified in the

Technical Instructions, the notification of such operator variations is made to ICAO for publication in the Technical Instructions.

2.6: Surface Transport. States should make provisions to enable dangerous goods intended for air transport and prepared in accordance with the Technical Instructions to be accepted for surface transport to and from aerodromes.

Chapter 3—Classification

The classification of an article or substance shall be in accordance with the provisions of the Technical Instructions.

See Note on the various classes of dangerous goods and potential risks.

Chapter 4—Limitation on the transport of dangerous goods by air

4.1: The transport of dangerous goods by air shall be forbidden except as established in the Annex and the detailed specifications and procedures in the Technical Instructions.

4.2: Dangerous goods specified below are forbidden for transport by air unless exempted by the States concerned or with valid approval by State of Origin (Defined):

(a) articles and substances identified and forbidden in the Technical Instructions for transport in normal circumstances;

(b) infected live animals.

4.3 deals with dangerous goods forbidden for transport by air under any circumstances, as identified in the Technical Instructions.

Chapter 5—Packing

This chapter deals with method, quality and other requirements of packing.

Chapter 6—Labelling and marking

This chapter deals with labelling and marking and the language to be used for markings.

Chapter 7—Shipper's responsibilities

7.1: A person offering a package or overpack of dangerous goods for transport by air shall ensure beforehand that such goods are not forbidden for such transport and are properly classified, packed, marked, labelled and accompanied by a properly executed dangerous goods transport document as specified in the Annex and Technical Instructions.

7.2–7.3 deal with provision of a dangerous goods transport document and its contents, declaration concerning the goods and the languages to be used.

Chapter 8—Operator's responsibilities

8.1: Operator shall not accept dangerous goods for transport by air:

(a) unless such goods are accompanied by completed documentation as required; and

(b) until package, overpack or container containing such goods has been inspected as required.

Note 1: Reporting of accidents and incidents
Note 2: Special provisions on overpacks.

8.2: Operator shall develop and use an acceptance checklist.

8.3.1–8.3.4 deal with inspection for damage or leakage of packs, overpacks, freight containers and ULDs containing dangerous goods and radioactive materials as specified; such inspection to be made prior to loading. It deals with the steps to be taken on discovery of damage or leakage.

8.4: Dangerous goods shall not be carried in the passenger cabin or on flight deck except as permitted by the Technical Instructions.

8.5 deals with removal of contamination from an aircraft; and withdrawal of such aircraft from service until the radiation level and the non-fixed contamination are within specified values.

8.6.1–8.6.3 deal with the separation and segregation of packages of dangerous goods. See provision on radioactive materials.

8.7: Securing of dangerous goods and cargo loads. The operator shall protect such goods from damage and secure them to prevent movement. See provisions on radioactive materials.

8.8: Loading on cargo aircraft. Packages of dangerous goods shall be loaded so that personnel can see, handle, and where size and weight permit, separate such packages from other cargo.

Chapter 9—Provision of information

9.1: Operator shall supply the pilot-in-command as early as possible before departure of the aircraft with the specified written information concerning dangerous goods to be carried.

9.2: Operator shall include necessary information concerning dangerous goods and emergencies in the Operations Manual for flight crew.

9.3: Operator shall warn passengers as to the types of goods forbidden to be transported on board an aircraft as checked baggage or carry-on articles.

9.4: Operators, shippers, and other organisations shall provide their personnel with information to enable them to carry out their responsibilities concerning dangerous goods and emergencies involving the same.

9.5: Information on dangerous goods should be provided by pilot-in-command to ATS unit for the information of aerodrome authorities in the case of an in-flight emergency.

9.6 deals with information to be provided by the operator carrying dangerous goods in the event of an aircraft accident or incident to the State where the accident or incident occurred.

Chapter 10—Establishment of training programmes

Dangerous Goods Training Programmes shall be established and updated.

Chapter 11—Compliance

11.1: Each State shall establish inspection, surveillance and enforcement procedures to achieve compliance.

11.2–11.4: Recommended practices concerning cooperation between States in respect of exchange of information on violations, penalties and establishment of procedures to control introduction of dangerous goods into air transport through postal services.

Chapter 12—Dangerous goods accident and incident reporting

12.1: With the aim of preventing the recurrence of dangerous goods accidents and incidents, each State shall establish procedures for investigating and compiling information concerning such accidents and incidents which occur in its territory and which involve the transport of dangerous goods originating in or destined for another State. Reports on such accidents and incidents shall be made in accordance with the detailed provisions of the Technical Instructions.

12.2: This Recommendation sets out similar provisions as in 12.1 but with regard to accidents and incidents occurring in the territory of a State in respect of dangerous goods which do not originate in or are not destined for another State.

(iii) Comments

(1) Technical Instructions for the safe transport of dangerous goods by air (doc. 9284–AN/905 "Technical Instructions").

The Technical Instructions are approved and published by decision of the Council of ICAO and are updated from time to time. They are detailed.

The Technical Instructions are based on the UN recommendations on the transport of dangerous goods (UN documents ST/SG/AC.10/1, as amended, and ST/SG/AC.10/11 also as amended), and the regulations for the safe transport of radioactive material of the International Atomic Energy Agency.

The basis of the packing requirements are also based on the recommendations of the UN committee of experts on the transport of dangerous goods.

In considering liability whether arising under the Warsaw Convention or otherwise, Part 4—Shippers' responsibilities, Part 5—Technical Instructions and Part 9—Provisions concerning passengers and crew, are important. They, however, cannot be read in isolation from the underlying technical requirements in other parts of the Technical Instructions.

Part 4, Chapter 1, sets out general requirements/duties of a person offering dangerous goods for transport by air which include the provision to the operator of two copies of the Dangerous Goods Transport document completed as required.

Part 5, Chapter 1, dealing with operator's responsibilities, provides in the Introductory Note the details of the responsibilities of operators with regard to acceptance, handling and loading of dangerous goods. However nothing contained in the chapter should be interpreted as requiring an operator to transport a particular article or substance or as preventing an operator from imposing special requirements on transport of a particular article or substances. See reference to ground handlers.

Part 9, Chapter 1, sets out provisions concerning passengers and crew. It states in 1.1 that except as provided in 1.2 dangerous goods must not be carried by passengers or crew, either in or as carry-on baggage or checked baggage or on their persons. Security-type attaché cases incorporating dangerous goods, for example lithium batteries or pyrotechnic material, are totally forbidden.

The exceptions include alcoholic beverages not exceeding 70 per cent. alcohol by volume when packed in receptacles of less than five litres.

(2) The general position is discussed by *S&B* in section VII(175); also refer to article by Dr N Matte on the "International Regulation of the responsibility for the transport by air of dangerous goods", *Annals of Air and Space Law* (Vol. XVI, 1991, McGill University).

(3) Both Annex 18 and the Technical Instructions set out requirements for training programmes.

(4) For domestic application of these regulations, see the US case of *NL Industries Inc* v. *Department of Transportation, FAA,* US Court of Appeals for District of Columbia No 89–1089 (1990); 22 AVI 17,930 1989–90. In this case the court upheld the decision of the FAA in finding that the manufacturer was liable for 370 violations of the Hazardous Materials Regulations and the $50,000 penalty was within the scope of the authority of the FAA. The manufacturer of a chemical product violated the Hazardous Materials Regulations Act when it delivered to an air carrier 79 drums of hazardous chemicals which were rejected by the carrier for failure to comply with applicable requirements. The drums were not properly marked, labelled, described, packaged or in the condition required for air transportation. There was no merit in the contention that the Hazardous Materials Regulations Act did not apply to the manufacturer because that Act applied only to shippers and carriers and it had performed in neither of those roles. The applicable regulations placed responsibility with one who transported hazardous materials or caused them to be transported, regardless of whether that person was a

shipper or a carrier. The FAA concluded the manufacturer knowingly offered the hazardous materials for air transportation.

(5) UK Air Navigation (Dangerous Goods) Regulations 1997 require that the consignor must in respect of dangerous goods furnish the operator of dangerous goods transport documents describing the goods as required by the Technical Instructions. They must also contain a signed statement that the instructions have been complied with in that the dangerous goods are fully and accurately described, correctly classified, packed, marked, and labelled and are in a proper condition for carriage.

(6) See (i) IATA Airport Handling Manual Items 316–319 on Special Load Notification to Captains (general). IATA members shall adopt a standard form to notify captains when dangerous goods and other special loads are included in the load; and (ii) IATA Dangerous Goods Regulations which "contain all provisions mandated by ICAO and all rules universally agreed by airlines to correctly package and safely transport dangerous goods by air".

CHAPTER 6

REGULATION OF CIVIL AVIATION IN EUROPE

This chapter summarises (i) the constitution and functions of the European Civil Aviation Conference (ECAC) and Joint Aviation Authorities (JAA) and (ii) the aviation activities of the European Union.

PART 1. ECAC

The founding of ECAC is described in the Historical Review appended to its Constitution and Rules of Procedure (ECAC, CEAC doc. No. 20 4th edition).

Following discussions between ICAO and the Council of Europe, ICAO constituted by Council Resolution the Conference on Coordination of Air Transport in Europe (CATE) in December 1953 (doc.7447–C/868). This Resolution was endorsed by the 7th Session of ICAO Assembly.

CATE first met in Strasbourg in April 1954 and recommended the establishment of a permanent European organisation of high-level aviation authorities to implement its recommendations and to carry out its work. Such organisation was constituted as ECAC by Resolution ECAC/1–Res 1 1955 and first met in 1955.

Relevant provisions of the ECAC Constitution are summarised below:

Article 1—Objective and functions

(1) The objective of ECAC shall be to promote the continued development of a safe, efficient and sustainable European air transport system.

(2) ECAC, shall bring within its scope all matters relevant to this objective, taking into account:
   (a) importance and interest of the subject to a large number of member states or other European organisations;
   (b) possibility of an acceptable solution to the problems involved;
   (c) cooperation with, and possibility of making an effective contribution to, the work of ICAO and other organisations.

(3) Functions: the functions of the conference shall be consultative and its resolutions, recommendations or other conclusions shall be subject to the approval of governments.

(4) ECAC may foster the conclusion and implementation of multilateral instruments or arrangements by a number of Member States in furtherance of its objective and functions. Such instruments may, where appropriate, establish joint procedures for carrying out some of the national responsibilities of Member States concerned in a coordinated manner.

Article 2—Membership

(1) Members are those States invited to the 1954 Strasbourg Conference on CATE and such other European States unanimously admitted as members. Members shall be ICAO Contracting States unless otherwise unanimously agreed in exceptional circumstances. See also Appendix to ECAC Constitution on application for membership.

(2) deals with the right of members to attend meetings.

Article 3—Relations with ICAO and other organisations

ECAC shall maintain close liaison with ICAO to help achieve its objectives. It shall establish relations with other governmental or non-governmental international organisations it considers necessary for achievement of its objectives.

Article 4—Bodies and associated bodies of the Conference

(1) Bodies of ECAC are:
The Plenary Conference;
The meetings of Directors General of Civil Aviation;
Groups established to carry out specific tasks;

(2) The associated bodies shall be any boards established under the terms of the multilateral instruments or arrangements referred to in Article 1(4), for the purpose of steering activities formed under such instruments or arrangements.

(3) The Coordinating Committee coordinates the activities of the bodies and associated bodies.

(4) Reports of all meetings of the bodies of ECAC shall be public documents unless the meeting in question otherwise decides.

Articles 5 and 6—Sessions

There shall be a triennial session and special sessions, it being understood that the chief delegates will normally be the Directors General of Civil Aviation or officials of high level.

Article 7—Meetings

This Article deals with meetings of directors of Directors General of Civil Aviation.

Subsequent provisions of the Constitution and the Rules of Procedure deal with methods of working, general constitutional matters and procedures such as meetings, committees and voting.

ICAO passed its own Resolution at the 10th session of the ICAO Assembly, Caracas, 1956, replaced by Resolution A27–17 in 1989, 27th session, dealing with its future relationship with ECAC. This Resolution not only dealt with ECAC but also with the African Civil Aviation Commission (AFCAC) and the Latin American Civil Aviation Commission (LACAC).

PART 2. JAA

(1) In 1979 13 European Civil Aviation Authorities signed an "Arrangement concerning the development and the acceptance of Joint Aviation Requirements". Twelve European Civil Aviation Authorities also signed a "Memorandum of Understanding on Future Airworthiness Procedures" in 1987 which expressed support for a more integrated structure to deal with civil aircraft safety in Europe.

(2) By decision of ECAC on 6 December 1989 JAA was accepted as an associated body of ECAC in accordance with Article 1(4) and 4(2) of the ECAC Constitution.

(3) On 11 September 1990 19 ECAC member states signed the document "Arrangements concerning the development, the acceptance and the implementation of Joint Aviation Requirements" ("Cyprus Arrangements"). This document sets out the history, constitution, aims and method of working of the JAA to achieve joint aviation requirements (JAR).

(4) A summary of certain provisions of the Cyprus Arrangements follows:

Paragraph "0"—Definitions

This paragraph sets out the Definitions which include as summarised:

(a) (i) "Product" means aircraft, engine, propeller or appliance.

(ii) "Appliance" means any instrument, equipment, mechanism, apparatus or accessory used or intended to be used in operating an aircraft in flight, which is installed in or intended to be installed in or attached to a civil aircraft, but is not part of an airframe, engine or propeller.

(iii) "Component" means a material, or part of sub-assembly not covered by (i) or (ii) for use on civil aircraft, engines, propellers or appliances.

(b) "Authority" means civil aviation Authority party to the Arrangements.

(c) "Findings" means a finding by the Authority of compliance with the certification requirements as specified.

(d) "Certification" is certification to applicable JARs unless otherwise specified; certification comprises the two activities of checking and certifying.

(f) and (g) define "Additional requirements for import", and "Special conditions" respectively. These requirements and conditions can be imposed by an Authority as necessary for certification of an imported product which has already been certificated in another country in the case of (f) and generally in the case of (g).

(h) "sole code" means a code used exclusively by a country to certificate products, services and organisations used by national operators (e.g. aircraft registered in the country used by the national operators, services provided to such aircraft, persons working for such aircraft or organisations contributing to their design, manufacture, maintenance or operation).

Footnote (1) comments:"The 'special conditions' defined in Article 4 of the Multilateral Agreement on Certificates of Airworthiness for Imported Aircraft of 22 April 1960 (ICAO doc. 8056) are included in this definition of additional requirements for import which corresponds to the definition contained in the bilateral agreements that most of the Authorities have with the USA."

Article 2 of such Multilateral Agreement provides that if a Contracting State receives an application for a Certificate of Airworthiness for an imported aircraft to be entered on its register, it shall, subject to the other provisions of such Agreement, either validate the existing Certificate of Airworthiness or issue a new certificate.

Article 4 provides that the Contracting State shall have the right to make the validation of the Certificate dependent on the fulfilment of any special conditions which are for the time being applicable to the issue of its own Certificates of Airworthiness and which have been notified to all Contracting States.

Paragraph 1—General

The Authorities commit themselves to cooperate in all aspects related to the safety of aircraft, in particular design, manufacture, continued airworthiness, maintenance and operation to ensure that a high consistent level of safety is achieved throughout the Member States, to avoid duplication of work between the Authorities and to facilitate exchange of products, services and persons between the Authorities and between the Authorities and others.

Paragraph 2—Functions of JAA

The functions of JAA are to:

(a) further develop, with adequate consultation, and publish JARs for use of the Authorities in the field of design, manufacture, maintenance and operations as stated in Appendix 1; JAA will also develop special conditions where applicable;

(b) define as soon as possible the general structure of the whole set of JARs and the scope of each JAR and to work to remove any national variants or national regulatory differences so that JAR becomes a uniform code for all JAA countries;

(c) establish procedures based on the use of the Authorities' resources that:

    (i) allow the use of any one set of technical findings in the field of design, manufacture, maintenance and operations;

    (ii) include practical measures for making technical findings only once for the benefit of all the Authorities (see Appendix 2);

    (iii) cover the initial certification (of products, services organisations or people) as well as the continuation of safety standards in service;

(d) establish administrative and technical procedures which would require a single administrative action from the applicant for each application as specified;

(e) make the technical findings needed to show compliance with JARs;

(f) perform for the benefit of a non-JAA importing country, in the case of products, services, persons or organisations certificated by a JAA Member Authority (exporting country) and requiring certification from a non-JAA country, the technical tasks which come under the duties of the Authority of the exporting country;

(g) explore the practicality and form of a European Joint Aviation Authority to cover the fields of design, manufacture, maintenance and operation of products.

Paragraph 3—Commitments of the Authorities

Paragraph 3 sets out the commitments of the Authorities who will:

(a) Participate in rule-making process and provide experts within the different groups involved in this process.

(b) Adopt the structure of the whole of future JARs and adopt the existing JARs as their sole codes as soon as possible. This sub-paragraph goes on to deal with interim arrangements and also deals with those situations where an Authority may deviate from JARs as a sole code, particularly on the request of an authority of a non-JAA country.

Note also the references to lease, charter or interchange of aircraft to be operated under Annexes 6 and 8 and as envisaged under Article 83bis of Chicago Convention 1944.

(c) Declare all their national regulatory differences to existing JARs and work towards the deletion of these national differences.

(d) and (e) Define, accept and exclusively use procedures enabling the technical findings to be made satisfactorily only once.

(f) Make without undue delay the legal findings for those products, services, organisations or persons found to comply with the relevant JARs (and, until they are removed, any remaining national regulatory differences).

(g) Pay their share of central JAA budget and provide staff for central JAA.

Paragraph 4—Organisation and procedures

JAA is controlled by a JAA Committee which works under the authority of the ECAC Plenary Conference and reports to the JAA Board of Directors General.

The paragraph sets out further provisions on policy, organisation, membership and procedures including (d) which provides that the relationship between JAA and ECAC will be in accordance with the ECAC constitution regarding ECAC associated bodies.

Paragraph 5—Budget

This paragraph deals with JAA's budget.

Paragraph 6—Membership

Membership is open to all the Authorities of ECAC Member States subject to the specified provisos.

Paragraphs 7–11

These paragraphs deal with constitutional and organisational questions.

Appendix 1—Development and publication of requirements

(a) The Authorities will cooperate to
  (i) produce common comprehensive and detailed requirements constituting the JARs and where necessary means of compliance and interpretation;
  (ii) define special conditions and agree on the applicable additional requirements for import.

(b) Those requirements cover all fields of aircraft safety and their safe operation and in particular design, manufacture, maintenance and operation of products etc. and competence of persons and organisations responsible for such manufacture, design, maintenance and operation.

(c) The Authorities will cooperate to produce administrative requirements also referred to as Joint Aviation Requirements (JARs) and procedures so that any applicant can finally use a single administrative document and one set of procedures and practices for any application to one of the Authorities.

(d) The JAA will, in developing the JARs:
- take into account duties and obligations under the Chicago Convention;
- consult the Parties to whom those requirements would be applied;
- take into account other aviation codes so as to facilitate exchange of products, services or persons or reliance on organisations between JAA countries and other countries.

(e) and (f) deal with the provision of experts and publication of JARs respectively.

Appendix 2—Joint implementation and joint performance

This appendix deals with joint implementation of JAR and joint performance of certification.

Appendix 3—Organisation of the JAA

This sets out how the objectives of the JARs are to be achieved and relevant technical administration. Among its provisions:

- Paragraph 8 deals with the relationship with the EC which will be handled within the framework of relations between ECAC and EC. See also 4(b) of the Arrangements.
- Paragraphs 9 and 10 deal with relationships with ICAO and other Authorities.

PART 3.   EUROPEAN UNION ("EU")

The European Economic Community was founded by the Treaty of Rome 1957. It is made up of four institutions:

(i) Parliamentary Assembly;
(ii) Intergovernmental Council;
(iii) Commission; and
(iv) Court.

The Treaty of Rome was one of three treaties; the other two being the Treaty of Paris 1951 setting up the European Coal and Steel Community and the EURATOM Treaty 1957 setting up the European Atomic Energy Community.

The Merger Treaty 1967 established a single Council and Commission for the three communities which were collectively called the European Community.

The Single European Act 1986 made important amendments to the various treaties particularly on the completion of a single European Market.

The Maastricht Treaty on European Union and Economic and Monetary Union 1992 made further changes aimed at economic and monetary union. It established a European Union (EU).

Starke comments (at page 115): "somewhat confusingly, since 1993, the term 'European Community' (EC) is now taken to refer only to the former EEC when it is necessary to refer to it separately; the three communities collectively have been absorbed within the European Union, created by the Maastricht Treaty . . . 1992."

The EU has the same institutional framework as the EEC. As at 1999 15 States are party to the EU.

Discussing international personality in international law *Starke* (at page 58) comments

"Perhaps the most outstanding current example is that of the European Union (or Community) which has become in the fullest sense an international entity with all the rights, duties and capabilities of a subject of international law—a position reinforced in a formal manner by the Single European Act (which entered into force in 1987) and by the Maastricht Treaty on European Union and Economic and Monetary Union (which entered into force in 1993), amending the Treaty of Rome of 25 May 1957. In particular, the European Community commonly participates in international conferences, enters into conventions or agreements with other states and conducts diplomatic relations with them through permanent missions."

For the purposes of this book the following are the main principles of EU law:

(1) Legislation of a Member State is subject to and must not be contrary to EU legislation;
(2) EU law can directly bestow rights and obligations on individuals in Member States provided certain conditions are fulfilled as provided by Articles 1 and 9 of the Treaty of Rome. Under Article 189 of the Treaty of Rome such law consists of:
　　(i) Regulations: "A regulation shall have general application. It shall be binding in its entirety and directly applicable in all Member States". This means that no domestic legislation is needed to make the regulation effective Domestic law in a Member State.
　　(ii) Directive: "A directive shall be binding, as to the result to be achieved, upon each Member State to which it is addressed,

but shall leave to the national authorities the choice of form and methods".

(iii) Decisions of the Council or Commission: "A decision shall be binding in its entirety upon those to whom it is addressed".

(iv) Recommendations and Opinions: "Recommendations and Opinions shall have no binding force".

In *Francovich and Bonifaci* v. *Italy* [1991] ECR I–5357; [1993] 2 CMLR 66, the European Court ruled that where an EC Directive was designed to confer rights on an individual, a Member State could be forced to pay damages for any harm caused to that individual as a result of the State's failure to implement the Directive properly.

Articles 84 and 75 of the Treaty of Rome give EU legal competence in aviation safety.

With effect from 1 January 1994 an Agreement came into force between EC and Member States of European Free Trade Area which created the European Community Area and extended most EC legislation to such area. An example of such legislation is the Council Regulation of 16 December 1991: the Harmonisation of Technical Requirements and Administrative Procedures in the Field of Civil Aviation (No. 3922/91).

In addition to Regulation 3922/91 examples of EU legislation referred to in this book are:

(i) Council Directive of 25 July 1985 on the Approximation of the Laws, Regulations and Administrative Provisions of the Member States concerning Liability for Defective Products, No. 85/374/EEC (see Chapter 11 below);

(ii) Council Directive of 21 November 1994 Establishing the Fundamental Principles Governing the Investigation of Civil Aviation Accidents and Incidents, No. 94/56/EC (see Chapter 13 below);

(iii) Council Regulation (EEC) No. 295/91 of 4 February 1991 Establishing Common Rules for a Denied-Boarding Compensation System in Scheduled Air Transport (see Chapter 7, Part 1, page 257);

(iv) Council Directive 90/314/EEC on Package Travel, Package Holidays and Package Tours. (see Chapter 7, Part 2, page 293).

A summary of the main provisions of Council Regulation on Harmonisation of Technical Requirements and Administrative Procedures in the Field of Civil Aviation follows:

Council Regulation of 16 December 1991 on the Harmonisation of Technical Requirements and Administrative Procedures in the Field of Civil Aviation (No. 3922/91)

Recitals

The Recitals set out the purpose of the Regulation, referring to the Chicago Convention, JAA, JARs and ECAC. They state that the accession of all EC Member States to the JAA and the participation of the EC Commission in its proceedings would facilitate harmonisation of technical requirements and administrative procedures relating to the safety of aircraft and their operation.

Article 1

1.1: The Regulation shall apply to the harmonisation of technical requirements and administrative procedures in the field of civil aviation safety as listed in its Annex II and in particular with respect to:

- the design, manufacture, operation and maintenance of aircraft;
- persons and organisations involved in these tasks.

1.2: The harmonised technical requirements and administrative procedures apply to all aircraft operated by operators as defined in Article 2(a), whether the aircraft are registered in a Member State or a third country.

Article 2

Article 2 defines the following eight words for the purposes of the Regulations: product, appliance, component, certification, operator, maintenance, national variant and arrangements.

The first four words follow the definitions in the JAA Cyprus Arrangements. The remaining four are defined thus:

(a) "operator" means a natural person residing in a Member State or a legal person established in a Member State using one or more aircraft in accordance with the regulations applicable in that Member State or a Community air carrier as defined in Community legislation.

(f) "maintenance" means all inspections, servicing, modification and repair throughout the life of an aircraft needed to ensure that the aircraft remains in compliance with the type certification and offers a high level of safety in all circumstances; this shall include in particular modifications imposed by the authorities party to the arrangements referred to in (h) in accordance with airworthiness checking concepts.

(g) "national variant" means a national requirement or regulation imposed by a country in addition to or instead of a JAR.

(h) "arrangements" mean the JAR arrangements developed under the auspices of ECAC concluded in Cyprus on 11 September 1990.

Article 3

Without prejudice to Article 11 the common technical requirements and administrative procedures applicable in the Community with regard to the fields listed in Annex II of the Regulation shall be the relevant codes referred to in the Annex and in force on 1 January 1992.

(Author's note: These requirements and procedures include, for example, Type certification of products and parts and certification of flight crew.)

Article 4

(1) With regard to the fields not listed in Annex II the EC Council shall adopt common technical requirements and administrative procedures on the basis of Article 84(2) of the Treaty of Rome, and of proposals of the EC Commission. In the meantime existing national regulations may be applied.

(Author's note: Article 84(2) of the Treaty of Rome empowers the Council to decide to what extent and by what procedure appropriate provisions may be laid down for air transport.)

Article 5

Member States shall ensure that their responsible civil aviation authorities shall meet the conditions for membership of the JAA specified in the Arrangements and shall sign such Arrangements without reservation before 1 January 1992.

Article 6

6.1: Member States shall, without further technical requirements or evaluation, recognise products designed, manufactured, operated and maintained in compliance with the common requirements and administrative procedures where such products have been certified by another Member State. When the original recognition is for a particular purpose, or purposes, any subsequent recognition shall cover the same purpose(s).

6.2 provides that existing products and derivatives not certified in accordance with common technical requirements and administrative procedures may be accepted by a Member State under their current national regulations pending adoption of such common requirements and procedures.

Article 7

Member States shall recognise certification granted under this Regulation by another Member State, or by a body acting on its behalf, to bodies or persons under its jurisdiction and who are concerned with the design, manufacture and maintenance of products, and the operation of aircraft.

Article 8

8.1: None of the above provisions described shall prevent a Member State from reacting immediately to a safety problem which becomes apparent from an accident, incident or service experience and involves either a product designed, manufactured, operated or maintained in accordance with this Regulation, or a person, procedure or body involved in such tasks. If the problem results from: an inadequate safety level corresponding to the application of the common technical requirements and administrative procedures, or shortcomings in the common technical requirements and administrative procedures, the Member State shall inform the Commission and other Member States immediately of the measures taken and the reasons therefor.

8.2: Following such action the Commission shall consult Member States and in special cases make appropriate proposals in accordance with the procedures provided for in Articles 4 and 11.

Articles 9–13

Article 9 deals with coordination and promotion of national research programmes.

Article 10 requires Member States to notify the Commission of changes and modifications of requirements, procedures or Arrangements as specified; and of results of consultations with industry and other interested bodies.

Article 11.1 gives the Commission power, following the Article 12 procedure, to make amendments to the specified common technical requirements and administrative procedures necessitated by scientific and technical progress.

Article 11.2 deals with any national variant contained in such amendments.

Article 12 establishes a Committee for the application of Articles 8, 9 and 11 empowered to deliver a majority opinion on the draft measure drawn up under these Articles for submission to the Commission. If no decision can be reached the Commission must pass the matter to the Council. If the Council has not acted on expiry of three months from the date of referral by the Commission, the proposed measures shall be adopted by the Commission, save where the Council has decided against the said measures by simple majority.

Article 13 deals with mutual assistance between member states, including the exchange of information on infringement and penalties.

Article 14

This Regulation shall enter into force on 1 January 1992 and shall be binding in its entirety and directly applicable in all Member States.

Annexes

Annex I defines the Cyprus Arrangements referred to in Article 1 above.

Annex II sets out the list of Codes in force containing the common technical requirements and administrative procedures referred to in Article 3.

European States are proposing to establish a new single European regulatory authority to replace existing arrangements. Its name will be the European Aviation Safety Authority and it will include both EU and non-EU States. Its function is intended to be an improvement on the ECAC/JAA/EU system. The final draft of the proposed treaty has been drawn up.

CHAPTER 7

LIABILITY OF THE AIR CARRIER FOR PASSENGERS, BAGGAGE, CARGO AND MAIL

PART 1—THE WARSAW CONVENTION 1929 AND RELATED TREATIES

Introduction

This Part summarises the liability of the air carrier in respect of international carriage of passengers, baggage and cargo as defined by the Warsaw Convention 1929 (the "Unamended Convention"), the Warsaw Convention as amended by the Hague Protocol 1955 (the "Amended Convention") and Montreal Additional Protocol 4 ("MP4"). Reference in this chapter to "Warsaw Convention" relates to the Warsaw Convention system generally or to particular provisions common to both the Unamended and the Amended Conventions. It also summarises the ICAO Convention for the Unification of Certain Rules for International Carriage by Air 1999 which, as between its Contracting States, will replace the Warsaw Convention, if and when it comes into force ("The ICAO Convention").

The reasons for the conclusion of the Warsaw Convention 1929 have been graphically stated by *S&B* (1st edition) quoted on page 19 above.

This position was also put in the English case of *Grein* v. *Imperial Airways Ltd* [1937] 1 KB 50 where Lord Justice Greene said: "The desirability of such an international code for air carriage [ie Warsaw Convention] is apparent. Without it, it is easy to imagine cases where questions of the greatest difficulty might arise as to which law or laws govern the contract and whether different laws might apply to different stages of the journey."

In that case the accident took place after the UK ratified the Warsaw Convention and the question was whether there was a single contract of carriage London–Antwerp–London where the Warsaw Convention would apply or two contracts of carriage London–Antwerp and Antwerp–London where the Warsaw Convention would not apply, Belgium not being party at that time to the Warsaw Convention; see Article 1.

The court held the Warsaw Convention applied. Therefore the limit of liability was, according to the Statement of Claim of the widow plaintiff, £1,670, being the then equivalent of 125,000 gold francs, see below.

Uncertainty as to the applicable domestic law would raise conflict of law questions on:

(i) the existence of liability;
(ii) how such liability could be proved;
(iii) whether a legal action could be brought and the place of such action;
(iv) how damages would be assessed.

The English case *Aslan* v. *Imperial Airways Ltd* (1933) 49 TLR 415; 149 LT 276; [1933] *US Aviation Reports* 6, concerned gold consigned from Baghdad to London. It travelled by aeroplane of the defendants from Baghdad to the Lake of Tiberius and was there transferred to a seaplane for on-carriage to Brindisi via Athens and then Brindisi to Paris by railway. Carriage from Paris to Croydon Airport was by air. The judge commented that the circumstances in which the gold was lost were wrapped in considerable obscurity.

As the contract of carriage was entered into before the Unamended Convention came into force, the court held that the defendant airline:

(i) effectively excluded its liability by the terms of contract of carriage; and
(ii) was not a common carrier and accepted no liability as such.

(A common carrier of goods is responsible for their safety, with certain exceptions, during the period from his acceptance of them till delivery by him.)

The Warsaw Convention imposes on the carrier a presumption of liability. This means that the passenger, or the cargo consignor or consignee, does not have to prove fault on the part of the carrier who is presumed liable unless it can prove that it has taken all necessary measures to avoid the damage or it was impossible to take such measures.

In return for this presumption, the carrier's liability is limited in the amount of damages except where:

• there is a special contract or declaration of value, as referred to below raising or removing the limit of liability; or
• there is defective carriage documentation; or
• the limit of liability is removed under the provisions of Article 25.

The Unamended Convention was amended by the Hague Protocol 1955 which increased the limit of liability for death or injury from 125,000 to 250,000 gold francs.

The US Government was not prepared to ratify the Amended Convention on the grounds that the proposed increase was inadequate and gave notice of denunciation of the Unamended Convention on 15 November 1965. This notice was withdrawn when a compromise was reached between the USA, ICAO and foreign airlines operating into the USA by means of the CAB 18900, commonly called Montreal Agreement. It should not be confused with the four Additional Montreal Protocols ("MP") signed in 1975 amending the Unamended and Amended Conventions.

MP1 and MP2 substituted the Special Drawing Right (SDR) for the Convention Gold Franc and have come into force. They are considered in Part 3 of this chapter. MP3 concerns increase of liability for passenger, death or injury and is unlikely to come into force. MP4 concerns amendments to the Amended Convention chiefly with regard to baggage and cargo liability and has come into force. The USA has ratified MP4 with its amendments to the Amended Convention with effect from 4 March 1999 but otherwise remains party with a few other States to the Unamended Convention only.

The limits of liability in respect of death or injury imposed by Article 22 of the Unamended Convention and then doubled by the Amended Convention are considered too low. Failure in the past to conclude a satisfactory amending treaty resulted in airlines increasing or abolishing limits of liability by contract with the passenger as described in Part 4 of this Chapter.

In May 1999 the ICAO Convention was concluded at a diplomatic conference. Its purpose is to replace entirely the Warsaw Convention system. While it has been signed by 53 States, it has to be ratified by 30 States before it comes into force.

In the text below, each Amended Convention Article is quoted in full and any minor differences between it and the corresponding Unamended Convention Article and Protocol are dealt with in the commentary.

Where the Amended Convention makes a substantial change to the Unamended Convention, the relevant provisions of both the Amended Convention, (a), and the Unamended Convention, (b), are quoted in full.

Where there is no reference in the texts to the Unamended Convention, it is because there is little or minimal difference from the Amended Convention text.

Further changes made by MP4, (c), or by the ICAO Convention, (d), are dealt with in the texts or in the comments.

The official language of the Unamended and the Amended Convention is French (Article 36). The English language version of the Unamended Convention in this book is that followed by the USA and used by IATA in their publication "Principal Instruments of the Warsaw System" ("IATA version"). Where necessary the phrase "English version" refers to the translation found in UK domestic legislation.

The English language text of the Amended Convention in the IATA publication usually follows the wording of the UK Carriage by Air Act 1961.

Help in interpretation of the provisions of the Warsaw Convention is given by the text of the working papers and records (*travaux préparatoires*) of both the conferences at Warsaw in 1928 and at The Hague in 1955.

Court decisions in Contracting States realise the importance of international uniformity in interpretation of the Warsaw Convention. See Comment 1.4 on Article 9, page 239.

The limited comments given in this Part relate to those aspects considered by the author to be useful and illustrative. They are not comprehensive. Books giving a more detailed analysis of the Warsaw Convention and its case law are mentioned below.

Each Article of the Hague Protocol is numbered with a Roman numeral. Chapter I of the Protocol contains the amendments to the articles of the Unamended Convention, each such article being numbered with an Arabic numeral. Chapter II deals with the Scope of Application of the Amended Convention, and Chapter III deals with the Final Clauses. A similar system of numbering applies to MP4. The ICAO Convention is completely new and stands alone. References in the comments to Articles refer to Warsaw Convention Articles; ICAO Convention Articles are clearly distinguished.

THE WARSAW CONVENTION
CHAPTER I

Scope—Definitions

(a) Amended Convention—Article 1

(1) This Convention shall apply to all international carriage of persons, baggage, or cargo performed by aircraft for reward. It applies equally to gratuitous carriage by aircraft performed by an air transport undertaking.

(2) For the purposes of this Convention, the expression *"international carriage"* means any carriage in which, according to the agreement between the parties, the place of departure and the place of destination, whether or not there be a break in the carriage, or a transhipment, are situated either within the territories of two High Contracting Parties or within the territory of a single High Contracting Party if there is an agreed stopping place within a territory of another State, even if that State is not a High Contracting Party. Carriage between two points within the territory of a single High Contracting Party without an agreed stopping place within the territory of another State is not international carriage for the purposes of this Convention.

(3) Carriage to be performed by several successive air carriers shall be deemed, for the purposes of this Convention, to be one undivided carriage if it has been regarded by the parties as a single operation, whether it has been agreed upon under the form of a single contract or of a series of contracts, and it does not lose its international character merely because one contract or a series of contracts is to be performed entirely within the territory subject to the same State.

(b) Unamended Convention—Article 1

Notable differences: none. The English version is shorter.

(d) ICAO Convention—Article 1

The Convention follows the Amended Convention wording but adds a fourth paragraph applying the Draft Convention to carriage governed now by the Guadalajara Convention 1961; see Part 2 of this chapter.

Comments

Article 1(1)

1. "Reward": The IATA version of the Unamended Convention refers to "hire". The French official text uses the word "rémunération", widely defined in Vocabulaire Juridique de Presses Universitaires. In other texts "hire or reward" are used together, for example in ICAO Annex 6; and EU Regulation 2407/92 (see page 78) refers to "remuneration and/or hire". The UK ANO requires the giving of valuable consideration for carriage to constitute public transport or aerial work.

These terms leave the question outstanding under the Warsaw Convention as to whether:

(i) money is essential or some other benefit is sufficient;
(ii) who provides the remuneration;
(iii) and who receives it so to fall within the terms of Article 1.

Giemulla comments that the commercial interest essential for Warsaw Convention operations does not mean pecuniary interest. "Thus for example the carriage of a lawyer on his client's private plane to a place where he is to act for his client may be carriage 'for hire' depending on how the flight is connected with the lawyer's action on behalf of his client even if it is not actually paid for" (BGHZ 62).

The criminal law UK case of *Corner* v. *Clayton* ([1976] 2 Lloyd's Rep 295; 3 All ER 212) is illustrative. Clayton was a member of a flying club and held a private pilot's licence which contained a prohibition from flying for the purpose of public transport. The UK Air Navigation Order 1974 provided that a flight is for the purposes of public transport if hire or reward is given or promised for the carriage of passengers or cargo in the aircraft on that flight. Clayton agreed to carry a family to a wedding and back in a club aircraft on payment to the club of £27.00.

The Court held on appeal that hire meant engaging the services of a person or the use of a chattel for payment, and it was immaterial whether there was a profit element in the hiring charge. Clayton was found guilty of an offence under the Air Navigation Order 1974 for flying without the appropriate licence. The wording of the ANO has since been modified; see Chapter 8 below.

S&B submit that "reward" should have the same meaning as "remuneration" in Articles 5 and 7 of the Chicago Convention, which refer to "remuneration or hire" (VII/363).

2. "Undertaking": The IATA version of the Unamended Convention refers to "enterprise". ANO defines "Air Transport Undertaking" as "an undertaking whose business includes the undertaking of flights for the purposes of public transport of passengers or cargo". The ANO defines public transport as generally requiring valuable consideration to be given for carriage of passengers and cargo.

Article 1(2)

3. There has to be a contract between the parties. This raises the question of who are the contracting parties, particularly where there is a tour operator or cargo consolidator involved; see Part 2 of this chapter on the Guadalajara Convention 1961.

4. "International carriage" is a term of art defined in the Warsaw Convention by reference to:

    (a) the agreement between the carrier and its customer;

    (b) the States party to the Warsaw Convention.

The following are examples of various contracts of carriage:

- Paris–Bangkok is not international carriage as Thailand is not party to the Warsaw Convention.
- Paris–Bangkok–London is governed by the Amended Convention.
- Tashkent–Bangkok–Tashkent is governed by the Unamended Convention, as Uzbekistan is party only to that Convention.
- New York–London: MP4.
- New York–Tashkent: Unamended Convention.

Generally, court decisions support the view that the contract of carriage is the journey comprised within the whole contract whether evidenced by one ticket or by more than one ticket as in the case of conjunction tickets. Therefore "destination" is the ultimate destination as shown on the ticket or tickets and not the point of arrival on any particular sector, see *Abdul Rahman Al-Zamil* v. *British Airways Inc*, 19 AVI 17,646 1985, the US Court of Appeals 2nd Circuit.

Where two tickets containing completely separate and distinct contracts of carriage had been issued, carriers could not be said to have regarded carriage as a single operation merely because both tickets are issued by the same travel agent (*Huxley & Others* v. *Aquila Air Ltd* [1995] 2 ASLR 364, British Columbia Supreme Court).

5. Articles XXI and XXIII in Chapter III of the Hague Protocol deal with Ratification of and Adherence to the Protocol by States not party to the Unamended Convention. In *Re Korean Airlines Disaster*, 1 September 1983 (District Court, District of Columbia), 19 AVI 17,578 1985–6, it was held that where South Korea did not ratify the Unamended Convention but ratified the Hague Protocol, such ratification effectively made it a party to the Unamended portions of the Warsaw Convention (Hague Protocol XXII) thus applying the Warsaw Convention to one way carriage USA–South Korea. This decision is understandably considered erroneous by Professor Bin Cheng ((1989) XIV *Air Law* 223).

Article 1(3)

6. Article 30 (below), which deals with successive carriers and apportionment of liability, must be distinguished from the positions of Contracting Carrier and Actual Carrier as referred to in the Guadalajara Convention 1961.

(a) Amended Convention—Article 2

(1) This Convention applies to carriage performed by the State or by legally constituted public bodies provided it falls within the conditions laid down in Article 1.

(2) This Convention shall not apply to carriage of mail and postal packages.

(b) Unamended Convention—Article 2

Article 2(2) reads "this Convention shall not apply to transportation performed under the terms of any international postal Convention".

(c) and (d) MP4 and ICAO Convention—Article 2

Article 2(2) is modified and Article 2(3) is added:

(2) In the carriage of postal items, the carrier shall be liable only to the relevant postal administration in accordance with the rules applicable to the relationship between the carriers and the postal administrations.

(3) Except as provided in paragraph 2 of this Article, the provisions of this Convention shall not apply to the carriage of postal items."

The ICAO Convention retains Article 2(1).

Comments

Article 2(1)

1. Carriage by the State itself either for reward or by way of an air transport undertaking is governed by the Warsaw Convention.

The Additional Protocol to the Warsaw Convention (page 287) reserves to the Contracting States the right to declare at the time of ratification or adherence that Article 2.1 shall not apply to international carriage by air performed directly by the State. The USA and Canada have, for example, exercised this right.

Article 2(2) and Article 2(3)

2. For the carriage of mail and postal packages, see page 308 of this chapter.

CHAPTER II
SECTION 1—PASSENGER TICKET

(a) Amended Convention—Article 3

(1) In respect of the carriage of passengers a ticket shall be delivered containing:

    (a) an indication of the places of departure and destination;

    (b) if the places of departure and destination are within the territory of a single High Contracting Party, one or more agreed stopping places being within the territory of another State, an indication of at least one such stopping place;

(c) a notice to the effect that, if the passenger's journey involves an ultimate destination or stop in a country other than the country of departure, the Warsaw Convention may be applicable and that the Convention governs and in most cases limits the liability of carriers for death or personal injury and in respect of loss of or damage to baggage.

(2) The passenger ticket shall constitute *prima facie* evidence of the conclusion and conditions of the contract of carriage. The absence, irregularity or loss of the passenger ticket does not affect the existence or the validity of the contract of carriage which shall, none the less, be subject to the rules of this Convention. Nevertheless, if, with the consent of the carrier, the passenger embarks without a passenger ticket having been delivered, or if the ticket does not include the notice required by paragraph (1)(c) of this Article, the carrier shall not be entitled to avail himself of the provisions of Article 22.

(b) Unamended Convention—Article 3

(1) For the transportation of passengers the carrier must deliver a passenger ticket which shall contain the following particulars:

(a) the place and date of issue;
(b) the place of departure and of destination;
(c) the agreed stopping places, provided that the carrier may reserve the right to alter the stopping places in case of necessity, and that if he exercises that right, the alteration shall not have the effect of depriving the carriage of its international character;
(d) the name and address of the carrier or carriers;
(e) a statement that the carriage is subject to the rules relating to liability established by this convention.

(2) The absence, irregularity or loss of the passenger ticket shall not affect the existence or the validity of the contract of carriage, which shall none the less be subject to the rules of this convention. Nevertheless, if the carrier accepts a passenger without a passenger ticket having been delivered he shall not be entitled to avail himself of those provisions of this convention which exclude or limit his liability.

(d) ICAO Convention—Article 3

Article 3.1 states that in respect of carriage of passengers an individual or collective document of carriage shall be delivered containing the same information as in Article 3(1)(a) and (b) of the Amended Convention.

Article 3.2 permits any other means which preserves the information referred to in Article 3.1 to be substituted for such document of carriage. If this is done, carrier shall offer to deliver to the passenger a written statement of the preserved information.

Article 3.3: A baggage identification tag shall be delivered for each piece of checked baggage.

Article 3.4: Written notice shall be given to the passenger that where the Convention applies, liability of carriers for death or injury and for destruction or loss of or damage to baggage, and for delay may be limited.

Article 3.5: Non-compliance with Article 3.1–3.4 shall not affect the existence or validity of the contract of carriage which shall none the less be subject to the rules of the ICAO Convention including those relating to limitation of liability.

Comments

1. Status and form of ticket

For convenience the passenger ticket and baggage check are combined into one document. GCC Pax Article 1 provides that "Ticket" means the document entitled "Passenger Ticket and Baggage Check" or the electronic ticket in each case issued by or on behalf of the airline concerned and includes the conditions of contract, notices and coupons.

IATA Resolutions 720 and 722 deal with the specification for the standard form of ticket, the automated ticket and electronic ticket.

2. IATA Resolution 724 sets out the Conditions of Contract on the ticket.

3. *Giemulla* observes that the ticket is a document of carriage, an accounting document and usually a receipt.

4. Failure to deliver a ticket

4.1 The Unamended Convention: Failure to deliver a passenger ticket results in the limit of liability not applying. It is likely that failure to include the obligatory details on the ticket will not result in loss of such limits; see paragraph 8 below.

4.2 Amended Convention: Failure to deliver a ticket containing the notice referred to in Article 3(1)(c) results in loss of limits of liability.

4.3 ICAO Convention: Failure to comply with the provisions of Article 3.1–3.4 does not result in loss of limit of liability.

4.4 If and when the ICAO Convention comes into force the comments in paragraphs 5–8 below will not be relevant to its application.

5. To whom must the ticket be delivered?

In *Ross* v. *Pan American Airways Inc* (New York Court of Appeals, 1949), 2 AVI 14,911 1946–50, it was held that delivery of a ticket made out in the passenger's name to the agent of a single passenger was sufficient. However, the judgment makes clear that the ticket was delivered to an agent and the passenger boarded the aircraft after the ticket had been laid before her on a table at the airport. *S&B* consider that this decision was correct and would be followed in England. This question has been considered in the USA in many cases in differing circumstances.

6. Is a single ticket adequate for a group of passengers?

In *Manion* v. *Pan American World Airways Inc,* (NY Sup Court, 1980) 15 AVI 18,337 1978–80 (on appeal 16 AVI 17,473) the Court considered (but without deciding) the question of whether delivery to a group leader would be constructive delivery of a ticket to each passenger. The court was reluctant to accept this argument "at least in the absence of authorisation or ratification by the individual passenger". While *S&B* submit such authorisation could be readily assumed, it is wondered how sympathetic the court would be in accepting this argument on constructive delivery if the airline concerned had not waived limits of liability for death or injury.

In view of the many different commercial circumstances surrounding the delivery of tickets there must be uncertainty as to how any court would decide the above question. However, both the Amended and Unamended Convention refer to "ticket" in the singular.

7. When must the ticket be delivered?

US case law has decided that a passenger must receive his ticket in time to give him a reasonable opportunity to protect himself against the limitation of liability provisions to which the notice alerts him. See *Domangue* v. *Eastern Airlines Inc*, (US District Court, Louisiana, 1981) 531 F Supp 334, 17 AVI 17,221 1982–3 and *Mertons* v. *Flying Tiger Line Inc*, 341 F 2d 851; 9 AVI 17,475, see also *Stratis* v. *Eastern Airlines Inc*, US Court of Appeals 2nd Circuit, 1982; 17 AVI 17,227 1982–3, where the court held the ticket was delivered adequately where the passenger was injured on a domestic sector of an international flight, holding only a domestic ticket for that sector but in adequate Warsaw Convention form.

8. Design and wording of the ticket

In *Lisi* v. *Alitalia Linee Aree Italiana SpA* (2nd Circuit 1966); 9 AVI 17,848, the US Court of Appeals held that liability was unlimited due to the inadequate print size, position and presentation of the relevant provisions in the ticket. Such shortcomings constituted failure by the ticket to contain the required information. This decision was affirmed by an equally divided Supreme Court.

As *S&B* point out the case is based on two propositions:

(1) The Unamended Convention removes the limit of liability if the required information is not included. This view was not followed in the Supreme Court in *Chan* v. *Korean Airlines*, 109 S Ct 1676 (1989); 21 AVI 18,221 1988–9.

(2) Inadequate size of print of statement or notice is failure to communicate the statement or notice.

This view was enthusiastically seized on by the US courts, in particular with regard to the size of print of the advice required by CAB 18900 (Montreal Agreement), which must be at least as large as 10 point modern type. However, with regard to such Montreal Agreement statement, the view was overruled by the US Supreme Court in *Chan* v. *Korean Airlines*. The Montreal

Agreement requires the relevant advice on the ticket to be in 10 point modern type in ink contrasting with the stock.

Following the *Lisi* case IATA adopted resolution 724 requiring the Amended Convention notice and the Unamended Convention statement and the other conditions of contract all to be of the type size and nature of print as specified.

In the light of the different wording in the two Conventions and the judgment of the US Supreme Court in *Chan* v. *Korean Airlines*, 21 AVI 18,221 1989, it is probably correct that under US law failure to include the particulars required by Article 3(1) of the Unamended Convention in the ticket will not result in the loss of the limit of liability for death or injury.

However, whatever is the current judicial analysis in whatever jurisdiction in respect of the ticket contents and print size, it remains in the carriers' interests that they should comply with IATA Resolution 724 on the contents of tickets and print size of the Unamended Convention statement, the Amended Convention notice, the Conditions of Contract and the Montreal Agreement advice (CAB 18900). For a useful discussion of *Lisi* v. *Alitalia* and *Chan* v. *Korean Airlines*, see the article of Rene Manckiewicz in (1990) XV *Air Law* 45.

While the Amended Convention has reduced the requirements for ticketing, requiring only that a passenger ticket and baggage check must be issued containing the essential Amended Convention notice, it is clear that under Article 3 of the Amended Convention failure to issue a ticket which contains the required notice under Article 3(1)(c) will result in loss of the liability limit.

9. Language

In *Legakis* v. *Olympic Airways* the Supreme Court of Appeal in Athens (Resolution No. 1142/1974) held that a ticket written only in the English language gave adequate notice as required by the Amended Convention to a Greek passenger.

In *Mahmoud* v. *Alitalia and KLM* (US District Court, SDNY, 1982; 17 AVI 17,598 1982–3) the Court held that liability was limited where the ticket stated in Dutch and English that liability would be limited.

From the standpoint of the carrier it is nevertheless desirable that notices and conditions of contract on tickets are written not only in English but also in the national language of the carrier. This is common practice in the case of tickets, but not in the case of air waybills.

10. Agreed stopping places

GCC Pax define "Agreed Stopping Places" as "those places, except the place of departure and the place of destination, set out in the ticket or shown in all timetables as scheduled stopping places on your route".

SECTION 2—BAGGAGE CHECK

(a) Amended Convention—Article 4

(1) In respect of the carriage of registered baggage, a baggage check shall be delivered, which, unless combined with or incorporated in a passenger ticket which complies with the provision of Article 3, paragraph 1, shall contain:

    (a) an indication of the places of departure and destination;

    (b) if the places of departure and destination are within the territory of a single High Contracting Party, one or more agreed stopping places being within the territory of another State, an indication of at least one such stopping place;

    (c) a notice to the effect that, if the carriage involves an ultimate destination or stop in a country other than the country of departure, the Warsaw Convention may be applicable and that the Convention governs and in most cases limits the liability of carriers in respect of loss of or damage to baggage.

(2) The baggage check shall constitute *prima facie* evidence of the registration of the baggage and of the conditions of the contract of carriage. The absence, irregularity or loss of the baggage check does not affect the existence or the validity of the contract of carriage which shall, none the less, be subject to the rules of this Convention. Nevertheless, if the carrier takes charge of the baggage without a baggage check having been delivered or if the baggage check (unless combined with or incorporated in the passenger ticket which complies with the provisions of Article 3, paragraph (1)(c)) does not include the notice required by paragraph (1)(c) of this Article, he shall not be entitled to avail himself of the provisions of Article 22, paragraph 2.

(b) Unamended Convention—Article 4

(1) For the transportation of baggage, other than small personal objects of which the passenger takes charge himself, the carrier must deliver a baggage check.

(2) The baggage check shall be made out in duplicate, one part for the passenger and the other part for the carrier.

(3) The baggage check shall contain the following particulars:

    (a) the place and date of issue;

    (b) the place of departure and of destination;

    (c) the name and address of the carrier or carriers;

    (d) the number of the passenger ticket;

    (e) a statement that delivery of the baggage will be made to the bearer of the baggage check;

    (f) the number and weight of the packages;

    (g) the amount of the value declared in accordance with Article 22(2);

    (h) a statement that the transportation is subject to the rules relating to liability established by this convention.

(4) The absence, irregularity, or loss of the baggage check shall not affect the existence or the validity of the contract of transportation, which shall none the less be subject to the rules of this convention. Nevertheless, if the carrier accepts baggage without a baggage check having been delivered, or if the baggage check does not contain the particulars set out at d), f) and h) above, the carrier shall not be entitled to avail himself of those provisions of the convention which exclude or limit his liability.

(d) ICAO Convention

Article 3 deals with documentation for checked baggage as well as for passengers; see comment 1 on page 229.

Comments

1. *Definitions*

1.1. "Baggage" (whether in English or French) is not defined in the Warsaw Convention. In the Definitions it is "Personal property of passengers or crew carried on an aircraft by agreement with the operator". The Warsaw Convention does not relate to liability towards crew.

1.2. IATA defines baggage in GCC Pax as "articles, effects and other personal property as are necessary or appropriate for wear, use, comfort or convenience in connection with [the passenger's] trip. Unless otherwise specified, it includes both [the passenger's] checked and unchecked baggage".

2. *Issue of baggage check*

2.1. The Amended Convention requires that a baggage check must be issued containing the required notice if liability is to be limited. The English Court of Appeal held in *Collins* v. *British Airways Board* [1982] 1 All ER 302; [1982] QB 734, that failure to fill in the baggage check with the number of pieces of registered baggage did not remove the limit of liability.

2.2. However, the Unamended Convention requirements for limitation of liability are more stringent. Unlike the passenger ticket, it is expressly stated that the limit of liability is lost if the particulars specified in sub-paragraphs d), f) and h) are not included. For discussion see *Chan* v. *Korean Airlines*. See also *Arkin* v. *NY Helicopter Corp* (NY Sup Court) 544 NYS 7343 (1989); 22 AVI 17,163 1989 which held that the Unamended Convention must be strictly applied if liability is to be limited.

3. *Courier baggage*

3.1. Sometimes a carrier will provide a personalised courier service for documents or small articles. It is important that the procedures for acceptance, carriage and delivery of "courier baggage" are analysed to check whether it is (1) registered baggage, or (2) objects of which the passenger takes charge himself, or (3) cargo. Once the status has been determined then the applicable Warsaw Convention procedures should be followed if liability is to be limited. See *Republic National Bank* of *New York* v. *Eastern Airlines Inc*, 815 F 2d 232 (1986); 20 AVI 7,920 1986–8. In this case a courier took currency in two bags as checked baggage. The first bag was covered by a baggage check and the second was not and contained US$2 million. It was stolen. The court found in favour of the carrier limiting liability to US$643. Following *Chan* v.

Korean Airlines the *Arkin* case should be presumed to apply and liability would not be limited now in similar circumstances. In the *Republic* case the court commented that the traveller was more like a commercial shipper than a passenger.

3.2. It is necessary to analyse the contractual position in view of the parties concerned, ie carrier, courier passenger and the parties interested in the "baggage". In certain cases the courier may be the contracting carrier; see Part 2 of this chapter on the Guadalajara Convention 1961 where the circumstances are all important.

3.3. The carriage of courier baggage is a recognised commercial activity, see Annex 17 (page 196 above).

4. and 5. Registered baggage

4. In *Collins* v. *British Airways Board* Kerr LJ also considered that registration "means the delivery of the articles to a carrier for carriage, and his acknowledgement of their acceptance by keeping some written record for himself and the delivery of the corresponding receipt to the consignor, who, in the context of carriage of passengers is likely to be the passenger himself."

5.1. See also conflicting cases, for example German Bundesgerichthof of November 1978 ((1979) IV *Air Law* 165) and *Schedlmayer* v. *Trans International Airlines* (New York City, Civil Court, 1979; 15 AVI 17,740 1978–80) as to the status of objects taken on board by the passenger and then handed over to the airline staff. Where the courts hold that such objects become registered baggage, there must be in existence a valid baggage check (usually part of the ticket) if the Warsaw Convention liability is to be limited. The Unamended Convention will also require the number and weight of pieces of baggage to be shown.

5.2. Where the Amended Convention applies and the weight of the bags is not shown on the ticket but only the free baggage allowance, the carrier can reasonably assert that in the absence of an excess baggage ticket, the weight of the bags is the free baggage allowance.

6. Pet animals

In *Newell* v. *Canadian Pacific Airlines Ltd* (1976) 74 DLR (3rd) 574 (Ontario County Court) two dogs were classified as baggage when their owners were passengers and the dogs were in the cargo compartment. For carriage of animals generally see IATA Live Animals Regulations and IATA Airport Handling Manual. (See Chapter 9.)

7. Baggage check and identification tag

The baggage check should not be confused with the baggage identification tag. Both are defined in GCC Pax.

8. Evidence of registration

Article 4(2) of the Amended Convention expressly states that the baggage check shall constitute *prima facie* evidence of registration of the baggage and also of the conditions of contract.

SECTION 3—AIRWAY BILL

(a) Amended Convention—Article 5

(1) Every carrier of cargo has the right to require the consignor to make out and hand over to him a document called an "air waybill"; every consignor has the right to require the carrier to accept this document.
(2) The absence, irregularity or loss of this document does not affect the existence or the validity of the contract of carriage which shall, subject to the provisions of Article 9, be none the less governed by the rules of this Convention.

(c) MP4—Article 5

(1) In respect of the carriage of cargo an air waybill shall be delivered.
(2) Any other means which would preserve a record of the carriage to be performed may, with the consent of the consignor, be substituted for the delivery of an air waybill. If such other means are used, the carrier shall, if so requested by the consignor, deliver to the consignor a receipt for the cargo permitting identification of the consignment and access to the information contained in the record preserved by such other means.
(3) The impossibility of using, at points of transit and destination, the other means which would preserve the record of the carriage referred to in paragraph 2 of this Article does not entitle the carrier to refuse to accept the cargo for carriage.

(d) ICAO Convention—Article 4

1. In respect of the carriage of cargo an air waybill shall be delivered.
2. Any other means which preserves a record of the carriage to be performed may be substituted for the delivery of an air waybill. If such other means are used, the carrier shall, if requested by the consignor, deliver to the consignor a cargo receipt permitting identification of the consignment and access to the information contained in the record preserved by such other means.

Comments

1. Definition

"Cargo" is not defined in the Warsaw Convention. Definitions define it as "Any property carried on an aircraft other than mail, stores and baggage". Annex 9 defines it as "Any property carried on an aircraft other than mail, stores and accompanied or mishandled baggage".

CC Cargo (Recommended Practice 1601), Article 1(4) defines cargo as: " 'Cargo' (which is the equivalent to the term 'Goods'). Anything carried or to be carried in an aircraft except mail, or baggage carried under a passenger ticket and baggage check, but includes baggage moving under an air waybill or shipment record."

2. *Importance*

The importance and substance of the air waybill is dealt with in considering Articles 5, 6 and 8 below.

3. *Form and contents*

See IATA Resolutions 600a, 600b and 600b(II) in current IATA Cargo Services Conference Resolutions Manual.

(a) Amended Convention—Article 6

(1) The air waybill shall be made out by the consignor in three original parts and be handed over with the cargo.
(2) The first part shall be marked "for the carrier," and shall be signed by the consignor. The second part shall be marked "for the consignee"; it shall be signed by the consignor and by the carrier and shall accompany the cargo. The third part shall be signed by the carrier and handed by him to the consignor after the cargo has been accepted.
(3) The carrier shall sign prior to the loading of the cargo on board the aircraft.
(4) The signature of the carrier may be stamped; that of the consignor may be printed or stamped.
(5) If, at the request of the consignor, the carrier makes out the air waybill, he shall be deemed, subject to proof to the contrary, to have done so on behalf of the consignor.

(b) Unamended Convention—Article 6

Article 6(3) reads "The carrier shall sign on acceptance of the goods".

(c) MP4—Article 6

(1) The air waybill shall be made out by the consignor in three original parts.
(2) The first part shall be marked "for the carrier"; it shall be signed by the consignor. The second part shall be marked "for the consignee"; it shall be signed by the consignor and by the carrier. The third part shall be signed by the carrier and handed by him to the consignor after the cargo has been accepted.
(3) The signature of the carrier and that of the consignor may be printed or stamped.
(4) If, at the request of the consignor, the carrier makes out the air waybill, the carrier shall be deemed, subject to proof to the contrary, to have done so on behalf of the consignor.

(d) ICAO Convention—Article 7

Article 7 substantially follows MP4 wording.

Comments

1. Where a cargo agent or consolidator acts for the shipper (or consignor), the former will often issue his house air waybill to the shipper of the cargo and will

then consolidate that cargo with cargo of other parties which will be shipped together. The air carrier will then issue a master air waybill to the consolidator. It is a matter of law and fact as to whether the consolidator or air carrier is "the air carrier". Where the Guadalajara Convention (see Part 2 of this chapter) applies this question is more easily answered from the point of view of the shipper in deciding on the basis of any claim and the party against whom such claim should be made.

2. The significance of the third part of the air waybill is explained by Article 12(3).

3. The limit of liability and associated provisions of the Warsaw Convention apply between carrier and consignor or consignee in respect of the loss, damage or delay of cargo. The relationship between carrier and consignor in respect of defective contents of an air waybill where Article 6(5) applies may well be governed by provisions of domestic law not found in the Warsaw Convention.

(a) Amended Convention—Article 7

The carrier of cargo has the right to require the consignor to make out separate waybills when there is more than one package.

(c) MP4—Article 7

The provision is added that the consignor has the right to require the carrier to deliver separate receipts when the other means referred to in Article 5(2) are used.

(d) ICAO Convention—Article 8

Article 8 follows the wording of Article 7 of MP4.

Comments

1. Exercise of this right may affect the limit of liability of the carrier.

(a) Amended Convention—Article 8

The air waybill shall contain:

(a) an indication of the places of departure and destination;
(b) if the places of departure and destination are within the territory of a single High Contracting Party, one or more agreed stopping places being within the territory of another State, an indication of at least one such stopping place;
(c) a notice to the consignor to the effect that, if the carriage involves an ultimate destination or stop in a country other than the country of departure, the Warsaw Convention may be applicable and that the Convention governs and in most cases limits the liability of carriers in respect of loss of or damage to cargo.

(b) Unamended Convention—Article 8

The air waybill shall contain the following particulars:

(a) the place and date if its execution;
(b) the place of departure and of destination;
(c) the agreed stopping places, provided that the carrier may reserve the right to alter the stopping places in case of necessity, and that if he exercises that right the alteration shall not have the effect of depriving the transportation of its international character;
(d) the name and address of the consignor;
(e) the name and address of the first carrier;
(f) the name and address of the consignee, if the case so requires;
(g) the nature of the goods;
(h) the number of the packages, the method of packing and the particular marks or numbers upon them;
(i) the weight, the quantity, the volume or dimensions of the goods;
(j) the apparent condition of the goods and of the packing;
(k) the freight, if it has been agreed upon, the date and place of payment, and the person who is to pay it;
(l) if the goods are sent for payment on delivery, the price of the goods, and, if the case so requires, the amount of the expenses incurred;
(m) the amount of the value declared in accordance with Article 22(2);
(n) the number of parts of the air waybill;
(o) the documents handed to the carrier to accompany the air waybill;
(p) the time fixed for the completion of the transportation and a brief note of the route to be followed, if these matters have been agreed upon;
(q) a statement that the transportation is subject to the rules relating to liability established by this Convention.

(c) MP4—Article 8

The air waybill and the receipt for the cargo shall contain:

(a) an indication of the places of departure and destination;
(b) if the places of departure and destination are within the territory of a single High Contracting Party, one or more agreed stopping places being within the territory of another State, an indication of at least one such stopping place; and
(c) an indication of the weight of the consignment.

(d) ICAO Convention—Article 5

Follows the wording of MP4 Article 8 except that in line 1 "or" replaces "and" and "include" is substituted for "contain".

(d) ICAO Convention—Article 6

The consignor may be required, if necessary to meet the formalities of customs, police and similar public authorities, to deliver a document indicating the nature of the cargo. This provision creates for the carrier no duty, obligation or liability resulting therefrom.

Comments

1. The result of failure to meet these requirements is dealt with under Article 9.

2. Article 6 of the ICAO Convention refers to the "formalities" of customs, etc., not to legal requirements. The Article does not specify who does the requiring, and must be contrasted with Article 16.

(a) Amended Convention—Article 9

If, with the consent of the carrier, cargo is loaded on board the aircraft without an air waybill having been made out, or if the air waybill does not include the notice required by Article 8, paragraph (c), the carrier shall not be entitled to avail himself of the provisions of Article 22, paragraph 2.

(b) Unamended Convention—Article 9

If the carrier accepts goods without an air waybill having been made out, or if the air waybill does not contain all the particulars set out in Article 8 (a) to (i) inclusive and (q), the carrier shall not be entitled to avail himself of the provisions of this Convention which exclude or limit his liability.

(c) MP4—Article 9

Non-compliance with the provisions of Articles 5 to 8 shall not affect the existence or the validity of the contract of carriage, which shall, none the less, be subject to the rules of this Convention including those relating to limitation of liability.

(d) ICAO Convention—Article 9

Follows MP4 Article 9, substituting Articles "4 to 8" for "5 to 8".

Comments

1.1. The simplified requirements of the Amended Convention have eased the burden of both the consignor and the carrier.

1.2. The effect of omission of certain of the listed particulars under the Unamended Convention was considered in *Maritime Insurance Co Ltd* v. *Emery Air Freight Corporation* (US Court of Appeals, 2nd Circuit 1993; 24 AVI 17,381 1992–5).

Where the Warsaw Convention text is clear the law as stated must be applied: omission of the particulars will result in the loss of the limit of liability; but where the text is ambiguous as in subsections (h) and (i) the court is free to employ traditional interpretative methods and find in favour of the carrier.

1.3. Strict interpretation of clear wording applied in *Chan* v. *Korean Airlines* in respect of passenger tickets was in favour of the carrier. Strict interpretation of clear wording in *Emery* was in favour of the consignee.

1.4. In *Emery* the Court of Appeals stated:

"The ambiguity in subsections (h) and (i) arises because the text does not make clear whether the items listed in each subsection should be read conjunctively or disjunctively. Moreover, differences among the French original and the English and American translations create further confusion. In *Exim Industries* v. *PanAm World Airways* 754 F 2d 106 2nd Circuit 1985, we resolved the ambiguity in accordance with decisions reached by several foreign courts. This was appropriate because where ambiguity exists the plain meaning rule does not apply and we are free to employ traditional interpretative methods."

In a similar English case of *Corocraft* v. *PanAm* [1969] 1 QB 616, Lord Denning held that the French text should prevail and that the Warsaw Convention should be given the same meaning throughout all countries who were parties to it.

1.5. In *American Smelting & Refining Co* v. *Philippine Airlines*, 4 AVI 17,413 1954 (New York Sup Court) the Air Waybill omitted the agreed stopping places required by Article 8(c). The Court applied a liberal interpretation holding that in the circumstances the omission did not remove the limit of liability as there was no doubt that the consignee had notice that the flight constituted international carriage. In *Brink's Ltd* v. *South African Airways* 93 F 3d 1022 (2nd Circuit, 1996) the Court held that incorporation by reference into an air carrier's timetable may satisfy Article 8(c) and that Article 8(e) was satisfied by identifying the airport of departure as the "address of the first carrier" on the Air Waybill. However, a more restrictive interpretation was imposed by *Tai Ping Ins Co* v. *Northwest Airlines*, 94 F 3d 29 (2nd Circuit, 1996) which held that Article 8(c) of the Warsaw Convention is not satisfied if the Air Waybill does not contain the correct flight information.

1.6. The Unamended Convention will still apply where the USA is one of the high contracting parties and the other such party remains party to both the Unamended Convention and the Amended Convention, but not party to MP4.

2. In *Bianchi* v. *United Air Lines*, 15 AVI 17,426 1978–80 (Washington Court of Appeals, 1978) the Court left open question whether judgment in *Lisi* on minimum type size could be adopted in cargo cases. This judgment indicated lack of enthusiasm for the *Lisi* argument. This is a pre-*Chan* v. *Korean Airlines* case.

3. Due to the changes brought about by Article 9 of MP4 (where it applies) non-compliance does not affect the limits of liability. The effect of Article 9 of the ICAO Convention is the same. Subject to a special declaration of value being made, the limit of liability for cargo applies in all cases and cannot be broken under either MP4 or the ICAO Convention.

(a) Amended Convention—Article 10

(1) The consignor is responsible for the correctness of the particulars and statements relating to the cargo which he inserts in the air waybill.

(2) The consignor shall indemnify the carrier against all damage suffered by him, or by any other person to whom the carrier is liable, by reason of the irregularity, incorrectness or incompleteness of the particulars and statements furnished by the consignor.

(b) Unamended Convention—Article 10

Under Article 10(2) the consignor shall be liable for all damages suffered by the carrier or *any other person* by reason of the irregularity, incorrectness or incompleteness of the said particulars and statements.

(c) MP4—Article 10

(1) The consignor is responsible for the correctness of the particulars and statements relating to the cargo inserted by him or on his behalf in the air waybill or furnished by him or on his behalf to the carrier for insertion in the receipt for the cargo or for insertion in the record preserved by the other means referred to in paragraph (2) of Article 5.

(2) The consignor shall indemnify the carrier against all damage suffered by him, or by any other person to whom the carrier is liable, by reason of the irregularity, incorrectness or incompleteness of the particulars and statements furnished by the consignor or on his behalf.

(3) Subject to the provisions of paragraphs (1) and (2) of this Article, the carrier shall indemnify the consignor against all damage suffered by him, or by any other person to whom the consignor is liable, by reason of the irregularity, incorrectness or incompleteness of the particulars and statements inserted by the carrier or on his behalf in the receipt for the cargo or in the record preserved by the other means referred to in paragraph (2) of Article 5.

(d) ICAO Convention—Article 10

Article 10 substantially follows MP4 Article 10 but adds to paragraph 1 the words "The foregoing shall also apply where the person acting on behalf of the consignor is also the agent of the carrier". Also, "Article 4" is substituted for "Article 5".

Comments

1. The consignor's obligations relate to particulars and statements. These obligations extend to his agent. The ICAO Convention makes clear these obligations apply where the agent is also agent of the carrier.

2. The Unamended Convention imposes a wider obligation on the consignor than the Amended Convention.

3. The liability of the consignor is for all damages and is strict. It is unlimited.

4. These obligations are determined under domestic law.

5. Omission of certain particulars or statements in carriage governed by MP4 or the ICAO Convention does not have the same importance as under the Amended or Unamended Convention.

(a) Amended Convention—Article 11

(1) The air waybill is *prima facie* evidence of the conclusion of the contract, of the receipt of the cargo and of the conditions of carriage.

(2) The statements in the air waybill relating to the weight, dimensions and packing of the cargo, as well as those relating to the number of packages, shall be *prima facie* evidence of the facts stated; those relating to the quantity, volume and condition of the cargo do not constitute evidence against the carrier except so far as they both have been, and are stated in the air waybill to have been, checked by him in the presence of the consignor, or relate to the apparent condition of the cargo.

(c) MP4—Article 11

Article 11 substantially follows the Amended Convention wording but includes wording to provide for statements in the cargo receipt.

(d) ICAO Convention—Article 11

Follows the wording of MP4 Article 11.

Comments

1. Article 11(1): The domestic law of evidence applies in interpreting these provisions. The air waybill is *prima facie* evidence of:

   (1) Conclusion of the contract: The court will have to apply the rules of domestic law in order to decide if there is a binding contract.
   (2) Receipt of cargo.
   (3) Conditions of carriage: These are the contractual conditions under which the goods are transported. They are found usually (i) on the reverse of the air waybill being the conditions of contract (being those found in IATA Resolution 600b(ii)) and (ii) the IATA Conditions of Carriage of Cargo (Recommended Practice 1601, see page 235 above). Whether these conditions are effectively incorporated into the contract is a matter of domestic law.

   2. The effect of Article 11(2) is that in the absence of checking by the carrier there is no presumption that he received the correct quantity and volume of the cargo in good condition.
   3. "*Prima facie* evidence" is defined in *Black* as "evidence good and sufficient on its face. Such evidence, as in the judgement of the law, is sufficient to establish a given fact, or a group or chain of facts constituting the party's claim or defence, and which if not rebutted or contradicted will remain sufficient".

(a) Amended Convention—Article 12

(1) Subject to his liability to carry out all his obligations under the contract of carriage, the consignor has the right to dispose of the cargo by withdrawing it at the airport of departure or destination, or by stopping it in the course of the journey on any landing, or by calling for it to be delivered at the place of destination or in the course of the journey to a person other than the consignee named in the air waybill, or by requiring it to be returned to the airport of departure. He must not exercise this right of disposition in such a way as to prejudice the carrier or other consignors, and he must repay any expenses occasioned by the exercise of this right.
(2) If it is impossible to carry out the orders of the consignor the carrier must so inform him forthwith.
(3) If the carrier obeys the orders of the consignor for the disposition of the cargo without requiring the production of the part of the air waybill delivered to the

latter, he will be liable, without prejudice to his right of recovery from the consignor, for any damage which may be caused thereby to any person who is lawfully in possession of that part of the air waybill.

(4) The right conferred on the consignor ceases at the moment when that of the consignee begins in accordance with Article 13. Nevertheless, if the consignee declines to accept the waybill or the cargo, or if he cannot be communicated with, the consignor resumes his right of disposition.

(c) MP4—Article 12

Article 12 of the Amended Convention is followed subject to the following:

12(1): "originally designated" is substituted for "named in the air way-bill".

12(3): "or the receipt for the cargo" is inserted after "air waybill".

12(4): "the waybill or" is deleted.

(d) ICAO Convention—Article 12

Article 12 of MP4 is followed.

Comments

1.1. For operation of Article 12(1) see the German case Oberlandesgericht Düsseldorf 18U 163/85, 31 July 1986 ((1987) 12 *Air Law* 41). The carrier shipped goods to Nigeria before instructions had been given as required by the contract and before an import licence was granted. The carrier was required to return the goods to the consignor at his own expense.

Air Law also refers to the freight forwarder concerned acting as the carrier (see Part 2 of this chapter on Guadalajara Convention, below).

1.2. *Giemulla* observes that the consignor can only require withdrawal of goods up to the time just before the goods have arrived at their destination when the rights of consignee arise under Article 13.

1.3. For further application of Article 12(1) see German decision of Bundesgerichtshof 1964, 1965 ZLF 167, where it was not possible to return the cargo immediately without prejudicing other consignors.

1.4. The French case of *Gulf Air v. Ste Romanaise de la Chaussure* (Lyons CA 1987); *S&B* AvR VII/265) considered Article 12.1 and also applied Article 20 in favour of the carrier, which is a rare event.

The court also held that the cargo, when in an airport warehouse awaiting collection, was still in the charge of the carrier thus bringing it within the period of presumption of carrier's liability under Article 18 of the Warsaw Convention. See also Article 13 of the Warsaw Convention and Article 8.2 of CC Cargo.

2. The Warsaw Convention official French text refers to "*aérodrome*" while the IATA version refers to "airport". The English version refers to "aerodrome"; see the comment on Article 18(3), Chapter 9, and the Definitions.

(a) Amended Convention—Article 13

(1) Except in the circumstances set out in the preceding Article, the consignee is entitled, on arrival of the cargo at the place of destination, to require the carrier to hand over to him the air waybill and to deliver the cargo to him, on payment of the charges due and on complying with the conditions of carriage set out in the air waybill.
(2) Unless it is otherwise agreed, it is the duty of the carrier to give notice to the consignee as soon as the cargo arrives.
(3) If the carrier admits the loss of the cargo, or if the cargo has not arrived at the expiration of seven days after the date on which it ought to have arrived, the consignee is entitled to put into force against the carrier the rights which flow from the contract of carriage.

(c) MP4—Article 13

Article 13 follows substantially Article 13 of the Amended Convention but deletes the two references to the air waybill in Article 13(1).

(d) ICAO Convention—Article 13

Article 13 of MP4 is followed.

Comments

1. For interpretation of Article 13(3) see the English case of *Gatewhite Ltd* v. *Iberia Lineas Aereas de España SA* [1990] 1 QB 326; *S&B* AvR VII/305; [1989] 1 All ER 944 and [1990] 1 Lloyd's Rep 160 where the court considered that the broad reference to the rights should be limited to the enforcement of those rights given to the consignee by the previous paragraphs of the Article.

2. Article 13(3): If the cargo eventually arrives the consignee is likely to be obliged to give the notice required by Article 26 if applicable.

3. *Giemulla* points out that although the consignee is not party to the contract of carriage between the carrier and consignor, "he has certain rights and duties which arise above all from Article 13".

4. In some jurisdictions "partial loss" constitutes damage, see *Fothergill* v. *Monarch Airlines Ltd* [1981] AC 251; [1980] 2 Lloyd's Rep 295; [1980] 2 All ER 696.

5. In view of Article 18 below the question of how loss arises after arrival is highly material. See *Gulf Air* v. *Ste Romanaise de la Chaussure* (Lyons CA 1987), page 243 above.)

(a) Amended Convention—Article 14

The consignor and the consignee can respectively enforce all the rights given them by Articles 12 and 13, each in his own name, whether he is acting in his own interest or in the interest of another, provided that he carries out the obligations imposed by the contract.

(c) MP4—Article 14

This follows the Amended Convention except that MP4 adds "of carriage" at the end.

(d) ICAO Convention—Article 14

Article 14 follows Article 14 of MP4.

Comments

1. The parties named on the air waybill such as freight forwarders can thus exercise those rights.
    2. See reference to *Gatewhite Ltd* v. *Iberia Lineas Aereas de España SA* under Article 18 below page 254.

(a) Amended Convention—Article 15

(1) Articles 12, 13 and 14 shall not affect either the relations of the consignor and the consignee with each other or the relations of third parties whose rights are derived either from the consignor or from the consignee.
(2) The provisions of Articles 12, 13 and 14 can only be varied by express provision in the air waybill.
(3) Nothing in this Convention prevents the issue of a negotiable air waybill.

(c) MP4—Article 15

Article 15 of the Amended Convention is followed subject to the following:

15(1): "mutual" is inserted before "relations of third parties".
15(2): "or the receipt for the cargo" is added.
15(3): is deleted.

(d) ICAO Convention—Article 15

The wording of Article 15 of MP4 is followed.

Comments

1. Article 15(1) is a reminder that the Warsaw Convention deals with the liability of the carrier only.

2. Article 15(1): Such relations will be governed by the provisions of any relevant contract which in turn may include INCOTERMS of the International Chamber of Commerce, for example CPT (Carriage Paid To (name place of destination))).

3. Article 15(2): Any intended variation will be subject to the provisions of Article 23 of the Warsaw Convention.

4. Article 15(2): *Giemulla's* commentary indicates this provision will be strictly applied by the courts. A variation not noted on the air waybill would be void.

5. Article 15(3) was added by the Amended Convention and removed by MP4.

(a) Amended Convention—Article 16

(1) The consignor must furnish such information and attach to the air waybill such documents as are necessary to meet the formalities of customs, octroi, or police before the cargo can be delivered to the consignee. The consignor is liable to the carrier for any damage occasioned by the absence, insufficiency, or irregularity of any such information or documents, unless the damage is due to the fault of the carrier or his agents.

(2) The carrier is under no obligation to enquire into the correctness or sufficiency of such information or documents.

(c) MP4—Article 16

Article 16 of the Amended Convention is followed subject in 16(1) to (i) the deletion of the words "attach to the air waybill" in line 1; (ii) the substitution of "his servants or agents" for "or his agents" at the end.

(d) ICAO Convention—Article 16

The wording of Article 16 of MP4 is followed, subject to the substitution of "any other public authorities" for "octroi".

Comments

1. In *Nowell* v. *Qantas Airways Ltd* (22 AVI 18,071 1989–90; US District Court, Western District of Seattle, 1990), limitation of liability provisions of the Warsaw Convention applied to determine the liability of an air carrier who negligently lost original air waybill and attached customs visas during transportation by air, resulting in delay and loss of profit. The delay was in the delivery of the cargo and not in the actual carriage by air. Losing the documents was an occurrence during the course of transportation by air.

2. Liability of the consignor to the carrier under Article 16(1) is strict and damages are unlimited.

3. In *Industrial Drugs Supplies Inc* v. *H&H Shipping Co Inc* (20 AVI 17,306 1986–8; New York Sup Court, 1986) the defendant's air freight agent

failed to obtain an indemnity from the third party carrier; the court held that the air waybill was not evidence of any contract between the two parties and there was no vicarious liability.

4. *Giemulla* comments that "formalities of . . . police" must be widely construed and include all relevant laws, regulations, police orders and decrees in force in the appropriate jurisdiction. "For example safety regulations governing the carriage of dangerous goods, radioactive substances, drugs, corpses or animals", see Annex 18 and in particular its Chapters 7–9, and Technical Instructions.

5. Annex 9 (Facilitation) and IATA Airport Handling Manual (Chapter 9) both refer to customs procedures.

6. Compare Article 16 with Article 6 of the ICAO Convention. The vagueness of the wording of the latter Article questions its *raison d'être*.

CHAPTER III
LIABILITY OF THE CARRIER

(a) Amended Convention—Article 17

The carrier is liable for damage sustained in the event of the death or wounding of a passenger or any other bodily injury suffered by a passenger, if the accident which caused the damage so sustained took place on board the aircraft or in the course of any of the operations of embarking or disembarking.

(d) ICAO Convention—Article 17

1. The carrier is liable for damage sustained in case of death or bodily injury of a passenger upon condition only that the accident which caused the death or injury took place on board the aircraft or in the course of any of the operations of embarking or disembarking.
2. The carrier is liable for damage sustained in case of destruction or loss of, or of damage to, checked baggage upon condition only that the event which caused the destruction, loss or damage took place on board the aircraft or during any period within which the checked baggage was in the charge of the carrier. However, the carrier is not liable if and to the extent that the damage resulted from the inherent defect, quality or vice of the baggage. In the case of unchecked baggage, including personal items, the carrier is liable if the damage resulted from its fault or that of its servants or agents.
3. If the carrier admits the loss of the checked baggage, or if the checked baggage has not arrived at the expiration of twenty-one days after the date on which it ought to have arrived, the passenger is entitled to enforce against the carrier the rights which flow from the contract of carriage.
4. Unless otherwise specified, in this Convention the term "baggage" means both checked baggage and unchecked baggage.

Comments

1. Sole cause of action

Both UK law (*Sidhu* v. *British Airways* [1997] 1 All ER 193) and US law (*Re Air Disaster at Lockerbie*, US Court of Appeals, 2nd Circuit, March 1991; 23

AVI 17,714 1991–2) make clear that the Warsaw Convention creates an exclusive cause of action and no domestic law remedies in tort or contract are also available. See the comment on *Sidhu* v. *British Airways* [1997] 1 All ER 193 (HL) under Article 24 (below). This decision is confirmed by Article 29 of the ICAO Convention. Such a view has not always been held in the USA.

Although founded on a contract of carriage the legal action is simply a "cause of action" created by statute. (*Proctor* v. *Jetway Aviation PGILT* [1982] 2 NSWLR 264.)

2. Passenger

The Definitions define "passenger aircraft" as an aircraft that carries any person other than a crew member, an operator's employee in an official capacity, an authorised representative of appropriate national authority or person accompanying a consignment.

It is considered that employees of the carrier travelling on business or leisure are passengers.

The Definitions also define "flight crew member" and "crew member", see pages 35 and 64 above. See the Scots case of *Fellowes (or Herd)* v. *Clyde Helicopters Ltd* (HL February 1997). Sergeant Herd was a member of the Police Helicopter Unit, Scotland. His duties were to carry out aerial surveillance and detection within Strathclyde. The helicopter was provided by the defendant Clyde Helicopters Ltd. During the flight in a snow storm the engine failed and Sgt Herd was killed. The UK law of non-international (domestic) carriage applied (see Part 5 of this chapter).

The duties of Sgt Herd were to direct surveillance operations. The pilot supplied by Clyde was solely responsible for flying the helicopter. The House of Lords held that although the police officer was on board the helicopter for the purpose of carrying out his police duties, he had no responsibility in respect of the operation of the aircraft which was solely under the control of the pilot, and consequently the activities which he carried out while on board could not be regarded as contributing to the carriage of himself or the other persons on board. He was therefore properly to be regarded as a passenger so far as the performance of the contract of carriage for reward was concerned.

3. *Giemulla* suggests that as the liability of the carrier under Warsaw Convention is based on contract, a stowaway has no contract and therefore no enforceable claim under such Convention. See comment 1 on Article 34, page 285 below.

4. Meaning of death and injury

"Death" is clear in its meaning. The only question may be whether the aircraft accident caused the death or whether it occurred for some other reason, either on the flight or subsequently. See *Air France* v. *Saks* below and Definitions in Chapter 1 of Annex 13 on page 155 above.

For a discussion on the meaning of "wounding . . . any other bodily injury" and the French official version "*mort, de blessure ou de toute autre, lesion corporelle*" see *S&B* VII (521).

The question arises whether under the official French version Article 17 covers psychological injury, mental stress or psychic injury.

Floyd v. *Eastern Airlines Inc*, 499 US 530, 111 S Ct 1489 held that damages for emotional distress flowing from physical injuries only could be recovered. Damages are not available for purely mental injury. "*Lesion corporelle*" did not cover such injuries.

In the Australian case *Kotsambasis* v. *Singapore Airlines Ltd* (Supreme Court of New South Wales, August 1997), the Court of Appeal held that

"the term 'bodily injury' for the purposes of the Warsaw Convention does not include a purely psychological injury . . . The general approach to the interpretation of an international convention is by application of the rules of interpretation recognised by customary international law. The words are first read literally and then, if the meaning is unclear, the courts are to give effect to the intention of the signatories to the convention including object and purpose of the convention . . . Municipal (domestic) Law can assist interpretation especially if the signatories had regard to the municipal law of particular contracting parties . . . courts are not at liberty to consider any word as superfluous or insignificant."

However the Israeli Supreme Court reached a different decision in *Daddon* v. *Air France* (1984) 1 S&B AvR VII/141; 38(3) PD 785 (1984) and 39 RFDA 232, (1985) under the name *Air France* v. *Teichner*. In view of the developing judicial views on mental injury both where the Warsaw Convention does and does not apply, this question needs to be kept under review.

5. Accident

5.1. The meaning of "accident" was discussed in *Air France* v. *Saks* 105 S Ct 1338 (1985); 18 AVI 18,538 1985 (US Supreme Court) where it was said: "Liability under Article 17 of the Warsaw Convention arises only if the passenger's injury is caused by an unexpected or unusual event or happening that is external to the passenger. This definition should be flexibly applied after assessment of all the circumstances surrounding a passenger's injuries." See reference to *Fenton* v. *J Thorley & Co Ltd* (page 446).

5.2. The English Court of Appeal agreed with this judgment in *Chaudhari* v. *British Airways* (1997). See also *Quinn* v. *Canadian Airlines International* where the Ontario Court of Appeal confirmed the lower judgment holding that where an elderly passenger with osteoporosis suffered a fracture of the vertebrae while still seated during mild turbulence, the damage was not covered by "an accident" within the meaning of Article 17. In both *Chaudhari* and *Quinn* the passengers in question had particular medical conditions.

5.3. Food poisoning may constitute an accident. See *Abdul Rahman Al-Zamil* v. *British Airways Inc.* 770 F 2d 3 (US Court of Appeals, 2nd Circuit,

1985); 19 AVI 17,646. In this case the Court applied Article 28 of the Warsaw Convention and dismissed the case for lack of jurisdiction.

5.4 Smoking.

(1) As *S&B* (IV (107)) point out, smoking prohibitions are primarily for safety reasons but the 29th ICAO Assembly adopted in 1992 a resolution calling for progressive smoking restrictions with the objective of implementing a complete smoking ban by 1 July 1996. The early case of *Ravreby* v. *United Airlines Inc*, Sup Court of Iowa, 18 June 1980; 15 AVI 18,235 1978–81 concerned non-international carriage. The Court held that the carrier did not breach its duty of care to a passenger in a no-smoking area of an aircraft by allowing passengers in the smoking area to smoke. Also the air carrier assumed no contractual duty to assure that a passenger was exposed to less smoke by the fact that the passenger was asked whether he preferred to be seated in a smoking or non-smoking section.

(2) In the Australian case of *Qantas Airways Ltd* v. *Cameron* (NSW District Registry) 66 FLR 246, 1996, the Appeal Court held that the carrier was under no liability for claims made in negligence and for unconscionable conduct under the Trade Practices Act in respect of "passive smoking". In respect of international carriage the Warsaw Convention was not mentioned in the Judgment. In most cases it is unlikely that a proven bodily injury from "passive smoking" could be proved to be due to a particular accident within the meaning of Article 17. Another question is whether in the absence of liability under Article 17 there is any cause of action available in respect of carriage by air (see *Sidhu* v. *British Airways* page 269 below).

(3) Australia, Canada and the USA entered into an agreement to ban smoking on international passenger flights in 1994 which entered into force on 1 March 1995.

5.5. In *Capacchione* v. *Qantas Airways Ltd* (US District Court, Central District, California, 1996; 26 AVI 17,340) it was held that a passenger had no claim against a foreign carrier for negligent exposure to insecticide or for failure to warn. Because the insecticide application was required by Australian regulations and the passenger's reaction was not an accident giving rise to Warsaw Convention liability recovery was barred under the terms of the airline's tariff (i.e. conditions of contract) which released it from liability arising out of compliance with government regulations.

6. *Extent of liability*

6.1. "On board the aircraft or in the course of any of the operations of embarking or disembarking . . . ". The original wording was probably intended to cover not only the risk of flight but also those risks associated with civil aviation operations such as the crossing of the apron to the aircraft from the terminal building. Many aircraft are now boarded through piers or gangways forming part of the terminal building. The courts take the view that there has to be an analysis of which particular enterprise has control of the passengers. Compare this with the carrier's duties under Annex 9 SARPS 3.31.1.

6.2. See *Maché v. Cie Air France* 17 RFDA 353, 20 RFDA 228, (1966); 21 RFDA 343, (1967); 24 RFDA 311, (1970) Cour de Cassation. In this case it was held that the physical injuries received as a result of the passenger falling into a manhole when crossing the apron to customs did not take place in the course of disembarkation.

6.3. The US Court of Appeals in *Day v. Trans World Airlines Inc*, 13 AVI 18,144 1975–6, adopted the tri-partite test based on (1) the activity of the passenger, (2) control of the passenger and (3) the place of the accident. In this case the passengers had checked in and were in the departure lounge when they were subjected to a terrorist attack—Article 17 applied to the terrorist attack. In *Adatia v. Air Canada* (1992), *The Times*, 4 June 1993, the English Court of Appeal held that in the circumstances an arriving passenger on a travelator was no longer in the course of disembarking even though she had not reached customs or immigration, and was following her mother who was being pushed in a wheelchair by an airline employee. See also *Adler v. Austrian Airlines* (Brussels Court of Appeal, 1986) where the passenger who slipped on ice disembarking from a bus in order to embark on the aircraft was in the course of embarking. Also *Ricotta v. Iberia Lineas Aereas de Espana* (District Court, 1979; 15 AVI 17,829 1978–80).

6.4. *Galvin v. Aer Rianta Air Charter* [1994] 1 ASLR 147 (Ireland High Court, October 1993) concerned the passenger processing agent of the carrier having knowledge of the special requirements of a charter flight of mainly middle-aged or elderly invalids who would have to ascend to an upper floor en route to the departure gate. The court held that embarkation commenced not later than the time when the flight was called and the passenger was instructed to proceed to departure gate.

6.5. Article 17 should be narrowly construed: "embarking" and "disembarking" connoting close and temporal and spatial relationship with the flight itself. Accordingly, the airline was not liable for a passenger accident occurring some considerable distance from the departure gate and well before any act of embarkation was possible and which took place in part of the terminal not restricted to passengers. The passenger was not under airline control (*McCarthy v. North West Airlines*, US Court of Appeals, 1st Circuit, May 1995, [1995] 2 ASLR 422).

6.6. The Definitions define embarkation as "The boarding of an aircraft for the purpose of commencing a flight, except by such crew or passengers as have embarked on a previous stage of the same through-flight", and Disembarkation as "The leaving of an aircraft after a landing except by crew or passengers continuing on the next stage of the same through flight". These Definitions draw attention to the status of a passenger who is injured during a transit stop.

Giemulla distinguishes between a transit stopover of the same flight where Article 17 liability will probably attach throughout the stopover, and a transfer stopover where such liability will not so attach throughout.

7. ICAO Convention—Article 17

7.1. Article 17.1 replaces the Warsaw Convention Article 17 and omits "woundings". While the provisions of both Articles are substantially the same, the provisions on limits of liability elsewhere in the respective Conventions are substantially different.

7.2. Article 17.2 deals both with checked and unchecked baggage.

With regard to checked baggage there must be an event which caused the destruction, loss etc which took place on board the aircraft or in the course of embarking or disembarking or during any period within which the baggage was in the charge of the carrier. However, the carrier is not liable to the extent that the damage resulted from the inherent defect, quality or vice of the baggage, see Article 23 of the Amended Convention below (page 268).

In the case of unchecked baggage, including personal items, the carrier is liable if the damage resulted from its fault. While this clarifies the basis of liability, *i.e.* fault, it does not impose any temporal or spatial restriction; see Comment 9 on Article 22 below (page 266). Article 17.3 imposes a waiting period of 21 days.

(a) Amended Convention—Article 18

(1) The carrier is liable for damage sustained in the event of the destruction or loss of, or of damage to, any registered baggage or any cargo, if the occurrence which caused the damage so sustained took place during the carriage by air.

(2) The carriage by air within the meaning of the preceding paragraph comprises the period during which the baggage or cargo is in charge of the carrier, whether in an airport or on board an aircraft, or, in the case of a landing outside an aerodrome, in any place whatsoever.

(3) The period of the carriage by air does not extend to any carriage by land, by sea or by river performed outside an aerodrome. If, however, such a carriage takes place in the performance of a contract for carriage by air, for the purpose of loading, delivery or transhipment, any damage is presumed, subject to proof to the contrary, to have been the result of an event which took place during the carriage by air.

(c) MP4—Article 18

The first three paragraphs read as follows:

(1) The carrier is liable for damage sustained in the event of the destruction or loss of, or damage to, any registered baggage, if the occurrence which caused the damage so sustained took place during the carriage by air.

(2) The carrier is liable for damage sustained in the event of the destruction or loss of, or damage to, cargo upon condition only that the occurrence which caused the damage so sustained took place during the carriage by air.

(3) However, the carrier is not liable if he proves that the destruction, loss of, or damage to, the cargo resulted solely from one or more the following:

    (i) inherent defect, quality or vice of that cargo;

    (ii) defective packing of that cargo performed by a person other than the carrier or his servants or agents;

    (iii) an act of war or an armed conflict;

    (iv) an act of public authority carried out in connection with the entry, exit or transit of the cargo.

"Destruction" is expressly included.

Paragraphs (4) and (5) follow the wording of paragraphs (2) and (3) of the Amended Convention.

(d) ICAO Convention—Article 18

1. The carrier is liable for damage sustained in the event of the destruction or loss of, or damage to, cargo upon condition only that the event which caused the damage so sustained took place during the carriage by air.

2. However, the carrier is not liable if and to the extent it proves that the destruction, or loss of, or damage to, the cargo resulted from one or more of the following:

    (a) inherent defect, quality or vice of that cargo;

    (b) defective packing of that cargo performed by a person other than the carrier or its servants or agents;

    (c) an act of war or an armed conflict;

    (d) an act of public authority carried out in connection with the entry, exit or transit of the cargo.

3. The carriage by air within the meaning of paragraph 1 of this Article comprises the period during which the cargo is in the charge of the carrier.

4. The period of the carriage by air does not extend to any carriage by land, by sea or by inland waterway performed outside an airport. If, however, such carriage takes place in the performance of a contract for carriage by air, for the purpose of loading, delivery or transhipment, any damage is presumed, subject to proof to the contrary, to have been the result of an event which took place during the carriage by air. If a carrier, without the consent of the consignor, substitutes carriage by another mode of transport for the whole or part of a carriage intended by the agreement between the parties to be carriage by air, such carriage by another mode of transport is deemed to be within the period of carriage by air.

Comments

1. *Fothergill* v. *Monarch* ([1981] AC 251; [1980] 1 Lloyd's Rep 160) establishes that partial loss constitutes notifiable damage.

2. Under the Warsaw Convention, there must be an occurrence during the carriage by air, see *Kinney Shoe Corporation* v. *Alitalia Airlines*, 15 AVI 18,509 1980. Accident is not required. The occurrence must be the cause of the damage. The ICAO Convention refers to an "event".

3. Who can claim? Common law cases suggest that not only the party to the contract of carriage but also the person who has beneficial interest in the goods

can claim. (See *Gatewhite Limited* v. *Iberia Lineas Aereas de Espana SA* [1989] 1 All ER 944; *S&B* AvR VII/305; [1990] 1 Lloyd's Rep 160; but see also the comments of the House of Lords on *Gatewhite* expressed in *Sidhu* v. *British Airways*.) In *Western Digital* v. *British Airways* (QBD, June 1999), the court concluded that the Warsaw Convention confines cargo loss and damage claims to proceedings instituted by the consignor, or the consignee or the person otherwise entitled to delivery under the Convention. The owner cannot claim if not one of those persons. Civil law limits the right of claim to the holder of the baggage tag (*SARL Ippo Sake International* v. *Air France*, 43 RFDA 257 (1989)).

4. For baggage and cargo handling procedures see Annexes 9, 17 and 18 and Chapter 9 of this book.

5. Warsaw Convention Article 18(1): Extent of damages depend on the applicable domestic law; damages for consequential loss can be awarded. See *Deere & Co* v. *Deutsche Lufthansa*, 21 AVI 17,513 1988.

6. Warsaw Convention Article 18(2): The facts of each case will determine whether the cargo or baggage is in the charge of the carrier. Factors include the ability of the carrier to exercise control, the site of the baggage or goods and the activities of the consignor, consignee, of the carrier or any agent. The English case *Swiss Bank Corp* v. *Brinks-MAT Ltd* 1986 *S&B* AvR VII/195; *S&B* 853, gives an analysis of when the goods come into the charge of the carrier. The court held that goods in the van, loaded and guarded and driven into the carrier's warehouse were not in charge of carrier, because in the circumstances the carrier still had no control over the contents of the van.

7. In *Bennett Importing Company* v. *Continental Airlines Inc* (US District Court, Mass 1988; 21 AVI 17,917 1988–9) the cargo remained in the charge of the carrier while held by the carrier in its customs bonded cargo facility.

8. Article 18(2): Decisions in a number of States hold that the goods remain in the charge of the carrier even after they have been delivered to customs until they have been delivered to the consignee. The decision must depend on the facts and other cases have held otherwise. See Article 8 of CC Cargo.

9. Warsaw Convention Article 18(3): The official French text refers to "aérodrome". See Comments, on Article 12, page 244 above.

For the meaning of "aérodrome" in this context see the Belgian case of *SA Cie Européene d'Assurances de Marchandises et de Bagages* v. *SA Sabena* (Brussels CA, April 1972; 1977 JT) and the US case of *Victoria Sales Corporation* v. *Emery Air Freight Inc* (Court of Appeals, 2nd Circuit, 1990; 22 AVI 18,502 1989–90). In the latter case the Warsaw Convention did not apply to loss of pharmaceutical products which were transported to an air freight forwarder's warehouse located outside the boundaries of an airport.

10. *Giemulla* gives examples of destruction or loss or damage:

> (1) Destruction must be total physical destruction. If dogs arrive at their destination dead this is destruction (*Dalton* v. *Delta Airways*,

US Court of Appeals, 5th Circuit, 1978; 14 AVI 18,425 1976–8). If an animal dies after arrival it is a case of notifiable damage in the circumstances (*Hughes-Gibb* v. *The Flying Tiger Line Inc.*, US District Court, Northern District, Illinois, 1981; 16 AVI 17,492 1980–2).

(2) Loss: In cases where [the consignee is a bank and] a shipment against a letter of credit is delivered to the "Notifying person" named without the bank's consent, one must work on the assumption that the goods have been handed over and lost, unless the collecting bank named as a consignee in air waybill has previously waived its rights of disposition.

(3) Damage occurs whenever the substance and thus the value of the goods is impaired. The distinctions between these categories are important. Damage requires notification to the carrier (Article 26(2) and (4)) but not in loss or destruction. It is therefore important to be aware of the case law where partial loss is assimilated by the court to damage.

11. The ICAO Convention: Article 18 applies only to cargo and does not include baggage. Liability is incurred during the period when the cargo is in the charge of the carrier. While MP4 18(3) gives a complete defence if the damage resulted solely from one or more of the four sets of circumstances, the ICAO Convention provides a defence if and to the extent that the destruction, etc. resulted from one or more of the same sets of circumstances.

12. The ICAO Convention: The last sentence of Article 18.4 applies the liability provisions of the Convention to other substituted modes of transport. It does not state whether its limits of liability should be applied in such cases where other modes of transport might have a higher limit of liability or no limit at all.

13. The ICAO Convention: Comments on the defences in Article 18.2 are—

(a) For inherent defect, etc., see Comment 5.1 on page 268;
(b) Defective packing can be by any person other than the carrier, its servants or agents;
(c) For consideration of "war or an armed conflict", see page 456;
(d) For possible acts of a public authority, see page 108 above.

(a) Amended Convention—Article 19

The carrier is liable for damage occasioned by delay in the carriage by air of passengers, baggage or cargo.

(d) ICAO Convention—Article 19

Follows the Amended Convention, adding the following final sentence:

Nevertheless, the carrier shall not be liable for damage occasioned by delay if it proves that it and its servants and agents took all measures that could reasonably be required to avoid the damage or that it was impossible for it or them to take such measures.

Comments

1. The Warsaw Convention limits of liability referred to in Article 22 apply to Warsaw Convention carriage.

2. There is no reference to accident or occurrence.

3. "Baggage" includes registered and hand baggage.

4. The claimant will be the passenger when he has suffered delay, but see *Pakistan Arts and Entertainment Corp* v. *Pakistan International Airlines*, 660 NYS App Div, 1997; 25 AVI 18,464 and *S&B* AvR VII/624. In the case of claims for delay of cargo and registered baggage, the nature of the proper claimant will depend on whether the court follows the judgment in *Gatewhite Ltd* v. *Iberia* or not. This case allowed the beneficial owner to claim irrespective of whether he is the ticket holder or is named on the air waybill as the consignor or consignee.

5. *S&B* wonder whether there is any argument that third parties damaged by delay can claim and consider that the legal authorities do not support this view.

6. Distinction must be drawn between delay in the contract of carriage governed by the Warsaw Convention and failure to carry. In the latter case, see Article 9 of GCC Pax and Article 6.3 of CC Cargo.

7. In *de Veira* v. *Japan Airlines* the US District Court applied the Warsaw Convention to a passenger who had purchased a round trip USA–Tokyo–Manila–New York. Delay in Tokyo occurred when Manila airport was closed, firstly due to typhoon and then to volcanic activity.

8.1. There is considerable argument as to the meaning of delay. Does it mean, (a) when not airborne, but otherwise falling within the periods covered by Warsaw Convention Articles 17 or 18 or, (b) delay while airborne or, (c) delay during carriage by air within the meaning of Article 18 or, (d) delay in the whole contract of carriage. Mankiewicz, in his book *The Liability Regime of the International Air Carrier*, suggests that delay means abnormal delay.

8.2. *S&B* suggest the carrier is bound to perform carriage within a reasonable time in the absence of any express obligation.

8.3. In considering the period of liability, *Giemulla* points out "that the only decisive factor in respect of damage caused by delay is the time the carriage ends. As far as the carriage of hand baggage is concerned this is determined in accordance with Article 17, and where cargo or registered baggage are in issue, the matter is determined in accordance with Article 18."

9. Where delay of a flight is caused by engine failure, under German law the passenger can claim under section 325 of the Civil Code and not under Article 19 which regulates compensation for damages caused by the inherent risk of air transport only. (Oberlandesgericht Düsseldorf, 19 June 1996; 18U 174/95, 1997; NJW RR 930; XXIII *Air Law* 40).

10. In *Bart v. British West Indian Airways Ltd* [1967] 1 Lloyd's Rep 239 (Guyana Court of Appeal) the plaintiff claimed £20,457.10 in negligence and/ or breach of contract for alleged delay in shipment of a winning football pools coupon from Guyana to UK. The Appeal Court overruled the judgment at first instance in favour of the plaintiff and held:

(i) there was bailment of the coupon by the plaintiff to the consignor, and sub-bailment by the consignor to BWIA; there was no physical loss or destruction of the goods and any claim lay in contract and not in tort;

(ii) the plaintiff lost his right to possession of the coupon when it was posted by the shipper and could only sue for permanent injury or loss to the coupon: there was no such material loss and BWIA could have relied on the limiting conditions in the Air Waybill;

(iii) negligence of BWIA could not amount to breach of fundamental term. BWIA could rely on Article 13(3) of the Unamended Convention as a further ground which was incorporated into the Carriage by Air (Non-International Carriage) (Colonies, Protectorates and Trust Territories) Order 1953, which imposed a period of seven days before a right to claim arose;

(iv) there was no privity of contract between the plaintiff and BWIA but even if the consignor was the plaintiff's agent then the plaintiff not being the consignor or consignee was deprived of the right by the 1953 Order to bring any suit against BWIA and liability would have been limited under such Order;

(v) the judge had awarded damages on the wrong basis and the plaintiff failed to prove that the pools operator would have paid a dividend.

11. Overbooking

Failure of the carrier to carry a passenger with a confirmed seat due to overbooking should not normally be "delay" within the meaning of Article 19. It should be governed by the law of the contract and any other applicable laws such as EC Council Regulation (EEC) No 295/91 establishing common rules for a denied boarding compensation system in scheduled air transport.

The EC Regulation:

(i) establishes uniform rules which give the passenger the choice to be reimbursed for the ticket or to be re-routed at the earliest opportunity or at a later convenient date and for payment of minimum compensation. This does not prejudice any claim for further compensation;

(ii) applies to all passengers with a confirmed reservation departing from an airport in an EU Member State irrespective of State where the carrier is established, nationality of the passenger and destination.

12. Domestic law will be applied in assessing damages payable for delay.

13. In certain cases Articles 18 and 19 may give concurrent remedies, e.g. damage caused to cargo through delay.

14. ICAO Convention: This defence, available in respect of delay only, is less severe from the carrier's point of view than the general defence provided by Article 20 of the Warsaw Convention, see below.

(a) Amended Convention—Article 20

The carrier is not liable if he proves that he and his servants or agents have taken all necessary measures to avoid the damage or that it was impossible for him or them to take such measures.

(b) Unamended Convention—Article 20

(1) The carrier shall not be liable if he proves that he and his agents have taken all necessary measures to avoid the damage or that it was impossible for him or them to take such measures.

(2) In the transportation of goods and baggage the carrier shall not be liable if he proves that the damage was occasioned by an error in piloting, in the handling of the aircraft or in navigation and that, in all other respects, he and his agents have taken all necessary measures to avoid the damage.

(c) MP4—Article 20

Article 20 is amended in the case of cargo by restricting the defence to damage caused by delay only.

(d) ICAO Convention—equivalent provisions

There is no defence identical to that provided by Article 20 of the Warsaw Convention.

Article 17.1 provides a defence in respect of checked baggage where the damage resulted from inherent defect, quality or vice of the baggage.

Article 17.2 dealing with destruction, loss or damage to cargo provides the four listed defences.

Article 21 deals with death or injury.

Comments

1. The burden of proof is on the carrier.

2. The defence can and must in certain cases be waived; see CAB 18900 (Montreal agreement), the IATA Inter-Carrier Agreement and EC Council Regulation No 2027/97 (see Part 4 of this chapter). The reference to Article 20(1) in CAB 18900 can only refer to the Unamended Convention as the Amended Convention deleted Article 20(2). However, CAB 18900 in many cases applies to carriage governed by the Amended Convention but nevertheless continues to refer to Article 20(1), for example carriage London/New York/London.

3. Article 20(1): In some States the courts have interpreted "all necessary measures" as "all reasonably necessary measures"; see for example the English

cases of *Chisholm* v. *British European Airways* [1963] 1 Lloyd's Rep 626 and *Goldman* v. *Thai Airways International* (1981) 125 Sol Jo 413 at first instance. See also *Manufacturers Hanover Trust Co* v. *Alitalia* (SDNY, 1977); 14 AVI 17,710; 1978 ZLW 291 where the court said that the phrase "all necessary measures . . . " cannot be read with strict literality but must be construed to mean "all reasonable measures", judgment in this case contains a vivid description of armed hold-up on the defendant carrier. In *Sana* v. *Palleron*, Rhone Court of Cassation [1938] AFLR 155, [1938] RDA 151 the court held that the necessary measures would be those as would be taken by the prudent and reasonable businessman or his crew in the special circumstances at hand.

4. This defence extends to the agents of the carrier. The official French text refers to "préposés". The Unamended Convention English translation refers to "agents" while the Amended Convention translation refers to "servants and agents". *Giemulla* suggests that the agents covered by Articles 20 and 25 are those persons used by the carrier in performance of the carriage.

5.1. Article 20(2) remains significant while USA is not party to the Amended Convention otherwise than in respect of carriage between States party to MP4. See *American Smelting & Refining Co* v. *Philippine Airlines*, 4 AVI 17,413 1954, where the cause of the accident was attributed to negligent piloting and defective air traffic control. The relevant part of the judgment is quoted in order to show how the court applied Article 20(2) in 1954 (the state of New York, New York County). The cargo was gold.

"The proof adduced upon the trial conclusively establishes that defendant took all possible precautions to ensure the safety of the flight and to avoid the crash of the aircraft. The record shows that defendant properly equipped, loaded and fuelled the plane, supplied an airworthy and duly licensed aircraft, a licensed and qualified pilot and crew who were given all necessary maps, charts and instructions, and that defendant adopted sound flight procedures in accordance with all applicable rules and regulations. The credible evidence proves that the crash of defendant's plane was caused by a combination of factors, including negligent piloting, faulty and erroneous instructions from Kai-Tak Airport control tower, possible failure of the pilot to obey instructions from the control tower and/or to follow defendant's established landing procedures, poor weather conditions, and a dangerous landing field and surrounding terrain. These factors entitle defendant to exclusion from all liability pursuant to the foregoing provisions of Article 20 of the Warsaw Convention."

5.2. Article 20(2) refers to piloting, handling, and navigation. It is arguable that the "handling" could apply to the aircraft while moving on the ground; the French word is "conduite".

(a) Amended Convention—Article 21

If the carrier proves that the damage was caused by or contributed to by the negligence of the injured person the court may, in accordance with the provisions of its own law, exonerate the carrier wholly or partly from his liability.

(c) MP4—Article 21

(1) In the carriage of passengers and baggage, if the carrier proves that the damage was caused by or contributed to by the negligence of the person suffering the damage the Court may, in accordance with the provisions of its own law, exonerate the carrier wholly or partly from his liability.

(2) In the carriage of cargo, if the carrier proves that the damage was caused by or contributed to by the negligence or other wrongful act or omission of the person claiming compensation, or the person from whom he derives his rights, the carrier shall be wholly or partly exonerated from his liability to the claimant to the extent that such negligence or wrongful act or omission caused or contributed to the damage.

(d) ICAO Convention—Article 20

Article 20 provides:

If the carrier proves that the damage was caused or contributed to by the negligence or other wrongful act or omission of the person claiming compensation, or the person from whom he or she derives his or her rights, the carrier shall be wholly or partly exonerated from its liability to the claimant to the extent that such negligence or wrongful act or omission caused or contributed to the damage. When by reason of death or injury of a passenger compensation is claimed by a person other than the passenger, the carrier shall likewise be wholly or partly exonerated from its liability to the extent that it proves that the damage was caused or contributed to by the negligence or other wrongful act or omission of that passenger. This Article applies to all the liability provisions in this Convention, including paragraph 1 of Article 21.

Comments

1. The burden of proof is on the carrier.

2. *Giemulla* defines contributory negligence as "fault on the part of the injured party: the injured party is at fault, if he or his servants or agents has or have not taken all necessary measures to avoid the damage, although he or they could have taken such measures" (Article 21 (page 5)).

3. *Giemulla* also quotes the definition of contributory negligence in the US Second Restatement of the Law of Tort. This defines contributory negligence, states its types and sets out the functions of court and jury.

4. Under Article 21, the Court applies its own law (*lex fori*) in determining the extent to which the carrier should be exonerated. The ICAO Convention is silent on this point, leaving it open to argument as to whether the law of the court or the law of the site of the accident applies.

5. The official French text refers to "*Faute*" as opposed to negligence. *Faute* is more widely defined. MP4 refers to negligence only in respect of passengers and baggage, and to negligence or other wrongful act or omission in respect of cargo. For "wrongful act" see Comment 1 to Article 6 on page 354. Under the ICAO Convention "negligence or other wrongful act or omission" is grounds for all exoneration of all liabilities.

6. In the USA the law applied by the court was held to be Federal common law rather than the law of an individual US state (*Eichler* v. *Lufthansa* 794 F Supp 127 (SDNY, 1994); 24 AVI 17,847 1992–5).

7. The IATA Inter-Carrier Agreement preserves all defences under the Warsaw Convention. In view of the unlimited liability accepted under this Agreement (see Part 4 of this chapter) there may be a tendency to attach more importance to this defence than previously.

8. Where the Warsaw Convention limit applies, the question arises whether the deduction from the damages is made from the full proven damages before the Warsaw Convention limit is applied or whether the limit is imposed on the damages which are then reduced according to the law and the facts. The better view is the first alternative (Drion, *Limitation of Liability in International Air Law*, (1954) section 110, page 123).

(a) Amended Convention—Article 22

(1) In the carriage of persons the liability of the carrier for each passenger is limited to the sum of two hundred and fifty thousand francs (16,600 SDRs). Where, in accordance with the law of the court seized of the case, damages may be awarded in the form of periodical payments, the equivalent capital value of the said payments shall not exceed two hundred and fifty thousand francs. Nevertheless, by special contract, the carrier and the passenger may agree to a higher limit of liability.

(2) (a) In the carriage of registered baggage and of cargo, the liability of the carrier is limited to a sum of two hundred and fifty francs per kilogramme (17 SDRs), unless the passenger or consignor has made, at the time when the package was handed over to the carrier, a special declaration of interest in delivery at destination and has paid a supplementary sum if the case so requires. In that case the carrier will be liable to pay a sum not exceeding the declared sum, unless he proves that that sum is greater than the passenger's or consignor's actual interest in delivery at destination.

(b) In the case of loss, damage or delay of part of registered baggage or cargo, or of any object contained therein, the weight to be taken into consideration in determining the amount to which the carrier's liability is limited shall be only the total weight of the package or packages concerned. Nevertheless, when the loss, damage or delay of a part of the registered baggage or cargo, or of an object contained therein, affects the value of other packages covered by the same baggage check or the same air waybill, the total weight of such package or packages shall also be taken into consideration in determining the limit of liability.

(3) As regards objects of which the passenger takes charge himself the liability of the carrier is limited to five thousand francs per passenger (332 SDRs).

(4) The limits prescribed in this Article shall not prevent the court from awarding, in accordance with its own law, in addition, the whole or part of the court costs and of the other expenses of the litigation incurred by the plaintiff. The foregoing provision shall not apply if the amount of the damages awarded, excluding court costs and other expenses of the litigation, does not exceed the sum which the carrier has offered in writing to the plaintiff within a period of six months from the date of the occurrence causing the damage, or before the commencement of the action, if that is later.

(5) The sums mentioned in francs in this Article shall be deemed to refer to a currency unit consisting of sixty-five and a half milligrams of gold of millesimal fineness nine hundred. These sums may be converted into national currencies in round figures. Conversion of the sums into national currencies other than gold shall, in case of judicial proceedings, be made according to the gold value of such currencies at the date of the judgment.

(b) Unamended Convention—Article 22

(1) In the transportation of passengers the liability of the carrier for each passenger shall be limited to the sum of 125,000 francs (8,300 SDRs). Where, in accordance with the law of the court to which the case is submitted, damages may be awarded in the form of periodical payments, the equivalent capital value of the said payments shall not exceed 125,000 francs. Nevertheless, by special contract, the carrier and the passenger may agree to a higher limit of liability.

(2) In the transportation of registered baggage and of goods, the liability of the carrier shall be limited to a sum of 250 francs (17 SDRs) per kilogram, unless the consignor has made, at the time when the package was handed over to the carrier, a special declaration of the value at delivery and has paid a supplementary sum if the case so requires. In that case the carrier will be liable to pay a sum not exceeding the declared sum, unless he proves that that sum is greater than the actual value to the consignor at delivery.

(3) As regards objects of which the passenger takes charge himself the liability of the carrier shall be limited to 5,000 francs (332 SDRs) per passenger.

(4) The sums mentioned above shall be deemed to refer to the French franc consisting of $65\frac{1}{2}$ milligrams of gold at the standard of fineness of nine hundred thousandths. These sums may be converted into any national currency in round figures.

(c) MP4—Article 22

MP4 removes "cargo" from Article 22(2)(a) and deals with it in a new Article 22(2)(b), renumbering the existing Article 22(2)(b) as (c). The new Article 22(2)(b) substitutes 17 SDRs for 250 francs (see Part 3 of this chapter).

MP4 inserts a new Article 22(6) which:

(i) defines the SDR and its conversion; and
(ii) enables States who are not parties to the IMF to limit liability to 250 monetary units per kilogram, such units having the same gold content as the Gold Franc.

(d) ICAO Convention—Article 21

1. For damages arising under paragraph 1 of Article 17 not exceeding 100,000 Special Drawing Rights for each passenger, the carrier shall not be able to exclude or limit its liability.

2. The carrier shall not be liable for damages arising under paragraph 1 of Article 17 to the extent that they exceed for each passenger 100,000 Special Drawing Rights if the carrier proves that:

(a) such damage was not due to the negligence or other wrongful act or omission of the carrier or its servants or agents; or

(b) such damage was solely due to the negligence or other wrongful act or omission of a third party.

(d) ICAO Convention—Article 22

Article 22 is summarised as follows:

22.1 Liability for damage caused by delay in the carriage of persons is limited to 4150 SDRs for each passenger.

22.2 For baggage, liability for destruction, loss, damage or delay is limited for each passenger to 1000 SDRs unless a special declaration of interest has been made in the same terms as set out in Article 22(2)(a) of the Amended Convention.

22.3 The limit of liability for destruction, loss, damage or delay of cargo is 17 SDRs per kilogram unless a special declaration of interest has been made in the same terms as set out in Article 22(2)(a) of the Amended Convention.

22.4 This follows the wording of Article 22(2)(b) of the Amended Convention except for express inclusion of "destruction" and the possibility that in certain cases an air waybill may not be issued.

22.5 The limits of liability stated in paragraphs 1 and 2 of this Article shall not apply to damage resulting from an act or omission of the carrier, its servants or agents done with intent to cause damage or recklessly and with the knowledge that damage would probably result; provided that in the case of such act or omission of a servant or agent it is also proved that such servant or agent was acting within the scope of its employment.

22.6 Limits of liability in Article 21 (100,000 SDRs) and in this Article shall not prevent the court from awarding, in accordance with its own law, court costs and other expenses of the litigation including interest. This provision will not apply if the amount of damages awarded, excluding such costs and expenses, does not exceed the sum which the carrier has offered in writing to the plaintiff within a period of six months from the date of the occurrence causing the damage, or before the commencement of the action, if that is later.

(d) ICAO Convention—Article 23

Article 23 is summarised as follows:

23.1 provides for conversion of the SDRs, as defined by the IMF, in the case of judicial proceedings, to be made according to the value of the relevant national currency in terms of the SDR at the date of judgment. Members of the IMF shall apply the IMF method of valuation then in effect. Non-Member

States of the IMF shall value national currency in the terms of the SDR in the manner determined by the relevant non-Member State.

23.2 States who are not members of the IMF and whose law does not permit the application of paragraph 1 of this Article may declare that the various limits of liability in Article 21 and 22 are fixed at the relevant sums of monetary units as specified. Such unit corresponds to $65\frac{1}{2}$ milligrammes of gold of millesimal fineness 900. Conversion into national currency in round figures shall be made according to the law of the State concerned. The units are:

Article 21	(in respect of judicial proceedings in the territory of the State concerned).
Article 22.1	62,500 units.
Article 22.2	15,000 units.
Article 22.3	250 units.

23.3 Calculation of a national currency, in terms of the SDR by a non-member of the IMF in accordance with Article 23.1, and conversion in accordance with Article 23.2 will be made in such manner as to express in the national currency of the relevant State party, as far as possible the same real value for the amounts in Articles 21 and 22 as would result from the application of conversion in accordance with the IMF method of valuation. States shall communicate as specified to the Depository (ICAO) the manner of calculation made pursuant to paragraph 1 and the reuslts of the conversion in paragraph 2 of this Article.

(d) ICAO Convention—Article 24

Article 24 is summarised as follows:

24.1 and 24.2 provide for review by the Depository ICAO at five year intervals of the limits of liability prescribed in Articles 21, 22 and 23. Review is by reference to an inflation factor corresponding to the accumulated rate of inflation since the previous revision or date of entry into force of the Convention. The measure of the rate of inflation shall be the weighted average of the annual rates of increase or decrease in the Consumer Price indices of those States whose currencies comprise the SDR. If the inflation factor exceeds 10%, the Depository shall notify States Parties of a revision to the limits of liability. Such revision will become effective six months after notification unless the majority of the States Parties register disapproval within three months then the question will be referred to a meeting of such States. The Depository shall immediately notify all States Parties to the coming into force of any revision.

24.3 provides for the above procedure to be applied any time provided that one third of the States Parties express a desire to that effect and also the inflation factor referred to in paragraph 1 has exceeded 30% since the previous revision or date of entry into force of the Convention if there has been no previous revision. Subsequent revisions take place at five year intervals.

(d) ICAO Convention—Article 25

The carrier may stipulate that the contract of carriage should be subject to higher limits of liability than those provided for in this Convention or to no limits of liability whatsoever.

(d) ICAO Convention—Article 28

In the case of aircraft accidents resulting in death or injury of passengers, the carrier shall, if required by its national law, make advance payments without delay to a natural person or persons who are entitled to claim compensation in order to meet the immediate economic needs of such persons. Such advance payments shall not constitute a recognition of liability and may be offset against any amounts subsequently paid as damages by the carrier.

Comments

1. Article 22(1): For increase of limit of liability by way of special contract see Part 4 of this chapter.

2. For consideration of the Gold Franc and the Special Drawing Right—see Part 3 of this chapter.

3. Article 22(2) does not specify that the special declaration of interest must be made in writing; compare this with Article 26. CC Cargo 5 states that if the sum entered on the face of the air waybill as "Declared Value for Carriage" exceeds applicable limits of liability and if any additional charge has been paid this constitutes a special declaration of value with liability being increased up to such value. *Giemulla* submits that a special declaration should be made in writing.

4. Where plaintiff made a special declaration of interest pursuant to Article 22(2)(a) he can recover in excess of the specified sum where limits of liability do not apply under the provisions of Article 25. (*Antwerp United Diamonds BVBA* v. *Air Europe* [1993] 4 All ER 469; English Court of Appeal: [1995] 3 All ER 424).

5. *BRI Coverage Corp* v. *Air Canada*, EDNY, 1989; 22 AVI 17,576 1989–90: Where the declared value is less than the liability limit, the claimant can recover only the declared value.

6. Article 22(2)(b) was inserted by the Amended Convention. Under the Unamended Convention the weight of the individual damaged package is applied (*Data Card Corporation* v. *Air Express International Corp* QBD [1983] *S&B* AvR VII/95; [1983] 2 All ER 639).

7. Where there are several pieces of registered baggage without their weight being individually recorded, the weight can be proved by the circumstance of the case, see *Bland* v. *British Airways Board* [1981] 1 Lloyd's Rep 289, CA.

8. The French Cour de Cassation held in *Cie Iberia* v. *Dufaud*, 39 RFDA 187, (1985) that freight charges cannot be claimed in addition to liability limits.

9.1. Objects of which the passenger takes charge. Article 22(3) of both the Unamended and Amended Conventions states that the limit of liability is 5,000 francs, now 332 SDRs, per passenger. These objects include hand baggage, clothing and jewellery.

9.2. Unlike Articles 17 and 18 which expressly impose liability in respect of passengers and registered cargo and baggage, there is no provision which imposes liability in respect of such objects. Article 22(3) leaves unanswered the questions on both the nature of liability, i.e. negligence or presumed liability, and when and where such liability can arise.

9.3. GCC Pax in Article 1 defines unchecked baggage as any baggage of the passenger other than checked baggage which in turn is defined as baggage of which carrier takes custody and for which carrier has issued a baggage check.

9.4. *S&B* suggest that "damage" within the context of Article 17 would cover loss or damage to unregistered baggage where there is also passenger death or injury.

9.5. GCC Pax Article 15.1.2(c) provides that where carriage is not subject to the liability rules of the Warsaw Convention, that the carrier is not liable for damage to unchecked baggage unless such damage is caused by negligence of the carrier.

9.6. Case law suggests that the period in which liability attaches corresponds to carrier's liability in respect of the passenger concerned, i.e. loss or damage arises on board the aircraft or in the course of any of the operations of embarking or disembarking. This includes loss or damage occurring as a result of security check on hand baggage, apparently after check-in but before boarding, at least in the case of *Baker* v. *Lansdell Protective Agency Inc* (US District Court SDNY, June 1984; 18 AVI 18,497 1983–5). Material aspects include:

(i) where the check took place;
(ii) on whose behalf was the security agent working; and
(iii) how did the damage occur.

9.7. If the personal effects are left on board and lost after disembarkation then this could well be outside the operations of embarking and disembarking and therefore there should be no presumption of liability.

9.8. Article 17.1 of the ICAO Convention expressly imposes liability on the carrier for damage to unchecked baggage caused by the carrier's fault. The Warsaw Convention position remains uncertain.

10. Does the limit of liability apply in all proceedings arising out of an incident covered by the Warsaw Convention? Suppose an injured passenger claims against a manufacturer and obtains unlimited damages under product liability. The manufacturer then claims against the carrier. Can the carrier limit his liability to Warsaw Convention limits not only against the manufacturer but possibly against a subsequent claim by the passenger? The Warsaw Convention does not deal with this expressly. The UK enabling legislation, the Carriage by Air Act 1961, expressly states in section 4(1) that the Article 22 limitations of liability apply whatever the nature of the proceedings.

The question in other jurisdictions must be answered on an individual basis.

11. Can interest be awarded by the court above the limit? In the English case *Swiss Bank Corporation* v. *Brinks-MAT Corporation* [1986] QB 853, Bingham J held that interest could not be awarded above Warsaw Convention limits. Judgment was based primarily on Article 22(4) of the Amended Convention which is not found in the Unamended Convention. The question is controversial in the USA in those cases where the Unamended Convention applies. In other States interest has been awarded above limits.

In *Maritime Insurance Co Ltd* v. *Emery Airfreight Corp* 24 AVI 17,381 1992–5 (Article 9, page 239 above) the US Court of Appeals (2nd Circuit) concluded their judgment stating: "Because nothing in the [Unamended] Convention prevents an award of pre-judgment interest where liability is not limited and because the amount in controversy is stipulated and therefore fixed and evident, pre-judgment interest should be awarded." Parties were ordered to pay their own costs.

Once the court has made its award inclusive of any interest within the Warsaw Convention limits, thus creating a judgment debt, interest can be awarded on that judgment debt irrespective of Warsaw Convention limits.

12. Article 22(4) dealing with costs was inserted by the Amended Convention and is therefore not applicable to the Unamended Convention.

13. Article 22(5) of Amended Convention and Article 22(4) Unamended Convention dealing with the conversion of the Gold Franc are dealt with in Part 3 of this chapter.

14. The ICAO Convention Article 21 switches the burden of proof and sense of the Warsaw Convention. Its effect is that, in respect of death or injury, the carrier is liable for unlimited damages above 100,000 SDRs unless it can prove that either Article 21.2(a) or (b) applies.

15. ICAO Convention: The limit of liability in Article 22.2 applies both to checked and unchecked baggage. The power to make a special declaration of interest applies only to checked baggage.

Under 22.5, the limits of liability in paragraphs 1 and 2 are removed in "Article 25 circumstances" of the Amended Convention, see page 270 below.

Article 22.6 clarifies the question of interest in favour of the plaintiff.

16. The ICAO Convention, Article 25 retains the capacity of the carrier to enter into special contracts, although the social requirement for so doing is not so strong.

(a) Amended Convention—Article 23

(1) Any provision tending to relieve the carrier of liability or to fix a lower limit than that which is laid down in this Convention shall be null and void, but the nullity of any such provision shall not involve the nullity of the whole contract, which shall remain subject to the provisions of this Convention.

(2) Paragraph (1) of this Article shall not apply to provisions governing loss or damage resulting from the inherent defect, quality or vice of the cargo carried.

(d) ICAO Convention—Article 26

The wording of Article 23(1) of the Amended Convention above is followed. Article 23(2) of the Amended Convention is transferred to Article 18 as one of the four defences.

(d) ICAO Convention—Article 28

This should be compared with Article 5 of EC Council Regulation 2027/97, see page 304 below.

Comments

1. Article 23(1) underlines the existence of a contract of carriage. That contract in standard airline procedure will include the conditions of contract on the ticket and baggage check or air waybill and also the general conditions of carriage.

2. Provisions which tend to relieve the carrier of liability or fix a lower limit include provisions altering the burden of proof or periods in which notice should be given or claims should be made.

3. For a clear summary of the effect of Article 23(1), see the UK case *Sidhu* v. *British Airways* (HL, 12 December 1996) and also its dicta on Articles 23 and 24.

4. Paragraph 2 was added by Amended Convention.

5.1. In *Attorney General of Canada* v. *Flying Tiger Line* (1987) 61 OR 673 ((1988) XIII *Air Law* 37), the court held that Article 23(2) could only be relied on where the loss or damage occurred because of some characteristic or aspect of the cargo carried and where the carrier was not at fault. A similar view was reached by the Paris Court of Appeal in holding the carrier liable for damage to garlic through delay (*Peronny* v. *Ethiopian Airlines* (Court of Appeal, 5th Chamber, 1975; 29 RFDA 395, (1976)).

5.2. In the decision of the Amtsgericht Frankfurt, 10 November 1995, 32 C1134/95–18, 1996 Transp R 348, the court held that the airline could exclude liability in respect of salmon, shipped as registered baggage, which were spoilt as a result of delay.

(a) Amended Convention—Article 24

(1) In the cases covered by Articles 18 and 19 any action for damages, however founded, can only be brought subject to the conditions and limits set out in this convention.
(2) In the cases covered by Article 17 the provisions of the preceding paragraph shall also apply, without prejudice to the questions as to who are the persons who have the right to bring suit and what are their respective rights.

(c) MP4—Article 24

(1) In the carriage of passengers and baggage, any action for damages, however founded, can only be brought subject to the conditions and limits set out in this Convention, without prejudice to the question as to who are the persons who have the right to bring suit and what are their respective rights.
(2) In the carriage of cargo, any action for damages, however founded, whether under this Convention or in contract or in tort or otherwise, can only be brought subject to the conditions and limits of liability set out in this Convention without prejudice to the question as to who are the persons who have the right to bring suit and what are their respective rights. Such limits of liability constitute maximum limits and may not be exceeded whatever the circumstances which gave rise to the liability.

(d) ICAO Convention—Article 29

In the carriage of passengers, baggage and cargo, any action for damages, however founded, whether under this Convention or in contract or in tort or otherwise, can only be brought subject to the conditions and such limits of liability as are set out in this Convention without prejudice to the question as to who are the persons who have the right to bring suit and what are their respective rights. In any such action, punitive, exemplary or any other non-compensatory damages shall not be recoverable.

Comments

1.1. *Sidhu* v. *British Airways* and *Abnett* v. *British Airways* were important consolidated cases arising out of the invasion of Kuwait by Iraq. The plaintiffs were passengers on a BA flight 149 London-Kuwait-Malaysia. The aircraft landed in Kuwait for refuelling after its invasion by Iraqi forces. Passengers while in the airport terminal were taken prisoner. They brought proceedings against BA in UK outside the two-year limit applied by Article 29 of the Warsaw Convention but within the three-year common law period for negligence. The claims were for personal injury alleging that by reason of BA's negligence in landing in Kuwait after hostilities had started they had suffered physical and psychological damage. They also claimed for loss of baggage.

The significant findings of the House of Lords as the ultimate UK Court of Appeal were:

(i) The Warsaw Convention provided an exclusive cause of action as sole remedy notwithstanding in certain cases that might leave the claimants without a remedy.

(ii) The purpose of Article 23 is to protect a passenger or other person dealing with a carrier against provisions of the kind it describes. Contracting out of liability in contracts is now widely regulated by statute but in the early 1920s carriers engaged in international carriage by air were free to contract on whatever terms they cared to select. The surrender of freedom on this issue was a concession by the carriers which made sense only in the context of the entire set of rules by which their conduct was to be regulated.

(iii) The counterpart of this compromise is to be found in Article 24. On the one hand the carrier surrenders his freedom to exclude or limit his liability. On the other hand the passenger or other party to the contract is restricted to the claims which he can bring subject to the conditions and limits set out in the Warsaw Convention.

(iv) Therefore, claims only lie within the terms of the Warsaw Convention and must be brought within two years and within the meaning of death, wounding or other bodily injury.

1.2. A number of passengers on BA flight 149 referred to above had bought tickets in France and litigated there. The Paris Court of Appeal in their judgment of 12 November 1996 in *Mohamed & Others* v. *British Airways* held that the passengers had valid claims outside the terms of the Warsaw Convention governed by the French Civil Code and they were awarded damages.

2. *Article 24(2)*

The law of the court handling the case regulates who has the right to bring the action.

3. The ICAO Convention makes its exclusivity of the right to bring an action absolutely clear. It supports the decision in *Sidhu v. British Airways*.

(a) Amended Convention—Article 25

The limits of liability specified in Article 22 shall not apply if it is proved that the damage resulted from an act or omission of the carrier, his servants or agents, done with intent to cause damage or recklessly and with knowledge that damage would probably result; provided that, in the case of such act or omission of a servant or agent, it is also proved that he was acting within the scope of his employment.

(a) Amended Convention—Article 25A

(1) If an action is brought against a servant or agent of the carrier arising out of damage to which this Convention relates, such servant or agent, if he proves that

he acted within the scope of his employment, shall be entitled to avail himself of the limits of liability which that carrier himself is entitled to invoke under Article 22.

(2) The aggregate of the amounts recoverable from the carrier, his servants and agents, in that case, shall not exceed the said limits.

(3) The provisions of paragraphs (1) and (2) of this Article shall not apply if it is proved that the damage resulted from an act or omission of the servant or agent done with intent to cause damage or recklessly and with knowledge that damage would probably result.

(b) Unamended Convention—Article 25

(1) The carrier shall not be entitled to avail himself of the provisions of this Convention which exclude or limit his liability, if the damage is caused by his wilful misconduct or by such default on his part as, in accordance with the law of the court seized of the case, is considered to be equivalent to wilful misconduct.

(2) Similarly the carrier shall not be entitled to avail himself of the said provisions, if the damage is caused under the same circumstances by any agent of the carrier acting within the scope of his employment.

(c) MP4—Article 25

The following is substituted in Article 25:

In the carriage of passengers and baggage, the limits of liability specified in Article 22 shall not apply if it is proved that the damage resulted from an act or omission of the carrier, his servants or agents, done with intent to cause damage or recklessly and with knowledge that damage would probably result; provided that, in the case of such act or omission of a servant or agent, it is also proved that he was acting within the scope of his employment.

Paragraph (3) of 25A shall be deleted and replaced by the following:

(3) In the carriage of passengers and baggage, the provisions of paragraphs 1 and 2 of this Article shall not apply if it is proved that the damage resulted from an act or omission of the servant or agent done with intent to cause damage or recklessly and with knowledge that damage would probably result.

(d) ICAO Convention—Article 22.5

5. The foregoing provisions of paragraphs 1 and 2 of this Article [Article 22] shall not apply if it is proved that the damage resulted from an act or omission of the carrier, its servants or agents, done with intent to cause damage or recklessly and with knowledge that damage would probably result; provided that, in the case of such act or omission of a servant or agent, it is also proved that such servant or agent was acting within the scope of its employment.

(d) ICAO Convention—Article 30

Follows substantially the wording of Article 25A of the Amended Convention, but referring to "conditions and limits of liability" in paragraph .1 and inserting at the beginning of paragraph .3 the words "save in respect of the carriage of cargo".

Comments

1.1. The application of Article 25 of both the Unamended and Amended Conventions illustrates differing interpretation by civil and by common law courts.

1.2. The official French version of Article 25 of the Unamended Convention removes the limit of liability if the damage arises from the "*dol*" (French word) of the carrier or from fault which, according to the law of the relevant court hearing the case, is considered as equivalent to "*dol*". "*Dol*" is defined by *Mankiewicz* at page 24 as "an unlawful act or non-fulfillment of a duty done with the intent to cause damage".

Giemulla writes "According to legal understanding in Civil law countries, the concept of 'dol' is defined as knowledge of the actual act and desire of the resulting damage" (Article 25 para 13 page 7).

1.3. French courts assimilated "*Dol*" to "*faute lourde*" which could be translated as "gross negligence", thus making it easier to break the limits of liability imposed by Article 22 (see *Cie Air France* v. *Nordisk Transport* 7 RFDA 105, (1953)). Both English and US decisions followed the "wilful misconduct" concept applied in the English case *Horabin* v. *BOAC* [1952] 2 All ER 1016. The court distinguished between "misconduct" and "wilful misconduct" in the following example:

"You may think that what is actually done matters less than the intention or state of mind of the person who did it. The same act may amount on one occasion to mere negligence, and on another to wilful misconduct. Two men driving motor cars may both pass traffic lights after they have changed from yellow to red. In both cases there are the same act, the same traffic lights, the same cross roads and the same motor cars. In the first case, the man may have been driving a little too fast and he may not have seen the lights until he was too close to them to stop, he did not intend to do anything wrong but he was careless in not keeping a proper look out and in going too fast as a result he committed an act which was clearly an act of misconduct. The second driver is also driving fast but he sees the lights in plenty of time and that they are changing from yellow to red, but he decides that he is not going to bother to stop and although he does not expect an accident to happen he knows that he is doing something wrong. This amounts to 'wilful misconduct'."

1.4. The Amended Convention version follows the common law view. Following the Hague Protocol conference laws enacted in France made clear that *dol* was the equivalent of *faute inexcusable*.

1.5. In the case of an act or omission done recklessly and with the knowledge that damage would probably result, the courts have to apply either the objective test or the subjective test. As Miller in her article "Unlimited Liability of the Air Carrier" explains:

"the subjective test is where the agent's behaviour is assessed in itself. The agent is not required to do what a reasonable man would have done, i.e. the plaintiff must prove that the pilot had actual knowledge that damage would probably result. The objective test is where the agent's behaviour is assessed through a comparison with the behaviour of a reasonable man, placed in similar circumstances, i.e. actual knowledge does not need to be shown. It is enough to show that the pilot should have known."

1.6. Generally the courts have adopted the subjective test. (See: *Tondriau* v. *Air India* (1977) *Pasicrisie Belge 1*, 574 (Cour de Cassation) and *Goldman* v. *Thai Airways International Limited* [1983] 1 WLR 1186 (English Court of Appeal); *Gurtner* v. *Beaton* [1993] 2 Lloyd's Rep 369 (English Court of Appeal)). On the other hand, the French courts have the applied the objective test in a number of cases, see *Emery* v. *Sabena*, RFDA 184, (1968) (Cour de Cassation) and others.

1.7. Under MP4 the legal right under Article 25 to unlimited liability in respect of cargo is removed, but is retained in respect of passengers and baggage.

1.8. Under the ICAO Convention the right of the carrier to limit liability in respect of death or bodily injury of passengers is removed, subject to the provisions of its Article 21, but the limit of liability in respect of delay of persons and in respect of baggage and cargo is retained and can be broken under Article 22.5 which replaces Article 25 of the Warsaw Convention.

2.1. Article 25(2) of the Unamended Convention provides that the limit of liability shall not apply where the agent of the carrier causes the damage by his wilful misconduct, etc. acting within the scope of his employment. Article 25A of the Amended Convention expressly applies the limits of liability unless Article 25 removes those limits.

2.2. When is the servant or agent acting within the scope of his employment? In common law the term "employment" applies to the employer and employee (servant) relationship. The official French version refers to *préposé* acting within the "*l'exercice de ses fonctions*". *Préposé* applies equally to an independent agent or employee, thus limiting the confusion engendered by Anglo-Saxon legal terminology. Theft by carriers' employees is treated in different ways in different jurisdictions. Under New York law theft was not committed within the scope of the employment of the employee of the carrier who is therefore not liable for unlimited liability in respect of theft of cargo on international flights (*Brink's Ltd* v. *South African Airways*, US District Court, Southern District, New York, 1995; [1995] ASLR 349).

2.3. In *Baker* v. *Lansdell Protective Agency*, 18 AVI 18,497 1983–5, the defendant cites the judge in *Denby* v. *Seaboard World Airlines Inc*, 18 AVI 17,494 1983–5, quoting an earlier judgment: "Under New York law, an employee acts within the scope of his employment 'when he is doing something in furtherance of the duties he owes to his employer and where the employer is, or could be, exercising some control, directly or indirectly, over the employee's activities'."

However, in the English decision of *Rustenburg Platinum Mines Ltd et al* v. *South African Airways and PanAmerican World Airways Inc* [1979] 1 Lloyd's Rep 19, CA, the Court of Appeal held that the carrier was liable with unlimited liability for theft by the employee.

2.4. Oberlandesgericht Stuttgart held that a carrier's liability is not unlimited if its employed security guards does not take care of a parcel with valuable watches during a strike, because he is not acting within the scope of his employment (1993, 3U 167/91; (1995) XX *Air Law* 4–5).

2.5. Most aviation activities are carried on by corporations who are artificial legal persons. Such legal persons can act only through servants (also known as employees) or independent agents.

2.6. Article 25A applies only to Amended Convention cases, theoretically leaving open the position of servants under the Unamended Convention. However in the US case of *Reed* v. *Wiser* the Court of Appeals applied the limitation of liability rules under the Unamended Convention to the employees of the carrier (2nd Circuit, 1977; 14 AVI 17,841). This was extended to independent agents in *Baker* v. *Lansdell Protective Agency*, 590 F Supp 165C (SDNY, 1984).

2.7. However the provisions of the Warsaw Convention concerning liability should not extend to agents of the carrier whose functions are not directly performed in relation to the carriage by air. See discussions both in *Giemulla* and *S&B*. There is also case law on the extent and in what circumstances the provisions of Warsaw Convention, other than Articles 25(2) and 25A, would cover servant or agent.

2.8. "Authorised Agent" is defined as "a responsible person who represents an operator and who is authorised or on behalf of such operator to act on all formalities connected with the entry and clearance of the operator's aircraft, crew, passengers, cargo, mail, baggage or stores". Where liability arises under the Warsaw Convention, such authorised agents should be protected by Warsaw Convention liability limits to the extent that their functions are directly related to carriage by air. However, the Definition indicates that the agent's function relates to commercial and official duties, rather than operational ones.

2.9. In the English House of Lords case of *Lloyd* v. *Grace, Smith & Co* [1912] AC 716 concerning liability of a firm of lawyers for dishonest conduct of its clerk, Lord MacNaghten said

"expressions 'acting within his authority', 'acting in the course of his employment' and 'acting within the scope of his agency' as applied to an agent, speaking broadly, mean one and the same thing. What is meant by those expressions it is not easy to define with exactitude. To the circumstances of a particular case one may be more appropriate than the other. Whichever expression is used, it must be construed liberally."

It is a pity that his Lordship did not have the opportunity to comment on Article 2(2)(b) of the Rome Convention 1952 on Surface Damage, see Chapter 10 page 352.

2.10. For further consideration of this topic, see Part 2 of this chapter.

(a) Amended Convention—Article 26

(1) Receipt by the person entitled to the delivery of baggage or cargo without complaint shall be *prima facie* evidence that the same has been delivered in good condition and in accordance with the document of carriage.

(2) In the case of damage, the person entitled to delivery must complain to the carrier forthwith after the discovery of the damage, and, at the latest, within seven days from the date of receipt in the case of baggage and fourteen days from the date of receipt in the case of cargo. In the case of delay the complaint must be made at the latest within twenty-one days from the date on which the baggage or cargo have been placed at his disposal.

(3) Every complaint must be made in writing upon the document of carriage or by separate notice in writing dispatched within the times aforesaid.

(4) Failing complaint within the times aforesaid, no action shall lie against the carrier, save in the case of fraud on his part.

(b) Unamended Convention—Article 26

Under Article 26(2) the number of days in which complaint must be made are:

- Damage to baggage   3 days;
- Damage to cargo   7 days;
- Delay   14 days.

(d) ICAO Convention—Article 31

Article 31 of the ICAO Convention follows Article 26 of the Amended Convention but with the following amendments:

(i) Paragraph 1 "checked baggage" is substituted for "baggage";

(ii) Paragraph 3 reads "every complaint must be made in writing and given or despatched within the times aforesaid."

(iii) Paragraph 4: "If no complaint is made" is substituted for "Failing complaint."

Comments

1. Article 26(1): "*Prima facie* evidence". Delivery without complaint is only *prima facie* evidence of good condition and compliance. Evidence may be advanced to the contrary.

2. Article 26(2): "Days" are current, not working days (Article 35) (see *Mystique Creations Inc* v. *North Star Airlines*, Civil Court, City of New York, 1990; 22 AVI 18,418 1989–90). GCC Pax defines "days" as:

"calendar days, including all seven days of the week; provided that, for the purpose of notification, the day upon which notice is dispatched shall not be counted; and provided further that for purposes of determining duration of validity of a Ticket, the day upon which the Ticket is issued, or the flight commenced shall not be counted."

3. Where the contracting carrier is not the actual carrier, Article 4 of the Guadalajara Convention (see Part 2 of this chapter) permits complaint to either carrier. Where such Convention does not apply then domestic law and facts need to be considered.

In the case of successive carriage (Warsaw Convention Article 30) complaint should be made to the carrier(s) from whom the complainant can claim or intends to claim damages.

4. Complaint does not have to be made where baggage or cargo is totally lost or destroyed. Where a horse became ill following the flight and subsequently died, the court held this was a case of damage where notice was necessary (*Stud* v. *Trans International Airlines*, US Court of Appeals, 9th Circuit, 1984; 18 AVI 17,684 1983–5).

5. "Partial loss" of contents of baggage constitutes damage and therefore appropriate notice should be given. See English case of *Fothergill* v. *Monarch Airlines Ltd* [1980] 2 All ER 696 and cases in other States.

6. There is varied case law as to the position on complaint where the nature of the complaint has changed. In *Bennett Importing Co.* v. *Continental Airlines Inc*, 21 AVI 17,917 (District Court Mass., 1988), the plaintiff notified the carrier of loss of the whole consignment. The consignment was then delivered and the plaintiff failed to complain for delay within the required period. He was therefore barred from claiming for delay.

7. Article 26(3): "Form of Complaint". Complaint in writing is essential. Completion of the carrier's standard property irregularity report may not suffice. In *Fothergill* v. *Monarch Airlines* the House of Lords approved the statement of the court at first instance "as to what Article 26 requires as a complaint": "the complaint must relate to the claim the passenger is seeking to enforce. It must give sufficient notice to the carrier to enable him to make the relevant enquiries". In *Western Digital* v. *British Airways* (see page 254) the court analysed the requirements of the adequacy of the form of complaint and the person by whom it should be made, holding on the facts that no criticism of the complaint's adequacy can be raised where the notice does lead to the appropriate enquiries.

8. Article 26(4): Suggestions on what could constitute fraud by the carrier is given in *Denby* v. *Seaboard World Airlines Inc*, US Court of Appeals, 2nd Circuit, 1984; 18 AVI 17,970 1983–5, where the court quoted with approval Dr N Matte that "the fraud . . . is not of a restrictive nature".

9. CC Cargo imposes a time limit of 120 days in which complaint is to be made in respect of loss. There are conflicting court decisions as to whether such limitation is void under Article 23.

(a) Amended Convention—Article 27

In the case of the death of the person liable, an action for damages lies in accordance with the terms of this convention against those legally representing his estate.

(d) ICAO Convention—Article 32

Follows Article 27 of the Amended Convention.

Comments

In most cases the principal defendant will be a legal person. However the Warsaw Convention extends to servants and agents who may be individuals, for example, flight crew killed in the relevant accident. Domestic law governs any claim against the estate.

(a) Amended Convention—Article 28

(1) An action for damages must be brought, at the option of the plaintiff, in the territory of one of the High Contracting Parties, either before the court of the domicile of the carrier, or of his principal place of business, or where he has a place of business through which the contract has been made, or before the court at the place of destination.

(2) Questions of procedure shall be governed by the law of the court to which the case is submitted.

(d) ICAO Convention—Article 33

1. An action for damages must be brought, at the option of the plaintiff, in the territory of one of the States Parties, either before the court of the domicile of the carrier or of its principal place of business, or where it has a place of business through which the contract has been made or before the court at the place of destination.

2. In respect of damage resulting from the death or injury of a passenger, an action may be brought before one of the courts mentioned in paragraph 1 of this Article, or in the territory of a State Party in which at the time of the accident the passenger has his or her principal and permanent residence and to or from which the carrier operates services for the carriage of passengers by air, either on its own aircraft, or on another carrier's aircraft pursuant to a commercial agreement, and in which that carrier conducts its business of carriage of passengers by air from premises leased or owned by the carrier itself or by another carrier with which it has a commercial agreement.

3. For the purposes of paragraph 2,

   (a) "commercial agreement" means an agreement, other than an agency agreement, made between carriers and relating to the provision of their joint services for carriage of passengers by air;

   (b) "principal and permanent residence" means the one fixed and permanent abode of the passenger at the time of the accident. The nationality of the passenger shall not be the determining factor in this regard.

4. Questions of procedure shall be governed by the law of the court seised of the case.

Comments

1. The action must be brought in the territory of a State party to the relevant Convention. A carrier may have his principal place of business in a State not party to the Warsaw Convention but may perform a contract of carriage subject to the Warsaw Convention. Whether or not the courts of such State will or should accept jurisdiction will depend on the domestic law of such State and the respect of such courts for international treaties.

2. While generally the jurisdictions established by Article 28(1) are considered exhaustive, some Japanese decisions appear to treat the Article as non-exclusive (e.g. *Yoshiko Inoue* v. *Aviacion y Comercio SA*, Tokyo DC, 8 May 1987).

3. *Forum non conveniens*: see Chapter 14 page 411.

4. Taking the four alternative Warsaw Convention jurisdictions in turn:

(a) Domicile of the carrier. The English version is "where the carrier is ordinarily resident". See *S&B* for the reason why (VII/139). Domicile and residence will be determined by the domestic law applied by the court. In the English case of *Rothmans of Pall Mall (Overseas) Ltd* v. *Saudi Arabian Airlines Corp* ([1981] QB 368 and *S&B* AvR VII/368 and on appeal) the court at first instance, confirmed by the Court of Appeal, held the defendant airline was not ordinarily resident in UK, a branch office was not sufficient. *S&B* submit that the location of the seat of Board of Directors is the most appropriate test of ordinary residence.

(b) Principal place of business. *S&B* suggest this is where the main part of the executive and managerial work is carried on.

(c) Place of business through which the contract has been made.

    (i) The official French version is *"où [le transporteur] possède un établissement par le soin du quel le contrat a été conclu"*. Some States interpret the wording strictly, thus not including travel agents and other airlines acting as agents. Courts in other States include such agents within the definition. (See *Eck* v. *United Arab Airlines*, 9 AVI 18,146 1966.)

    (ii) The court must first decide the legal system to be applied in deciding whether a contract has been made or not (see Chapter 3, page 19). There should be no problem where a ticket or air waybill is issued direct to the passenger or consignee. However, where a flight is booked and a "pre-paid ticket advice" is issued in one State and the ticket is issued in another State the contract may well be made in the State of booking.

(d) (i) Destination: It is generally accepted that it is the ultimate destination which is material when interpreting or applying Article 28, not the end of a particular sector. Usually the court will determine the destination from the ticket (*McCarthy* v. *East African Airways*, SDNY, 1974; 13 AVI 17,385 1974–6; *Duff* v. *Varig Airlines Inc SA*, Illinois Appellate Court, 1989; 22 AVI 17,367 1989–90).

    (ii) In the case of successive carriage the ultimate destination is the place of destination (*In Re Alleged Food Poisoning Incident, Al Zamil* v. *British Airways Inc*, US Court of Appeals, 2nd Circuit, 1985; 19 AVI 17,646 1985–6).

5.1. Once jurisdiction is selected in accordance with Article 28 domestic law governs the question of other aspects of litigation, for example service of proceedings, and whether such proceedings should be brought in any specific court or venue.

5.2. UK and USA case law hold that any jurisdiction within the State is adequate, leaving the relevant court in that State to determine which part of such State is the proper forum. (See *Abnett* v. *British Airways plc* [1994] 1 ASLR 1 and *Smith* v. *Canadian Airlines Inc* (Court of Appeals, 2nd Circuit, 1971) 12 AVI 17,143 1972–4.)

5.3. See contrary view in *Swissair Air Transport Co Ltd* v. *African Continental Bank Ltd* [1971] 1 ALR Comm 213 (Nigerian Supreme Court) and also French cases.

6. Article VIII of the Guadalajara Convention (Part 2 of this chapter) permits an action to be brought before the court having jurisdiction at the place where the actual carrier is ordinarily resident or has his principal place of business.

7. ICAO Convention: the fifth jurisdiction (Article 33.2) would increase the opportunity of passengers to sue in their own jurisdiction, for example, the USA where damages can be substantial. Carriers, who code share or who are members of an alliance may find themselves held within such jurisdiction. The fifth jurisdiction resembles option (ii) of the agreement on measures to implement the IATA Inter-Carrier Agreement, see Part 4 of this Chapter, page 299.

(a) Amended Convention—Article 29

(1) The right to damages shall be extinguished if an action is not brought within two years, reckoned from the date of arrival at the destination, or from the date on which the aircraft ought to have arrived, or from the date on which the carriage stopped.
(2) The method of calculating the period of limitation shall be determined by the law of the court to which the case is submitted.

(d) ICAO Convention—Article 35

The wording of Warsaw Convention Article 29 is followed with minor amendments.

Comments

1. As a result of failure to bring the action "the cause of action is now non-existent—extinguished, finished, gone forever" (*Proctor* v. *Jetway Aviation* [1982] 2 NSWLR 264). As observed by *S&B* it follows that the expired cause of action cannot be relied upon by way of defence to an action brought by the carrier.

2. *Korba* v. *Trans World Airlines*, 508 Ne 2d 48 (Ind App, 1987) deals with the relevant date in respect of actual carriage preceding the scheduled date; the actual carriage date was applied.

3. Where the dates as specified in Article 29 differ the latest date applies (*Alltransport Inc.* v. *Seaboard World Airlines* (New York City, Civil Court) 349 NYS 2d 277 (1973); 12 AVI 18,163 1972–4).

This case also deals with the date when carriage stopped in relation to cargo.

4. The applicable limitation period in domestic law for a claim for contribution by the carrier against a third party or vice versa requires consideration. Does the Article 29 two-year period apply? While UK law makes the position clear by section 5 of the Carriage by Air Act 1961 (as amended), this is not so in every jurisdiction. Both French and US cases have held that Article 29 does not apply to claims by carriers against their handling agents. However, in *Connaught Laboratories Ltd* v. *Air Canada* (Ontario High Court of Justice, 1978; 15 AVI 17,705 1978–80; 230 R (2d) 176) the court held Article 29 applies only to claims against the carrier flowing from liability under Articles 17–19 and does not apply to claims arising from the provisions of Articles 10, 12(3) and 16. This case concerns a claim by first carrier against a successive carrier.

5. Generally, it is considered that it is not possible to waive or extend the Article 29 two-year limitation period, as is possible with certain other limitation periods. However, Article 29(2) suggests alternative interpretations:

(i) limited interpretation: The method of calculating the period of limitation relates to questions of when the two-year period starts to run; for example, does the two-year period include the day on which transportation stopped or does it run from midnight that day; also if the two-year period expires on a public holiday or a weekend does the period expire on the first day legal proceedings can be issued; thereafter?

(ii) broad interpretation: The general law of the State may permit the limitation period to be broken or to be extended or, as in the case of infancy, not to start running until the infant comes of legal age. Such provisions of domestic law would make inroads into the concept of the two-year period. Courts in most States have not interpreted Article 29(2) to allow such an extension. However, the French Court of Cassation permitted the suspension of the two-year period in accordance with French law (*Lorans* v. *Air France*, D.89.1977; 31 RFDA 268, (1977)).

6. When bringing the action within the two years it is necessary to bring the action in a competent court (*Giemulla*). See also case law where the action is brought by a person who is not so entitled at first or who seeks to amend the action through change of or addition of a party.

7. In certain States a claim for damages in private law can be linked with criminal proceedings (adhesive procedure). This applies where the examining judge decides to open the case after the preliminary investigation. Whether this adhesive procedure is adequate depends on the domestic law of the State

where the proceedings are taking place. (See Chapter 13 on Accidents and their Investigation.)

8.1. The Dutch Supreme Court held in *FATUM/De Nederlanden van 1845, Schadeverzekering NV* v. *Bondaire Petroleum Company NV* (1995) NJ 20 (Hoge Raad, 7 January 1994) that Article 29 is not a provision limiting liability on which the carrier cannot rely if a ticket has not been issued.

8.2. A similar view was reached in *Asif Sahi* v. *British Airways* (Quebec, 17 November 1997; RFDA 166, (1998)) in respect of conduct depriving the carrier of limits of liability within the meaning of Article 25.

9. ICAO Convention: Article 35 suggests the defence of expiry of the two year period can be waived.

(a) Amended Convention—Article 30

(1) In the case of carriage to be performed by various successive carriers and falling within the definition set out in the third paragraph of Article 1, each carrier who accepts passengers, baggage or cargo is subject to the rules set out in this Convention, and is deemed to be one of the contracting parties to the contract of carriage in so far as the contract deals with that part of the carriage which is performed under his supervision.

(2) In the case of carriage of this nature, the passenger or his representative can take action only against the carrier who performed the carriage during which the accident or the delay occurred, save in the case where, by express agreement, the first carrier has assumed liability for the whole journey.

(3) As regards baggage or cargo, the passenger or consignor shall have a right of action against the first carrier, and the passenger or consignee who is entitled to delivery will have a right of action against the last carrier, and further, each may take action against the carrier who performed the carriage during which the destruction, loss, damage or delay took place. These carriers will be jointly and severally liable to the passenger or to the consignor or consignee.

(d) ICAO Convention—Article 36

The wording of the Amended Convention is followed substantially.

Comments

1. Article 1.3 states the requirements for successive carriage. Article 30 provides the remedy. Article 30 and the Guadalajara Convention deal with different legal relationships although a successive contracting carrier might arrange for its flight to be performed by an actual carrier. See Part 2 of this chapter.

2. The parties must regard the whole journey as one undivided carriage; compare *Bafana* v. *Commercial Airways (Pty) Ltd* (1990) (1) SA 368 (Witwatersrand Loc Div), where an internal trip to Kruger National Park was held part of a contract for international carriage, with *Huxley* v. *Aquila Air Ltd* (page 226 above).

3. See *S&B* VII para 156 for delay on the first sector causing the passenger to miss the flight on the next sector with a successive carrier; the carrier on the first sector bears the liability.

4. In *Kelechian* v. *Air France* the Court of Appeal of Aix-en-Provence (36 RFDA 349, (1982)) held that the tickets produced by the plaintiff were not in the circumstances adequate proof of the existence of an express agreement referred to in Article 30(2).

5. Where Article 25 applies in respect of passengers the contracting carrier is subject to unlimited liability in respect of acts or omissions of the actual carrier under the Guadelajara Convention. In the cases of successive carriage the first carrier is not normally responsible for the acts or omissions of the successive carrier (*Vassallo & Clare* v. *Trans Canada Airlines* (1963) 38 DLR (2nd) 383). The Court rejected the consignee's argument that Article 30(3) gave a new statutory right of action not dependent on contract and not bound by contractual rules for calculations of damage. The Court held that the Warsaw Convention placed the consignee in the position of the consignor and the principles of contract applied (*S&B* VII/624).

6. Successive carriage is brought about in many cases by application of the IATA multilateral interline traffic agreements for passengers and cargo. Non-IATA carriers may participate in these agreements.

CHAPTER IV
PROVISIONS RELATING TO COMBINED CARRIAGE

(a) Amended Convention—Article 31

(1) In the case of combined carriage performed partly by air and partly by any other mode of carriage, the provisions of this Convention apply only to the carriage by air, provided that the carriage by air falls within the terms of Article 1.
(2) Nothing in this Convention shall prevent the parties in the case of combined carriage from inserting in the document of air carriage conditions relating to other modes of carriage, provided that the provisions of this Convention are observed as regards the carriage by air.

(d) ICAO Convention—Article 38

Article 38 of the ICAO Convention follows the wording of Article 31 of the Amended Convention, subject to the application of Article 18.4 of the ICAO Convention.

Comments

1. "Carriage by air" is defined by Article 18 and corresponds to the circumstances in which liability arises under Article 17. See *Arctic Electronics Co (UK) Ltd* v. *McGregor Sea & Air Services Ltd* [1985] 2 Lloyd's Rep 510 as an

example. Any other mode of carriage in any combined carriage will be governed by the applicable domestic law and treaty law. The main question is "How and where did the damage or loss occur?"

2. *S&B* (VII 368) discuss the question of liability where the road vehicle containing the goods is carried on board the aircraft without the goods being unloaded from the vehicle and consider that the Convention on the Contract for the International Carriage of Goods by Road (Geneva) 1956 applies.

3. The conditions of contract on a ticket or air waybill and general conditions of carriage usually incorporated into the contract may also be relevant. For example Condition 6.3.2 of the CC Cargo provides that the carrier is authorised to carry the consignment without notice wholly or partly by any means of surface transportation or to arrange such carriage.

4. The UN Convention on International Multimodal Transport of Goods 1980 is not yet in force. *S&B* comment "Commercial practice is to use, where necessary, one of a number of published sets of conditions of contract, especially those prepared by the International Chamber of Commerce based in part on earlier drafts of the Conventions" (VII 307).

MP4—Article 30A and ICAO Convention—Article 37: Rights of recourse

Both these Articles provide "Nothing in this Convention shall prejudice the question whether a person liable for damage in accordance with its provisions has a right of recourse against any third party."

Comments

There is no similar provision in either the Amended or the Unamended Convention. Its intention is to clarify the position.

GENERAL AND FINAL PROVISIONS

(a) Amended Convention—Article 32

Any clause contained in the contract and all special agreements entered into before the damage occurred by which the parties purport to infringe the rules laid down by this Convention, whether by deciding the law to be applied, or by altering the rules as to jurisdiction, shall be null and void. Nevertheless for the carriage of cargo arbitration shall be allowed, subject to this Convention, if the arbitration is to take place within one of the jurisdictions referred to in the first paragraph of Article 28.

(d) ICAO Convention—Articles 49 and 34

Article 43 follows the first sentence of Article 32 of the Amended Convention.

Article 34 on arbitration provides that parties to the contract of carriage for cargo may agree in writing to settle any dispute on liability under this convention by arbitration which shall, at the option of the claimant, take place within one of the jurisdictions referred to in Article 33. The arbitrator shall apply the provisions of the convention. Any provision in the arbitration agreement to the contrary shall be null and void.

Comments

The provision that "the arbitration proceedings shall, at the option of the claimant, take place within one of the jurisdictions referred to in Article 33" may give rise to misunderstanding. Presumably the option given to the claimant is to choose one of the four mandatory jurisdictions.

(a) Amended Convention—Article 33

Nothing contained in this Convention shall prevent the carrier either from refusing to enter into any contract of carriage, or from making regulations which do not conflict with the provisions of this Convention.

(c) MP4—Article 33

Article 33 of MP4 follows the wording of Amended Convention but inserts the words at its beginning "Except as provided in paragraph 3 of Article 5".

(d) ICAO Convention—Article 27

Follows in substance Article 33 of the Amended Convention with slightly different wording, and expressly gives the carrier the power to waive any defences.

Comments

IATA Resolution 724 establishes the conditions of contract for the passenger ticket. Condition 3(3) incorporates into the conditions of contract "carrier's conditions of carriage and related regulations which are made part [of the contract] . . . ".

(a) Amended Convention—Article 34

The provisions of Articles 3 to 9 inclusive relating to documents of carriage shall not apply in the case of carriage performed in extraordinary circumstances outside the normal scope of an air carrier's business.

(b) Unamended Convention—Article 34

This convention shall not apply to international transportation by air performed by way of experimental trial by air navigation enterprises with the view to the establishment of regular lines of air navigation, nor shall it apply to transportation performed in extraordinary circumstances outside the normal scope of an air carrier's business.

(c) MP4—Article 34

The wording of Article 34 of the Amended Convention is followed but substitutes figure 8 for 9.

(d) ICAO Convention—Article 51

The provisions of Articles 3 to 5, 7 and 8 relating to the documentation of carriage shall not apply in the case of carriage performed in extraordinary circumstances outside the normal scope of a carrier's business.

Comments

1. In the Canadian case of *Johnson Estates* v. *Pischke* (1989), 1 *S&B* AvR VII/ 337, [1989] 3 WWR 207 (Sask) the court applied Article 34 of the Amended Convention. The pilot was a licensed instructor but not licensed to carry passengers internationally and therefore the flight had been performed in extraordinary circumstances outside the normal scope of an air carrier's business. The three others on board were J, J's daughter C and son-in-law D who was under instruction. J intended to pick up a dog in Idaho. D wanted more flying hours. The aircraft crashed in the mountains. The court also stated that the contractual concept of consideration is irrelevant as is apparent from the use of the phrase "gratuitous carriage" in the Article. By way of illustration, a "stowaway cannot attain the benefits of the Convention . . . not because there is a lack of consideration for his flight but rather, because there is no agreement of carriage".

2. Unamended Convention: *Karfunkel* v. *Cie Nationale Air France* (SDNY, 1977), 14 AVI 17,674 1976–8. Hijacking is an accident within the meaning of Article 17 and does not bring the carriage within Article 34. The court held that Article 34 was adopted to protect a carrier who for benevolent purpose undertakes a flight which from its inception is to be performed in extraordinary circumstances outside the normal scope of the carrier's business.

3. ICAO Convention: Failure to issue properly completed documents has lost much of its importance in this Convention.

(a) Amended Convention—Article 35

The expression "days" when used in this Convention means current days not working days.

(d) ICAO Convention—Article 52

Follows Article 35 of the Amended Convention subject to substituting "calendar" for "current".

(b) Unamended Convention—Articles 36–41

These are the Final Provisions of the Unamended Convention. They apply also to the Amended Convention unless modified by the Hague Protocol.
   For Articles 36–38 see Chapter 2 pages 8–9.

Comments

Under UK law, an Order in Council issued under section 2 of the Carriage by Air Act 1961, and certifying who are the High Contracting Parties, is conclusive in the UK to the matters so certified.

(b) Unamended Convention—Article 39

(1) Any one of the High Contracting Parties may denounce this convention by a notification addressed to the Government of the Republic of Poland, which shall at once inform the Government of each of the High Contracting Parties.
(2) Denunciation shall take effect six months after the notification of denunciation, and shall operate only as regards the party which shall have proceeded to denunciation.

Comments

For denunciation see *Starke* page 433 and Article 56 of Vienna Convention.

(b) Unamended Convention—Article 40

(1) Any High Contracting Party may, at the time of signature or of deposit of ratification or of adherence, declare that the acceptance which it gives to this convention does not apply to all or any of its colonies, protectorates, territories under mandate, or any other territory subject to its sovereignty or to its authority or any territory under its suzerainty.
(2) Accordingly any High Contracting Party may subsequently adhere separately in the name of all or any of its colonies, protectorates, territories under mandate or any other territory subject to its sovereignty or to its authority or any other territory under its suzerainty which has been thus excluded by its original declaration.
(3) Any High Contracting Party may denounce this convention, in accordance with its provisions, separately or for all or any of its colonies, protectorates, territories under mandate, or any other territory subject to its sovereignty or to its authority, or any territory under its suzerainty.

(a) Amended Convention—Article 40A

(1) In Article 37, paragraph 2 and Article 40, paragraph 1, the expression *High Contracting Party* shall mean State. In all other cases, the expression *High Contracting Party* shall mean a State whose ratification of or adherence to the Convention has become effective and whose denunciation thereof has not become effective.

(2) For the purposes of the Convention the word territory means not only the metropolitan territory of a State but also all other territories for the foreign relations of which that State is responsible.

Comments

Article 40A was added by the Hague Protocol and forms part of the Warsaw Convention only for those States party to such Protocol.

(b) Unamended Convention—Article 41

Any High Contracting Party shall be entitled not earlier than two years after the coming into force of this convention to call for the assembling of a new international conference in order to consider any improvements which may be made in this Convention. To this end it will communicate with the Government of the French Republic which will take the necessary measures to make preparations for such conference.

This Convention, done at Warsaw on 12 October 1929, shall remain open for signature until 31 January 1930.

ADDITIONAL PROTOCOL

The High Contracting Parties reserve to themselves the right to declare at the time of ratification or of adherence that the first paragraph of Article 2 of this Convention shall not apply to international transportation by air performed directly by the State, its colonies, protectorates, or mandated territories, or by any other territory under its sovereignty, suzerainty, or authority.

Comments

This protocol applies to both the Amended and Unamended Conventions. See Comments on Article 2, page 227.

(d) ICAO Convention—Article 50

The Convention contains the following new provision:

Article 50
States Parties shall require their carriers to maintain adequate insurance covering their liability under this Convention. A carrier may be required by the State Party into which it operates to furnish evidence that it maintains adequate insurance covering its liability under this Convention.

(a) Amended Convention

Chapter II—Scope of Application of the Convention as Amended by the Hague Protocol

Article XVIII

The Convention as amended by this Protocol shall apply to international carriage as defined in Article 1 of the Convention, provided that the places of departure and destination referred to in that Article are situated either in the territories of two parties to this Protocol or within the territory of a single party to this Protocol with an agreed stopping place within the territory of another State.

Comments

This Article casts doubt on the decision in *Re Korean Air Lines Disaster*, see Comments, page 226.

(a) Amended Convention

Chapter III—Final Clauses of the Hague Protocol

Article XIX: As between the Parties to this Protocol the Unamended Convention and the Protocol shall be read and interpreted together as one single instrument and shall be known as the Warsaw Convention as amended at The Hague 1955.

Article XX: Deals with the Protocol remaining open for signature.

Article XXI: Ratification of the Protocol.

Article XXII: Coming into force of the Protocol.

Article XXIII: Adherence by non-signatory states to the Protocol.
Paragraph 2 provides that adherence by any State which is not a Party to the Convention shall have the effect of adherence to the Convention as amended by this Protocol.

Article XXIV: Denunciation of the Protocol.
Paragraph 3 provides that as between Parties to the Protocol denunciation of the Unamended Convention in accordance with its Article 39 shall not be construed in any way as a denunciation of the Convention as amended by the Protocol.

Article XXV: Application of the Protocol for all territories for the foreign relations of which a State Party to the Protocol is responsible subject to any declaration or denunciation made in accordance with this Article.

Article XXVI: No reservation may be made to the Protocol except that a State may at any time declare by notification addressed to the Polish Government that the Convention amended by the Protocol shall not apply to the carriage of persons, cargo and baggage for its military authorities on aircraft, registered in that State, the whole capacity of which has been reserved by or on behalf of such authorities.

Article XXVII: The Polish Government shall give immediate notice to the States as specified and to ICAO of signature, ratification, adherence, denunciation, declaration and notifications made under Articles XXV and XXVI and of the date the Hague Protocol comes into force.

(c) MP4

MP4 Article XIV provides that the Warsaw Convention as amended at the Hague in 1955 and by MP4 shall apply to international carriage as defined in Article 1 of the Convention provided that the place of departure and destination referred to in that Article are situated either in the territories of two parties to MP4 or within the territory of a single party to MP4 with an agreed stopping place in the territory of another State.

Articles XV–XXV are the Final Clauses.

(d) ICAO Convention—Chapter 7

This chapter contains the Final Clauses of which the more important Articles are summarised below.

Article 53.2

The Convention is open for signature by not only all States under Article 52.1 but also for signature by Regional Economic Integration Organisations which means an organisation constituted by sovereign States of a given region which has competence in respect of certain matters governed by the ICAO Convention and has been duly authorised to sign and ratify, accept, approve or accede to the Convention. Except for specified Articles, a reference to "State Party" applies equally to a Regional Economic Integration Organisation. For the purposes of Article 24, references to a majority of the States Parties and one-third of States Parties shall not apply to such an organisation.

Article 53.5

Designates ICAO as the Depositary.

Article 53.6

Provides that the Convention shall enter into force on the 60th day following the date of deposit of the 30th instrument of ratification, acceptance, approval or accession.

Article 55—Relationship with other Warsaw Convention Instruments

Convention shall prevail over any rules applied to international carriage by air:

1. between States Parties to this Convention by virtue of those States commonly being Party to:

     (a) the Unamended Convention;
     (b) the Amended Convention;
     (c) the Guadalajara Convention 1961;
     (d) the Guatemala City Protocol 1971;
     (e) Additional Montreal Protocols 1 to 4.

2. Within the territory of any single State Party to the Convention by virtue of that State being Party to one or more of the Conventions or Protocols referred to in 1(a) to (e).

Comments

1. The title to Article 55 acknowledges the kinship which the ICAO Convention has with "other Warsaw Convention Instruments". It nevertheless stands alone.

2. When the ICAO Convention comes into force but is not widely accepted, applicability of the relevant convention, Protocol or special contract will remain an important and complicating factor.

Article 56—States with more than one system of law

If a State has two or more territorial units in which different systems of law apply to the matters dealt with in the Convention, it may declare at the specified times that the Convention shall extend to all or any one or more of the units. This declaration can be modified. Articles 23, dealing with national currency, and 28, dealing with national law, shall be construed accordingly.

Article 57—Reservations

No reservation may be made to the Convention except that a State Party at any time may declare by notification addressed to the Depository that the Convention shall not apply to:

(a) international carriage performed and operated directly by that State Party for non-commercial purposes in respect to its functions and duties as a Sovereign State; and/or

(b) the carriage of persons, cargo and baggage for its military authorities on aircraft registered in or leased by that State Party, the whole capacity of which has been reserved by or on behalf of such authorities.

The Convention was signed in English, Arabic, Chinese, French, Russian and Spanish languages, all text being equally authentic.

PART 2—GUADALAJARA CONVENTION 1961

"The Convention, supplementary to the Warsaw Convention, for the Unification of Certain Rules Relating to International Carriage by Air Performed by a Person other than the Contracting Carrier", Guadalajara 18 September 1961 ("Guadalajara") came into force on 1 May 1964.

Its preamble states "Noting that the Warsaw Convention does not contain particular rules relating to international carriage by air performed by a person who is not a party to the agreement for carriage . . . it is desirable to formulate rules to apply in such circumstances".

Neither the Unamended nor the Amended Conventions define what is meant by carrier. What would be the legal liability position where one carrier entered into the contract of carriage but carriage was performed by another carrier possibly by chartered or interchanged aircraft?

Professor Manckiewicz describes the background to Guadalajara in his article in (1989) XIV *Air Law* 252, where he refers to it as "The unnecessary Guadalajara Convention". His views and the position generally are summarised:

(a) The official French version of Articles 20 and 25 of the Warsaw Convention refers to *"préposé"* which in the Unamended Convention is officially translated as "agent" in both the US and English translations, and in the Amended Convention as "servant or agent".

(b) It is strongly arguable that *"préposé"* or "agent" covers the actual carrier, i.e. the operator of a chartered or interchanged aircraft, thus applying the provisions of the Warsaw Convention to such carrier as well as the contracting carrier.

(c) Article 25(2) of the Unamended Convention provides that the liability of the carrier will be unlimited where the *"préposé"* in the scope of his employment acted with wilful misconduct. On the other hand Article 25A of the Amended Convention expressly extends the limit of liability to the *"préposé"*. The gap in Article 25(2) of the Unamended Convention was closed in the USA at least with regard to the employees by the US case of *Reed* v. *Wiser*, US Court of Appeals, 2nd Circuit, 1977; 14 AVI 17,841 1976–8. In this case the personal representatives of passengers killed in an accident sued employees of the carrier Trans World Airlines arguing that such employees were not governed by the provisions of the Unamended Convention and therefore their liability was not limited. The Court held that the liability limitation contained in Article 22 did apply in favour of the employees. Liability limitations were subsequently extended to independent agents of the carrier; see *Baker* v. *Lansdell Protective Agency* 590 F Supp 165 (SDNY, 1984).

(d) It was considered incorrectly, originally in the USA, that "carrier" meant actual carrier who performed the carriage and who would be liable in tort not contract.

(e) ICAO legal committee set up a sub-committee to review "the legal aspects of hire, charter and interchange of aircraft with regard to the Warsaw Convention".

(f) Guadalajara came into force in 1964 dealing with "contracting" and "actual" carrier.

(g) In *Benjamins* v. *British European Airways*, (US Court of Appeals, 2nd Circuit, 1978; 14 AVI 18,369 1976–8) it was held that the Warsaw Convention carrier is the contracting carrier and overruled a 1952 decision that the Unamended Convention provided no independent cause of action.

(h) In March 1999 MP4 applying and amending the Amended Convention as between MP4 States came into effect in the USA, who continues not to be a party to Guadalajara.

(i) The ICAO Convention retains the provisions of Guadalajara in Chapter V, Articles 39–48, and replaces Guadalajara as between Party States if and when it comes into force.

A summary of Guadalajara follows:

Article I

Article I Guadalajara applies to both Unamended Convention and Amended Convention carriage.

The German decision of the Landgericht Offenborg 1986, 1986 Transp R 151 ((1986) XI *Air Law* 177) ruled that Guadalajara applies only where State of departure and State of destination are party to that Convention. However, the Belgian decision of *Alliance Insurance Co Ltd* v. *Air Express International USA* (Brussels, 4 March 1991; 26 Eur Tr L 556) ruled that Guadalajara applies if either the country of departure or that of destination has ratified it.

Article I(b) "Contracting carrier" means a person who as a principal makes an agreement for carriage governed by the Warsaw Convention with a passenger or consignor or with a person acting on behalf of the passenger or consignor.

Article I(c) "Actual carrier" means a person, other than the contracting carrier, who, by virtue of authority from the contracting carrier, performs the whole or part of the carriage contemplated in Article I(b) but who is not with respect to such part a successive carrier within the meaning of the Warsaw

Convention. Such authority is presumed in the absence of proof to the contrary.

Comments

1. These definitions beg the questions of what types of persons and transactions fall within the definition of "contracting carrier"? Travel agents, tour operators, freight forwarders and charterers may all in the course of their business be persons who as principals make agreements for carriage governed by the Warsaw Convention. This may happen when a cargo consolidator, having received a number of individual cargo consignments in respect of which he issues his own house air waybill, then consolidates the cargo and the actual carrier issues the master air waybill under which the consolidator can be both consignor and consignee.

Georgette Miller in "Liability in International Air Transport" deals with different possible relationships under both civil and common law.

According to the authorities cited by *Giemulla*, "Travel Agencies, forwarders and other persons can only become contracting carriers where they undertake to perform the carriage, but not where they merely enter into the contract on behalf of a third party in their capacity as agents, sales officers or employees".

2. Condition 5 of IATA Passenger Conditions of Contract (Resolution 724) provides that "An air carrier issuing a ticket for carriage over the lines of another air carrier does so only as its Agent".

3. In addition to the possibility of a tour operator being liable under Guadalajara, he may also be subject to liability provisions of EC Council Directive 13 June 1990 (90/314/EEC) on package travel, package holidays and package tours; Article 5.2 of the Directive provides that compensation may be limited in accordance with the applicable Conventions, which would include the Warsaw Convention.

4. The following cases illustrate the application of Guadalajara:

    (i) *Osman Erdem* v. *Germanair*, Landgericht Düsseldorf, 3 July 1971; ZLW 290. The court held that the Warsaw Convention applied to a travel agency who issued a return ticket Düsseldorf–Istanbul–Düsseldorf indicating Germanair on the ticket as air carrier. Through overbooking the plaintiff took a flight with KLM and arrived for his work a day late. The court held the travel agency was responsible for the delay as contracting carrier while Germanair was the actual carrier.

    (ii) In *Bandelloni et al* v. *Icomsa, Air 70* (Tribunal of Padua, 5 November 1982) the defendant Icomsa organised a trip with an air charter operator Air 70 for a group of technicians to fly Trieste–Algiers. The aircraft crashed. As Icomsa had organised the trip and paid for it, there was no relationship between the carrier Air 70 and the passengers. Therefore both Icomsa and Air 70 were liable under Guadalajara as contracting carrier and actual carrier respectively.

5. While the USA is not a party to Guadalajara, in *Hitachi Data System Corp et al* v. *Nippon Cargo Airlines et al* (US DC North District of California, January 1995; 24 AVI 18,433 1992–5), the court extended Warsaw Convention limits protection to the freight forwarder on the grounds that Federal common law makes clear that a freight forwarder by contracting with a direct air carrier for transportation services assumes the responsibility of the air carrier and is thus deemed to be an air carrier under the Warsaw Convention.

Article II

Article II applies the Warsaw Convention for the whole of the carriage to the contracting carrier, and to the actual carrier for only that part of the carriage performed by it except as otherwise provided in Guadalajara.

Comments

The provisions of Guadalajara must be distinguished from Article 30 of the Warsaw Convention dealing with "successive carriage".

Article III

Article III(1) provides that the acts and omissions of the actual carrier and of his servants and agents acting within the scope of their employment shall be deemed to be those of the contracting carrier also.

Correspondingly, Article III(2) provides that the acts and omissions of the contracting carrier, his servants and agents, acting within the scope of their employment, shall be deemed to be those of the actual carrier in relation to carriage performed by the actual carrier, provided that no such act or omission shall subject the actual carrier to liability exceeding the limits specified in Article 22 of the Warsaw Convention.

Any special agreement entered into by the contracting carrier under which he assumes obligations not imposed by the Warsaw Convention, or waives rights conferred by such Convention or any special declaration of interest in delivery at destination contemplated by Article 22 shall not affect the actual carrier unless agreed to by the latter.

Comments

1. "Scope of employment" will be construed in accordance with the domestic law applied by the court, see page 273 above.

2. The actual carrier is not bound by any contractual increase in or abolition of the limit of liability in respect of death or personal injury. However, where two carriers contemplate a code-sharing arrangement they should consider carefully its impact on any passenger special contract (see Part 4 of this chapter) in the "contractual" and "actual" carrier relationship.

Code sharing is a form of joint venture marketing where one airline agrees with another that the first may use its designator code on flights operated by such other.

Code sharing cannot overrule the liability provisions of the Warsaw Convention and will not overrule the ICAO Convention. It remains therefore necessary to analyse the rights and liabilities of the respective carriers, passengers or cargo interest.

In analysing the position the following should be considered:

   (i) Warsaw Convention and Guadalajara provisions;
  (ii) Conditions of contract on tickets or air waybills;
 (iii) General conditions of carriage, e.g. GCC Articles 2.3, 15.1.2(b);
 (iv) The terms of the code-sharing agreement.

Articles IV–X

Article IV deals with complaints or orders as given under the Warsaw Convention which may be given either to the contracting carrier or actual carrier except that orders given under Article 12 of the Warsaw Convention shall be addressed to the contracting carrier to be effective.

Article V applies the limits of liability under the Warsaw Convention to the servant or agent of the actual carrier acting within the scope of his employment unless he acted in such a way which prevents the limits of liability being invoked. The wording follows Article 25A of the Amended Convention.

Article VI limits the total amount recoverable from both carriers and their servants and agents to the amount which could be recovered from one carrier, i.e. Warsaw Convention limits, but no person shall be liable for any sum in excess of the limit applicable to him.

Article VII gives the plaintiff the right to claim against either or both contracting and actual carrier where carriage is performed by the actual carrier. The carrier against whom the claim is made can require the other carrier to be joined in the proceedings.

Article VIII applies the provisions of Article 28 of the Warsaw Convention to jurisdiction and also permits an action to be brought before the court having jurisdiction at the place where the actual carrier is ordinarily resident or has his principal place of business, thus providing a fifth jurisdiction.

Article IX(1) provides that any contractual provision tending to relieve either carrier of liability or to fix a lower limit than that applicable under Guadalajara shall be null and void but such nullity shall not involve the nullity of the agreement as a whole.

Article IX(2): In the case of the carriage performed by the actual carrier, the provisions of Article IX(1) do not apply to carriage performed by the actual carrier in respect of contractual provisions governing loss or damage resulting from inherent defect, quality or vice of the cargo carried.

Article IX(3): Any provision in the contract of carriage and all special agreements entered into before the damage occurred purporting to infringe the rules of Guadalajara, whether by deciding the law to be applied or by altering the rules on jurisdiction, shall be null and void. Cargo arbitration clauses are permitted as specified.

Article X provides that except as provided in Article VII nothing in Guadalajara shall affect the rights and obligations of the carriers between themselves.

Comments

Guadalajara leaves open the question of the applicable law, for example in respect of a claim for any indemnity by one of the contracting carriers.

Giemulla considers the effect of endorsing a ticket by carrier to another. Does the endorsement constitute a new contract of carriage between the passenger and endorsee or is this an example of the situation Guadalajara is intended to cover?

Articles XI–XVIII

These Articles deal with the coming into effect of Guadalajara.

PART 3—THE GOLD FRANC AND SPECIAL DRAWING RIGHT

The purpose of the Warsaw Convention is to provide a uniform system of regulating liability in international carriage by air.

Liability under both the Unamended and Amended Conventions was, at the time of their negotiation, and still is in many cases, expressed in the currency unit consisting of $65\frac{1}{2}$ milligrams of gold of millesimal fineness 900. This currency unit was selected for the Unamended Convention in 1929 when currencies were either expressed in gold or were easily converted to gold at official rates. Such currency unit was intended to give stability to the various domestic limits of liability which would therefore be unaffected by currency fluctuations. It was called the Poincaré gold franc in the Unamended Convention and is referred to in this book as the "Gold Franc".

The content of the Gold Franc and its conversion into local currency are dealt with in Article 22(4) of the Unamended Convention and Article 22(5) of the Amended Convention.

The subsequent changes in the status of gold raised questions as to the practicality of using the Gold Franc as the measure of liability. These questions are illustrated in two common law cases in the USA and Australia. They are *Trans World Airlines Inc* v. *Franklin Mint Corp* (US Supreme Court, 17 April 1984; 18 AVI 17,778 1983–5) and *SS Pharmaceutical Co Ltd* v. *Qantas Airways Ltd* (Supreme Court of New South Wales, 22 September 1988).

Franklin Mint sued TWA for US$250,000 for the loss of numismatic materials weighing 714 pounds being carried from Philadelphia to London, alleging unlimited liability on the basis that the Warsaw Convention limits were unenforceable in the USA.

SS Pharmaceutical sued Qantas for $AUS111,837, alleging that the current market price of gold applied in converting the Gold Franc to local currency.

The elements taken into account by the courts in reaching their differing decisions are summarised as follows:

Year

1928: France returned to a devalued national franc which was convertible into gold. This franc was accepted as the measure of liability under the Unamended Convention. The Gold Franc was defined not by its national origin but by its gold content.

1929: Conclusion of the Unamended Convention.

1944: Bretton Woods Conference established the International Monetary Fund (IMF). Members of the IMF (including Australia and the USA) undertook to maintain a par value of their currencies, not to change the value of their currencies by more than 10 per cent without approval of the Fund and to buy and sell gold at the official price.

1955: Conclusion of Hague Protocol amending Warsaw Convention 1929.

1968: Two-tier gold standard was instituted. Thereafter the official gold transactions were conducted at the official price and private transactions at the floating free-market price.

1970: Market price of gold began to increase substantially over official price. Special Drawing Rights (SDR) were created by IMF and increasingly became the IMF reserve currency unit. Gold was then the unit of value of the SDR.

1972: USA: Par Value Modification Act 1972 was passed, increasing the official price of gold. Consequentially, the US Civil Aeronautics Board directed air carriers to increase dollar-based liability limits in respect of their liabilities under the Warsaw Convention, such limits to be increased in their tariffs as filed in the USA.

1974: US Civil Aeronautics Board Order 74–1–16 provided the minimum acceptable figures in US dollars for the various limits of liability applicable to international carriage in respect to passengers, baggage and cargo.

1975: Legal Committee of ICAO passed a resolution condemning the use of commodity (market) price of gold for the purpose of converting Gold Francs into national currencies pursuant to Article 22 (Legal Committee 21st Session Minutes 84, ICAO doc. 901 LC/173–1).

1975: IMF Member States formulated Jamaica Accord to eliminate gold as basis of international monetary system.

1975: Warsaw Convention Contracting States drew up in Montreal four Montreal Additional Protocols: 1 and 2 specifically dealing with the Gold Franc:

(1) Montreal Additional Protocol No. 1 amended the Unamended Warsaw Convention by substituting 8300 SDRs for 125,000 Gold Francs for the death or injury limit; 17 SDRs for 250 Gold Francs for each kilogram in respect of registered baggage and cargo; and 332 SDRs for objects of which the passenger takes charge himself.

(2) Montreal Additional Protocol No. 2 amended the Amended Convention by substituting 16,600 SDRs for 250,000 Gold Francs in Article 22 for death or injury and the same SDR values as in Montreal Additional Protocol 1 for the other heads of damage.

Both these Protocols are in force.

1978: IMF Second Amendment. With effect from 1 April 1978 the SDR became the sole reserve asset that IMF nations would use in their mutual dealings. The official price of gold was abolished. The US Par Value Modification Act ceased to be effective.

Various dates: US Civil Aeronautics Board confirms that CAB Order 74–1–16 is still effective.

The SDR is an international reserve asset created by the IMF and is also the unit of account of the IMF. Its value is calculated daily on the basis of five leading national currencies.

In the light of the above events, the US Supreme Court concluded in *Franklin Mint* v. *TWA* that CAB Order 74–1–16 remained in force with a limit of US$9.07 per pound, giving thus a limit of US$20 per kg. Such order applies to all Warsaw Convention limits expressed in Gold Francs. Therefore the limit of liability for death or injury is US$20,000.

However in *SS Pharmaceutical Co Ltd* v. *Qantas Airways Ltd*, the Supreme Court of New South Wales (affirmed by the New South Wales Court of Appeal) held in 1988 that the free market price of gold applied in that particular case taking into consideration statements made in the Australian Parliament at the time that the matter was subject to review by the legislature.

The administrations and courts in various States have dealt with the question in a number of ways:

(1) The court may be obliged to apply the official price of gold under executive order or delegated legislation, e.g. in the USA CAB Order 74–1–16 or in the UK the Carriage by Air (Sterling Equivalents) Order 1996. These laws usually apply values based on the most recent official price of gold, but sometimes increased to take account of changing economic circumstances.

(2) The courts may apply the market price of gold, being substantially higher than the former official price.

(3) In several cases the French courts have applied a conversion from the current French franc, see for example the decision of the Court of Appeal in Paris (1980) in the case of *Egypt Air* v. *Chamie*; later overruled.

(4) Conversion into the local currency may be taken from the SDR as set out in Montreal Protocols 1 and 2, even where such Protocols either had not come into effect internationally or had not become domestic law within the State concerned. See particular cases such as the marine case of *State of Netherlands* v. *Giants Shipping Corporation* (*The Blue Hawk*) (Ref SC 1 May 1981) and the aviation case of *Alitalia* v. *Riccioli* (Rome Civil Court, 14 November 1978). The Italian viewpoint has been confirmed by Law 274 (see Part 4 of this chapter).

(5) SDR is applied in accordance with the domestic law following ratification of or adherence to the Montreal Protocols 1 and 2 by the State concerned after the Protocols had come into force internationally.

Montreal Protocols 1 and 2 only apply between States party to them.

In the meantime in those States where the law is uncertain, the controversy will continue, particularly as long as limits of liability are applied to claims for death or personal injury. However, if and when that aspect of carriers' liability is finally resolved, the question will continue to be an important one in such States for cargo claims, as is shown by the two cases considered above.

When the ICAO Convention comes into effect, it will, as between its parties, bring order to a confused situation. It seeks to tie up its one loose end by its Article 23.2 and 23.3.

PART 4—MEASURES TO INCREASE CARRIER'S LIMIT OF LIABILITY IN RESPECT OF DEATH OR INJURY OF PASSENGERS

The Unamended Convention and the Amended Convention are international treaties. Generally, amendments to treaties cannot be made unilaterally by one State.

In 1955 when the Hague Protocol was concluded, the limit of liability of 125,000 Gold Francs for death, wounding or other bodily injury ("death or injury") was equal to about US$8,300. This limit was doubled by the Amended Convention.

Governments subsequently sought to increase these limits of liability. The Guatemala Protocol 1971 proposed an increased limit to 1,500,000 Gold Francs and an imposition on the carrier of absolute liability for death or injury subject to defences of contributory negligence or state of health of the passenger.

The Montreal Additional Protocol 3 (1975) was drafted to replace the Guatemala Protocol. It substituted 100,000 SDRs for the limit of liability of 1,500,000 Gold Francs. The US Government suggested the implementation of a compensation plan supplemental to the Protocol.

Neither the Guatemala Protocol, nor Montreal Additional Protocol 3 nor any other treaty has come into effect increasing the Warsaw Convention liability limit in respect of death or injury.

The ICAO Convention waits to be ratified.

Article 22 of the Warsaw Convention which imposes the limits of liability provides, "Nevertheless by special contract the carrier and the passenger may agree to a higher limit of liability". The nature of such contract is a private law agreement between the two parties and is not imposed directly by international treaty although government influence and, in the EU, law may prevail upon, or oblige the carrier to enter into a special contract. The contract which provides for a higher limit or abolishes any limit is usually included in the general conditions of carriage.

In the absence of any international treaty the limits of liability have been increased on an *ad hoc* basis by way of special contract under Article 22. The main steps taken to date are set out below:

1. USA Civil Aeronautics Board 18900 (Montreal Agreement) 1966

Due to dissatisfaction of the USA with the limits of liability for death or injury, it not only refused to ratify the Hague Protocol but threatened to denounce the Unamended Convention. Before denunciation became effective a compromise was reached in the Montreal Agreement 1966 filed in the USA under designation Civil Aeronautics Board 18900.

Every non-US airline who requires a permit to operate into the USA and every US airline operating international flights must adhere to the provisions of CAB 18900 under which the carrier must include in the contract of carriage a special provision under Article 22 whereby the limit of liability is increased to US$75,000 in respect of death or injury. Any defence under Article 20 that the carrier took all necessary measures to avoid the damage or that it was impossible for him to take such measures must be waived. Where legal costs are payable in addition the limit is US$58,000. For ticket advice provision see page 230 and in particular comments on *Chan* v. *Korean Airlines*.

2. UK

The CAA as regulatory authority only grants a UK carrier an Air Transport Licence for operation of international services on the condition that such carrier includes in its contract of carriage a special contract increasing the

Warsaw Convention limit of liability to the sterling equivalent 100,000 SDRs exclusive of costs. This practice does not apply to non-UK carriers.

3. Italy

In 1985 the Italian Constitutional Court declared the limits of liability imposed by the Warsaw Convention in respect of death or injury unconstitutional. In order to preserve the integrity of the Warsaw Convention system the Italian legislature passed Law 274 (1988) which provided that

"In the case of international air carriage of persons performed by either Italian or foreign carriers, and also in the case where the contract envisages only a stopover in Italian territory, the carrier may avail itself of the limit of liability provided in the Warsaw Convention as amended by the Hague Protocol on condition that . . . the carrier has established a limit of compensation for each passenger for death or personal injury of not less than 100,000 Special Drawing Rights".

The carrier must also take out adequate insurance cover. For full text and requirements see article by Guerreri in *Air Law*, Vol XIV, Number 4/5 (1989).

4. Japan

The liability limits for domestic air transportation were abolished in Japan in 1982. In order to bring international carriage into line, the principal Japanese carriers abolished the Warsaw Convention limit of liability by way of amendment to their Conditions of Carriage which came into effect on 20 November 1992. The waiver of such limit of liability applies only with respect to passengers travelling on those Japanese airlines, and not to passengers travelling to or from Japan, or elsewhere, on non-Japanese airlines.

The Japanese carriers concerned will not apply any limit of liability to proven damages in respect of death or injury, provided that in a claim for damages above 100,000 SDRs these carriers have retained the defence under Article 20 of the Warsaw Convention.

5. Australia

On 18 October 1994 the carrier's limit of liability for domestic carriage in Australia was increased from Australian $180,000 to Australian $500,000. On 27 July 1995 in respect of Australian international carriers a new passenger liability limit of 260,000 SDRs became effective. The intention of the Australian Department of Transport was to bring liability in international carriage into line with the new domestic limit. The Department of Transport has sought agreement from foreign carriers for voluntary compliance with this limit by way of special contracts although this appears to have been overshadowed by the advent of the IATA inter-carrier agreement on passenger liability.

6. IATA Intercarrier Agreement on Passenger Liability ("IIA")

The IIA is a multi-party agreement between a substantial number of carriers. It waives limits of liability altogether but preserves the Warsaw Convention system.

The IIA is an "Umbrella Agreement" which was endorsed at the IATA Annual General Meeting in Kuala Lumpur on 30 October 1995. While it came into force on 1 November 1996, it did not become effective until 14 February 1997 after it had received the necessary EU and US consents.

The legal rights and responsibilities of the signatory carriers are implemented in their conditions of carriage and tariff filings. These conditions and tariffs are established by the Agreements on Measures to implement the IIA ("MIA").

These Agreements are summarised as follows:

(1) *IIA*: The carriers party to the agreement agree:

1. To take action to waive limitation of liability on recoverable compensatory damages as to claims for death, wounding or other bodily injury for passengers within the meaning of Article 17 of the Warsaw Convention ("Convention"), so that recoverable compensatory damages may be determined and awarded by reference to the law of the domicile of the passenger.

2. To reserve all available defences under the Warsaw Convention, nevertheless any carrier may waive any defence including any waiver up to a specified amount of recoverable damages.

3. To reserve all rights of recourse against any other person including rights of contribution or indemnity.

4. To encourage other airlines to apply the terms of IIA.

5. To implement the provisions of IIA no later than 1 November 1996 or upon receipt of the required Government approvals.

6. Nothing in IIA shall affect the rights of the passenger or claimant otherwise available under the Convention.

7. The Agreement may be signed in counterpart.

8. Any carrier may withdraw on 12 months' notice.

(2) *MIA*:

1. The carriers agree to incorporate in their conditions of carriage and tariffs the following:

1.1 The limitation of liability under Article 22(1) of the Convention will not be invoked in any claim for recoverable compensatory damages under Article 17.

1.2 Carrier shall not avail itself of any defence under Article 20(1) of the Convention with regard to that portion of the claim which does not exceed 100,000 SDRs unless the option in 2.2 below is applied.

1.3 Subject to 1.1 and 1.2, all defences available under the Convention are reserved. All rights of recourse against third parties are reserved including, without limitation, rights of contribution and indemnity.

2. The carrier may include the following provisions in the conditions and tariffs:

2.1 Subject to applicable law compensatory damages may be determined by reference to the law of domicile or of permanent residence of the passenger.

2.2 Carrier shall not avail itself of any defence under Article 20(1) of the Warsaw Convention, in respect of that portion of such claim which does not exceed 100,000 SDRs except that such waiver is limited for the routes and amounts as indicated, subject to any government authorisation.

2.3 Neither the waiver of limits nor waiver of defence shall apply in respect of claims made by public social insurance or similar bodies to which the limit in Article 22(1) and the defence in Article 20(1) will apply. The carrier will compensate the passenger or his dependants for recoverable compensatory damages in excess of such social security payments.

MIA includes further ancillary provisions including the right of any carrier to withdraw from the agreement on 12 months' notice. It should be noted that the provisions of MIA 2.1. are discretionary.

The provisions concerning earlier special contracts referred to in paragraphs 1–5 above remain applicable where the carrier concerned is not party to the IIA and MIA.

7. EC Council Regulation (EC) 2027/97 on Air Carrier Liability in the event of accidents ("Regulation")

The Regulation was adopted on 9 October 1997 and came into force on 18 October 1998.

The effect of the Regulation is summarised as follows:

Article 1

Article 1 describes the purpose of the Regulation which regulates the liability of a Community air carrier arising out of an accident causing death, wounding, or other bodily injury which takes place on board the aircraft or in any of the operations of embarking or disembarking.

Article 2

Article 2 defines the relevant terms including "Community Air Carrier", which means an air carrier with a valid operating licence granted by a Member State in accordance with the provisions of Regulation EC No 2407/92.

Article 3

The following is covered in Article 3:

1. (a) Liability of a Community air carrier for damages in respect of death, wounding or any other bodily injury sustained by a passenger shall be subject to no financial limit.
   (b) Community air carrier shall be insured to up to 100,000 SDRs per passenger and thereafter up to a reasonable level.

2. For damages up to 100,000 SDRs the Community air carrier shall not exclude or limit liability by proving he and his agents took all necessary measures to avoid the damage or it was impossible to take such measures.

3. Contributory negligence is a partial or total exoneration from liability in accordance with the applicable law.

Article 4

Article 4 provides that nothing in the Regulations shall imply that a Community air carrier is the sole party liable to pay damages or shall restrict rights of recourse of the Community air carrier to seek contribution or indemnity.

Article 5

Advance payments for compensation are dealt with thus in Article 5:

1. and 2. Not later than 15 days after the identity of the natural person entitled to compensation has been established advance payments shall be made to meet immediate economic needs "on a basis proportional to the hardship suffered" and shall be not less than 15,000 SDRs in the event of death

3. An advance payment shall not be a recognition of liability and may be offset against subsequent sums paid on the basis of Community air carrier liability. Such payment is not returnable except:

   (i) in the case of negligence as specified in Article 3.3; or
   (ii) where the person who received the advance payment caused, or contributed to the damage by negligence; or
   (iii) where it is proved that the payee was not the person entitled to compensation.

Article 6

The following information on the provisions in Articles 3 and 5 is covered by Article 6:

1. The provisions contained in Articles 3 and 5 shall be included in the Community air carriers' conditions of carriage.

2. Adequate information on the provisions in Articles 3 and 5 shall be available on request to passengers at the Community air carriers' agencies, travel agencies, check-in counters and points of sale. A ticket document or equivalent shall contain a summary of the requirements in plain and intelligible language.

3. Air carriers established outside the Community but operating to/from or within the Community and not applying the provisions referred to in Articles 3 and 5 shall inform the passengers thereof, at the time of purchase of the ticket at the agencies, travel agencies and check-in counters in Member States specified. They shall provide the passenger with a form setting out their conditions. The fact that only a liability limit is indicated on the ticket document or an equivalent shall not constitute sufficient information.

Article 7

The Commission is required by Article 7 to draw up a report on the application of the Regulation not later than two years after its entry into force taking into account electronic developments and developments in international fora.

Comments

1. The Regulations apply to all accidents of Community air carriers and whether the contract of carriage is for international carriage or not.

2. None of the 15,000 SDRs or other funds payable under Article 5 is repayable if for any reason it is an overpayment of damages under the applicable domestic law.

3. The Regulation imposes duties of disclosure of information on non-Community air carriers.

PART 5—AIR CARRIERS' LIABILITY FOR NON-INTERNATIONAL CARRIAGE OF PASSENGERS, BAGGAGE AND CARGO

There are two types of non-international carriage:

(i) carriage which is *international* in the commonly accepted sense of the word, i.e. carriage between States but which is not "international carriage" as defined in the Warsaw Convention;

(ii) domestic air carriage, i.e. the contract of carriage for an internal flight within one State.

In the event of death, injury or delay to passengers or destruction, loss, damage or delay of baggage or cargo under a contract of carriage by air between two States not governed by the Warsaw Convention, each State has its own domestic law regulating the position of the parties. It is therefore necessary for the court to decide the applicable domestic law. Therefore there may be a "conflict of laws". This can be solved by the parties' express choice of law or by applying rules which take into account factors such as the law of the place where the contract was made.

Where for example there is a contract of carriage for a flight from London to Bangkok, if the accident occurred in Thailand and the claim is brought there, the Thai courts may well apply Thai law. If the claim is brought in the UK the applicable law is set out in Schedule 1 to the Carriage by Air Acts (Application of Provisions) Order 1967 which applies provisions similar to the Amended Convention but with a statutory limit of liability of 100,000 SDRs in respect of "death or wounding" of a passenger. Corresponding provisions apply to cargo and baggage.

It is therefore not possible under UK law for an air carrier to exempt itself from liability in respect of passengers, baggage or cargo. To the extent liability can be regulated by contract rather than by State law, see Article 15 of GCC Pax.

In the UK similar provisions apply where the contract is for a domestic flight (e.g. London–Manchester) where Schedule 1 to the 1967 Order also applies. In other States liability may either follow Warsaw Convention principles or be strict or arise in negligence. Liability may be unlimited.

The current position can be contrasted with the earlier common law position in the Canadian domestic carriage case of *Ludditt* v. *Ginger Coote Airways Ltd* [1947] AC 233 where the Judicial Committee of the Privy Council held that the contract of carriage effectively excluded the carrier's liability for bodily injury caused by negligence of the carrier. However, in *Fosbroke-Hobbes* v. *Airwork Ltd and British American Air Services Ltd* [1937] 1 All ER 109 the condition excluding liability was not incorporated in the contract of carriage for the UK domestic flight. Goddard J found the carrier guilty of negligence on the basis of *res ipsa loquitur* (a thing speaks for itself, i.e. negligence is assumed from the facts). The damages of £10,000 were awarded to the widow and daughter on the death of the passenger who had a life expectancy of 30 years and good prospects.

In the USA in domestic carriage the carrier may be liable in negligence as a common carrier for unlimited liability. Principles of negligence are considered in Chapter 11 on product liability. Sometimes the court is prepared to assume negligence from the circumstances without the claimant having to prove lack of care, i.e. *res ipsa loquitur*.

For example, in *Andrews* v. *United Airlines Inc*, US Court of Appeals, 9th Circuit 1994; 24 AVI 18,072, the plaintiff was injured by a briefcase falling from an overhead compartment. The parties agreed that the defendant was a common carrier and as such "owes both a duty of utmost care and the vigilance of a very cautious person towards its passengers". The defendant was refused summary judgment.

On the other hand in *Sheffer* v. *Springfield Airport Authority, American Airlines Inc et al* (Illinois Appellants Court, 1994; 24 AVI 18,094 1992–5), neither the airline as common carrier, nor the airport authority owed a passenger a duty of care to warn her against slipping on the ice when disembarking. Compare this with Warsaw Convention cases discussed in paragraph 6.3 of the comments on page 251 above.

Therefore the relevant law may:

(1) Be uniform for both domestic carriage and carriage between sovereign States not being "international carriage" within the meaning of the Warsaw Convention;

(2) Apply provisions similar to the Warsaw Convention; or

(3) Apply a general law on carriage as in the two US cases above.

The following decisions illustrate the conflict of laws position:

1. *Barkanic and Fox* v. *Civil Aviation Administration of the People's Republic of China (CAAC)* (US Court of Appeals, 1991; 23 AVI 17,253 1991–2). This was an action by the widows of Mr Barkanic and Mr Fox who booked with a travel agent in Washington DC tickets for a domestic flight in the People's Republic of China from Nanjing to Beijing. The two men were killed in an accident. The resultant litigation established:

(i) There was sufficient nexus between the commercial activity in the USA of the aviation agency of the People's Republic of China and the accident to give subject matter jurisdiction in the USA under the Foreign Sovereign Immunities Act.

(ii) Choice of law rules under FSIA dictated that the law of the People's Republic of China applied in the wrongful death action. The airline's motion for partial summary judgment limiting its liability to $20,000 per passenger pursuant to Chinese law was granted.

2. The UK decision of *Holmes* v. *Bangladesh Biman Corp* ([1989] 2 WLR 481, House of Lords, 1989) illustrates both application of the law of non-international carriage and the extent of the power of a State to legislate on matters outside its territory:

Mr Holmes was killed in an accident to the defendant's aircraft on which he was travelling under a domestic contract of carriage within Bangladesh from Chittagong to Dhaka. The widow plaintiff sued in England and asserted her claim was governed by the UK 1967 Order with a limit of liability of 100,000 SDRs (£83,763) as opposed to the Bangladesh limit of liability, being approximately £913.

The House of Lords held that despite the wide wording of section 10(1) of the enabling Carriage by Air Act 1961, the section should be construed as authorising delegated legislation which should be limited to carriage wholly within the UK, or non-Warsaw Convention carriage involving a place of departure or destination or an agreed stopping place in the UK or other British territory.

While the above case law refers to passengers it applies equally to cargo.

Jurisdiction

This question will be covered by the law of the State where the action is brought. Where Article 28 of the Warsaw Convention does not apply, the carrier may be more exposed to being made a co-defendant or third party in multi-party litigation, for example where a US manufacturer is also a defendant. See also Chapter 14.

PART 6—MAIL

The Definitions define mail as "Dispatches of correspondence and other objects tendered by and intended for delivery to postal administrations".

The Unamended Convention states that it shall not apply to carriage performed under the terms of any international postal convention.

The Amended Convention states that it shall not apply to carriage of mail and postal items.

MP4 and the ICAO Convention state that in the carriage of postal items the carrier shall be liable only to the relevant postal administration in accordance with the rules applicable to the relationship between the carriers and the postal administrations.

The international carriage of mail by air is performed by the air carrier usually under agreement with the postal administration of the State concerned. Such carriage is regulated at government level by the Universal Postal Union (UPU) which was originally established by the Treaty of Berne in 1874. UPU is now regulated by its Constitution concluded at Vienna in 1964. The Constitution, General Regulations, Detailed Regulations and the Universal Postal Convention make up the Acts of the UPU. This structure is explained in the Australian case of *WestPac Banking Corporation & Another* v. *Royal Tongan Airlines, Qantas Ltd & Others* (Supreme Court of New South Wales, Commercial Division, 1996).

The Postal Parcels Agreement and the Money Orders Agreement were concluded in 1994 at Seoul.

Under the Universal Postal Convention ("UP Convention") letter post items may be sent Registered, Recorded Delivery, Insured and Express.

Under Articles 34 and 35 of the UP Convention postal administrations exempt themselves from liability except for registered mail for which there is a limited liability of 30 SDRs for each item.

Refund of charges paid can be made in respect of loss of recorded delivery items.

Postal administrations are liable for loss, damage or theft of an insured item up to its value as specified.

The Postal Parcels Agreement 1994 provides under Article 26 that, subject to certain exceptions, postal administrations shall be liable for loss, theft or damage for insured parcels up to their insured value as specified expressed in SDRs and for uninsured parcels up to a limit of a combined rate of 40 SDRs per parcel and 4.5 SDRs for each kilo; consequential losses and loss of profits shall not be taken into account.

Article 27 specifies the circumstances where the administrations shall not be liable.

In accordance with standard treaty procedures, the relevant provisions of the UPU should be incorporated into domestic law.

The following cases demonstrate the position:

1. UK: *Moukataff* v. *BOAC* [1967] 1 Lloyd's Rep 396. The plaintiff instructed his bank in London to despatch £20,000 in bank notes by registered airmail from London to Kuwait. The registered packet was delivered to BOAC and stolen by a BOAC loader.

The court held that although BOAC was acting as agent for the Crown (the UK postal administration) it was not exempt from full liability as was the administration. BOAC owed the sender a common law duty.

The court classified the relationship between the sender and the postal administration as one of bailment and, if the relationship between the postal administration and BOAC was sub-bailment, BOAC owed a duty to the sender as bailee.

Bailment is delivery by the bailor to the bailee of goods for a specific purpose. The goods should be redelivered or disposed of in conformity with instructions. It is an ancient form of legal relationship in England pre-dating general contractual principles and liability in tort.

Following this case section 29(3) the Post Office Act 1969 was enacted extending the immunity of the postal administration to its servants and agents, except at the suit of the administration itself.

Subsequent to the change in law, the court held in the English case of *American Express Co & Another* v. *British Airways Board* [1983] 1 All ER 557 (QBD) that British Airways was immune from suit and that exemption from suit in tort also extended to bailment.

Although Article 4 of Carriage by Air Acts (Application of Provisions) Order 1967 extended "Warsaw Convention" liability to the carriage of mail or postal packages, section 29(3) of the Post Office Act 1969 protected the air carrier in the circumstances.

2. USA: In the US case of *Lerakoli Inc & Other* v. *Pan American World Airways Inc* (19 AVI 18,131 1986), the US Court of Appeals ruled that the defendant Pan American World Airways Inc was an agent of the US postal service and was entitled to liability limitations attaching to the postal administration. The

amount claimed was US$4.8 million and the limit of liability which applied was US$173.36.

The court referred to *Moukataff* v. *BOAC* and confirmed that the concept of bailment would be applied in US law.

Pan American World Airways was entitled to the exemption without any express provision under US domestic law concerning such entitlement.

In reaching its decision the court drew an analogy from the Warsaw Convention, referring both to *Reed* v. *Wiser* (page 291) and to *Baker* v. *Lansdell Protective Agency Inc* (page 292) where the Warsaw Convention limitations were extended to employees and independent agents respectively (see paragraph (c) on page 291).

3. Australia: In *WestPac Banking Corp & Another* v. *Royal Tongan Airlines, Qantas Airways Ltd & Another* the court accepted the relationship of bailment and exemption of liability available under the UPC. However, the defendant Qantas was not entitled to the exemption as it could not prove that the loss occurred when it was acting as the mail handler of the postal administration.

4. France: In *Cie Nationale Air France* v. *Bureau d'Etudes Techniques Atelier* (Versailles CA, 14 December 1995) the court held that the air carrier was entitled to the exemption from liability of the French postal administration, as the person used by the administration to fulfil its mission. The claim was for the loss of a "chance to win" competition due to delay in delivery of a parcel consigned from France to the Wallis and Futuna Islands. The court exonerated Air France from all liability, even in the case of *faute lourde* ("gross negligence"). Wallis and Futuna Islands are a French overseas territory.

Chapter 4 of the Airport Handling Manual (page 324 of this book) and Annex 9 paragraphs 2.10 (page 102), 4.59 (page 112), 6.1 (page 112) and 7.4 (page 116) deal with documentation and procedures for the shipment and handling of mail.

CHAPTER 8

GENERAL AVIATION AND
AERIAL WORK

Annexes 6, 9 and 15 define a general aviation operation as "an aircraft operation other than a commercial air transport operation or an aerial work operation".

Annex 6, Part I defines a commercial air transport operation as an aircraft operation involving the transport "of passengers, cargo or mail for remuneration or hire".

The Definitions define aerial work as "an aircraft operation in which an aircraft is used for specialised services such as agriculture, construction, photography, surveying, observation and patrol, search and rescue, aerial advertisement, etc.".

The SARPS apply to general aviation and aerial work, for example Annex 2 on Rules of the air, unless otherwise expressly provided as for example in Annex 6.1.

General aviation hovers between the definition of "commercial air transport" and an "etcetera" of aerial work; it is helpful to consider briefly these concepts.

PART 1. COMMERCIAL AIR TRANSPORT

Chapter 2 of Annex 6, Part I provides that its SARPS shall apply to all operations of aircraft by operators authorised to conduct international commercial air transport operations. These SARPS therefore apply not only to specific operations for remuneration or hire but also to gratuitous operations by an operator authorised to conduct operations for remuneration or hire. These provisions correspond to the definition of carriage to which the Warsaw Convention applies, i.e. carriage for reward or gratuitous carriage by an air transport undertaking.

4.2.1.1 of Annex 6, Part I provides that the operator shall not engage in commercial air transport operations without a valid air operator's certificate or equivalent document issued by the State of Operator.

Carriage for remuneration or hire could still remain commercial air transport operation even if the carrier did not have the requisite authority. However, such carriage is likely to be unlawful under domestic law.

The terms *"rémunération"* (French), "remuneration", "reward", "hire", "remuneration and/or hire" and latterly in the UK "valuable consideration" are mentioned elsewhere in this book.

PART 2.   AERIAL WORK

The Definition of "aerial work" is followed in the main by the ICAO Manual on Aerial Work, First Edition, 1984 (doc. 9408) which lists seven main classes of aerial work:

  (i)   aerial application;
 (ii)   aerial survey;
(iii)   aerial observation and patrol;
 (iv)   aerial construction;
  (v)   aerial communication;
 (vi)   production of air turbulence;
(vii)   emergency operations (e.g. fire fighting, SAR and medical evacuation).

The Manual subdivides each of these seven classes into different activities but deals almost exclusively with aerial application.

In dealing with the "etc." not much help is given by the Foreword to Annex 6, Part II which deals with international general aviation. It states that in 1986 the "Air Navigation Commission . . . concluded that the definition of general aviation should be revised to exclude aerial work thus recognising that aerial work was a distinct aspect of civil aviation", and also that the Commission "was not aware of any degree of international aerial work operations which would necessitate the development of International Standards and Recommended Practices".

This view has not inhibited ICAO from issuing its Manual on Aerial Work.

The ICAO Definition of aerial work specifies that the aircraft is used for specialised services. It is therefore likely that the "etc." is intended to refer to other forms of specialised services.

The type of activities which general aviation should cover would be the use of corporate aircraft, all aspects of private flying and training including club and competitive flying.

In the USA neither "General Aviation" nor "Aerial Work" appear in the definitions in Part 1 of the Federal Aviation Regulations while "Commercial Operator" and "Air Carrier" are so defined.

However, in the US General Aviation Revitalisation Act 1994 a general aviation aircraft is for the purposes of such Act defined as:

"any aircraft for which a type certificate or an airworthiness certificate has been issued by the Administrator of the FAA, which, at the time such certificate was originally issued, had a maximum seating capacity of fewer than 20 passengers, and which was not, at the time of the accident, engaged in scheduled passenger-carrying operations as defined under the regulations in effect under the Federal Aviation Act of 1958 (49 USC App 1301 *et seq.*) at the time of the accident".

The Act imposes a limitation period of 18 years running from the date of delivery of the aircraft or from replacement with a new component for an old component in respect of any civil action for damages for death, injury or property damage. The Act was made law to give some support to general aviation manufacturers who had suffered severely from high jury awards for damages and consequential substantial increase in insurance premiums.

For application of the Act see *Attseimer* v. *Bell Helicopter Textron* (US District Court, East District California, 1996; 25 AVI 17,272), when summary judgment was given in favour of the manufacturer.

Under UK domestic law there are for the purposes of regulation by way of the issue or withholding of the AOC three operational categories:

(i) public transport;
(ii) aerial work;
(iii) private flight.

An aircraft in flight shall, for the purposes of the ANO, be deemed to fly for the purposes of public transport

(a) if valuable consideration is given or promised for the carriage of passengers or cargo in the aircraft on that flight;
(b) if the passengers (as specified and defined) or cargo are carried gratuitously by an air transport undertaking on that flight; or
(c) for the purposes of Part III of the ANO dealing with airworthiness and equipment if valuable consideration is given or promised for the primary purpose of conferring on a particular person the right to fly the aircraft on that flight (not being a single seat aircraft as specified) otherwise than under a hire purchase or conditional sale agreement.

However, the definition continues at length to treat certain operations as exceptions which would unrealistically be caught within the definition of public transport (ANO Article 119).

"Air transport undertaking" is defined as an undertaking whose business includes the undertaking of flights for the purposes of public transport of passengers or cargo (ANO Article 118).

The definition underlines the importance of whether working personnel on board the aircraft are passengers or not; see *Fellowes (or Herd)* v. *Clyde Helicopters Ltd* (page 248 above), Definition of crew, and *S&B* (IV) (50).

JAR 1 states that "commercial air transportation" means the transportation by air of passengers, cargo or mail for remuneration or hire.

JAR follows the ICAO Definition of Aerial Work.

ANO Article 119 defines aerial work as any purpose (other than public transport) for which an aircraft is flown if valuable consideration is given or promised in respect of the flight, or the purpose of the flight. If the only valuable consideration consists of remuneration for the services of the pilot, the flight shall be deemed to be a private flight.

Again there are a substantial number of definitions and exceptions to cover different operational situations where the legislature does not consider that the operation should fall into the categories of public transport or aerial work, thus constituting the particular flight as a private flight.

"Private flight" means a flight which is neither for the purpose of aerial work nor public transport. Therefore the ICAO Definition of general aviation covers both UK "private flight" and some aspects of UK "aerial work".

Whatever the uncertainty attributable to the term "general aviation", people believe they know what they mean when they talk about it. ICAO devotes Part II of Annex 6 to it; CAA issue a series of General Aviation Safety Sense and Safety Information leaflets; safety committees, trade associations and journals are dedicated to it. It is not, however, a term which appears in UK legislation.

Whatever the terminology and regulatory position as between ICAO SARPS and domestic law systems, it is the applicable domestic law which is important in any given situation. Therefore, if in doubt, the operator or pilot who proposes to undertake a flight must ask himself:

(i) How is the proposed operation classified under the appropriate domestic law?

(ii) Do I or my enterprise need an AOC or other form of authority, e.g. Aerial Application Certificate, for the operation?

(iii) Does the operation need an air transport licence or an EC operating licence or similar authority?

(iv) Are the categories of crew licences and maintenance adequate?

(v) Is the Certificate of Airworthiness adequate?

(vi) Should a ticket or airway bill be issued to limit liability?

(vii) Would any liability against me or my enterprise be based on negligence, strict liability, presumed liability or otherwise?

(viii) Does my or my enterprise's insurance cover the selected activity and has full disclosure been made to my insurers?

PART 3. ICAO MANUAL ON AERIAL WORK

While the Manual is titled Aerial Work, a substantial part of it is taken up with Aerial Application (see Foreword). A few comments on the Manual follow:

Chapter 5: This deals specifically with safe operating procedures including the ICAO 11-point safety guide for agricultural operations which are described in an abbreviated form as follows:

(i) Special selection and training of the pilot;

(ii) Pilot abides by common sense personal practices concerning food, drink, drugs etc.;

(iii) Special design or modification of the aircraft for the task is required;

(iv) Take-off and landing area conform to minimum safety standards;

(v) Structural limitations of the aircraft are known and taken into account and aircraft is maintained in an airworthy condition;

(vi) Physical limitations of pilot are assessed and taken into account, e.g. fatigue;

(vii) Protective helmet and harness are used at all times;

(viii) Local obstacles are ascertained and taken into account;

(ix) Local meteorological conditions are studied and taken into account;

(x) Aircraft operating data is ascertained and taken into account;

(xi) A study is made of toxic characteristics of chemicals to be used.

Chapter 6 deals with the responsibilities of States; the introductory note refers to an example of State regulations contained in Attachment B.

Article 6.1:   Normally the protection of persons from the consequences of their employer's or their own disregard of safety precautions is subject to the State's industrial regulations. However, it is quite common to have additional regulations applying specifically to the aerial application industry.

Article 6.1.2:   There is a considerable amount of movement involved in international agricultural operations.

Article 6.1.4:   Substantially repeats paragraph 1.2.5 of the ICAO Manual of Procedures for Operations, Inspection, Certification and Continued Surveillance (doc. 8335 AN–879), see page 77.

The rest of the chapter goes on to deal with specific regulatory practices concerning:

- Aerodromes;
- Certification of operations;
- Training and licensing of personnel;
- Flight time limitations.

Attachment B sets out suggested regulations concerning approval of agricultural operators and pilots.

For an example of domestic law Regulations on aerial application, see Article 50 of the ANO, which deals with the requirements for an aerial application certificate, the procedures for its issue and the provision of an aerial application manual.

CHAPTER 9

AIRPORTS AND GROUND HANDLING

PART 1. DEFINITIONS

The Definitions of "Aerodrome", "Apron" and "Manoeuvring area" are on page 164 above. Other Definitions include "International Airport": An airport designated by the Contracting State in whose territory it is situated as an airport of entry and departure for international air traffic, where the formalities incident to customs, immigration, public health, animal and plant quarantine and similar procedures are carried out.

"Heliport": An aerodrome for use by helicopters only.

The term "Airport" is used in this chapter.

PART 2. PUBLISHED DETAILS

Aeronautical Information Publication (AIP)

Details of the operational characteristics of an airport and the services it provides are given in the AIP (see Annex 15 in Chapter 5 above). Such characteristics and services are often material in a liability situation.

London Gatwick Airport in the UK AIP is an example. Its entry consists of 20 pages of written material and a list of 29 related charts.

The following is a list of 24 headings in the entry:

AD2.1: Name of city and aerodrome—EG KK London Gatwick;
AD2.2: Location, elevation, administration, address and traffic permitted (IFR/VFR) and similar topics;
AD2.3: Operational hours;
AD2.4: Handling services and facilities including type of fuel, hangar space, de-icing and repair facilities;
AD2.5: Passenger facilities, hotels, restaurants, medical, transportation and other facilities;
AD2.6: Rescue and fire-fighting facilities including capability for removal of disabled aircraft;
AD2.7: Seasonal availability—clearing;
AD2.8: Aprons, taxiways and location data;

AD2.9:   Surface markings;

AD2.10:   Aerodrome obstacles;

AD2.11:   Meteorological information provided;

AD2.12:   Runway physical characteristics;

AD2.13:   Declared distances;

AD2.14:   Approach and runway lighting;

AD2.15:   Other lights, secondary power supply;

AD2.16:   Helicopter landing area;

AD2.17:   ATS airspace (this entry for example includes limits and airspace classification of the London Gatwick Control Area, and Traffic Zone);

AD2.18:   ATS communication facilities;

AD2.19:   Radio navigation and landing aids;

AD2.20:   Local traffic regulations (these are broken down into six sections: airport regulations, ground movement, category II/III operations, warnings, helicopter operations, and use of runways);

AD2.21:   Noise Abatement Procedures (this sets out the Gatwick Airport/ London interim (noise abatement requirements) Notice 1997 made under section 78 of the Civil Aviation Act 1982);

AD2.22:   Flight procedures (this sets out 15 sections on various aspects of such procedures);

AD2.23:   Additional information (currently blank);

AD2.24:   A list of 29 charts related to the aerodrome.

PART 3. LIABILITY OF PERSONS INVOLVED IN AIRPORT OPERATIONS

(i) Regulatory authorities

In order to comply with domestic regulatory procedures, it is usually necessary that the airport should be licensed by the regulatory authority to ensure that it meets national standards which should correspond at the least to the Annex 14 SARPS; see ANO Articles 90 and 92 and comments on *West* v. *FAA* at the end of Annex 14, page 173. Liability is most likely to arise in tort, including breach of statutory duty (where such remedy is available).

(ii) Airport operator

The operator may be the State, statutory corporation, local authority or private enterprise. The regulatory authority should not be the same person as the operator. The legal obligations of the operator will be assessed in the light of the Annexes, the AIP, the Aerodrome Licence and domestic law.

Liability of the operator can arise both in contract and tort.

(a) Contract

In certain cases the operator may try to exclude his liability towards users of the airport. Sometimes an exculpatory clause is included in General Conditions of Use of the Airport which may be contained in the relevant AIP, or issued in some other manner. Whether these conditions have been brought properly to the notice of the party concerned or whether they are enforceable wholly or partly depends on the domestic law.

In *British Airports Authority* v. *British Airways Board* (QBD 1981), the court applying English law held that British airports (a) had the right to impose a condition excluding liability in respect of damage to aircraft unless done with intent or recklessly and with the knowledge that damage would probably result, but (b) could not impose an obligation on the air carrier to indemnify it against any claim by any person using or being in an aircraft, including any claim arising from any act or default of the British Airports Authority unless done intentionally or recklessly. This case is a pointer to the effectiveness of such an exculpatory clause.

(b) Tort

Tortious Liability may arise:

    (i) for defective premises including leased premises and operating areas.

    (ii) from services provided at the airport, e.g. ground movement control, bird scaring, navigation aids, surface motor vehicles.

Liability can arise both on airside and landside.

Not all services available at an airport are necessarily provided by its operator, for example ATS and meteorological services. Information in this respect should be given in the AIP.

Liability may also be incurred through environmental damage caused by noise, vibrations or spillage or inadequate drainage of harmful chemicals and other substances.

(iii) Aircraft operator

Liability is considered elsewhere in this book. The aircraft operator may also be in an unenviable position where his aircraft is blocking the runway with an ever-increasing number of aircraft holding or being diverted; see AD2.6 in Section 2 above. Questions of legal liability for economic loss and insurance for such liability can arise; see page 449.

(iv) Security services provider

Security services against acts of unlawful interference may be provided by a number of different persons, see Chapter 12. Liability can arise in contract or tort.

(v) Operator of surface vehicles

Examples of operators of surface vehicles are catering, baggage or cleaning vehicles. Liability can arise in contract and in tort.

(vi) Ground handler

Ground handling services may be provided by the airport operator, a carrier or other enterprises. Liability can arise in contract and in tort. See reference to IATA Standard Ground Handling Agreement, page 335.

(vii) Providers of warehouse and customs clearance facilities

Liability can arise in contract and in tort. The legal nature of services provided by customs clearing and cargo agents is important in considering whether delivery of the cargo has taken place for the purposes of Article 13 of the Warsaw Convention and Article 8 of the CC Cargo.

   The provision of secure storage for precious cargo or baggage and the ensuing legal obligations raise important questions as between the carrier, the consignee and the provider of such storage.

(viii) Fuelling enterprise

The terms under which a fuel supplier carries on business at an airport and provides fuel to the aircraft operator raises legal questions such as:

   (i) defective fuel storage
   (ii) supply of the wrong type of fuel
   (iii) environmental damage and fire caused by fuel spillage
   (iv) the terms of any fuel supply contract.

For guidance see IATA "Fuel Quality Control and Fuelling Service Guidance Material".

(ix) Caterers

A number of questions arise including:

   (i) Supply of defective food to passengers and crew. The courts have treated food poisoning as an "accident" within the meaning of the Warsaw Convention. See *Abdul Rahman Al Zamil* v. *British Airways Inc* (1985) 19 AVI 17,646 1985–6 (US Court of Appeals, 2nd Circuit).

(ii) The provisions of any supply contract between the caterer and the aircraft operator, for example the exculpatory clause; see IATA Standard Catering Services Agreement (AHM 814), page 343.

PART 4. PUBLIC LAW REGULATIONS

Apart from the public law applicable to airport licensing and matters such as security, the day-to-day management of the airport may be subject to general regulations on matters such as access and the operation of surface vehicles (see Annex 14, 9.6.6 on page 170). Breach of these regulations may constitute a criminal offence.

PART 5. IATA AIRPORT HANDLING MANUAL (19th EDITION) (AHM)

A brief summary and comments on selected AHM topics follow. Bold numbers refer to AHM topic headings. This summary leaves out certain topics, in particular recommendations concerning transmission of information and the format of such transmission. Furthermore, in the full text there are sometimes gaps in numbering. The AHM is regularly revised.

Introduction

This refers to the development of standards for airport handling under the auspices of IATA. These standards arose from the necessity for airlines to arrange handling contracts with each other. Note (i) the reference to the IATA Airport Services Committee and Ground Handling Council; and (ii) the abbreviations, conversions, tolerances, and service codes.

The standards take the form of recommendations. See also Appendix 4 to this book.

019 recommends that stowage for aircraft documents, as specified, is provided.

030 deals with designation and definition of holds, compartments, bays and cabin.

050–052 deal with electronic data processing exchange for semi-permanent data for check-in and load control and related topics.

071: Emergency Procedures.

Section **071.1** sets out the 3 ICAO emergency phases: INCERFA, ALFERFA and DISTRESFA, which can only be declared by ATS. It repeats the Annex 13 Definition of "accident".

Sections **071.2–071.8** set out recommendations for the following:

2. Each airline shall establish a central accident/emergency control centre and sets out certain of the primary responsibilities of such centre.
3. Local Accident/Emergency Control Centre (facilities/organisation). A suitable area at each airport shall be nominated as such a centre. The section then lists the facilities, duties and responsibilities, organisation and documentation. It gives a typical example of an emergency rescue chart.
4. Local accident/emergency (facilities) for dead and injured.
5. Emergency Procedures (Alarm).
6. Action in the event of an accident.
7. Handling of rescued load, i.e. passengers, crew, baggage, cargo and mail.
8. Emergency check lists and forms (text suggested).

Comment

See Annexes 12 (SAR), 13 (Accident Investigation) and 14 (Aerodromes) in Chapter 5, and Chapter 15 on Risk Management.

072: Aircraft/Airport Security Procedures are set out in sections 1 to 4. These procedures are developed from the IATA Security Manual and are designed to run parallel to, and in conjunction with airport authority procedures, as defined in ICAO Airport Services Manual.

Section **072–1**: It should be ensured that an anti-sabotage programme provides for preventive measures to be taken in the following areas:

- aircraft ground security
- baggage security
- cargo and mail security

Recommendations on a wide and detailed range of security procedures then follow.

073 sets out guidelines for the establishment and proceedings of airline operators committees at all international airports to facilitate clearance and handling of passengers, crews, baggage, cargo and aircraft. It refers to the IATA Technical Policy Manual and to Airport Terminals Reference Manual.

073.2 lists the purposes of the committee.

074 deals with minimum aircraft ground times.

091 provides a functional specification for a standard departure control system. Its purpose is to define User Requirements, to assist in providing standard departure control systems to user airlines.

092 recommends adoption of a handling company evaluation checklist.

094 Airport Handling Quality Audit. This provides carriers with a standard procedure for inspecting/auditing airport handling activities in relation to the industry's commonly accepted standard practices and procedures. The document primarily focuses on ground safety activities. Each activity is inspected/audited by using a checklist covering specified aspects. It is a detailed and important document. In any investigation of an accident, the question of whether such audit had been carried out and the result of such audit would be significant.

100 deals with classification and numbering for members' airport handling manuals.

175 deals with arrangements for transit passengers remaining on board and their embarkation and disembarkation during refuelling.

176 recommends the procedures when handling passengers with reduced mobility. These are defined as those passengers with a physical disability or with a medical condition, which require individual attention or assistance on enplaning/deplaning and during ground handling which is normally not extended to other passengers.

Chapter 2—Baggage Handling (272, 276–280)

This chapter deals with hold loading of duty-free goods, security procedures, wheelchairs, interline and on-line transfer, local baggage committees, establishment of local rules and procedures, transfer baggage delivery times, and theft prevention.

Chapter 3—Cargo

316–319: Standard forms of notification to captains and messages when dangerous goods and other special loads are included in the load.

330: Preparation for loading of cargo, including procedures for:

- Bulk Cargo;
- Unit Load Device (ULD);
- Dangerous Goods, Live Animals and other Special Cargo.

330.8: The carrier or its handling company shall ensure that the specified procedures are carried out by qualified personnel and the signature of the responsible person be recorded.

The AHM Glossary includes the following definitions:

"Bulk": Loading piece by piece.
"Unit Load Device": A unit in which deadload is bulk loaded and subsequently loaded as a unit into the aircraft.
"Deadload": Baggage, cargo, mail, ballast and equipment in compartments not included in dry operating weight of the aircraft.

331: Tagging of ULD

332: Collection sacks and bags to be used for small loads which should be colour coded as specified.

337: Handling of damaged cargo.

338: Handling of pilfered cargo.

340: Handling and loading dangerous goods as defined in the IATA Dangerous Goods Regulations—see last paragraph of Appendix 4 of this book.

345: Handling wet cargo.

346: Handling of perishable cargo, e.g. meat, hatching eggs, flowers, vaccines.

350: Handling and protection of valuable cargo.

352: Handling and stowage of live animals in accordance with the IATA Live Animals Regulations. Live animals shall only be loaded into suitable aircraft compartments authorised by the carrier, *taking into account the needs of the animals*. See procedures for ramp handling and stowage.

353: Human remains. Note distinction between remains cremated and uncremated.

374, 375, 376, 385 and **388** deal with the use of, and handling and procedures for ULDs. **376** contains useful sketches.

(Author's comment: The brief reference to these sections by way of their titles must not detract from their importance in promoting proper standards essential for the efficient handling and loading of cargo and the safety of the aircraft and the occupants.)

Chapter 4—Mail handling

(See Chapter 7, Part 6 on Mail)

415.1 lists the 15 airmail documents specified by the Universal Postal Union Convention which are used for transportation and are necessary for accounting of airmail. They include the AV7 Delivery Bill airmail as referred to in Annex 9 (2.10 on page 102).

Examples of the format of these documents are given in 415.

415.2: All documents are completed by the Post Office.

415.3: Distribution

   3.1   Point-to-point Operation.

   3.2   Additional documents for through-going mail.

415.4: Stowage—Documents handed to airlines by Post Offices or handed over at point of transfer should be stowed in the flight portfolio, or other special pouch in which flight documents are kept and extracted immediately on arrival of the aircraft at its destination.

415.5: Use of three-letter codes to minimise risk of misrouteing.

430, 435, 436 and **437** all deal with handling of mail, including missing and damaged mail.

450 deals with mail security:

450.1: When mail is in the care of airlines it must be given maximum protection. See recommendations as to procedures.

450.2 deals with damaged or pilfered mail.

451: Mail safety: deals with hazardous items control.

480: Mail irregularity message procedure and format.

Chapter 5—Load Control

510 Lists the handling/load information codes to be used on traffic documents and messages.

513: Aircraft structural loading limitations.

513.1 Introduction. An aircraft is a flexible structure. In particular, the fuselage contorts during flight according to the load it contains, so that the fuselage contortion does not exceed at any point the maximum allowed limits, which would result in a risk of permanent damage, the airframe manufacturer defines airframe structural loading limitations.

The Airframe Manufacturers Weight and Balance Manual is the authority that specifies the allowable limits on aircraft loading. The data contained in this manual reflects the design limits established by the airframe manufacturer and approved by the aviation regulatory authorities. The presentation of these structural loading limitations used by the manufacturer usually precludes direct use in the operational environment.

513.2. Structural load limitations. The following structural loading limitations are known within the airline industry:

- running (linear) load limitation
- compartment load limitation
- area load limitation
- contact load limitation
- point load limitation
- asymmetrical load limitation
- combined load limitation
- cumulative load limitation
- barrier net load limitation.

513 then deals individually with the above nine structural loads in paragraphs **2.1** to **2.9**.   **2.10** deals with the development and completion for each flight of a check sheet for structural loading limitations for full flight and combi aircraft.

514–515: Recommendations for the issue of EDP (Electronic Data Processing) and Manual Loading Instruction/Reports respectively.

The Glossary defines: "Loading Instruction" as "instructions given by Load Control to the person responsible for loading"; and "Loading Report" as "signed loading instructions, with any deviations recorded, passed back to Load Control for action as required".

516: "Manual Loadsheet" sets out the procedures for the completion of the Manual Loadsheet. It deals with:

516.1: forms;
516.2: colour;
516.3: preparation;
516.4: completion with table of format.

516.5: IATA Members may combine into a single document, the loadsheet, loadmessage and balance chart provided it conforms with 516 and 519.

516.6 deals with the loadmessage, referring to 583, and is followed by examples of loadsheets and loadmessages.

The AHM Glossary states "A completed loadsheet contains all weight data pertaining to a particular flight, i.e. the weight of the aircraft, crew, pantry, fuel, passengers, baggage, cargo and mail. It also contains where necessary details of the distribution of this load in the aircraft".

517 gives Recommendations for loadsheet produced by EDP machine.

518: Captain's weight and balance information:

518.1: ACARS (Aircraft Communications Addressing and Reporting System) loadsheet with format;
518.2: Verbal transmission of data. It is recommended that a standard verbal transmission format be used to avoid error as specified. An example is provided.

519: Balance calculation methods. This recommends that the aircraft trim shall be determined either by manual methods or automatically by an EDP method. It states how the respective methods shall be applied.

520: ULD/Bulk Load Weight statement. This recommends that members use a ULD and Bulk Load Weight statement to provide:

(i) a record of the ULD and bulk load weights as a basis of load planning and aircraft weight and balance calculations;
(ii) a means of advising Load Control about items requiring special attention; and
(iii) to provide a basis for equipment control.

Specification, distribution and completion provisions are set out.

The AHM Glossary defines "Load Control" as " A function to ensure the optimum utilisation of the aircraft capacity and distribution of load as dictated by safety and operational requirements".

530: Standard weights for passengers and baggage. It is recommended that the procedures in 531 are adopted for weight and balance purposes. See further recommendations.

531: Procedures for establishing standard weights for passengers and baggage.

531.1.1 points out that it is of considerable significance to the safe performance of a flight to determine the take-off weight precisely and to ensure that the actual weight does not exceed performance limits. Standard passenger weights, as specified, may be used. National legislation may require official approval.

531.1.4: Standard passenger weight figures published by the carrier shall be used unless carrier has permitted otherwise.

531.2 deals with checked baggage.

531.3 deals with non-standard passenger/baggage weight, e.g. fully equipped military personnel or athletic teams.

The loadsheet must be endorsed to show whether actual weights or weights provided by passengers were used. See rest of 531.3 for further procedures.

533: Passengers occupying crew seats; note the difference between passenger and "all cargo" aircraft.

534: Weight control of load. This sets out the procedures to be adopted when weighing and handling load in order to achieve a correct load distribution and carrier weight control. The IATA commentary states: "The above AHM has been developed to eliminate any discrepancies which may occur when loadsheet entries are solely based on weights from manifests, flight coupons, etc."

536: This sets out "Equipment in Compartments" procedures which is defined in the Glossary as "Equipment which is carried on the aircraft but which is not manifested and which is not elsewhere included in the weight composition, such as additional flight kit".

537: Ballast:

> **537.1:** General Ballast may be required to bring the centre of gravity within operational limits.
>
> **537.2:** Two methods of carrying ballast: ballast (hold loaded) and ballast fuel.
>
> **537.3:** Loadsheet procedures.
>
> **537.4:** Flight crew information procedures.

The Glossary defines "Ballast" as "Deadload weight carried to achieve a particular balance condition".

540: This provides Aircraft ULD—weight and balance control procedures as specified.

550: Captain's signature on the loadsheet: it is recommended that this is not required, although a loadsheet check by the captain remains a useful safety precaution. This should be included in the cockpit checklist, the task to be completed before commencement of the take-off run, and an appropriate certificate for signature should be included in an alternative document such as a flight plan.

551: Last minute changes on loadsheet. The procedures include:

> **551.4:** Correction of balance conditions
>
> **551.5:** The responsibility of load control agent
>
> **551.6:** Information of flight crew

580, 581, 583, 584 and 587 deal with various messages and signals in connection with loads.

588: Statistical load summary. This deals with the preparation and dispatch of the Summary.

590: Load control procedure, responsibility, training and qualifications. It is recommended that members shall in the interest of flight safety establish procedures for an efficient load control and ensure a high level of proficiency for all staff engaged in load control work. 590 has five main sections:

> **590.1**: Load control procedure;
> **590.2**: Responsibility;
> **590.3**: Training and qualification;
> **590.4**: Standards of competence;
> **590.5**: Reference regulations. This lists the applicable regulations.

590 includes test example questions and a load control process flow diagram.

591: Signature procedures in airport handling/cargo (responsibility and accountability). The procedures begin with a statement "A full compliance with aircraft loading procedures is an essential element in ensuring aircraft safety", and end with "Aircraft safety relies on actions being properly carried out and documented".

Chapter 6—Aircraft loading and handling on the ramp

625: Provision and carriage of loading accessories should normally be provided by the operating carrier. 625 continues with recommendations on loading accessories and comments that observance of the recommendations as stated will improve the chances of IATA negotiations to free the airlines from restrictive customs documentation and controls. Many countries subject this equipment to import/export control procedures and thus the speedy movement of valuable equipment is impeded.

629: Recommendations for production and maintenance of ballast bags.

635: Operating of aircraft doors. This recommends members adopt a specified procedure to define areas of responsibility with regard to aircraft doors operation.

640: Aircraft loading and off-loading precautions. It is recommended that members shall instruct their loading staff or handling agents to apply the stated procedures.

640.1: General. Preparation and loading of bulk-load and load in ULDs shall always be performed in accordance with current instructions. Where there are more passengers and load than seats, weight or space on the aircraft, they shall be accepted for carriage according to the sequence given load/off-load priority list. See the further provisions concerning the list. (Author's comment: This is the operational "face" of bumping; see Comment 11, page 257).

640.2: Loading of bulk load. The condition of the load shall be checked prior to loading in order to detect leaking or otherwise damaged shipments. Note the importance in the case of live animals, dangerous goods, wet cargo etc. Packages which are damaged or with leaking contents must not be loaded.

640.3: Loading of ULDs. Inspection prior to loading is required. ULDs must not be loaded in the case of leakage or damage as specified.

640.4: Unloading. On completion of the off-load, the cargo compartments shall be checked to ensure all load has been removed. Any traces of leakage shall be inspected at once to establish its source. The compartment in which goods were carried shall be inspected for contamination.

640.5: Remedial action. In the event of leakage or suspected leakage of dangerous goods or other substances (specified) which might affect the structure of the aircraft or damage goods or property, immediate action will be taken to establish the source. Necessary specialised assistance shall be requested in accordance with instructions.

640.6: provides procedures for reporting leakage or damage to dangerous goods and possible leakage of seafood or other wet cargo.

641: Aircraft ground stability—tipping. A critical aft centre of gravity situation may lead to tail tipping of the aircraft, therefore precautions must be taken to eliminate this possibility. Various types of aircraft are mentioned. Precautions are set out.

645: Loading precautions for incompatible loads. See the table of incompatibilities and reference to IATA Dangerous Goods Regulations.

IATA notes that animals that are natural enemies, such as cats and dogs, should not be loaded in sight, sound, smell or reach of each other.

650: Potable water servicing. The procedures include a reference to the World Health Organisation publications "WHO International Standards for Drinking Water" and "Guide for Hygiene and Sanitation in Aviation".

670: Standardisation of gravity forces against which load must be restrained. This recommends that Members base their load securing instructions and requirements of lashing equipment to meet the specified gravity (G) forces. This is not applicable to large capacity aircraft.

See:

(a) The definition of "G Forces" in the Glossary.

(b) AHM commentary which refers to (i) differences in restraint requirements (G forces) for each type of aircraft by national aviation authorities and aircraft manufacturers; (ii) aircraft Weight and Balance Manual; (iii) uniformity.

671: Securing of load. This refers to

(1) certified aircraft holds and ULDs;

(2) non-certified ULDs;

(3) securing of ULDs;

(4) number of lashings as required by company manuals;

(5) lashing equipment and rings; and

(6) definition of breaking strength.

672 deals with procedures on discovery of technical malfunctions limiting load on aircraft. The AHM commentary states "Technical Malfunctions can cause limitations to the carriage of load on an aircraft and must be considered as an important safety factor. Handling company must ensure that, whenever observed, they are immediately brought to the attention of the carrier."

673: Bulk compartment load limitation.

673.1: Aircraft structure limitations.

673.1.1.1 defines running (linear) load limitation as follows:

"An aircraft is a flexible structure. In particular, the fuselage contorts during flight according to the loads it contains. So that the fuselage contortion does not exceed at any point the maximum allowed limit, which would result in a risk of permanent damage, the manufacturer defines a running (linear) limitation, ie a maximum load acceptable on any given fuselage length. This limitation is expressed in kg per m (lb per in) of fuselage length.

The linear limitation applies to the whole of the load located in a given part (on a given length) of the hold."

673.1.1.2 and **1.1.3** deal with the load limitations in the general case and for heavy packages respectively

673.1.2: Area load limitation.

673.1.2.1 states that the hold area load limitation (expressed in kg/m^2 or lb/ft^2) is to prevent the weight of the load (expressed in kg or lb) resting upon a certain area of the compartment floor (expressed in m^2 or ft^2) to exceed the capability of the aircraft structure underneath the floor (beams, cross-beams, attachments to the aircraft body).

673.1.2.2: The hold area load limit is provided by the aircraft manufacturers in the appropriate chapter of the Weight and Balance Manual. The rest of 673.1.2 deals further with the application of the limitation.

673.2: Floor panels limitations.

673.2.1: Contact load limitations.

673.2.1.2 to **673.2.1.3**: The floor contact load limitation (expressed in kg/m^2 or lb/ft^2) is used to prevent the weight imposed by those parts of the load in direct contact with the floor from exceeding the capacity of the horizontal floor panels. The limit is provided by some manufacturers in the Weight and Balance Manual. The topic is developed in the remainder of 2.1.

673.2.2: Point load limitation.

673.2.2.1: This defines the resistance to puncture (by a heavy load bearing onto a very small surface) to the material used in a bulk hold floor. It is equivalent to a pressure, and is expressed in kg/cm^2 (lb/in^2). See reference to application of precautions.

673.2.2.2.1 deals with package handling.

676: Handling bulk loading of heavy items. This recommends that when a heavy item exceeding 150 kg weight is to be loaded into a bulk compartment the specified procedures apply.

677: Handling and loading of big overhang items. See definitions, general procedures, and special procedures for automobiles.

680: Airside safety performance audits. The Introduction states that safety standards and procedures are fundamental to the efficient and effective performance of ramp operations. Organisations that have established performance criteria require a process to measure compliance with these standards and procedures. This process is undertaken in the form of an audit. The recommendation sets out procedures of the audit, stating that the audit and actions taken as a result of it can provide significant benefits to an organisation, listing certain of them. 680 sets out a pro-forma report form including a checklist.

682: Recommendations for airside safety investigations set out procedures and reasons for carrying out internal investigations into airside incidents/accidents. Any company report would not normally be privileged under common law rules of disclosure (see Chapter 14 page 416). (Author's Note: the accident or incident may also fall within the ICAO Definition of an accident and be investigated by the Annex 13 authority.)

683: Guidelines for a due diligence programme. This recommends that members shall, in the interests of safety, establish guidelines for a due diligence programme that may assist in reducing the number of accidents, personnel injuries, property damage and costs. The generic definition of due diligence is: "take every precaution reasonable in the circumstance to avoid a particular event in the circumstance". In other words, to do everything reasonable to prevent an accident from occurring that could result in a personnel injury or property damage. 683 states that due diligence is a legal defence for a corporation as well as its employees in many countries.

683 goes on to set out the important purposes of the due diligence programme.

690: Airside safety training objectives. This recommends members shall, in the interest of safety, establish minimum airside safety training requirements in the training of personnel from all departments involved in airside activities. The recommendation is divided into two parts:

(1) Airside safety; and
(2) Management of airside safety.

692: Ramp handling and loading procedures, training and qualifications. It is recommended that "Members shall, in the interests of flight safety, establish procedures for efficient Ramp Handling and Loading and ensure a high level of proficiency of all staff engaged in Ramp Handling and Loading work".

692.1: Ramp handling and loading procedures. Ramp handling and loading covers all functions in connection with the safe and efficient preparation of the load and handling of the aircraft on the ramp and includes the following:

- Assembly of load in ULD and in bulk.
- Efficient management of resources, such as personnel, loading and servicing equipment etc.
- Loading/off-loading of aircraft according to written loading instructions reports.
- Catering requirements and cabin appearance.
- Coordination between the carrier's departments/functions involved in the handling of the aircraft at departure and arrival.

692.2: Training. Certain minimum requirements shall be recognised in the training of personnel engaged in supervising of ramp handling and loading functions. They shall be:

(i) assessed on recruitment on their ability to do simple arithmetic;
(ii) trained in theory and practice; and
(iii) trained and qualified in load control functions as per AHM 590.

The 17 items for which a good knowledge is required are listed.

692.3: Qualifications. This covers the assessment and qualifications of ramp handling supervisory personnel and of cargo handling and loading personnel for each aircraft type or group of types. Personnel shall be continuously up-dated and reassessed as specified.

692.4: Handling agent qualifications. Member airlines may accept handling agent's staff for handling and loading provided they have the qualifications listed in 692.2. and 692.3. The airline may require additional type training.

Note: Commentary states that "ramp handling covers all functions in connection with the safe and efficient handling of aircraft. This includes the loading of the aircraft and prior assembly of ULDs or bulk cargo in the cargo warehouse. The limit of responsibilities varies widely depending on the organisation of the carrier/agent and personnel concerned. However, compliance with the above procedure is essential."

693: Ramp Incident/Accident Form. It is recommended that where a ground incident/accident occurs as defined by the carrier and damage, however minor, is caused to an aircraft, the Accident/Incident Damage Report shall be completed and forwarded to the carrier according to 694. (Author's comment: The list of possible factors contributing to accidents is instructive. Note the inclusion of "jet blast" and "prop wash". For "Vandalism/Malign Mischief" see the comments on AVN 48B in Chapter 16 on Insurance, page 456).

694: Recording of damage to aircraft caused by ground support equipment. It is recommended that Members use the definitions and methods to record all incidents when damage is caused to an aircraft on the apron by ground support equipment.

Note the definitions in **694.1** which include:

"Foreign object damage": Any damage caused to an aircraft on the apron, through engine ingestion or otherwise by a mobile object which is not a piece of ground support equipment (except jet blast damage).

"Jet Blast damage": Any damage to an aircraft on the apron caused by jet blast interference from another aircraft.

"Operator": Synonym for "Carrier".

694.2 deals with the method of recording such damage.

695: Safety precautions in aircraft handling operations.

695.1: Introduction.

695.1.1: "Safety in aviation is a permanent requirement and its first commandment. In the air and on the ground, safety first is the rule. Airside safety rules and procedures ensure safe handling, therefore safety regulations should be understood and always applied on the apron, on and around aircraft, in hangars and workshops."

695.1.2: "Should even the slightest scratch or dent in the aircraft occur or be noticed it must immediately be reported to permit technical evaluation. As aircraft have to withstand very great forces at high altitudes, personnel should be made aware that even minor deformations, apart from detracting from performance, could be the direct cause of serious accidents."

695.2: Recommendation. These five recommendations deal with:

695.2.1: Training of personnel.

695.2.2: Enforcement by companies of application of all safety rules, procedures and requirements connected with aircraft handling.

695.2.3: Ground support equipment must be operated with great care as specified.

695.2.4: Consideration be given to aircraft being fitted whenever practical with mechanised in-plane loading systems.

695.2.5: Though safety should be a prime requirement in all activities connected with loading and unloading aircraft, the following minimum measures, as specified, should be taken in order to ensure as high a safety standard as possible.

695.3: Ground support equipment operation: 30 minimum measures.

695.4: Chocking of Aircraft: 14 minimum measures.

695.5: Aircraft loading/unloading operations. 15 minimum measures.

695.6: Aircraft equipment. Eight minimum measures.

695.7: Mobile ground-level aircraft walkway operations: seven minimum measures.

695.8: Baggage and material handling: seven minimum measures.

695.9: Personnel: 28 minimum measures.

695.10: Fire protection and prevention. 13 minimum measures.

695.11: Apron markings. The use of standard apron marking forms an integral part of the overall requirements at an airport to ensure a safe operation.

696: Safety considerations for aircraft movement operations. This section sets out safety factors to be taken into consideration; it deals in particular with pushback, powerback and towing, all Defined.

697: Recommendations for apron markings and signs. The Introduction observes that "although standards and recommended practices for aircraft ground movement have been developed, only limited guidance material is available for ground support equipment movement and parking on the apron. It is anticipated that implementation of worldwide standards for airport apron markings will be a significant contribution to a safe apron environment."

See also sections **697.2**: Definitions, **697.3**: Requirements, and **697.5**: Recommendations.

The definitions include "apron" (ramp)—"a paved area on the airside of the terminal building where aircraft are manoeuvred and parked and where activities associated with handling of flights can be performed". This definition is slightly different from the ICAO Definition on page 164.

698: Guidelines for aircraft ground accident cost assessment. The purpose of this recommendation is to detail standard elements for cost assessment. Guidelines need to be established to distinguish direct and consequential costs. Direct costs are directly associated with the accident. Consequential costs describe the financial impact of an accident/incident other than direct costs. The recommendation sets out provisions on direct costs, consequential costs, calculation of labour costs and material costs.

699: Recommendations for an industry risk control programme for apron operations.

Introduction: "All organisations face risk. The management of risk is a critical component to the commercial survival of organisations. The key step in managing risk is to identify the risks facing the organisation. Once a risk has been identified then it can be dealt with, either by removing the risk or bringing it to an acceptable level. In the airside operations environment risk control is required in order to prevent injury to people, damage to property and/or loss to process".

699 then recommends the following methods:

699.1: Management control of loss (risk control);
699.2: Assessment of hazards and risks;
699.3: Action on findings.

Each of the three methods is broken down into separate recommedations. There follows a Risk Activity Assessment Flow Chart.

Chapter 7—Aircraft movement control

780, 781, 782 and **783** deal with aircraft, fuel and information messages.

785 deals with *ad hoc* schedules message procedure taken from Chapter 5 and Appendix H of the Standard Schedules Information Manual.

Chapter 8—Ground handling agreements

801 is an introduction to the IATA Standard Ground Handling Agreement (SGHA) and is summarised as follows.

A Ground Handling Agreement is a "Standard Ground Handling Agreement when, and only when, the wording of its Main Agreement and of its Annex A corresponds exactly to the text in 810".

Differences from the standard text are to be recorded in its Annex(es) B.

801.1: The SGHA consists of :

801.1.1: Main Agreement containing legal and administration clauses.

801.1.2: Annex A listing and describing the ground handling activities.

801.1.3: Annex B includes items such as the location, fees and any deviations from SGHA.

801.2: Use of the agreement.

801.2.3: sets out an alternative simplified procedure for the SGHA.

802 sets out IATA comments ("IATA Comments") on the SGHA.

802.1: General: Interpretation of the SGHA should be governed by the underlying principle that the carrier should not be required to perform any handling or coordinating task with regard to the contracted services.

802.2: The term "services" is intended to refer to activity/work as well as the use of resources such as equipment or facilities.

Other IATA comments relate to specific Articles in the SGHA some of which are dealt with below under the Article headings.

803 sets out the Recommended Text Memorandum of Understanding (MoU) on Service Delivery Standards dealing with the listed service elements: general, passenger handling, ramp handling and cargo and any additional items. It is followed by description of service delivery standards.

804 sets out a system for performance measurement of airport handling standards. Such a system is AHS 1000.

810 sets out the SGHA text. Comments on certain provisions follow. Some provisions are summarised. For brevity the word "the" has been omitted before "Carrier" and "Handling Company". The text is preceded by Definitions and Terminology.

Main Agreement

Article 1—Provision of services
1.1 General. The services will be made available within the limits of the possibilities of Handling Company and in accordance with applicable IATA and/or ICAO rules, regulations and procedures.
The text states that not every detail of the services will be specified.

Comment

ICAO SARPS are public law international standards and should be part of domestic law subject to Article 37 of the Chicago Convention. IATA rules etc. are contractual obligations accepted by its members. Presumably it is intended that the MoU in 803 and the above limits of possibilities should correspond.
The other provisions in Article 1 deal with:

- 1.2 The documents for ground handling.
- 1.3 Scheduled flights.
- 1.4 Extra flights.
- 1.5 Priority in the case of multiple handling.
- 1.6 Emergency assistance, for example forced landings, accidents or acts of violence.
- 1.7 Additional services.
- 1.8 Other locations.

Article 2—Fair Practices
This deals with maintenance of confidentiality of information received by the parties in operation of the Agreement. It refers expressly to protection of carrier's sales information.

Article 3—Sub-contracting of services
3.1: Handling Company can sub-contract with Carrier's consent, not to be unreasonably withheld. Handling Company remains responsible for the proper rendering of services.
3.2: Carrier shall not appoint any other person etc. to provide the services the Handling Companies agree to provide except as mutually agreed.

Comment

Article 3.2 makes this SGHA an exclusive agreement. In some States there may only be one possible ground handler at an airport. Other airports have given franchises to a number of competing companies to provide ground handling services.

Within the EU see Council Directive (EC) 96/67 on access to the ground handling market at Community airports.

Article 4—Carrier's representation

4.1: Carrier can appoint its own representative(s) at the relevant location who, with representative(s) from the Carrier's head office, may inspect the services furnished by Handling Company and provide such assistance as specified and as shall not interfere with the furnishing of services by Handling Company.

4.2: Carrier may also appoint a supervisor to supervise the services of Handling Company.

4.3: The assistance performed by such representative(s) or supervisor(s) will be the sole responsibility of Carrier unless requested by the Handling Company.

Article 5—Standard of Work

5.1: Handling Company shall carry out all technical and flight operations services in accordance with Carrier's instructions receipt of which must be confirmed in writing to Carrier by Handling Company.

In the case of absence of instructions by Carrier, Handling Company shall follow its own standard practices and procedures.

Other services also having a safety aspect, for example load control, loading of aircraft and handling of dangerous goods, shall be carried out in accordance with the applicable IATA and/or ICAO rules, regulations and procedures.

5.2: All other services shall be in accordance with the standard practices and procedures usually followed by Handling Company and in accordance with worldwide industry standards. Reasonable requests of Carrier not conflicting with applicable orders or regulations of the appropriate authorities will be complied with.

5.3: Handling Company shall take all possible steps to ensure Carrier's aircraft, crews, passengers and load shall receive treatment no less favourable than that given by Handling Company to other carriers or to its own comparable operations at the same location.

5.4: Authorisations for specialised personnel shall be kept up-to-date by Handling Company. Carrier shall be informed immediately if requested authorised personnel cannot be provided.

5.5: Carrier shall supply Handling Company with sufficient information and instructions.

5.6: In provision of the services as a whole, due regard shall be paid to safety, security, local and international regulations, applicable IATA and/or ICAO and/or other governing rules, regulations and procedures and the aforementioned request(s) of Carrier in such a manner that delays and damage to Carrier's aircraft and load are avoided and the general public is given the best impression of air transport.

5.7: Handling Company must report to Carrier's representative imme-diately all loss of or damage, threatened or actual, to aircraft and loads noticed in the course of handling or which otherwise comes to the knowledge of Handling Company.

5.8: The parties shall reach mutual agreement on the quality standards for any services, not excluding those covered by 5.1 above. Such standards for a specific location may form part of Annex B. Handling Company agrees to take all possible steps to ensure that with regard to contracted services, the agreed quality standards will be met.

Comment

Presumably agreement under Article 5.8 relates to the MoU in 803. Article 5.8 wording indicates an obligation on the parties to reach agreement. In the absence of agreement does a dispute situation arise or is the second paragraph of Article 5.1 sufficient to resolve the question?

Article 6—Remuneration
The charges set out in Annex B and specified additional expenditure payable by Carrier to Handling Company do not include (i) the charges, fees or taxes imposed by Airport, Customs or other authorities for the provision of the services, and (ii) expenses in connection with stop-over and transfer pas-sengers and handling of passengers with interrupted, delayed or cancelled flights, which are to be borne ultimately by Carrier.

Article 7—Accounting and settlement
Settlement shall be effected through the IATA Clearing House unless other-wise agreed in Annex B.

Article 8—Liability and indemnity
(The text is set out in full).
In this Article all references to:

(a) "Carrier" or "Handling Company" shall include their employees, servants, agents and sub-contractors.
(b) "ground support equipment" shall mean all equipment used in the performance of ground handling services included in Annex A, whether fixed or mobile, and
(c) "act or omission" shall include negligence.

8.1: Except as stated in Sub-Article 8.5, Carrier shall not make any claim against Handling Company and shall indemnify it (subject as hereinafter provided) against any legal liability for claims or suits, including costs and expenses incidental thereto, in respect of:

(a) delay, injury or death of persons carried or to be carried by Car-rier;

(b) injury or death of any employee of Carrier;

(c) damage to or delay or loss of baggage, cargo or mail carried or to be carried by Carrier; and

(d) damage to or loss of property owned or operated by, or on behalf of, Carrier and any consequential loss or damage

arising from an act or omission of Handling Company in the performance of this Agreement unless done with intent to cause damage, death, delay, injury or loss or recklessly and with the knowledge that damage, death, delay, injury or loss would probably result.

PROVIDED THAT all claims or suits arising hereunder shall be dealt with by Carrier; and PROVIDED ALSO THAT Handling Company shall notify Carrier of any claims or suits without undue delay and shall furnish such assistance as Carrier may reasonably require. PROVIDED ALSO THAT where any of the services performed by Handling Company hereunder relate to the carriage by Carrier of passengers, baggage or cargo direct to or from a place in the United States of America then if the limitations of liability imposed by Article 22 of the Warsaw Convention would have applied if any such act or omission had been committed by Carrier but are held by a Court not to be applicable to such act or omission committed by Handling Company in performing this Agreement then upon such decision of the Court the indemnity of Carrier to Handling Company hereunder shall be limited to an amount not exceeding the amount for which Carrier would have been liable if it had committed such an act or omission.

8.2: Carrier shall not make any claim against Handling Company in respect of damage, death, delay, injury or loss to third parties caused by the operation of Carrier's aircraft arising from an act or omission of Handling Company in the performance of this Agreement unless done with intent to cause damage, death, delay, injury or loss or recklessly and with knowledge that damage, death, delay, injury or loss would probably result.

8.3 (a) Notwithstanding the provisions of Sub-Article 8.1 in the case of claims arising out of surface transportation which is provided on behalf of Carrier and is part of the operation of loading/embarking or unloading/disembarking and/or is covered by Carrier's Contract of Carriage the indemnity shall not exceed the limits specified in the said Contract of Carriage.

(b) In the case of claims arising out of surface transportation which is not provided on behalf of Carrier and/or is not part of the operation of loading/embarking or unloading/disembarking and/or is not covered by Carrier's Contract of Carriage the waiver and indemnity herein contained shall not apply.

8.4: Handling Company shall not make any claim against Carrier and shall indemnify it (subject as hereinafter provided) against any legal liability for claims or suits, including costs and expenses incidental thereto, in respect of:

(a) injury to or death of any employees of Handling Company, its servants, agents or sub-contractors; and

(b) damage to or loss of property owned or operated by, or on behalf of, Handling Company and any consequential loss or damage

arising from an act or omission of Carrier in the performance of this Agreement unless done with intent to cause damage, death, delay, injury or loss or recklessly and with knowledge that damage, death, delay, injury or loss would probably result.

8.5: Notwithstanding Sub-Article 8.1(d), Handling Company shall indemnify Carrier against any physical loss of or damage to Carrier's Aircraft caused by Handling Company's negligent operation of ground support equipment PROVIDED ALWAYS THAT Handling Company's liability shall be limited to any such loss of or damage to Carrier's Aircraft not exceeding the limits stated in Annex(es) B which shall not, in any event, exceed USD 1,500,000 except that loss or damage in respect of any incident below USD 3,000 shall not be indemnified.

For the avoidance of doubt, save as expressly stated, this Sub-Article 8.5 does not affect or prejudice the generality of the provisions of Sub-Article 8.1 including the principle that Carrier shall not make any claim against Handling Company and shall indemnify it against any liability in respect of any and all consequential loss or damage howsoever arising.

IATA Comments

The text may have to be replaced in Annex B as different legal systems and conditions prevailing worldwide make it very difficult to present an Article 8 universally acceptable and workable. The text is offered as a basis on which a specific Article 8 may be built.

Author's Comments

1. Preamble:

(i) All references to Carrier or Handling Company shall include their employees, servants, agents and sub-contractors. Both "employees" and "servants" have been included, and it may need to be considered whether those words have separate meanings.

(ii) "act or omission" includes negligence, in the case of Articles 8.1 and 8.2, of Handling Company and in the case of 8.4 of Carrier.

Whether it is possible under the relevant domestic law for those employees, etc., to be given enforceable rights is a complex question. Perhaps sub-contractors' position can be strengthened if consent is obtained under Article 3.1.

2(i): Article 8.1: the exception relating to "an act or omission . . . done with intent to cause damage . . . or recklessly and with the knowledge that damage . . . would probably result" repeats the wording of Article 25 of the Amended Warsaw Convention (see 270 above). The arguments in respect of subjective and objective interpretation of these provisions can be advanced here. It is likely the burden is on the Carrier to prove that the exception applies.

2(ii): On the basis that this is an enforceable provision, Handling Company is exempt subject to the third provisos. Certain parallels can be drawn with *British Airports Authority* v. *British Airways* (page 319 above), although that case concerned the airport operator rather than a ground handler. The enforceability of this type of exculpatory clause is subject to domestic law, as indicated by the IATA Comments (page 340).

2(iii): Carrier includes agents and sub-contractors. Article 8.1(b) presumably extends the exclusions of liability and indemnity to employees of those persons.

2(iv): The reason for the third proviso may be as follows:

(a) The USA was party only to the Unamended Warsaw Convention when this was drafted.

(b) The Unamended Warsaw Convention does not state expressly that the servants and agents ("*préposés*") of the Carrier are protected by the limits of liability; the Amended Warsaw Convention expressly so states.

(c) Therefore theoretically a US court is more likely in any situation to find the Ground Handler is not protected by the Warsaw Convention, but see *Baker* v. *Lansdell Protective Agency* (page 292).

Whatever is the correct interpretation, the question could have been dealt with more clearly by limiting the proviso to those cases governed by the Unamended Warsaw Convention and where there is jurisdiction in the USA.

In any event the court in any jurisdiction has to decide as to whether such agents are protected or not.

3. Article 8.2 excludes the right of Carrier to make a claim for contribution or indemnity against Handling Company where a third party makes a claim against the Carrier in respect of damage, death etc. as specified. This provision applies only to the operation of the aircraft where the damage has been caused by act or omission of Handling Company. If the third party claims directly against Ground Handler there is no express provision requiring Carrier to indemnify Ground Handler.

4. Article 8.3(a) refers for example to the case where a passenger is injured during surface transportation provided by the Ground Handler as part of the embarking or disembarking of a passenger of Carrier. In such a case the claim against Carrier would be limited to Warsaw Convention limits or any other applicable limit and the indemnity in favour of the ground handler would not exceed such applicable limits. The reference to "and/or is covered by Carrier's Contract of Carriage" may extend to liability arising outside the embarkation/disembarkation. Presumably where there is no limit, then there is no limit to the indemnity. The gradual elimination of the limit in respect of death or injury affects the application of this provision.

5. On the basis that the words " the waiver and indemnity herein contained" in Article 8.3(b) refers to the surrender of rights given by Carrier in Article 8, this provision is logical; Carrier should not waive its rights in respect of its passengers where Handling Company causes injury to such passengers when not providing services to Carrier. However, the use of "and/or" confuses the issue.

6. Article 8.4(a) refers to employees, servants, agents or sub-contractors of Handling Company. In the preamble "Handling Company" includes employees, servants, agents and sub-contractors. If an employee of a maintenance sub-contractor of Handling Company is injured, this should be covered by the exclusion in favour of Carrier. The waiver by Handling Company should cover employees etc. of Carrier.

7. Article 8.5 is an exception to the general tenor of Article 8. The indemnity to be given by Handling Company to Carrier relates only to physical loss of or damage to the aircraft of Carrier caused by negligent operation of ground support equipment. The modest monetary limits apply.

Article 9—Arbitration
Any dispute or claim concerning the scope, meaning, construction or effect of the agreement or arising therefrom shall be subject to arbitration in accordance with the specified procedures including the appointment of arbitrator(s). The Arbitral Tribunal shall settle its own procedure and if necessary shall decide the law to be applied. The award shall be final and conclusively binding on the parties.

IATA Comments

The person who appoints the arbitrator(s) can in the alternative be the International Chamber of Commerce.

Author's Comments

The applicable law, particularly in the case of Article 8, may be important.

Article 10—Stamp duties and registration fees.

Article 11—deals with duration, modification and termination of the Agreement.

Comments

Article 11.3: IATA comments on the notice provisions that due consideration should be given to mail delivery.

Under Article 11.8 both parties are exempt from obligation if prompt notification is given by either party in respect of any failure to perform obligations arising from labour disputes involving complete or partial stoppage of work or delay in the performance of work; or *force majeure* or any other cause beyond the control of either party.

Article 11.10 sets out the terms on which Handling Company can vary the charges payable by the Carrier.

Annex A sets out at length the ground handling services. It covers 14 separate sections dealing with the following:

1. Representation and accommodation
2. Load control communications and departure control system
3. Unit load device control
4. Passengers and baggage
5. Cargo and post office mail
6. Ramp
7. Aircraft servicing
8. Fuel and Oil
9. Aircraft maintenance
10. Flight operations and crew administration
11. Surface transport
12. Catering services
13. Supervision and administration
14. Security.

The Annex sets out a list of services under each of the 14 sections.
    Annex B sets out the locations, agreed services and charges.

813 deals with (i) the definition of truck-handling and truck service; and (ii) liability. All subsections in Annex A to the SGHA will apply to loads to be carried on a truck service. In the Main Agreement and Annex A the terms "aircraft" will read "truck", and "flight" will read "truck service".

Catering Service Agreement

814 sets out the IATA Standard Catering Services Agreement consisting of the Main Agreement, Annex A catering services; and Annex B location, agreed services and charges. Space does not permit the catering agreement to be dealt with in detail. Some procedures resemble those in the SGHA. Reference is made to the following summarised Articles:

5.9 Caterer undertakes that it shall:

(a) Ensure that all premises and equipment (as specified) used for storage, preparation, production and transportation of meals and beverages provided to Carrier's aircraft meet the standards of hygiene specified by all applicable local and international laws, regulations, procedures and requirements.

(b) Take all reasonable steps to ensure food and water delivered to Carrier's aircraft, and the utensils or vessels used for the provision of the contracted services shall be free from both living organisms of disease and toxic substances of any origin to the extent required by all applicable local and international laws, regulations, procedures and requirements.

(c) Ensure that evidence that the above standards have been and continue to be monitored on a regular basis is maintained and available for inspection.

(d) Ensure the services are provided in a timely manner.

(e) Ensure additional standards specified in Annex B are met.

Comments

Article 5.9(a) is an obligation "to ensure" while Article 5.9(b) is an obligation "to take all reasonable steps". Both provisions are subject to local and international laws, regulations etc, which shall include any ICAO and WHO requirements.

8. Liability and indemnity
In this Article all reference to Carrier or Caterer shall include employees, servants, agents and sub-contractors.

Comments (Article 8.1)

(This exculpatory wording is the same as 8.1 in the SGHA except that in 8.1(c) of the catering agreement the exculpatory provisions apply to delay but not to damage or loss of baggage, cargo or mail. Might not a catering vehicle collide with a baggage trolley prior to loading?)

Proviso 3 in 8.1 of the SGHA concerning US operations is not included.

Article 8.2: Notwithstanding 8.1, Carrier may claim against Caterer in respect of death, injury, illness or disease of persons carried by Carrier or any employee of Carrier arising from Caterer's failure to comply with the 5.9(a) and (b) and Caterer undertakes to indemnify Carrier against legal liability.

Comments (Article 8.2)

In respect of the essential catering duties, the exculpatory clause therefore does not apply even where there is no intent or recklessness with knowledge. This is a major difference from the SGHA.

Comments (Articles 8.3 to 8.6)

8.3: This wording is similar to 8.2 of SGHA, making allowances for the different functions. It defines third parties as "being parties other than the Carrier and the Caterer and other than persons carried or to be carried by the Carrier . . . ".

   8.4 (a) is substantially the same as 8.3(a) of the SGHA, making allowance for the different functions. It envisages the type of claim where a passenger might be injured by a catering ground vehicle where Caterer might be regarded as a servant or agent of the carrier so as to fall within the provisions of the Warsaw Convention and its limitation of liability. It expressly refers to "surface transportation provided in the execution of this Agreement". However, while the indemnity given by Carrier is limited to the liability limit of the Carrier, a direct claim against Caterer may not be so limited. While Caterer may be an agent, it is arguably not performing functions directly concerned with the operation of the flight.

        (b) invokes the same comments as are given in respect of Article 8.3(b) of SGHA above.

   8.5 is substantially the same as SGHA 8.4 except in the catering agreement "death" has been omitted after "with knowledge that".

   8.6 requires Caterer to maintain at its own expense such insurances as are necessary to cover its liabilities and obligations arising under the agreement and in particular under sub-article 8.2 for the amount of and upon the terms specified in Annex B.

12: General.

   12.1 deals with notices.

   12.2 states that the rights of either party shall not be prejudiced or restricted by any indulgence or forbearance.

   12.3: Caterer shall act as an independent contractor and shall not be, nor shall hold itself out as an agent, partner or authorised representative of the carrier.

Comments (Article 12.3)

A provision of this kind will be taken into account in deciding whether Caterer is a *préposé* (servant or agent) of the carrier for the purposes of the Warsaw Convention. On the basis that it is not, Caterer may be more exposed than

Handling Company in SGHA. This may be logical, as Caterer is supplying a product which is not essential to the operation of the aircraft.

Article 13 specifies that the agreement shall be governed by the law referred to in Annex(es) B.

815–816: IATA Transportation Documents Service Agreement.
   There are two standard agreements:

1. Between Carrier and Handling Company (815)
2. Between airlines (816)

Under the agreements Handling Company or airline providing the service undertakes to issue air transportation documents for carriage on Carrier's service.

817: Standard Training Agreement
   Article 1. Provision of aviation training.
   1.1: Provides that the Training will be made available within the limits of possibility of the Training Company and the Customer's reasonable request in accordance with the IATA and/or ICAO Rules, Regulations and Procedures.
   1.2: Training Material will be provided by:

(a) the Training Company;
(b) the Customer;
(c) others;

and should comply with the standards established under IATA and/or ICAO Rules, Regulations, Procedures and Customer's or the Training Company's reasonable request if applicable.
   1.3 and 1.4 deal with the Training Schedule and duration of training.

Comments

Training will be provided in accordance with the IATA and/or ICAO Rules, Regulations and Procedures. If for example in the carriage of dangerous goods the IATA Procedures are more restrictive than the ICAO Technical Instructions, the parties should decide as to which provisions should be used.

Article 2—Fair Practices
This corresponds to Article 2 of the SGHA. However, in the SGHA, 2.1 requires that Handling Company will take all practicable measures to ensure that sales information contained in Carrier's flight documents is made available for the purposes of Carrier only and 2.2 requires neither party to the agreement to disclose any information contained in Annex(es) B to outside parties without the prior consent of the other party, unless such information is specifically required by the applicable law or regulations.

In the standard Training Agreement there is no corresponding obligation on the Training Company although the Customer will be providing training material.

Article 3—Sub-Contracting of Services
This is similar to 3.1 of the SGHA. There is no equivalent in the Training Agreement to 3.2 of the SGHA.

Article 4—Standard of Work
4.1 and 4.2 resemble 5.1 and 5.2 of the SGHA.
  4.3 of the Training Agreement resembles 5.4 of the SGHA.
  4.4 of the Training Agreement requires the Training Company to provide the reports, as mutually agreed, such as individual evaluation reports.

Article 5 deals with agreement of charges for the training.

Article 6—Liability and indemnity
In this Article all references to the Customer or the Training Company shall include their employees, servants and sub-contractors.
  6.1: Neither party shall make any claim against the other party and shall indemnify it (subject as hereinafter provided) against any legal liability for claims or suits, including costs and expenses incidental thereto in respect of:

  (a) injury or death to any employee of the either party; and
  (b) damage or loss of property and/or operated by, or on behalf of either party and any consequential loss or damage;

arising from any act or omission of either party in the performance of this Agreement, unless done with intent to cause damage, death, delay or loss or recklessly and with the knowledge that damage, death, injury or loss would probably result.

Comments

The intent is that each party, in respect of its own employee or property, should not make any claim against the other party and will indemnify such other party as specified. However, whether the wording reflects this intent is not clear.

  6.2: Neither party shall make any claim against the other party in respect of damage, death, injury or loss caused by third parties during the provision of training services.

Comments

Loss lies where it falls. Presumably 6.2 does not extend to employees, servants and sub-contractors.

Both paragraphs raise questions as to the rights and duties of the employees, servants and sub-contractors.

The agreement is silent as to damage caused to third parties as a result of defective training.

Article 7—Arbitration
All disputes shall be subject to the Rules of Conciliation of the International Chamber of Commerce.

Article 8—Duration, Modification and Termination
8.1: Either party may terminate in whole or part on 60 days' notice.
8.2 gives the Customer the right to terminate the agreement if any necessary permit of Training Company is revoked, cancelled or suspended.
8.3 exempts both parties, if prompt notification is given, in respect of failure to perform their obligations arising from:

  (a) Labour disputes as specified;
  (b) *Force majeure* or any cause beyond the control of either party.

8.4: Termination is without prejudice to accrued rights and liabilities of either party.
818: Standard Ground Support Equipment Procurement Agreement
This Agreement was introduced into the 19th edition of the AHM. Its object is to establish a standard agreement for deliveries of ground support equipment and support service for such equipment. The Agreement is intended to form an industry standard for the business of purchase and supply between suppliers and members of IATA.

The 34 Articles of the Agreement deal with contractual terms for the supply of goods and the provision of related services. They include Articles dealing with risk of loss, delivery and inspection, insurance and indemnification. The Agreement is not further described in this book.
830 sets out IATA recommended Ground handling Charge Note which includes a written acceptance on behalf of the Aircraft Owner of SGHA Article 8 which is set out in full.
832: Form of Message for casual aircraft handling.
840: Model Handling Agreement for Electronic Data Interchange.

The remainder of the AHM contains mainly Specifications and IATA Directives. It includes a useful Glossary.

SUMMARY

The summary of Annex 14 and this chapter indicate the personnel involved in airport operations and the standards and procedures which they should apply. Subject to Articles 37 and 38 of the Chicago Convention, the obligatory nature of ICAO SARPS has already been considered. While AHM refers to its standards and procedures, these are recommendations which only apply between contracting parties and should not be confused with the SARPS; they may, however, in some cases be regarded by the court as minimum standards, breach of which would constitute a tort of negligence.

Pages 635 onwards of the AHM deal with specifications for airport handling ground support equipment and are not dealt with at all in this book.

The 19th Edition contains important additional material on maintaining and monitoring airside standards of handling.

CHAPTER 10

LIABILITY FOR DAMAGE CAUSED BY AN AIRCRAFT OTHER THAN TO PASSENGERS, BAGGAGE, CARGO AND MAIL CARRIED ON IT

INTRODUCTION

Damage caused by an aircraft other than to its passengers, baggage, cargo or mail falls into three categories which are considered in turn:

1. Damage to persons or property on the surface caused by aircraft in flight.
2. Damage caused by aircraft in flight to persons or property resulting from an aerial collision.
3. Surface damage caused by aircraft operating on the surface.

Liability for such damage usually arises in tort or under an Act in the absence of any contract. It is possible that a contractual relationship also exists where for example an aircraft damages by jet blast a surface vehicle providing ground handling services to it under contract.

PART 1. DAMAGE TO PERSONS OR PROPERTY ON THE SURFACE CAUSED BY AIRCRAFT IN FLIGHT

Convention on Damage caused by Foreign Aircraft to Third Parties on the Surface, Rome 1952

The International Convention for Unification of Certain Rules relating to Damage caused by Aircraft to Third Parties on the Surface, Rome 29 May 1933 ("1933 Convention") applies where damage was caused on the surface in the territory of one High Contracting Party by an aircraft registered in the territory of another High Contracting Party. In substance it has been replaced by the Convention on Damage caused by Foreign Aircraft to Third Parties on the Surface, Rome 1952 ("1952 Convention").

A summary of the main Articles of the 1952 Convention follows. In some cases the Articles have been paraphrased:

Article 1

(1) Any person who suffers damage on the surface shall, upon proof only that the damage was caused by an aircraft in flight or by any person or thing

falling from it be entitled to compensation. There is no right to compensation where the damage is not a direct consequence of the relevant incident, or if the damage results from the mere fact of passage through airspace in conformity with existing air traffic regulations.

(2) An aircraft is considered to be in flight from the moment when the power is applied for the purpose of actual take-off until the moment when the landing run ends. In the case of an aircraft lighter than air the expression "in flight" relates to the period from the moment when it becomes detached from the surface until it becomes again attached thereto.

Comments

(1) Damage must be "a direct consequence". *Black* defines "direct" as "immediate; proximate; . . . operating through an immediate connection or relation instead of operating through a medium . . . ".

(2) Compare the definition of "in flight" to section 76(2) of the UK Civil Aviation Act 1982, (see page 363). See also "Flight time" in the Definitions: "The total time from the moment an aircraft first moves under its own power for the purpose of taking-off until the moment it comes to rest at the end of the flight". This definition is followed by a note "flight time as here defined is synonymous with the term 'block-to-block' time or 'chock-to-chock' time in general usage which is measured from the time the aircraft moves from the loading point until it stops at the unloading point."

The significance of these differing definitions is that strict liability of the 1952 Convention only applies while the aircraft is "in flight" as defined by such Convention. Liability for other damage may be in negligence only.

(3) Liability under the 1952 Convention attaches to commercial air transport, aerial work and "General Aviation".

Article 2

(1) The liability for compensation shall attach to the operator of the aircraft.

(2)(a) The "operator" shall mean the person who was making use of the aircraft at the time the damage was caused provided that if control of the navigation of the aircraft was retained by the person from whom the right to use the aircraft was derived, whether directly or indirectly, that person shall be considered the operator.

(2)(b) A person shall be considered to be making use of the aircraft when he is using it personally, or when his servants or agents are using the aircraft in the course of their employment, whether or not in the scope of their authority.

(3) The registered owner of the aircraft shall be presumed to be the operator, and shall be liable unless he proves some other person was the operator and takes appropriate measures to join that other person in the relevant legal proceedings.

Comments

(1) Definitions define "operator" as: "A person, organisation or enterprise engaged in or offering to engage in an aircraft operation".

(2) Article 2(2)(b) makes a distinction between "course of employment" and "scope of authority"; a distinction not found in Article 25A of the Amended Warsaw Convention. An example might be where a pilot authorised to act as co-pilot only positions the aircraft as pilot-in-command to another aerodrome across the State border. It is submitted the pilot is acting in the course of his employment but not within the scope of his authority. See Comments (2.1) *et seq.* on page 273.

Article 3

If the operator at the time the damage was caused had not the exclusive right to use the aircraft for a period of more than 14 days, then the person from whom such a right was derived shall be liable jointly and severally with the operator, each being bound by the provisions and limitations of the Convention.

Comments

The registered owner will only escape liability if he proves that he has given the exclusive right to use the aircraft to a person who is the operator within the meaning of Article 2(2)(a); such exclusive right would usually preclude the registered owner from using the aircraft.

Article 4

This deals with a person making use of the aircraft without the consent of the person entitled to its navigational control. The latter will be jointly and severally liable with the user unless he can prove he exercised due care to prevent such use.

Article 5

Any person who would be liable under the provisions of the Convention shall not be liable if the damage is a direct consequence of armed conflict or civil disturbance or if such person has been deprived of the use of an aircraft by act of public authority.

Comments

(1) "Direct": see Comment (1) to Article 1.

(2) Many States have the legal right to requisition aircraft on their register in times of international crisis. See section 62(b) of the UK Civil Aviation Act

1982. Requisition by public authority of aircraft registered in other States raises questions of war-risk and political-risk insurance cover.

Article 6

(1) Damage caused solely or partly by negligence or other wrongful act or omission of the person who suffers the damage or of his servants or agents will either remove or reduce liability. This does not apply if such servants or agents acted outside the scope of their authority.

(2) This principle extends to a legal action by one person to recover damages arising from the death of another person whose negligence or other wrongful act or omission or that of his servants or agents is involved.

Comments

(1) For "negligence" see Chapter 11 on page 369. *Black* defines "wrongful act" as "Any act which in the ordinary course will infringe upon the rights of another to his damage, unless it is done in the exercise of an equal or superior right". This definition would extend to breach of a property right; perhaps it should be construed restrictively only to cover for example breach of an air navigation regulation.

(2) The qualification in the last sentence of Article 6(1) refers only to "scope of authority", it does not mention "course of employment", see Article 2(2)(b) and Comments (2.1) *et seq.* on page 273.

Article 7

Where two aircraft have collided or interfered with each other in flight and have caused damage contemplated by Article 1, each shall be liable within the provisions and limits of the Convention.

Comments

This relates only to surface damage. The legal position between the two aircraft is dealt with under Part 3 of this chapter. See also Article 24 below.

Article 8

extends the defences available to operators to those persons referred to in Articles 2(3), 3 and 4.

Article 9

Neither the operator, owner, or any person liable under Articles 3 and 4 nor their respective servants or agents shall be liable for damage on the surface caused by an aircraft during flight or any person or thing falling from the aircraft otherwise than expressly provided in the 1952 Convention. This rule shall not apply to any such person who is guilty of a deliberate act or omission done with intent to cause damage.

Comments

Perhaps this provision permits another cause of action or claim in respect of indirect damage caused by such a deliberate act or omission; compare this Article with Article 12(1) which removes the limit of liability.

Article 10

The Convention does not prejudice the question of whether a person liable under the Convention has a right of recourse against any other person.

Article 11

(1), (2) and (4): This Article, which is subject to Article 12, imposes a limit of liability dependent on the weight of the aircraft. Such liability limit is calculated according to the weight of the aircraft and expressed in francs which are a currency unit consisting of $65\frac{1}{2}$ mg of gold of millesimal fineness 9,000. This is the same Gold Franc which is found in the Warsaw Convention referred to in Chapter 7, Part 3 above. Conversion into national currencies shall be made according to the gold value of such currencies at the date of judgment or allocation under Article 14.

The limit of liability is 500,000 francs for an aircraft weighing 100,000 kg or less and is 10,500,000 francs plus 100 francs per kg over 50,000 kg for aircraft weighing more than 50,000 kg, with intermediate limits depending on the weight of the aircraft.

Liability in respect of loss of life or personal injury shall not exceed 500,000 francs per person killed or injured.

(3): "Weight" means the maximum weight of the aircraft authorised by the certificate of airworthiness for take-off, excluding the effect of lifting gas when used.

Article 12

(1) If the injured person proves that the damage was caused by the deliberate act or omission of the operator, his servants or agents done with intent to cause damage, the limit of liability shall not apply provided it is also proved in the case of servant or agent that he was acting in the course of his employment and within the scope of his authority.

(2) If a person wrongfully takes and makes use of an aircraft without the consent of the person entitled to use it his liability shall be unlimited.

Comments

(1) Under Article 12(1) Corporations, i.e. legal persons, can only act through servants or agents who must be proved to have acted both within the *course of their employment* and the *scope of their authority*. In Article 25A of the Amended Warsaw Convention it must be proved that the servant or agent acted within the scope of his employment. Comment 2 on Article 2(2)(b) applies here.

(2) Under Article 12(2) there could be a number of cases where an aircraft is taken wrongfully without the consent of the owner; see comment on "wrongful" above. What would be the position where the owner had terminated a charter agreement on breach of a major term by the lessee (charterer). The charterer then takes the aircraft and flies it. This is a private law wrong but does the operation fall within the terms of Article 12(2)?

Article 13(1) and (2)

provide for apportionment of damages and the limit of damages to apply overall where two or more persons are liable for the damage under the provisions of the 1952 Convention. Where more than one aircraft is involved, each aircraft has its own limit of liability unless there are circumstances where that limit does not apply.

Comments

(1) Each aircraft would have to be registered in Contracting State(s) other than the Contracting State where the damage occurred. Interesting questions of burden of proof and limits of liability would arise, e.g. if an accident in Contracting State A occurred between one aircraft registered in Contracting State B and a second aircraft registered in non-Contracting State C. The first aircraft would be liable under the 1952 Convention and the second aircraft would be liable under the applicable domestic law. This problem would not arise within States who are not party to the 1952 Convention, e.g. the UK.

Article 14

deals with the *pro rata* reduction of more than one claim in excess of liability limits taking into account the limit imposed by Article 11(2) in respect of death or injury. If the claims are exclusively in respect of death or personal injury or exclusively in respect of damage to property, the claims shall be reduced in proportion to their respective amounts. If the claims are both in respect of death or injury and in respect of damage to property then half the total sum distributable will be appropriated preferentially to death and injury claims with the balance being proportionally distributed in respect of the property.

Comments

See proposed amendments to Article 14 by the Montreal Protocol 1978 (see page 361).

Article 15

(1) Any Contracting State may require that an operator of an aircraft registered in another Contracting State shall be insured in respect of his liability for the compensation existing under Article 1. Insurance shall be up to the limits applicable under Article 11.

(2) and (3) deal with the terms under which the insurance shall be accepted, or may not be accepted, as satisfactory.

(4) deals with provision of security alternative to insurance.

(5) and (6) require certification of the insurance or provision of security.

(7) specifies the procedures where the State overflown has reasonable grounds for doubting the financial responsibility of the insurer or bank providing the security. Any dispute concerning the adequacy of evidence on financial responsibility shall be submitted to an arbitral tribunal which shall be ICAO Council or person or body mutually agreed by the parties.

(8) deals with notification to ICAO of any requirement made pursuant to this Article, who shall inform Contracting Parties accordingly.

(9) provides definitions.

Article 16

(1) deals both with the defences available to the person who provided insurance or security and also with the continuation of insurance or security in certain circumstances.

(2) deals with the obligations of the State who has issued a certificate of insurance or security to notify the termination or cessation, otherwise than by expiry, of the insurance or other security, to the interested Contracting States as soon as possible.

(3) deals with change of operator during the validity of the security.

(4) deals with continuation in force of the security that shall apply only for the benefit of the person suffering damage.

(5) and (6) deal with further rights and duties of the relevant parties.

Article 17

(1) deals with the specific and preferential assignment of security furnished pursuant to Article 15(4) for payment of claims.

(2) deals with sufficiency of the security in the case of one or more aircraft.

(3) deals with the increase and maintenance of security in the case of notice of a claim being made against the operator.

Article 18

exempts moneys due from insurer to operator from seizure and execution by creditors of the operator until the claims of third parties under the 1952 Convention have been satisfied.

Article 19

If a claimant has not brought an action to enforce his claim, or if notification of such claim against the operator has not been given within six months of the date of the relevant incident, the claimant shall only be entitled to compensation out of the amount for which the operator remains liable after all claims made within the six months period have been met in full.

Comments

The claimant claims under the 1952 Convention, but the Article does not expressly state that all the other claims must be made under the 1952 Convention; they might be passenger claims.

Article 20

This deals at length with jurisdiction and the procedures for bringing and enforcing claims. An action can only be brought before the court of the Contracting State where the incident occurred, subject to any agreement of the parties concerned. It gives the claimant the right to bring a new action outside the two-year limitation period referred to in Article 21 where execution of an earlier judgment has been refused as specified.

Article 21

imposes a two-year limitation period. Grounds for suspension or interruption of the period is determined by the court trying the action, but in any case the right to bring action is extinguished on expiry of three years from the date of the incident which caused the damage.

Comments

Compare these provisions with Article 29 of the Warsaw Convention, see page 279.

Article 22

In the event of the death of the person liable, action in respect of such liability shall lie against those legally responsible for his obligations.

Article 23

The 1952 Convention applies only to damage contemplated under Article 1 caused in the territory of a Contracting State by an aircraft registered in the territory of another Contracting State. A ship or aircraft on the high seas shall be regarded as part of the territory of the State in which it is registered.

Comments

This important provision limits the application of the Convention.

Article 24

The 1952 Convention shall not apply to damage caused to an aircraft in flight or to persons or goods on board such aircraft.

Comments

See page 362 below.

Article 25

The 1952 Convention shall not apply to damage on the surface if liability for such damage is regulated by contract, or by law relating to workmen's compensation applicable to a contract of employment between the relevant persons.

Comments

This Article underlines the fact that the purpose of the Convention is to protect third parties. A possible contract might be between an air display organiser and a foreign exhibitor.

Article 26

The 1952 Convention does not apply to damage caused by military, customs or police aircraft.

Comments

These aircraft are the same as in Article 3(b) of the Chicago Convention.

Article 27

Contracting States will as far as possible facilitate payment of compensation in the currency of the State where the accident occurred.

Article 28

If legislative measures are necessary to give effect to the Convention, ICAO is to be advised of such measures when taken.

Article 29

The 1952 Convention shall supersede the 1933 Convention as between those Contracting States who have ratified both.

Article 30

Definitions:

> "person" means any natural or legal person, including a State.
> "Territory of a State" means the metropolitan territory of a State and all territories for the foreign relations of which that State is responsible, subject to the provisions of Article 36.
> "Contracting State": see text and also provisions of Article 36.

Articles 31–39

These Articles deal with the coming into force of the 1952 Convention and its application, ratification and denunciation. Articles 36 and 37 deal with the application or non-application of the 1952 Convention to such territories as the relevant State may declare or notify. In particular Article 37 deals with the effect on the 1952 Convention of transfer of territory and also territories achieving independence.

The 1952 Convention was done in the English, French and Spanish languages, each text being of equal authenticity.

Annex

The Annex to the 1952 Convention sets out provisions on various certificates relating to insurance, financial responsibility, guarantee, deposit and government guarantee.

Montreal Protocol 1978

The Montreal Protocol 1978 ("The 1978 Protocol") will amend the 1952 Convention if and when the former comes into force. The proposed amendments to the Articles of the 1952 Convention are taken in turn:

Article 2

Concerning aircraft registered as property of a State, liability devolves on the person entrusted with the operation of the aircraft.

Article 11

The limits of liability are expressed in SDRs, or in monetary units of gold content where the Contracting State cannot measure liability in SDRs.

Article 14

The wording is amended on apportionment where claims exceed the limit of liability. The total sum distributable, as opposed to half such sum, shall be appropriated preferentially to meet proportionately claims in respect of death and personal injury.

Articles 15–17

"Guarantee" is substituted for security, and other provisions are amended.

Article 20

The provisions on Rules of Procedure are amended in a number of ways.

Article 23

The following replaces the existing paragraph.

"This convention applies to damage contemplated in Article 1 caused in the territory of a Contracting State by an aircraft registered in another Contracting State or by an aircraft, whatever its registration may be, the operator of which has his principal place of business or, if he has no such place of business, his permanent residence in another Contracting State."

Article 26

This Article is replaced by the following:

"This Convention shall not apply to damage caused by aircraft used in military customs and police services".

Article 27

This is a new Article stating the Convention shall not apply to nuclear damage.

Article 29

This Article, dealing with the supersession of the 1933 Convention, is deleted.

Article 30

Under the existing Article 30 the new definition of "Contracting State" is substituted for the existing definition; the definition "Territory of a State" is deleted; a new definition of "State of the Operator" is included which substantially conforms to the corresponding ICAO definition; it is not identical.

The existing Articles 36 and 37 are deleted with consequential amendment to Article 38.

Comments

(1) Possible sources of 1952 Convention claims are "blue ice bombs". The cause is usually a leaking lavatory waste valve: the leak builds up into external ice which separates during descent into warmer air on approach.

(2) The 1952 Convention has not been widely adopted; at the time of going to print 41 States are party to it. Where the Convention does not apply States have developed their own laws. Many but not all States have adopted strict liability where negligence does not have to be proved. On the other hand, for example under Dutch law and the laws of some US states, negligence has to be proved. Where the limitation of liability under the 1952 Convention does not apply, damages are likely to be unlimited, subject to proof of loss.

(3) Belgium applies the 1952 Convention to domestic flights wherever the aircraft is registered. In the case of a balloonist and a dead cow there was no liability on the former for the latter as there was no evidence of direct damage (Court of Appeal, Gent, (1994) *Air and Space Law* XXI No. 1 1996).

UK law

The UK is party neither to the 1933 Convention nor to the 1952 Convention. Liability is dealt with in its Civil Aviation Act 1982, as follows:

Section 76(1)

No action shall lie in respect of trespass or in respect of nuisance, by reason only of the flight of an aircraft over any property at a height above the ground which, having regard to wind, weather and all the circumstances of the case is reasonable, or the ordinary incidents of such flight, so long as the provisions of any Air Navigation Order and of any orders under Section 62 above have been duly complied with and there has been no breach of Section 81 below.

Comments

1. Section 62 deals with control of aviation in time of war or emergency. Section 81 imposes a criminal penalty for dangerous flying.

2. Trespass and nuisance are common law torts. Trespass is an unjustifiable interference with persons, land and goods. Nuisance is a tort, the essence of which is interference with use or enjoyment of land.

Section 76(2)

Subject to sub-section (3) below, where material loss or damage is caused to any person or property on land or water by, or by a person in, or an article, animal or person falling from an aircraft while in flight, taking off or landing, then unless the loss or damage was caused or contributed to by the negligence of the person by whom it was suffered, damages in respect of the loss or damage shall be recoverable without proof of negligence or intention or other cause of action, as if the loss or damage had been caused by the wilful act, neglect or default of the owner of the aircraft.

Section 76(3)

Where material loss or damage is caused as aforesaid in circumstances in which:

(a) damages are recoverable in respect of the said loss or damage by virtue only of sub-section (2) above; and
(b) a legal liability is created in some person other than the owner to pay damages in respect of the said loss or damage,

the owner shall be entitled to be indemnified by that other person against any claim in respect of the said loss or damage.

Section 76(4)

provides that where the aircraft has been *bona fide* demised, let or hired out for any period exceeding 14 days to any other person by its owner, and no pilot, commander, navigator or other operative member of the crew is in the employ-ment of the owner, section 76 shall have effect as if for references to the owner there were substituted references to the person to whom the aircraft has been so demised, let or hired out.

Section 77

This section deals with noise and vibration caused by an aircraft on an aerodrome and provides for the regulation of such noise and vibration. No legal action shall lie in respect of nuisance by reason only of noise and vibration caused by aircraft on an aerodrome as long as the relevant regula-tions are complied with.

Section 78

In this section the regulation by the Secretary of State for Transport of noise and vibration from aircraft is dealt with at length.

Comments

The position of a UK owner or operator can be summarised as follows:

(1) UK is not party to the 1952 Convention. Therefore wherever UK registered aircraft fly and cause the surface damage under consideration, liability is likely to be regulated by the law of the place of the accident which may be strict, or based on negligence, or possibly on some other grounds. Damages are likely to be unlimited.

(2) UK law imposes a strict unlimited liability for material loss or damage on the owner, subject to the provisions of section 76 of the Civil Aviation Act 1982.

(3) No legal action can be brought against the owner or operator in the UK for trespass or nuisance provided that the conditions in section 76(1) are met. If they have not been met then implicitly such action can be brought.

Case law

Domestic case law is extensive. Three examples follow:

(1) UK: A landowner's rights in airspace above his land are restricted to such height as is necessary for the ordinary use and enjoyment of his land and the structures on it. Aerial photography of his house did not infringe his rights (*Bernstein v. Skyviews and General Ltd* [1978] 1 QB 479).

(2) Australia: An operator may be liable for injury to a rider caused by falling from a horse startled by an aircraft (*Southgate v. Commonwealth of Australia* (1987) 13 NSWLR 188).

(3) USA: Operator was strictly liable for damage caused to fish by chemicals in aerial crop spraying (*Green v. Zimmerman*, South Carolina Sup Court 1977; 14 AVI 18,199 1976–8).

PART 2. DAMAGE CAUSED BY AIRCRAFT IN FLIGHT TO PERSONS OR PROPERTY IN THE AIR

Aerial collisions

There is currently no international treaty dealing with liability arising out of aerial collisions. Where two aircraft collide an analysis has to be made of the circumstances to ascertain the applicable domestic law. Where a collision takes place over the territory of a State then the law of that State should apply as the *lex loci delicti*.

If the collision takes place over the high seas, it is possible that the applicable law will be that of the State most closely connected with the provision of air traffic services for the aircraft concerned. However, if the collision takes place between aircraft with the same State of Registration then it may be argued that the law of the State of Registration will apply.

Once the applicable domestic law is determined, then the nature of the liability needs to be considered. This is most likely to be in negligence or possibly strict.

Passengers carried on one of the colliding aircraft are likely to have a claim against their own carrier, subject to the provisions of the Warsaw Convention or other applicable law, and possibly a claim in tort against the other aircraft operator for unlimited liability.

Both operators are likely to be liable for damage caused on the surface by wreckage.

In the case of an accident over the high seas between aircraft registered in different States, the question arises as to which State has the primary obligation to investigate the accident under Annex 13. However, 4.7–4.8 of Annex 13, (page 157) does not provide for this.

While most systems of law apply the law of tort, in aerial collisions there may be an element of contract in certain cases such as flying displays, club operations or a joint venture relating to crop spraying.

Applicable domestic law must be considered where a parachutist and an aircraft collide in the air.

Wake turbulence

This turbulence is described by Mr Bruce Byron in his article "Wake Turbulence" in *Asia-Pacific Air Safety* (February 1996):

"Rather than being a haphazard region of turbulent air behind an aircraft, wake turbulence consists of two predictably shaped vortices that are shed by the wing tips of a fixed wing aircraft. The forces that create lift are the same as those that create these vortices. Consider wake turbulence as the price we pay for generated lift. A lift-producing wing moving forward through the air creates an area of relatively low pressure above the wing compared to that below the wing. At the wing tips, the relatively high-pressure air below surges around the wing tip. This circulation of air, combined with the downwash induced by the wing, causes the air leaving the trailing edge of the wing tip to form a vortex flow that rolls itself up into a swirling spiral of disturbed air behind each wing tip. The complete wake consists of two counter-rotating vortices."

The article comments that "in a controlled traffic the particular problem of wake turbulence should be largely resolved by the application of published separation standards". For an example of separation requirements to be adopted by ATS, see the UK Manual of Air Traffic Services Chapter 3 (CAP 493).

Thus in assessing any liability situation concerning wake turbulence the involvement of ATS may be very material. See *Yates* v. *USA* referred to in Comment (3) at the end of Annex 11 summary, page 148.

PART 3. DAMAGE CAUSED BY AIRCRAFT OPERATING
ON THE SURFACE

Damage can be caused by an aircraft, when taxiing, taking-off or landing by colliding with people, other aircraft, airport vehicles or buildings, or by "prop wash" or by jet blast.

The definition of "in flight" in Article 1(2) in the 1952 Convention or in corresponding domestic law will determine the applicable legal regime for liability arising out of propeller wash and jet blast accidents. See also references in the IATA Airport Handling Manual, (AHM 693) pages 332–334 above.

Where the aircraft is not in flight and in the absence of any contract, liability will almost certainly be governed by the law of the place of accident and more likely to arise in negligence rather than in strict liability. It is therefore important to distinguish between damage caused by an aircraft in flight and aircraft not in flight according to the applicable law. In certain cases liability for damage may be governed by terms of contract, for example where there is collision between a catering or re-fuelling vehicle providing services to the aircraft in question.

Elements to be considered also in any claim for loss, contribution or indemnity are (i) the provision of ground movement control, (ii) airport equipment, and (iii) surface markings.

CHAPTER 11

PRODUCTS LIABILITY

PART 1. INTRODUCTION

Products liability arises from the design, manufacture, modification, supply and other forms of dealing with a product. Such liability is governed by domestic law. Due to the international nature of civil aviation, conflict of laws questions can arise.

Products liability must be distinguished from liability arising out of the provision of services. For example, the supply of an aircraft containing a defective component can give rise to product liability while the careless fitting by a maintenance organisation of an airworthy component into an aircraft already in use constitutes the defective provision of services. Sometimes the distinguishing line may be hard to draw.

In those cases where the Warsaw Convention continues to apply a limit of liability to damages, products liability will (where it arises) provide a safety valve for the interests of the travelling public as generally it applies no such limit unless by contract or under Article 16 of the EC Directive, see below.

A distinction between air carrier's liability and products liability is that even in respect of strict products liability, the claimant must prove the defect. Under the Warsaw Convention proof of fault is not required.

PART 2. THE BASIS OF PRODUCTS LIABILITY AND CONTRACT

Both common law and civil law systems distinguish between breach of contract and the torts of negligence and strict product liability.

Members States of the EU are subject to the EC Council Directive 85/374 of 25 July 1985 on the Approximation of the Laws, Regulations and Administrative Provisions of the Member States concerning Liability for Defective Products ("EC Directive").

PART 3. CONTRACT AND EXCULPATORY CLAUSES

The nature of the contractual relationship has been considered in Chapter 3. The contract and its formation are governed by domestic law. Such law in many States recognises that the seller of goods should be liable to the buyer for the supply of defective goods. Therefore, in the absence of an express obligation in the contract to supply goods of a satisfactory quality, the relevant law may imply a term into the contract that the goods will be of such quality and fit for the purpose for which they are sold.

In US law such a provision concerning fitness and quality is called a warranty, either express or implied. In English law a distinction is made between contractual terms of different legal strength which are classified as conditions or warranties; a breach of the former gives the injured party the right to repudiate the contract, while a breach of the latter gives a right to damages only.

In many legal systems it is possible for the seller to exclude his liability by way of an express clause in the contract, called in the USA an "exculpatory clause". The purpose of the clause is often to exempt the supplier from liability for the supply of the defective product itself and all liability caused by the defect. Exculpatory clauses are applied in other legal relationships; see page 338 on discussion of Article 8 of the Standard Ground Handling Agreement.

Exculpatory clauses are strictly construed by the court against the party who seeks to rely on them. Their wording has therefore become increasingly complex. See *Keystone Aeronautics Corporation* v. *R J Enstrom Corporation* 499 F 2d 146 (US Court of Appeals, 3rd Circuit, PA, 1974); 14 AVI 18,185 1976–8.

A more simple example in English law is *White* v. *John Warwick & Co Ltd* [1953] 2 All ER 1021. The plaintiff was injured by a defective bicycle he hired from the defendants under a contract which provided that "Nothing in this agreement shall render the owner liable for personal injury". The court held that the wording excluded strict liability in contract but not liability for negligence in tort.

The law in some States removes or limits the effectiveness of exculpatory clauses for social policy reasons. For example, in French law an exculpatory clause will probably be ineffective against the buyer where the defect in the goods is a "*vice caché*", that is a hidden or latent defect.

The purpose of such policy is to protect the consumer and prevent abuse of a dominant commercial position.

In English law the position is dealt with in the Unfair Contract Terms Act 1977, Consumer Protection Act 1987 and the Unfair Terms in Consumer Contracts Regulations 1994. The Consumer Protection Act 1987 applies the EC Directive.

Exculpatory clauses are in many States ineffective where liability to be excluded relates to death or personal injury.

In the USA para 2–302 of the Commercial Code empowers the court to refuse to enforce any unconscionable contract or clause. Para 2–719 provides that limitation of consequential damages to the person in the case of consumer goods is *prima facie* unconscionable but limitation of damages where the loss is commercial is not.

Where there is an international element in the contract it is necessary to decide which law governs the contract ("the proper law") and effect of that law on the contract. Where the contract does not expressly designate the proper law the court must decide on the question.

A contract of sale of an aviation product may contain an exculpatory clause seeking to exclude all liability in respect of its defects but at the same time providing an express warranty that the product is of satisfactory quality. Such warranty often will only (i) apply for a certain period of time of use after delivery of the product, and (ii) provide the purchaser with a limited remedy such as replacement or repair free of charge of the defective component; the component may be of minimal value when compared with the loss of a new aircraft due to, or liability arising from, such defective component.

It is a matter of bargaining power whether a prospective purchaser is willing to enter into a contract which contains an exculpatory clause in return for a limited "warranty".

While the doctrine of privity of contract (Chapter 3) generally allows only a party to the contract to benefit from it, a more liberal view has been taken in the USA in some courts with regard to sub-contractors. In *Aeronaeves De Mexico SA* v. *McDonnell Douglas Corp*, 677 F 2d 771 (9th Circuit, 1982) the court ruled that the manufacturer's exculpatory clause was extended to protect the sub-contractor manufacturer of a landing gear, apparently on the basis that if the sub-contractor was liable to the buyer, AeroMexico, in the particular circumstances the sub-contractor could claim indemnification from McDonnell Douglas. This would "nullify the contractual allocation of risks" between McDonnell Douglas and AeroMexico; McDonnell Douglas would be "denied the benefit of its bargain".

All cases are decided on their own facts and law. The French Court of Cassation in *Besse et autre* v. *Protois et autre* (Cass Fr (Ass) 12 July 1991) held that where there was no contractual link existing between the owner of a house and the sub-contractor of the builder, the owner had no remedy in contract against the sub-contractor.

One of the distinctions between these two cases is that the *AeroMexico* case was a dispute between commercial enterprises while the French plaintiff was a consumer.

Another aspect of privity of contract is whether under domestic law an exculpatory clause will extend to cover servants and agents; see comments on the IATA Ground Handling Agreement in Chapter 9.

PART 4. THE TORT OF NEGLIGENCE

Where there is no contract between the person who manufactured the defective product and the injured person, the latter may have a claim by way of the tort of negligence against the manufacturer. The principles of the tort of negligence in the UK were established by the House of Lords, the highest court of appeal, in the Scottish case of *Donoghue* v. *Stevenson* [1932] AC 562.

In this case two ladies went into a restaurant in Edinburgh. The first lady bought a bottle of ginger beer from the restaurant proprietor for her friend, the second lady. The bottle was opaque. The second lady poured out half the ginger beer and drank it. She then poured out the rest of the ginger beer and alleged that with the ginger beer came out the remains of a decomposed snail. She alleged that the effect of drinking the ginger beer caused illness.

The second lady had no contractual relationship with the restaurant proprietor because it was the first lady who bought the ginger beer. Instead she sued the manufacturer of the ginger beer who was responsible, she alleged, for letting the snail get into the bottle.

The court established that it is necessary to have three essential elements in the tort of negligence:

(i) the duty of care;
(ii) the breach of that duty; and
(iii) damage caused by the plaintiff.

Lord Atkin in his judgment said:

"A manufacturer of products, which he sells in such a form as to show he intends them to reach the ultimate consumer in the form in which they left him with no reasonable possibility of intermediate examination, and with the knowledge that the absence of reasonable care in the preparation or putting up of the product will result in an injury to the consumer's life or property, owes a duty to the consumer to take reasonable care."

In the USA liability based on the negligence of the manufacturer was established in the case of *MacPherson* v. *Buick Motor Co*, 217 NY 382, 111 NE 1051 (1916) where the court stated "We have put aside the notion that the duty to safeguard life and limb, when the consequences of negligence can be foreseen, grows out of contract and nothing else. We have put the source of the obligation where it ought to be. We have put its source in law."

This duty of care extends to component manufacturers, assemblers, designers and others.

Products liability doctrine applies when a product is placed in a stream of commerce.

Depending on domestic law, defences include intermediate inspection, contributory negligence and comparative negligence law. See *Northwest Airlines* v. *Glenn L Martin Co*, US Court of Appeals (6th Circuit, 1955); 4 AVI 17,682 1953–6.

The tort of negligence applies not only to the supply of goods but also to the provision of services and other acts or omissions.

Compared with contract, a claim in negligence has the following disadvantages:

  (i) the plaintiff has to prove breach of a duty of care which in a technical case may be difficult and expensive;

  (ii) in tort contributory fault, i.e. negligence on the part of the plaintiff, can result in the reduction or removal of damages. In some legal systems, contributory negligence is not a defence which can be used by the defendant in a claim in contract to reduce the damages claimed against it.

However, the tort of negligence has the advantage that it is usually impossible for the negligent party to contract out of his obligation where such party has no contractual relationship with the person injured, but see the *AeroMexico* case above.

An example of the civil law approach is found in the article "An Overview of Italian Product Liability Law" by Giuseppe Guerreri in the *German Journal of Air and Space Law* (ZLW 44 JG 1/1995). Prior to the EC Directive coming into force, Italian law was illustrated not by a snail in a ginger beer bottle but by a box of mouldy biscuits sold to the plaintiff, an Italian lawyer. Although the plaintiff claimed damages both from the manufacturer and the retailer, only the manufacturer Saiwa was ordered to pay compensation. In this particular case the retailer was not liable in breach of contract because the biscuits were contained in a sealed box which prevented any checking, thus strict contractual liability was not applied and the remedy in tort was sufficient. Product liability in tort in Italy prior to the EC Directive was governed by the general principles of negligence in the Civil Code.

In Decision No 1270 of 25 May 1964, the Italian Supreme Court laid down two main guidelines:

  (i) negligence of the manufacturer is founded on article 2043 of the Civil Code;

  (ii) the consumer is relieved of any evidentiary burden when the manufacturer's negligence is presumed on account of the dangerous nature of the product (*culpa in re ipsa*).

Guerreri compares the wording of the Italian decree bringing the EC Directive into force with the corresponding wording of the Directive itself concerning design defect. The article also discusses the penal litigation in Italy arising out of the ATR 42 aircraft accident near Milan in October 1987 (see Chapter 13, pages 397–398).

PART 5. STRICT PRODUCTS LIABILITY IN TORT

This liability developed firstly in the USA and subsequently in the EU.

In view of the possible difficulties which face an injured party who can only sue in the tort of negligence, both US courts and legislation developed a strict theory of liability outside the framework of contract. These developments were:

     (i) implied warranty;

    (ii) the tort of strict product liability.

(i) Implied warranty

Implied warranty is a legal fiction. The contractual theory of the warranty which denotes an undertaking by one contracting party to the other was transposed to a non-contractual tortious situation. Dean Prosser stated in "The Assault upon the Citadel" (1960) 69 Yale LJ 1099, "The adoption of this particular device was facilitated by the peculiar and uncertain nature and character of warranty, a freak hybrid born of the illicit intercourse of tort and contract".

    In *Middleton* v. *United Aircraft Corp*, 6 AVI 17,975 1958–60 (US District Court SDNY, 1960) the court commented: "With liability of the manufacturer to one not in privity with him on a negligence theory established, it is but one logical step forward to allow recovery against the manufacturer on a breach of warranty theory by one not in privity with him."

(ii) Strict product liability

In the case of *Greenman* v. *Yuba Power Products Inc* 377 P 2d 897; (1962) 27 Cal Rptr 697 the court said that, "A manufacturer is strictly liable in tort when an article he places on the market knowing that it is to be used without inspection for defects, proves to have a defect that causes injury to a human being". The California Supreme Court held the defendant liable not in negligence nor on express or implied warranty but in strict liability. In this case the plaintiff had been injured by a piece of wood which flew out of a power tool given to him as a present. The court specified the three elements necessary for strict product liability:

    (i) the existence of a defect;

    (ii) the defect existed at the time the product left the manufacturer's control;

    (iii) the defect caused the injury.

Following the development of the tort of strict product liability in *Greenman* v. *Yuba Power Products Inc* (1962) the legal fiction of the implied warranty might cease to serve any useful purpose; nevertheless state law in the USA continues to grant breach of warranty remedies where there is no privity of contract (*Fullerton Aircraft Sales & Rentals Inc* v. *Beech Aircraft Corporation*, US Court of Appeals, 4th Circuit, (1988); 21 AVI 17,120 1988–9). There is however no reference to strict product liability in this case where Kansas law applies.

    The theory of strict product liability was set out in section 402A of the US Restatement (Second) of Torts published in 1966 as follows:

"(1) one who sells any product in a defective condition unreasonably dangerous to the user or consumer or to his property is subject to liability for physical harm thereby caused to the ultimate user or consumer or to his property if:

(a) the seller is engaged in the business of selling such product, and
(b) it is expected to and does reach the user or consumer without substantial change in the conditions in which it is sold.

(2) the rule stated in sub-section (1) applies although:

(a) the seller has exercised all possible care in the preparation and sale of his product, and
(b) the user or consumer has not bought the product from or entered into any contractual relationship with the seller."

Such Restatement states that the product is to be in a defective condition "unreasonably dangerous to the user . . . ". However, the Restatement has no legislative effect in itself and therefore the courts are not obliged to accept the requirement of the product being "unreasonably dangerous", see *Cronin* v. *J B E Olsen Corp*, 501 R 2d 1153 (Cal 1972). The publication *"Products Liability"* by Frumer and Friedman considers how the various US states have dealt with this question.

While the EC Directive applies strict product liability, such liability is best illustrated in the copious US case law, each state applying its own law.

The social reasons supporting the doctrine of strict liability are stated in *Nesselrode* v. *Executive Beechcraft Inc and Beechcraft Aircraft Corp* Missouri Sup Court No. 67428, (1986); 20 AVI 17,224 1986–8 where the court commented that the imposition of strict tort liability is justified on the grounds that the manufacturer or seller is almost always better equipped than the consumer to endure the economic consequences of accidents caused by defective products. In this case the Maintenance Manual did not warn of the possibility of reverse installation of visually identical left and right actuators. These social reasons are echoed in the EC Directive.

Strict products liability attaches to the carrying on the business of selling products for use or consumption. It applies to all persons in the production process, manufacturer, designer, wholesaler, retailer or distributor.

Products usually include items such as manuals and charts.

Defects include design defects, and defects involving inadequate warning.

Defences may include conduct of the claimant being:

(1) abnormal use;
(2) contributory negligence (a complete bar to recovery);
(3) comparative negligence (damages are apportioned according to law).
(4) voluntary assumption of risk.

Strict products liability is governed by US state law. See *Alexander & Others* v. *Beech Aircraft Corp & Others*, US Court of Appeals, 10th Circuit, (1991); 23 AVI 18,130 1991–2 (see Chapter 14, page 414 of this book).

The case of *SA Empresa de Viacao Aerea (Varig)* v. *Boeing Co and Weber Aircraft Corporation* (US District Court WD, Washington N9C76–169M, 17 January 1977) is instructive:

(1) Varig sued Boeing for recovery for the hull loss on the grounds of strict liability, negligent misrepresentation and post-delivery negligence. The court held that the liability of Boeing was effectively excluded by the exculpatory clause.

(2) On the strict liability issue the court stated that the doctrine of strict liability "grew out of a need to protect the average consumer who was thought unable to protect himself and unable to distribute the risks of loss to others when dealing with a large manufacturer . . . " Although there were sound reasons why this doctrine should not apply to the transactions of two large corporate powers, as here, it was unnecessary to decide the issue because Varig waived by disclaimer any claim it had against Boeing.

However, in subsequent litigation arising out of the same accident, when Varig sued the component manufacturer Walter Kidde & Co, the US Court of Appeals 9th Circuit held that strict liability did not apply to negotiated transactions between large commercial enterprises where the airline, manufacturer and component manufacturer have negotiated from a position of relatively equal economic stance (*Varig* v. *Walter Kidde & Co Inc* 669 F 2d 1337, US Court of Appeals, 9th Circuit 1982; 16 AVI 18,476). See also *Tokyo Marine & Fire Insurance Co* v. *McDonnell Douglas Corp* (US Court of Appeals, 2nd Circuit 1980; 15 AVI 18,050 1978–80), where the court reached the same decision. Both decisions were governed by Californian law which would not necessarily be followed in other states. This limitation does not apply to negligence.

S&B indicate that it is possible to exclude strict liability by way of exculpatory clause. On the basis of *Varig* v. *Walter Kidde,* this could only apply in a contract not between large commercial enterprises; in such case social policy law, such as para 2–719 of the US Commercial Code, may have to be taken into account, see page 368.

A further defence in US law is Government Contractor Defence where it has been held that manufacturers of military products cannot be held liable for injuries to servicemen on active duty caused by design defects in military equipment. In *McKay* v. *Rockwell International Corporation* (US Court of Appeals, 9th Circuit 1983; 17 AVI 18,247 1982–3), the court held that strict product liability for design defects did not apply where:

(i) the US is immune from liability under Federal Tort Claims Act;

(ii) the supplier proves the US established or provided reasonably precise specification;

(iii) the equipment conformed to a specification;

(iv) the supplier warned the US about patent errors in the specifications or dangers involved in the use of the equipment known to the supplier but not to the United States.

See also *Miller* v. *UT Corporation* where the defence applies to military equipment resold by the US Government to a foreign Government (233 Conn 732 Ad 1995).

Logically, "state of the art" defence should not be a defence to strict product liability, but see *Bruce* v. *Martin Marietta Corp*, 544 F 2d (1966 Okla) where the court allowed such a defence.

The majority of US state jurisdictions accept liability based on crashworthiness. The plaintiff has to prove that the crash was survivable.

In *Perin Gobhai* v. *KLM Royal Dutch Airlines*, NY Court of Appeals, 1982; 17 AVI 17,589 1982–3, the airline who distributed slippers to its passengers was not held liable under a strict product liability to the mother of a passenger who was injured when she slipped and fell in a friend's apartment when wearing the slippers.

PART 6. EC DIRECTIVE

The EC Directive establishes a uniform concept of strict product liability in EU Member States who are obliged to incorporate the Directive into their domestic law.

The second recital to the EC Directive establishes its social reason: "Whereas liability without fault on the part of the producer is the sole means of adequately solving the problem, peculiar to our age of increasing technicality, of a fair apportionment of the risks inherent in modern technological production."

A summary of the principal articles of the Directive follow:

Article 1:   The producer shall be liable for damage caused by defect in his product.

Article 2:   "Product" means all moveables except for primary agricultural products and game, even though incorporated into another moveable or into an immoveable. "Primary agricultural product" is defined. "Product" includes electricity.

Article 3:   (1): "Producer" means the manufacturer of the finished product, the producer of any raw material or the manufacturer of any component part and any person who, by putting his name, trademark or other distinguishing feature on a product presents himself as its producer.

(2): Without prejudice to the liability of the producer, any person who imports into the European Community a product for sale, hire, leasing or any form of distribution in the course of his business shall be deemed to be a producer within the meaning of the Directive and be responsible, as a producer.

(3): Where the producer cannot be identified, each supplier of the product shall be treated as its producer unless he informs the injured person of the identity of the producer or person who supplied him with the product. (Similar provisions apply to an importer.)

Article 4:   The injured person shall be required to prove the damage, defect and the causal relationship between defect and damage.

Article 5:   Where due to this Directive two or more persons are liable for the same damage they shall be jointly and severally liable without prejudice to the national (domestic) law concerning rights of contribution or recourse.

Article 6:   (1): A product is defective when it does not provide the safety which the person is entitled to expect taking all circumstances into account including:

(a) the presentation of the product;

(b) reasonably expected use of the product;

(c) the time when product was put into circulation.

(2): A product shall not be considered defective for the sole reason that a better product is subsequently put into circulation.

Article 7:   Producer shall not be liable if he proves that:

(a) he did not put the product into circulation; or

(b) it is probable that the defect did not exist when the product was put into circulation by him, or this defect came into being afterwards; or

(c) the product was neither manufactured by him for sale or any form of distribution for economic purpose nor manufactured or distributed by him in the course of his business; or

(d) the defect is due to compliance of the product with mandatory regulations issued by public authorities; or

(e) the state of scientific and technical knowledge at the time he put the product into circulation was not such as to enable the existence of the defect to be discovered; or

(f) in the case of the manufacturer of a component, the defect is attributable to the design of the product in which the component has been fitted or to the instructions given by the manufacturer of the product.

Article 8:   (1): Without prejudice to national law on contribution or recourse, the liability of the producer shall not be reduced when the damage is caused both by a defect in the product and by the act or omission of a third party.

2: Deals with reduction or disallowance of liability in the case of damage caused by both product defect and fault of the injured person or any person for whom he is responsible.

Article 9:   Damage means:

(a) damage caused by death or personal injuries;

(b) damage to, or destruction of, any item of property other than the defective product itself, with a lower threshold of 500 ECU, provided that such item:

(i) is of a type ordinarily intended for private use or consumption; and

(ii) was used by the injured party mainly for his own private use or consumption.

This Article shall be without prejudice to national provisions relating to non-material damage.

Article 10:   (1): Provides a 3–year limitation period running from the day when the plaintiff became aware, or should reasonably have become aware, of the damage, defect and identity of the producer.

(2): Laws of Member States on interruption or suspension of the limitation period shall not be affected by this Directive.

Article 11:   Rights conferred on the injured person by the Directive shall be extinguished on the expiry of 10 years from the date on which the producer put into circulation the actual product which caused the damage, unless the injured person has in the meantime instituted proceedings against the producer.

Article 12:   Liability of the producer arising from the Directive may not be limited or excluded in relation to the injured person.

Article 13:   The Directive shall not affect any rights the injured person may have according to the rules of the law of contractual or non-contractual liability or a specified liability system existing at the moment when this Directive is notified.

Article 14:   The Directive shall not apply to nuclear accidents covered by international conventions ratified by Member States.

Article 15   gives Member States the powers of derogation from Article 2 (exclusion of primary agricultural products and game) and Article 7(e) ("state of scientific and technical knowledge" defence). Note the consequences of the exercise of such powers in respect of Article 7(e) and ensuing procedures.

Article 16   (1): Any Member State may provide that a producer's total liability for damage resulting from a death or personal injury and caused by identical items with the same defect shall be limited to an amount which may not to be less than 70 million ECU.

(2): Ten years after notification of the Directive the Commission shall report to the Council as specified on the limit of

liability referred to in Article 16(1) so that the Council shall
decide whether to repeal paragraph 16(1).

Articles 17–22 deal with the Directive coming into force, the definition of
ECUs, revision of amounts in the Directive and duties of the
Member States and of the Commission.

Comments

1. Articles 1 and 9 make clear that the type of damage covered is that
essentially suffered by the consumer. The EC Directive does not apply to
commercial disputes between corporations.

2. Article 3: For an analysis of the effect of this Article on a European airline
importing an aircraft into the EU, see the views in *Aviation Quarterly* of J-M
Fobe and Arnold Kean in Fobe's article "Aviation Products Liability Law in
Europe—an Update" ([1996–97] TAQ 159).

3. The interpretation of the defences in Article 7 are particularly important
in the light of different defences available in the USA.

4. Article 13 permits the retention of rights arising under pre-existing law
and thus provides a system of dual remedies.

5. There has been little case law:

   (a) a Monza court awarded the plaintiff damages for personal injuries for
a defective bicycle component (20 July 1993, RG 4963/91);

   (b) In *AB & Others* v. *South West Water Services Ltd* [1993] 2 WLR 507
it was accepted that inadvertent water pollution came within the UK
enactment of the Directive; the case was fought only on the amount
of damages.

6. Translation into domestic law by a Member State may not be slavish.
S&B point out that, unlike Article 2 of the EC Directive, the UK Consumer
Protection Act 1987 "is silent on the effect of the incorporation of a product
into a piece of immovable property, for example the building of radar equipment into a ground station" (*S&B* V(35.4)).

7. The European Commission brought proceedings against the UK in the
European Court of Justice on the grounds that the Consumer Protection Act
1987 did not implement Article 7(e) accurately because the Article applied an
objective test while section 4(1)(e) of the 1987 Act applied a more subjective
test where the domestic court could apply rules of negligence and liability
based on fault. The European Court found in favour of the UK. However, the
UK courts still have to decide this question.

In considering EU product liability, it is necessary to take into account EEC
General Product Safety Directive of 29 April 1992 (92/59/EEC) which
imposes an obligation on the producer to place only safe products on the
market. Such Directive is without prejudice to the EC Directive. See defini-

tion of "safe product" in Article 2(6). There are also EU controls on import of unsafe products into the EU from third countries. See Council Regulation (EEC) No. 339/93.

The EC Directive has also been adopted by the European Free Trade Members and has been influential in other States.

Other States have developed their own systems of product liability often as part of their consumer protection legislation. For example the Russian Federation has developed no fault liability under the Civil Code and Resolution No 7 of the Supreme Court 1994 (as amended) "On the Procedure of Examination by the Courts of Consumer Rights Protection Cases".

Conflict of laws questions arise in product liability, see *S&B* V(44), and, in particular, *Skyrotors Ltd* v. *Carrier & Technical Industries Ltd* (1979) 26 Ont (2nd) 207. Certain conflict of law questions in product liability are dealt with in the Hague Convention on Product Liability 1973.

CHAPTER 12

ACTS OF UNLAWFUL INTERFERENCE AGAINST CIVIL AVIATION

INTRODUCTION

The Chicago Convention 1944 contains no Article specifically relating to acts of unlawful interference with civil aviation ("unlawful acts") which only quite recently earned their Annex 17 in 1974.

Article 64 of the Chicago Convention states that ICAO may, with respect to air matters within its competence directly affecting world security, by vote of the Assembly, enter into appropriate arrangements with any general organisation set up by the nations of the world to preserve peace. Article 64 does not apply to most unlawful acts.

Article 3bis of the Chicago Convention deals with interception of civil aircraft. This amendment was introduced following the shooting down of the Korean Airlines Boeing aircraft after it strayed into USSR territory in 1983. It came into force on 1 October 1998.

The Attachment to Annex 17 lists those SARPS in other Annexes and ancillary documents which are directly affected by unlawful acts. Annex 8 must now be added to the list (see page 96 above).

AHM 072 sets out security procedures (page 332 above) and refers to the IATA Security Manual.

The following treaties deal with unlawful acts:

- Tokyo Convention 1963—on Offences and Certain Other Acts Committed on Board Aircraft ("Tokyo 63").
- Hague Convention 1970—for the Suppression of Unlawful Seizure of Aircraft ("Hague 70").
- Montreal Convention 1971—for the Suppression of Unlawful Acts against the Safety of Civil Aviation ("Montreal 71").
- Montreal Protocol 1988—for the Suppression of Unlawful Acts of Violence at Airports Serving International Civil Aviation, supplementary to the Convention for Suppression of Unlawful Acts Against the Safety of Civil Aviation, Montreal 1971 ("Montreal 88").
- Montreal Convention 1991—on the Marking of Plastic Explosives for the Purposes of Detection ("Montreal 91").

McWhinney, when considering piracy as an unlawful act falling within the provisions of Tokyo 63 or Hague 70, observed that piracy was clearly an offence under customary international law.

Article 15 of the Geneva Convention of the High Seas 1958 provides that piracy consists of any of the following acts:

"(1) Any illegal act of violence, detention or any act of depredation, committed for private ends by the crew or passengers of a private ship or a private aircraft and directed:

(a) on the high seas against another ship or aircraft, or against persons or property on board such ship or aircraft;

(b) against a ship, aircraft, person or property in a place outside the jurisdiction of any State."

Article 19 gives every State the right on the high seas, or any other place outside the jurisdiction of any State, to seize a private ship or aircraft, or a ship taken in piracy and under the control of pirates, and arrest the persons and seize the property on board.

While Article 19 provides an opportunity for intercepting and seizing, *McWhinney* points out that the High Seas Convention is of limited application as the unlawful act must be committed for private ends.

The following paragraphs summarise the main provisions of the Conventions on unlawful acts.

TOKYO 63

Chapter I—Scope of the Convention

Article 1(1): The Convention applies in respect of (a) offences against penal law; (b) acts which, whether or not they are offences, may or do jeopardise the safety of the aircraft or of persons or property therein or which jeopardise good order or discipline on board.

Article 1(2): Except as provided in Chapter III Tokyo 63 shall apply in respect of such offences or acts done by any person on board an aircraft registered in a Contracting State, while that aircraft is in flight or on the surface of the high seas or of any other area outside the territory of any State.

Article 1(3): The aircraft is in flight the moment when power is applied for the purpose of take-off until the moment when the landing run ends.

Article 1(4): Tokyo 63 shall not apply to aircraft used in military, customs or police services ("the State aircraft exception").

Comments: Tokyo 63 does not create a new offence to be applied in domestic law.

Article 2: Without prejudice to Article 4 and except when the safety of the aircraft or persons or property on board so requires, Tokyo 63 shall not be interpreted as authorising or requiring any action in respect of offences against penal laws of a political nature or those based on racial or religious discrimination.

Comments: In considering offences against these penal laws reference can be made to the wording used by Articles 9.2 and 10.2 of the European Convention on Human Rights.

Chapter II—Jurisdiction

Article 3(1) and 3(2) affirm the rights and duties of the State of Registration concerning jurisdiction over such offences and acts.

Article 3(3) provides that the Convention does not exclude any criminal jurisdiction exercised in accordance with national domestic law.

Comments: Articles 2 and 3 are intended to make clear that the intention of Tokyo 63 is to preserve safety of persons and property, rather than assisting, or detracting from the application of domestic criminal law.

Article 4: A Contracting State not being State of Registration, may not interfere with an aircraft in flight in order to exercise its criminal jurisdiction over an offence committed on board except in the following cases:

(a) the offence has effect on its territory;
(b) the offence has been committed by or against one of its nationals or permanent residents;
(c) the offence is against its security;
(d) the offence consists of a breach of rules or regulations relating to flight or manoeuvre of aircraft in force in such State;
(e) the exercise of jurisdiction is necessary to ensure the observance of any obligation of such State under a multilateral international agreement.

Comments: 1. This Article relates to offences only and not to the other acts referred to in Article 1(1).

2. Are the rules in Article 4(d) intended to cover, for example, Instrument Flight Rules or regulations on drunkenness? See also the comments of the court in *McClean* v. *McClean* on regulations (Chapter 16 page 459).

Chapter III—Powers of aircraft commander

Article 5(1): The provisions of this Chapter do not apply to offences and acts committed or about to be committed by a person on board an aircraft in flight in the airspace of the State of Registration or over the High Seas or any other area outside the territory of any State, unless the last point of take-off or the next point of intended landing is situated in a State other than that of registration, or the aircraft subsequently flies in the airspace of a State other than that of registration with such person still on board.

Article 5(2): For the purposes of this chapter "in flight" means any time from the moment when all the aircraft external doors are closed following embarkation until the moment when any such door is opened for disembarkation. In the case of a forced landing, the provisions of this chapter shall continue to apply with respect to offences and acts committed on board until competent authorities of a State take over the responsibility for the aircraft and for the persons and property on board.

Comments: 1. The "acts" referred to in Article 5(1) must no doubt be the acts described in Article 1(1)(b).

2. Article 5(1) emphasises the authority of the State of Registration. See footnote 13 of *S&B* VIII(5): "Thus it would appear that an Air France commander en route from Paris to Martinique cannot exercise his powers unless after the commission of the offence he makes a detour into Dominican or St Vincent airspace."

3. The State mentioned in Article 5(1), other than the State of Registration, is not designated as a Contracting State.

4. Article 5(2): This is another definition of "in flight", intended to extend control over the wrongdoer.

Article 6(1): The aircraft commander may, when he has reasonable grounds to believe that a person has committed, or is about to commit, on board the aircraft, an offence or act contemplated in Article 1, paragraph (1), impose upon such person reasonable measures including restraint which are necessary:

(a) to protect the safety of the aircraft, or of persons or property therein; or

(b) to maintain good order and discipline on board; or

(c) to enable him to deliver such person to competent authorities or to disembark him in accordance with the provisions of this Chapter.

Article 6(2): The aircraft commander may require or authorise the assistance of other crew members and may request or authorise, but not require, the assistance of passengers to restrain any person whom he is entitled to restrain. Any crew member or passenger may also take reasonable preventive measures without such authorisation when he has reasonable grounds to believe that such action is immediately necessary to protect the safety of the aircraft, or of persons or property therein.

Comments: 1. In *Levy* v. *American Airlines et al* (SDNY 1993; 24 AVI 17,581 1992–5) the plaintiff sued American Airlines and Swissair alleging injury, false imprisonment and other wrongs as a result of events on flights Cairo–Zurich, and Zurich–New York, when he was held in the custody of Drug Enforcement Agency officials following extradition.

As a result of struggles, and attempted suicide of the plaintiff on the flight, a passenger, who was a licensed anaesthesiologist, injected him with the sedative Valium.

The judgment of the court included:

(i) There was no accident within Article 17 of the Warsaw Convention, which did not therefore apply, leaving the plaintiff free to bring a common law claim under state law.

(ii) However, because American Airlines was subject to Federal Rules, those Rules pre-empted the state principles and in the circumstances the case was dismissed.

(iii) The false imprisonment and assault and battery allegations against Swissair were precluded on the grounds of Tokyo 63. The use of Valium was reasonable.

(iv) With regard to the claims against Swissair for failure to provide safe passage, failure to provide medical treatment, and negligence in releasing him to the DEA agents, the court held that the wording of Tokyo 63 did not extend to protect airline employees from liability when they failed to act to protect a prisoner being extradited by police officials. The claims were however dismissed.

The finding (iv) is a reminder that a treaty will only apply to cases contemplated by its wording.

Article 7(1): Measures of restraint upon a person in accordance with Article 6 shall not be continued beyond any point at which the aircraft lands unless:

(a) such point is in the territory of a non-Contracting State and its authorities refuse to permit disembarkation or those measures have been imposed in accordance with Article 6(1)(c) in order to enable that person's delivery to the competent authorities;

(b) the aircraft makes a forced landing, and the commander is unable to deliver that person to the competent authorities; or

(c) that person agrees to onward carriage under restraint.

Article 7(2) requires the commander to notify as soon as practicable, and if possible before landing in the territory of a State, with a person on board placed under restraint, the authorities of such State of the fact that a person on board is under restraint and the reasons therefor.

Comments: Articles 6, 8 and 9 all give the commander powers which he *may* take while Article 7(1) requires that the measures of restraint *shall* not be continued beyond any point at which the aircraft lands, subject to the stated exceptions. Thus the commander has a discretion as to whether he should exercise these powers or not, where their exercise might increase any danger to the aircraft and those on board. Another aspect of this possible situation is found in 5.6.2 of Annex 11, page 145.

Article 8.1: For the purposes of safety and the maintenance of good order and discipline as provided in Article 6(1), as specified, the commander may disembark in the territory of any State in which the aircraft lands any person he reasonably believes has committed or is about to commit an act referred to in Article 1(1)(b).

Article 8(2): The commander shall report to the authorities of such State any such disembarkation and the reasons for it.

Comments: 1. Note the reference to "any State", which is not limited to any Contracting State. As a non-Contracting State is not bound by Tokyo 63 and in the case of any argument, it might be necessary to look at customary international law or seek refuge in the more general provisions of the Chicago Convention, e.g. Article 25. (See Chapter 5, Annex 12 above, page 148).

2. This Article concerns only those acts, whether offences or not, relating to safety, good order and discipline on board the aircraft.

Article 9(1): The commander may deliver to the authorities of Contracting State in which the aircraft lands any person he reasonably believes has committed on board the aircraft an act which in his opinion is a serious offence according to the penal law of the State of Registration.

Article 9(2) and 9(3) deal with notification of the authorities to whom the person is delivered and provision to them of evidence and information which under the law of the State of Registration are lawfully in the possession of the commander.

Comments: 1. The commander must not only fly the aircraft but must also have sufficient knowledge of the criminal law of the State of Registration.

2. Article 9 applies only to a Contracting State as opposed to a mere State in Articles 7 and 8.

Article 10: For actions taken in accordance with Tokyo 63, neither the commander nor the other specified persons including crew and passengers shall be held responsible in any proceedings on account of treatment undergone by the person against whom such actions were taken.

Comments: "Treatment"—this could cover rough handling on the aircraft, interrogation by the authorities, defective medical treatment, imprisonment or repatriation. The person will usually be a passenger; one of the purposes of this Article may be intended to override the presumed liability under the Warsaw Convention. However the court in *Levy v. American Airlines* found there was no accident.

Chapter IV—Unlawful seizure of aircraft

Article 11(1): When a person on board has unlawfully committed by force or threat thereof an act of interference, seizure or other wrongful exercise of control of an aircraft in flight or when such an act is about to be committed, Contracting States shall take all appropriate measures to restore control of the aircraft to its lawful commander or to preserve his control of the aircraft.

Article 11(2): In the cases contemplated in Article 11(1), the Contracting State in which the aircraft lands shall permit its passengers and crew to continue their journey as soon as practicable, and shall return the aircraft and its cargo to the persons lawfully entitled to possession.

Comments: 1. *McWhinney* makes the following points:

(i) Article 11(1) specifically deals with hijacking where a person on board has unlawfully committed by force or threat an act of interference etc. The act in itself must be unlawful. Tokyo 63 does not make the act a criminal offence which each Contracting State must translate into its domestic law.

(ii) Steps to be taken by Contracting States are already established in the existing international customary law, such as that on distress, that all members of the international community should respect.

2. Distress is mirrored by Article 25 of the Chicago Convention 1944 "Aircraft in Distress" which is put into effect by Annex 12 (SAR) and Annex 11 (ATS).

3. Article 11(1): the act must be "about to be committed"—reasonable grounds of belief (Article 6(1)) is not enough.

Chapter V—Powers and duties of States

Article 12: Any Contracting State shall allow the commander of an aircraft registered in another Contracting State to disembark any person pursuant to Article 8.

Comments: This puts into effect the powers given to the commander by Article 8 as between Contracting States only.

Article 13 imposes on Contracting States obligations with regard to:

(1) taking delivery of any person delivered by the commander, under Article 9(1);

(2) taking (a) such person into custody; or (b) other measures as specified; such custody and measures may only be continued for such time as is reasonably necessary to enable any criminal or extradition proceedings to be instituted;

(3) provision of certain facilities to any person in custody;

(4) making a preliminary enquiry into the facts; and

(5) notification of detention and its circumstances to State of Registration and State of Nationality of detained person and to any other interested State, reporting to them the results of any preliminary enquiries and indicating whether it intends to exercise jurisdiction.

Comments: The obligations of the relevant Contracting State under this Article have to be read in conjunction with the provisions of Articles 14, 15 and 16. There is no strict obligation to bring criminal or extradition proceedings. The specified measures may only be continued for such time as is reasonably necessary for such proceedings to be instituted.

Article 14(1) deals with the return of any person, disembarked or delivered up in accordance with Articles 8(1), 9(1) and 11 (and who cannot or does not want to continue his journey) and where the State in which he landed refuses to admit him. Return may be to the territory of his nationality or permanent residence, or the territory of the State in which he began his journey by air.

Article 14(2) requires that neither disembarkation, nor delivery nor taking into custody or any other measures contemplated by Article 13(2) shall be considered as admission to the territory of the Contracting State concerned for the purposes of its law relating to entry or admission and nothing in Tokyo 63 shall affect the law concerning expulsion from the territory of a Contracting State.

Article 15(1): Without prejudice to Article 14(1) any person who has been disembarked in accordance with Article 8(1) or delivered in accordance with Article 9(1) or has disembarked after committing an act contemplated in Article 11(1) and who desires to continue his journey shall be at liberty as soon as practicable to proceed to any destination of his choice unless his presence is required by the law of the State of landing for the purpose of extradition or criminal proceedings.

Article 15(2): The treatment to be accorded by a Contracting State to such person shall be no less favourable for protection and security than that accorded to nationals of the Contracting State concerned in like circumstances.

Chapter VI

Article 16: Offences committed on aircraft registered in a Contracting State shall be treated for the purposes of extradition as if they had been committed not only in the place where they occurred but also on the territory of the State of Registration. Without prejudice to this provision, nothing in Tokyo 63 shall be deemed to create an obligation to grant extradition.

Article 17: In investigating, or arresting or exercising jurisdiction in respect of any offence, Contracting States shall pay due regard to safety and other interests of air navigation and avoid unnecessary delay of the aircraft and its crew or cargo.

Comment: Both Articles 17 and 18 refer to "offences" only.

Article 18 deals with the application of Tokyo 63 in respect of joint air transport operating organisations or international operating agencies where aircraft are not registered in any one State. A designated State shall be considered as the State of Registration and ICAO shall be notified.

Articles 19–26 deal with the coming into force, ratification, denunciation and notification of Tokyo 63 with the exception of Article 24 dealing with dispute resolution.

Article 24 provides that if any dispute between Contracting States which cannot be settled through negotiation, it shall at the request of one of the Contracting States be submitted to arbitration. If organisation of the arbitration cannot be agreed within six months, then the dispute may be referred to the International Court of Justice.

Article 24(2) and (3) deal with any reservation by any Contracting Party to be bound by Article 24(1).

Signature provisions: Tokyo 63 is drawn up in three authentic texts in the English, French and Spanish languages.

HAGUE 70

Article 1 provides that any person who on board an aircraft in flight:

(a) unlawfully, by force or threat thereof, or by any other form of intimidation, seizes, or exercises control of, that aircraft, or attempts to perform any such act; or
(b) is an accomplice of a person who performs or attempts to perform any such act;

commits an offence ("the offence").

Article 2: Each Contracting State shall make the offence punishable by severe penalties.

Comments: In view of the weakness of Tokyo 63, Hague 70 makes clear that hijacking is an offence and each Contracting State is obliged to incorporate Hague 70 into its own domestic criminal law. However, the act must be unlawful, i.e. not the exercise of a right to seize control of the aircraft.

Article 3(1): The definition of "in flight" follows that in Article 5(2) of Tokyo 63.

Article 3(2) applies the State aircraft exception in Article 1(4) of Tokyo 63.

Article 3(3): Hague 70 applies only if place of take-off or actual landing of the aircraft is situated outside the territory of the State of Registration. It is immaterial whether the aircraft is engaged in an international or domestic flight.

Article 3(4) deals with application of Hague 70 where there is a joint air transport operating organisation or international operating agency concerned, as specified.

Article 3(5): Articles 6, 7, 8 and 10 apply (see below) whatever the place of take-off or place of actual landing, if the alleged offender is found in the territory of a State other than the State of Registration.

Comment: Article 3(5): It is the place of "actual" not "intended" landing.

Article 4(1): Each Contracting State shall take necessary measures to establish its jurisdiction over the offence and any other act of violence against passengers or crew committed in connection with the offence in the following cases:

(a) when the offence is committed on board an aircraft registered in that State;
(b) when the aircraft on board which the offence is committed lands in its territory with the alleged offender still on board;
(c) when the offence is committed on board an aircraft leased without crew to a lessee who has his principal place of business or, if the lessee has no such place of business, his permanent residence, in that State.

Article 4(2): Each Contracting State shall take necessary measures to establish jurisdiction over the offence where the alleged offender is present in its territory and it does not extradite him to any of the States mentioned in paragraph 1 of this Article.

Article 4(3): Hague 70 does not exclude criminal jurisdiction exercised in accordance with national law.

Article 5 deals with the joint air transport operating organisations or international operating agencies and is similar to Article 18 of Tokyo 63.

Article 6 deals with action to be taken by the Contracting State where the offender or alleged offender is in its territory. The action is: (a) taking into custody of the offender or taking such other measures to ensure his presence; (b) making a preliminary enquiry into the facts; (c) assisting the person in custody to communicate with his national State; (d) notifying the State of Registration and other States as specified concerning the person taken into custody, reporting the findings of any preliminary enquiry and indicating if it intends to exercise jurisdiction.

Article 7: Any Contracting State in whose territory the alleged offender is found, shall, if it does not extradite him, without exception, submit the case to its competent authorities for prosecution as specified. Such authorities shall decide in the same manner as for any other serious ordinary offence under the law of that State.

Comments: 1. Article 7 makes the obligation on the Contracting State concerned absolutely clear, unlike Tokyo 63.

2. P. St. J. Smart in his note "The China Airlines Incident: Political Offenders and the Hague Convention 1970" ((1986) *Air Law*, Vol XI, page 258) comments that neither the wording of this Article nor its application indicates that it does not apply to politically motivated acts. While States do exercise criminal jurisdiction, the political motive of the unlawful act can be reflected in the light sentence given in certain cases by the Court.

Article 8(1)–(3): For the purposes of extradition paragraphs (1)–(3) deal with the status of any offence both where there is, and where there is not, an extradition treaty between the Contracting States concerned.

Article 8(4) establishes that the offence shall be treated, for the purposes of extradition, as being committed not only in the place where it occurred but also in the territories of the States required to establish their jurisdiction in accordance with Article 4(1).

Article 9(1): In the case of any acts mentioned in Article 1(a), Contracting States shall take all appropriate measures to restore control of the aircraft to its lawful commander or to preserve such control.

Article 9(2): Contracting States shall facilitate the continuation of the journey of the passengers as soon as practicable and shall without delay return the aircraft and its cargo to the persons lawfully entitled to its possession.

Comments: The wording of Article 9 is stronger than that in Article 11, Tokyo 63.

Article 10 deals with the provision of mutual assistance between Contracting States in connection with the relevant criminal proceedings.

Article 11 requires each Contracting State in accordance with its national law to report to the ICAO Council with information concerning the offence, action taken under Article 9, and measures taken in relation to the offender.

Comments: "In accordance with its national law . . . ": This phrase suggests application of law in addition to that found in Hague 70, perhaps the law on "subjudice" questions, or security.

Article 12: Dispute resolution provisions follow Tokyo 63.

Articles 13 and 14 deal with the coming into operation and denunciation of Hague 70.

Signature provisions: Hague 70 is drawn up in four authentic texts in the English, French, Russian and Spanish languages.

MONTREAL 71

As unlawful acts became more outrageous yet another international treaty was needed, "Montreal 71".

Article 1(1) provides that a person commits an offence if he unlawfully and intentionally:

(a) performs an act of violence against a person on board an aircraft in flight if that act is likely to endanger the safety of that aircraft;

(b) destroys an aircraft in service or causes damage to such an aircraft which renders it incapable of flight or which is likely to endanger its safety in flight;

(c) places or causes to be placed on an aircraft in service, by any means whatsoever, a device or substance which is likely to destroy that aircraft, or to cause damage to it which renders it incapable of flight, or to cause damage to it which is likely to endanger its safety in flight;

(d) destroys or damages air navigation facilities or interferes with their operation, if any such act is likely to endanger the safety of the aircraft in flight; or

(e) communicates information which it knows to be false, thereby endangering the safety of an aircraft in flight.

[*Article 1(1)bis* (Added by Montreal Protocol 1988): Any person commits an offence if he unlawfully and intentionally, using any device, substance or weapon:

(a) performs an act of violence against a person at an airport serving international civil aviation which causes or is likely to cause serious injury or death; or

(b) destroys or seriously damages the facilities of an airport serving international civil aviation or aircraft not in service located thereon or disrupts the services of the airport, if such an act endangers or is likely to endanger safety at that airport.]

Article 1(2) extends the offence to attempts to commit, and acting as accomplice.

Comments: As in Hague 70, the act must be unlawful and intentional if it is to constitute an offence. It is difficult to see how an act of violence could in fact not be an offence. The act of violence in Article 1(1)(a) must be likely to endanger the safety of that aircraft. Thus an assault by a drunken passenger on another passenger would not usually constitute an offence under Article 1(1)(a) but a similar assault against a member of the flight crew is likely to constitute such an offence.

Article 2(a) applies the "in flight" definition found in Article 5(2) of Tokyo 63.

Article 2(b) provides that an aircraft is considered to be in service from the beginning of the pre-flight preparation of the ground personnel or by the crew for a specific flight until 24 hours after any landing; period of service shall extend, in any event, for the entire period during which the aircraft is in flight as defined.

Article 3: Each Contracting State shall make the offences in Article 1 punishable by severe penalties.

Article 4(1) applies the State Aircraft Exception (Article 1(4) of Tokyo 63).

Article 4(2): In the cases contemplated in sub-paragraphs (a), (b), (c) and (e) of Article 1(1), the Convention shall apply, irrespective of whether the flight is international or domestic only if:

(a) the place of take-off or landing, actual or intended, of the aircraft is situated outside the territory of the aircraft's State of Registration; or

(b) the offence is committed in the territory of a State other than the State of Registration.

Article 4(3): Notwithstanding paragraph 2 above, in the cases contemplated in sub-paragraphs (a), (b), (c) and (e) of Article 1(1) the Convention shall also apply if the offender or alleged offender is found in the territory of a State other than the State of Registration.

Article 4(4): In the case of States establishing joint operating organisations or international agencies (Article 9) and in the cases mentioned in sub-paragraphs (a), (b), (c) and (e) of Article 1(1) the Convention shall not apply if the places mentioned in paragraph (2)(a) of this Article are situated within the territory of the same State where that State is one of those States referred to in Article 9, unless the offence is committed, or the offender or alleged offender is found in the territory of a State other than that State.

Article 4(5): The Convention applies to cases contemplated in Article 1(1)(d) only if the air navigation facilities are used in international air navigation.

Article 4(6): Paragraphs (2), (3), (4) and (5) of this Article apply to attempts or acting as an accomplice contemplated in Article 1(2).

Article 5(1): Each Contracting State shall take necessary measures to establish jurisdiction over the offences when:

(a) the offence is committed in its territory;

(b) the offence is committed against or on board an aircraft registered in such State;

(c) the aircraft on which the offence is committed lands in the territory of such State with the alleged offender still on board;

(d) the relevant aircraft is leased without crew to a lessee with his principal place of business, or if he has no such place of business, permanent residence in that State.

Article 5(2): Each Contracting State shall likewise take necessary measures to establish jurisdiction over the offences mentioned in Article 1, paragraph (1)(a), (b), and (c) and Article 1, paragraph (2) where the alleged offender is present in its territory and it does not extradite him to the State as specified.

Article 5(2)bis (added by "Montreal 88") obliges each Contracting State to take measures necessary to establish its jurisdiction in respect of offences mentioned in Article 1(1)bis and Article 1(2) in so far as Article 1(2) applies to such offences where the alleged offender is present in its territory and it does not extradite him as specified.

Article 5(3): Montreal 71 does not exclude criminal jurisdiction exercised in accordance with national law.

Articles 6, 7 and 8 correspond to the Articles bearing the same numbers in Hague 70 except in respect of certain consequential cross-references.

Article 9 corresponds to Article 5 of Hague 70.

Article 10(1): Contracting States shall in accordance with international and national law endeavour to take all practicable measures for the purposes of preventing the offences mentioned in Article 1.

Article 10(2) corresponds to Article 9(2) of Hague 70 with certain changes.

Article 11 corresponds to Article 10 of Hague 70.

Article 12: Any Contracting State having reason to believe that one of the offences mentioned in Article 1 will be committed shall, in accordance with its national law, furnish any relevant information in its possession to those States which it believes would be the States mentioned in Article 5(1).

Comments: Article 12: Note again the reference to "in accordance with its national law".

Article 13 corresponds to Article 11 of Hague 70.

Article 14 corresponds to Article 12 of Hague 70 for dispute resolution.

Comments: For the effect of UN Security Council Resolutions on the rights and duties of Contracting States, see decision of the International Court of Justice, April 1992 in *Libya* v. *UK* (see *S&B* AvR VIII/17).

Articles 15 and 16 deal with the coming into force and denunciation of Montreal 71.

Signature provisions: Montreal 71 is drawn up in four authentic texts in the English, French, Russian and Spanish languages.

MONTREAL 91

Article I sets out the applicable definitions including: "Explosives" "Detection Agent" and "Marking".

Article II provides that each State Party shall take the necessary and effective measures to prohibit and prevent the manufacture in its territory of unmarked explosives.

Article III(1): Each State Party shall take the necessary and effective measures as to prohibit and prevent the movement into or out of its territory of unmarked explosives.

Article III(2) deals with exceptions to this principle in the case of State Party use, for example in the performance of military, or police functions.

Article IV sets out the necessary measures to be taken by each State Party to comply with their obligations under Articles II and III.

Article V establishes an International Explosives Technical Commission.

The remainder of the Articles and the Technical Annex deal with the consequential provisions of putting into effect Montreal 91 which are not dealt with here for the sake of space.

Montreal 91 was drawn up following UN Security Council Resolution 635 of 14 June 1989 and the UN General Assembly Resolution 44/29 of 4 December 1989 urging ICAO to intensify its work on devising an international regime for marking of plastic or sheet explosives for the purposes of detection.

GENERAL COMMENTS

1. Public law. For details of prosecutions under Australian and New Zealand law applying these Conventions, see case note (1995) XX *Air Law* 268 (Margaret Vennell). *R. v. Whiteman* concerned a domestic ambulance flight. *R. v. Takaheshi* concerned an international flight.

2. For domestic legislation on unlawful acts, see for example the UK Aviation Security Act 1982 and the Aviation and Maritime Security Act 1990.

3. Unlawful acts, whether the subject of treaty or not, give rise to breach of private law rights. Some aspects of these are considered:

  (i) In most cases unlawful acts constitute an accident within the terms of Article 17 of the Warsaw Convention. In *Husserl v. Swiss Air Transport Co Ltd* SDNY 1972; 12 AVI 17,637 1972-4, and SDNY 1975; 13 AVI 17,603 1974-6, the plaintiff sued for psychosomatic injuries arising from the hijacking at Dawson's Field. The court decided that the bodily injury arose out of the hijack which constituted an accident, and in that case awarded damage for psychological injuries. The latter part of the judgment on psychological injuries was later overturned by the US Supreme Court in *Floyd* v. *Eastern Airlines Inc* (see page 249 above). See also *Rein* v. *Pan American World Airways Inc*, US Court of Appeals, 2nd Circuit, 1991; 23 AVI 17,714 1991–2 (*Re Air Disaster at Lockerbie*) where the monetary limit of liability was removed by Article 25 of the Warsaw Convention.

(ii) In *Stanford & Others* v. *Kuwait Airways & Others* (25 AVI 17,511 1996) the US Court of Appeals had to consider the position of Middle East Airlines who had sold airline tickets to suspicious-looking passengers who had interlined from the MEA flight onto the flight of Kuwait Airways which was later hijacked. The court remanded the case for a new trial holding that an airline in the position of MEA could be liable in appropriate circumstances to other passengers on the Kuwait Airways flight in the absence of any contract.

4. Unlawful acts are now an unwelcome part of aviation operations and the SARPS. They cannot be dismissed as an independent criminal act for which no innocent party can be responsible. Claims are made, successfully fought or settled by individuals against enterprises and authorities who are innocent of any involvement in an unlawful act other than having failed to prevent it.

5. Potential defendants can include:

(i)   the air carrier;
(ii) the ground handling agent;
(iii) security agents;
(iv) airport operator;
(v)   government agencies and authorities charged with collecting and disseminating intelligence and also monitoring and providing security procedures;
(vi) contractors providing equipment used for security;
(vii) enterprises indirectly concerned with the effect of unlawful acts, see *Stanford* case above.

6. For insurance, see Chapter 16, page 456.

CHAPTER 13

ASPECTS OF AIRCRAFT ACCIDENT INVESTIGATION

Annex 13 has been summarised in Chapter 5. Three topics are considered below:

(1) Other forms of investigation and the EU Investigation of Accidents Directive.
(2) The general application of Annex 13 and the Investigation Directive in the UK.
(3) The status of Annex 13 reports and related information in private law litigation.

PART 1. OTHER FORMS OF INVESTIGATION AND THE EU INVESTIGATION OF ACCIDENTS DIRECTIVE

The Annex 13 SARPS were first adopted in 1951. However, there have long been and continue to be other types of investigation in respect of sudden death or serious physical injury.

In common law countries, as in other States, there is a criminal police investigation, the purpose of which is to ascertain whether any crime has been committed and if a prosecution should be brought.

In England in the case of death there will usually also be a coroner's inquest. The duty of the coroner, as representative of the Crown, is to establish the cause of death where violent or sudden death has occurred or in certain other circumstances. In civil aviation accidents the coroner will usually be guided by evidence available both to the Air Accidents Investigation Branch of the Department of the Environment, Transport and the Regions and to the police. Coroners' inquests are regulated by Coroners Act 1988 and Regulations.

Coroners Act 1988, section 42, provides that no verdict shall be framed in such a way as to appear to determine any question of (a) criminal liability on the part of a named person, or (b) civil liability.

In Scotland an investigation may be carried out by the local sheriff under the Fatal Accidents and Sudden Death Inquiry (Scotland) Act 1976. Its section 6(3) provides that the sheriff's determination shall not be admissible as evidence in any judicial proceedings.

It is, however, in civil law countries where the judicial inquiries have been and are most significant in their relationship to the Annex 13 investigation. Where there has been a death, or serious injury, a judge will carry out a preliminary judicial inquiry. If there is *prima facie* evidence of a crime having been committed, the judge may open the case to a full trial. If there is no such evidence or if, in some States, the possible wrongdoer has died, the case will probably be closed. This may happen where the available evidence points to the cause of the accident being an error of the aircrew who have died in the accident.

This criminal inquiry in some civil law States takes precedence over the Annex 13 investigation. This can lead to delay suffered by the Annex 13 investigators in obtaining access to essential evidence obtainable from flight data recorders, wreckage, or examination of bodies of victims. This delay may hinder the investigators both in finalising their report and in making recommendations under Chapter 7 of Annex 13. 5.10 of the Annex requires coordination between the Annex 13 investigator-in-charge and the judicial authorities.

To meet problems over conflicting interests between the judicial inquiry and the Annex 13 investigation, and also to introduce other improvements, EU Council issued Directive 94/56/EC in 1994 establishing fundamental principles governing the investigation of accidents and incidents ("the Investigation Directive").

A summary of the principal provisions of the Investigation Directive follows.

Article 1: The purpose of the Investigation Directive is to improve air safety by facilitating the expeditious holding of investigations, the sole objective of which is the prevention of future accidents and incidents.

Article 2: Additionally to investigations into civil aviation accidents and incidents within the territory of the Community, the Directive applies outside Community territory to investigations into (i) accidents involving aircraft registered in a Member State; (ii) serious incidents involving aircraft registered in a Member State or operated by an undertaking established in a Member State, when in (i) or (ii) such investigations are not carried out by another State.

Article 3 sets out the definitions which substantially follow those of Annex 13.

Article 4(1) imposes an obligation to investigate accidents or serious incidents. Member States may take measures to enable incidents to be investigated when safety lessons may be expected to be drawn from such investigations.

Article 4(2): The extent of investigations and procedure to be followed shall be determined by the investigating body taking into account the Investigation Directive and the lessons on safety improvement it hopes to draw from the accident or serious incident.

Article 4(3) states that such investigations shall in no case be concerned with apportioning blame or liability.

Article 5(1) requires Member States to define within their internal legal systems a legal status of the investigation which will enable the investigators-in-charge to carry out their tasks in the most efficient way and within the shortest time.

Article 5(2) provides that in accordance with legislation in force in the Member States and where appropriate in cooperation with the authorities responsible for the judicial inquiry, investigators shall have adequate authorisation for access to all necessary information, witnesses and evidence as specified.

Article 6(1) requires that the technical investigations are conducted or supervised by a permanent civil aviation body which shall be functionally independent of national aviation regulatory authorities as specified or any other party with possible conflicting interests.

Article 6(2) provides that the activities entrusted to the body may be extended to the gathering and analysis of air safety related data, as long as these activities do not affect its independence and entail no responsibility in regulatory, administrative or standards matters.

Article 6(3) requires the body to be given the means and status required to carry out its responsibilities independently.

Article 6(4): The body may request the assistance of bodies or entities from other Member States to supply installations, facilities, equipment and experts which should be made available, as far as possible, free of charge.

Article 6(5) permits delegation of tasks of investigation to another Member State.

Articles 7, 8, 9 and 10 deal with the issue of reports and safety recommendations by the investigating body. A safety recommendation shall in no case create a presumption of blame or liability.

The Annex sets out a list of examples of serious incidents.

The Investigation Directive is mandatory for EU Member States. While it is a shorter and less detailed document than Annex 13, nevertheless it includes many principles and aspects of the Annex which therefore become compulsory within Member States, without the discretionary effect of Articles 26 and 37 of the Chicago Convention.

PART 2. APPLICATION OF ANNEX 13 AND THE INVESTIGATION DIRECTIVE IN THE UK

In the UK accidents are investigated by the Air Accidents Investigation Branch (AAIB) of the Department of Environment, Transport and Regions in accordance with the Civil Aviation (Investigation of Air Accidents and Incidents) Regulations 1996 ("Regulations"), made under the Civil Aviation Act 1982. AAIB is therefore part of the central government.

As regulatory functions are performed by the CAA, the AAIB should be independent of any person who in an official capacity may have participated in any act or omission causative to an accident. This independence is recognised as essential by Annex 13 para 5.4 and by Article 6(1) of the Investigation Directive.

Such independence reflects one of the two essential rules of natural justice: no man, or in this case no regulatory authority, should be judge in its own cause. It is essential that not only justice should be done but that it should be seen to be done.

Although Annex 13 procedure is *not* a judicial procedure, nevertheless the findings of an Annex 13 investigation often have a serious impact on personal welfare and commercial reputation as is recognised by Regulation 12.

A summary of the Regulations follows. Any reference to "accident" usually includes "serious incident". The bold numbers refer to regulation numbers:

1: The Regulations are cited as the Civil Aviation (Investigation of Air Accidents and Incidents) Regulations 1996 and came into force on 21 November 1996.

2: Those definitions found in the Regulations and in Annex 13 and the Investigation Directive are substantially the same.

3: The Regulations apply only to civil aviation accidents and incidents.

4 follows 3.1 of Annex 13.

5(1): Where the Chief Inspector is required to carry out an investigation under regulation 8(3), the relevant person, which includes the aerodrome authority where the accident occurs on or adjacent to an aerodrome, shall notify (i) the Chief Inspector of the AAIB and (ii) in the case of an accident occurring in or over the UK the relevant police officer.

5(2) defines relevant person which includes in the case of a serious incident occurring in a country other than a Member State or Contracting State to an aircraft registered elsewhere than in the UK, but operated by an undertaking established in the UK, that undertaking.

5(3): The notice to the Chief Inspector shall contain those items listed in 4.2(a)–(i) of Annex 13 (see page 157).

5(4): In the case of an incident, other than a serious incident, the owner, operator, commander or hirer of the aircraft shall, if required by notice given to him by the Chief Inspector, provide such information as may be specified in the notice.

6: Subject to regulations 11(4)(b) (requiring any investigation report on an incident to protect anonymity of persons involved), and 18 (dealing with the disclosure of relevant records), the Chief Inspector may at any time publish information relating to an accident or incident, whether or not subject of an investigation by an Inspector.

7(1): Subject to regulations 7(2) and 9 (powers of Inspector(s)), where an accident occurs in or over the UK resulting in withdrawal from service of an aircraft no person other than an authorised person shall have access to the aircraft, neither shall it nor its contents be removed or otherwise interfered with except with the authority of the Secretary of State.

7(2): Subject to the specified provisions of the Customs and Excise Management Act 1979 the aircraft may be removed or interfered with as far as may be necessary for the purpose of specified reasons including the extricating of persons or animals.

8(1) and **(2)** deal with the appointment of inspectors, including a Chief Inspector, by the Secretary of State who shall form that part of the Department of Transport (now the DETR) known as the Air Accidents Investigation Branch.

8.3: The Chief Inspector shall carry out or cause an Inspector to carry out investigations into (a) accidents in or over the UK; (b) accidents occurring in or over any country which is neither a Member State (of the EU) nor a Contracting State (to the Chicago Convention) to aircraft registered in the UK when such investigation is not carried out by another State; (c) serious incidents occurring in a country which is not a Member State nor a Contracting State to aircraft registered elsewhere than in the UK but which are operated by an undertaking established in the UK when such investigation is not carried out by another State; and (d) accidents to aircraft in the UK in the circumstances described in 5.3 of the Annex (page 158 above).

8(4): The Chief Inspector may, when he expects to draw air safety lessons from it, carry out an investigation into an incident, other than a serious incident, occurring in or over the UK, or anywhere else to an aircraft registered in the UK.

8(5)–(7) deals with delegation of tasks of investigation by the Chief Inspector, to Member States and Contracting States and vice versa.

8(8): Without prejudice to the power of an Inspector to seek advice or assistance, the Secretary of State may at the request of the Chief Inspector appoint persons to assist inspectors in a particular investigation who shall have the powers as specified.

8(9) and **(10)** deal with delegation by the Chief Inspector of his powers and obligations to an Inspector and nomination of an Inspector to be in overall charge of any investigation.

9(1) follows substantially the provisions of Article 5 of the Investigation Directive concerning the authority of the investigator.

9(2) sets out the powers of the Inspector enabling him to exercise the authority given under regulation 9(1).

9(3) deals with expenses of those summoned to give information under regulation 9(2).

9(4): On request by the investigating body of another Member State, the Chief Inspector may supply installations, facilities, equipment and experts as specified to such Member State.

9(5) applies the meanings in the Investigation Directive of "operator" and "in cooperation with the authorities responsible for the judicial enquiry" to this Regulation.

10 empowers the Chief Inspector to determine the extent and procedure of investigations. The Chief Inspector shall take into account Regulation 4, the Investigation Directive and the lessons he expects to draw from the accident or incident for the improvement of safety.

11(1) requires the inspector to prepare a report upon completion of the investigation appropriate to the accident or incident.

11(2) provides where there is a military element in the accident or incident and the investigation has been completed apart from investigation of the matters affecting discipline or internal administration of the military forces concerned, the inspector may finalise his report which shall state the matters to which his investigation has not extended.

11(3)–(4) provide that (a) the report in the case of an accident shall state the sole objective of the investigation as described in 4, and contain appropriate safety recommendations; (b) in the case of an incident the report shall contain the recommendations, protect the anonymity of persons involved in the incident and be circulated to parties likely to benefit from its findings with regard to safety.

11(5): A safety recommendation shall in no case create a presumption of blame or liability.

11(6): A copy of every report shall be submitted to the Secretary of State without delay.

12(1)–(7): No report which is required to be published under regulation 13 shall be so published if, in the investigating inspector's opinion, it is likely to affect adversely the reputation of any person until the inspector has (a) served a notice on the person or his estate which shall include the adverse material; and (b) made such changes as the inspector thinks fit following his consideration of any representations made to him by or on behalf of the person whose reputation may be so affected. The Regulation specifies various procedures for periods for notice and reply.

12(5) prohibits disclosure of the information by the person notified, without prior written consent of the Chief Inspector.

13 requires the Chief Inspector, subject to regulation 12(1), to publish the report, other than in the case of delegation by a Member State to UK of investigation of an incident, in the shortest time possible (and if possible within 12 months of the date of the accident) in such manner as he thinks fit.

14(1): The Chief Inspector shall communicate the reports referred to in regulation 13 to the undertakings and national authorities concerned and also to the Commission of the EU. Such reports shall include those not required to be published under regulation 13, and also the safety recommendations.

14(2) deals with the obligations of the undertaking or authority to whom a safety recommendation is communicated, see 7.5 and 7.6 of Annex 13.

15 deals with the re-opening of the investigation where new important evidence has been disclosed or where there is ground for suspecting the reputation of any person has been unfairly and adversely affected.

16 deals with the rights of participation in the investigation of accredited representatives of the five States specified in Annex 13; Registry, Design, Manufacture, Operator and a State which has furnished information, facilities or experts to the investigating Inspector.

17 prohibits any person from (i) obstructing the investigation and (ii) failing to comply with any summons of an Inspector.

18 deals with the disclosure of records and is summarised as follows:

(1) Subject to (2) and (4)–(6) below, the Secretary of State shall not make available any relevant record to any person for purposes other than the investigation.

(2) The Secretary of State may make available a record to any person who is party to or otherwise entitled to appear at judicial proceedings where the court has ordered the record shall be made available to him for the purpose of such proceedings, or in any other circumstances where the court orders the records shall be made available for the purposes of those circumstances.

(3) defines "judicial proceedings", "relevant court", "relevant record" and "Secretary of State".

(4) No order shall be made by the relevant court unless it is satisfied that the interests of justice outweigh any adverse domestic or international impact which disclosure may have on the investigation to which the record relates or any future accident or incident investigation in UK.

(5) A record or part of a record shall not be treated as having been made available where it is included in the final report or appendices of the final investigation report.

(6) The provisions of this regulation shall be without prejudice to any rule of law which authorises or requires the withholding of any relevant record or part of record on the grounds of public interest.

(For further consideration of this question see Part 3 of this chapter.)

The Annex 13 Report and the activities of the AAIB can be challenged in England by way of judicial review.

Since the Regulations extend to accidents of British registered aircraft in the UK they are therefore wider than the provisions of Article 26 of the Chicago Convention, see section 75 of the Civil Aviation Act 1982.

PART 3. STATUS OF THE ANNEX 13 REPORT AND RELATED INFORMATION IN PRIVATE LAW LITIGATION

The position concerning the Annex 13 Report in many States is similar to that stated by the court (Walsh DJ) in the Canadian case of *Swanson* v. *R* (Federal

Court of Canada, 1989/90; *S & B* AvR, Issue 2, see also Annex 6 above, page 78):

"In the present case, the report [of the Canadian Aviation Safety Board] was made by the chairman . . . and seven board members . . . It would not appear to be feasible or necessary in the present case to call on all of the many witnesses who testified. It is nevertheless a public document . . . I believe that the report should be admitted on the understanding that the court will not accept as proven any facts contained therein which are not before the court as a result of admissible evidence and that the decision of the court will not be influenced by the opinions and recommendations in the report, which are not binding on it. On this basis, the report has limited value but neatly summarises considerable portions of the evidence established by those who testified (at the time) and the documents produced."

In short, the Annex 13 Report can be produced in court in private law proceedings, but binds neither the court nor the parties.

However, in the USA, section 1441(e) of the Federal Aviation Act (49 USC) provides, "No part of any report or reports of the National Transportation Safety Board relating to any accident or the investigation thereof, shall be admitted as evidence or used in any suit or action for damages growing out of any matter mentioned in such report or reports". This provision was in substance repeated in section 1903(e) of the Independent Safety Board Act 1974.

These US provisions were applied in *Re Air Crash Disaster at Sioux City*, Iowa, 19 July 1989, MDL 817.

The Arizona Court of Appeals held in *Davis* v. *Cessna Aircraft Corporation* that the trial court erred when it admitted into evidence a report from the NTSB concerning its belief about the probable cause of the accident (24 AVI 18,242 1994). The Court of Appeals applied section 1441(e). The case concerned liability of the manufacturer for an accident in which a pilot and passenger were killed following a collision with unmarked power lines. The Court of Appeals remanded the case to the trial court. The court accepted that most Federal courts admitted factual findings contained in the NTSB reports.

(*Author's Note*: The NTSB report in *Re Air Crash Disaster at Sioux City*, the subject matter of this case, is recommended reading. It is illustrative of the various elements found in an airline accident and in particular questions concerning the use of materials in manufacture and operation of power plants; see Chapter 17.)

In *John Christ* v. *International Business Machines & Others* (Pennsylvania Court of Common Pleas, 1989 No. 3601; 22 AVI 18,290 1989–90) the court considered that there were parts of the NTSB report which would be disclosable but that Pennsylvania law prohibited such disclosure. The National Transportation Safety Board being the Federal agency charged with the duty to investigate accidents produced two reports, one detailing the facts and circumstances surrounding the crash (factual report) and the second determining the probable cause of the accident. The defendants, Messerschmitt-

Bölkow-Blohm GmbH (MBB), wished to introduce the factual report, arguing that its introduction was supported by previous cases. For example, in *Beiguido* v. *Eastern Airlines*, 17 F 2d 628 (3rd Circuit, 1963) the court ruled that 49 USC, section 1441(e) did not bar admission of the "facts, conditions and circumstances" relating to the accident. The court limited the application of section 1441(e) to the finding of probable cause. In the circumstances the court held that portions of the report offered by the parties were not excludable under sections 1441(e) but were excludable under Pennsylvania law because portions of the factual report offered by MBB were double hearsay and untrustworthy.

With regard to Annex 13 generally, and in particular its paragraph 5.2, the judgment of the New Zealand Court of Appeals in *New Zealand Airline Pilots Association Inc* v. *Attorney General* (Court of Appeal, Wellington, 1997, page 269) is illustrative of questions which can arise in this field. The case concerned two sets of proceedings in which the appellant plaintiffs sought an order to prohibit:

(i) the police from obtaining a search warrant for the cockpit voice recorder, its transcript and the digital flight data recorder;
(ii) the Transport Accident Investigation Commission (TAIC) from annexing to their report extracts from the cockpit voice recorder transcript.

The enforcement in New Zealand of Annex 13 and in particular 5.12 were considered. The court reached the following conclusions:

(i) New Zealand constitutional law requires incorporation of a treaty into domestic law. Currently, in respect of the Chicago Convention, this is done by the Civil Aviation Act 1990. The wording of such Act made clear that different parts of the Convention were implemented into New Zealand law in a variety of ways. The Convention does not as a whole form part of New Zealand law.
(ii) While, for example, Article 12 (Rules of the Air) of the Chicago Convention was mandatory and was treated as such by New Zealand legislation, both Article 26 and 37 of the Chicago Convention allowed a discretion to the State not to apply Annex 13 strictly in all its terms.
(iii) Parliament had not made Annex 13 part of New Zealand law and in any event New Zealand had filed an Article 38 notification indicating that the records listed in 5.12 might be disclosed.
(iv) 5.12 did not place any limit under New Zealand law on the power to issue a search warrant, which power was not limited by public interest immunity for the reasons specified.
(v) A report on an investigation aimed at preventing further accidents, determining the causes of an accident, and prepared by a qualified and experienced body include a statement of relevant facts as an

integral part of determination of the facts. For TAIC to publish its report, including the information, in terms of its statutory function, was not to "disclose" it. It was simply to carry out its statutory role. The inclusion in the Appendix of extracts from the transcript came within the power of TAIC under the Transport Accident Investigation Act.

The plaintiff's appeals failed.

The court also observed that it was important for commission reports to be published early.

CHAPTER 14

ASPECTS OF LITIGATION AND CLAIMS INCLUDING DAMAGES

This chapter considers some topics found in international aviation litigation.

PART 1. FORM OF LITIGATION

Litigation is the bringing, defending and conduct of legal actions ("action" or "proceedings") whether by way of action in the State or international courts, or arbitration or alternative dispute resolution. This chapter deals only with private law litigation.

(1) Procedure in State courts

All proceedings are subject to their own rules of procedure imposed by domestic law such as the English Civil Procedure Rules 1999 ("CPR") or Codes of Civil Procedure in civil law States.

The State judicial organisation in some former communist States includes litigation procedures applicable to commercial or foreign enterprises which are sometimes designated as "arbitration", although the courts concerned form part of the standard judicial system.

(2) Arbitration

The parties may agree to submit a dispute to arbitration, either before or after the dispute arises. See for example Article 9 on Arbitration in the IATA Standard Ground Handling Agreement (Chapter 9).

The justification for arbitration is that it allows the parties to control resolution of their disputes (party autonomy). It is also sometimes stated to be quicker, less expensive and more confidential than standard court procedure. It is unlikely to be cheaper in most cases as the parties have to pay the fees of the arbitrators as well as of their own lawyers. State judges are usually supplied free of charge. It can be quicker. It should be confidential unless the parties do not treat it as such.

The extent to which arbitration proceedings and awards are subject to review by the ordinary courts of the State of arbitration depends on the domestic law and the arbitration agreement between the parties. The site of arbitration proceedings will not be a popular one in the international commercial community where either party can "replay the match" by going to the ordinary courts of the land following the arbitration award. However, a modest right of the ordinary courts to intervene on the grounds of procedural irregularity and in extreme cases to overrule the arbitrator's award, is a useful fallback position.

An example of arbitration is found in *Re Keenair Services Ltd and Norwich Union Fire Insurance Society Ltd* (Arbitration Re Policy No A. 8203/218, 29 July 1983) concerning failure to issue a ticket; see page 453.

For a further example of arbitration see *Coleman v. Youell*. This concerns arbitration between hull all risk and war risk re-insurers; the report is found in *S&B Reported Air Law Cases*, see page 457.

The procedure for arbitration will either already be in place, for example the Rules of the International Chamber of Commerce, or will be set by the arbitrators, usually in discussion with the parties. The arbitrator's award may be enforced under the New York Convention on the recognition and enforcement of foreign arbitral awards 1958 or possibly by some other method.

(3) Alternative dispute resolution

Alternative dispute resolution (ADR) describes a variety of informal methods of resolving disputes which avoid the courts and arbitration, in particular mediation, which is a non-binding process until recorded by the parties in a settlement agreement.

PART 2. WHY AVIATION LITIGATION CAN BE COMPLEX

Aviation disputes may contain complicating elements including:

    (i) Different domestic laws may apply to different aspects of the same case. For example where an air carrier of State A using defective equipment purchased under contract in State B crashes in State C due partly to the defective equipment and partly due to the defective provision of ATS, the issues in any passenger litigation may include:

        (a) the Warsaw Convention;

        (b) the proper law of contract for the supply of the equipment and its effect;

        (c) the domestic law on defective provision of ATS.

    (ii) Many accidents have several causes and the court must analyse the technical arguments in order to attribute legal responsibility.

(iii) There may be a number of parties in the action whose places of business are in different jurisdictions. This may give rise to proceedings in different States (or states within a State) arising out of the same accident.

PART 3. JURISDICTION AND INITIATION OF PROCEEDINGS

Jurisdiction is the power of a particular court to hear a case and to control the parties by its rules. Jurisdiction also describes the place where the court is situated.

The claimant chooses the jurisdiction most advantageous to him. Once the jurisdiction in the appropriate State has been selected, then the particular court (often depending on the amount claimed) and also the physical location of such court has to be chosen.

In selecting jurisdiction factors to be considered are:

   (i) the availability of the defendant and any other parties
  (ii) the applicable limitation (prescription) period
 (iii) nature of damages available
 (iv) availability of evidence
  (v) enforcement of any judgments.

Under conflict of laws rules it may be necessary to answer some of these questions either by application of the law of the court seised of the case (*lex fori*) or by the substantive law of the State applicable to the dispute (*lex causae*).

In potential multi-party litigation the plaintiff and the defendant need to keep in mind the joining of other parties and their accessibility to the jurisdiction.

(1) Service

Sometimes in selecting jurisdiction the choice of the plaintiff may be limited, for example by Article 28 of the Warsaw Convention; see page 277.

Once a claimant has selected his jurisdiction he will start proceedings in accordance with the applicable rules. For example, in England Part 7 of the CPR states that proceedings in the High Court or County Court are begun by claim form. Details of the claim form will be entered on the court register. It will then be necessary to serve the claim form on the defendant within the required period and in accordance with the applicable rules. Service is carried out by the plaintiff or his agent which is usually his lawyer or process server.

In France, proceedings are usually started by the issue of a summons (assignation) which is served by a sworn bailiff (*huissier de justice*).

Where the defendant is within the jurisdiction, then no problem usually arises with regard to service. If the defendant is outside the English jurisdiction, then in English law both English rules and the rules of the country in which service is to be effected will apply. Service may be made under a bilateral Civil Procedure Convention or the Hague Convention on Service Abroad of Judicial and Extra-Judicial Documents in Civil and Commercial Matters 1965. Schedule 1, Rule 11 of CPR gives the court discretion to give leave to serve a claim form outside the jurisdiction on a number of grounds. For example, in sub-para (c) it may be given where the claim is brought against a person duly served within or out of the jurisdiction and a person out of the jurisdiction is a necessary or proper party thereto.

While under English law valid service of proceedings is the basis of jurisdiction, the plaintiff must, where service on the defendant is outside the jurisdiction, bring his case within certain specific rules in order to establish jurisdiction of the English courts.

In Western Europe questions of jurisdiction, service of proceedings and enforcement of judgment are uniformly dealt with under the Brussels Convention on Jurisdiction and the Enforcement of Judgments in Civil and Commercial Matters 1968 and the Lugano Convention 1988 (having the same title).

Where there is jurisdiction in England under Article 28 of the Warsaw Convention and the defendant is not within the jurisdiction then the RSC automatically allow service to be made on him outside the jurisdiction.

Once service has been made on the defendant the latter must choose whether:

(1) He accepts service;
(2) He accepts jurisdiction;
(3) He intends to defend the case or not.

If he has been validly served and does not take steps to defend the action, then he runs the danger of judgment being given in default against him.

The growing network of international treaties concerning civil procedure and the international nature of civil aviation, increasingly limits the opportunity for the defendant to ignore judgment given against him in default.

(2) Jurisdiction

If the defendant decides to resist jurisdiction he will need to take into account the procedure for so doing. For example, in proceedings in the USA, the plaintiff will have to satisfy the court that: (1) it has subject matter over jurisdiction, that is to say there is no immunity or other reason why the court cannot hear the action; and (2) there is adequate personal jurisdiction over the defendant which is satisfied by the defendant having minimum contacts with the state concerned.

Contesting the question in the USA of whether a particular defendant has minimum contacts or not may lead to prolonged discovery by the plaintiff against the defendant (see page 416).

Both parties should take into account whether the court will treat the issue of jurisdiction as a preliminary issue to be dealt with before the main trial starts or whether dispute on jurisdiction and trial on the substance of the case run in tandem. In some States an appeal on jurisdiction can follow the main trial.

Apart from disputing jurisdiction of the court to hear the case generally and also exercise jurisdiction over the defendant, there are a number of other aspects of jurisdiction:

(i) Forum non conveniens

The principle of *forum non conveniens* is where a court, which has valid jurisdiction over a case which has been started before it, recognises there is an alternative jurisdiction which is more appropriate to hear the case, and orders its transfer to that alternative jurisdiction.

Forum non conveniens was developed by the Scottish courts, adopted in the US courts and later accepted by the English courts (*Dicey* page 398). The application for transfer is normally made by the defendant.

In *Piper Aircraft Co.* v. *Reyno*, 548 US 235 (1981); 16 AVI 17,986 1980–2, the estates of British nationals sued Piper and Hartzell Propeller Inc. for wrongful death damages arising out of an air taxi service crash in Scotland. The US Supreme Court, in upholding the decision of the District Court, ordering the transfer of the case to Scotland, stated

"The District Court concluded that the relevant public interests also pointed strongly towards dismissal. The court determined that Pennsylvania law would apply to Piper and Scottish law to Hartzell if the case were tried in the Middle District of Pennsylvania. As a result, 'trial in this forum would be hopelessly complex and confusing for a jury.' In addition, the court noted that it was unfamiliar with Scottish law and thus would have to rely upon experts from that country. The court also found that the trial would be enormously costly and time-consuming; that it would be unfair to burden citizens with jury duty when the Middle court of Pennsylvania has little connection with the substantial interest in the outcome of the litigation."

While US courts apply the doctrine of *forum non conveniens* to the Warsaw Convention regime, English courts do not.

In *Re Air Crash Disaster near New Orleans*, Louisiana, 9 July 1982 (US Court of Appeals, 5th Circuit, 1987; 821 F 2d 1147; 20 AVI 18,179 1986–8) the Court held that while Article 28(1) of the Warsaw Convention vested the absolute choice of forum in the plaintiff, this did not prevent a District Court from considering and applying *forum non conveniens*. It was not applied in the case in point because the USA was a party to the litigation and the only forum available was in the USA.

However, the doctrine of *forum non conveniens* was successfully applied in *Feng Zhen Lu* v. *Air China International Corp* (US DC EDNY, 1992; 24 AVI 17,369 1992–5). The United States District Court in 1992 ordered the case to be transferred from New York to Beijing, despite there being jurisdiction in the USA under Article 28 of the Unamended Warsaw Convention. The claimant and the airline were both resident in the People's Republic of China, the alleged accident took place in Beijing and the witnesses were in China. The court ordered that the case should be transferred to China.

In both this case and *Piper* v. *Reyno* the plaintiffs were not US citizens.

However, in England in *Milor SRL* v. *British Airways* [1996] 3 All ER 537 the Court of Appeal confirming judgment in the lower court held that the plaintiff's choice of forum under Article 28(1) is absolute and that *forum non conveniens* does not apply to the Warsaw Convention. Two elements which the Appeal Court took into account were:

(1) The Warsaw Convention was a self-contained code within the terms of Article 28 on jurisdiction. When the Warsaw Convention was concluded in 1929 not every common law country recognised *forum non conveniens* and also the court believed that *forum non conveniens* was and is not part of the jurisprudence of civil law countries.

(2) The Court rejected the defendant's argument that "bringing an action" under both Articles 28 and 29 meant merely starting the action following which, in the case of Article 28, the doctrine of *forum non conveniens* could be applied. The court observed that in the official French version the French words "porté" was used in Article 28 and "intentée" was used in Article 29.

At the time the case is restarted in the appropriate transferee court, the applicable limitation period in such court may have expired. It will therefore usually be a condition of dismissal of the original action that the defendant should waive the time bar in the foreign jurisdiction. Where the Warsaw Convention applies it is suggested that the transferring court may have to keep the case alive in view of the strict wording of Article 29 (see page 279).

(ii) Sovereign immunity

Sovereign immunity is the immunity of foreign States and heads of States from legal action in the territorial (domestic) courts of another State. This is a principle of public international law reflecting comity of nations. *Starke* comments: "In English courts, as distinct from the courts in a number of continental countries, the rule of absolute jurisdictional immunity prevailed, without exception, for the case of involvement of foreign States in transactions of a commercial or non-governmental nature" (page 191).

Due to the development of commercial activities of foreign States and their wholly owned agencies or corporations, legislation has been passed in some States clarifying and limiting immunity. See for example the US Foreign Sovereign Immunities Act 1976 (FSIA) and the UK State Immunity Act 1978. Generally speaking, under such legislation immunity will not apply to commercial activities.

The FSIA applies to foreign States and to any entity, which is more than 50 per cent owned by a single foreign State, with certain exceptions. Once it is shown that full immunity does not apply, probably because of commercial activities, the State entity can require any action against it to be brought in the Federal court as opposed to the state court.

(iii) Injunction against plaintiff to restrain foreign proceedings

A recent development in common law civil aviation litigation is an application (usually by a defendant) against a plaintiff claiming an injunction (an order) from the court prohibiting the plaintiff from taking proceedings in a particular State which has no proper connection with the circumstances of the case. See *Société Nationale Industrielle Aerospatiale* v. *Lee Kui Jak & Another* [1987] AC 871.

The administrators of the estate of the deceased passenger started proceedings within the applicable limitation period both in Brunei and in Texas (both common law jurisdictions) against the French manufacturers. Texas was not the natural forum for the action, but it was and is attractive to claimants because of the high damages awards made by juries there. The UK Judicial Committee of the Privy Council, the ultimate court of appeal for Brunei, ordered the plaintiffs to desist from their action in Texas.

This procedure must be distinguished from an application for *forum non conveniens*. In the case of *forum non conveniens* the court which is exercising jurisdiction, transfers the case to another jurisdiction. In *Aerospatiale* v. *Lee Kui Jak* the court of one State (Brunei) orders the plaintiff within its jurisdiction not to proceed with litigation in the courts of another sovereign State (USA) which is prepared to accept jurisdiction.

Failure of the plaintiff to obey the injunction is contempt of court and is subject to sanctions by the latter.

(iv) Lis alibi pendens

Where proceedings are started in one jurisdiction when there are already current proceedings between the same parties on the same subject matter in another jurisdiction, each court will have to decide on application of whichever party whether it should continue to hear the case and what order to issue to the parties following its decision.

(3) General procedure

As soon as the preliminary questions such as jurisdiction or service are resolved the action will proceed. It will be normally conducted on the basis of written pleadings and oral arguments although common law and civil law procedures differ as to the emphasis put on these two ways of presenting arguments. Civil law puts more emphasis on written pleadings.

A defence will need to be served. The court procedure should provide for the joining of co-defendants and claims by the defendant against other parties who contributed to the damage.

The speed with which the case comes to trial depends on the local procedural law and the complexity of the case. Once judgment has been given then the question of an appeal by either party who is dissatisfied with the judgment has to be considered.

(4) Limitation (or prescription)

Most legal systems apply the principle that there should be an end to litigation and stale claims should not drag on. Domestic laws have therefore developed their laws on limitation (or in civil law terms, prescription) of actions. Each cause of action has its own period of limitation. If a claimant has not taken the steps necessary to stop time running by the time such period has expired, the claimant will be time barred from bringing his action.

The following comments are of a general nature:

While the applicable domestic law specifies the period of limitation and the legal effect of its expiry, in cases involving an international element, the court will decide in accordance with the domestic law whether it should apply the limitation period of the court hearing the case (*lex fori*) or the limitation period of the law governing the case (*lex causae*).

In certain States the court is obliged to apply a foreign limitation period by Act, see, for example, the English Foreign Limitation Periods Act 1984 and US state "borrowing" statutes.

Domestic law determines the effect of expiry of a limitation period. Expiry may, as in certain common law cases, merely stop the claimant from enforcing his rights as a plaintiff. If he can enforce those rights in any other way, for example by way of appropriation of funds, then he is at liberty to do this. Expiry of other limitation periods may fully extinguish the rights of the claimant.

As limitation periods differ according to the State in which the action is brought, the claimant may be able to forum-shop, going to the court most favourable to his case once the limitation period has expired in another jurisdiction. However, this will not help if the court in which he finally brings his case applies a foreign limitation period which has expired.

In some US states and also in the EU Product Liability Directive (Article 11) there is in product liability, in addition to the standard limitation period, an additional long-term period imposed by the "Statute of Repose".

See also the US General Aviation Revitalization Act 1994 (Chapter 8, page 312).

In *Alexander & Others* v. *Beech Aircraft Corp & Others* the plaintiffs brought proceedings in Kansas for wrongful death based on products liability arising out of an accident in Indiana. The US Court of Appeals' findings included the following: the Kansas Borrowing Statute applied the Indiana 10–year

Statute of Repose. Therefore, although the action was brought against Beech within the two–year limitation period running from the accident, the action was time barred because it was brought more than 10 years after delivery of the product to the initial user or consumer (US Court of Appeals, 10th Circuit, December 1991; 23 AVI 18,130 1991–2).

Sometimes the period of limitation is uncertain, for example in an action against a manufacturer in France based on *"vice caché"* ("latent defect") the claim must be brought *"à bref delai"* ("within a short time") after the defect becomes known. This time will vary from case to case although there are a considerable number of cases dealing with application of this period.

There is often doubt under the law as to when the period of limitation starts running.

How the period of limitation is broken so that the rights of the claimant are preserved depends on the domestic law.

Limitation periods and how they work is definitely not one of the "do it yourself" areas of the law.

(5) Evidence

(i) Importance of documentary evidence

Evidence is defined in *Black* as any species of proof, or probative matter legally presented at the trial by act of the parties and through the medium of witnesses, records, documents, exhibits, concrete objects etc. for the purpose of inducing belief in the minds of the court or jury as to their contention (*Taylor* v. *Howard*).

Part 32.2 of the English CPR states that the general rule is that any fact which needs to be proved by the evidence of witnesses is to be proved at trial by their oral evidence given in public and at any other hearing by their evidence in writing. Oral evidence can be supported by documents, for example maintenance records.

Evidence in international civil aviation litigation can be extensive and complex. While the position of the consumer plaintiff has become easier due, for example, to the law on strict product liability or waiver by many airlines on the limits of liability for death or injury, nevertheless technical evidence remains important, particularly so with regard to claims among the defendants themselves such as the carrier, manufacturer and aerodrome operator.

(ii) Production of documents

Generally speaking in civil law jurisdictions the party is free to produce those documents only which are beneficial for his case (subject to particular circumstances). However, the position generally under common law is that the parties have to produce all documents which relate to the matters in question, whether in the interests of the producing party or not.

A reason for this distinction is that the role of most civil law judges is inquisitorial, requiring them to seek out the facts while on the other hand the role of common law judges is adversarial; they must consider the evidence as submitted by the parties.

The procedures for the production of documents and, in the USA, the taking of oral evidence by way of deposition, apply before trial thus giving both parties a much clearer idea of the merits of their respective cases. This leads to many cases being settled before reaching trial.

(iii) England

Documents

In England CPR Part 31 requires where standard disclosure is ordered by the court that each party must serve on the other party a list of documents which are or have been in his control. For this purpose a party has or has had a document in his control if it is or was in his physical possession, he had a right to possession or a right to inspect or take copies. Standard disclosure requires disclosure of the documents on which a party relies or which adversely affect either party's case or support the case. Mutual inspection of documents by the parties then proceeds.

"Documents" is widely construed and includes information stored on a computer.

Certain documents are privileged from production which are broadly categorised as: (i) documents protected by legal professional privilege; (ii) documents tending to incriminate or expose to a penalty the party who would produce them; (iii) documents privileged on the grounds of public policy, and (iv) documents created on a "without prejudice basis".

The case of *Waugh v. British Railways Board* [1980] AC 521 is useful in considering the English law of privilege. In this case an internal report produced by the defendant on an accident was not considered to have legal privilege because it was not brought into existence primarily for the purposes of litigation and therefore protected by legal professional privilege.

CPR also provide for documents to be produced by a person who is not a party to the litigation. Such party can only be compelled to produce documents at full trial.

Where under CPR a party fails to disclose facts, as opposed to documents, the other party should apply to the court for an appropriate order.

Other forms of pre-trial discovery include medical examination in a personal injury case, and inspection of objects and places.

(iv) USA

Pre-trial discovery in the USA is more varied and lengthy than in England; it includes:

(a) Production of documents on request (whether favourable to the producing party or not) and inspection of objects and places material to the case;

(b) Wide use of Interrogatories. They may be used at an early stage to try to find out contacts which the defendant has with the relevant jurisdiction;

(c) Depositions: Depositions are oral examinations taken under oath before a reporter or on videotape. Depositions may be made against representatives of the other party or against third parties, where it may be necessary to issue a subpoena (an order for the witness to appear). The use of depositions enables the deposing party to obtain information not recorded in writing. Once the depositions have been committed to writing, they are agreed by the parties and they can be used at trial.

Discovery procedures also deal with exchange of statements of witnesses and of experts prior to trial.

(v) Protection of witnesses and privileged information

In both England and USA there are various rules protecting witnesses, restricting discovery to relevant issues, and protecting certain types of confidential or privileged information.

(vi) Hague Convention on the Taking of Evidence

Where a party to an action in one State requires evidence in another State, the Convention on the Taking of Evidence Abroad in Civil and Commercial Matters signed at The Hague on 18 March 1970 may apply. The Convention is translated into UK law by the Evidence (Proceedings in other Jurisdictions) Act 1975. Rule 70.1–70.6 of Schedule 1 to CPR deals with practical application of this Convention. For a detailed consideration of this Convention see the decision of House of Lords in *Rio Tinto Zinc Corporation & Others* v. *Westinghouse Electric Corp* where the US applicant sought to compel production of evidence concerning a possible uranium cartel ([1978] AC 547).

(6) Protection of assets

Courts in many domestic legal systems have the power to grant orders on application of one party which prevents the other party from dealing with his own assets including documents and other evidence to the detriment of the applicant party pending judgment in the action or solution of an interim (interlocutory) question prior to full trial. Such orders can extend to assets in the hands of a third party. In England the *Mareva* injunction and the *Anton Piller* order are examples of such orders.

(7) Damages

"Damages" in common law terminology is the sum of money paid by one person to another for a wrong done. They must be distinguished from "damage" which is the word describing the result of the wrong done.

McGregor on Damages (16th edition) states that damages are the pecuniary compensation obtainable by success in an action for a wrong which is either a tort or a breach of contract, the compensation being in the form of a lump sum awarded at one time unconditionally and generally but not necessarily expressed in English currency. *McGregor* goes on to point out that English courts can now award periodic and also provisional damages.

The US Second Restatement of the Law of Torts provides in paragraph 12(a) that damages are "A pecuniary compensation or indemnity which may be recovered in the courts by any person who has suffered loss, detriment or injury, whether to his person, property or rights through the unlawful act or omission, or negligence of another. A sum of money awarded to a person injured by the tort of another."

The use of the word "damage" in the English translation of the Warsaw Convention attracted comment from Lord Wilberforce in *Fothergill* v. *Monarch Airlines* (HL, 1980): "Sometimes [damage] means 'monetary loss', e.g. in Article 17 or Article 19. Sometimes it means 'physical damage', e.g. in Article 22(2)(b). In some Articles it is used with both meanings, e.g. Article 18."

Some aspects of damages, principally in common law jurisdictions, are set out below.

(i) Common law damages can be either compensatory or punitive

The purpose of compensatory damages is to compensate the injured party by payment of money with the purpose of putting him in the same position he would have been, if he had not suffered the wrong for which he is being compensated. Damages cover pecuniary and non-pecuniary loss.

The purpose of punitive or exemplary damages is to punish the defendant and deter him from similar conduct in the future. They are awarded in England: (i) where there is oppressive, arbitrary or unconstitutional action by servants of the Government; or (ii) where the defendant's conduct has been calculated by him to make a profit for himself which may well exceed the compensation payable to the plaintiff.

In the USA punitive damages are awarded much more frequently. For example, they may be awarded by way of punishing the defendant where he is guilty of fraud, oppression or malice.

The law of some US states prohibits the insurance of the risk of punitive damages. The claiming of punitive damages therefore may raise important questions both of the law governing the insurance policy and conduct of the defence of the aviation enterprise.

A number of US decisions hold that punitive damages cannot be awarded under the Warsaw Convention (*Re Air Disaster at Lockerbie*, 21 December 1988; *Rein* v. *Pan American World Airways Inc*, 23 AVI 17,714 1991; *S&B* AvR VII/1579).

The insurance policy considered in Chapter 16 covers only compensatory damages.

Compensatory damages in contract and tort are pecuniary or non-pecuniary.

(ii) Contract

The purpose of an award of damages by the court is to restore the plaintiff to the position he would have been in had the particular damage not occurred.

It is not always easy to determine what the plaintiff has actually lost and a distinction has to be made between "expectation loss" and "reliance loss".

"Expectation loss" is the loss that the plaintiff would have received if the contract had been properly performed. This would include loss of profit.

On the other hand "reliance loss" is the expenditure incurred by the plaintiff in his reliance on the defendant honouring the contract. See Cheshire, Fifoot and Furmston, *Law of Contract* (12th edition, page 596) and also Fuller and Perdue, "The Reliance Interest in Contract Damages" (1936–37) 46 *Yale Law Journal* page 52.

A further question—"for what kind of damage may the plaintiff recover compensation?"—was considered in the English cases of *Hadley* v. *Baxendale* (1854) 9 Exch 341 and *Victoria Laundry (Windsor) Ltd* v. *Newman Industries Ltd* [1949] 2 KB 528. In the latter case the court said:

"In cases of breach of contract, the aggrieved party is only entitled to recover such part of the loss actually resulting as was at the time of the contract reasonably foreseeable as liable to result from the breach.

What was at that time reasonably so foreseeable depends on the knowledge then possessed by the parties or, at all events, by the party who later commits the breach.

For this purpose, knowledge 'possessed' is of two kinds; one imputed, the other actual. Everyone, as a reasonable person is taken to know the 'ordinary course of things' and consequently what loss is liable to result from a breach of contract in that ordinary course. This is the subject-matter of the 'first rule' in *Hadley* v. *Baxendale*. But to this knowledge, which a contract-breaker is assumed to possess whether he actually possesses it or not, there may have to be added in a particular case knowledge which he actually possesses of special circumstances outside the 'ordinary course of things', of such a kind that a breach in those special circumstances would be liable to cause more loss. Such a case attracts the operation of the 'second rule' so as to make additional loss also recoverable."

Where the parties agree beforehand as to what sum a party will pay if he fails to perform his obligations, English common law distinguishes between liquidated damages and a penalty. Payment of the former is enforceable and payment of the latter is not.

(iii) Tort

The main principle applies in tort as in contract:

"where any injury is to be compensated by damages, in settling the sum of money to be given for reparation of damages you should as nearly as possible get that sum of money which will put the party who has been injured, or who has suffered, in the same position as he would have been in if he had not sustained the wrong for which he is now getting his compensation or reparation" (*Livingstone* v. *Rawyards Coal Co* (1880) 5 App Cas 25, 39).

Such a principle can be followed in the case of pecuniary damages, for example loss of salary or loss of certain profits, but is not so easy to apply to damages for pain and suffering in the case of personal injury. In the latter case compensation is notional, i.e. theoretical compensation.

Aspects of pecuniary loss in the case of personal injury include questions such as whether payment of damages is by lump sum or by periodical payments, loss of earnings, social security payments received and tax implications.

The result of payment by authorities of social security payments to injured parties may well form the basis of a subrogation action by the authority against the wrongdoer, an aspect which is taken into account, for example, in the IATA Inter-Carrier Agreement which expressly does not waive the Warsaw Convention limits of liability in respect of such subrogation. (See page 302).

Where a breadwinner has been killed leaving a widow and children, factors to be taken into account will include:

(a) the net income of the breadwinner;
(b) the amount of money which the breadwinner would have spent on himself;
(c) the duration of dependency of the family on the breadwinner if he had survived;
(d) the Social Security payments which the family have received as a result of death;
(e) the financial prospects of the breadwinner;
(f) expenses such as funeral or medical expenses.

Non-pecuniary damages in respect of pain and suffering, loss of amenities and moral damages are payable in most States in respect of personal injury and bereavement. The method in which they are assessed and the heads of damage recoverable vary.

Generally, damages for pain and suffering are payable to those who are injured while damages for bereavement are payable to the family of the deceased. In certain civil law countries certain of these non-pecuniary damages are designated as "moral damages", see Article 1099–1101 of the Russian Civil Code.

Under English law the estate of the deceased can claim for pain and suffering and loss of amenities and earnings from the date of injury to the date of death.

Fear of impending death in the case of fatal injury does not give a right to claim damages for anguish under English law. However, some US states award damages for mental anguish in death cases both prior to and post impact.

Damages for psychological or mental damage to family members of the deceased is governed by domestic law.

Private rights created by treaty must be interpreted under the applicable domestic law. The nature of injury, and damages awarded under the terms of the Warsaw Convention were considered by the House of Lords in *Abnett* and *Sidhu* v. *British Airways*. The Paris Court of Appeal reached a differing conclusion (page 270). Another treaty example is Article 1 of the Rome Convention 1952, page 351, which imposes liability for direct damage only.

In tort the question of remoteness of damage arises, as it does in contract. The plaintiff will not necessarily be compensated for all damage or loss suffered by him or his estate from the wrongful act.

In the English tort of negligence damages can only be recovered if the damage was such a kind as the reasonable man should have foreseen as being likely to occur to the plaintiff (*The Wagon Mound* [1961] AC 388). Damage can include economic loss depending on facts. While this principle appears to be simple, it is in fact quite complicated, taking into account factors such as:

(a) how narrowly or broadly "damage" is defined; and
(b) the defendant wrongdoer must take the plaintiff "as he finds him", for example with an egg-shell thin skull.

In *Saxton* v. *McDonnell Douglas Aircraft Co* 428 F Supp 1047 (CD Cal, 1977); 14 AVI 18,163 1976–8, the personal representatives of a mother who committed suicide after her son and daughter-in-law were killed in an air crash, were unable to recover damages.

Damages are not the only remedy awarded by courts. In common law the court may order a party to do something by way of an order for specific performance or order him not to do something by way of injunction.

(iv) Conflict of laws

Damages are governed by domestic law. Where there is a foreign element in the case the court applies its own conflict of law rules. The question arises whether the law of the case (*lex causae*) or law of the court (*lex fori*) applies.

In England, in those cases where legislation such as the Contracts (Applicable Law) Act 1990 does not apply, questions of substance such as remoteness of damage or heads of damage will be governed by *lex causae* and questions of quantification will be governed by *lex fori*. For example, the House of Lords held in *Boys* v. *Chaplins* [1973] AC 356, that the question of whether damages were recoverable for pain and suffering was a question of substance.

(v) Mitigation of loss

In most legal systems the plaintiff has a duty to take reasonable steps to mitigate his loss.

(vi) Damages paid as annuities

If the parties agree, settlement of a claim in some jurisdictions may be structured so that damages are paid by way of annuities to take advantage of the domestic system of taxation.

(vii) Property

Damages can include market value, repair and replacement costs and loss of use; see Chapter 9, AHM 698 dealing with accident cost assessment.

(viii) Interest

Domestic law will govern the question of time from which any interest on damages are payable. Relevant dates may be:

    (i) the date the cause of action arose;
    (ii) the date legal proceedings are started;
    (iii) date of any judgment.

(ix) Death or bodily injury

Damages for death or bodily injury in tort can be substantial, particularly in the state courts in the USA where jury awards for compensatory and punitive damages may run into many millions of dollars in a single case. It is awards of this nature which gave rise to the General Aviation Revitalisation Act 1994 (see page 312 of Chapter 8).

(8) Enforcement of foreign judgments

Each State has its procedures for enforcement of a judgment given by its own courts.

The enforcement in one State (the enforcing State) of a judgment obtained in another State (the original State) is a matter of domestic law for the enforcing State although such domestic law may have originated in a Treaty.

In England, for example, judgments may be enforced at common law or under UK Acts which are themselves the result of treaties or similar international arrangements. The relevant three UK Acts are the Administration of

Justice Act 1920 ("the 1920 Act"), the Foreign Judgments (Reciprocal Enforcement) Act 1933 ("the 1933 Act") and the Civil Jurisdiction and Judgments Act 1982 which gives effect to the Brussels Convention ("the 1982 Act").

The most basic system of enforcement is the start of proceedings in the common law courts to enforce the foreign judgment on the basis that it is a debt owed to the successful litigant.

Enforcement under the three Acts requires registration of the judgment.

Before enforcing a judgment at common law or under the 1920 Act or 1933 Act, the court has to be satisfied that certain essential requirements are fulfilled. For example, enforcement provisions apply to money judgments only; the court of the original State must have been competent; and the judgment in the original State must be final.

The judgment in the original State must not be contrary to UK public policy nor to the principles of natural justice. Furthermore, the English court must be satisfied that the person against whom the judgment is being enforced was either resident in the original State or submitted to the jurisdiction of the court in such State.

The difference between enforcement in common law and the 1920 and 1933 Acts is that at common law, enforcement requires a full legal action while judgments under the two Acts need only be registered, although the party against whom the judgment is to be enforced may object to registration and the manner in which judgment in the original State was obtained.

The powers of enforcement under the Brussels Convention contained in the 1982 Act are much wider and present fewer obstacles to the successful litigant.

CHAPTER 15

RISK MANAGEMENT

British Standard 8444 dealing with risk management defines:

(i) Risk as "Combination of the frequency, or probability, of occurrence and the consequence of a specified hazardous event";

(ii) Risk analysis as "systematic use of available information to identify hazards and to estimate the risk to individuals or populations, property or the environment"; and

(iii) Risk management as "systematic application of management policies, procedures and practices to the tasks of analysing, evaluating and controlling risk".

The three main activities in a risk management programme are therefore identification, assessment and control of risk. See also "Guidelines on Risk Issues" produced by the Engineering Council of UK and Lloyd's Register (1993) and its bibliography.

The primary objective of risk management is to anticipate, plan for and prevent a loss rather than to wait for a loss to occur, and then to react and cure.

The Institute of Risk Management of London suggests in its brochure that the responsibilities of a risk manager are likely to include:

(i) The identification and quantification of risks facing an enterprise;

(ii) Proposals for the optimum allocation of scarce resources to control risk;

(iii) The drawing-up, with line management, of contingency and disaster plans;

(iv) Proposals for the financing of risk, whether by retention or transfer;

(v) The purchase of insurance and/or creation and management of in-house (captive) insurance companies;

(vi) Providing reports to the management on the actual and potential cost of risk.

These suggested responsibilities are considered in turn.

425

PART 1. IDENTIFICATION AND QUANTIFICATION OF RISKS FACING AN ENTERPRISE

Each type of civil aviation activity runs its own risk.

Sources of information on these risks, external to the enterprise, include the following:

(1) ICAO: Aircraft Accident Digests.

(2) ICAO Accident/Incident Reporting (ADREP) Circulars – Annual Statistics.

(3) IATA: Safety Information Exchange (members only).

(4) NASA: Administered Aviation Safety Reporting.

(5) FAA/NTSB Systems (ASRS).

(6) State analyses such as those carried out by: NTSB (Annual Review of Aircraft Accidents); Bureau of Air Safety Investigation of Australia; Transportation Safety Board of Canada; and Civil Aviation Authority UK.

(7) Corporate systems, e.g. British Airways Safety Information System (BASIS) (members only).

(8) National Confidential Reporting Programmes, such as CHIRP in the UK: i.e. Confidential Human Factors Incident Reporting Programme, see Comment (5) to Annex 15 (page 182).

(9) Flight Operations Quality Assurance (FOQA).

(10) Publication of Statistical Summary of Commercial Jet Accidents World-wide Operations (published by Boeing).

(11) Mandatory Occurrence Reporting Programme.

(12) Operational Monitoring Programme.

(13) Use of Internet, for example FAA Safety Information Website.

(14) Publications of Flight Safety Foundation, Inc. and similar institutions.

(15) Air Miss/Air Proximity reporting.

(16) ICAO Circulars such as Continuing Airworthiness of Aircraft in Service (No 95) and Human Factors Digests 1–13.

(17) GAIN. The FAA initiated in 1996 the concept of Global Analysis and Information Network (GAIN) the purpose of which is to collect, analyse and disseminate aviation safety information and thus to provide a significantly improved operational early warning capability. GAIN is currently in its planning stage.

ICAO Annex 13 Chapter 7 provides:

7.3: States should establish formal incident reporting systems to facilitate collection of information on actual or potential safety deficiencies.

7.4: Where practicable States should establish database systems to facilitate effective analysis of the information obtained from its investigation of accidents and incidents wherever they occurred.

The database systems should use standardised formats to facilitate data exchange.

Product integrity: Example of serious failure in product integrity are likely to be included in the sources of data referred to above. Good advice on product integrity programmes abounds. Publications such as the CAA paper 96004 "Study into potential sources of Human Error in the maintenance of large civil transport aircraft" are helpful.

Sources of information within the enterprise depend on the commitment and efficiency of its management.

See AHM 699, page 334.

PART 2. PROPOSALS FOR THE OPTIMUM ALLOCATION OF SCARCE RESOURCES TO CONTROL RISK

Budgetary and management decisions include the following:

(1) Appointment of risk management personnel to promote awareness of risk, and its management;
(2) The provision of statistics and other information for in-house use;
(3) Creation of an open atmosphere within the enterprise to encourage the reporting of incidents;
(4) Promotion of awareness of those elements which influence safety including:
  (a) money
  (b) training
  (c) communication;
(5) Provision of funds and time for conferences and courses;
(6) Participation in external databases.
(7) Drawing up of risk management plans, e.g. Annex 6, Part 1, para 3.6 and AHM 683—Due Diligence Program (page 331).

Identification of risk may lead to the conclusion that existing equipment including aircraft should be replaced with more modern equipment, and maintenance and training should be improved. In such circumstances risk management may require both substantial funds, and management decisions at the highest level.

The activities in (1) to (6) above apply as much to the provision of ATS and to manufacturing activities as they do to air transport operations.

PART 3. THE DRAWING-UP WITH LINE MANAGEMENT OF CONTINGENCY AND DISASTER PLANS

Annex 6, Part 1, para 3.6 requires an operator to establish and maintain an accident prevention and flight safety programme. However, this particular risk management heading deals with what happens or what may happen after the accident has occurred.

Not every accident or catastrophe in civil aviation falls within the strict definition of an Annex 13 accident. Accidents at manufacturing plants and certain accidents at airports may be investigated by other types of government inspectors as well as by examining judges and others.

Disaster and contingency plans have to deal with many problems and responsibilities which follow a major accident including:

(1) In the case of an airline the relationship which it has with airport operators and emergency services, at base and "on-line" stations.
(2) The relationship between the enterprise and the investigating and judicial authorities.
(3) Liaison with the insurance broker and insurers of the enterprise and their technical and legal representatives.
(4) Care for passengers, employees and others and their relatives in the case of death and injuries, and an understanding of handling bereavement and of counselling. In this context note the provisions of the USA Aviation Disaster Family Assistance Act 1996 and Foreign Air Carrier Family Support Act 1997 imposing an obligation on the carrier to draw up and file a plan for addressing the needs of the families of the victims of an aviation disaster.
(5) Repatriation of deceased and injured.
(6) Preservation of evidence.
(7) Relationship with the media.

Other factors may include security procedures, airworthiness and the continuing financial health of the enterprise depending on the particular circumstances.

Some major airlines have their own crisis management centre which can be made available to other airlines.

In the case of an aerodrome, Annex 14 requires emergency plans to be prepared and tested.

Annex 17 requires the drawing up of a national security plan.

IATA Airport Handling Manual (19th edition) sets out emergency procedures in AHM 071 (see page 321).

PART 4. PROPOSALS FOR THE FINANCING OF RISK, WHETHER BY RETENTION OR TRANSFER

In addition to spending more on safety and on improving procedures, financing of risk can be by way of: (i) creating a captive insurance company; (ii) purchase of insurance; or (iii) establishment of a fund within the enterprise to pay for losses. Whether in (iii) such a fund is effective from a tax point of view and whether it is also susceptible of being "raided" by other divisions of the enterprise depend on the circumstances.

Transfer of risk can be by way of commercial contract or insurance. The exculpatory clauses in an aircraft sale agreement or ground handling agreement are examples of risk transfer. Whether they are effective depends both on the domestic law concerned and the financial position of the party who agrees to accept the liability.

Transfer of certain financial risks by way of hedging fuel prices or foreign currency prices are outside the scope of this book.

PART 5. THE PURCHASE OF INSURANCE AND/OR THE CREATION AND MANAGEMENT OF IN-HOUSE (CAPTIVE) INSURANCE COMPANIES

The purchase of insurance is dealt with in Chapter 16 below.

Captives

A "captive" is an insurance company within the corporate group of the enterprise. A captive may also be owned by a number of enterprises as in the case of Airline Mutual Insurance Ltd.

The captive provides insurance cover to the extent of its assets. It receives a premium which is retained within the group to the extent that the claims record is good. It can therefore demonstrate a tangible benefit.

Risks insured by the captive can be reinsured in the insurance market. Conversely risks or portions of risks not insured by the captive can be insured directly in the market.

The object of a captive is to contribute towards reduction in the total cost of risk.

Factors in deciding whether or not to establish a captive include:

(1) the state of the market, for example capacity and rates;
(2) the loss experience and risk management of the enterprise;
(3) financial management of the enterprise including cash flow and tax considerations.

Once the decision to establish a captive has been taken, these three factors should remain under constant review. Furthermore, a suitable domicile must be selected. Choice of domicile depends on a number of elements including:

(1) regulatory requirements;
(2) corporate structure;
(3) tax;
(4) political stability of the domicile;
(5) accounting procedures and law;

(6) legal requirements on reserve and solvency.

Lloyd's Corporation now admits captive insurance subsidiaries of multinational companies as underwriting members of Lloyd's.

PART 6. PROVIDING REPORTS TO THE MANAGEMENT ON THE ACTUAL AND POTENTIAL COST OF RISK

Management must have regular reports to enable it to make the correct decisions on risk management. Cost of risk includes legal liability, loss or damage to property including aircraft, equipment and buildings, and consequential and economic loss as well as the cost of risk management.

While the risk manager's responsibilities may include the six items considered above, risk management is a joint operation between the enterprise, and the regulatory and investigating authorities, brokers, insurers and their respective advisors.

For example, section 85 of the UK Civil Aviation Act 1982 establishes the Airworthiness Requirements Board whose functions concerning airworthiness are to advise the CAA and to consult such persons as the Board considers appropriate. The CAA shall appoint to the Board representatives of manufacturers, operators, insurers and pilots of aircraft as well as members of CAA.

There are few accidents which are attributable to one cause. Risk management in all aspects of civil aviation is essential.

The Boeing Company projected in April 1996 that unless the global accident rate is reduced, by the year 2015, an airliner will crash somewhere in the world almost weekly. (Final Report of White House Commission on Aviation Safety and Security 1997 (Gore Report)).

Significant publications include those listed in Comment 4 on Annex 6 (page 78).

PART 7. INSURANCE RISK MANAGEMENT

Even insurers and reinsurers need to manage their risks. Lord Mustill, a Lord of Appeal in Ordinary (that is an appeal judge of the House of Lords) in his address to the 1997 Annual General Meeting of the Association of Average Adjusters ("Humpty Dumpty and Risk Management" [1997] LMCLQ 488) proposed the following:

(1) The parties must be agreed about the result they wish to achieve, whether as between insurer and insured, or insurer and reinsurer.

(2) The agreement must be written down in a way (i) which accurately reflects what has been agreed, so that no doubts can later arise between the parties as to the distribution of the perils; (ii) which can

be correctly understood by those who are not parties to it but who need to know about it; (iii) the writing must be such that when (a) the law, and (b) the interpretative methods of whoever will rule on disputes, are applied to it the results it produces are what the parties intended.

Insurers may instruct surveyors to carry out a survey of safety standards of the enterprise which they insure.

CHAPTER 16

AVIATION INSURANCE

PART 1. INTRODUCTION

The purchase of insurance is a major element in risk management. This chapter deals with insurance for:

(i) loss of or damage to property such as aircraft; and
(ii) legal liability.

Most law mentioned in this chapter comes from common law systems which apply to much of the activity of the market.

In the UK the market consists of:

(i) Incorporated insurance companies which may be owned by:
    (a) various shareholders or holding companies;
    (b) a State or other authority.
(ii) Pools or groups of insurers trading together under the same manager.
(iii) Lloyd's syndicates ("Syndicates").

Until recently Syndicates were made up of individuals ("names" or "underwriters") who underwrote for profit but with unlimited liability in respect of losses. Following reconstruction of the Lloyd's market, corporate members can now invest with limited liability in Syndicates. The Syndicates are managed by managing agents which are limited liability companies.

Equitas is a group of limited liability reinsurance companies independent of Lloyd's. It is authorised only to reinsure and run-off the non-life liabilities of the Syndicates for 1992 and prior years.

The insurance industry in the UK is regulated by the Insurance Companies Act 1982 ("1982 Act") and the Lloyd's Acts 1871–1982.

The 1982 Act applies mainly to companies although the Syndicates must also comply with certain of its provisions. It requires companies and Syndicates to comply with rules on maintenance of solvency margins, auditing and filing of accounts and other regulatory requirements. It also applies certain EC Directives.

Subject to the 1982 Act, the Lloyd's Acts 1871–1982 currently control Lloyd's including the functioning of its council and the Syndicates.

The 1982 Act also regulates insurance companies whose principal places of business are in other States both within and outside the EU, and who carry on business in the UK.

Certain court decisions held that an insurance contract entered into by an insurance company in breach of the 1982 Act was illegal and void. This situation was rectified by section 2 of the Financial Services Act 1986.

While London is the centre of the market, other important aviation insurance centres exist in France, Germany, Italy, Japan, Switzerland and USA.

Schedule 2 to the 1982 Act classifies four types of insurance business as falling within "aviation" business: accident, aircraft, goods in transit and aircraft liability.

Ivamy in his *Dictionary of Insurance Law* defines aviation insurance as "a type of insurance" covering:

   (i) Loss of or damage to an aircraft;
   (ii) Third party liability;
   (iii) Liability to passengers.

PART 2. NATURE OF INSURANCE

In order to understand the law of insurance it is necessary to distinguish it from other contracts. Volume 25 of *Halsbury* para 2 states as follows:

"Every insurance, whatever its nature, postulates that a sum of money will be paid by the insurers on the happening of a specified event. There must be uncertainty as to the happening of the event, either as to whether it will happen or not, or if it is bound to happen, like the death of a human being, uncertainty as to the time at which it will happen. There must also be an insurable interest in the assured which is normally, that the event must be one which is *prima facie* adverse to his interest."

The English case of *Lucena* v. *Craufurd* (1806) 2 Bos & PNR 269 states "insurance is a contract by which the one party in consideration of a price paid to him adequate to the risk becomes security to the other that he shall not suffer loss, damage or prejudice by the happening of the peril specified in certain things which may be exposed to them".

These two definitions contain the requirements of an English contract of insurance, namely:

- There must be at least two parties to the contract; the insured and the insurer;
- Consideration is provided by the insured to the insurer who will be obliged to pay a sum of money on the happening of a certain event;
- The event is uncertain;
- The insured has an insurable interest which is normally that the event must be adverse to the insured's interest.

Other English rules on formation of contract apply, for example offer and acceptance, privity of contract and capacity.

Under the doctrine of privity only the insured can sue to recover the indemnity. The Third Parties (Rights Against Insurers) Act 1930 is an exception in the case of insolvency of the insured.

While the contract of insurance provides a financial service, such contract, as pointed out by Malcolm Clarke in his book *The Law of Insurance Contracts (Clarke)*, must be distinguished from "a guarantee contract whereby A guarantees that B will repay B's debt to C". This must be contrasted with "an insurance contract, especially credit or guarantee insurance, whereby A promises to indemnify C, if B fails to pay or repay the debt".

PART 3. PROPER LAW OF CONTRACT

In the English marine hull insurance case of *Amin Rasheed Shipping Corp* v. *Kuwait Ins Co* [1984] AC 50, Lord Diplock said: "Contracts are incapable of existing in a legal vacuum. They are mere pieces of paper devoid of all legal effect unless they were made by reference to some system of private law which defines obligations assumed by the parties to the contract."

While the 1982 Act applies the EC Long Term Directive which establishes the proper law of certain insurance contracts, nonetheless in respect of direct insurance of aviation risks, choice of law is left to the parties. In reinsurance the parties are also free to choose their law under the UK Contracts (Applicable Law) Act 1990.

In the absence of choice by the parties the court seised of the case will have to decide according to its own rules as to the proper law of the contract.

PART 4. LAW AND PRACTICE IN THE LONDON MARKET

Aviation risks are substantial. One new wide body aircraft may cost in the area of US$200 million. The aggregate liabilities arising out of a major air carrier's liability can be heavy. Liability reserves for accidents can be in the area of US$750 million or more.

Liability Insurance can be offered to major airlines by the market sometimes in the area of "US$2,000,000,000, Combined Single Limit any one accident". This means that insurance cover is provided up to that figure in respect of all liabilities arising out of one accident, thus covering passenger, cargo and third party liability.

Liability insurance has to provide for the possibility of a mid-air collision between wide-bodied aircraft full of passengers over an urban area or installation such as a nuclear power station.

Therefore, most aviation risks are shared by insurers. In some States 100 per cent of a major risk may be insured within that State, for example where the insured is a State enterprise and the insurer is a State insurance company;

however, a substantial part of such risk will probably be reinsured on the market.

A few risks can be insured with one insurer in one State which will require no reinsurance, for example certain minor general aviation risks.

Insurers working in the market both insure and reinsure.

Under English law it appears that there is no legal requirement for an aviation insurance contract to be in writing although common sense dictates that it should be so. In any event this position definitely does not apply world-wide and care should be taken to conform with any domestic law requirements, where they are applicable, to ensure direct and reinsurance contracts are valid.

In this chapter "insurance contract" means a binding obligation to pay a premium for insurance and a corresponding obligation to provide such insurance. "Policy" means a written policy of insurance, when prepared, which constitutes the contract and replaces any other written document such as the slip.

English law on policy interpretation and contractual validity is mostly established by case law. While the Marine Insurance Act 1906 applies to marine insurance only, it codifies many common law principles also applicable to other types of insurance including aviation, see *Highlands Ins Co* v. *Continental Ins Co* [1987] 1 Lloyd's Rep 109.

PART 5. PARTIES TO THE CONTRACT OF INSURANCE

In the case of Hull insurance the parties would be:

(1) Insurer: In view of the risk sharing, insurer usually consists of the leading insurer who is selected by the broker, with the rest of the insurers constituting the "following market". (See page 438 below.)

(2) Insured (Assured): In the case of aircraft hulls or other high value equipment, there may be several insured; owner of the aircraft, the lessee, mortgagee or other persons having a financial interest in the aircraft.

In the case of complex financing agreements insurers now use the standard Airline Finance/Lease Contract Endorsement (AVN 67B).

AVN 29 adds the manufacturer as an additional assured but only in so far as its interests arise as owner.

AVN and its number denotes a specific standard clause used in the London market which may be included in the contract. See Part 11, page 442, below.

In the case of liability insurance the identity of the insured will depend on the nature of the operation and the risk—

(1) Aircraft operators: The principal insured will be the air carrier. Other insured on the policy may be persons who can be subject to a liability arising out of the operation, for example ground handler or tour operator under the Guadalajara Convention 1961. The owner, if not the air carrier, is likely to be an insured.
(2) In the case of product or aerodrome liability policies, the manufacturer or operator will be the principal insured respectively.
(3) A single policy may cover several insured who in certain circumstances may have valid claims against each other. In the circumstances the policy may include a cross liability clause such as AVN 63.

Policies may expressly include employees of the insured including air crew as joint assured.

AVN 67B also gives liability cover to persons having an interest in the aircraft.

Policies sometimes include general wording covering all those corporate entities associated with the principal insured such as its holding or subsidiary or associated companies.

PART 6. INSURANCE BROKERS

The insurance broker is an intermediary used to place business in the market. Risks may only be placed with Lloyd's underwriters by approved Lloyd's brokers. Brokers who are not Lloyd's-approved brokers are restricted to placing risks with insurance companies only.

Lloyd's Act 1982, section 83, defines, a Lloyd's broker as a partnership or body corporate permitted by the Council of Lloyd's to broker insurance business at Lloyd's.

The UK and EU have substantial bodies of laws and codes governing the qualification, conduct and powers of insurance brokers.

Whether the broker is the agent of the insured or of the insurer is determined by domestic law. In the UK the broker is generally the agent of the insured. The case of *African Merchants Ltd* v. *Bayley* ([1969] 1 Lloyd's Rep 268) established that if a broker receives a report from an adjuster or lawyer, representing insurers, it should only be on the basis that the report may be disclosed to the insured. This question is now dealt with in the Code of Practice for Lloyd's Brokers.

While the broker acts solely as the agent of the insured in placing insurance business, if the broker who makes a claim on the insurers on behalf of the insured wishes to be free to take instructions from the insurers investigating the claim he is obliged to obtain the consent of the insured.

In some specific cases the broker is clearly acting for the insurer, for example where he is authorised as agent to bind the insurer for certain types of insurance contracts.

For an analysis of the role of the broker, particularly in the London market, see *Margo* and *Clarke*.

The broker's functions include: negotiation of rates and policy terms, liaising between insured and insurers, and often advising the insured on risk management.

The broker must be distinguished from an agent of insurers whose job may be to find business for his principal.

PART 7. FORMATION OF THE CONTRACT OF INSURANCE IN THE LONDON MARKET

In the London market the broker will write down on a piece of paper called "the slip" details of the risk and the principal terms and conditions of the insurance cover required by the prospective insured. These terms and conditions include the risk to be insured, period of cover, fleet details, the identity of the insured, the standard clauses, e.g. AV48B (exclusion of War Risks), a reference to the wording to be used in the policy, premium and commission.

Where only one insurer is needed for minor risks, the broker selects the insurer and offers the risk to him. When the terms have been negotiated the contract is concluded and the policy is issued.

Where the risk is spread among a number of insurers the broker selects the insurer he decides should be first offered the risk ("the leading insurer"). This selection assumes that the proposed leading insurer will (a) quote a reasonable premium, (b) accept a reasonable percentage of the risk and (c) be accepted as a suitable leading insurer by the "following market". When the leading insurer and the broker have agreed the terms of the contract, the broker will then go on to another insurer offering him the risk until the full 100 per cent is insured. These other insurers make up the "following market". This placing of the risk can be done personally or by electronic means.

Where competitive rates can be obtained, the broker may:

- before finally placing the risk on the slips sound out different possible leading insurers to obtain a competitive premium; or
- divide the 100 per cent risk into different tranches, each tranche having a different leading insurer and probably with a different premium rating; these tranches will constitute the "main" and "off-line" slips.

The terms "insurer" and "underwriter" are used interchangeably in this book although, as *Margo* points out, the job title "underwriter" is used to describe the person exercising an underwriting function in both companies and syndicates.

See *Margo* for more details on slips generally and particularly in respect of amendment, endorsement, renewal, line slips and also over-subscription of the risk.

As the English common law rules on contract offer and acceptance usually apply, it is not always clear as to when the contract is concluded where there is a leading insurer and following market. In the English Court of Appeal case of *General Reinsurance Corporation* v. *Forsakringsaktiebolaget Fennia Patria* ([1982] QB 1022; [1982] 1 Lloyd's Rep 87; varied [1983] QB 856; [1983] 3 WLR 318; [1983] 2 Lloyd's Rep 287) Kerr LJ said: "Each line written on a slip gives rise to a binding contract *pro tanto* between the underwriters and the insured or reinsured for whom the broker is acting when he presents the slip. The underwriter is therefore bound by his line, subject only to the contingency that it may fall to be written down on closing to some extent if the slip turns out to have been over-subscribed." This means that usually acceptance of the risk by each insurer constitutes a separate contract.

This must be read subject to the case where the insurer accepts the risk on the condition that the slip is subscribed 100 per cent.

Where a contract of insurance is concluded without a broker or without a slip, the rules of offer and acceptance also apply, where for example the contract of insurance will come into being on acceptance of the proposal.

In the UK a contract of insurance will be void if the contract was made with an enemy alien when a state of war existed between the UK and the alien's country (*Janson* v. *Dreifontein Consolidated Mines Ltd* [1902] AC 484).

It is usual under a common law contract for the parties to agree on all material terms for there to be a binding contract. However, in the London market, sometimes the premium or wording of the policy remains to be agreed by the leading insurer even where the risk has been 100 per cent subscribed. The abbreviation "TBA L/U" is used. This means: "To be agreed by the leading underwriter." However, the extent to which terms can remain to be agreed when insurance is in place depends on commercial practice and contractual law.

Margo comments, "In the case where premium is to be agreed by the leading underwriter, it will depend on the circumstances whether the underwriters are on risk immediately on issuing the Slip, or whether no risk is undertaken, pending agreement of the premium by the leading underwriter".

In the case of *American Airlines Inc* v. *Hope* [1974] 2 Lloyd's Rep 301, the slip provided for the deletion of the war risks exclusion clause (see page 456 below) in respect of the aircraft hulls covered. The relevant wording was ". . . AP and Geographical Limits tba L/U . . . ". The abbreviation stood for "at an additional premium and geographical limits to be agreed by the leading underwriter". The court held it was obvious from the context the insured was not covered in respect of war risks in the absence of the agreement of the leading underwriter, since it made no sense to extend that cover until the geographical limits of such cover had been agreed.

Once the contract has been concluded, the broker may issue a "cover note" to the insured with details of the insurance which should reflect what is shown on the slip. The slip is the contract, the cover note is not.

The insurance policy will then be issued which will take the place of the slip. Where, for whatever reason, there is a conflict between policy and slip, then it may be necessary to apply to the court for rectification of the policy.

The procedures for preparation and issue of the policy and accounting depend on the practice of the particular insurance market. In London these functions are performed by the parties with the involvement of Lloyd's Policy Signing Office or Institute of London Underwriters.

While the London market applies English contractual rules to formation of a contract, reinsurance contracts concluded in the market may nevertheless apply the law of the underlying policy, thus possibly raising a conflict of law question on conclusion of the contract.

PART 8. INSURABLE INTEREST

The English law of insurance requires the insured to have an "insurable interest" in the subject matter of the insurance; otherwise it will be a wager and unenforceable. This is a rule of public policy based on precedent and on various Acts such as the Gaming Act 1845, Marine Insurance Act 1906 and Life Insurance Act 1774.

For example, in the case of property insurance such as an aircraft hull, the insured must show he has a present right to a legal or equitable interest in the aircraft or right under a contract.

With regard to liability insurance the general rule is that a person has an insurable interest in the potential liability to which he may be exposed (*Prudential Insurance Co* v. *Inland Revenue Commissioners* [1904] 2 KB 658). For further information on this subject in the market refer to *Margo*.

A hirer (bailee) of an aircraft has an insurable interest in his liability to the person who hires out the aircraft (bailor) for its loss or damage.

PART 9. DUTY OF DISCLOSURE

In English law a contract of insurance is classified as a contract of "utmost good faith". The Latin phrase "*uberrima fides*" is used to describe the relationship between the insurer and the insured. This means that the proposer seeking insurance must disclose all facts relevant to the risk to the prospective insurers. Such disclosure may be done on the slip, in a proposal, or by some other document.

Section 18(1) of the Marine Insurance Act 1906 provides that the assured must disclose to the insurer, before the contract is concluded, every material circumstance which is known to the insured, and the insured is deemed to know every circumstance which, in the ordinary course of business, ought to be known by him.

Scrutton LJ stated in the English case of *Rozanes* v. *Bowen* (1928) 32 Ll L R 98 that, "It is the duty of the assured . . . to make a full disclosure to the underwriters without being asked of all the material circumstances . . . that is expressed by saying that it is a contract of the utmost good faith—*uberrima fides*".

However, in *Mutual and Federal Ins Co Ltd* v. *Oudtshoohorn Municipality* (1985) (1) SA 419, 433A, cited by *Margo*, the Appellate Division of the Supreme Court of South Africa held that while affirming the basic duty on the part of the insurer and insured to disclose facts material to the risk, the term *uberrima fides* (utmost good faith) is an "alien, vague and useless expression without any particular meaning in South African law". South African law is a civil law system.

A material fact is "one which would influence the judgement of a prudent insurer in deciding whether to assume the risk, and if so at what premium and on what terms and conditions" (*Container Transport International Inc* v. *Oceanus Mutual Underwriting Assoc (Bermuda) Ltd* [1984] 1 Lloyd's Rep 476, CA).

In *Lambert* v. *Co-operative Ins Soc Ltd* [1975] 2 Lloyd's Rep 485 the English Court of Appeal held that the duty of disclosure on renewal was the same as when applying for the original policy; and that the rules on disclosure in marine insurance were the same as rules in other forms of insurance.

The insured need not disclose circumstances actually known to the insurer or of which the insurer is presumed to know; he is presumed to know matters of "common notoriety or knowledge, and matters which an insurer in the ordinary course of business, as such, ought to know".

Failure under English law to disclose material facts which could have been ascertained by reasonable enquiry will render the policy voidable by the insurers.

These duties of disclosure are imposed on the insurance broker when acting as agent of the insured.

Margo points out that while the duty of disclosure usually terminates when the contract is made, the policy may include a continuing obligation on the insured during the policy period to notify any material change in the circumstances or nature of the risks which are the basis of the contract. (See General Condition 3 in the Policy Form AVN 1C considered below, page 461).

PART 10. MISREPRESENTATION UNDER ENGLISH LAW

If the insured has made a false or inaccurate representation as to material fact and which induced the insurers to enter into the contract, the policy will be voidable at the instance of the insurers (section 24 of the Marine Insurance Act 1906).

The insurer may waive the requirement to disclose material circumstances and misrepresentation by the insured.

The non-disclosure or misrepresentation must induce the insurer to enter into the contract; if it does, the insurer may elect to avoid the policy and return the premium and until he so elects, the policy remains in effect, but is voidable (*Pan Atlantic Insurance Co Ltd* v. *Pine Top Insurance Co Ltd* [1994] 3 All ER 581, HL).

Margo considers two cases on misrepresentation:

(1) The Canadian case of *Shepherd* v. *Royal Insurance Co Ltd* ((1951) 4 DLR 316), concerned completion by a pilot of an insurance proposal form. The pilot had disclosed to insurers a crash on overshooting but had stated that his licence had never been suspended. Due to the accident the licence was suspended but the pilot had not received notice of suspension until after the six-month suspension had expired. The court held the failure to disclose the suspension was not a material misrepresentation.

(2) In *Opossum Exports Ltd* v. *Aviation & General (Underwriting Agents) Pty Ltd* (Annals ASL (XII) 483, High Court NZ, 1984) the New Zealand High Court found that "representations by the insured that the pilot flying the insured helicopter had 700 hours of flight experience in helicopters, when in fact he had only 116 hours of experience in helicopters, and that the pilot had more experience in live deer recovery operations than he actually had, were material misrepresentations which entitled the insurer to avoid the policy under section 6(2) of the New Zealand Insurance Law Reform Act 1977".

PART 11. POLICY, FORMS AND CONTENT

Various market policy forms, endorsements and AVN and other clauses are found in Lloyd's Aviation Underwriters Association book *Standard Policy Forms, Proposal Forms and Clauses Etc.* ("LAUA Book"). The Association expressly makes no recommendation as to whether or when use of the forms and clauses is appropriate.

Attachment of special terms, clauses or endorsements after the insurance contract has been included follows the usual requirements for English law of contract; there must be consideration provided by persons receiving benefit. In some cases the following market may authorise the leading underwriter to agree on behalf of all the insurers amendments after the contract is made.

A standard policy form and its terms are discussed at Part 15, page 445 below.

PART 12. REINSURANCE

The insurer often "lays off" the risk of insurance by reinsuring part or sometimes all of the risk with other insurers ("reinsurers").

Case law establishes that the 1982 Act applies to reinsurance (*Re NRG Victory Reinsurance Ltd* (1994, unreported)).

Types of reinsurance include the following:

(a) Reinsurance of a single direct insurance, known as facultative reinsurance.

(b) Reinsurance of a series of risks, known as Treaty Reinsurance, see *Margo* (pages 341–342) for discussion of various types of treaties.

(c) Reinsurance of reinsurers, known as a retrocession agreement, as in *Highlands Ins Co* v. *Continental Ins Co* [1987] 1 Lloyd's Rep 109.

Other forms of laying off the risk include "excess of loss", being the loss reinsured from a bundle of insurance contracts above a certain aggregate sum retained by the insurer. Excess of loss can also relate to only one underlying contract of insurance.

The contract of insurance and the contract of reinsurance are separate contracts between separate parties. The reinsurance may apply the same proper law as the original insurance or its own proper law.

Sometimes in the case of aircraft financing, the underlying policy may contain a "cut through" clause which in turn should be reflected in the reinsurance policy. This requires hull reinsurers to pay direct the original insured finance company their entitlement of the hull moneys. Without this arrangement the finance company as assured would be entitled to claim only against the original insurers. However, cut-through clauses are usually subject to the domestic law of the original insurance which sometimes forbids such clauses.

In the case of facultative reinsurance it is quite possible to have a full insurance policy and then a full form reinsurance policy. However, often reinsurance is done by way of "slip reinsurance" incorporating many terms and conditions of the original insurance policy into the reinsurance contract.

Subject to any express provision in the contract, English law imposes on the reinsured the burden of proving that the reinsurer is liable to indemnify him.

In reinsurance the alternative claims handling procedures are:

(a) "Full RI" (full reinsurance) which leaves the original insurer free to handle the claims of the original insured subject to any contractual obligations imposed by the reinsurance contract;

(b) "Claims cooperation clause". This provides that it is a condition precedent to reinsurers' liability that:

(i) the reinsured shall upon knowledge of any loss which may give rise to a claim under this policy advise reinsurers within seven days; and

(ii) the reinsured shall furnish reinsurers with all information available and shall cooperate with reinsurers in any adjustment and settlement (AVN 21).

(c) "Claims control clause". It is a condition precedent to reinsurers' liability that:

(i) the reinsured shall, upon knowledge of any loss or losses which may give rise to a claim, advise reinsurers within 72 hours; and

(ii) furnish reinsurers with all information available and the reinsurers shall have the right to appoint adjusters, assessors and/or surveyors and to control all negotiations, adjustments and settlements in connection with such loss or losses (AVN 25).

(d) "Reinsurance and underwriting claims control clause". This has more stringent provisions additionally giving reinsurers the sole right to appoint adjusters, assessors, or surveyors and/or lawyers and to control all negotiations, adjustments and settlements in connection with the loss. No amendment of the original policy shall be binding on reinsurers without their prior agreement (AVN 41).

The amount of the risk retained by the insurer, before reinsurance cover applies, is known as "the retention".

Under English law the various obligations considered above in respect of insurance apply also to reinsurance, for example duty to disclose and the necessity of insurable interest.

PART 13. DEDUCTIBLE

The deductible is that part of the liability or hull risk which is retained and paid for by the insured with the insurance cover being provided only when the liability or loss has reached a certain amount. Deductibles on hulls can be substantial and the prospective insured can buy insurance cover for this deductible exposure.

PART 14. PREMIUM AND COMMISSION

The price paid by the insured for insurance is called the premium. The amount of the premium should normally be included in the contract of insurance. It may be included on the slip. Sometimes the premium may remain "TBA", i.e. "to be agreed".

Method of payment depends on the terms of the contract and market practice.

The effect of late or non-payment of the premium will be dealt with expressly in the insurance contract or by the governing domestic law.

Premiums for hull insurance are calculated often as a fixed sum or percentage of the total value of the aircraft.

In the case of passenger liability, the premium can be assessed on an amount per passenger seat or in the case of airlines on the basis of the revenue passenger miles flown by the airline.

The policy may require an additional premium to be paid on increase of risk or for reduction of the premium on certain occasions.

In certain other cases the insured may be entitled to claim repayment of all or part of the premium, see *Margo*, pages 110–111.

Where the broker is the agent of the insured, his commission may be deducted from the premium, usually before it is paid.

In the London market a Lloyd's broker is liable to the Syndicates for the payment of premium on default by the insured.

PART 15. LONDON AIRCRAFT INSURANCE POLICY AVN 1C 21.12.98

A study of the London Aircraft Insurance Policy AVN 1C ("Policy") dated 21 December 1998 illustrates law and practice.

The Policy is included in the LAUA Book. From the viewpoint of the insured its wording is stricter than that usually found in most airline fleet policies, which are often drafted by the broker and negotiated with the leading insurer. It reflects a number of points considered in this book.

Only certain provisions of the Policy are considered below, which are summarised. The full text is in Appendix 5.

Section I—Loss of or damage to aircraft

Paragraph 1(a)

The insurers will at their option pay for, replace or repair, accidental loss of or damage to the Aircraft described in the Schedule for the risks covered, not exceeding the specified amount. Loss includes disappearance if the Aircraft is unreported for 60 days.

Comments

1. The "insured" is named in the policy Schedule.

2. Column 5 of Part 2 of the Schedule sets out the amount insured. The insured can choose to insure the aircraft either for "an insured value" or "an agreed value".

The "insured value" is the estimated market value of the aircraft and is the maximum amount the insured can recover. The amount payable is the value of the aircraft at the date and place of loss, which may be less than such maximum.

The "agreed value" is the amount agreed by the parties which will take into account the value of the aircraft to the insured and the cost of replacement. It is important that the Policy makes clear whether the aircraft is insured for an "insured" or "agreed" value. The agreed value applies also to a partial loss. An "agreed value" cover is more usual.

AVN 61 provides that in the case of total hull loss at an agreed value there is no right of replacement. In the absence of AVN 61, see the case of *Trimble-Waterman Associates* v. *Certain Underwriters at Lloyd's* (New York Sup Court, 1975; 13 AVI 17,986), where the court held that there was a right of replacement where the aircraft was insured for an agreed value.

3. Whether there is a loss, as opposed to damage or not, is important for the insured and his financing bank. Loss includes:

   (i)   Total loss, see *Ranger Ins Co* v. *Lee Kidd*, 12 AVI 17,471 1972–4 (Texas Court of Civil Appeals, 1972). The aircraft was a total loss when there remained no substantial remnant which a reasonably prudent owner, uninsured, desiring to restore the aircraft to its original condition, could utilise as a basis for such restoration. The Marine Insurance Act 1906, s. 60 defines a total loss.
   (ii) Constructive total loss: where an aircraft is so damaged that it is beyond economical repair having regard to its value, whether it is an insured or agreed value (*Margo* page 147).
   (iii) Arranged total loss is a compromised settlement where a total loss has not in fact occurred (*Witherby's Dictionary of Insurance*, 3rd edition).

4. Loss or damage must be accidental to the insured, although not necessarily from the point of view of any third party who may have caused the accident, for example in the case of an unlawful act against civil aviation (in such case "war risk" cover may be involved). In the English case of *Fenton* v. *J Thorley & Co Ltd* [1903] AC 443 it was held that an accident is "an unlooked for mishap or an untoward event which is not expected or designed".

5. The risks are described in the Schedule.

Paragraph 1(b)

Paragraph 1(b) provides for payment by the insurers of up to 10 per cent of the amount insured for emergency expenses necessarily incurred if the aircraft is insured for risks of flight.

Comments

1. Policy definition of "Flight": "From the time the Aircraft moves forward in taking off or attempting to take off, whilst in the air, and until the Aircraft

completes its landing run. A rotary-wing aircraft shall be deemed to be in Flight when the rotors are in motion as a result of engine power, the momentum generated therefrom, or autorotation."

Paragraph 2

The exclusions to hull cover detailed in this paragraph are:

  (a) wear and tear, deterioration, breakdown, defect or failure howsoever caused in any Unit of the Aircraft and the consequences thereof within such Unit;
  (b) damage to any Unit by anything which has a progressive or cumulative effect but damage attributable to a single recorded incident is covered under Policy paragraph 1(a).

Accidental loss or damage to the aircraft consequent upon paragraph 2(a) or (b) is covered under paragraph 1(a).

Comments

1. "Wear and Tear" is not defined in the policy definitions in section IV(D) but section 55(2)(c) of the Marine Insurance Act 1906 refers to insurers not being liable for losses caused by ordinary wear and tear.

2. Unit is defined in the Policy as a part or assembly of parts (including any sub-assemblies) of the aircraft which has been assigned an Overhaul Life as part or an assembly. Engines shall constitute a single Unit in the terms specified in the definitions. WATOG (see Appendix 1) also has its definition of Unit. For consideration of this exclusion, see *Rural Helicopters (Australia) Pty Ltd* v. *Ryan* [1985] ANZ Ins Cases 78,956, see also *Margo* at page 158: "The insured aircraft was damaged in a forced landing in rough terrain because of loss of engine oil due to a crack which had opened in the aircraft oil cooler in the wing causing engine oil to be pumped into the outside air." The court held that the oil cooler was not such a unit but the engine was a unit for such purposes. However, the court held that the damage was attributable to a single recorded incident and was covered.

3. Paragraph 2(b) refers to incident. Neither incident nor accident are in substance defined in the Policy as they are in Annex 13.

Paragraph 3

Paragraph 3 imposes conditions applicable to hull cover only.

  (a) Damage to the aircraft is dealt with and the cost of its dismantling, transport and repair.
  (b) If insurers pay for or replace the aircraft,
      (i) they may take the aircraft and title to it as salvage;
      (ii) cover afforded by the hull section of the policy is terminated;

      (iii) any replacement aircraft shall be of the same make and type and in reasonably like condition unless otherwise agreed.

  (c) Except where insurers pay for or replace the aircraft there shall be deducted

      (i) the deductible specified in Part 6(B) of the Schedule;

      (ii) such proportion of the Overhaul Cost of any unit repaired or replaced as the used time bears to the Overhaul Life of the Unit.

  (d) Unless the insurers should elect to take the aircraft for salvage, it shall remain at all times the property of the insured who shall have no right of abandonment to the insurers.

  (e) No claim is payable if the insured has effected other insurance without the knowledge or consent of insurers which is payable for loss or damage payable under this Section.

Comments

1. In assessing the damage and other costs referred to in paragraph 3(a) insurers will be guided by their appointed hull surveyor.

2. Paragraphs 3(b)(i) and 3(d) concern salvage.

Hardy Ivamy in *General Principles of Insurance Law* (6th edn, Butterworths Tolley) comments that it is the duty of the insured on receiving payment in full to hand over to the insurers the salvage. Title of the insurers thereupon relates back to the date when the loss took place who become owners of the salvage from that date.

Hardy Ivamy also raises the questions of whether the property in the salvage passes to insurers from the date of the loss by the fact of payment, or whether insurers are entitled to exercise an option in the matter so that the property does not pass to them unless they think fit to take over the salvage. He comments that under English law it is probable that the latter alternative is correct, and they may therefore refuse to take over the salvage, if, by doing so they would be incurring liabilities to third persons. Here the Policy expressly gives insurers the right to choose.

If insurers take the aircraft as salvage, then they have the responsibility for dealing with the wreckage of the hull. This may impose both responsibilities and expense particularly where the aircraft has crashed at an airport. See for example paragraph 4.5.1 in Annex 12 concerning "wreckage removal" (page 150). Wreckage removal can be expensive; a prospective insured should consider whether it requires insurance for expenses incurred, in case insurers do not take the salvage.

Whether insurers take over the salvage or not, a number of questions arise:

  (a) all or part of the wreckage will probably remain under the control of the investigating authorities until they have finished with it;

  (b) in negotiating any sale of the wreckage/salvage the following should be taken into account:

(i) possible removal of the aircraft from its register.

(ii) passing of property.

(iii) taxes and export duties.

(iv) conditions of sale.

Even if the wreckage is sold under the most scrupulous conditions, the vendor should be aware of the fact that unscrupulous dealers may choose to sell rogue parts which are unairworthy.

An accident may result in spillage of fuel and other substances giving rise to pollution, see page 450 below.

3. Paragraph 3(c)(i) refers to the hull deductible.

4. Paragraph 3(c)(ii) deals with the question of "betterment". Overhaul Cost and Overhaul Life are defined in the Policy. If, for example, as the result of the repair of a lifed component, it becomes zero lifed, the insured has to make good such "betterment" by way of deduction from the claim.

Section II—Legal liability to third parties (other than passengers)

Paragraph 1

The Insurers will indemnify the Insured for all sums which the Insured shall become legally liable to pay, and shall pay, as compensatory damages (including costs awarded against the Insured) in respect of accidental bodily injury (fatal or otherwise) and accidental damage to property caused by the Aircraft or any person or object falling therefrom.

Comments

1. This liability is considered in Chapter 10.

2. Cover is only in respect of compensatory damages and therefore punitive damages are not covered.

3. There must be liability in respect of accidental bodily injury or property damage.

Suppose an aircraft crashes on approach to land, damaging ground navigation aids and blocking the runway so that other aircraft have to divert and the airport is closed. The airport operator claims repair costs and loss of revenue; the diverted aircraft operators may seek to claim additional operating costs or loss of revenue. Any damages payable to the airport operator for repair costs would be covered. Any valid claims by the diverting aircraft operators would not be covered. The claim by the airport operator for loss of profit might possibly be covered if, under the domestic law, such damages could be tacked on to the property damage claim. However, the property damage relates to the ground aids, not to the blocked runway; such cover is unlikely.

Paragraph 2

Express exclusions apply to:

(a) any director, employee or partner of the Insured whilst acting in the course of his employment with or duties for the Insured;

(b) any member of the flight, cabin, or other crew while engaged in the operation of the aircraft;

(c) passengers when entering, on board, or alighting from the aircraft;

(d) loss of or damage to any property belonging to or in the care, custody or control of the Insured;

(e) claims excluded by the Noise and Pollution and Other Perils Exclusion Clause.

Comments

1. Paragraph 2(a): For judicial comment on "course of employment" see page 273. Although the Policy is subject to English law it is unlikely that English law would be applied to the interpretation of "course of employment" in the case of a foreign insured.

2. Paragraph 2(b): The crew must be engaged in the operation of the aircraft for the exclusion to apply. See the Definitions in Annex B and reference on page 248 above to *Fellowes (or Herd)* v. *Clyde Helicopters Ltd* (HL, 1997).

3. Paragraph 2(c): This wording is marginally different from Article 17 of the Warsaw Convention which establishes legal liability in respect of passengers suffering injury "on board the aircraft or in the course of any of the operations of embarking or disembarking", see comments on page 452 below.

4. Paragraph 2(d): In respect of this excluded cover see the comments on the Ariel "Airport Owners and Operators Liability Policy" referred to at page 462 below.

5. Paragraph 3: this paragraph is subject to the "Noise and Pollution and Other Perils Exclusion Clause" (AVN 46B) which excludes from cover in its paragraph 1 "claims directly or indirectly occasioned by, happening through or in consequence of:

(a) noise (audible to the human ear or not), vibration, sonic boom and associated phenomena;

(b) pollution and contamination of any kind whatever;

(c) electrical and electromagnetic interference;

(d) interference with the use of property

unless caused by or resulting in a crash, fire, explosion, collision or a recorded inflight emergency causing abnormal aircraft operation".

Paragraphs 2 and 3 of AVN 46B deal with insurers' obligations in respect combined claims as defined.

Paragraph 4 of AVN 46B provides that nothing in AVN 46B shall override any radioactive contamination or other exclusion clause attached to or forming part of the policy.

In respect of exclusion (b) of AVN 46B, pollution and contamination, see the Aircraft and Aerial Application Liability Policy (LPO417D 1 October 1996) in the LAUA Book which covers liability for bodily injury and property damage wherever there is an occurrence (defined) and arising out of ownership, maintenance or use of the aircraft including aerial application. Aerial application is defined as "the spraying or dropping of chemical or seed" (see also Chapter 8 above). The exclusions include "4. Injury to or destruction of any crops, pastures, trees or tangible property to which the Aerial Application is deliberately made whether in error or not."

Exclusion (d) in such Policy could be interpreted to exclude from cover a wide range of commercial risks.

Paragraph 4

This paragraph deals with the limits of indemnity given in Part 6(C) of the Schedule, any third party deductible (Part 6(B)), and legal costs.

Section III—Legal liability to passengers

Paragraph 1

"The Insurers will indemnify the Insured in respect of all sums which the Insured shall become legally liable to pay, and shall pay, as compensatory damages (including costs awarded against the Insured) in respect of

(a) accidental bodily injury (fatal or otherwise) to passengers whilst entering, on board, or alighting from the Aircraft and
(b) loss of or damage to baggage and personal articles of passengers arising out of an Accident to the Aircraft

Provided always that (i) before a passenger boards the Aircraft the insured shall take such measures as are necessary to exclude or limit liability for claims under (a) and (b) above to the extent permitted by law; (ii) if such measures include the issue of a passenger ticket/baggage check, the same shall be delivered correctly completed to the passenger a reasonable time before the passenger boards the Aircraft."

In the event of failure to comply with these documentary precautions in proviso (i) or (ii), the liability of insurers under this section shall not exceed the amount of legal liability which would have existed had the proviso been complied with.

Paragraph 2. Exclusions

Insurers shall not be liable for injury or loss sustained by any (i) director, employee or partner; (ii) member of crew, both exclusions as described in the exclusions 2(a) and 2(b) in Section II.

Comments

1. "Bodily injury": see the comments on Article 17 of the Warsaw Convention (Chapter 7, page 247).

2. If "entering" and "alighting" are more limited than "the course of any of the operations of embarking or disembarking" in Article 17 of the Warsaw Convention, questions may arise on the extent of cover if a passenger is injured when crossing the apron. Furthermore the proviso to paragraph 1 of Section III uses the words "boards the Aircraft". It is hoped that any arbitrator (General Condition 7) will take a realistic approach.

3. With regard to baggage and personal articles referred to in paragraph 1(b) an accident to the aircraft is required while it is not so in the case of the passenger injury cover. In the policy definitions, "accident" is defined as meaning "any one accident or series of accidents arising out of one event". However, must "accident" in the policy meet the criteria of accident in the ICAO Definition, or in UK domestic law (see *Fenton* v. *J Thorley & Co Ltd* ([1903] AC 443) (page 446 above))?

The wording suggests that if a passenger entering an aircraft stumbles on defective embarkation steps, breaking his ankle and his spectacles, the insured's liability for the ankle but not for the spectacles will be covered, unless the breaking of the ankle can be construed as an accident to the aircraft, which is unlikely.

4. The Policy provides no cargo liability cover which can be added by agreement. If there were such cover, there might be provisions requiring issue of air waybills in the required forms similar to those provisions on passenger tickets. The distinction between baggage and cargo, and the documentation required in each case, may become blurred, particularly in general aviation. When an oil-rig worker stows equipment on the aircraft for a journey from A to B is this baggage or cargo where an air waybill would be needed in respect of "International carriage"? Changes either made by MP4 or to be made by the ICAO Convention remove the importance of issuing an air waybill.

5. The proviso requiring issue of tickets/baggage checks covers two situations:

(a) where the Warsaw Convention or similar provisions in respect to "non-international" carriage apply;
(b) where the Warsaw Convention or such provisions do not apply.

The need to issue a passenger ticket/baggage check for Warsaw Convention carriage in order to limit liability, and the changes in the law proposed by the ICAO Convention have already been considered. To the extent that a special contract (Chapter 7, Part 4) has removed limits of liability for death or injury then this provision ceases to be of significance as no doubt the insured will have advised the insurers of the special contract concerned. However, failure to issue a ticket where death or injury liability limits have been waived may still result in an unintentional unlimited liability in respect of baggage or delay. This could prove expensive for the insured where the baggage of the oil-rig worker includes an essential drilling component.

In respect of non-Warsaw Convention situations, there may be some States where it is still possible to limit or exclude liability in respect of death or bodily injury by contract. However, this is a diminishing possibility.

See *Margo* (page 166) on the arbitration case of *Re Keenair Services Ltd and Norwich Union Fire Insurance Society Ltd* (Arbitration Re Policy No A. 8203/218, 29 July 1983). This case concerns not only failure to issue a ticket where a similar policy requirement applied but also the question of insurer's agreement by way of policy endorsement to an increased limit of liability by way of special contract. Such increase would have been dealt with in the ticket which was not issued. The arbitrator held that the insurer's liability extended to the increased limit.

These Policy ticketing provisions are strict. Standard airline fleet policies usually have more liberal provisions.

6. The exclusions apply to directors or employees acting in the course of their employment. Thus the insured is unlikely to be covered in respect of the death of an in-house accountant when travelling as a passenger from London to Paris for a meeting with insured's local handling agents. See *Fellowes (or Herd) and Another* v. *Clyde Helicopters Ltd* (HL, 1997): page 248 above. The transport of corporate employees is an element in distinguishing "public transport" and "aerial work" under the ANO. (See Chapter 8.)

Paragraph 3

Paragraph 3 refers to the limits of liability in the Schedule and insurance cover in respect of legal costs and expenses.

Section III is not subject to the Noise and Pollution and other Perils Exclusion Clause.

Section IV

Section IV sets out: (A) General Exclusions, (B) Conditions Precedent applicable to all sections of the Policy, (C) General Conditions applicable to all sections of the Policy, and (D) Definitions. Some of these are considered below:

(A) General Exclusions

The Policy does not apply in the situations listed:

Ex 1: Use of the aircraft for any illegal purpose or for any purpose other than those stated in the Schedule and as defined in the Policy Definitions.

Comments

1. "Illegal" is defined, as by *Black*, as "Against or not authorized by law". The purpose rather than the operation must be illegal. It is submitted that "illegal" in this case is a breach of the criminal law. The distinction should be clear when compared with Condition Precedent 2 which requires the Insured to comply with all air navigation and airworthiness orders and requirements as specified; failure to comply with certain of these orders may constitute an offence, see ANO (Article 111). The unlawful carriage of narcotics would be an illegal purpose outside cover under Section IV(A)1. However continuation of the flight into night conditions when the pilot's night rating had lapsed would probably be an illegal operation. In *Nel* v. *Santam Insurance Co Ltd* (1981) (2) SA 230T; [1980] *US Aviation Reports* 1901, the Supreme Court of South Africa held that insurance cover for a charter flight without the required temporary air service permit was not excluded. The distinction may not always be clear.

2. Purpose. Part 3 of the Schedule sets out the purposes for which cover is provided. The Policy definitions include private pleasure, business, commercial and rental. These are "standard uses" and do not include those other flying activities listed, such as instruction, aerobatics, fire-fighting etc.

Neither "private pleasure" nor "business" include cover for use for hire or reward while "commercial" does so, thus raising the possible applicability of the Warsaw Convention. The fact that the Insured may operate for hire or reward may make it an air transport undertaking, under domestic laws. Therefore gratuitous carriage of the in-house accountant could give rise to an uninsured Warsaw Convention liability. No doubt the Insured will have issued a ticket! (See Chapter 8 on General Aviation.)

Ex 2: Whilst the aircraft is outside the geographical limits stated in the schedule unless due to *force majeure*.

Comments

Cover applies where the aircraft is outside the geographical limits due to *force majeure*. Compare this with Ex 10(g) where cover applies only where the aircraft shall be deemed to have been restored to the control of the insured on safe return of the aircraft at an airfield not excluded by the geographical limits of the Policy and entirely suitable for the operation of the aircraft.

Ex 3: Whilst the aircraft is being piloted by any person other than as stated in the schedule except the aircraft may be operated on the ground by any person competent for that purpose.

Comments

1. Where the pilot is named specifically there should be no confusion. Where the pilot(s) are generally described by reference to employment or approval, for example, problems of interpretation can arise, see cases referred to by *Margo* (page 123).

   2. If a pilot is not an insured, insurers are legally entitled to subrogate against him.

Ex 4: Whilst the aircraft is being transported by any means of conveyance except as a result of an accident giving rise to a claim under Section 1 of the Policy.

Ex 5: Whilst the aircraft is landing or taking-off or attempting to do so from a place which does not comply with the recommendations laid down by the manufacturer of the aircraft except as the result of *force majeure*.

Comments

The wording of Ex 5 is less strict than the earlier version in the Policy which excluded cover "whilst the aircraft is using unlicensed areas unless due to *force majeure*". This current exclusion does not require that the aircraft must use an aerodrome. It merely excludes a place "which does not comply with recommendations laid down by the manufacturer".

Ex 6: To liability assumed or rights waived by the Insured under any agreement (other than a passenger ticket/baggage check issued under Section III hereof) except to the extent that liability would have attached to the insured in the absence of such agreement.

Comments

1. Generally speaking, if the insured issues a ticket for a flight which it then sub-contracts, as contracting carrier, to another operator, as actual carrier, so that the Guadalajara Convention may apply, any passenger liability will attach to the insured as a result of a contract evidenced by the ticket but not as a result of any accident to the insured contracting carrier. The wording would suggest that this situation is expressly exempt from this exclusion. However, this situation is most unlikely to arise under the Policy where cover is restricted to specific aircraft and pilot(s).

   2. *Margo* suggests that the exclusion would apply where an aircraft operator signs waiver or release in favour of an airport operator in respect of damage to an aircraft operating in or out of an airport. (See for example the case of *British Airports Authority* v. *British Airways Board* (QBD, May 1981) referred to in Chapter 9, page 319.)

Ex 7: When passengers carried exceed the declared maximum in the schedule.

Comment

The distinction between passengers and crew is important; see *Fellowes (or Herd)* v. *Clyde Helicopters Ltd* (page 248 above).

Ex 8: Non-Contribution: To claims payable under any other policy except in respect of any excess beyond the amount which would have been payable under such other policy had this insurance not been effected.

Comments

This must be read in conjunction with paragraph 3(e) of Section I. It will apply alone in any event to Sections II and III.

Ex 9: Nuclear Risks Exclusion Clause applies AVN 71 in the LAUA Book.

Comments

AVN 71 excludes cover for loss, destruction or damage to property and any legal liability of whatsoever nature caused or contributed by, or arising from, any nuclear explosive assembly or component or other radioactive source.

Ex 10: Claims caused by war risks as listed which copies AVN 48B.

Comments

The wording of AVN 48B excludes claims not only caused by war and other forms of hostilities in the generally accepted sense but also by "(c) strikes, riots, and civil commotions or labour disturbances . . . ; and (e) any malicious act or act of sabotage; (f) confiscation . . . ; (g) hijacking or any unlawful seizure . . . ". *Margo* analyses the various words and phrases. See also AHM 693 of the Airport Handling Manual (page 332 above) dealing with the item "Vandalism/Malign Mischief".

The standard procedure in the market is that where there is a policy covering hull and liabilities risks, AVN 48B is applied, but certain war risk cover for liabilities is written back into the policy by way of AVN 52C "Extended Coverage Endorsement (Aviation Liabilities)". However, this written back cover automatically terminates, for example, on the outbreak of war between two or more of the five named powers or, on "hostile detonation of weapon of war employing atomic or nuclear fission . . . ", in respect of the written back cover excluded by AVN 48(a) which excludes war in the generally accepted sense and similar activities.

While war risk hull cover can be "written back", it is usually insured with different insurers in the market. Therefore disputes can arise between "all risk" insurers and "war risk" insurers as to which insurance cover should respond to the claim. In order to meet the commercial needs of the insured, both sets of insurers can include the "50/50 Provisional claims settlement clause" in their respective policies. This obliges the two sets of insurers to pay in equal shares a valid claim in case of doubt as to the applicable cover and then to arbitrate among themselves later as to which insurance should respond. For an example of this see the arbitration *Coleman* v. *Youell* (1991) reported in 1 *S&B* AvR VIII/5 1991.

For further information see *Margo*; also *PanAmerican World Airways Inc* v. *Aetna Casualty and Surety Co* [1974] 1 Lloyd's Rep 207, SDNY, 1973; 13 AVI 17,340 1974–6; affirmed [1975] 1 Lloyd's Rep 77, and *Boden* v. *Hussey* [1988] 1 Lloyd's Rep 423, CA.

If an exclusion clause as considered above is an exception to the general cover given by the insurer, the burden of proof on the application of the clause is on the insurer. If, however, such exclusion clause defines the limited cover given by the insurer, the burden of proof is on the insured.

Thus the burden of proof in applying an exclusion clause depends on the answer to the question whether it creates "a promise with exceptions", or "a qualified promise". See *Munro, Brice & Co* v. *War Risks Assoc Ltd* [1918] 2 KB 78 and [1920] 3 KB 94.

(B) Conditions Precedent applicable to all sections

It is necessary that the insured observes and fulfils the following conditions before the Insurers have any liability to make payment under this Policy.

Comments

1. In interpreting the rights and obligations under an insurance policy, English law classifies the contractual provisions of the policy as conditions, warranties or other terms.

A condition precedent is usually a condition to be fulfilled prior to the validity of the policy; a condition subsequent must be fulfilled otherwise the policy ceases to exist. A condition may also be precedent to a loss, as is the case in this Policy.

In *Bond Air Services Ltd* v. *Hill* [1955] 2 QB 417 the court held that the burden of proof is on the insurers to prove a breach of condition.

A warranty can be described as a term in a contract of insurance upon the exact compliance with which the liability of the insurers depends, and upon breach of which, however trivial, the insurers may repudiate the policy (*DeHahn* v. *Hartley* (1786) 1 Term Rep 343, 99 ER 1130; affirmed (1787) 2 Term Rep 186n).

If a warranty is an affirmative warranty affirming the existence of a state of particular facts, then its breach will entitle the insurers to void the whole policy regardless of materiality or whether it caused or contributed to the loss.

If the warranty is a promissory warranty as to a future state of affairs, breach will entitle the insurer to repudiate the policy from the date of the breach.

If the legal status of these terms is uncertain, it will be the duty of the court to construe the policy and to assess such status and to apply the applicable law to any breach.

2. Does this wording release the insurers from payment of any future claims or only the claim under immediate consideration? It is likely that the court would construe any ambiguity against the party seeking to rely on it, i.e. the insurers.

Con (1): "The Insured shall at all times use due diligence and do and concur in doing everything reasonably practicable to avoid or diminish any loss hereon."

Comments

Condition (1) can be construed as imposing four obligations on the insured:

  (i) to use due diligence to avoid accidents;
  (ii) to do and concur in doing everything reasonably practicable to avoid accidents;
  (iii) to use due diligence to avoid or diminish any loss hereon; and
  (iv) to do and concur in doing everything reasonably practicable to avoid or diminish any loss hereon.

An English common law interpretation of due diligence is given in the shipping case of *Riverstone Meat Co Pty Ltd* v. *Lancashire Shipping Co Ltd* [1960] 1 All ER 193, page 219 (Court of Appeal) where Willmer LJ said "an obligation to exercise due diligence is to my mind indistinguishable from an obligation to exercise reasonable care". On this basis the obligation of the insured under the Policy is to exercise reasonable care and do and concur in doing everything reasonably practicable to avoid accidents and to diminish any loss hereon. However, the *Riverstone* case was reversed by the House of Lords on appeal which held that under the marine Hague Rules an obligation was imposed on the marine carrier to exercise due diligence "to make the ship seaworthy", which was an obligation that there should be due diligence in the work concerned, and the ship having been entrusted by the ship owners to the repairers for survey, the negligence of the fitter employed by the repairers was a lack of due diligence for which the ship owner was responsible. On the basis that this interpretation could be applied in interpreting Condition (1), the requirement for due diligence imposes a substantial obligation on the insured.

In the case of *Fraser* v. *B N Furman (Productions) Ltd* [1967] 3 All ER 571, the policy contained a condition, described as a condition precedent, which provided that "the insured shall take all reasonable precautions to prevent accidents and disease". As *Margo* points out, the English Court of Appeal held that the condition "had to be construed in the context of the commercial purpose of the insurance contract to which it related . . . the test whether the insured had taken "reasonable" steps to prevent the accident would not have been whether he failed to do what a hypothetical reasonable insured would have done, but whether he had deliberately courted a danger, the existence of which he had recognised, by failing to take measures to avert it or by taking measures to avert it which he knew were inadequate". In considering this provision, *Margo* comments that the various decisions suggest that there are limited circumstances in which conditions in this form could be used by insurers to avoid liability based on the insured's acts or omissions.

However, under the Policy the insured must also use due diligence.

The current Policy wording is in line with *Margo's* suggestion (page 143). In a hypothetical case of careless controlled flight into terrain, this Condition raises the questions:

(1) Are the flight crew joint assured?

(2) If not, are their acts attributable to their insured employer?

(3) Will the Insured have discharged its obligations by proper crew training?

Due to the uncertain meaning of due diligence, it is arguable that there is no cover.

Con (2):

"The Insured shall comply with all air navigation and airworthiness orders and requirements issued by any competent authority affecting the safe operation of the Aircraft and shall ensure that:

(a) the Aircraft is airworthy at the commencement of each Flight;

(b) all Log Books and other records in connection with the Aircraft which are required by any official regulations in force from time to time shall be kept up to date and shall be produced to the Insurers or their agents on request;

(c) the employees and agents of the Insured comply with such orders and requirements."

Comments

1. Article 111 of the ANO states that any person who contravenes any provisions of the ANO and other specified regulations commits an offence.

2. It is necessary to analyse the meaning of "all air navigation and airworthiness orders and requirements issued by any competent authority affecting the safe operation of the aircraft". The UK legislation includes Civil Aviation Act 1982, ANO and Rules of the Air Regulations 1996. Requirements could refer to JAR and the British BCAR.

In the Australian case *McClean* v. *McClean* (1977) 15 SASR 306 the insured had to comply under the policy with "all air navigation and airworthiness orders and requirements issued by the Department of Civil Aviation or other competent authority". It was alleged the insured failed to comply with the policy terms in that he had flown the aircraft in breach of the Air Navigation Regulations. The Court held that these Regulations did not fall within the description of "air navigation and airworthiness orders and requirements" issued by the DCA or other competent authority. The court considered that the Regulations were made by the Governor-General in his executive function pursuant to section 26 of the Air Navigation Act 1920, and were therefore part of the law of the land, and were not such orders and requirements. This is a strict interpretation in favour of the insured.

3. The insured has to comply with the orders and requirements and also shall ensure in Condition (2)(c) that his employees and agents do likewise. Most insured in civil aviation are limited liability corporations, i.e. artificial legal personalities which have no physical existence and come into existence by compliance with certain procedures and documentation. Such corporations can only act through natural persons such as directors, employees and agents. *Margo* considers this point in citing the case *Aviation Insurance Co of Africa Ltd* v. *Burton Construction (Pty) Ltd* (1976) (4) SA 769. In this case the insured undertook (i) to comply with all air navigation and airworthiness orders and requirements and (ii) had to take all *reasonable* steps to ensure such orders and requirements were complied with by its agents and employees and the aircraft would be airworthy at the commencement of each flight. The court pointed out that if the insured were a natural person the position would be clear. He would personally have to comply with the orders and requirements. He employed an agent and merely had to take all reasonable steps to ensure he had complied with the orders and requirements. The court asked why the insurer should be in a better position merely because the insured is a company.

In *Bates & Lloyd Aviation (Pty) Ltd* v. *Aviation Insurance Co Ltd* (1985) (3) SA 918, CA the court held with regard to (i) any breach must properly be committed by the directing mind of the corporation and with regard to (ii) the company discharged its duties to take all reasonable steps by employing a qualified and responsible pilot.

The Policy does not include the words "and shall take all reasonable steps to" and therefore imposes a strict obligation on the insured to ensure that the employees and agents comply with all orders and requirements. On the basis that the policy is strictly construed, this could in many cases be a severe limitation on cover provided. *Margo* wonders whether it is arguable that the insured cannot for practical reasons be expected to do more than take "reasonable steps to ensure his servants and agents comply". However, he cites against this argument the South African case of *Improefed (Pty) Ltd* v. *American International Insurance Co Ltd* (1981) (2) SA 68; affirmed on appeal. Views have been expressed elsewhere that it has been common ground that the duty under the contract is not to be read literally as an absolute duty to ensure but that it means a duty to take all reasonable steps to ensure compliance.

The combined effect of Conditions (1) and (2) imposes strict obligation on the insured, particularly if the applicable domestic law does not apply the distinctions made by the court in *McClean* v. *McClean* in respect of regulations and orders and requirements.

Con (3) requires the insured (1) to give immediate notice of and information on any event likely to give rise to a claim including any impending prosecution, (2) render such further information and assistance as insurers may reasonably require, (3) not to act in any way to the detriment or prejudice of insurers, (4) not to make any admission of liability or payment or offer or promise of payment without the written consent of the insurers.

(C) General Conditions applicable to all sections

Con (1): "The Insurers shall be entitled (if they so elect) at any time and for so long as they desire to take absolute control of all negotiations and proceedings and in the name of the Insured to settle, defend or pursue any claim."

Comments

Condition (5) elucidates the provisions in Sections II (third party liability) and III (passenger liability) that the insurers will indemnify the insured for all sums which the insured shall become legally liable to pay and shall pay as compensatory damages. In practice insurers instruct their professional advisors to handle the claims and where appropriate settle them, using insurers' funds.

Con (2): Subrogation. See page 465 below.

Con (3): Variation in risk. The insured shall give immediate notice to insurers if there is any change in the circumstances or nature of the risks which are the basis of this contract. No claim arising subsequent to such change shall be recoverable unless such change has been accepted by the insurers.

Comments

Any change in the circumstances or nature of the risks must be notified. There are no words limiting the exclusion of cover to claims arising as a result of the change of circumstances.

Con (4): Deals with cancellation of the Policy, and any consequential return of premium. Insurers only have a discretion to return any premium when the insured cancels.

Con (5): Prohibits assignment of the Policy by the insured except by the consent of the insurers.

Con (6): The Policy is not, and the parties expressly agree that it shall not be construed as, a policy of marine insurance.

Comments

While the Marine Insurance Act 1906 embodies general principles of law of insurance nevertheless there are aspects of marine insurance not appropriate to aviation.

Con (7): The Policy is subject to English law and any dispute or difference shall be submitted to arbitration in London.

Con (8): Where two or more aircraft are insured the Policy terms apply separately to each.

Con (9): Policy limits of indemnity apply where there is more than one insured.

Con (10): False and fraudulent claims. If the insured knowingly makes a false or fraudulent claim, the Policy shall become void and all claims under the Policy shall be forfeited.

Part (D) sets out the Policy definitions.

PART 16. OTHER POLICIES IN THE LAUA BOOK

The following policies are also included in the LAUA Book:

1. The Ariel "Airport Owners and Operators Liability Insurance Policy"

This policy gives liability cover for bodily injury including death and loss of or damage to property of others caused by accident occurring during the policy period and arising out of the hazards set forth in sections 1, 2 and 3.

Section 1 covers bodily injury and property damage

   (a) in or about the premises specified in the schedule as a direct result of services granted by the insured, and
   (b) elsewhere in the course of work or performance of duties carried out by the insured or his employees in connection with the business or operation specified in the schedule

caused by fault or negligence of the insured or defect in premises, ways, works, machinery or plant used in the insured's business.

Section 2 covers loss or damage to aircraft or aircraft equipment not owned, rented or leased by the insured whilst on the ground, in the care, custody or control of or whilst being serviced, handled or maintained by the insured or any servant of the insured.

Section 3 covers bodily injury or property damage arising out of the possession, use, consumption or handling of any goods or products manufactured, constructed, altered, repaired, serviced, treated, sold, supplied or distributed by the insured or his employees, but only in respect of such goods or products which form part of or are used in conjunction with aircraft, and then only after such goods or products have ceased to be in the possession or under the control of the Insured.

Each section is subject to its own important exclusions which distinguish the cover given in that particular section from cover under the other sections. There are also general exclusions and conditions applicable to all sections.

In the light of Condition Precedent (2) of the Policy AVN 1C considered above, it is interesting to note that General Condition (6)(d) of the Ariel policy provides that "The Insured shall comply with all international and Government Regulations and Civil Instructions".

2. Cargo insurance

There are two types:

(i) Cargo liability insurance to protect the carrier against the type of liability considered in Chapter 7.
(ii) Cargo "all risks" insurance usually taken out by consignor or consignee of goods.

These are taken in turn.

(i) Cargo legal liability insurance

The prospective insured should make clear that this cover is required (for example it is not included in the Policy). If provided it may form part of the liability policy covering passengers, their baggage and cargo. The parties are free to agree the extent of the cover but from the point of view of the insured it is prudent to make sure that the cover should extend to unlimited liability including the case where there is a special value declared under Article 22 of the Warsaw Convention or removal of limits on the grounds of Article 25 of the Warsaw Convention, where that Convention still applies. Cargo liability cover limits are likely to be part of the "combined single limit" cover in respect of any one accident.

It is in the interests of the insurers to impose on the insured an obligation to procure the issue of an Air Waybill in the required form where such issue is necessary to limit liability.

An important question is the extent of cover for each consignment. Cover may commence from the time of issue of the Air Waybill or other contract of carriage and terminate upon delivery by the insured or its agent to the consignee or upon handing over to the succeeding carrier.

(ii) Cargo all risks insurance

This insurance covers the person interested in the cargo against all risks independently of whether there is a liability on the air carrier for the loss or damage.

The insurance cover may be effected by the consignor or consignee. It may be arranged with the insured air carrier.

The terms of the cover may apply the Institute (of London Underwriters) Cargo Clauses (Air), the Institute War Clauses (Air Cargo) and the Institute Strike Clauses (Air Cargo). The air carrier may indicate on the Air Waybill that insurance has been provided to cover the consignment. This can take the place of issuing a certificate of insurance.

The form currently in use is LPO 359B (10.96).

> Section 1 covers legal liability.
> Section 2 covers all risks.
> Section 3 sets out the General Conditions which include clauses similar to those in the Policy.
> Section 4 deals with the premium.

3. Products liability insurance

Product liability insurance may be provided to a single manufacturer on negotiated terms or possibly under a collective scheme such as the British Aerospace Companies (SBAC) Scheme or the Aircraft Builders Council Inc (ABC) Scheme in the USA.

The LAUA Book contains "London Market Aviation Products Liability", Policy Wording AVN 66 1 October 1996. No further comments are made here.

PART 17. POLITICAL AND FINANCIAL RISKS INSURANCE

Types of insurance available in the market include:

> (i) Political risk covering certain of those risks excluded by AVN 48B(f);
> (ii) Financial risk insurance for aircraft non-repossession.

PART 18. COMPULSORY INSURANCE

The Rome Convention 1933 and the Rome Convention 1952 require compulsory liability insurance for surface damage covered by those Conventions (see Chapter 10 above).

EC Council Regulation (EEC) No 2407/92 on licensing of air carriers; Article 7 requires that an air carrier shall be insured to cover liability in the case of accidents.

Article 50 of the ICAO Convention imposes compulsory insurance. See page 287.

Various States or authorities may also require compulsory insurance in respect of operators. For example (i) possibly as a condition for the granting of an Air Operators Certificate (see ICAO Manual of Procedures for operations, inspections, certification and continued surveillance (doc. 8335—AN/879), page 77 above), or (ii) as a condition for the granting of permission for operation of a non-scheduled flight to an operator from another State.

Some States require operators to take out automatic personal accident insurance for passengers up to a specified sum: in Germany such sum is DM 35,000.

PART 19. DATE RECOGNITION EXCLUSION AND LIMITED COVERAGE CLAUSES

In view of anticipated problems over recognition by computers of change of year or date during the period 1999–2000 the Market has issued AVN 2000—Date Recognition Clause. However, on adequate completion of the Application for Date Recognition Limited Coverage Clause, insurers are prepared to provide cover in accordance with AVN 2001 for hull and aircraft liability coverage and with AVN 2002 for non-aircraft liability only.

PART 20. SUBROGATION

Subrogation is widely recognised and applied in the international community. Each State has its own domestic laws on subrogation.

General

Subrogation in the English law of insurance is "a doctrine in favour of underwriters or insurers in order to prevent the insured from recovering more than a full indemnity; it has been adopted solely for that reason".

It was stated in *Castellain* v. *Preston* (1883) 11 QBD 380: "Once the insurers have indemnified the insured under the policy they step into his shoes in relation to any rights of recovery which may be available to the insured against third parties."

The English common law doctrine of subrogation applies to indemnity insurance which includes hull and liability insurance. It does not apply in the case of personal accident or life insurance.

Subrogation under English law takes place automatically when insurers have admitted and paid the insured's claim. The right is exercisable in the name of the insured.

However, if under English law there has been an express assignment of rights by the insured to insurers then it is very likely that any action will have to be started by insurers in their own names. This may also be necessary where right of subrogation arises by Act.

The insured has an implied duty to assist insurers and not to prejudice their position.

While the English common law doctrine of subrogation applies to aviation, the principle is stated in section 79 of the Marine Insurance Act 1906 as follows:

"Where the insurer pays for a total loss, either of the whole, or in the case of goods of any apportionable part, of the subject-matter insured, he thereupon becomes entitled to take over the interest of the insured in whatever may remain of the subject-matter so paid for, and he is thereby subrogated to all the rights and remedies of the assured in and in respect of that subject-matter as from the time of the casualty causing the loss."

In other legal systems, subrogation is dealt with in the State's Civil Code; see for example Article 965 of the Civil Code of the Russian Federation.

It is a matter of the relevant domestic law as to whether subrogation rights have to be exercised in the name of the subrogated insurers or in the name of the insured. Furthermore, domestic law will determine whether a written document in some form is required in order to preserve rights of subrogation.

Where the right of subrogation accrues to the insurer automatically on payment of the claim, no document may be necessary to create that right. While most payments made by insurers will be done by banking transaction which provides evidence of payment, it may nevertheless be prudent to have some form of receipt or agreement as evidence both (i) of the payment giving rise to the right of subrogation and (ii) of the parties, the amount and the purposes of the payment; such document may also include possible additional provisions dealing with the right of subrogation and its exercise. In the market, payment to the insured will usually be made by its broker who will have collected funds from the insurers.

The principles of subrogation may cover not only the insurer stepping into the shoes of the insured to make a recovery against a third party, but also the exercise of the insurer of a right to recover from the insured moneys received by the latter from the third party in respect of an insured loss already paid by insurers. In the latter case in English common law the moneys would be held on trust for the insurers.

Aviation insurance policies often contain a clause setting out the insurer's rights of subrogation. The court concerned must apply the applicable domestic law rules of construction in interpreting an express subrogation clause when the question of subrogation is already regulated either by the Civil Code, as in the case of Russia mentioned above, or by legal precedent, as generally in England.

General Condition (2) of the Policy states, "Upon an indemnity being given or a payment being made by the Insurers under this Policy, they shall be subrogated to the rights and remedies of the Insured who shall co-operate with and do all things necessary to assist the Insurers to exercise such rights and remedies".

In the case of a major hull subrogation the duties of the insured to assist its insurers may be extensive and costly, for example the provision of witnesses, and the production of evidence and technical information. It may save both misunderstanding and time if these questions are dealt with expressly in the policy.

Sometimes the policy may contain words limiting the powers of subrogation, for example where the insured has to give its consent to the subrogation action. A fierce and arduous subrogation action in the name of the insured against a defendant with whom it does business regularly is not always welcome to the insured.

An insured should not take any step in respect of a third party which would prejudice the insurer's subrogation rights.

Loan Receipt

The use of a loan receipt is a method adopted by insurers where they wish to indemnify their insured under the relevant policy, but also to also reserve their position as against him. The insurers make an interest-free loan of an amount equal to what should be paid to the insured under the policy. This is repayable only to the extent that any recovery is later made from any third party or the facts ultimately show that the insured has no right to indemnity under the policy, or for some other reasons.

Subrogation in liability claims

Where a liability risk is insured, and principles of subrogation apply to such insurance, then substantially the same rules apply as in a hull case. For example, if insurers indemnify an airline against passenger liability claims, they will take over the right of the airline to make a claim against a third party such as a manufacturer.

In some cases a party such as an airline will discharge its liability to the injured party such as a passenger and will take over the rights of that passenger to make a claim against a third party such as the manufacturer. In broad terms in certain legal systems the airline can be regarded as being "subrogated" to the rights of the injured party. In certain States this may be referred to as a "regress claim". In common law it would be regarded as a third party claim for contribution or indemnity by the airline or its subrogated insurers. The nature of such claim is determined by domestic law and might not only be in tort but also in contract where, for example, the airline purchased a defective aircraft from the manufacturer. The nature of any documentation required in this type of claim depends on the domestic law.

Any subrogation claims by Social Security agencies should be taken into account by the airline when applying any limit of liability under the Warsaw Convention. See MIA para 2.3, page 303 dealing with this in the IATA Inter-carrier Agreement.

CHAPTER 17

STRUCTURES AND MATERIALS

AIRCRAFT STRUCTURES

A convenient, if arbitrary, way of classifying the parts of an aircraft is to consider the airframe, the engines, and the equipment as separate groups. The airframe consists of fuselage, wings and empennage.

Engines do not require definition.

Equipment covers a multitude of items such as hydraulics, electrics, electronics, navigational and fire detection and suppression equipment. Some equipment falls into more than one of these classes: undercarriages are usually regarded as equipment but could also be considered as part of the airframe. Fuel systems, including pumps and tanks, fall on the boundary between all three groups.

AVAILABLE AIRCRAFT MATERIALS

The general requirements of aircraft materials are strength, stiffness, toughness and durability. Special properties are required for components that operate at high temperatures and in hostile environments, e.g. turbine blades and other engine components. Since reduction of weight is of great importance in aircraft there is a strong preference for low density materials. While cost of raw materials is not of the first importance, because of the high value added in manufacture, this factor needs to be considered.

Aerospace materials can be classified, again rather arbitrarily, into four broad groups:

(a) Metals and alloys;
(b) Ceramics;
(c) Plastics (polymers);
(d) Composites.

Metals and alloys

Metals are crystalline solids that can be strengthened by mixing (alloying) with other metallic or non-metallic elements. Alloys and pure metals can be strengthened by cold working and a small number of alloys can be greatly strengthened by heat treatment, steel being the best-known example. The predominance of metals and alloys in engineering is due to the unique combination of strength, stiffness and toughness they can provide. They are also reasonably easy to fabricate into useful shapes by casting, forging, rolling and extrusion. Their disadvantages include relatively high densities, a tendency to react with certain environments (corrosion) and loss of strength and toughness at elevated temperatures.

Ceramics

Ceramics are generally crystalline solids formed by chemical reaction between a metal and a non-metallic element. Aluminium oxide, tungsten carbide, and silicon nitride are examples. Non-crystalline (amorphous) ceramics are called glasses. Crystalline ceramics are hard, stiff and potentially very strong. Many of them have low densities and their high melting points give good high temperature strength. Unfortunately, ceramics are inherently brittle which means that their strength is degraded by very small sharp cracks. Their low ductility and high hardness make their fabrication and machining difficult. The same comments are broadly true of the glasses.

Plastics

This term covers a wide range of man-made polymers that are generally amorphous although crystalline and partially crystalline polymers can be made. Stiffness and strength are generally modest compared with metals and ceramics. This is largely offset by their very low densities. Other advantages are the ease with which polymers can be fabricated into complex shapes, modest cost and excellent corrosion resistance. Unfortunately, there are no current polymers that can withstand prolonged exposure to temperatures above 200°C.

Composites

These are man-made materials that combine two or more materials to provide properties not possessed by either constituent alone. The principle is ancient, since ice reinforced with straw and mud reinforced with wood or straw are building materials that pre-date history. Modern composites date from the discovery in the 1950s of the fact that fine "whiskers" of metals and other solids have extremely high strengths. In the 1960s it was discovered that textile fibres could be converted to graphite fibres of high strength and stiffness. This led to the development of carbon fibre reinforced plastics (CFRPs) that have mechanical strengths superior to the earlier glass fibre reinforced plastics (GFRPs). In these materials the fibres provide most of the strength and stiffness while the matrix protects fibre surfaces and transfers loads between fibres.

Composites reinforced with particles, composites made by lamination and composites with metallic or ceramic matrices are of interest to the aircraft engine industry.

AIRFRAME STRUCTURES

The structure of the fuselage of a commercial transport aircraft is like the hull of a boat. Its section is roughly circular and varies in diameter along its length with the maximum diameter near the wing root position. This portion of the fuselage contains a massive central structure, often a forging, to which the fuselage belly skin and the wing roots attach. Heavy gauge booms attach to the forging and run fore and aft. These booms and the forging form an immensely strong spine equivalent to the keel of a boat.

The fuselage skin is attached to regularly spaced circumferential frames by rivets. The frames are made from sheet material fabricated into a "Z" shaped cross section. The skin is longitudinally stiffened by fore and aft stringers attached by rivets and spaced at regular intervals around the fuselage. Stringers are also made from sheet formed into a "top hat" cross section. Additional strength and stiffness is achieved by joining stringers and frames together with brackets sometimes called stringer clips. Frames are numbered sequentially from front to rear while stringers are numbered in both circumferential directions from the crown of the fuselage using the letters R and L. Any position on the fuselage can thus be identified by quoting the frame and stringer number of that body station.

If the aircraft is pressurised, airtight bulkheads are fitted near the front and rear of the fuselage. Both forward and rear pressure bulkheads (FPB and RPB) are dish-shaped structures made of sheet with substantial radial and circumferential stiffening members. Substantial transverse beams carry the cabin floor and the floors of cargo holds which are also normally pressurised.

Wings are fabricated from spanwise spars, each spar being made up of booms, often extrusions, joined by webs. These spars are connected by a series of chordwise ribs. Wing skin made of sheet or plate covers upper and lower surfaces. The gauge of the materials used increases from wing tip to wing root. Most of the structural joints are made by riveting but the wings are attached to the fuselage by very substantial pin joints which permit the removal of wings when this is necessary. The space inside the wings is utilised to accommodate fuel tanks. The structure of the wing must also be strong enough to permit the attachment of engines.

The empennage (horizontal stabiliser and rudder) use the same form of construction as the wings and again attach to the fuselage by pin joints capable of disassembly.

AIRFRAME STRESSES

When an aircraft is parked all loads are reacted by the undercarriage legs which are compressed in response to the weight of the aircraft. The wings and fuselage sag under their own weight and this induces tension in the top surface of wings and the top of the fuselage. When the aircraft is taxiing the stresses are essentially of the same sign but bumpy surfaces induce cyclic loads which may be significant with respect to fatigue (see Liquid Metal Embrittlement at page 486 below).

When airborne the situation changes dramatically. The hull is pressurised with respect to the outside environment inducing substantial circumferential (hooped) and longitudinal tensions in the hull. Wings and horizontal stabilisers are bent upwards, putting their lower surfaces in tension and upper surfaces in compression. Each flight thus imposes a very large load cycle on the airframe and this is of the first importance with respect to fatigue life.

Manoeuvres, changes of configuration (lowering of landing gear, deployment of flaps etc.) and gust loading all impose additional cyclic loads.

AIRFRAME MATERIALS

The age-hardening aluminium-copper alloys discovered in 1911, usually containing some magnesium, provide the combination of strength, stiffness, toughness and low density ideal for aircraft structures. In addition, the alloys can be produced in many shapes by rolling, extruding and forging. They are easy to machine, simple to heat treat and have good corrosion resistance. Importantly, they can readily be joined by bolting or riveting.

In the 1930s a second group of age-hardening aluminium alloys, the aluminium–zinc–magnesium alloys, began to be developed. These had potentially higher strengths than the aluminium–copper alloys and were widely used in the 1950s and 1960s for both civil and military aircraft. Unfortunately, the penalty of using these alloys at their highest strengths was their low fracture toughness and susceptibility to stress corrosion failure. This was overcome by the use of cleaner materials and revised heat treatments, which resulted in some loss of yield and tensile strength.

The most recently developed group of high strength aluminium alloys are the aluminium-lithium alloys. These have a higher stiffness and lower density than other aluminium alloys and have the potential to save up to 15 per cent of airframe components weight when replacing either aluminium–copper or aluminium–zinc–magnesium alloys.

These three groups of alloys account for more than 60 per cent of the airframe weight of current commercial transport aircraft. There is a trend for aluminium–lithium alloys to be more widely used, especially in military aircraft.

Titanium and titanium alloys are increasingly used in airframes and represent about 10 per cent of the airframe weight of a modern transport aircraft. This proportion is rather higher in military aircraft. Pure titanium is a soft and ductile material with excellent corrosion resistance and a high melting point and can be joined by welding. It is thus a useful material for firewalls and hot air ducting. Titanium alloys containing aluminium and vanadium develop high strengths and have high stiffness and good corrosion resistance. These alloys retain their strength at high temperature very much better than the competing aluminium alloys and are thus strong candidate materials for supersonic airframes. Unfortunately, these high strength alloys cannot be welded, are not easy to fabricate and their cost is high.

Composite materials, notably CFRPs currently make up some 10 per cent of the airframe weight of a commercial aircraft and it is predicted that this proportion will double in the foreseeable future. Flaps, airbrakes and tabs as well as helicopter blades are all moderately stressed components often made from composites. Cabin floors of large commercial passenger aircraft also make use of CFRP and GFRP. "Kevlar" fibre reinforced plastics (KFRP) are increasingly used as an alternative to CFRP in applications where the slight reduction of stiffness is acceptable and the slightly higher strength and lower density of KFRP offers an advantage. Kevlar is a synthetic textile fibre.

Other materials, notably steels, magnesium alloys, copper alloys, zinc alloys and polymers make up a small percentage of airframe weight. The choice is often based on some specific property that the material possesses.

ENGINES

The internal combustion engine used in propeller-driven light aircraft is very similar to a car engine. The major difference is that the aircraft engine uses aluminium alloys and composites to replace steel where this is possible so as to save weight.

The gas turbine, in one of its forms, is widely used in aviation. Every gas turbine consists of a shaft rotating within a tubular casing. A fan or compressor fixed to the front of the shaft sucks in large volumes of air. This is further compressed by a series of compressors mounted on the shaft one behind the other. Each compressor stage consists of a disc or wheel, often with a "U" section rim, to which blades are attached, often by pin joints. It is the rotating blades that force the air through the engine. Fixed stator blades project inwards from the casing between each compressor stage and duct the airflow rearwards.

The compressed air, now heated by the compression, passes into an array of combustion chambers. The chambers are short tubes arranged around the shaft with their long axes parallel to the shaft but with their exits inclined slightly inwards. Fuel, generally kerosene, is injected into each chamber where it mixes with the air and is burnt to produce large volumes of extremely high pressure hot gas.

The hot gasses pass into a turbine mounted on the shaft. The sole object of the turbine is to drive the shaft, and hence the compression stages, and draw in more air. The hot gasses pass out of the engine through the tail pipe at high velocity and temperature to provide the thrust of the engine.

Jet engines can conveniently be divided into three broad classes:

(a) The *straight jet* as described above, using axial flow compressors. A limitation of this arrangement is that increasing the intake of air by increasing rotational speed or increasing intake diameter leads to problems as the compressor blade tip speed reaches the speed of sound.

(b) A solution to this problem is to increase the diameter of the intake, installing a large diameter fan that rotates at relatively low speeds. This low speed requires a secondary drive shaft driven by the main shaft via a system of gears. A tubular main shaft with the secondary shaft running down its centre is a usual solution. The formidable engineering problems have been solved and the so-called "*Fan Jets*" are the usual powerplants of large commercial aircraft.

(c) The *turbo-prop*, in which the turbine output drives a conventional propeller via a gear box. Such power units are fairly widely used on small and medium sized commuter and short haul aircraft.

STRESSES IN ENGINES

Aircraft engines are subjected to an even more demanding stress environment than airframes. This is essentially because all engines involve components that rotate at high speed and components that are subjected to very high temperatures. In addition to the mechanical forces imposed on an engine, each engine start and shutdown or "flight" imposes a thermal cycle on engine components. Since different materials have different coefficients of thermal expansion, and because temperature gradients are inevitable in the heating and cooling cycle, so called thermal stresses are inevitable and are important. An additional complication is that the largest mechanical loads are imposed when the engine is at full power for take off and this coincides with the large temperature gradients of an engine that is warming up.

ENGINE MATERIALS

The major materials problems that occur in gas turbine engines arise from the fact that the inlet temperature can be sub-zero, rises to some hundreds of degrees Centigrade at the final compressor stage and rises abruptly to some 1400°C at the turbine inlet. All materials lose strength and stiffness with increase in temperature and high temperature increases the risk of chemical reaction with the environment (dry corrosion). Creep deformation, creep fracture and thermal fatigue are also problems of high temperature operation. These degradation mechanisms are discussed on page 479.

These problems are additional to the general aerospace material requirements of maximum strength, stiffness and toughness coupled with minimum weight and reasonable cost.

Jet engines of the 1950s used aluminium alloys for the early compressor stages and steels for the hotter stages. Current engines use titanium alloys for early stages and need to use the nickel based super alloys for the final compressor stages. Some cobalt based alloys are used for flame tubes.

The development of the jet engine has depended critically on the development of the nickel based super alloys over the last fifty years especially for use in the turbine. Since the turbine is the region where the highest temperatures are experienced, retention of high temperature strength and creep resistance are vital. Current alloys contain:

(a) from 11–15 per cent chromium which ensures oxidation resistance by the formation of a continuous surface film of inert chromium oxide;

(b) from 7–16 per cent cobalt;

(c) 3–6.5 per cent molybdenum;

(d) 2–5 per cent aluminium;

(e) 2.5–4.5 per cent titanium as well as a small quantity of carbon which provides strength. This is because these alloys develop a structure consisting of a nickel rich matrix strengthened by a dispersion of fine intermetallic particles such as nickel aluminide. This structure confers high strength at very high temperatures and excellent creep resistance. The current alloys are difficult to fabricate by the conventional casting–forging–machining route. This has led to fabrication from metal powders compacted to near the final component geometry and size followed by sintering at high temperature.

The turbine blade is perhaps the most critical jet engine component since it is directly subjected to the impingement of hot gasses at the turbine inlet temperature. In the 1960s inlet temperatures were below 900°C; they now exceed 1400°C. Increasing inlet temperature is vital to engine development since its increase raises engine thrust and at the same time reduces fuel consumption. While better materials have played a large part in permitting higher inlet temperature a great deal of the improvement stems from designs that permit blade cooling. This involves the cooling of blades, externally and internally, with air bled from the compressor.

Turbine blades are made from super alloys usually by precision casting to near final size and shape. If allowed to solidify normally each blade would consist of an aggregate of grains randomly orientated with respect to each other and separated by grain boundaries. It is unfortunate that ground boundaries are favoured sites for creep deformation and creep fracture if stresses act across the boundaries. This problem can be avoided by the expensive and difficult process of solidifying the blades as single crystals. The alternative is to produce blades consisting of an array of long columnar crystals with all boundaries running parallel to the long axis of the blade. This is achieved by lowering the mould full of molten metal through a temperature gradient to achieve directional solidification. Grain boundaries parallel to the tensile axis of the blade experience:

(i) no shear stresses that are the cause of boundary sliding; and
(ii) no tensile stress across the boundary that cause creep fracture. This is analogous to stressing wood parallel to its grain and not across it.

In addition to the main engine components discussed, such items as shafts, gears and bearings are of vital importance. These are manufactured from medium and high strength steels of very high quality. Flame tubes are made from cobalt or nickel based alloys. The engine casing is important since blade failure in an engine rotating at high speed must not result in fragments damaging the aircraft. The casing must therefore have sufficient strength and toughness to contain these high energy fragments. Metal casings reinforced with Kevlar reinforced plastic is one method of achieving this.

EQUIPMENT

Current aircraft have, in addition to airframe and engines, a multiplicity of "systems" employing special equipment. Hydraulics, electrics, electronics, air conditioning, navigation, fire detection and suppression, catering and sanitation are only a few examples. The range of materials employed is vast but in every case the basis of selection is adequate properties, minimum weight and reasonable cost. It is only possible to consider a few of these systems as examples.

Undercarriages are clearly essential but are only space-consuming dead weight when an aircraft is airborne. Minimum weight and volume are therefore important. The high strength aluminium and titanium alloys and high strength steels are widely used.

Hydraulics are used to power movement of control surfaces, lower and raise undercarriages and operate brakes. Hydraulic jacks, reservoirs and filter bowls are generally made from aluminium alloys and much of the extensive piping made from stainless steel.

Heating, ventilating and air conditioning the pressure cabin of a large passenger jet is complex. Hot air is bled from engine compressors through titanium ducting to air conditioning packs. These cool the compressor air and mix it with air taken from the cabin and filtered. This is fed to the cabin by aluminium and polymer ducting. The correct pressure is maintained within the cabin by complex pressure relief valves at the rear of the fuselage.

The fuel management system is a vital part of engine equipment and must permit fuel to be moved from tank to tank to permit the trim of the aircraft to be maintained as well as delivering the fuel to the engine. The engine fuel pump pressurises the fuel and injects it into the flame tubes via a burner which itself is a complex device. The system must also provide for the dumping of fuel in an emergency.

These are brief examples of the enormous complexity of aircraft equipment and systems and the wide variety of materials needed to build them.

MECHANICAL PROPERTIES OF AIRCRAFT MATERIALS

The materials currently used in airframes, engines and equipment are now discussed and perhaps more importantly the factors that govern selection are considered. In this context the bulk of the materials in an aircraft are "structural", i.e. they are load carrying. Some items such as cabin trim and insulation blankets do not carry much load and are considered non-structural.

The most important single group of properties of materials are those that concern mechanical strength. They include the information obtained from the simple tensile test in which a bar of uniform cross section is pulled under smoothly increasing load with the extension of the specimen being monitored. The results can be plotted as a graph of load against extension or more usually as stress (load divided by cross sectional area) against strain (increase in specimen length divided by original length).

Such tests provide the following data:

(a) The stiffness of the material referred to as its modulus of elasticity or Young's modulus. It is denoted by the symbol "E" and the units are those of stress;

(b) The yield stress which is the stress at which permanent or plastic behaviour begins (it is often denoted by the Greek letter sigma and the subscript y);

(c) The tensile strength (TM) which is the maximum stress the material can carry in tension without breaking. The term ultimate tensile strength or UTS is sometimes used or the Greek letter sigma with the subscript ult or ts;

(d) The elongation to fracture and the reduction of area at fracture are expressed as percentages. The usual abbreviations are El and R of A. Both quantities indicate the ductility of the material.

Many materials suffer drastic reductions of strength if small cracks are present. Glass is a familiar example. In contrast, other materials, such as rubber are only slightly weakened by small cracks. The materials sensitive to small cracks are described as "brittle" while those that are relatively insensitive to cracks as "tough". In general it is the strongest and stiffest materials that are the most brittle. Toughness is measured by loading sharply notched or pre-cracked specimens and using the data to calculate a quantity, Kc, which is the stress at fracture multiplied by the square root of the crack length.

Hardness tests involve indentation of a flat specimen with a standard indenter acting under a known load. Either the depth or the superficial area of the indentation is used to calculate the hardness from standard tables. The Vickers Hardness Number derived from tests using a pyramidal diamond indenter and the Rockwell Number are the most common measures of hardness.

The range of mechanical properties of materials available to the aircraft designer are listed in the table below. Density, which is a physical rather than a mechanical property, is included because of the enormous importance of weight saving in aerospace applications.

Range of mechanical properties of materials

Material	Density	Stiffness	Yield Strength	Ultimate Tensile Strength	Toughness
Aluminium alloys	2.7	70	100–630	300–700	15–45
Titanium alloys	4.5	110	180–1,300	300–1,400	50–120
Steels	7.8	200	250–1,900	400–2,400	50–200
Ceramics	3–4	380–500	–	3,000–10,000*	1–5
Plastics	1–1.5	1–7	6–50	20–300	1–20
CFRPs	1.5–1.6	70–200	–	700†	30–45

Note: Stiffness values are in giga Pascals (Gpa), yield and ultimate strengths in mega Pascals (Mpa). Toughness is in mega Pascal root metres (Mpa/m) and density in mega grams per cubic metre.
* The ultimate strength in tension of ceramics cannot be measured because brittle fracture by extension of pre-existing cracks occurs at low stresses. The potential UTS of ceramics is extremely high. The yield stress values of ceramics are measured in compression which prevents the spread of pre-existing cracks.
† The yield and ultimate strengths of CFRPs are essentially the same since such composites are elastic. In common with all other composites strength properties depend critically on the volume fraction of fibres, their orientation and whether or not they are continuous.

All materials used in aircraft have to conform to a material specification issued by an appropriate national or international body such as the International Standards Organisation (ISO), the American Society for Testing Materials (ASTM) or the British Standards Institution (BSI). The particular specification must also be approved by the appropriate certifying authority (e.g. FAA or CAA) for use in aircraft. A material specification details chemical composition, and mechanical properties. It may also require particular methods of manufacture and heat treatment.

THE DEGRADATION OF AIRCRAFT MATERIALS AND STRUCTURES

Service life and the passage of time cause aircraft structures to deteriorate until they ultimately reach a condition when they are no longer airworthy. The life-span of an aircraft, like that of a house or a human being, depends critically on how well it is inspected and maintained.

The main life threatening illnesses of aircraft are:

(a) Corrosion, which is degradation of a material by chemical reaction with the environment. The classic and familiar example is the rusting of motor car bodies.

(b) Fracture of a structure or component. Fracture by simple overstress is rare in aircraft except where collision is involved. However, there are a number of fracture mechanisms that involve the initiation and slow growth of cracks. When such a crack reaches a critical length, defined by the toughness of the material and the applied stress, the unbroken ligament fractures by catastrophic overload. The slow growth of a crack in a windowpane or a drinking glass that leads to final fracture is a familiar example of this behaviour. Fatigue, stress corrosion cracking, creep, liquid metal embrittlement, solid metal embrittlement and hydrogen embrittlement are all processes that generally involve slow crack growth.

(c) Both corrosion and slow crack growth processes can occur in polymers, ceramics and composites as well as in metals and alloys. These processes are now considered in some detail.

WET CORROSION

Wet corrosion is an electrolytic process that involves a liquid, usually water, containing dissolved substances that make it a conductor of electricity. In the case of aircraft, water containing chlorides is the most common problem, with sodium chloride (common salt) the main contaminant. However, nitrates, sulphates, carbonates and alkalis can all cause problems.

Such corrosion may be general with the whole surface of a specimen or component being attacked. It may also be extremely localised at crevices and other moisture traps. Pitting corrosion occurs when small areas of a specimen have a different composition from the bulk material. In the presence of an electrolyte small corrosion cells are formed and the very localised corrosion resulting in pits occurs. Compositional differences at and near grain boundaries in metals can lead to rapid intergranular corrosion.

General corrosion is less damaging than the localised form. This is because the corrosion product can provide protection against further corrosion by acting as a barrier to the aggressive environment.

Localised corrosion is a special problem because it can be very difficult to prevent and to detect. Localised corrosion damage can decrease toughness and act as initiation sites for a number of cracking processes, notably fatigue and stress corrosion cracking.

DRY CORROSION

This occurs when a material is heated to a temperature where it can react chemically with the, usually gaseous, environment in which it is operating. In aircraft the important case is the reaction of hot engine components with atmospheric oxygen. Sulphur and vanadium contamination of fuel can also cause problems.

CORROSION PROTECTION

Corrosion cannot be totally prevented but it can be reduced and controlled. Effective control depends upon the choice of material, taking account of the conditions that occur in service, good design and the provision where necessary of adequate corrosion protection. Above all, corrosion control depends on regular and careful inspection.

Clearly, inherent corrosion resistance is not the only parameter governing choice of material but it is generally an important consideration. So far as wet corrosion is concerned metals and alloys are the biggest problem simply because they are good electrical conductors and wet corrosion requires the passage of an electric current. Polymers and ceramics are immune from electrolytic corrosion but polymers may be attacked by organic solvents and molten salts can dissolve some ceramics.

The corrosion resistance of some metals and alloys depends, in some cases, on the nature of the corrosion product generated. When iron and steel suffers general corrosion a layer of rust is produced and this provides some protection against further corrosion. This is because further corrosion requires the active constituent in the environment to diffuse through the rust layer to reach the metal or, conversely, for iron atoms to diffuse through the rust to reach the environment. These are slow processes so that film formation produces a decrease in the corrosion rate. However, iron corrosion products have a very high volume compared with the iron that produces them and this means that stresses develop in the rust film as it thickens. These stresses cause cracking and flaking of the rust layer exposing fresh metal to the corrosive environment. This sequence is very familiar to the owners of elderly motor cars!

A few metals, for example aluminium, titanium and chromium, exhibit excellent corrosion resistance because of the nature of the oxide surface films they produce. In these materials oxide films are thin, strong, chemically inert, impervious and highly adherent. These films form naturally in air but in the case of aluminium better films are produced by electrolytically anodising the material.

It is the chromium content of stainless steels and the nickel based super-alloys that gives them their corrosion resistance again by the formation of a chromium oxide film. Similarly the copper–aluminium alloys, known as aluminium bronze, form corrosion resistant aluminium oxide films. An advantage of corrosion protection by oxide films is that a mechanically damaged film is "self healing".

Susceptibility to wet corrosion can be reduced by careful design. Geometries that permit the accumulation of moisture by condensation or by drainage should be avoided. The special problem of moisture traps is that if the moisture is contaminated with a corroding species such as a chloride, drying out merely concentrates the damaging salt. Hollow sections should be totally hermetically sealed or have adequate drainage and ventilation. Again corrosion due to moisture entrapment is a phenomenon well known to car owners.

Lavatory and galley spillage was a source of severe corrosion problems in early jet airliners. Re-designing these facilities as discrete units that can be removed from the aircraft has reduced this problem.

Joints that have dissimilar metals in contact almost inevitably cause corrosion problems in the presence of moisture. Clearly, such joints cannot be entirely avoided and special measures may be needed to protect and inspect them.

Most of the components of an aircraft are protected from corrosion by coating with a suitable material. Electroplating and painting are everyday examples of protective coating and both are used in the aerospace industries. Virtually all steel components are electroplated. Cadmium was, until recently, the most usual coating but its high toxicity has led to a decline in its use. Zinc, nickel, chromium silver and even gold coatings are, or have been, used in the industry, especially for engine and equipment components.

All aluminium alloy components are artificially anodised to ensure a continuous oxide film of the required thickness. All internal airframe surfaces are painted with zinc chromate rich paint which has the familiar khaki-green colour. External surfaces are generally left unpainted.

Special care is taken with joints and riveted seams which are often "wet assembled" using a chromate rich jointing compound. Pinned joints, e.g. wings to centre section, use steel pins generally cadmium plated and the aluminium alloy spars are usually bushed with plated bronze. Wet assembly is usual. An important feature of these joints is reasonable ease of disassembly at major overhauls.

Corrosion resistance in engines also involves the use of highly complex coatings. For example, turbine blades may be sprayed with molten aluminium which is converted to nickel aluminide by reaction with the blade material by post-coating heat treatment.

Inspection and maintenance are vital in preventing aircraft deterioration by corrosion to a point where safety is prejudiced. To this end manufacturers lay down stringent inspection and repair procedures that are enforced by the regulatory bodies concerned with safety. Regular visual inspection can detect corrosion on accessible components. Corrosion at lap joints can be detected by the joint swelling. This occurs because the corrosion product has a large volume and forces the joint apart and can cause rivet fracture. Inside surfaces of wings and around pressure bulkheads are not easily accessible, making visual inspection less easy. Major overhauls and maintenance involve considerable disassembly and this includes the dismantling of major joints for detailed inspection.

Corrosion is one of the most important factors governing the useful life of an aircraft. This is because corrosion not only degrades the structure but corrosion damage provides easy initiation sites for a number of fracture processes.

FRACTURE

It is self evident that any material loaded to its ultimate tensile strength will fracture. Such simple overload fracture in aircraft is most unusual except in the case of heavy landing or collision. This is because design calculations and testing provide good safety margins. There are a few materials that show a ductile–brittle fracture transition with decrease in temperature.

Of much more concern are a number of fracture processes that involve the initiation of a small crack followed by its slow and generally accelerating growth. When such a crack reaches its critical length, defined by the applied stress and the fracture toughness of the material, the remaining uncracked ligament breaks by overload. Slow growing cracks are generally very fine and hence difficult to detect. The final overload failure generally occurs without warning and can be catastrophic as was the case with the Comet airliners.

The following slow crack growth processes are important:

(a) Fatigue and corrosion fatigue;
(b) Stress corrosion cracking (SCC);
(c) Liquid metal and solid metal embrittlement (LME and SME);
(d) Hydrogen embrittlement;
(e) Creep.

Of these processes fatigue (including corrosion fatigue) is by far the most common, accounting for more than 80 per cent of all engineering failures. It occurs most commonly in metals and alloys but also occurs in polymers and composites.

OVERLOAD FRACTURE

Although overload failures are unusual in aircraft they are worth mentioning briefly. Overload in ductile metals always occurs by a process of plastic deformation. Toughness values are moderate to high and ductility is also high. Many plastics also fail in a ductile manner.

Ceramics and glasses fail in a brittle manner. In polycrystalline ceramics brittle transcrystalline fracture along crystal planes often occurs and this is called "cleavage". Brittle intercrystalline also occurs in ceramics. Ductile fracture in ceramics is possible but only at temperatures near to their melting points.

Of special engineering importance are those metals and alloys that are ductile at ordinary temperatures but show a transition to transgranular cleavage or brittle intergranular fracture at lower temperatures. The low temperature brittle behaviour is encouraged by notches and by high rates of loading. Low carbon steels are the most important class of materials showing this transition and many ships have been lost as the result of catastrophic brittle fracture. When a cleavage crack propagates it does so at high speed with little energy absorption and is only arrested when it reaches a free surface or interface. Fortunately, mild steels are not much used in aircraft construction.

However, both titanium and magnesium alloys show a ductile–brittle transition and these are used in aircraft. In practice, the brittle fracture of these materials has not been a serious problem.

Fortunately, aluminium alloys, like all other metals with a face centred cubic crystal structure (copper, nickel, silver, gold), do not suffer this ductile–brittle transition. It is confined to some metals with the body centred cubic or close packed hexagonal structure.

FATIGUE

Fatigue is fracture caused by the repeated application of small loads each of which is below the stress that would cause failure as a single load. In general the smaller the amplitude of each cyclic load (S) the larger the number of cycles (Nf) required to cause failure. Some materials, notably low and medium carbon steels, show a value of S below which failure does not occur however large N becomes. This is called the fatigue limit (Slim). Other materials, including the aluminium alloys, do not show such a limit and design is based on the value of S that causes failure at a particular value of N (generally 10 million or 100 million cycles). Such a value of S is called the endurance limit at N cycles. Fatigue limits, and endurance limits at 10 million cycles are generally between 0.25 and 0.5 of a material's tensile strength. Fatigue was recognised and the first fatigue S/N data published before 1870. However, the mechanisms involved were not understood for another ninety years.

Work between 1950 and 1965 involving metallographic examination using both optical and electron microscopy, combined with careful fatigue testing methods, established the following facts about fatigue that are now generally accepted:

(a) If the specimen is smooth, localised cyclic plastic deformation initiates a surface crack. This may be associated with some special micro structural inhomogeneity such as a grain or twin boundary or a quench band. This stage takes less than 5 per cent of Nf;

(b) The small crack grows on a plane of high shear stress usually on a specific crystal plane. This is called Stage I crack growth. While Stage I may take up to 95 per cent of Nf it generates only a minute fraction of the total area of the final fatigue fracture;

(c) The Stage I crack turns through 45 degrees and continues to grow as a Stage II crack on a plane at right angles to the axis of maximum tension. Stage II growth is relatively fast and accelerates rapidly until the crack reaches its critical length and the unbroken ligament fails by overload. Stage II generates most of the area of a fatigue fracture but may take only a few per cent of Nf.

Fatigue crack initiation almost always begins at a free surface or a weak interface that intersects a free surface (e.g. a grain boundary or inclusion matrix interface). Because of this the fatigue lives of smooth specimens and components are extremely sensitive to surface condition. Grooves, changes of section, machining marks, mechanical damage and some surface coatings can all reduce fatigue life by assisting surface initiation of cracks. Conversely, strengthening surfaces or introducing residual compressive stresses into surface layers increases life. The case hardening of steel, the nitriding of steel and the shot peening or vapour blasting of surfaces of metals are examples of surface treatments that improve fatigue properties and all are used in the aerospace industries.

Generally, fatigue cracks initiate in the first few per cent of the fatigue life of a smooth specimen but they are so small that they can only be detected by special laboratory techniques such as electron microscopy. In many practical cases there are surface features present in a component that can be considered as crack like defects so that no fatigue crack initiation stage is necessary and the whole fatigue process is one of crack growth.

Stage I crack growth in metals and alloys generally follows specific crystal planes or a favourably orientated grain boundary. The shear stress on the growth plane appears to control the process. The rate of crack growth is sensitive to both microstructure and environment. This process may occupy more than 90 per cent of the total fatigue life but only generate a small area of fracture. In acutely notched specimens, especially if the cyclic stresses are high, there may be no Stage I and the whole fatigue life may consist of Stage II crack growth.

Stage II crack growth generates the vast majority of the surface area of most fatigue fractures even when it takes as little as 10 per cent of the total fatigue life of the specimen. Stage II fracture surfaces are at right angles to the major axis of tension and often show macroscopic beach markings. Finer "striations", each generated by a single stress cycle, may also be present on the fracture but these can only be detected by high power optical microscopy or by electron microscopy. Both sorts of fracture markings are important in diagnosing fatigue failures.

The rate of Stage II growth depends on the stress opening the crack multiplied by the square root of the crack length raised to the power of 3 or 4. This quantitative law (the Paris law) is important since it permits calculation of the remaining life of a cracked structure and calculation of the reduction in stress that would stop further growth.

Most of the understanding of fatigue described resulted from work on metals. The ductile crystalline solids (silver chloride, lithium fluoride) show similar behaviour. In polymers, fatigue cracks generally initiate at surface defects followed by Stage II growth of the sort described. Composites with polymer matrices show rather similar behaviour with cracks initiating and growing along fibre matrix interfaces.

There are a number of special cases of fatigue that deserve brief mention. Fretting, the attrition between surfaces in contact and under pressure, can cause premature fatigue failure. Rolling contact fatigue of roller bearings is unusual in that sub-surface cracks are initiated and lead to material spalling from the surface.

STRESS CORROSION CRACKING (SCC)

Stress corrosion cracking can occur in virtually every engineering material and requires the combination of a steady tensile stress and exposure to a chemical environment that is damaging. The tensile loads may arise from applied stress, residual stress induced in manufacture or from stresses generated in assembly. The stresses involved are usually high and generally some 75 per cent or more of the materials yield strength.

The mechanism of failure involves the initiation then the slow growth of a crack or cracks that may follow either transgranular or intergranular paths in metals and alloys. When the slowly growing crack reaches a critical length the unbroken section fails by overload.

SCC can be very sensitive to microstructure and a well-known example is that the austenitic stainless steels if heated in the range 400–700°C develop regions adjacent to grain boundaries that are depleted of chromium. These depleted zones, which are preferred sites for SCC, were once a severe problem with welded stainless steels since regions adjacent to the welds had inevitably been heated within the critical temperature range. This problem was called "weld decay" and is now prevented by additions of titanium to the steel that inhibit the formation of chromium depleted zones.

Heat treatments that develop very high strengths at the expense of reduced toughness may be especially susceptible to SCC. The ultra high strength steels and the strongest forms of the aluminium–zinc–magnesium alloys are examples of this. Currently used aluminium–zinc–magnesium alloys are generally aged beyond peak hardness to confer extra toughness at the expense of some loss of strength. Boiling water quenching is also usual when solution treating these alloys so as to minimise thermally induced residual stresses. The high strength aluminium alloys when in the form of extrusions and forgings may have a marked fibre structure and poorer SCC resistance must be expected in components loaded across the fibre direction. The improved heat treatments have greatly reduced the incidence of SCC failures in the high strength aluminium alloys.

Titanium alloys, until the 1960s believed to be immune from this form of failure, suffer SCC in the presence of chlorides especially if they are pre-cracked. The austenitic stainless steels can suffer catastrophic and rapid failure by this mechanism in water containing low concentrations of chlorides. High strength steels can suffer this sort of failure under any of the conditions of corrosion that generate hydrogen and this is discussed in the section on hydrogen embrittlement below.

Non-metallic materials also fail by stress corrosion. Glass is susceptible in the presence of water vapour and many polymers suffer this form of failure in the presence of organic solvents.

LIQUID METAL EMBRITTLEMENT (LME)

A solid metal under stress, and in contact with a second metal that is liquid, may suffer slow crack growth leading to catastrophic failure. The liquid metal penetrates the solid material generally along grain boundaries, reducing its strength to that of the liquid.

There is no method of predicting which solid metal–liquid metal couples will be susceptible to such behaviour but there are some empirical rules of thumb. Embrittlement does not occur unless the liquid metal wets the solid. If the two metals tend to react chemically or dissolve in one another embrittlement is not likely. Tensile stresses, applied and residual, and geometric stress concentrators (notches and sharp corners) promote this mode of failure.

The only common metal that is liquid at room temperature is mercury and it readily causes failure of aluminium and its alloys. This is the reason why mercury thermometers may not be included in airline passengers' luggage. Mercury also embrittles many copper alloys and titanium but not steels and magnesium alloys.

Gallium, with a melting point of only 30°C, readily embrittles aluminium alloys and has caused at least one major problem to an aircraft.

Perhaps more importantly, a great many low melting point metals and alloys are used as solders, coating and seals in engine and equipment components that may be exposed to elevated temperatures in service. Cadmium, tin and zinc coatings are commonly used to prevent corrosion and all have low melting points; there are cases where their melting has caused service failures. Lead, copper and indium have all caused the liquid metal embrittlement of high strength steels.

Once a solid material has suffered LME it is impossible to salvage it so that great care must be taken to avoid situations where it can occur.

SOLID METAL EMBRITTLEMENT (SME)

Solid metals, generally when present as coatings, can cause embrittlement by penetration along the grain boundaries of the coated material. Temperatures above about half of the coatings melting point are required and the mechanism involves surface diffusion to transport the embrittling species to the tip of the growing crack. This generally results in the rate of crack growth decreasing as the crack gets longer, leading to crack arrest at a length that is generally below about 5 mm.

HYDROGEN EMBRITTLEMENT

Free hydrogen exists abundantly in the atmosphere as hydrogen molecules (H_2) each consisting of two hydrogen atoms. Under certain conditions the molecules can dissociate into separate atoms and these may each lose an electron to become positively charged hydrogen ions. Since water is a combination of hydrogen and oxygen, corrosion and electroplating processes are an important source of atomic hydrogen and hydrogen ions liberated at the surfaces of conductors.

Because the hydrogen atom is very small it can fit in the spaces between metal atoms so that it is readily dissolved in substantial quantities and has the ability to migrate through the metal at high rates. The hydrogen molecule is generally too large to behave in this fashion.

Some metals react with hydrogen to form a hydride of the metal and this can cause embrittlement. Titanium and zirconium are important examples of this behaviour.

Iron and the steels do not form a hydride but hydrogen embrittlement is a serious problem in these materials. This is especially so since the highest strength steels, favoured by the aerospace industry, are the most susceptible to hydrogen damage.

Large quantities of hydrogen occluded in steel can cause blistering and serious loss of ductility. These are not problems in aircraft quality steels since carefully controlled steelmaking and tight quality control ensures that hydrogen contents are low.

Unfortunately, very small quantities of hydrogen (around 1–2 parts per million by weight) can cause hydrogen induced delayed failure (HIDC) in high strength steels that are highly stressed. The stress to cause failure must exceed a threshold value that depends on the properties of the steel and on hydrogen concentration.

The major sources of the hydrogen that causes this mode of failure are processes such as welding, pickling and electroplating which generate hydrogen which enters the metal and segregates to regions where there are high triaxial stresses. The mechanism of embrittlement is not fully understood but it is currently believed that the hydrogen ions can reduce the strength of the bonds between iron atoms. This can initiate cracks that grow slowly until they reach the critical length at which catastrophic overload failure is inevitable.

Hydrogen generated by in-service corrosion especially at pits and notches can enter a steel component and cause slow crack growth and ultimate failure. This is generally classified as SCC cracking and can occur in a very wide range of steels.

Hydrogen picked up by steels during processing can be reduced by post-process heat treatments. For example, electroplated components should be heated at 250°C for a suitable period and it is important that this is done immediately after plating. In aircraft components most HIDC failures occur in electroplated components such as pins, bolts, undercarriage bogies, jacks, washers, etc. The hydrogen related SCC failures, caused by corrosion generated hydrogen, are best prevented by adequate corrosion protection.

CREEP

This mode of failure can occur in any material simultaneously subjected to a tensile force and an elevated temperature for a period of time. In this context elevated temperature is more than about 0.4–0.5 the material's melting point in degrees absolute. (The absolute temperature is degrees Centigrade plus 273 and is often called degrees K or Kelvin in honour of Lord Kelvin who devised this scale. 0 degrees K is the absolute zero that can never be achieved.)

A material subjected to a tensile stress and elevated temperature suffers an immediate increase in length as the load is applied. It may, if stress and temperature are high enough, be followed by a steady increase in extension with time. The rate of extension is proportional to stress and temperature.

This deformation is permanent and called steady state creep. This mode of deformation gives way to accelerated deformation at some point and this leads to accelerating creep and fracture.

Lead, because of its low melting point can creep readily at room temperature. This can be seen in such items as the lead guttering and downspouts of ancient buildings. Glasses and polymers, which do not have sharply defined melting points, soften with increase of temperature and creep by flow that is characteristic of high viscosity liquids. Pitch and Brie cheese show this behaviour in hot weather.

Both creep rate and total creep life are extremely sensitive to temperature and the magnitude of the applied stress. There are two ways in which creep can destroy the integrity of a component or structure:

(a) Creep fracture may occur.
(b) Creep deformation may alter the geometry or the dimensions of a component so as to make it unfit for further service. In some cases, such as a turbine blade, the clearances between blades and adjacent components is so small that minute deformations can lead to high speed contact between components that can cause potentially catastrophic damage.

Creep is not a problem in the airframe materials of subsonic aircraft because the temperatures are not high. It is a consideration in supersonic aircraft where kinetic heating can raise skin temperatures into the creep regime and this is one of the reasons for the increased use of titanium in these aircraft. This is an example of the case where the shape changes caused by creep deformation can degrade the aerodynamic efficiency of the aircraft and so reduce service life.

Creep is clearly a problem in engines where temperatures and stresses are high and especially so in jet engines where performance and fuel consumption improve as operating temperatures are raised. The need for higher operating temperatures provides the drive for current research on nickel based super-alloys, the titanium aluminides, ceramics and composites.

THE CONTROL OF STRUCTURAL AND MATERIAL DEGRADATION

Degradation of materials and structures is inevitable but it can be controlled to extend useful life. Much more importantly it must be monitored to prevent failures that could be catastrophic. The major degradation processes are the slow crack growth mechanisms already considered and environmental effects, most notably corrosion. While design and good material selection can help in preventing a single component failure from causing a catastrophe, non-destructive testing plays a vital part in detecting cracks and monitoring the rate at which they are growing.

The nightmare scenario is the situation in which a structure containing a short crack fails catastrophically by fast fracture in at most a few seconds. This was the case with the accidents to the early Comet aircraft, the first all-welded "Liberty Ships" of the Second World War and a number of bridges and welded pipelines. Such failures have been largely eliminated by developments since the mid 1950s that have involved the following methods:

(a) Fail-safe design which ensures that if a single component fails there is another component that can take the loads. For example an engine may be fixed to an aircraft's wing by, say, three fittings so designed that if one breaks the other two can hold the engine in place. The use of dual circuit braking systems in current motor cars is an example of fail-safe design. There are of course penalties of cost and weight attached to this design philosophy.

(b) The use of "damage tolerant" materials and components in which the critical crack length for fast fracture is as long as possible. This increases the chances of detecting a crack before it has grown to its critical length. Since critical crack length is defined by the fracture toughness of the material involved and the applied stress, the use of high toughness materials and moderate working stresses are of vital importance.

(c) Both of these philosophies require regular inspection of components and structures to detect corrosion and to detect the presence of cracks and to monitor the rates at which such cracks are growing. Crack detection involves the use of non-destructive testing methods capable of finding cracks that cannot be seen. A summary of the techniques used are set out in the next section. It is these two design philosophies and adequate inspection procedures which have reduced the incidence of catastrophic failures of aircraft structures to extremely low levels.

NON-DESTRUCTIVE TESTING

These are procedures for detecting cracks and crack-like defects before they can cause a risk of complete failure. The problem is simpler in those situations where the likely location of such defects can be predicted. Notches, changes of section and joints fall into this category. Conversely, the problem is more difficult if the cracks are fine and "hairlike" as is generally the case with fatigue and stress corrosion cracking. Each of these procedures, which has its own advantages and disadvantages, is summarised below:

(1) Visual inspection can detect fairly obvious cracks that intersect a free surface especially if the cracks gape. The probability of detecting a fine fatigue crack with the naked eye under field conditions is extremely low. The probability of detection increases if a hand lens or low power microscope can be used and the specimen is clean and adequately illuminated.

There are two widely used techniques for improving the visibility of surface breaking cracks:

(a) Magnetic crack detection which can only be used on ferromagnetic materials which include iron and ferritic steels. The sample is magnetised by a magnet or by an electric current. It is immersed in, or sprayed with, fine iron particles suspended in a liquid. A crack-like defect concentrates the lines of magnetic force causing the iron particles in the "magnetic ink" to be strongly attracted to their vicinity. The concentration of particles greatly improves the visibility of the defect. Even better visibility is obtained if the component is sprayed with a white coating before magnetising.

(b) Dye penetrant crack detection uses a high wettability penetrating liquid as the carrier for a dye. The specimen must be clean and free from grease before being sprayed with the dye penetrant. The surplus dye is removed from the surface which is then sprayed with a fine suspension of chalk. The coated component is then allowed to stand for some 30 minutes to permit dye trapped in cracks to seep out and stain the chalk so making them visible.

(2) Radiography can detect both surface and internal flaws. Both X-rays and gamma rays can be used and the radiation penetrates the specimen to produce an image on a fluorescent screen or a photographic film. Defects, such as cracks appear on the image but sensitivity of the method depends on many factors.

(3) Ultrasonic flaw detection is a powerful technique that operates on the same principle as radar and sonar. It requires an ultrasound generator and a probe that is placed on the top surface of the specimen and permits short pulses of ultrasound to enter the specimen. These are reflected by the bottom surface of the specimen and by any defect within the specimen. The reflected wave pulses are detected by a receiver probe and the output from this displayed on the vertical axis of a cathode ray tube (CRT). The horizontal axis of the CRT indicates the time taken for the transmitted wave to be reflected from the back surface and from any defect. The relative positions on the time axis of a blip due to a defect and the blip from the lower surface indicate how far the defect is below the surface. The lateral position and size of the defect is determined by sliding the probes over the specimen surface.

(4) Eddy current flaw detection uses a small coil carrying an electric current to induce "eddy currents" in a specimen that must be a conductor of electricity. The eddy currents are measured and any crack-like defect disturbs their magnitude. The technique can be useful for detecting cracks formed on the internal surfaces of drilled holes and for monitoring their growth.

(5) All of the methods outlined above are carried out with the aircraft on the ground and generally out of service. There are now methods being used to monitor the in-service degradation of components by continuous "on-board" monitoring procedures. These depend on the fact that the vibration characteristics of a component change as it degrades and on the fact that a major event, like a burst of crack growth, gives rise to "acoustic emission". Vibration

monitors (transducers) can detect these effects and store them in computer memories or vibration measurements can be indicated directly in the cockpit. Subsequent computer analysis of the stored data can detect both gradual changes in vibration characteristics and any sudden changes in the vibration pattern such as would arise from cracking.

FUTURE DEVELOPMENTS

Predictions beyond the next decade are dangerous. History suggests that there will be steady progress in the materials field rather than any dramatic and revolutionary breakthrough. It is reasonably certain that more aluminium–lithium alloys, titanium alloys and composites will be used in airframes. Improved manufacturing methods, especially of composites and polymeric materials should lead to worthwhile weight saving.

On the engine side improvements of nickel base superalloys will probably come from better alloy powders and new ways of fabricating powder metallurgy components. If the titanium-aluminides are successfully developed for hot components their use should provide a substantial increase in engine power-to-weight ratio and an improvement in specific fuel consumption. Metal matrix composites may well be used more and ceramic turbine blades become common if their low toughness can be improved or the problem circumvented. Improvements in non-destructive testing are essential if low toughness materials are to be used more widely because of the extreme reduction of their strength induced by very small cracks.

Progress in materials research and development depends very much on adequate funding. It should be remembered that high strength fibres, age hardening and the transistor all resulted from basic research on the structure of solids.

CONCLUSIONS

It seems clear that engineering progress has always depended heavily on the development of new materials and the improvement of existing ones. It has also required engineers to exercise great ingenuity in design and manufacture of components using the newer materials of higher strength but lower ductility and toughness than the familiar low strength steels and aluminium alloys. There can be little doubt that the development of materials and engineering will continue as long as the industrial society exists.

For those who wish to explore this subject more thoroughly the following texts are suggested. Two books by J. E. Gordon, *The New Science of Strong Materials* and *Structures or Why You Don't Fall Through the Floor* are published by Penguin. The series "Engineering Materials" by M. F. Ashby and D. R. H. Jones published by Pergamon Press are also excellent. Volume I of the series

Engineering Materials, *An Introduction to Their Properties and Applications*, is especially recommended.

Finally, for those wishing to go a little further in understanding of the subject, "strength of materials" is important. There are many books carrying this title and it is important to choose one at first-year undergraduate level. J. P. Den Hartog's *Strength of Materials*, published by Dover, is excellent.

CHAPTER 18

FLIGHT CREW: TRAINING, FLIGHT TIME LIMITATIONS, NEW TECHNOLOGY

INTRODUCTION

The public's awareness of airline safety has been heightened over recent years. This is demonstrated by intense media coverage of accidents, by passengers' reluctance to patronise certain airlines, by their refusal to board aircraft which they perceive to be unsafe, and by regulatory authorities taking unilateral discriminatory action against States and airlines whose standards they believe to be deficient.

One should never forget the saying "The pilot always gets to the scene of the accident first". The number one concern of any professional pilot, reputable airline or manufacturer is always safety. In the words of one US airline president: "If you think safety is expensive, try an accident."

One of the fundamental elements of flight safety is the thorough and consistent training of flight crew to the highest standards. The training of pilots and flight engineers has evolved from its military origins through two world wars into the internationally regulated civil airline procedures of today.

While the ICAO SARPS remain in place worldwide, the situation in Europe is changing rapidly due to the advent of the Joint Aviation Authority (JAA), and increasing application of the Joint Aviation Requirements (JARs). Under the supervision of national authorities, individual airlines are gradually transferring their operations across to JARs.

The UK legislation is contained in Schedule 8 (Licences) and Schedule 10 (Operations) to the ANO. The JAA Regulations can be found in JAR—FCL (Flight Crew Licensing), JAR—OPS (Operations) and JAR—STD (Simulators).

The following sections set out the steps taken by a responsible airline to ensure that the necessary high standards of pilot training and testing are achieved and maintained.

SECTION 1. OPERATIONS AND TRAINING MANUALS

The benchmark, so far as flight crew are concerned, is an airline's Operations Manual, which incorporates all the relevant legislation and regulations, and is regularly amended by the airline. The Operations Manual includes: general regulations, sometimes known as flight crew orders; aircraft type specific Manuals, also described as Flying or Technical Manuals; type specific Navigation and Performance Manuals; and Training Manuals, both general and aircraft type specific. All these Manuals with any amendments must be approved by the relevant authority.

SECTION 2.   RECRUITMENT AND BASIC TRAINING

Airlines can no longer fill their vacancies with flight crew leaving the armed services. The services are today much smaller, whilst the civil airline industry is much larger than it was in the late 1950s. Airlines have been obliged to turn to other sources—primarily sponsored cadets, other airlines and general aviation.

At the time of writing, it is possible in the UK for aspiring pilots to follow the "self-improvement" route, by obtaining a Private Pilot's Licence, then building up a total of 700 flying hours, either paying for it themselves, or, more probably, taking low-paid casual work as a light aircraft instructor. This exempts them from the requirement to follow an "approved course" at a CAA approved flying training school, and they are thereafter merely required to pass written exams and practical tests to obtain a Commercial Pilot's Licence. When the JAR Flight Crew Licensing regulations come into effect, this option will cease.

Sponsored cadets, and many private individuals undertake "approved courses" at a limited number of recognised and licensed training schools which involve a minimum period of classroom instruction, and a much reduced flying hours requirement of 150 hours for "integrated" and 200 hours for "modular" courses.

The competition for sponsored *ab initio* training enables airlines to demand high academic and personal standards. A higher secondary education or a university degree are normally required. The upper age limit is around 28. Natural aptitude is very important, and sophisticated tests are used to assess it. Although it is expensive, the airlines favour this route since the entire course can be tailored to their requirements, and "quality control" is to that extent assured. Sponsored cadets are usually contracted to remain with their airline for a number of years, and either to repay a proportion of the cost of training or accept a lower starting salary. In practice, by virtue of the rigid seniority system, the majority remain with their sponsoring airline for their entire career and represent a sound investment.

In order to maintain a reasonable age profile, airlines recruit both sponsored *ab initio* pilots, and more experienced licence holders, from general aviation, the armed services or other airlines. Pilots tend to gravitate from the fringes of the industry towards the larger operators where pay and conditions are usually better.

SECTION 3. AIRLINE CONVERSION TRAINING

On joining an airline, or on transferring from one aircraft type to another, pilots undertake a type-specific conversion course, the content of which must be approved by the CAA. A typical course will begin with a period of classroom training, most probably making use of audio-visual aids and procedures trainers, which, dependent on the complexity of the aircraft, may last up to a month. This phase will concentrate on the technical aspects of the aircraft; its limitations, systems and performance, and trainees must pass a written technical examination approved or set by the CAA, before they move on to the next part of the course.

If the aircraft type is small and simple, all training will be conducted on the aircraft itself. Normally, however, about three weeks will be spent on a simulator learning normal operating procedures for the aircraft type concerned, and becoming familiar with its flying characteristics. Abnormal and emergency procedures practice, covering all significant potential failures including engine and system failures and fire and smoke drills will be progressively introduced during the 50 or so hours the average pilot will spend on the simulator course, half of which will be spent handling the controls and half acting as co-pilot to his or her colleague. Flight engineers would, of course, be at their station for the whole time. The simulator syllabus is also approved by the CAA, and a wide variety of manoeuvres must be satisfactorily performed and approved by a CAA authorised examiner before the next training phase is undertaken.

This phase is aircraft or "base" training. In some instances, it may be carried out in a "zero flight time" simulator approved by the CAA, but this depends upon the experience of the pilot concerned, the nature of the aircraft and the quality of the simulator. Assuming a base training detail is necessary, an empty aircraft will be flown to a suitable airfield and the pilot under training will be required to demonstrate an acceptable standard of take-offs and landings, including engine failures on take-off, engine-out approaches, go-arounds and landings. The minimum requirement for experienced pilots is three take-offs and landings, but most will practise half a dozen or more, whilst cadet entry pilots require a minimum of three hours aircraft training. A qualified base training captain will occupy the other pilot's seat so that he can take control immediately, should a dangerous situation develop. A type qualified "Safety Pilot" will also be carried to keep a look-out.

"Base" training completes the minimum requirements to enable a pilot to have an aircraft type endorsed on his or her licence by the CAA, in accordance with Schedule 8 to the ANO. This requires a course completion certificate from the ground school, a fully signed CAA Form 1179 confirming that all required tests and manoeuvres have been successfully completed, and an Instrument Rating Pass Certificate.

For airline operations the pilot must now complete "on the job" route training; this entails operating normal passenger or cargo flights, with an instructor in the other pilot's seat, and an observing "Safety Pilot", for a minimum of four sectors for experienced pilots, and a minimum of 30 sectors for sponsored cadets. The Safety Pilot will alert the instructor in the event of dangerous situations developing, or of mistakes and/or omissions on the part of either operating pilot. Further route training, without the Safety Pilot, will continue for between 10 and 15 sectors for the average experienced pilot and between five and 20 sectors for most sponsored cadets. Additional sectors will be required if progress is slow. Instructors must be satisfied that the route training syllabus, including numerous discussion items and mandatory types of approaches, has been completed and that an individual's standard of operation is safe, competent, and up to the standard expected for a Final Route Check, as required by Schedule 10 to the ANO. This final test will be conducted by a Senior Check pilot on a normal line flight, after which the pilot will be cleared to operate unsupervised as a qualified crew member.

Even then, the newly qualified pilot will be "tagged", and will not be rostered to operate with a newly qualified colleague for a minimum of three months. Conversion training can last between two and six months, depending on the complexity of the aircraft type, and whether the operation is long or short haul.

SECTION 4. AIRLINE RECURRENT TRAINING

Once qualified, pilots face a series of tests and checks to maintain the validity of their licences and their standard of operation. There cannot be many other occupations where individuals must face up to the theoretical possibility of losing their livelihood five times a year!

In addition to stringent medical examinations by a CAA authorised medical examiner every six months (for pilots over 40), airline crews have to pass a two-day simulator check twice a year, together with an annual Route Check on a normal line flight. These practical flying tests are conducted by Training or Route Check captains appointed by the airline. Training captains also hold the office of "authorised examiner" and conduct these checks on behalf of the CAA. In order to achieve instrument rating and type rating examiner status, pilots must have attended and passed a CAA course, and are regularly "observed" by CAA training inspectors, who ensure that standards are maintained. Training captains must renew their examiner's authorisation every four years. There are moves in the UK for airlines to train their own instructors and training pilots "in house", with only the final check conducted by the CAA.

The framework for recurrent checks laid down in the ANO will be superseded by JAR—OPS, JAR—FCL and JAR—STD. Although the details vary, the basic requirements are similar. In order to maintain the validity of their licences, flight crew must renew their instrument rating every year, either in an aircraft fitted with blind flying screens or, more usually, in an approved simulator. The instrument rating consists of a flight conducted under IFR in icing conditions including an en route "airways" section, a holding pattern, an ILS approach and a go-around procedure flown from MDA (Minimum Decision Altitude).

Additionally, every six months, pilots must also complete what was formerly known as a Certificate of Test and Base Check, but is retitled an Operator's Proficiency Check (OPC) under JAR—OPS. This typically consists of a rejected take-off, an engine fire or failure on take-off, followed by an engine-out ILS approach and go-around leading into an engine-out non-precision instrument approach (using a VOR or NDB procedure). The whole exercise is conducted under IFR, with cloudbase at or below the relevant minima. A wide variety of abnormal and emergency drills are also regularly tested; these include fire and smoke drills, total or partial electrical and hydraulic failures, decompression and pressurisation problems, landing gear and instrument faults. The object is to review at least once every three years every significant failure which could occur on the aircraft type, thereby testing and refreshing the knowledge and expertise acquired during the type conversion course. A specimen recurrent training form is reprinted here.

JAR—OPS requires that pilots undergo All Weather Operations Category 2/3 Autoland training in the simulator every six months, and that they fly a LOFT (Line Orientated Flight Training) exercise in the simulator to practise their Crew Resource Management (CRM) skills at least once a year on every other check. Pilots must attend annual classroom and practical training and testing in safety and emergency procedures (including fire-fighting, use of life-saving equipment such as oxygen, lifejackets and rafts, aircraft evacuation and emergency use of doors and exits) and they must also receive classroom training in aviation medicine and aviation security matters once a year. Pilots are, lastly, required to complete and pass an aircraft type specific technical exam and questionnaire, on an annual basis.

The final element of recurrent training is the Annual Route Check which is normally conducted on a regular flight by a designated Route Check Captain. The Route Check function is often additional to and separate from the training establishment within an airline, with the Route Check Captain reporting to the Chief Pilot of a Fleet, and not to the Training Section. All aspects of the operation are included, from pre-flight preparation through aircraft handling to customer service and commercial awareness, as shown on the specimen form. Pilots are also required to maintain their airfield, route and area qualifications at the same time, be it by a written or audio visual briefing or a practical test.

SECTION 5. CURRENT ATTITUDES TO TRAINING AND CHECKING

This volume of checks was a daunting prospect for pilots 25 years ago. They were often conducted in an intimidating atmosphere, but times have changed

AREA / AERODROME QUALIFICATION & ROUTE CHECK REPORT

Date	A/C Type	Base	Staff No.	Rank	Name

Checking Official	Other Crew (Rank & Name)

Date	Sector	T/O Ldg A/L Circle when completed	Date	Sector	T/O Ldg A/L Circle when completed

Management Capabilities

Levels	M	G	P	A	I	Remarks
Leadership						
Managing Performance						
Valuing Others						
Customer Focus						
Business Competence						
Communication						M – *Minimum.* G – *Good.* P – *Proactive.* A – *Advanced.* I - *Inspired*

Final Assessment and Recommendations (including APIC/Command Suitability as necessary)

	1
	2
	3
	4
	5

Circle Grade

FLIGHT CREW AREA / AERODROME QUALIFICATION CERTIFICATE
I certify that I have briefed myself for Areas and Aerodromes as required by FCO 2010 et seq. and associated briefing requirements in the Route Information Manual. Written Area Briefings are required for the areas listed below. There are additional requirements for North America and Polar Areas – refer to the Route Information Manual. Before operating into a specific Area / Aerodrome covered by these requirements, I acknowledge that I must re-brief using written briefings, audio / visual briefings or visits as applicable.

Delete those not applicable	Short Haul Operations in OCAs	Eastern Europe to Siberia
North America	Polar	South America & Caribbean
Africa	Middle East / Far East	Australia

Signature: Date:

I certify that I have read the comments contained in this report and understand the Final Assessment above.

Signature: Date:

I certify that this Officer was tested in accordance with JAR OPS (Subpart N) and British Airways SOPs, and that *he/she *has/has not satisfied me that *he/she is competent to carry out the duties required of *him/her.
* *Delete as applicable*

Signature: Appointment: Date:

Flight Management Certification
I certify that the Officer has been tested in accordance with JAR OPS (Subpart N) and FCOs.

Signature: Appointment: Date:

Revision 6

British Airways Area/Aerodrome Qualification Certificate and Route Check Report (revision 6), © British Airways plc

Summary of flight including weather and any unusual circumstances:

Handling / Procedures	
Scan Checks / Engine start Taxi / Parking Take-Off / Power Settings Acceleration / Climb Cruise Descent / Deceleration Approach Landing analysis Use of FD / AP Adherence to SOPs FMS/INS Procedures Adverse Wx Procedures R/T Procedures Management of Flight Accuracy / smoothness	

Non-Handling / Technical	
Pre-Flight Preparations Fuel Planning Tech & Cabin Log/DDM/MEL Pre-flight chks – Ext / Int T/O calculations Standard Calls Checklists / Monitoring Wx & terrain considerations Situational awareness Flight path monitoring Fuel management & checks Company comms / ACARS Scans / leaving panel c/list In-Flight Paperwork Troubleshooting / Manuals	

C R M	
First Impressions Appearance Proactive Briefing Prioritises / Communicates Identifies potential problems Sets operational guidelines Key task & time management Shares plans Alert to unexpected Cabin / Ground Crew Liaison Free & open communications Speaks up / assertiveness Effective use of resources Supportive – Objective Inter-Personal Awareness Encourages Feedback	

and whilst an element of "checking" is required by both UK and JAR Regulations, the emphasis is now on training to ensure that the required standard is achieved, after suitable practice and refresher training where appropriate. Old-style "checking" concentrated on the handling abilities of the individual pilot, often in very difficult circumstances, with minimal assistance from his fellow crew members. This "one-man-band" approach achieved very little other than to test a pilot's flying under stress. Today, the airline crew is treated as a team, who pool their skills and resources of knowledge, delegating tasks to one another in order to jointly deal with and solve a problem. Their flying ability will still be assessed, but in a more realistic environment.

LOFT and CRM hold the key to this new approach. A LOFT training session aims to make the exercise as close to a real flight as possible, flying a fully documented route from one airport to another, with the instructor playing the role of air traffic control, ground staff, cabin crew etc. Within this scenario, the instructor will introduce the training items at an appropriate moment, be they air traffic or weather related, aircraft system or powerplant failures, or even situations developing on the simulated aircraft itself, such as sickness or security problems. The instructor will assess the crew's performance and decision-making, possibly with the help of a video recording, but he will not intervene, nor debrief and give feedback to the crew until the exercise is complete. LOFT training is designed to enable a crew to practise dealing with abnormal and emergency situations in familiar—as opposed to examination—surroundings, making full use of all the human and technical resources which would be available to a regular crew "flying the line".

Inseparable from LOFT is CRM, which has been defined as the effective use of all resources including hardware, software and human factors to achieve safe and efficient flight operations. Over the years, the airline industry world-wide has generally established an impressive record which testifies to the safety of multi-crew aircraft. When accidents do happen, however, they are most often the result of a breakdown in crew coordination and management. Almost three-quarters of airline accidents are caused by errors on the part of the crew, and most of these can be put down to poor crew management, as opposed to breakdowns in technical skill. The basic resources which the flight crew manages are people—fellow crew members including cabin crew, passengers, ATC and ground staff,—and Equipment—instruments and controls together with crew interface with complex computerised Flight Management Systems, and such diverse items as charts, checklists and company/manufacturer's Manuals.

Major accidents in the 1970s and 1980s led to the establishment of formal CRM courses by some of the world's leading airlines. Their objective was to improve crew performance in decision-making, teamwork, stress and fatigue management, leadership and interpersonal communications. So successful were they that CRM training is now a required element of *ab initio* training and crews are regularly assessed on their CRM skills during six-monthly recurrent checks.

The advent of LOFT and CRM has brought a great change from the rigid and structured approach of earlier years. Nowadays all crew members seek to communicate frankly and openly with their colleagues, listen to and take proper account of their opinions, consider one another's feelings, and work together naturally as a crew in order to achieve a safe and efficient operation. Whilst the captain remains in overall charge, it is appropriate for him to delegate so as to manage the operation, and for the whole crew to show leadership traits and skills in voicing their views, concerns and suggestions at an appropriate time.

Everyone agrees that this change has been for the better. Training, not "checking" is the new order; Training Captains are no longer seen as the remote and austere authority figures of the past, but as approachable colleagues with an interest in solving fellow crew members' queries and problems, helping them to maintain and improve their standards.

SECTION 6.   THE USE OF SIMULATORS IN TRAINING

Rudimentary simulators have been used for the training of crews since the earliest days of flying. From the Link Trainer in widespread use with Allied Air Forces to teach and practise instrument flying and radio navigation, procedures trainers were developed which reproduced the cockpits, controls and instrumentation of specific aircraft types. Whilst these had no visual systems, and either very restricted or no motion whatsoever, they represented a significant step towards modern technology, and their successors remain in use for basic instruction in systems management and cockpit familiarisation.

Since the Second World War, simulators have developed into the highly sophisticated training tools used today. The most advanced full flight simulators are remarkable machines costing many millions of dollars, which, to the crew member sitting at the controls with their artificial "feel", are indistinguishable from flying the real aircraft. They move on hydraulic jacks in all three axes; they have day and night wrap-around visual systems which can portray airports and surrounding terrain with an accuracy limited only by cost. They faithfully reproduce the sounds made by an aircraft—from engine noise to the sound of the landing gear being raised or extended, or the squeal of the tyres on touchdown. The controls and instruments all function exactly as in the aircraft itself.

Cost and safety are the prime reasons why almost all airline training nowadays is conducted in flight simulators. As aircraft become ever larger, more complicated and more expensive, a simulator, even with a price-tag of many million dollars, is a far cheaper option than training in the aircraft itself. Simulators do not require airport slots, do not cause noise disturbance and can operate 24 hours a day. They do not consume fuel or need major overhauls in scarce and expensive hangar space, or servicing by teams of mechanics. All that is required is a reliable electricity supply, a "bay" for the simulator cab and its associated bank of computers, a small number of computer engineers and some mechanics to service the hydraulic motion and other systems. Hour-for-hour, flying time in a simulator costs about 25 per cent of aircraft time for a small and relatively simple modern jet, decreasing to 10 per cent or less for large wide-bodied types.

Flight simulators represent an enormous advance in terms of safety and training convenience. They provide an ideal means of enabling crew to rehearse emergency drills and failures, as required by training schedules, in total safety. Engine failure and fires, smoke in the cockpit and multiple or total hydraulic and other system failures can be realistically reproduced.

Weather on the simulator can be varied at will to simulate fog, strong winds, low cloud or freezing temperatures. The simulator can be set at almost any airport and at any total weight and fuel load. The simulator can be frozen in operation when the instructor wishes to emphasise a point or prevent a potentially hazardous situation or crash.

The most sophisticated simulators not only faithfully mirror the handling qualities of the aircraft type, but also have visual and ancillary systems to match these standards. They are often designated as "zero flight time" simulators and are approved for base training. There are other simulators, which will never be approved for "zero flight time", useful as they may be for general training to a lower standard.

Within the UK, classification of and annual approvals for all flight simu-lators are the responsibility of inspectors from the CAA who have developed great expertise in this field, and have set the standards which the rest of the world aspires to follow.

SECTION 7.   FLIGHT TIME LIMITATIONS

Flight crews are subject to legal restriction and regulation in respect of their working hours, rest periods and days off. The ANO requires that the operator shall have a scheme for the regulation of flight times of crews, which must be approved by the CAA, and included in the Company Operations Manual. Since 1975 in the UK, the rules which regulate such schemes have been set out in Civil Aviation Publication CAP 371, which was the result of the Bader report, and the work of the Flight Time Limitations Board.

While companies may negotiate agreements with their crews which restrict working hours to less than the limit imposed by CAP 371, commercial pressures create an inexorable trend towards the maximum number of hours allowed.

The table reproduced below sets out the effect of the CAP 371 Rules for a two-pilot operation which allows duty periods up to the maximum number of hours shown.

Local time of Start	Sectors							
	1	2	3	4	5	6	7	8 or more
0600–0759	13	$12\frac{1}{4}$	$11\frac{1}{2}$	$10\frac{3}{4}$	10	$9\frac{1}{2}$	9	9
0800–1259	14	$13\frac{1}{4}$	$12\frac{1}{2}$	$11\frac{3}{4}$	11	$10\frac{1}{2}$	10	$9\frac{1}{2}$
1300–1759	13	$12\frac{1}{4}$	$11\frac{1}{2}$	$10\frac{3}{4}$	10	$9\frac{1}{2}$	9	9
1800–2159	12	$11\frac{1}{4}$	$10\frac{1}{2}$	$9\frac{3}{4}$	9	9	9	9
2200–0559	11	$10\frac{1}{4}$	$9\frac{1}{2}$	9	9	9	9	9

Cumulative duty hours limits allow 55 hours in one week, 95 hours in any two consecutive weeks and 190 hours in four consecutive weeks.

The growth in charter holiday operations, together with the introduction of aircraft with extended operating capacity subsequent to the implementation of these rules, has resulted in an increase of consecutive night duty periods (despite some additional restrictions), single sector ultra-long haul operations, and more flights crossing multiple time zones.

It is therefore necessary to keep these rules under constant review to provide for any necessary revision.

CAP 371 is frequently held up as a model set of regulations bearing in mind that a number of JAA States have no flight time limitations regulations whatsoever.

The JAA recently sought to promote its own flight time limitation rules, but these have been held in abeyance in the light of objections from the EU, on the grounds that the JAA was not accountable to the EU and that these were matters of social policy.

Proposals to extend the principles of the EU Council Directive 93/104/EC (the Working Time Directive) to flight time limitations are currently under consideration.

There can be no doubt that the general public expects that air crews should not be fatigued, and therefore that there should be sensible rules governing duty and rest periods.

SECTION 8. NAVIGATION AIDS AND NEW TECHNOLOGY

In the 1950s and 1960s, at the threshold of the age of jet transport, aircraft still carried Flight Navigators in their crew and fixed their position by reference to sextant star shots, radio navigation systems such as Consol, LORAN or Decca, and manual tuning of radio beacons. Course information was derived from rudimentary magnetic or gyro compasses, with pitot and static airspeed and altitude data, and gyro attitude and turn information.

The advent of wide-bodied aircraft in the 1970s coincided with introduction of Inertial Navigation Systems (INS) and the disappearance, for the most part, of the Flight Navigator. These very sophisticated INS gyro platforms are aligned with the known latitude and longitude of the stationary aircraft at the departure airport; their associated navigation computers thereafter measure lateral accelerations so as to (a) determine the aircraft's precise position at all times; (b) calculate the distance, time and course to any desired location; and (c) provide additional information including inertially-derived track and groundspeed information, drift and wind velocity and such like.

Aircraft have navigated very accurately and generally most satisfactorily by this method, for many years, with two or three independent INS sets on board, and the majority still do.

Currently the worldwide Global Positioning System (GPS) has not been fully approved for airline use. Airlines continue with their tried and tested INS systems, albeit with updated laser gyros and associated Flight Management Systems.

Similarly, while passengers have satellite telephones available at their seats, crew continue to communicate with ATC with the same type of HF radio equipment as has been used since the demise of the radio operator with his morse key. Satellite communications have not yet been approved for ATC.

Given the proven accuracy of GPS, and the reliability and clarity of satellite communications, all this will change in the fullness of time when international agreement can be reached. Much debate has taken place and much research undertaken to arrive at a common standard for FANS—otherwise known as Future Air Navigation Systems.

The airline industry will undoubtedly make massive use of GPS and satellite communications, in harmony with other developments which will include (a) aircraft continually broadcasting their height, course, speed and position by automated data link; and (b) air traffic controllers possibly having the facility of transmitting navigational instructions directly to the aircraft's Flight Management System, with no requirement to relay this information through to the crew on board.

Such a quantum leap in both custom and practice and in technology naturally requires the greatest care in setting the optimum standard specification at the outset, and it has already taken many years to arrive at the outline position being worked on today. It will also be many years before all aircraft are so equipped, and therefore today's status quo and FANS will have to co-exist as best they can. The ultimate goal is the establishment of worldwide "free flight", which would allow all aircraft to fly wherever they want, whenever they want, with no slot times, holding patterns, air traffic control delays or circuitous routings imposed at the whim of the military or controlling authorities. An ideal well worth striving for.

Of course, some airlines may complain of the cost of making these changes, the benefits of "free flight" notwithstanding. However, over the years airlines have been compelled to install additional equipment which was not part of the aircraft's original specification. Thus the last 30 years have seen the arrival of

DME (Distance Measuring Equipment), weather radar and air traffic transponders, i.e. secondary surveillance radar (which broadcasts a discrete code enabling a read-out of aircraft height and flight number on a controller's radar screen), to name but a few. Two further compulsory "fits" of equipment have come about directly as a result of past accidents: GPWS (Ground Proximity Warning System) and TCAS (Traffic Alert and Collision Avoidance System), otherwise referred to as ACAS in the Annexes.

GPWS was developed following numerous CFIT (Controlled Flight into Terrain) accidents which might have been avoided had GPWS equipment been on board. Based on information derived from the radio altimeter, GPWS monitors Excessive Rates of Descent approaching the Ground (Mode 1) or Excessive Terrain Closure Rate (Mode 2). Both of these generate what are known as "hard" warnings, sounding an alarm with the words "Pull Up". If the aircraft is below the Minimum Safety Altitude in the area, most airline procedures require the pilot to immediately apply full power and rotate the aircraft to a "Go-Around" attitude until the warning ceases and he is above the relevant Minimum Safety Altitude. GPWS also monitors Altitude Loss after Take-off (Mode 3), Landing Gear or Flaps not in position approaching the ground (Mode 4), or Descent below the Glidepath (Mode 5). These generate "soft" warnings such as "Don't sink" or "Too low, Gear" to which the pilot must respond. From early unreliability and false warnings, GPWS has developed into one of the industry's most important tools in the quest for air safety.

TCAS is designed to complement ATC and not to replace it. The system uses range and altitude data obtained by interrogating the transponders of other aircraft to determine the possibility of collision. It also presents bearing information of aircraft intruding into the TCAS aircraft's airspace, but uses this information for information on the map display only, to help the crew visually identify the intruder. When the change of range and change of altitude rates of the intruder are computed and a collision is predicted, TCAS will declare the intruder a "threat" and give a manoeuvre advice in aural and visual form. Avoidance manoeuvres commanded by TCAS are in the vertical plane only ("Climb" or "Descend") since bearing information is not sufficiently accurate to determine horizontal avoidance advice. A pilot will respond to a "hard" warning or RA (Resolution Advisory) which may well conflict with the instructions and expectations of ATC.

TCAS was originally made mandatory by the FAA and all aircraft flying to US airports were required to carry the equipment. Despite the fact that the system is less than perfect it can be said that the risk of mid-air collision has been significantly reduced thanks to TCAS, and most air traffic controllers have witnessed situations where TCAS has proved very useful. Improved TCAS equipment has encouraged a large number of aviation authorities worldwide to consider making the system mandatory in their national airspace. The UK will mandate TCAS in the near future, and from 1 January 2000, TCAS will be mandatory for all members of ECAC.

With the advent of FANS and "free flight", civil aviation stands on the threshold of another era of great change. In a "high tech" industry, continual change is something which flight crew and others have to learn to live with and accept; modern flight decks bear only a superficial resemblance to those which pilots now approaching retirement were originally trained to operate. The control column has disappeared from the new Airbus family of aircraft, to be replaced by an electronic sidestick which directly signals computers to operate hydraulically powered flying controls in a "fly-by-wire" system. Conventional electro-mechanical instruments have been replaced by electronic flight instrument displays containing information previously obtained from dozens of dials. Typically six or eight CRT displays (TV screens) can replace between five and ten times that number of instruments. The whole aircraft—instruments, navigation, flight controls, engines—is increasingly managed by highly sophisticated computers. The flight crew, however, remain firmly in control—monitoring, planning, commanding and overriding where necessary, but their role today and into the future is now much more one of systems management, as opposed to the "drivers—airframe" of the past.

CHAPTER 19

AIRCRAFT MAINTENANCE PROCEDURES

SECTION 1. INTRODUCTION

Annexes 6 and 8 include SARPS on maintenance. Annex 1 sets out the SARPS on licensing of aircraft maintenance (technician engineer mechanic) personnel. Both the Cyprus Arrangements (page 209) and EC Regulation 3922/91 include provisions on harmonisation of maintenance procedures.

For the definition of maintenance in Regulation 3922/91 see page 216.

SECTION 2. MAINTENANCE PROGRAMMES

All aircraft need inspecting, repairing and servicing in accordance with approved maintenance procedures. These procedures depend on the requirements of the manufacturer and of the authority for each type of operation and on the legislative framework of use, i.e. public transport, aerial work, or private flight.

This chapter deals principally with transport category aircraft (as provided in the ANO) and their maintenance programme.

The operator is required to maintain his aircraft in accordance with the Approved Maintenance Programme ("AMP").

The origin of the AMP lies in the analysis by the manufacturer of its product. The manufacturer draws up a list of inspections, tests and replacements he considers necessary to ensure the safe and economic operation of the aircraft.

The process of drawing up the AMP begins when the manufacturer first makes a formal application for a Type Certificate of Airworthiness; much of this process runs concurrently within the time scale of the designing and production of the first aircraft. Consequently, production of the AMP is closely aligned with the construction and testing of the aircraft, thus allowing a realistic assessment of necessary maintenance.

The body primarily responsible for drawing up the AMP is the Maintenance Review Board ("MRB") which consists of the manufacturer and the air worthiness authority ("authority"). The MRB takes into account the views and suggestions of the maintenance steering committee which consists not only of the manufacturer and authority but also prospective operators.

This phase of activity produces a programme acceptable to all parties, subject to their recognising the lack of operating experience of the aircraft type concerned.

This procedure was first applied in the production of the maintenance programme for the Boeing 747; it was adopted by the Air Transport Association of the USA and is known as the Maintenance Steering Group.

The progressive updating of this process has led to Version 3 and is currently the accepted way by which all commercial public transport aircraft achieve an AMP at the time of entry into service.

The MRB deals with the smallest detail of the proposed programme, checking the logic analysis applied to tasks and bringing to bear the practical knowledge of how best to perform the tasks in the programme. The MRB may set up specialist subgroups for power plants, systems and structures.

The final review is managed by the authority responsible for issuing the Type Certificate of Airworthiness for the aircraft. In practice, MRBs frequently include representatives from several authorities to facilitate acceptance of the type into the States of customers for the aircraft. The whole process may take several years and is so arranged that the MRB draw up their final report, termed the Maintenance Review Board Report ("MRBR"), sufficiently prior to entry into service of the new type, so as to enable operators to plan for the provision of adequate maintenance.

The manufacturer turns the MRBR into a practical document known as the Maintenance Planning Document from which operators implement their maintenance by way of the AMP. In most cases, regulatory approval is required and this is provided by the operator's national authority.

The AMP will provide for all inspections of structure, systems and equipment considered necessary by the manufacturer. It will also prescribe tests devised to detect failures not readily evident to crews or maintenance personnel where such failure could adversely affect airworthiness.

The intervals between such tests are arrived at by theoretical calculation which raises the question of how determination of the interval is made so as to provide a safe margin. This is dealt with by setting a safe margin between the calculated maximum interval and that called for in the AMP. While rig and flight testing will reduce this margin by verifying calculations, a margin will always be necessary in the absence of operating experience.

Within the AMP several concepts for control of "lives" of items (parts) can apply. The first is "Hard Time", the second "On-Condition" and the third "Condition Monitoring". The modern aircraft and its operating environment depend heavily on the Condition Monitoring approach. These terms are explained below:

Hard Time	A primary maintenance process under which an item must be removed from service at or before a previously specified time. (WATOG definition)
On-Condition	A primary maintenance process having repetitive inspections or tests to determine the condition of units, systems, or portions of structure with regard to continued serviceability (corrective action is taken when required by item condition). (WATOG definition)
Condition Monitoring	This is not a preventative process, having neither Hard Time nor On-Condition elements, but one in which information on items gained from operational experience is collected, analysed and interpreted on a continuing basis as a means of implementing corrective procedures.

(For WATOG see Appendix 1, "Definitions".)

After production of the AMP the first stage in its implementation is the production of the work card (or task card) which expands a single task or group of tasks into a form which mechanics and engineers can use. The source for the text is often cards produced by the manufacturer but many maintenance companies vary these as their experience and capability permits. Problems can arise if the manufacturer's words differ in principle or intent from those used by the maintainer. The Aircraft Maintenance Manual ("AMM"), as required for example by BCAR A7–4 and ICAO Annex 6 Chapters 8 and 11.3, is the authoritative source of how to perform a task and is itself a controlled and certificated document. A wise maintenance organisation draws heavily on this source when producing its own workcard.

Check cycles and their content

A work pack prepared for the maintenance team may vary from a dozen sheets up to a pack containing 5,000 individual documents. The disparity is clear when comparing a simple frequent maintenance service on a small commuter aircraft with a heavy maintenance package on an elderly wide-body. Considerable use is made of computer tracking of material, manpower and progress on large checks. In many cases, the workcards are produced at the work station by a "controller" and issued in a predetermined sequence to staff.

A check cycle comprises packages of work with intervals between the packages from the smallest, the pre-departure inspection, to the largest, commonly the D Check. While terminology varies, the term "A through to D Check" is universally understood. A typical example is that for the Boeing 757, below. This cycle recognises the maturity that the Boeing 757 has reached in its life cycle development.

Pre-Departure	—	Prior to every flight.
A Check	—	Every 500 flight hours/300 flights.
B Check	—	Not required on the Boeing 757.
C Check	—	6,000 flight hours/every 3,000 flight cycles or 18 months.
D Check	—	24,000 flight hours/12,000 flights or 72 months.

The Pre-Departure check can, where necessary, be performed by the flight crew but all larger checks will be carried out by certificated maintenance organisations.

The A Check comprises minor inspections and replenishment of fluids and gases and a few system tests.

The B Check is the first check that will require housing the aircraft under cover and is a more comprehensive inspection, this time including cleaning, lubrication, inspections and replacement of time limited components. It can include performing some portion of the anti-corrosion programme and deeper attention to aircraft structure in defined areas.

The C Check involves a more comprehensive inspection and more extensive repairs and replacements. It is due on the basis of hours or flights. It can be scheduled to suit the flying programme of the operator either at the maximum limit specified in the AMP or earlier.

The C Check is carried out at the specified intervals until the largest check, the D Check, becomes due. This important check requires the performance of modifications, structural inspections and anti-corrosion measures, and an extensive renovation of passenger accommodation and colour schemes. The amount of work required by a D Check is not of itself the measure of the workload. The totality of the work however requires high levels of coordination.

A major check (or D Check) usually includes:

- Rectification of incoming minor defects;
- Removal of access panels and defuelling the tanks;
- Carrying out the inspection as specified in the workpack;
- Removal of cabin interior including seats, galleys, toilets and sidewall trim;
- Removal of time limited components such as landing gears;
- Carrying out repairs found necessary as a result of the inspection;
- Refurbishing various systems;
- Carrying out such modifications and directives as laid down or as needed by the operator;
- Reprotecting structure against corrosion;
- Refitting all equipment and parts;
- Carrying out extensive system testing;
- Re-weighing the aircraft and perform a flight test.

There is some flexibility in the maximum interval between checks but this is subject to agreement by the authority and can be applied only to overcome some unforeseen technical or operational problem.

In any event as an aircraft matures in service operators may seek to escalate the original intervals. The process for this is well-established and concerns primarily the operator and its authority.

The escalation of programmed check intervals is a major factor in reducing direct maintenance man-hours, total direct maintenance costs, and aircraft maintenance downtime.

The ideal scheduled maintenance programme is one which has escalated the intervals between the various maintenance checks to a point which takes maximum advantage of the reliability and serviceability of the airframe, engines, systems and components without compromising airworthiness or generating excessive maintenance or repair costs.

The Corrosion Control Programme becomes effective on aircraft largely on a calendar basis, i.e. number of years from build, and is made mandatory by Airworthiness Directives. Corrosion control requires resolute implementation.

SECTION 3. AIRWORTHINESS DIRECTIVES

From time to time in the life cycle of an aircraft type, action is required to correct an unsatisfactory or unsafe condition. In most cases the condition will be remedied as a result of action taken by the operator following an issue of a Service Bulletin from the manufacturer. The Service Bulletin ("SB") will summarise the problem, recommending how and when it should be dealt with. In a few cases, the urgency or gravity of the unsatisfactory or unsafe condition will induce the authority to issue an Airworthiness Directive.

The phrase Airworthiness Directive is universally understood although national versions exist such as a "Consigne de Navigabilité" (the DGAC of France) or Mandatory Modifications and Inspections (CAA). The basis for issue of Airworthiness Directives in the USA is FAR 39; in the UK is BCAR A6–6; and throughout the JAA States it is JAR 39.In theory the airworthiness authority has the absolute discretion whether or not to order a mandatory modification or inspection but in practice consultation with industry is usual. In the USA the practice of "Notice of Proposed Rule Making" ("NPRM") is used for most Airworthiness Directives. A similar practice is followed in Europe.

The CAA procedures for the consultation process are as follows:

Where the CAA, in consultation with the Type Design Organisation decides that a modification, inspection or change to approved documentation is essential for airworthiness, it will initiate mandatory status by raising a provisional Airworthiness Directive.

The CAA shall be satisfied that the Type Design Organisation, in the development of the modification/inspection, change, has consulted representative operators of the aircraft type to which the provisional Airworthiness Directive applies.

Where action essential for airworthiness involves engine(s), propeller(s), or equipment, the CAA shall be satisfied that the Type Design Organisation has involved the Type Design Organisation of the aircraft into which the equipment may be installed.

When satisfied that the development of the material essential for airworthiness is complete, the CAA will provide the Type Design Organisation with an Airworthiness Directive number.

At the same time as the CAA allocates an Airworthiness Directive number, the Type Design Organisation will be provided with a draft of the Airworthiness Directive to be promulgated by the CAA.

Where possible, the CAA and the Type Design Organisation will endeavour respectively to promulgate the Airworthiness Directive, and the Service Bulletin, Flight Manual amendment or equivalent document on a mutually agreed date.

The CAA has a duty to promulgate an Airworthiness Directive without the agreement of the Type Design Organisation if it believes this is essential for airworthiness.

Some typical examples of Directives which have been issued in the past are:

(1) Boeing 737 (Issued by FAA)
    Airworthiness Directive 90–25–01
    This requires implementation of the manufacturer's Corrosion Control Document
    The numbering system of ADs gives the year of issue (1990)
    The bi-weekly sequence number (25)
    The individual item in that sequence (01).

(2) Airbus A320 (Issued by French DGAC)
    Consigne de Navigabilité 93–123–046
    This requires compliance with a manufacturer's Service Bulletin concerning lightning strike protection of certain flight controls, the bulletin number being *A320–29–1058*.

(3) Rolls Royce RB211 (Issued by CAA)
    Mandatory Inspection 005–07–95
    This requires compliance with a manufacturer's service bulletin involving the engines combustion section. An inspection is required of the front combustion liner head section and meterpanel assembly.

(4) McDonnell Douglas DC10 (Issued by FAA)
    AD 80–11–05

Issued to ensure integrity of the wing engine pylon structure and attachment.

The majority of Service Bulletins do not need to be classified by the certifying authority as "mandatory"—that is an "Airworthiness Directive" —however, this does not imply that many bulletins do not merit implementation. Bulletins are categorised by their impact on safety, reliability, economy or maintainability. Many bulletins on safety would no doubt come within the mandatory Airworthiness Directive category although both the authority and the manufacturer would strive to avoid anomalies. These can occur and hindsight has been a prodigious legislator in aviation.

Considerable effort is made by the manufacturer in framing and publishing Service Bulletins for he has the dual purpose of correcting a shortcoming and, at the same time, in minimising its impact on his customer. Indeed, in a few cases, the manufacturer will defray the cost by allowing material and embodiment cost to be passed back to him. Such an instance would be when a major design flaw has become apparent. The operator would expect in such cases to recoup some or all of his embodiment cost depending on the time since original construction of the aircraft. The matter is often dealt with in warranty clauses in the contracts of sale.

SECTION 4.   LICENSING AND SUPERVISION OF ENGINEERS

Inspection and certification of maintenance is carried out by engineers licensed—in most countries—by the national authority. The SARPS for maintenance engineers is specified by ICAO Annex 6, Chapter 8, which also contains the SARPS for provision of a maintenance organisation to maintain aircraft in an airworthy condition.

Member States of JAA have taken steps to institute a requirement (JAR 66) for a standardised licence for maintenance staff (see Section 5 below).

The path to a licence begins with a sound technical education blended with a practical involvement, possibly an apprenticeship, for some two to five years. In that time, the individual would be receiving training on the basics of his trade plus such other necessary items as aviation legislation, human factors and broad principles on troubleshooting and inspection techniques.

On applying to his authority and provided the requirements are met, the applicant will be examined on his knowledge of the subject in written and oral form. The successful candidate then receives a licence issued by the airworthiness authority which at this point does not confer rights to certify work. It serves only as proof that he has met minimum standards. The next stage is to obtain a "type rating". This involves specific type training and examination.

A level of practical experience is also necessary. It is at this point that traditional and "newer" (including JAR 66) policies differ. Up until the early 1970s those who undertook type ratings were examined by the CAA; however, for various reasons, the responsibility for the type exam moved to the employer under rules laid down by the CAA. This method operates very successfully in practice and is the process nearest to the current JAR 66 regulation. The development of JAR 66 has been subject to widespread consultation and scrutiny bearing in mind the EU basic requirement for freedom of employment opportunity together with introduction of a JAA-wide scheme at grass roots level.

Constant supervision of all maintenance staff, be they licensed engineers, mechanics or indirect workers (planners for example), is carried out by the organisation by various methods. The most obvious being the department quality audit. This is a planned activity in which independent technical staff (in practice from the same enterprise) survey the staff, facilities and performance within a given area. In addition, random product samples are performed. Furthermore, at intervals, all certifying staff are expected to undergo continuation training. The authority in discharging its duties also performs audits to check that the standards of performance are met by organisations and its employees.

During the performance of an aircraft check, a team of mechanics will be allocated to an individual engineer. It is likely that this team will remain intact during the duration of the check, giving the engineer adequate time to carry out the specified inspection as well as the direction of the mechanics in repair and replacement activity. Most tasks require the certification of completion by both the mechanic and the engineer, whilst a few of the more critical items, for example, flight and engine controls require a second and entirely independent engineer to duplicate the inspection performed by the first.

SECTION 5.   THE RELEVANCE OF FAR AND JAR

The primary code for British civil aviation has, up to this time been BCAR —British Civil Airworthiness Requirements, most of which still apply to aircraft built and operated in the UK. However, for US-built aircraft Federal Airworthiness Requirements (FAR) apply. While there has been general similarity between these two codes, sometimes differences have emerged which can be far from academic. At times they have led to two aircraft of the same type operating in parallel competition in Europe, one operated by a British operator, the second by a mainland European operator, the British operator having more severe operational rules.

In the 1970s with the emergence of Airbus Industrie as a major international manufacturer committed to the US market, Europe resolved to establish its own joint certification rules which had as a major aim convergence with the FAR code. Thus, Joint Aviation Requirements (JAR) began to be developed within ECAC.

One of the first Joint Aviation Requirements to be issued was JAR 25 and equated to FAR Part 25, laying down the certification minima for large aeroplanes.

A large portfolio of requirements has since been drafted and, in many cases, adopted as the only code for aviation manufacture and maintenance both among JAA members and in the EU.

By way of example, JARs include:

JAR 1	Definitions	Adoption: July 1979
JAR 25	Large Aeroplanes	Adoption: July 1979
JAR 27	Small Rotorcraft	Adoption: September 1993
JAR 29	Large Rotorcraft	Adoption: November 1993
JAR 21	Certification Procedure for Aircraft and Related Procedure and Parts	Adoption: June 1994
JAR—OPS	Operations	Part 1: April 1995 Part 3: April 1995

SECTION 6. MAINTENANCE OF TECHNICAL RECORDS

Incumbent on an operator is the duty of maintaining the record of his aircraft, its operations, maintenance and service history, this duty originating in Annex 6, Chapter 11.

The simplest way to portray this activity is to liken it to a road vehicle where mileage and services performed are recorded in the service log.

In air transport, the process is somewhat magnified. First, the Maintenance Programme (see Section 2 above) together with the "Time Limits" Chapter of the Maintenance Manual provide a complete list of all items which have time constraints. These have to be controlled by the operator by whatever system he chooses. The regulator does not mandate, for example, a computer system over a manual one but merely that proper control is kept. However, it would be a virtual impossibility to control the requirements of a fleet of modern aircraft without technology. This technology becomes increasingly sophisticated when the operator keeps details of his flights, aircraft maintenance, workshop maintenance, engine overhaul, parts traceability and human resources on one integrated system. It is when organisations take steps down the road of IT integration that good internal disciplines and the oversight by the authority is necessary.

Some seemingly insignificant error in programming or operator action could have enormous consequences for a large fleet. An example could be the life applied to an engine turbine disc. Should this be done incorrectly, perhaps applying too high a service life, then this incorrect life would be applied to all like engines in the fleet. The persons responsible for ensuring that the software prevents such mistakes must have deep experience of control of lifed items with all their pitfalls.

An integrated system described above would, in addition to providing the mandatory records of lifed items, tasks and processes, also serve an organisation as its logistic control. This enables the organisation to repair, modify and where necessary re-life the parts using centralised engineering and, at the same time, enforcing the maximum permitted service life. It will also support logistics allocation to work stations and remote bases so that essential parts are held where required. Early warning of shortages is provided and through linkage of costing data, stock valuation becomes easy.

One other part of record keeping is the traditional "dirty finger records", that is the actual task cards which have been used by maintenance people to perform and certify work. Rigid requirements are laid down in both FARs and JARs on the subject, e.g. FAR 121.380 (FAR 121 is the principal US operational requirement for air carriers).

Some extracts from FAR 121.380 are shown below:

   (a) Each certificate holder shall keep the following records for the periods specified in paragraph (b) of this section:
      (1) All the records necessary to show that all requirements for the issuance of an airworthiness release have been met.
      (2) Records containing the following information:
         (i) The total time in service of the airframe.
         (ii) The current status of life-limited parts of each airframe, engine, propeller, rotor and appliance.
         (iii) The time since last overhaul of all times installed on the aircraft which are required to be overhauled on a specified time basis.
         (iv) The identification of the current inspection status of the aircraft, including the times since the last inspections required by the inspection programme under which the aircraft and its appliances are maintained.
         (v) The current status of applicable Airworthiness Directives, including the method of compliance.
         (vi) A list of current major alterations to each airframe, engine, propeller, rotor and appliance.
   (b) Each certificate holder shall retain the records required to be kept by this section for the following periods:
      (1) Except for the records of the last complete overhaul of each airframe, engine, propeller, rotor and appliance, the records specified in paragraph (a)(1) of this section shall be retained until the work is repeated or superseded by other work or for one year after the work is performed.

    (2) The records of the last complete overhaul of each airframe, engine, propeller, rotor and appliance shall be retained until the work is superseded by work of equivalent scope and detail.

    (3) The records specified in paragraph (a)(2) of this section shall be retained and transferred with the aircraft at the time the aircraft is sold.

  (c) The certificate holder shall make all maintenance records required to be kept by this section available for inspection.

In the retention of records, technology is also playing a role. The traditional method was the archiving of all the paper records with the inconvenience associated with this. The next stage of progress was to utilise microfilming. This vastly reduced the storage requirements whilst permitting quicker access when old documents were sought. Currently, the latest method, the CD-ROM, is beginning to make its presence felt. Some organisations have moved on to permanent retention of all records on this format which provides even larger storage capacity and enhanced access whilst retaining the document quality of the original.

CHAPTER 20

HELICOPTER OPERATIONS

INTRODUCTION

Although helicopters vary widely in layout and size, they all essentially work the same way. They have a rotor or rotors consisting of airfoil-section blades rotating in the horizontal plane to generate a vertical thrust (lift). The most familiar helicopters have a single main lifting rotor and a small, vertical rotor at the tail. The tail rotor counteracts the torque required to drive the main rotor and so prevents the helicopter spinning in the opposite direction. Although the most common, this type of helicopter is comparatively inefficient because the power required to drive the tail rotor does not contribute to the lift. The alternative types, with contra-rotating main rotors, allow all the power to be used to lift the helicopter but at the cost of extra complication. Contra-rotating helicopter rotors can be tandem (Boeing-Vertol), co-axial (Kamov) or inter-meshing (Kaman). All these types are used extensively in the heavy-lift business where their efficiency is of greatest value.

DIFFERENCES BETWEEN AEROPLANES AND HELICOPTERS

Lift generation and control

Aeroplanes and helicopters both obtain their lift from the movement of air over their airfoils. Aeroplanes use their forward speed to obtain airflow over their wings; helicopters rotate their rotor blades through the air, allowing them to obtain lift without requiring forward speed.

The lift generated by an airfoil is dependent on its speed through the air and the angle that it presents to the air—the *angle of attack*. If the angle of attack is increased the lift will increase, until the stalling angle is reached. This is the angle where the lift suddenly reduces because the airflow can no longer follow the airfoil's upper surface. Aeroplanes change the angle of attack of their wings by changing the aircraft's attitude while helicopters do so by changing the pitch of the main rotor blades.

Aeroplanes can vary their lift by changing their angle of attack or their airspeed but since helicopter rotors, for strength reasons, have to rotate at a very closely governed speed, helicopter lift can only be controlled by changing the blade pitch and not by varying rotor speed. Changing the pitch of all the blades together to increase or decrease lift is known as a *collective pitch* change and is achieved by raising or lowering a flying control called the *collective lever*. Conventionally, this control is positioned on the left side of the pilot.

Accurate control of the rotational speed of the rotors within the range defined in the Flight Manual is critical to safe flight. In modern turbine helicopters, this is usually achieved with a fully automatic governing system although a manual backup system may be provided for emergency use. However, in piston-engined machines, rotor speed control is accomplished manually by the pilot using a throttle twistgrip mounted on the collective lever.

Method of propulsion

While aeroplanes are propelled by the thrust of propellers or jet engines aligned with the direction of flight, helicopters obtain their propulsion by tilting their lifting rotors in the direction of travel, thus sharing the total rotor thrust between lift and propulsion. The rotor is tilted by varying the pitch of each rotor blade throughout each revolution. This is called *cyclic pitch* change and is achieved by the pilot moving his cyclic stick in the required direction. It is equivalent to the control stick in an aeroplane cockpit and is usually operated by the helicopter pilot's right hand.

Speed limitations

When a helicopter is in forward flight, as the main rotor blades rotate, some blades will be moving rearward as their opposite blades are moving forward. The forward speed of the helicopter will increase the airspeed of the forward-moving blades and reduce the airspeed of the rearward-moving ones. If the pitch of the blades remained the same throughout their rotation, this difference in airspeed would cause the lift of the forward-moving blades to increase while that of the rearward-moving blades to decrease which would make the helicopter roll in the direction of the rearward-moving blades. To compensate for this, the pitch, and thus the angle of attack, of the advancing blade is reduced, and that of the retreating blade increased. As the helicopter's forward speed increases, this compensation eventually causes the rearward-moving blades to reach their stalling angle, resulting in loss of control. This problem, known as *retreating blade stall*, largely determines the maximum forward speed of conventional helicopters. So, while aeroplanes stall if they fly too slowly, helicopters stall if they fly too fast.

Altitude control

The pitch altitude of a conventional aeroplane is controlled through the elevators. These are hinged control surfaces at the rear of the horizontal tailplane that are moved by fore or aft displacements of the pilot's control stick. If he pulls the control stick back, the elevators are deflected up into the airflow generating a downward force on the tail, thus raising the nose of the machine. When the helicopter pilot takes the same action on his cyclic stick, the input is passed through a *mixing unit* up to the rotor head where *pitch change rods* force the pitch angle of each rotor blade to vary around each revolution in such a way that a rearward tilt of the rotor disc occurs. Inertia and drag effects cause the helicopter's fuselage to follow the plane of the main rotor, so the fuselage also tilts in the same direction and a nose-up altitude change occurs. This means that a helicopter pilot flies his machine by controlling the fuselage altitude in the same way as an aeroplane pilot. Because the rotor can be tilted in any direction, helicopters can move forwards, backwards or sideways, but aerodynamic factors limit the safe speed in any other than the forward direction to about 30 mph (50 kph).

The pitch angle of the tail rotor blades, and hence the thrust of the tail rotor, may be varied by the pilot over a wide range of positive and negative values using his foot-operated *yaw pedals*. This allows him to turn the helicopter in the hover and to maintain balanced flight as main rotor torque changes occur during flight manoeuvres.

Performance comparison

If a helicopter's ability to take-off vertically is to be used, its performance will be far more weight restricted than an aeroplane's. Given a long enough runway, an aeroplane can take-off almost regardless of its weight, but if a helicopter cannot lift off at full power its weight must be reduced until it can.

Mechanical complexity

The combination of collective and cyclic control inputs, and the effects of the helicopter's forward speed on the rotating airfoils, result in very complex airflows and motions of the blades throughout each revolution. To cope with this, considerable mechanical complexity is required in the rotor hub of a helicopter, a component which is subjected to very high rotational stresses and vibration. With their multiple rotors and complex transmissions to combine and convey the power from the engines to the rotors, helicopters are truly "flying machines" in contrast to aeroplanes which are structures carrying machinery.

Cost

The high rotational stresses and the vibration caused by the complex airflows mean that all the major components of a helicopter are subjected to fatigue loading. Metal rotor blades, for instance, have fixed safe lives (typically 6,000 flying hours) on completion of which they must be scrapped. Engines and transmissions have far shorter overhaul lives than their aeroplane counter-parts, often as low as 3,000 flying hours, because they are subjected to frequent large power changes while aeroplane engines spend many hours at constant power. Helicopters also require more frequent maintenance and more detailed inspections than aeroplanes because they are more complex and more highly stressed.

The price the helicopter pays for its versatility is a heavy one in terms of extreme mechanical complication, low efficiency and comparatively low max-imum forward speed. These lead to low reliability, low service lives of expensive components, high fatigue loading, high fuel consumption and lim-ited range. Thus it is always significantly more expensive, more hazardous and more time consuming to travel by helicopter if the same journey can be made by aeroplane.

HELICOPTER CONFIGURATIONS

Helicopter designers have a choice between the efficient contra-rotating rotors, where all the engine power is directed to the lifting rotors at the cost of considerable mechanical complication, and the more common single-main-rotor layout which "wastes" power in driving a non-lifting tail-rotor but is less vulnerable to mechanical failure. However, a tail rotor is very exposed when operating in small clearings or close to obstructions and is a danger to people moving around a running helicopter on the ground.

Contra-rotating rotors

Helicopters with contra-rotating rotors are particularly dependent on the integrity of their transmissions, highly stressed complex machinery which requires impeccable maintenance. This is not to say that single-main-rotor helicopters are invulnerable to transmission failures, but the consequence for them is not usually disastrous as it almost always is for contra-rotating types. The three different types of contra-rotating rotors are discussed below.

Tandem-rotor

Tandem-rotor helicopters have a number of gearboxes, connecting shafts and couplings to transmit engine power and to ensure that the two rotors are synchronised. The failure of any component in this transmission train will allow the rotors to de-synchronise, causing the rotor blades to strike each other catastrophically. It will also result in a total loss of power to one rotor while still driving the other. The loss of lift from the undriven rotor will cause a major pitch-up or down of the helicopter and loss of control. Transmission failures in tandem rotor helicopters have invariably proved fatal.

Intermeshing rotor

Intermeshing rotor helicopters combine the drive and synchronisation of their rotors into one gearbox and are thus dependent on fewer components. The failure however of any transmission component will cause the rotors to destroy each other, with fatal results.

Co-axial rotor

Co-axial rotor helicopters also combine the drive of both rotors in one gearbox but do not have to maintain synchronisation. However, loss of drive to one rotor means that the helicopter will rotate rapidly due to the drive to the other rotor and autorotation must be entered quickly to stop this. An *engine-off landing* must then be carried out. The control of both rotors is also achieved through a very complicated mechanism, failure of which would be disastrous.

Single-main-rotor

Single-main-rotor helicopters, as has been mentioned before, are vulnerable to loss of drive to, or control of, the tail rotor and this could be compared to transmission failures in the contra-rotating types. The loss of tail rotor effectiveness is not however catastrophic since it can be overcome by auto-rotating to the surface and making an engine-off landing. This is still a serious emergency and its success will depend on the surface the helicopter is flying over, but a safe landing has been achieved many times throughout the history of helicopter flight.

A recent improvement in the design of single-main-rotor helicopters has been the elimination of the exposed tail rotor in the *Notar* design by McDonnell-Douglas. This replaces the tail rotor by a ducted fan in the tail boom, with axial slots which induce an airflow around the boom and a variable outlet at the tail to provide control. This design is now in production and has shown great safety improvements in confined area operations and to other possibilities of in-flight contact dangers, as well as providing a welcome reduction in the helicopter's noise.

HOVER PERFORMANCE

Helicopters require more power to hover than for forward flight. Helicopter Approved Flight Manuals contain performance graphs which allow a pilot to calculate the maximum aircraft weight at which he can hover depending on his height above the ground, and the atmospheric conditions in which he will be operating. The maximum power available for use is determined by the power the engines can produce and the strength of the transmission components.

The power required to hover is determined by the weight of the loaded helicopter, its height above the ground, the altitude and air temperature. The graphs take all these aspects into account and also include an allowance for windspeed.

When a helicopter is very close to the ground it requires less power to hover. This is known as hovering *inside ground effect* (IGE). This *ground effect* is greatest when the helicopter is just touching the ground, becoming negligible at about $1\frac{1}{2}$ rotor diameters above the ground. Above this height the helicopter is said to be *outside ground effect* (OGE) or in a *free-air hover*. For a typical large helicopter, hovering at 10 feet above the ground requires 13 per cent less power than an OGE hover, while hovering at 20 feet the saving is only 9 per cent.

As has already been mentioned, helicopters require more power to hover than to maintain forward flight. This is because rotor efficiency increases as forward airspeed is gained, and so the power required to maintain level flight decreases. This continues up to about 70 mph (110 kph) which is known as *minimum power speed* (often referred to as V_y or V_{broc}). Any further increase in forward speed above V_y requires increased power to overcome the increase in drag. To maintain level flight at *minimum power speed*, a typical helicopter requires about half the power it would need in order to hover in the same conditions.

When a helicopter is hovering, the pilot normally heads into the wind because this gives the helicopter "free" forward airspeed and improves its performance. Rearwards manoeuvring will, of course, negate any wind effect and thus require greater power and so will a transition into forward flight that has to be made out-of-wind.

Although the power requirement reduces as airspeed is gained, moving out of the hover requires additional power for a short time. To ensure adequate performance for transition to forward flight, take-off weight is usually calculated as the mean of OGE and IGE hover weight. A good rule-of-thumb in the absence of a performance calculation is to have 15 per cent power available over the power required to hover.

MULTI-ENGINE HELICOPTERS

Multi-engine helicopters are normally operated to Category "A" (FAA/JAA), or Group "A" (CAA), take-off performance rules. These restrict the aircraft's weight so that continued flight or a safe landing is always possible if one engine fails, using the phenomenon of a reducing power requirement up to *minimum power speed*. The helicopter will be able to hover comfortably with both engines operating but will probably not be able to maintain level flight below 30 mph airspeed on one engine (OEI—one engine inoperative).

The take-off is the most critical phase of flight because the helicopter is at its heaviest, having not used any fuel. If an engine fails while a helicopter is hovering it sinks back onto the ground or heli-deck, but once the transition from the hover to forward flight has started, there may be a period during which the helicopter cannot safely fly away on one engine and a landing must be made. This is called a *rejected take-off* and requires a cleared area to be available along the take-off path. A *take-off decision point* (TDP) during the take-off profile determines the course of action; if an engine fails before decision point the helicopter must land, after decision point it can safely fly away, but allowance must be made for the lower angle of climb because of the reduced power available.

Despite the emphasis placed on training for engine failures during take-off, they are comparatively rare and more accidents probably occur while training for them.

AUTOROTATION

Helicopters developed from the autogyro, the difference between them being that engine power is used to force air down through the helicopter's rotor, while the airflow through the autogyro's unpowered rotor is always upward. Autogyros cannot hover and need a conventional propeller for propulsion.

If a helicopter loses all engine power it can be flown as an autogyro but, lacking propulsion, it must descend. This condition is known as *autorotation* since the rotors rotate of their own accord. It relies on the pilot reducing collective pitch to its minimum setting as soon as power is lost otherwise the rotors will slow down rapidly. If the rotor speed is allowed to fall below the *autorotative range*, it cannot be regained without engine power; the rotors will stop turning and the helicopter will fall out of control.

In autorotation a helicopter will descend at about 1,000 to 1,500 feet per minute. The descent will normally be made into wind in order to reduce ground speed and at an airspeed of 60 to 90 mph to obtain the minimum rate of descent, although higher or lower speeds can be used if required. The angle of glide is fairly steep and, from normal cruising height, will limit the choice of landing place to within a radius of a mile or so. On approaching the ground, the helicopter's forward speed and rate of descent can be reduced to zero by adopting a nose-up attitude in a flare manoeuvre. If correctly judged, this will place the helicopter about 10 feet above the surface and the remaining rotor energy can then be used to cushion the touchdown by increasing collective pitch.

The resulting landing will be smooth and, with little or no forward speed, requires a level space little larger than the helicopter itself but, although theoretically possible, autorotative landings should not be attempted to elevated helipads or offshore platforms since the price of misjudgement would be disaster. However, with the assistance of fixed or inflatable emergency floats, autorotative landings can be made successfully onto water.

If a zero or low forward speed autorotation has to be made, airspeed must be increased before reaching a low altitude in order to provide sufficient energy for the flare. The dive to increase airspeed must not be left too late, as it causes the rate of descent to increase dramatically.

Autorotative landings are very skill- and judgement-dependent and require regular practice. This forms part of the routine competency check for pilots of single-engined helicopters. Although a total engine failure in a multi-engined helicopter is unlikely, autorotative landings may still be necessary under certain circumstances, such as a tail-rotor drive or control failure, so pilots should remain in practice. The normal multi-engined practice procedure is to descend in autorotation to the final flare height, at which point the engines are restored and the helicopter brought to the hover or climbed away. In this way the handling of the descent and judgement of the landing site can be practised without the danger of damaging the aircraft in a poorly judged autorotative touchdown.

Autorotations would be required in the event of a transmission failure or, more likely, effective loss of the tail rotor due to a drive shaft or control system failure or damage to a tail rotor blade, with the resulting vibration causing the entire tail rotor assembly to detach. Without a tail rotor to counteract the main rotor drive torque, the helicopter will spin uncontrollably unless it is put into autorotation.

MULTI-ENGINE VERSUS SINGLE-ENGINE

The obvious advantage of multi-engined helicopters is that they can continue to fly after an engine fails, provided they are operated to Group A or Category A rules. This is of greater importance if the helicopter is being operated over water or inhospitable terrain such as jungle or mountains, or over densely populated areas. There are however some commercial disadvantages to operating multi-engined helicopters which should be borne in mind.

The first is cost. Powerplants and transmissions form a high proportion of the cost of a helicopter and the duplication of these items in a multi-engined helicopter increases the purchase price considerably.

Secondly, the price of multi-engined safety is a reduced payload compared to the equivalent single-engined helicopter. If a multi-engined helicopter is operated as if it were a single, its payload will be no bigger but its likelihood of an engine failure, and an accident, will be greater simply because it has more engines. Since there is no question of a single continuing to fly if its power-plant fails, its load, unlike a Group A or Category A multi-engined helicopter, is only restricted by the maximum power available and, with only one power-plant, the probability of an engine failure is less.

THE VERSATILE HELICOPTER

Advantages

The nature of the helicopter allows it to carry out tasks that no other single vehicle can. As more powerful and efficient engines, transmissions and rotor blades are designed, so the helicopter's radius of action (range) and capability at that radius increases. If the helicopter cannot land at its destination, it can hover at a reduced weight and transfer its load by hoist or long-line. The capabilities of the helicopter are almost limitless provided that proper planning is used, the performance rules are obeyed, and excessive skill and judgement is not required of the crew. The advantages of using helicopters for many of the most common tasks are those of speed over difficult terrain to inaccessible locations (Search and Rescue), access without damaging environmentally sensitive areas (logging), relatively comfortable transportation over difficult routes (oil and gas exploration) and time saving transport into city centres.

HELICOPTER ROLES

Overland operations

A variety of *onshore* helicopter roles, and some of their operating characteristics are described below:

Private

Helicopters flown in the *private* category include the relatively cheap, economical, and lightweight single-engine types such as the piston-engined Robinson R22 Beta and R44 Astro, Schweizer 300, Enstrom F280 Shark, and Bell 47. These machines are often owned by the pilot and flown from small helipads for pleasure and business travel. In general, both their performance and equipment standards are modest and they are best suited to short-range day VFR flying in reasonably good weather.

Air taxi and corporate work

This group includes the faster turbine machines such as the single-engine Eurocopter AS350 Squirrel and the ubiquitous turbine-engined Bell 206 Jet Ranger. For longer range routes, including cross-Channel and trans-European work, corporate users may prefer the additional safety and the IFR capability offered by twin turbine machines. These include the Eurocopter AS355 (Twin

Squirrel), Eurocopter BO105 and the Agusta 109, all of which may be flown *single-pilot*. The role requires the crew to be both flexible to meet the changeable demands of their clients, and resolute in resisting pressures to fly in conditions beyond the capabilities of the aircraft. Landing and take-off areas may include international airports, race courses, factory sites and hotel grounds.

Pilot training—civil and military

Civil helicopter operators provide *ab initio* training for both civil and military pilots. In the UK, the low purchase and operating costs of the piston-engined Robinson R22 Beta make it a popular choice for low-budget training up to Private Pilot's Licence (PPL) or Commercial Pilot's Licence (CPL) standard. Military *ab initio* training favours the use of single turbine machines such as the Eurocopter AS 350 Squirrel. Prior to commencing any flying training, military organisations are able to filter their trainee pilots by the use of ground aptitude testing. By contrast, a civil training school may find itself occasionally in the more hazardous position of attempting to teach a self-funded pilot with inadequate natural skills.

The training role makes heavy demands on both the flying instructor and the helicopter. The former must remain alert at all times for unexpected student reactions and the latter should be tolerant of mishandling and occasional abuse. Exercises such as landing on sloping ground, landing from an autorotation following a simulated engine failure, and confined area operation must be introduced into the student pilot's repertoire but all require extremely precise handling and fine judgement.

Transmission line and pipeline inspection

Regular inspection of electricity transmission lines and pipelines from a helicopter is an efficient means of identifying faults, leaks or encroaching building developments. Smaller single or twin types with a crew of one pilot and an observer are employed in this role. The unique nature of this work dictates that the pilot fly at low level (a typical operating height for checking low voltage transmission lines is 50 feet), at a relatively slow groundspeed to allow adequate inspection time, and in a direction dictated by the line taken by the cables or pipes. Depending on the prevailing wind, this may mean operating under conditions which require an exceptionally high degree of flying skill to effect a safe recovery or landing following an engine failure, and the pilot attempts continuously to update his mental contingency plan for such an event.

Other VFR overland roles

Other VFR roles well-suited to the smaller helicopter are photography and aerial sequence filming, crop spraying, livestock herding, traffic information services, Emergency Medical Services (EMS), and police support. General underslung cargo work includes the short range lifting of fish fry, forestry seedlings, stones, animal feed, ski lift supports, transmission line poles, buckets of concrete, air conditioning units, and many other items.

Each role has its associated hazards. For instance, crop spraying involves continual vigorous manoeuvring at low level, often in the vicinity of wires, whilst the police support helicopter may be required to work at low airspeed over built-up areas at night. Many tasks require the helicopter to operate in hilly terrain where the ground contours can create turbulence and unexpected changes in wind strength and direction. The advantage of carrying loads underslung beneath the helicopter under these circumstances is that, as a last resort, the pilot can jettison it immediately if a sudden loss of performance occurs.

Larger twin-engined machines are used for logging and the support of oil exploration work in remote areas. Where forest fires are a natural hazard and a source of water is readily available, authorities use specially adapted machines for fire suppression. The helicopter hovers low over a lake and water is pumped rapidly into a large internal tank via a suspended pipe dipped under the surface. The contents of the tank are dumped on to the fire in a controlled manner to provide optimum suppression.

Offshore operations

The primary offshore role of the civil helicopter is the support of the oil industry although other tasks, such as lighthouse re-supply, ship/shore transfer of harbour pilots, Search and Rescue (SAR), and support of naval exercises, are carried out by civil operators.

Non-hostile sea areas

For economic reasons, single turbine-engined machines equipped with emergency floats are used for supporting offshore oil fields located in waters regarded as *non-hostile* in terms of sea state, temperature, and weather predictability (for example, the Gulf of Mexico). The flights are made under VFR, enabling significant cost savings in equipment and crew training to be made.

Hostile sea areas

Oil fields located in *hostile* sea areas (e.g. North Sea, Atlantic, and the South China Sea), are supported by medium sized twin-engined helicopters equipped to operate under IFR and fitted with a variety of emergency survival and location aids. The most economical machine for the job will depend on the range and payload required by the chartering company. In the North Sea, the Eurocopter AS332L Super Puma dominates the long range market and is capable of transporting 18 workers and their baggage a distance of 300 miles.

Offshore approaches in poor visibility and/or low cloud

Many airfields are equipped with an *Instrument Landing System* (ILS). This is an accurately calibrated radio beam guidance system which may be used by the IFR helicopter pilot in conditions of poor visibility and/or low cloud to fly his aircraft down to a point 200 feet above, and just short of, the runway threshold. Except in conditions of thick fog, the pilot will see the runway approach lights at this point and will be able to transfer his attention from the cockpit instruments to the outside visual references to complete the landing. However, at the present time, no precision system similar to ILS is available to provide a helicopter pilot with approach guidance to an offshore installation in bad weather.

A non-precision approach can be made in IMC using the helicopter's weather radar, providing other rigs or vessels are not close enough to confuse the radar picture. Most offshore installations are equipped with a non-directional beacon (NDB). The pilot will use his on-board automatic direction finding (ADF) to obtain a bearing to the NDB and crosscheck this with the rig's relative position given by the area navigation equipment. Providing that this information ties up with a return on the weather radar display, and there are no obstructions within a specified area around the rig, the pilot may carry out the airborne radar approach (ARA) procedure. The crew uses the radar display continuously to derive the approximate range and bearing of the destination during the final approach.

Offshore operating problems

Having established visual contact with his destination installation, the offshore helicopter pilot is faced with a number of operating problems to consider during the landing and take-off phases. Almost every offshore installation has a different configuration and each presents a unique operating environment to the pilot.

Deck motion on mobile installations presents the pilot with additional difficulties. First, the pilot must synchronise the movement of the helicopter with that of the deck and then choose the optimum moment for touchdown. At night, with limited outside visual cues, this is a demanding task. Secondly, once on the deck, and before the disembarkation of passengers commences, the pilot must ensure that the helicopter is secure and will not slide if the deck rolls or pitches.

Shuttling

When a pilot makes a series of landings and take-offs to a number of decks in the same general area, this is known as a *shuttling*. In some multi-platform oilfields, passengers are flown from land to one of the platforms by a long range helicopter, and then shuttled to their individual destinations by a small twin machine based offshore. In addition, the small machine will often provide a daily *bus service* to transfer personnel between installations around the field.

Commercial air transport winching

There are occasions when it is not possible to land a helicopter on an installation but the transfer of personnel is deemed to be essential. For instance, a mechanical breakdown on the installation may require the immediate attention of a specialist engineer but its deck motion may be excessive. Alternatively, the deck may be blocked by an unserviceable helicopter, or a vessel's helideck may be too small for the only machine available. In these cases, personnel are winched up and down from a helicopter but strictly in accordance with a set of *Commercial Air Transport* rules. Since these are not emergency situations, the helicopter must be able to suffer an engine, hoist or hoist cable failure during the transfer without causing serious injury to personnel.

Other offshore tasks

Other tasks the offshore pilot may be called upon to perform include underslung load work (e.g. changing a flare tip), *open-door* photography and emergency missions. Emergency tasks might require a casualty with a head injury to be transferred rapidly at night and low level to an onshore hospital or the mass evacuation of all personnel from an installation in the path of a typhoon in the South China Sea.

Miscellaneous helicopter roles

Search and Rescue

The role of a civil Search and Rescue (SAR) team is characterised by long periods of boredom punctuated by short bursts of extreme excitement. Both aircraft and crews must be in a continuous state of readiness to react to a call-out within the agreed response time. Typically, a unit providing 24-hour SAR cover will be required to be airborne within 15 minutes during the day and 45 minutes at night but much shorter times are often achieved. Some SAR units have an *operating patch* that includes mountains, coastal cliffs and large sea areas. Crews must be conversant with a variety of specialised rescue techniques, and must work closely as a team to choose and execute the most appropriate course of action as soon as they arrive on the scene. The rescue plan may be constrained by the helicopter's performance in adverse weather conditions or by the close proximity of an obstruction such as a cliff face or violently oscillating yacht mast. Compromises must be considered quickly and comparative risks must be assessed before deciding on the best option.

Test flights

The civil helicopter pilot is often required to carry out post-maintenance test flights. This requirement may arise after a major component change (e.g. a main gearbox) to diagnose an elusive intermittent system fault, or to assess the effect on vibration of an adjustment to the rotor system. Additionally, there may be a requirement by the local regulatory body to perform a periodic airworthiness test flight on each machine in the fleet to check that engine and rotor performance levels have been retained, and that handling characteristics and systems operating standards have not degraded with the passage of time.

Support roles

The civil operator may be contracted to provide a variety of support roles including:

- Support of Antarctic research work;
- Stores resupply for military exercises and missile firing ranges;
- Support of United Nations peace-keeping work;
- Support of offshore fishing fleets.

HELICOPTER EQUIPMENT

The equipment fitted to a helicopter is dictated by the role in which it is to be used. The following paragraphs are intended to give an overview of equipment in current use.

Automatic flight control systems

Helicopters do not have the natural stability associated with fixed wing aeroplanes. If an automatic flight control system (AFCS) is not fitted, the pilot continually must apply small control corrections on the cyclic stick, the collective lever, and the yaw pedals to prevent the machine diverting from the desired flight condition.

Modern multi-engined transport machines are fitted with electronic "autopilots" which enable the pilot to fly "hands-off" for extended periods. These AFCS provide *attitude* stabilisation where the equipment retains in memory the exact attitude and heading set by the pilot and, in the event of an external disturbance, automatically returns the aircraft smoothly to this datum condition.

Navigation systems

In the past, navigating helicopters has been achieved using a map, conventional aeronautical beacons (VORs, DME and NDBs), or relatively complicated, quirky and expensive area navaids such as DECCA, OMEGA/VLF, or LORAN. Today, the trend is towards the use of Global Positioning Satellite (GPS) systems which provide worldwide coverage and extremely high accuracy at an amazingly low cost. GPS receivers are small, lightweight and require little electrical power to function so they are very attractive to all categories of helicopter operations.

CVFDR

Cockpit Voice and Flight Data Recorders (CVFDR) are a mandatory requirement for medium-sized public transport helicopters in the UK. Typically, these crash-resistant digital *black box* recorders provide accident investigators with at least five hours of pre-accident flight data and one hour of cockpit voice recordings. All vital parameters are recorded, each at an appropriate sampling rate, including all control positions, attitudes, accelerations, airspeed, altitude, engine and rotor speeds, landing gear position, navigational information, fuel state, etc. In offshore helicopters, an acoustic beacon is attached to the CVFDR to facilitate its location underwater.

Icing

Helicopters are susceptible to various adverse icing effects at temperatures below around +5°C whenever moisture is present.

Under critical temperature and humidity atmospheric conditions, piston engines are liable to *carburettor icing* and are protected by a carburettor air heating system. The pilot must monitor conditions carefully to ensure that heat is selected "on" before carb icing occurs and "off" before demanding a high power setting.

Similarly, ice may build up inside the air intakes of turbine engines due to the drop in temperature that occurs in a venturi. If this ice subsequently breaks off in sizeable chunks and passes into the engine, flame-out may occur. Preventative design measures include heated surfaces inside the intake to prevent accretion, sharp bends in the intake duct with "escape paths" to allow ice chunks to be expelled, and continuous ignition that immediately reignites the engine in the event of flame-out.

When flying at temperatures below 0°C in cloud or freezing rain, super-cooled water droplets freeze instantly on contact with main and tail rotor blades. As the ice forms around the leading edge of the blade, its aerofoil shape is changed and its ability to produce thrust is reduced.

In addition to rotor icing, ice may build up on any forward facing surface of the airframe causing a gradual increase in the weight of the helicopter. Ultimately, the combined icing effects of reduced lift and increased weight may lead to an enforced descent.

Health and Usage Monitoring Systems (HUMS)

Health and Usage Monitoring Systems (HUMS) have been installed in many UK public transport helicopters although, at the present time, they are not mandatory. Each aircraft is fitted with a number of sensors which enable gearbox vibration, rotor track and balance characteristics, and any parameter exceedences to be recorded automatically during every flight. After each flight, the data are downloaded and processed to provide the engineers with a clear picture of any changes in the helicopter's mechanical *signature*.

Since HUMS can detect the vibration characteristics of every gearbox shaft and bearing, any deterioration in condition beyond a predetermined threshold (e.g. a chip in a gear tooth or a worn bearing) is highlighted. Complex rotor diagnostics computer programs analyse the recorded rotor track and balance data and indicate when maintenance actions are required. To minimise the risk of human error, the diagnostics program also quantifies the amount of adjustment required and where it should be applied.

Exceedences are logged to ensure components damaged inadvertently are not allowed to continue in service without inspection.

Safety equipment

As the offshore helicopter business has evolved, the emphasis on safety, survivability and minimisation of risk has increased. Numerous safety systems have been developed and some of these in current use are:

- Automatic tracking of helicopters using satellite communications;
- Automatically deployed emergency location transmitters (ADELT) and crash position indicators (CPI). These are ejected from the helicopter in the event of a ditching and radiate emergency radio signals;
- Automatically deployed flotation systems (AFDS) to prevent capsize after ditching;
- Automatically activated emergency lighting to assist the location of escape exits underwater;
- "Reversible" liferafts that cannot inflate upside down;
- Effective lifejackets for crew and passengers that will hold a survivor's head above the water;
- Well-sealed survival suits for crew and passengers;
- Compulsory realistic sea survival training for all crew and passengers including the use of helicopter underwater escape trainers (HUET).

HELICOPTER ACCIDENT—MAIN CAUSES

In recent years, the causes of UK commercial air transport helicopter accidents have been established with increased confidence due to the availability of pre-crash flight data and cockpit voice recordings obtained from the CVFDR. Invariably, several contributing factors may be revealed during the investigation and the absence of any one of them may have prevented the accident. As a very over-simplified guide, the primary cause of helicopter accidents is likely to fall into one of two categories:

- Those due to one or more *human factors*; and
- Those due to a technical failure.

Human factors may include fatigue, frustration, indisciplined flying, poor crew cooperation in a multi-crew environment, over-reliance on inadequate visual cues, and physical discomfort. Typically, these factors may lead to controlled flight into terrain (CFIT), misjudgement of power requirements, wire strikes and loss of control in marginal weather conditions.

Where possible, critical systems and components are duplicated to provide *redundancy* in the event of a single *technical failure*. However, it is not feasible to duplicate the transmission and rotor systems, and failures in these areas may be catastrophic. In order to meet the defined airworthiness requirements, the designer must convince the authorities by statistical argument that a failure in these critical systems will be *extremely improbable*.

FUTURE DEVELOPMENTS

Areas in which technological advances will bring benefits to the helicopter industry in the future are impossible to predict with any accuracy. The introduction of new aviation technology involves costly and lengthy research and development programmes followed by extensive flight testing to demonstrate safety and reliability.

Helicopter airframe manufacturers are faced with difficult decisions when considering the specification of their next production model:

(1) They must anticipate what the market will require many years ahead. The gestation period of a new machine will depend on its complexity and the maturity of its technology but somewhere between five and 15 years would be typical. Experience has shown that attempts to introduce too many innovative ideas into a new machine have led either to over-extended development periods or an under-developed helicopter. Either way, customer dissatisfaction is assured. Manufacturers have realised that although "new" machines must offer an incremental improvement over their previous model, they must combine proven design and technology with

just a few innovative features. For example, it would be extremely risky for a manufacturer to introduce a new airframe and install a new engine design.

(2) For maximum sales, they must produce a multi-role machine suitable for both military and civil applications. However, the ensuing and inevitable design compromises must not degrade significantly its capabilities in any single role.

(3) They must exploit the advantages of new technology and materials but minimise the associated risks.

(4) A manufacturer is obliged to build its helicopters to airworthiness standards specified by their regulating authority (e.g. FAA, JAA). However, there may be variations in these standards according to whether it is deemed to be a "new" type or merely a variant of a previous model. This decision has both cost and development time implications and does not necessarily encourage an innovative approach.

(5) New helicopters are extremely expensive. Old helicopters can be maintained in excellent airworthy condition for many years and many thousands of flight hours. Therefore, new helicopters must provide operators with convincing economic and performance benefits to justify large investments in their purchases.

In recent years, the evolution of the civil helicopter has been gradual. Each new helicopter has yielded small improvements in hover performance, forward speed, cruise economy and reliability but there have been no giant steps. The helicopter world has not seen its equivalents of the Concorde (for speed), of the Boeing 747 (for range, comfort and capacity), and of the Airbus family of "fly-by-wire" machines (for technical sophistication). The civil tilt-rotor may be on the horizon and holds some promise, but such a large technology jump will be accompanied by great risks through its maturing years.

In comparison with the huge worldwide market for fixed wing aeroplane equipment, the potential market for equipment specifically designed for use in helicopters is tiny and fraught with risk for manufacturers with new ideas. Hence the funding of new helicopter technology is entirely dependent on a guarantee that it will provide an adequate return on the investment within the accountants' prevailing definition of a reasonable time. In the past, such guarantees have often proved elusive.

Some of the possible future improvements might include the following:

EFIS

Electronic Flight Instrument Systems (EFIS) replace the conventional electro-mechanical instruments that have provided pilots with flight and systems information ever since the inception of the helicopter. EFIS displays are based on colour CRT or LCD technology and enable many flight parameters to be presented together within a small area. No common standard has yet evolved for the format of these displays and work has to be done to realise their full potential.

Lightning protection

With the increased use of composite materials in rotor blades and structures, parallel work on the understanding of lightning strike mechanisms, and the protection of critical components from catastrophic damage, must be carried out.

DGPS

Differential Global Positioning Satellite (DGPS) systems offer the civil aviation industry a relative cheap means of enhancing the accuracy of GPS navigation to provide precision flight guidance throughout an approach to a landing. In essence, a differential system requires two GPS receivers; one in the aircraft and one in a known position on the ground, plus some form of data link between the two. This arrangement enables most of the position errors inherent in the data to be removed and guidance accuracies within a few metres are feasible. Such an arrangement would appear to offer the offshore helicopter industry the basis for developing a much safer and more accurate means of approaching a rig in poor visibility. There is a possibility that GPS accuracy may be degraded in the vicinity of large metal structures and the level of approval given to an offshore DGPS-based approach system will depend upon the confidence with which any adverse effects can be quantified.

DEFINITIONS

Definitions are used to achieve accuracy and brevity. Their application may be mandatory, as in ICAO Annexes, or may be agreed by two parties to a commercial agreement. An awareness of different sets of definitions is important in order to avoid conflict in their use.

Examples of definitions in civil aviation include the following:

1. ICAO

Definitions as used in the Annexes are part of the Material comprising the Annex proper. They are "definitions of terms used in the SARPS which are not self explanatory in that they do not have accepted dictionary meanings. A Definition does not have an independent status but is an essential part of each SARP in which the term is used, since a change in the meaning of the terms would affect the specification."

On 13 April 1948 ICAO Council adopted a resolution inviting the attention of Contracting States to the desirability of using in their own national regulations, as far as is practicable, the precise language of those ICAO standards that are of a regulatory character.

The ICAO publication "International Civil Aviation Vocabulary" (doc. 9317) contains ICAO definitions found in the ICAO Lexicon (doc. 9294–1) and ICAO Definitions (doc. 9569).

2. IATA

IATA uses definitions in a number of its documents, for example in the GCC Pax and also in the CC Cargo. The Airport Handling Manual has its own glossary.

3. Airline Industry Standard World Airlines Technical Operations Glossary (WATOG)

This glossary is produced by ATA, IATA and ICCAIA. It defines terms such as those used in maintenance procedures and contractual documents.

4. Contractual definitions applied on an ad hoc basis

An example of such definitions is found in the Aircraft Insurance Policy AVN 1C 21.12.98 given in Appendix 5 below.

RESOLUTION A23–13 OF ICAO ASSEMBLY ON LEASE, CHARTER AND INTERCHANGE OF AIRCRAFT IN INTERNATIONAL OPERATIONS

Whereas it is in the general interest of international civil aviation that arrangements for lease, charter and interchange of aircraft, particulary aircraft without crew, be facilitated;

Whereas the international provisions in force contain no absolute impediment to the implementation of such arrangements;

Whereas inter alia, Annex 6 to the Convention on International Civil Aviation does not prevent the State of Registry from delegating to another State the authority to exercise the functions incumbent upon it pursuant to that Annex;

Whereas such delegation may facilitate the implementation of arrangements for lease, charter and interchange of aircraft, particularly aircraft without crew;

Whereas such delegation may only be made without prejudice to the rights of third States;

Whereas the Convention on International Civil Aviation was developed prior to the widespread application of international lease, charter and interchange of aircraft, particularly aircraft without crew;

Whereas the Convention on International Civil Aviation places on a State of Registry responsibilities that it can fulfil when the aircraft is operated by an operator of that State, as is normally the case, but it may be unable to fulfil adequately in instances where an aircraft registered in that State is leased, chartered or interchanged, particularly without crew, by an operator of another State;

Whereas the Convention on International Civil Aviation may not adequately specify the rights and obligations of the State of an operator of the aircraft leased, chartered or interchanged, in particular without crew, until such time as the amendment to the Convention (Article 83bis) enters into force;

Whereas the safety and economics of international air transportation may be adversely affected by the lack of clearly defined responsibilities for aircraft leased, chartered or interchanged, in particular without crew, under the existing provisions of the Convention on International Civil Aviation;

Whereas the instances of lease, charter and interchange of aircraft have substantially risen in number, thus presenting serious problems;

Whereas the provisions in the Annexes to the Convention on International Civil Aviation relating to the delegation of authority from one State to another to exercise certain functions may only be invoked without prejudice to rights of third States;

Whereas the law of certain Contracting States is not further adapted to this situation; and

Whereas the basic problem of ultimate responsibility of the State of Registry in this matter remains unresolved until such time as the amendment to the Convention (Article 83bis) enters into force;

The Assembly:

1. *Commends* the Council for the measures taken thus far in order to facilitate the lease, charter and interchange of aircraft, on the one hand by adopting various amendments to the Annexes to the Chicago Convention and on the other by commissioning the study of an appropriate agreed text by a working group and then by a special subcommittee of the Legal Committee;

2. *Declares* that the matter of lease, charter and interchange of aircraft continues to present various problems which need solution;

3. *Urges* that, where arrangements for the lease, charter and interchange of aircraft—particularly aircraft without crew—would be facilitated, the State of Registry of such an aircraft, to the extent considered necessary, delegate to the State of the Operator its functions under Annex 6 to the Convention on International Civil Aviation;

4. *Urges* that in such cases, the State of the Operator change, if necessary, its national regulations to the extent required to empower it both to accept such delegation of functions and to oblige the operator to fulfil the obligations imposed by Annex 6;

5. *Invites* all Contracting States, the provisions of whose laws inhibit the lease, charter or interchange of aircraft, to review in due time such provisions with a view to removing those inhibitions and extending their powers in order to better enable them to exercise the new functions and duties which could be placed upon them as State of the Operator; and

6. *Declares* that this resolution supersedes Resolutions A18–16, A21–22 and A22–28.

APPENDIX 3

ICAO ANNEX 14: TABLE OF CONTENTS

APPENDIX 4

IATA

1. IATA was incorporated in 1945 by Canadian Act of Parliament. It has its head office in Montreal, Canada and its executive office in Geneva, Switzerland.

2. Under Article 3 of the Act of Incorporation, its purposes, objects and aims are:

   (a) to promote safe, regular and economical air transport for the benefit of the peoples of the world, to foster air commerce and to study the problems connected therewith;
   (b) to provide means for collaboration among air transport enterprises engaged directly or indirectly in international air transport service;
   (c) to co-operate with the International Civil Aviation Organization and other international organizations.

3. The activities of IATA are regulated by its Articles of Association which include the following:

   (a) Article V.1 establishes categories of membership which are:
      (i) Active Member: any airline operating an international air service; and
      (ii) Associate Member: any airline operating an air service other than an international air service.
      The Article contains further qualifications and rules for membership.
   (b) Article VI empowers the Board of Governors to establish a class of membership known as "IATA Affiliates".
   (c) Article VIII.1 establishes that a General Meeting of members of IATA is vested with the ultimate authority to exercise all the powers of IATA.
   (d) Article VIII.2 establishes an executive committee to be known as the "Board of Governors". Such Board is authorised to exercise all such powers of IATA which are not by law, the Act of Incorporation or these Articles required to be exercised by a General Meeting. The Board is accountable to a General Meeting.
   (e) Article IX.3.c empowers Annual General Meetings to establish Standing Committees, Conferences and such other groups and subordinate bodies as it considers appropriate and to confirm the membership of the standing committees.
   (f) Article XII.3 sets out the functions of the Board of Governors. In particular in (c) the Board shall be vested with executive powers and duties, including the general management and control of the business affairs, finance and property of IATA.

4. There are four Standing Committees: Cargo Committee; Industry Affairs Committee; Financial Committee and Operations Committee. Special and Other Committees include Information Management Committee, Environment Task Force and Council on Human Resource Development.

5. Many decisions relating to the achievement of the aims and objects of IATA are taken by the IATA Traffic Conferences. The conduct of the Conferences is set out in the Provisions for the Conduct of the IATA Traffic Conferences, certain of which are referred to below:

I   1. The Traffic Conferences for passenger matters are:
    (i) Passenger Procedures Conference comprising:
        • Passenger Services Conference;
        • Passenger Agency Conference;
    (ii) Passenger Tariff Co-ordinating Conferences comprising the Conferences for the designated geographical areas.
   2. The Traffic Conferences for cargo matters are:
    (i) Cargo Procedures Conferences comprising:
        • Cargo Services Conference;
        • Cargo Agency Conference;
    (ii) Cargo Tariff Co-ordinating Conferences comprising the Conferences dealing with the tariffs for the designated geographical areas.

II   deals with the rights and duties relating to membership of Active Members and non-voting membership of Associate Members.

IV   The aims and objects of the Traffic Conferences shall be those of IATA.
IV.3(i) provides that the Passenger Services Conference shall take action on matters relating to passenger services including passenger and baggage handling, documentation, procedures, rules and regulations . . . ; IV.3(ii) provides that the Passenger Agency Conference shall take action on all matters between airlines and recognised passenger sales agents and other intermediaries, but excluding remuneration levels.
IV.4(i) and (ii) deal with responsibilities and functions of the Cargo Services and Cargo Agency Conferences.
IV.5–9 deal with the duties and functions of the Tariff Co-ordinating Conferences.

X   deals with Committees and Working Groups. For example, the terms of reference of the Airport Services Committee is to develop recommendations to simplify and improve passenger and baggage handling and other procedures and systems, and to provide overall policy, direction and general management for airport standards and procedures. It shall publish its recommendations concerning ramp services in the IATA Airport Handling Manual (Recommended Practice 1690).

XII   deals with compliance of the IATA Members with the provisions of the Regulations and the Resolutions of the various Conferences as specified.
Examples of Resolutions and Recommendations of the Conferences are: Resolution 724: Passenger Ticket—Notices and Conditions of Carriage; and Recommended Practice 1724: General Conditions of Carriage (Passenger and Baggage).

6. While IATA uses the term "Recommended Practice", this phrase must not be confused with the recommended practices of the SARPS. SARPS are applied under treaties between sovereign States and to the extent of Articles 37 and 38 of the Chicago Convention impose an obligation on all member States. IATA Resolutions, Standards and Practices apply only to its members or to those who otherwise agree to be bound by them.

7. Publications of IATA are listed in its Products and Services Catalogue. They include those publications considered in this book such as Dangerous Goods Regulations 37th Edition effective 1 January 1996. Section 1 of such Regulations explains in

1.1.4 that they contain all the requirements of the ICAO Technical Instructions. (See Annex 18, comment 6, page 205 above.) IATA has included additional requirements which are more restrictive than the Technical Instructions and reflect industry standard practices or operational considerations.

APPENDIX 5

POLICY AVN 1C 21.12.98

LONDON AIRCRAFT INSURANCE POLICY

Headings and marginal captions* are inserted for the purpose of convenient reference only and are not to be deemed part of this Policy.
Certain words and phrases used in this Policy have special meanings which can be found in Section IV(D) Definitions.

The Insurers agree to insure against loss, damage or liability, arising out of an Accident occurring during the Period of Insurance to the extent and in the manner provided in this Policy.

SECTION I LOSS OF OR DAMAGE TO AIRCRAFT

1. Coverage

(*a*) The Insurers will at their option pay for, replace or repair, accidental loss of or damage to the Aircraft described in the Schedule arising from the risks covered, including disappearance if the Aircraft is unreported for sixty days after the commencement of Flight, but not exceeding the Amount Insured as specified in Part 2(5) of the Schedule and subject to the amounts to be deducted specified in Condition 3(c).

(*b*) If the Aircraft is insured hereby for the risks of Flight, the Insurers will, in addition, pay reasonable emergency expenses necessarily incurred by the Insured for the immediate safety of the Aircraft consequent upon damage or forced landing, up to 10 per cent of the Amount Insured as specified in Part 2(5) of the Schedule.

2. Exclusions applicable to this Section only

The Insurers shall not be liable for

Wear and Tear, Breakdown
(*a*) wear and tear, deterioration, breakdown, defect or failure howsoever caused in any Unit of the Aircraft and the consequences thereof within such Unit;
(*b*) damage to any Unit by anything which has a progressive or cumulative effect but damage attributable to a single recorded incident is covered under paragraph 1 (*a*) above.

HOWEVER accidental loss of or damage to the Aircraft consequent upon 2 (*a*) or (*b*) above is covered under paragraph 1 (*a*) above.

---

 * Captions that appear in the margin in the original document have been set as italic shoulder headings in this Appendix.

3. Conditions applicable to this Section only

(*a*) If the Aircraft is damaged

Dismantling Transport and Repairs
(i)   no dismantling or repairs shall be commenced without the consent of the Insurers except whatever is necessary in the interests of safety, or to prevent further damage, or to comply with orders issued by the appropriate authority;

(ii)   the Insurers will pay only for repairs and transport of labour and materials by the most economical method unless the Insurers agree otherwise with the Insured.

Payment or Replacement
(*b*)   If the Insurers exercise their option to pay for or replace the Aircraft

(i)   the Insurers may take the Aircraft (together with all documents of record, registration and title thereto) as salvage;

(ii)   the cover afforded by this Section is terminated in respect of the Aircraft even if the Aircraft is retained by the Insured for valuable consideration or otherwise;

(iii) the replacement aircraft shall be of the same make and type and in reasonably like condition unless otherwise agreed with the Insured.

Amounts to be deducted from the claim
(*c*)   Except where the Insurers exercise their option to pay for or replace the Aircraft, there shall be deducted from the claim under paragraph 1 (*a*) of this Section

(i)   the amount specified in Part 6 (B) of the Schedule and

(ii)   such proportion of the Overhaul Cost of any Unit repaired or replaced as the used time bears to the Overhaul Life of the Unit.

No Abandonment
(*d*)   Unless the Insurers elect to take the Aircraft as salvage the Aircraft shall at all times remain the property of the Insured who shall have no right of abandonment to the Insurers.

Other Insurance
(*e*)   **No claim shall be payable under this Section if other Insurance which is payable in consequence of loss or damage covered under this Section has been or shall be effected by or on behalf of the Insured without the knowledge or consent of the Insurers.**

See also Section IV

SECTION II   LEGAL LIABILITY TO THIRD PARTIES (OTHER THAN PASSENGERS)

1. Coverage

The Insurers will indemnify the Insured for all sums which the Insured shall become legally liable to pay, and shall pay, as compensatory damages (including costs awarded against the Insured) in respect of accidental bodily injury (fatal or otherwise) and accidental damage to property caused by the Aircraft or by any person or object falling therefrom.

2. Exclusions applicable to this Section only

The Insurers shall not be liable for

Employees and Others
 (*a*) injury (fatal or otherwise) or loss sustained by any director or employee of the
  Insured or partner in the Insured's business whilst acting in the course of his
  employment with or duties for the Insured;

Operational Crew
 (*b*) injury (fatal or otherwise) or loss sustained by any member of the flight, cabin or
  other crew whilst engaged in the operation of the Aircraft;

Passengers
 (*c*) injury (fatal or otherwise) or loss sustained by any passenger whilst entering, on
  board, or alighting from the Aircraft;

Property
 (*d*) loss of or damage to any property belonging to or in the care, custody or control
  of the Insured;

Noise and Pollution and Other Perils
 (*e*) claims excluded by the attached Noise and Pollution and Other Perils Exclusion
  Clause.

3. Limit of Indemnity applicable to this Section

The liability of the Insurers under this Section shall not exceed the amount stated in
Part 6 (C) of the Schedule, less any amounts under Part 6 (B). The Insurers will defray
in addition any legal costs and expenses incurred with their written consent in defending any action which may be brought against the Insured in respect of any claim for
compensatory damages covered by this Section, but should the amount paid or
awarded in settlement of such claim exceed the Limit of Indemnity then the liability of
the Insurers in respect of such legal costs and expenses shall be limited to such
proportion of the said legal costs and expenses as the Limit of Indemnity bears to the
amount paid for compensatory damages.

See also Section IV

SECTION III LEGAL LIABILITY TO PASSENGERS

1. Coverage

The Insurers will indemnify the Insured in respect of all sums which the Insured shall
become legally liable to pay, and shall pay, as compensatory damages (including costs
awarded against the Insured) in respect of

(*a*) accidental bodily injury (fatal or otherwise) to passengers whilst entering, on
board, or alighting from the Aircraft and

(*b*) loss of or damage to baggage and personal articles of passengers arising out of an
Accident to the Aircraft.

Provided Always that

Documentary Precautions
(i) before a passenger boards the Aircraft the Insured shall take such measures as are necessary to exclude or limit liability for claims under (*a*) and (*b*) above to the extent permitted by law;

(ii) if the measures referred to in proviso (i) above include the issue of a passenger ticket/baggage check, the same shall be delivered correctly completed to the passenger a reasonable time before the passenger boards the Aircraft.

Effect of Non-Compliance
In the event of failure to comply with proviso (i) or (ii) the liability of the Insurers under this Section shall not exceed the amount of the legal liability, if any, that would have existed had the proviso been complied with.

2. Exclusions applicable to this Section only

The Insurers shall not be liable for injury (fatal or otherwise) or loss sustained by any

Employees and Others
(*a*) director or employee of the Insured or partner in the Insured's business whilst acting in the course of his employment with or duties for the Insured;

Operational Crew
(*b*) member of the flight, cabin or other crew whilst engaged in the operation of the Aircraft.

3. Limits of Indemnity applicable to this Section

The liability of the Insurers under this Section shall not exceed the amounts stated in Part 6 (C) of the Schedule, less any amounts under Part 6 (B). The Insurers will defray in addition any legal costs and expenses incurred with their written consent in defending any action which may be brought against the Insured in respect of any claim for compensatory damages covered by this Section, but should the amount paid or awarded in settlement of such claim exceed the Limit of Indemnity then the liability of the Insurers in respect of such legal costs and expenses shall be limited to such proportion of the said legal costs and expenses as the Limit of Indemnity bears to the amount paid for compensatory damages.

See also Section IV

SECTION IV

(A) GENERAL EXCLUSIONS APPLICABLE TO ALL SECTIONS

This Policy does not apply:

Illegal Uses
1. Whilst the Aircraft is being used for any illegal purpose of for any purpose other than those stated in Part 3 of the Schedule and as defined in the Definitions.

Geographical Limits
2.   Whilst the Aircraft is outside the geographical limits stated in Part 5 of the Schedule unless due to force majeure.

Pilots
3.   Whilst the Aircraft is being piloted by any person other than as stated in Part 4 of the Schedule except that the Aircraft may be operated on the ground by any person competent for that purpose.

Transportation by other Conveyance
4.   Whilst the Aircraft is being transported by any means of conveyance except as the result of an Accident giving rise to a claim under Section I of this Policy.

Landing and Take-Off Areas
5.   Whilst the Aircraft is landing on or taking off or attempting to do so from a place which does not comply with the recommendations laid down by the manufacturer of the Aircraft except as a result of force majeure.

Contractual Liability
6.   To liability assumed or rights waived by the Insured under any agreement (other than a passenger ticket/baggage check issued under Section III hereof) except to the extent that such liability would have attached to the Insured in the absence of such agreement.

Number of Passengers
7.   Whilst the total number of passengers being carried in the Aircraft exceeds the declared maximum number of passengers stated in Part 2(4) of the Schedule.

Non-Contribution
8.   To claims which are payable under any other policy or policies except in respect of any excess beyond the amount which would have been payable under such other policy or policies had this Policy not been effected.

Nuclear Risks
9.   To claims excluded by the attached Nuclear Risks Exclusion Clause.

War, Hijacking and Other Perils
10.   To claims caused by

(*a*)   War, invasion, acts of foreign enemies, hostilities (whether war be declared or not), civil war, rebellion, revolution, insurrection, martial law, military or usurped power or attempts at usurpation of power.

(*b*)   Any hostile detonation of any weapon of war employing atomic or nuclear fission and/or fusion or other like reaction or radioactive force or matter.

(*c*)   Strikes, riots, civil commotions or labour disturbances.

(*d*)   Any act of one or more persons, whether or not agents of a sovereign Power, for political or terrorist purposes and whether the loss or damage resulting therefrom is accidental or intentional.

(*e*)   Any malicious act or act of sabotage.

(*f*)   Confiscation, nationalisation, seizure, restraint, detention, appropriation, requisition for title or use by or under the order of any Government (whether civil military or de facto) or public or local authority.

(*g*)   Hijacking or any unlawful seizure or wrongful exercise of control of the Aircraft or crew in Flight (including any attempt at such seizure or control) made by any person or persons on board the Aircraft acting without the consent of the Insured.

Furthermore this Policy does not cover claims arising whilst the Aircraft is outside the control of the Insured by reason of any of the above perils.

The Aircraft shall be deemed to have been restored to the control of the Insured on the safe return of the Aircraft to the Insured at an airfield not excluded by the geographical limits of this Policy, and entirely suitable for the operation of the Aircraft (such safe return shall require that the Aircraft be parked with engines shut down and under no duress).

(B) CONDITIONS PRECEDENT APPLICABLE TO ALL SECTIONS

It is necessary that the Insured observes and fulfils the following Conditions before the Insurers have any liability to make any payment under this Policy.

Due Diligence
1.   The Insured shall at all times use due diligence and do and concur in doing everything reasonably practicable to avoid accidents and to avoid or diminish any loss hereon.

Compliance with Air Navigation Orders, etc.
2.   The Insured shall comply with all air navigation and airworthiness orders and requirements issued by any competent authority affecting the safe operation of the Aircraft and shall ensure that

(*a*)   the Aircraft is airworthy at the commencement of each Flight;
(*b*)   all Log Books and other records in connection with the Aircraft which are required by any official regulations in force from time to time shall be kept up to date and shall be produced to the Insurers or their Agents on request;
(*c*)   the employees and agents of the Insured comply with such orders and requirements.

Claims Procedure
3.   Immediate notice of any event likely to give rise to a claim under this Policy shall be given as stated in Part 8 of the Schedule. In all cases the Insured shall

(*a*)   furnish full particulars in writing of such event and forward immediately notice of any claim with any letters or documents relating thereto;

(*b*)   give notice of any impending prosecution;

(*c*)   render such further information and assistance as the Insurers may reasonably require;

(*d*)   not act in any way to the detriment or prejudice of the interest of the Insurers.

The Insured shall not make any admission of liability or payment or offer or promise of payment without the written consent of the Insurers.

(C) GENERAL CONDITIONS APPLICABLE TO ALL SECTIONS

Claims Control
1. The Insurers shall be entitled (if they so elect) at any time and for so long as they desire to take absolute control of all negotiations and proceedings and in the name of the Insured to settle, defend or pursue any claim.

Subrogation
2. Upon an indemnity being given or a payment being made by the Insurers under this Policy, they shall be subrogated to the rights and remedies of the Insured who shall co-operate with and do all things necessary to assist the Insurers to exercise such rights and remedies.

Variation in Risk
3. Should there be any change in the circumstances or nature of the risks which are the basis of this contract the Insured shall give immediate notice thereof to the Insurers and no claim arising subsequent to such change shall be recoverable hereunder unless such change has been accepted by the Insurers.

Cancellation
4. This Policy may be cancelled by either the Insurers or the Insured giving 10 days notice in writing of such cancellation. If cancelled by the Insurers they will return a pro rata portion of the premium in respect of the unexpired period of the Policy. If cancelled by the Insured a return of premium shall be at the discretion of the Insurers. There will be no return of premium in respect of any Aircraft on which a loss is paid or is payable under this Policy.

Assignment
5. This Policy shall not be assigned in whole or in part except with the consent of the Insurers verified by endorsement hereon.

Not Marine Insurance
6. This Policy is not and the parties hereto expressly agree that it shall not be construed as a policy of marine insurance.

Arbitration
7. This Policy shall be construed in accordance with English Law and any dispute or difference between the Insured and the Insurers shall be submitted to arbitration in London in accordance with the Statutory provision for arbitration for the time being in force.

Two or More Aircraft
8. When two or more Aircraft are insured hereunder the terms of this Policy apply separately to each.

Limit(s) of Indemnity
9. Notwithstanding the inclusion herein of more than one Insured, whether by endorsement or otherwise, the total liability of the Insurers in respect of any or all Insureds shall not exceed the Limit(s) of Indemnity stated in this Policy.

False and Fraudulent Claims
10. If the Insured shall make any claim knowing the same to be false or fraudulent as regards amount or otherwise this Policy shall become void and all claims hereunder shall be forfeited.

(D) DEFINITIONS

1. "ACCIDENT" means any one accident or series of accidents arising out of one event.

2. "UNIT" means a part or an assembly of parts (including any sub-assemblies) of the Aircraft which has been assigned an Overhaul Life as a part or an assembly. Nevertheless, an engine complete with all parts normally attached when removed for the purpose of overhaul or replacement, shall together constitute a single Unit.

3. "OVERHAUL LIFE" means the amount of use, or operational and/or calendar time which, according to the Airworthiness Authority, determines when overhaul or replacement of a Unit is required.

4. "OVERHAUL COST" means the costs of labour and materials which are or would be incurred in overhaul or replacement (whichever is necessary) at the end of the Overhaul Life of the damaged or a similar Unit.

5. "PRIVATE PLEASURE" means use for private and pleasure purposes but NOT use for any business or profession nor for hire or reward.

6. "BUSINESS" means the uses stated in Private Pleasure and use for business or professional purposes but NOT use for hire or reward.

7. "COMMERCIAL" means the uses stated in Private Pleasure and Business and use for the carriage by the Insured of passengers, baggage accompanying passengers and cargo for hire or reward.

8. "RENTAL" means rental, lease, charter or hire by the Insured to any person, company or organisation for Private Pleasure and Business uses only, where the operation of the Aircraft is not under the control of the Insured. Rental for any other purpose is NOT insured under this Policy unless specifically declared to Insurers and the detail of such use(s) stated in Part 3 of the Schedule under SPECIAL RENTAL USES.

Definitions 5, 6, 7 and 8 constitute Standard Uses and **do not include** Instruction, Aerobatics, Hunting, Patrol, Fire-fighting, the intentional dropping, spraying or release of anything, any form of experimental or competitive flying, and any other use involving abnormal hazard, but when cover is provided details of such use(s) are stated in Part 3 of the Schedule under SPECIAL USES.

9. "FLIGHT" means from the time the Aircraft moves forward in taking off or attempting to take off, whilst in the air, and until the Aircraft completes its landing run. A rotary-wing aircraft shall be deemed to be in Flight when the rotors are in motion as a result of engine power, the momentum generated therefrom, or autorotation.

10. "TAXIING" means movement of the Aircraft under its own power other than in Flight as defined above. Taxiing shall not be deemed to cease merely by reason of a temporary halting of the Aircraft.

11. "MOORED" means, in the case of aircraft designed to land on water, whilst the Aircraft is afloat and is not in Flight or Taxiing as defined above, and includes the risks of launching and hauling up.

12. "GROUND" means whilst the Aircraft is not in Flight or Taxiing or Moored as defined above.

SCHEDULE

SCHEDULE

PART 1

Policy No.	Proposed dated

Name of Insured

Address

Period of Insurance

From   To   both days inclusive

PART 2

Particulars of Aircraft

(1)	(2)	(3)	(4)	(5)	(6)
Make & Type (Insert "Land", "Sea", "Amphibian" or "Rotor Wing" (as applicable)	Year of Manufacture	Registration Marks	Declared Max. No. of Passengers at any one time	Amount Insured	Risks covered (Insert "Flight", "Taxiing", "Moored", "Ground", "Rotors in Motion", "Rotors not in Motion" as applicable)

PART 3

Purpose of Use Standard Uses (Insert "Private Pleasure" "Business", "Commercial", "Rental for Private Pleasure and Business only" as applicable)	Special Uses	Special Rental Uses

PART 4

Pilots

PART 5

Geographical Limits

AVN 1C 21.12.98

SCHEDULE—continued

PART 6

Limits and Deductibles (Appropriate boxes to be completed – others to be marked "not applicable")

(A) Policy Section & Risk	(B) Amounts to be deducted		(C) Limit of Indemnity from which must be deducted the amount in column (B)	
I Loss of or damage to Aircraft listed in Part 2 above		each Accident	See Part 2 Column (5)	
II Liability to Third Parties	Bodily Injury Damage to Property	NIL each Accident	Bodily Injury and Damage to property – Combined	 each Accident
III Liability to Passengers	Bodily Injury Baggage and Personal Articles each person	NIL	Bodily Injury Baggage and Personal Articles	each person each Aircraft/Accident each person each Aircraft/Accident
II/III Combined Liability to Third Parties and Passengers - Combined	Bodily Injury Damage to Property Baggage and Personal Articles	NIL each Accident each person	Bodily Injury and Damage to property – Combined including Baggage and Personal Articles limited to	 each Accident each person each Aircraft/Accident

PART 7

Premium	Section I
	Section II
	Section III

	TOTAL -------------------

PART 8

Immediate notice of any claim pursuant to Section IV(B) Paragraph 3 to be given to:

Dated in London, the

INDEX